Children of the Blood

EXPLORATIONS IN ANTHROPOLOGY
A University College London Series

Series Editors: Barbara Bender, John Gledhill and Bruce Kapferer

Children of the Blood

Society, Reproduction and Cosmology in New Guinea

Bernard Juillerat

Translated by Nora Scott

BERG

Oxford • New York

FIRST PUBLISHED IN ENGLISH BY BERG.

EDITORIAL OFFICES:
150 COWLEY ROAD, OXFORD, OX4 1JJ, UK
70 WASHINGTON SQUARE SOUTH,NEW YORK,NY 10012,USA.

ORIGINALLY PUBLISHED IN FRENCH AS 'LES ENFANTS
DU SANG' BY EDITIONS DE LA MAISON DES SCIENCES DE
L'HOMME,PARIS,1986. COPYRIGHT EDITIONS DE LA
MAISON DES SCIENCES DE L'HOMME,1986.
ENGLISH EDITION COPYRIGHT BERNARD JUILLERAT 1996

Berg is an imprint of Oxford International Publishers Ltd.

Library of Congress Cataloging-in-Publication Data

A catalogue record for this book is available from the Library of
Congress.

British Library Cataloguing-in-Publication Data

A catalogue record for this book is available from the British
Library.

ISBN 1 85973 161 9 (Cloth)

Typeset by JS Typesetting, Wellingborough, Northants.
Printed in the United Kingdom by WBC Book Manufacturers,
Bridgend, Mid Glamorgan.

Afwêeg taf na ruwar, kagêri aranêri ogohôk
Sa taf na ruwar, kagêri angwanêri ogohôk
Kagêri Yafar ba taf na ruwar

Children of the blood of the *afwêeg* sago palm
that's us, the Araneri ('male' moiety)
Children of the blood of the coconut palm
that's us, the Angwaneri ('female' moiety)
We the Yafar are the children of the blood.

Contents

Foreword

Never have anthropological field studies so prospered since, twenty or twenty-five years ago, some anthropologists condemned small-society and 'village monographs'. They were desperate for comparative and theoretical studies, and wanted never to have to read ethnography again. Today we are still waiting for these comparative regional studies, and specialists are still as divided over how to go about determining the laws, or more modestly, the universal factors behind sociocultural phenomena. Instead of developing, or even outlining, major new theoretical directions that might draw the various extant theoretical propositions together in a pluralistic spirit, combining them, in a complementary fashion, by means of synthesis and a broader reflection, we have seen anthropologists harden their respective positions, defending the unity of their theoretical convictions against all foreign elements. Some have gone so far as to advertise their categorical scorn for any approach to social facts that they saw, often wrongly, as irremediably incompatible with their own. Any attempt at theory was fragmented not only by the multiplication of scientific specializations, which is normal and beneficial, but by that of ideologies as well. This trend does not date from the last thirty years, but this does seem to be when it began to pick up speed. And so we continue to hear anthropologists of the historical school maintaining that there is no heuristic value in studying myths or symbolic systems or, conversely, mythologists pouring scorn on the extremely down-to-earth questions that interest technologists and analysts of subsistence-based economies. At the same time, and alongside a few excellent if rare pieces of research in ethnopsychoanalysis, a few psychoanalytically inclined anthropologists are still turning a blind eye to social and historical factors, while specialists in kinship or power structures remain silent on the subject of psychic representations. Still others would explain everything in terms of a post-Jungian cluster in which man, entirely divorced from his material context, is reduced to his imaginary represent-ations, while for yet others this same man historically constructs his society merely by reacting to stimuli or adopting a strategy that is both unconscious and utilitarian. As this English edition goes to press structuralism is almost dead, and we are witnessing a dangerous enthusiasm for cognitivism, compensated, of course, by a relative rebirth of psychoanalytical anthropology. These con-tradictory extremes could be seen as indicating a diversity of thinking characteristic of the human sciences and thus be a cause for celebration. They are this too, but the problem is the compart-mentalization of these orientations rather than their disparity. One obstacle that sometimes arises is anthropologists' tendency to identify their own perfectly legitimate scientific interests (resulting from personal tastes and, in some cases, their pre-anthropology training) with the only orientation or the sole object of research worth pursuing. That each person's subject-ivity selects from among the vast array of realities offered up by the human sciences is only normal, but to claim to be in pos-session of the only truth is at once to underrate the intellectual subjectivity of others, to reduce the objective richness of the sociocultural phenomenon and to foster a unilateral determinism where, behind the diversity of levels of interpretation, one should be capable of seeing a plurality of causes.

But parallel, and no doubt in reaction to this ill-managed diversity, the number and quality of field studies have been growing. Some anthropologists have set out in search of the mat-erial they need to develop their theory further, others have gone on seeking facts, with no clear idea of what they hoped to find or prove. The hesitations, disparities, fashions and ever-growing fragmentation of anthropology, the feeling of having reached a point of saturation in the formulation of theories, and also the rapid transformation of the last third-world societies which still have something to say about their own identity, all of this has favoured a massive return to facts and has been enriched by the necessity – after the fashion of a few famous precursors but with new problematics – of 'digging' longer, and therefore deeper, in the same spot rather than coming back with just one more ethnographic sample to add to the already well-stocked inventory of our library shelves.

The present work is in the same vein. The fruit of thirty-three months of intensive fieldwork spread over a period of twelve years, it proposes what I would like to be a global analysis of the structures and social organization as well as the symbolic representations of the Yafar of West Sepik Province, a small society in Papua New Guinea. While it is no longer possible to reconstruct this all-inclusiveness of social facts in our own Western societies, 'tribal'-type communities still lend themselves particularly well to holistic analysis, for they continuously produce such coherence in their technical, economic, social and spiritual life, ensuring the circulation of meaning between the material and the non-material, between their social practice and their vision of the universe. Naturally, I am not going to present a society dressed up in some all-pervasive principle of harmony: consistency of meaning does not signify ironclad cohesion or social solidarity or systematic symbolic equivalences, nor does it mean roles perfectly adapted to each institution or type of behaviour. But it so happens that, over the course of their history, the culture and social system of these groups were produced in the absence of any kind of specialization: those who devised and fashioned a tool, perfected an agricultural technique or domesticated animals were also those who situated society within the cosmos and reinvented the cosmos in their symbolic order. A material fact is no more the prisoner of an exclusively material causality than a belief is captive to a single concatenation of ideas. On the contrary, an attempt must be made to resituate the former within a system of thought and the latter in the concrete world. Human beings intervene in their natural environment in order to satisfy their needs, but at the same time they integrate this environment and symbolize it with the help of their own psychic materials: inside and outside meet in culture. I have sought to show something of these correlations here.

This book contrasts with an earlier study of mine on a society in Cameroon.[1] My experience as an Africanist laid the preliminary foundations for my approach to the Yafar. In the beginning, I felt, literally, on foreign ground, since I was going from the Sahel to the tropical rain forest and from a dense population of sorghum farmers, with a scattered pattern of settlement, to a group of slash-and-burn cultivators living in isolated hamlets.

---

1. *Les bases de l'organization sociale chez les Mouktélé. Structures lignagères et mariage.* Paris, Institut d'Ethnologie, 1971.

Later, I was just as disconcerted by a social organization and culture that did not fit my familiar African paradigms, but whose lineage organization, curiously enough, I eventually recognized as a variant form of the Cameroon Muktele segmentary system.

Yafar life-style – dispersal in the forest, villages deserted during the day, minimal social communication – and their psychological defensiveness towards others, their refusal to let outsiders glimpse the inner workings of their society and the founding ideas of their culture, the antagonism between the sexes as well as a sort of strategy of silence enveloping everything having to do with fertility, all force the investigator to adopt a pace marked by long stretches of waiting. Progress was therefore slow during my first two stays (1970–1971 and 1973); I took advantage of these pauses to collect plant specimens, draw up genealogies, visit neighbouring groups in search of elements of comparison and make a film on the horticultural cycle (CNRS 1977). In 1976 came the first breakthrough, and in 1978 my right-hand informant, May Promp, became caught up in the study and from then on (in 1981 and 1986) found growing pleasure in holding forth on his own culture. Observation, data collection and difficult question-and-answer interviews enriched my fund of information with what had been lacking: spontaneous commentaries, but also the revelation of unspoken aspects of the culture governed by strict social control.

The present work is an ethnographic monograph in the sense that I wanted to present the material gathered in the field in sufficient detail. Despite the small size of the society, it seemed indispensable, to the best of my ability, to suggest interpretations which I would not venture to generalize. The suggestions formulated remain in the realm of the particular; they are not based on a comparative study, but result from confronting the fact under examination with other elements of the culture, from an effort to integrate these elements under the common denominator of a single representation. This attempt at intracultural interpretation will contribute an overall image of local culture, the component parts of which are not kept separate in the analysis but as far as possible appear with their links and pave the way for a future synthesis. The ethnographic field study thus seeks to go beyond its purely descriptive and even analytical functions to discover what emerges of the latent level of culture that was not initially apparent in its social realization or in the verbal expression of its representatives.

This work will appear to dwell too heavily on the symbolics of reproduction and its expression in myth and ritual for some. This insistence is not due to Western nostalgia for 'precolonial' societies, nor to an old-fashioned attachment to the study of 'natural philosophies'. As this book is being published, other peoples of Melanesia are fighting for international recognition of their right and capacity to control their own history. It is important for anthropology to contribute a point of view free of former prejudices, but without taking upon itself the burden of post-colonial guilt which, in order to locate societies better within the process of change imposed on them by history, seeks to strip them of their imaginary representations on the pretext of increasing the credibility of their demands. At a time when we are discovering that European societies, present and past, lend themselves to ethnographic study as much as 'exotic' societies do, and turn out to be much closer to these than had been thought,[2] – at a time, too, when our Western cultures are giving free expression to symbolic thinking in their own literature, art, cinema, advertising or fringe movements (youth groups, sects, green movements) – it would be contradictory, with the praiseworthy aim of breaking with colonial ethnography, to reduce third-world societies to their response, whether adaptive or reactive, to colonial or neo-colonial impact, or to retain only that part of their culture which is 'rational' (in the Western sense of the word).

As the last chapter will indicate, the Yafar also belong to a region which had only been administered for some ten years when I first arrived. Colonization had therefore been short lived, and missionary influence, even today, remains singularly limited. Over the course of this study, the ethnographic enquiry continually uncovered non-material elements which, after endless cross-referencing, eventually built up a form of latent symbolic 'discourse' on the world, a global representation of the universe including society, which, while obeying its own logic, in no way impeded the implementation of a pragmatic rationality and which developed its specificity using conceptual materials that

2. Returning to our home turf has enabled ethnography to attenuate, though not to eliminate entirely, the Western/non-Western polarity and to extend the comparative perspective to European societies: see, for example, Bachelard 1975; Favret-Saada 1978; Darmon 1977; Héritier 1984.

were universal. This is the perspective in which this aspect of the present work must be placed.

The first four chapters deal with the units of society, not merely their structure, but also the basic rules of organization, presenting them from the outset as the loci of sociopolitical dynamics and symbolism. Carrying this analysis further, Part Two (Chs 5–8) studies the juridical and practical organization of the various forms of production, while leaving proper space for the representations that duplicate and sometimes modify technical behaviours and social relations. Part Three illustrates the concepts of 'reproduction' and social continuity with the help of ethnographic material, working from the social management of sexuality (Ch. 9) through to the organization of a defensive violence for ensuring social continuity. The final chapter uses Yafar history and a nascent messianic movement to examine the fractures and forms of 'adaptation' that can be observed in the Yafar community since it has stepped irrevocably into the contemporary era.

A Warning

My Yafar informants who, especially during my last visits, chose to reveal secret aspects of their religious representations and their ritual have given me permission to publish this information on the condition that it does not get back to them by some circuitous route. This applies to all exegetical elements of myths and rites, notions about sexuality and procreation, cosmology and religious offices, as well as representations attaching to the Cargo Cult. I therefore ask any reader who might happen to travel or work in West Sepik, and particularly in Amanab District, or who might come into contact with other parties having business in these regions to observe the utmost discretion in these matters. To divulge, even partially, some of the information in this book among those groups concerned could not fail to disturb social relations within the group and to engender feelings of shame.

Acknowledgments

My five stays with the Yafar were funded by the Centre National de la Recherche Scientifique (RCP 259 and 587) and by the Direction Générale des Relations Culturelles, Scientifiques et Techniques of the French Ministry of Foreign Relations, by the Wenner Gren Foundation for Anthropological Research in New York, and by the Maison des Sciences de l'Homme in Paris.

In Papua New Guinea, I would like to thank the Institute of Papua New Guinea Studies and the anthropology department of the University of Papua New Guinea for their cooperation. I am grateful to Professors T.M. Berra and J.I. Menzies of the biology department of this university for the identification of animal specimens, and to Professors J.S. Wormersley, M. Galore and E.E. Henty, under whose supervision the plant specimens collected on my earlier trips were identified at the Division of Botany (Department of Forests). I would also like to thank the West Sepik (*Sandaun*) provincial government at Vanimo for their permission to work in this border region, and the Amanab administration and its successive district officers who, from 1970 to 1981, received me warmly whenever I called at the post.

In France I would principally like to thank professor Louis Dumont and Françoise Héritier-Augé, Professor at the Collège de France, for their valuable comments on the present work, which led me to reconsider certain formulations, and to express my gratitude to André Haudricourt. I am indebted to my wife Michèle Juillerat for giving me the possibility of discussing the material collected on many occasions, especially during our joint stay in 1978.

Lastly, my heartfelt gratitude goes to the Yafar themselves who, although this was the first time they had been confronted with the prolonged presence of a stranger in their midst, put up with the constraints of an ethnographic enquiry. I am particularly indebted to my informants (to use the traditional term) Waya

Warey, Kofay, Buwô and Wagif Promp, Wïy Afas, Subwen and Kabyo Nuwas, Pweney Kuray, Awêr Anmay, Yow Wampi, Mawyan Saywe, Now Koboy, Woy Wafyo, Awpiy Nahwey, Ibniy Wampi and Gafnaw Afas, and also to a few women like Tuay, Hwan or Afwey and her daughter Amo, most of whom are no longer living. But the richest part of the present work would still be lacking had I not enjoyed the continual aid, since 1971, of May Promp, friend, informant and gainsayer, whose intellectual and human qualities can be glimpsed throughout this book.

Note to the English Translation

The present English edition contains few changes with respect to the original French published some ten years ago, apart from a line added here and there and an updated bibliography. As I have not visited the Yafar since 1986, it seemed difficult to envisage a total revision. I can only say that, from the few letters I have received, the society seems to have changed somewhat as the older generation has given way to younger men concerned more with possibilities for local development (a little native gold has been found in the streams) than with maintaining tradition. Christianity in its Protestant form has no doubt intrigued some young people, and one or two may have left for the Mission in the Many Lands Bible School in Amanab, though it can certainly not be said that the Yafar have undergone a collective conversion. Job possibilities on the outside are still closed, and the plantations are not hiring. The road between Amanab and Yafar is now open, but the Yafar are still cut off from Vanimo and the north coast. This situation is no doubt not to their liking, but at least it gives them some protection from the not always legal progress of foreign logging companies.

The translation was funded by the Centre National du Livre at the Ministry of Culture and by the Maison des Science de l'Homme, both in Paris. I would also like to thank Nora Scott for the particular care she has taken with this translation.

Bernard Juillerat

General Introduction

The Geographical and Cultural Setting

The upper course of the Sepik River, where it forms the border between eastern and western New Guinea, had been explored as early as 1914 by Richard Thurnwald, but further penetration of the riverine area and its administration by Australia did not occur until after 1950. Also, for reasons given in the last chapter, the hilly massif called the Border Mountains, running the length of the frontier on the left side of the river, although fairly populous, did not come under the complete control of the colonial administration until the beginning of the 1960s. This is a border region in terms not only of political divisions but also of geographical boundaries, since, although it faces mainly on to the Sepik flood plain, its waters drain towards the west, that is towards the Idenburg Valley and, lower down, towards the Mamberamo Valley in what is today Indonesia. From a maximum altitude of 1,120 metres in its southernmost part, this modest massif slopes gently off to the north to high points of 750 metres with inhabited areas at around 400 metres. To the east, the hills drop sharply to the Sepik plain, partially flooded some nine months of the year; to the west the massif extends across the international border, which, although not patrolled, has been closed since western New Guinea (Irian Jaya) was incorporated into Indonesia.[1] Like most of the New Guinea lowlands, the plain and the hills are entirely covered in tropical rain forest where, year in year out, the populations wield axe and fire to clear gardens which, the harvest barely in, begin reverting to fallow, then to forest (Barrau 1958). Even though these slash-and-burn societies are attached to fixed territories and settled in relatively

1. When the Dutch withdrew in 1962, the new situation was 'legitimized' in 1969 by the Act of Free Choice. Western New Guinea has a population of around 1.2 million inhabitants (Tapol ed. 1983; Osborne 1985).

stable hamlets, they are by no means unfamiliar with hunting; indeed, this is the men's activity *par excellence*, while men and women without distinction add to the family's daily fare by gathering and sometimes fishing.

Although they face on to the Sepik, with its immense alluvial plain stretching to the eastern horizon, the Border Mountains seem to have been populated, at least in part, from the west or northwest, and the cultures found there contrast sharply with those of the nearby plain.[2] Without venturing to define a 'culture area', the unity of which would be contradicted by the diversity of linguistic families and difficult to demarcate to the west for lack of information on Irian Jaya groups,[3] it is possible to identify the dominant cultural features which, although they contrast with those of the plain and Sepik regions in general, seem to place these societies in a group that we propose to call 'Border Mountain peoples'.

On the ecological level the more broken terrain entails a number of consequences, particularly economic, the main ones being the absence of large swamps, restricting the natural stands of sago palms, which the hill dwellers are therefore forced to cultivate; a modest hydrographic system, which considerably reduces fishing and keeps the crocodiles in the plain (where the skins provide a sporadic source of income); and the fact that the climate in the hills is marginally better and more healthy, which can be seen as favouring the greater human density found there.

For reasons of both ecology and defense, village houses are clustered on hill tops, whose summit, once levelled, forms the village square, the centre of public and ceremonial life. Hill houses are smaller than plains dwellings and, with the exception of certain Waina groups to the north, are built according to the same basic plan: a floor on stilts into which are set two or four suspended cooking fires, and access via a veranda or simple defensive porch reached by a notched tree trunk that can be lowered into place or removed at will.[4] The single room is a family space,

2. The nearby plain is occupied by groups speaking Baibai, Kwomtari and Nagatman, whose cultures have not been studied. I paid a brief visit to the Kwomtari in 1973 (Juillerat 1975c); some information can also be found in Craig 1969.

3. But see Galis 1956–1957.

4. The journalist Willey, who walked from Vanimo to Amanab in the early 1960s, remarks that the villages of Babuk and Yafar 'were the most advanced we had seen since leaving Vanimo' (1965: 189). When he wrote these words, he had just crossed the Waina region, where the houses were still built directly on the ground.

and despite the fact that there is frequently a 'bachelors' house' for adolescent boys, the village does not have anything like a 'men's house', whereas in the plain (Kwomtari), one finds fairly spacious houses for the unmarried men containing ritual objects and which, forbidden to women, appear as a euphemized form of the *haus tambaran* of the lower Sepik. In addition, the inhabitants of the southern and central Border Mountains – extending north of the Amanab (Eri) groups – organize ceremonial cycles over several years (up to ten) for the guardian spirits of game, at which time the village builds an enclosure, at the centre of which they erect a hut called the 'spirit house'.[5]

Collective initiations of the type found farther down the Sepik are not attested here and, as a general rule, nothing like the institution of personalized political authority or competitive exchanges between big men can be isolated from social life as a whole. It is this type of organization that has given rise to such terms as 'loose structure' or 'anarchy' in the ethnographic literature on New Guinea (Pouwer 1960). But it is more an absence of functional coherence at the level of the social group, to the advantage of a dynamic articulated mainly by individual relations. The social life of the individual is only weakly determined by membership in a clan, a 'moiety' or a village; rather, it is organized through repeated communication and exchanges with certain kinsmen or allies. In particular, it is the policy of marriage alliances that allows this permanent quest for new ties, which are highly dependent upon the 'mechanics' of kinship, but determined too by unforeseen attractions and affects. This individualistic bent is not specific to the Border Mountains (see, for instance, Lawrence 1984; Schieffelin 1976), but it is typical.

And yet social groups are not wholly transparent, and our opening chapters are devoted to this problem. With the exception of their exogamy, the clans appear more as a projection *in abstracto* of patriliny as it is experienced by the individual; and moieties, there where dual organization is found, have only a symbolic or ritual role. As for the villages, these are often the temporarily frozen expression of a residential dynamic that, over the long term, seems to consist of mobility, scissions and regroupings. Even the expression of violence is organized without the aid of corporate groups: no one is going to draw up a map of friendly

5. See Ch. 7, and Huber 1973, 1990.

or enemy tribes in the Border Mountains. The atomism of the tribal groups goes a long way to explaining the lack of well-defined, operational institutions in the social system. A society of 100 or 200 individuals does not need institutions to establish an internal structure, and should the numbers increase beyond a certain threshold, the group will split. But, as it is too small for sufficiently diversified exchanges within the society, it simultaneously extends its network of communications to the neighbouring tribes, thus creating a 'social space' in which links between the groups result from the development of individual relations and marriages. Folded back on to its own inalienable identity, the tribe also overspills its boundaries because of the abundance of kinship ties and sometimes because of the transmission of ties between non-related trading partners. The availability of land is such that demographic pressure is still not a problem, which has until now ensured the tribal territory a high degree of stability.

In contrast to the techniques found in the plain, Border Mountain societies used to employ traditional adzes for wood-cutting and still use sago scrapers fashioned from a hafted piece of flaked stone, not a piece of wood with a sharpened edge.[6] The penis sheaths are ovoid (a type found west of the border: Galis 1956) and contrast with the elongated shapes found in the plain and at the eastern limit of the hills. The hour-glass shaped drums are some of the longest attested in New Guinea and have no handles; but the hills also use trumpets made from wood (not bamboo), played by groups of two, or, in the north, five men (Juillerat 1993b). The contrast is visible, too, in the structure of the ceremonial masks; always made from highly perishable materials, with new masks being produced for each rite, they are smaller and less skilfully decorated than those in the plain or in the vicinity of Telefolmin (Craig 1988).[7]

Despite these shared features, there is a diversity within the Border Mountains that manifests itself either by slight cultural variations from one village to the next or in sharply differentiated zones. For example, there seem to be no dual organizations in the southern half of the massif, and mediumism is not found in the north, among the Waina. On the other hand, the latter have developed an altogether original totemic fertility cult, which will

6. See Ch. 6 and Juillerat 1975c, 1983b, 1984a.
7. See Juillerat 1975c and objects on exhibition at the Musée de l'Homme in Paris.

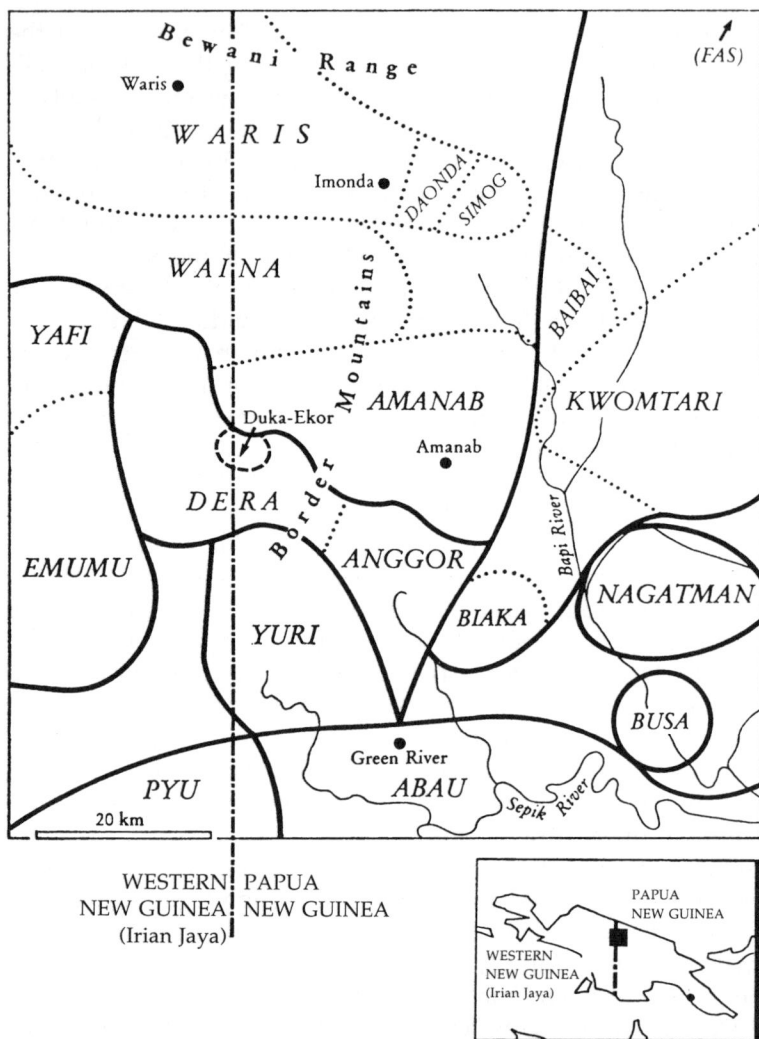

Map 1. Linguistic map of the Border Mountains and Adjoining Plain (After Wurm and Haltori eds 1981)

be discussed in this work; in addition, they have a stable settlement pattern based on the nucleation of former clan hamlets (Gell 1975). Lastly, the villages on the eastern slope have been strongly influenced by plain groups (Baibai and Kwomtari) and have adopted some of their cults, as well as the now-abandoned use of bridewealth in the form of shellrings.

This rapid survey of features common to the Border Mountains suggests a culturally dominant form, but the 'atomized' structure of these societies is a barrier to the development of any 'ethnic sentiment'. The linguistic groups have no proper name for themselves or for other groups, and the term 'Border Mountains' is unknown, being rarely used by the Administration. The world is viewed from a sociocentric standpoint and in relation to the kinship security zone determined by exchanges. In effect, it is at a level below that of cultural and linguistic units that the coherent set of relations and behaviours is organized into what we call a 'society'.

The Linguistic Setting: The Eri (Amanab)

The group we will be studying, the Yafar, speak a non-Austronesian language, Amanab (Maps 1 and 2), which has the most speakers of any Border Mountains language[8] and is the southernmost of the Border Stock (Laycock 1975), which extends across the frontier to the northwest.[9] Linguistic boundaries do not constitute social barriers or stand in the way of exchange and marriage. Marriage across linguistic frontiers gives rise to a form of limited bilingualism, more particularly among women who marry into another group and among their close kin and affines. Furthermore, the neo-Melanesian version of Pidgin English is used as a lingua franca by everyone but elderly men and the women, especially north of the Amanab patrol post. Amanab sports a number of dialectal variants, which do not follow clear-cut boundaries and do not hamper mutual understanding. The strongest contrast seems to be between the Eri in the south and those in the northwest, the Yafar belonging to the latter.

I have retained the term Amanab (a deformation of the toponym Amaraf, referring to the clearing in which the patrol post

8. Around 2 ,950 speakers reported in 1965, nearly 3 ,700 in 1984 and 4,000 today, for a territory of some 500 km². A further 2,800 live in Irian Jaya (source: Summer Institute of Linguistics). See also Graham and Graham 1980, Juillerat 1994.

9. For the classification of the languages of the region, see Loving and Bass 1964; Voorhoeve 1971; Laycock 1975; Wurm and Haltori (eds) 1981.

was built in 1960) in speaking of the language, but I prefer to designate the speakers by the term Eri (*êri*, 'person', 'human'), most tribe and clan names also being marked by the ending -*neri* (*na êri*, 'people of. . .').

From the outset the Administration dropped the village names in favour of tribal names, and simply numbered the hamlets when there were several for one society. This practice was adopted by the inhabitants themselves, with the result that the toponyms or former village names have all but fallen into disuse. In their stead, members of a given group speak of '*namba wan*' or '*namba tu*' to designate their hamlets. Most tribes have a maximum of three or four villages, and a number have only one. On this basis there should be as many tribes (named cohesive

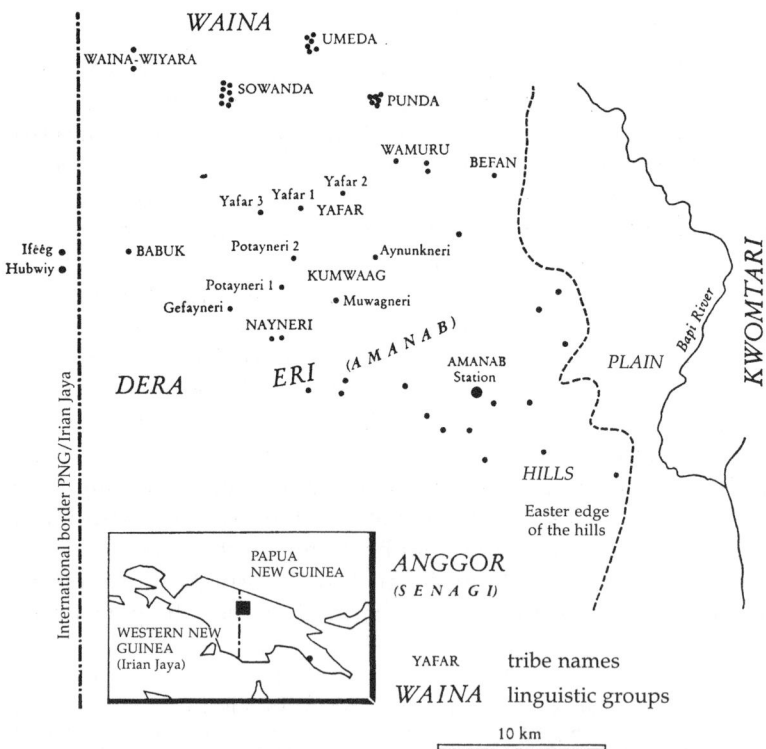

Map 2. The Amanab region. Linguistic groups and location of the Yafar

sociopolitical groups exploiting a common territory) as there are names, in this instance 28 for the Eri (or an average of 128 individuals per group in 1981). But it turns out that several of these societies form or once formed a larger unit, composed of some of the present-day groups whose bonds have gradually dissolved but which still carry the same name. These 'confederations' (a term applied by some authors to other parts of New Guinea) are in this case tribes in the process of breaking up following an increase in population.

Comparison of population figures for 1965 and 1981 shows an average annual growth rate of 1.33%. But the 1970 census indicates a rate of 1.6% for the past year, or a 3.78% birth rate against a 2.18% death rate. The sex ratio shows a persistent discrepancy to the disadvantage of females, which affects the life of society by restricting the choice of wives. However, the phenomenon does not seem to have any connection with the practice of infanticide in the region (Ch. 9, p. 276). This imbalance must be attributed to two other causes, one of which is genetic, appearing in the slightly lower number of girls born. In the case of the other, it is hard to say if it is of a genetic or a cultural order,[10] but it can be detected from an increase in the discrepancy during the first five years of life. In the census we consulted, the numbers listed in Figure 1 for the 1–5-year-old group (85.3 girls for 100 boys) can in fact be broken down into two subgroups:

0–1 year	92.98 girls for 100 boys
1–5 years	83.60 girls for 100 boys

This drop is significant and seems to show that girls are more likely to die in infancy.

1965	1968	1970	1973	1981
2848	2979	3066	3250?	3489

Table 1. Global population figures for Amanab District – Eri groups minus the Babuk tribe: approximately 100 (*Government Census*, Amanab)

---

10. In the latter case, we need detailed studies if we are to determine whether the discrimination is expressed only through a difference in diet or whether it is also or only the mother's behaviour that differs.

Age group	Men	Women	Sex ratio*
Totals	1680	1386	82,5%
Over 45	102	110	107,8
16–45	841	647	76,9
11–15	213	180	84,5
6–10	217	187	86,2
1–5	307	262	85,3

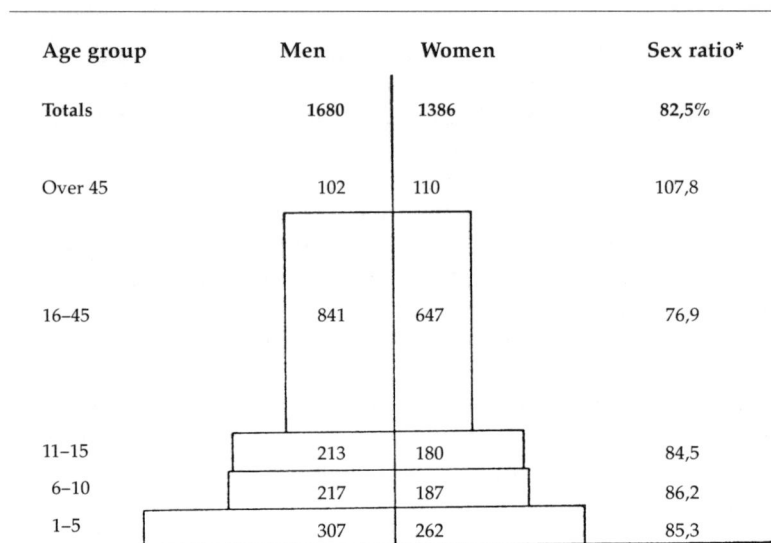

* Number of women per 100 men

Figure 1. Age pyramid for the Eri living in Amanab District, October–November 1970 (*Patrol Report*, Amanab)

	Men	Women
Under 18 years old	894	650
Over 18 years old	1095	850
Total	1989	1500
Sex ratio[11]	100	75.4

Table 2. Census of the Eri Living in Amanab District (minus the Babuk) in February 1981 (*Government Census*, Amanab)

11. The population figures for the entire West Sepik District showed, in 1980, 59,168 men for 54,951 women, or a sex ratio of 100/92.87; for Amanab District these were 10,422/8,914, or 100/85.53, respectively. The same imbalance between the sexes is found in the statistics of all districts of the country, with the exception of Southern Highlands Province, no doubt because the men emigrate to find work (National Census 1980).

The Eri population is subject to wide fluctuations over time, as is suggested by Figure 1. This is due in particular to the high variation in the mortality rate caused by epidemics ('influenza' or tuberculosis) which periodically sweep through the area (the last was in the late 1970s).

The Yafar society, clustered at the time of my fieldwork into three hamlets, is one of the 28 tribes mentioned above. The tribe occupies a territory of around 45 km² in the northern band of the Amanab linguistic group and numbers some 200 people. While linguistically a part of the whole Eri group, it also falls within the Waina culture (some 1,000 members) zone of influence, located immediately to the north, an influence felt particularly as far as the totemic fertility cult is concerned. Communication with the Waina flows mainly through the kinship and marriage ties maintained with the Punda (Map 2). On the Eri side, Yafar territory abuts on to the Babuk to the west, the Potayneri and the Aynunkneri to the south and the Wamuru to the east. All these groups and, to a lesser extent, a few non-adjoining ones exchange women and goods with the Yafar, who in this way are integrated into a much vaster space. The same is true for each of their neighbours.

Transcription of Amanab Terms

The results of a phonological study of the Amanab language, carried out by H. Tourneux, are summarized in Appendix A; I have added a few comments on the verb and noun systems. Below I have listed only those signs that need defining.

Vowels

ê	closed *e*
e	open *e*
ə	schwa. This sound is not a separate phoneme but results from the weakening of another vowel.
ô	closed *o*
o	open *o*
ö	rounded *o*

The unvoiced *i* in final position has been left as '*i*'.
A double vowel indicates a long syllable.

Consonants

b	very often prenazalized [*mb*]
f	unvoiced bilabial fricative [the voiced form is not attested]
w, y	semi-vowels
r	apico-alveolar. Sometimes pronounced, e.g. between vowels, like an *l*.
	The *d*, from which it derives, has disappeared.
h	moderately aspirated

Part I

Social Groups: Structures, Dynamics and Representations

The first part of this work analyses the various stable social units that make up Yafar society. By 'stable social units', I mean permanently constituted groups whose coherence is assured by descent, residence or, more formally, by a conceptual principle, in this instance dual organization. Descent and residence give rise to units whose reality is based on their demographic content alone. This is the case for the unilateral descent group, the household, the hamlet and the tribe as a whole. Dual organization, on the other hand, engenders units that may be termed symbolic or formal, in the sense that they exist independently of their human content; should one of these lose its population, a readjustment will be made, and the weakened or empty unit will be restocked with individuals or groups. The formal unit is part of a coherent structure and cannot be eliminated or forgotten without the whole structure crumbling: even emptied of its members, the unit continues to exist (see also Gell 1975, Ch. 2). The opposition between these two types of group is also expressed in their denominations: the name of the former is tied to a specific human group and in principle dies with it, while moiety names are independent of their social content.

Further, Yafar social units are organized inclusively, and it is in that order that we will define them, beginning with the broadest and gradually focusing down to the narrowest. These are the tribe (or confederation), hamlet, moiety, submoiety, clan, lineage and household.

Theoretically, we should add to these the natural groups based on sex and age, in so far as they are the poles of antagonistic relations and constitute operational units. But they cannot be dealt with in the same way as groups created by society, for they derive their value only from the relations that spring up between their poles and from the determination of individual status, established at birth for sex and evolving over a lifetime for age. Nevertheless we can already call attention to these categories, which announce the fundamental role they play in Yafar social relations.

Other, less stable types of social groupings play a role in the everyday workings of society: occasional work groups, gardening groups, sago-working groups, hunting groups, ritual groups, etc. These units come together and dissolve in response to need or personal ties. They have a purely temporary function. As a result, I will deal with them only from the angle of the socioeconomic circumstances that condition them (Chs. 5–8).

In these opening chapters I will attempt to define the units in question, both diachronically and synchronically, for it is through their processes of transformation that we will come to understand just what makes a clan, a hamlet, a tribe. When the temporal dimension is taken into account, the first of these two approaches leads to two theories of the way in which social time may be apprehended. One is to analyse how the system changes over the short term and what principles govern this evolution. The other leads to the historical reconstruction of events which could have produced the present situation. We know that in studying societies without writing, especially small remote ones, historical reconstruction still has serious limitations. Yafar historical tradition goes back no further than genealogical memory, in other words a few generations. Consequently, readers will perhaps be surprised at the scarcity of information on migrations and on the origin of this society, but they will understand that the material collected has more to say about social dynamics than about history proper. The search for pieces of the tribe's past has led me to understand those factors which have determined the displacement of a village or its scission, the segmentation of clans and the appropriation or loss of land.

1

Society and Local Groups

The people came and built a platform around the iron tree. They took their adzes and climbed up and chopped away at the trunk. The tree cracked and threatened to fall in every direction; its blood spurted out. The people who were frightened ran off and founded the Walsa, Fêr, Twêf, Fangri, Ohoruf, Yiyi, Gersap, Yabro, Akmari, Wofna. . . tribes. But those who were standing next to the tree stayed and were not afraid. These are the Yafar, Wamuru, Kumwaag, Sowanda, Waina, Umeda, Punda, Babuk. . .Koow! They made a ritual ring around the base of the iron tree and sang the *popwamôk*: 'What water? Blood of the *mara* tree! Yee! Blood of the *Ficus ahômp*, yee! Yee! Water of the armpit, water of the groin, water of the thigh!' The tree then fell with its blood. The people looked into the fallen trunk. They saw that beneath the water was hidden the blood. The water flowed out first, the blood followed behind: clear to the top of the tree, which touches the Ocean.

(From a myth)

If we have chosen to deal with two apparently very different social units in the same chapter, it is because many Eri tribes are made up of only one village, entire societies all together in a single residential unit. And where there are two or three hamlets, it is because these used to be a single village which later split due to conflict or an increase in population. The tribal unit is therefore divided spatially into mobile and structurally fragile local groups.

The 'Tribe'

Each Eri tribe is set in a wider social space, made up of itself and the neighbouring tribes, of which it is the centre. Thus exchanges and social life are sociocentric and radiate outwards (see also Ch. 8). Figure 2 illustrates this concentric structure.

5

The social unit we call the 'tribe'[1] can be defined objectively by no other term than its own name. A Yafar will sometimes use the word *awaanǝga* to designate the other Yafar, but lexically speaking this term should signify 'classificatory fathers'.[2] Besides having a name, the tribal group builds its identity on the sharing of a common territory, on its dual structure, and on a sort of solidarity 'contract'. Let us look at these different points.

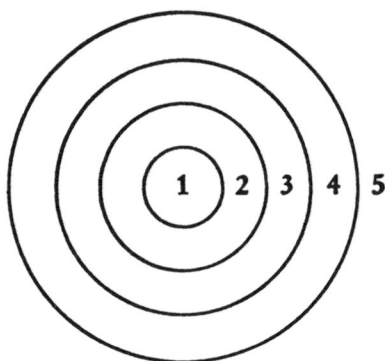

1. Local group: agnates, cognates, affines (*heheeg*)
2. Tribe: agnates, cognates, affines
3. Multitribal social space: affines, cognates, non-kin
4. Peripheral social space: known non-kin, a few isolated affines and cognates
5. Tribes known by name: foreigners (*angôruwaag*)

Figure 2. Sociocentric organization of kinship and residence

1. In all likelihood, 'Yafar' means 'Yafay's people' (*Yafay na êri*),[3] Yafay being a mythical ancestor, apparently Kumwaag's brother, from whom descended the confederation of the same name immediately to the south of the Yafar (see below). As a means of identification and differentiation, the name Yafar is often used in such formulas as *Kagêri Yafar*, 'we Yafar'. In its exclusive form, the same 'we' serves as an identity marker for various levels of social integration: tribes, moieties, clans, villages.

1. Concerning the relativity of the term 'tribe', see Fried 1975, Godelier 1973.
2. Even though this relationship is normally designated by the term *hmon* or *hmonik* (Juillerat 1977).
3. The other tribes of the region also carry patronymic names: Potayneri (*Botay na êri*, 'people or descendants of Botay'), Muwagneri (*Muwag na êri*), Aynunkneri (*Aynunk na êri*), etc. These are mythical figures who do not feature in genealogies.

2. Sharing a common *territory*. Tribal lands are the best-defined territorial unit in terms of both politics and land-holding, for the group defends its land against neighbouring tribes (irrespective of any kinship ties there might be). The territory is more clearly circumscribed than 'clan' lands, which are a stable intratribal unit in theory, but in fact derive from the dynamics of kinship (Ch. 5).

3. *Dual structure*. This type of organization, characteristic of northern Border Mountains societies, does nothing to reinforce social solidarity or to alter relations between individuals. But it does structure society by subdividing it in such a way as to ensure its unity. To divide an object into two parts and call them halves or 'moieties' is to define the unity of a whole. Neither the Eri nor the Waina have a term for 'moiety', however; they describe their dual groups as 'male' and 'female', which is the best way of imposing duality and keeping it from turning into a ternary system, for instance. In the next chapter we will see the meaning of Yafar dual organization, but here we need to point out its integrating function and its place among the factors that define the tribe: each society in the region has its own dual organization, not only discrete and irreducible, but independent of demographic fortunes and clan segmentations.

4. *Solidarity* is of a different nature and corresponds to a set of relations that often defies clear-cut definition and remains fairly informal; it is also subject to transgressions and personal interpretations. For the Yafar, solidarity is the result of an accumulation of kinship ties and sometimes a shared residence in the context of being part of the same tribal group. The normative resolution of internal conflicts through stick fights instead of murder (Ch. 14), could be held up as one of the clearest realizations of the sentiment of tribal solidarity.

The Tribe: An Alliance Group?

The chapters that follow study the descent and marriage systems. They will show how Yafar society functions with respect to these two dimensions, which have determined two orientations of ethnological theory (Dumont 1971); they will also show, in the societies under examination, the dominance of one or the other of these organizing principles. The Yafar social system partakes of both dimensions simultaneously, but segmentation of patri-lineages is often carried out by founding a collateral branch in another tribe, and marriage occurs both within the society and with outside groups: patriclans, submoieties, villages and tribes may or may not find themselves allied by intermarriage. The relative instability of agnatic groups and the practice of marrying in as much as out mean that neither of these two complementary principles can be used as a criterion for defining the tribe. The most that can be said is that the patriclan, as a group, tends to remain attached to its tribe and that there is a preference for marriages within the society. Only with these reservations can the tribe be termed an alliance group, that is to say the conjoining of a certain number of exogamous patriclans which intermarry (see Chapter 10, 'exogamic solidarities'). But that is not the founding principle, since some Yafar clans are not allowed to intermarry, and the network of marriages extends well beyond the social limits of the tribe.

The idea, sometimes expressed by my informants, that one day spatially isolated clans gathered into multiclan villages in order to be 'stronger', less vulnerable to the murderous raids of neighbouring groups, should therefore be interpreted as a hypothesis concerning a modification in the organization of local groups and not as the society's founding principle. And yet the principle of the clan as residential group (hamlet) prevails among the neighbouring Waina-speaking societies, and the Yafar themselves used to live in one vast village composed of several hamlets (see below). Looking at the different synchronic cross-sections of Eri history, one can only imagine a set of tribes that were already constituted but whose individual component clans were subject to modification from one cross-section to the next and whose membership, respective numerical importance and even name varied. We shall see that Yafar 'residential history' is one long string of dispersals and concentrations. This Eri model of mobility contrasts with the stability of the Waina-speaking hamlets and clans.

The insufficiency of historical documents obliges us to attempt a reconstruction of the historical process that gave rise to the present situation by seizing it in the making, completing in the extended present which constitutes today's situation by recollections of recent events (over several generations). What was this process?

Chapter 3 will discuss patrilineal units in more detail, but here we already need to discuss lineage segmentation, which appears as the mainspring of tribal renewal. From a synchronic point of view, Yafar society is made up of:

a) former 'founding' clans or lineages (*moog* 'base or stump of a tree'), which may have broken off to join other tribes in which collateral branches can be found;
b) collateral branches descended from 'founding' lineages residing in another tribe (the inverse of the preceding), which may be in various stages of assimilation;[4]
c) in some cases a man from a neighbouring tribe as yet without descendants; he will become the founder of a 'foreign' line within his host group.

These various situations can be seen as different moments of a single process of assimilation, which means they should not be regarded as the definitive state of the group concerned, but again as synchronic cross-sections of its evolution. On the basis of this information, we can advance the hypothesis that the early history of these groups consists of successive incorporations of 'foreign' lines, of the extinction of certain lineages replaced by others from neighbouring tribes, and of segmentations giving rise to the implantation of a local line in another tribe. We see that the tribe – the society – only appears to be a fixed nucleus on to which secondary elements accidentally graft themselves, and that in reality we have, over the long term, a nucleus which undergoes a gradual but thorough transformation, the external elements working their way bit by bit to the centre to replace others that have become demographically weakened or extinct (Juillerat 1992b).

So much for the formal process of assimilation. But for what reasons do some lineage segments find themselves uprooted from their original tribe? The most frequent is remarriage or widows returning home with one or several young male children. Sometimes the agnates want the children back, but not always, and they are often adopted by their new community, which may be the home tribe of their mother, who has returned to remarry or to

---

4. Inversely, five Yafar clans dispersed to other areas (mainly to the west: Babuk, Hubwiy, Ifêêg), and four branches are still represented there.

live with her brothers, or by yet a third tribe in which she finds a husband; as we shall see (Ch. 10), both eventualities stem from her rejection of a secondary, leviratic type marriage. The 'migrant mother' is almost always a widow, but although exceptional, can also be fleeing ill-treatment by her husband and taking refuge in her home village with her young children. In this case, it is the mother who is the vehicle of the future founders of the 'transplanted' segment (see Haudricourt 1964). There is an obvious parallel with shifting agriculture, in which cuttings and sprouts are transplanted from one garden to another. Furthermore, allegorical figures in Yafar mythology refer to the mother as the representation of the cutting or the seed, and to her son as the new shoot or sprout. Just as the cutting or seed must rot to give birth to a new plant, so the widow is sentenced to extinction as her son founds a new patriline in his host land (group).

But a man can also go to live in his wife's village at the invitation of her family. This uxorilocality can also lead to collateral lineage segments being founded outside the home tribe, but this is usually only temporary. In the case of land-holding, we shall see the importance of the phenomenon of land-based uxorilocality. Lastly, the adoption of a male child by a matrilateral relative residing in another tribe can also lead to the founding of a new patriline. In every case, the migrant will be said to have been 'raised', *yuguk*, by his host group.

It is the social life of *individuals*, then, that is the main determinant of lineage dynamics and its relation with residential groups and tribes. And yet the latter two units – sometimes fused into a single entity – are the object of another dynamic: mobility. There is no link between these two principles; they are of two different orders: kinship in the first case, and locality in the second.

A Tentative Historical Reconstruction of Yafar Group Mobility

The processes of splitting, segmentation, incorporation of linages and morphological transformation of tribes all go on independently of the movements of hamlets.[5] Local history is also made

---

5. I use 'village' and 'hamlet' interchangeably to designate the local or residential group, i.e. a group of houses built around an open space on cleared ground.

up of social events, but here I will restrict my presentation to the succession of moves, splits and reformations of residential groups. This mobility is the reflection and the consequence of a strategy either for managing the natural resources of an available territory or for protecting the group and resolving its internal and external conflicts. This reconstruction harks back to the period immediately before the oldest ancestors on genealogical record (four generations before today's mature adults), in other words some 120 years ago. The first reported changes of residence were temporary and explained as being for economic reasons; home base was the ancestral village of Sahya, located a few kilometres southwest of present-day Yafar 2, on a steep ridge. Two other hamlets lay near by: Meteber, home of the ancestors of the present-day Potayneri, and Mwasya, occupied by those of the present-day groups Aynunkneri, Muwagneri and Gefayneri. Sahya village no longer exists, but the site, although completely overgrown by secondary forest, can still be identified from the mounds on which the houses stood, divided into several hamlets and representing a total population of some 300 individuals (not including the Babuk group, which subsequently separated from the Yafar). This figure, distinctly higher than today's population, as well as the size of the local unit suggest a tribe that was demographically and socially strong. The settlement pattern seems to have been stable and morphologically similar to present-day Waina societies (Gell 1975; Juillerat 1981), that is to say, several close-set hamlets made up of one or several clans, each of which belonged to only one moiety. The clans were the same as those of today, which indicates the slow pace of internal change; only the Yafwayneri, Sawayneri and Esnaneri segments (Ch. 3) were not present at this time. Yafar lands extended mainly to the north, while immediately to the south lay the Kumwaag territory. In mythology, Sahya was the first village of the society, and as such it is imbued with a sacred nature. Even in recent times, periodic rites were still performed there, particularly on one cordyline supposed to have come from the penis of the god W. . ., having sprung up after he coupled with his earthly partner B. . . (see Ch. 2). At that time nothing but grass grew on the earth. A mythical 'father' is supposed to have chosen the Yafar as the guardians of W. . .'s penis after rejecting a previous group of men because he did not like their language, with all its apical sounds (i.e. the present dialectal form of Amanab spoken in the centre, south and east). And that was how, according to legend, the Yafar came to take up residence at Sahya.

1. From Sahya to *Kergona*[6] (on the Ohompi River, near present-day Wamuru, 7 km as the crow flies). The whole tribe takes up residence with the Babuk, in a temporary village on the far northeast border of their lands, to work the numerous wild sago palms that grow there. No genealogical reference (around the 6th ascending generation, beyond genealogical record). A relatively short stay (less than a year?), then back to *Sahya*, which remains home base.

2. From Sahya to *Hôn-Burwô* (near the Api River, which drains towards western New Guinea and flows through present-day Kumwaag land). The whole tribe goes this time to set up hunting camps. Menaneri, Wamawneri and Wiyneri clans are the first to return to Sahya, followed by the rest. No genealogical record, or at best at the time of the earliest generations (+5).

3. From Sahya to *Haô* (on Yafar land near present-day Potayneri 2, west of Sahya). The whole tribe establishes a new but short-lived village, the place being judged unfavourable. Back to Sahya.

4. From Sahya to *Pakim* (same area as Haô). All Yafar clans go to work sago and to hunt (land not exploited at the time, not yet occupied by the Kumwaag). This happens in the third or fourth generation. Then back to Sahya.

5. From Sahya to *Buu* (same area as Pakim). All clans go: sago palms and hunting. Second ascending generation before old men, around 1900. Two Yafar are killed by Potayneri for reasons unclear, whence back to Sahya.

6. From Sahya to *Safwahana* (slightly north of Sahya). After a number of deaths, followed by accusations of sorcery and murders of Yafar by the Potayneri, the Yafar decide to move away, finally abandoning the old village of Sahya. This is the generation of the fathers and grandfathers of today's oldest Yafar.

7. From Safwahana to *Hwagimp* (near Safwahana) and on to *Tahway kəbik* (near present-day Yafar 2). A murder was the cause of this move: men from different clans kill Kney, of the Menaneri lineage, who was accused of having committed

6. Nearly all hamlets are named after rivers. The word kəbik, which is often added to the river name, means 'village, place'.

adultery with the wife of Nahwey, of the Biyuneri lineage: a classificatory father of the victim seeks vengeance, which precipitates the departure of a man from the Ifêêg clan and another from Sumneri clan, later followed by other Yafar from the 'male' moiety, then by three Biyuneri. These men, soon joined by a Suwê-enunguruk man and a few Wamawneri (two Yafar clans), found Hwagimp. Some time later, the clans of the 'female' moiety (with the exception of the Biyuneri) found their own new hamlet, Tahway kəbik.

8. From Tahway kəbik to *Faywe-moog kəbik*. Tahway kəbik is soon abandoned for reasons unknown, and the same group founds Faywe-moog kəbik ('village of the tree-fern stump'). A few years later, the large number of deaths in the village sparks a dispersal into the forest, a group of Amisneri founding *Kay kəbik*, where the epidemic continues. Two Amisneri men return to Hwagimp, then the rest of the scattered clans finally come together to form a new hamlet, again called Faywe-moog; in the interim, an intermediate hamlet is constructed and immediately abandoned, *Momsaf kəbik*.

A new feud causes Faywe-moog kəbik to be abandoned by the remaining members of Amisneri clan. These families rally to Hwagimp, where the clans of the 'male' moiety are living: one night Rabwey (an Amisneri man), 'possessed by a ghost', comes knocking at Raw's (an Ifêeg man's) door, who, taking him for a foreign sorcerer, wounds him with an arrow shot through a slit. Rabwey dies. The victim's elder brother, Rumwaw, provokes the Amisneri men by shooting arrows at their houses. Then, together with his kinsmen, he surrounds four Amisneri men and a woman, who manage to escape into the forest where they hide for some months before returning to Hwagimp. The other Amisneri soon join them.

These events can be dated to around 1920 because they happened shortly before some Indonesian bird-of-paradise hunters paid a visit to Hwagimp, which we have been able to place in the 1920s.

9. From Hwagimp to *Waô kəbik* (next to present-day Yafar 1). The Wamawneri, Wiyneri, Menaneri, Bwasneri and Fuwaneri clans and one Amisneri lineage remain in Hwagimp. The other clans found two hamlets side by side at Waô kəbik, a few kilometres west of Hwagimp: Waô kəbik proper, with Ifêêg, Ifêaroog and Biyuneri clans as well as one man

from another Amisneri lineage and two Suwê-enunguruk men; and nearby, at the foot of the same hill, Uwag Komohraag hamlet, comprising the other clans.

It was at Waô kəbik that one day the Yafar saw a plane drop hundreds of leaflets, no doubt announcing the end of the Second World War. A few years later, the same village received the visit of a Dutch administrative patrol, which appointed some village headmen and was never seen again, the border having subsequently been more clearly established (Ch. 15).

10. From Faywe-moog kəbik to New *Sahya* (a new village built close to the first Sahya). The generation of the present-day elders, who were children at the time, took part in this move by the 'female' moiety clans. The Amisneri leave Hwagimp to join their moiety clans at Sahya. No particular reason: just a return to ancestral lands.

11. From Waô kəbik to *Saybəga* (1–2 km to the east, between the present-day hamlets of Yafar 1 and 2). Biyuneri, Ifêêg, Ifêaroog, Sumneri and Amisneri clans found this new hamlet, as Waô kəbik does not have room for the whole group.

12. From Saybəga to *Yihbiy* (very near Saybəga). Saybəga is destroyed by an accidental fire shortly after it is built, and the group establishes a new hamlet nearby, Yihbiy.

13. From New Sahya to *Habrif* (200 m from present-day Yafar 2). The reason for this new move is once again a problem of insecurity in the face of presumed Kumwaag sorcery, particularly on the part of the Muwagneri. The latter are held responsible for the deaths of two Yafar men, whence the revenge by the victims' kinsmen (present generation), who kill a Muwagneri. The murderers hide out for some time in a bush encampment; for reasons of security, other New Sahya Yafar also disperse for a few months, then join forces once more and build Habrif.

14. From Yihbiy to *Hopwan kəbik* and to *Nef*. A quarrel arising from accusations of sorcery following the suspicious deaths of several men initiates the fragmentation of Yihbiy and the founding of two new hamlets, one near by to the west, Hopwan kəbik, corresponding to present-day Yafar 1,[7] and the other several kilometres westward, Nef.

---

7. In 1983, following the 1979–1980 epidemic, this village split.

Hopwan kəbik brings together the Biyuneri, Amisneri and Sumneri clans (except for two men); Nef brings together a group of men from a variety of clans, including Ifêêg, Ifêaroog and Suwê-enunguruk. Nef is sited on land that had been little exploited except for hunting. This hamlet will change place once more for reasons of terrain and will become present-day Yafar 3, the toponym of which is *Sangweri kəbik wa-inaag* 'hamlet in the big forest'.

While Yihbiy was in the process of splitting but still had some Yafar in residence, they were visited by an Australian doctor on patrol in the region, having set out from Abau (present-day Green River, near the Sepik Loop); the Amanab air-strip did not yet exist. This patrol can be dated to 1958. This was the first contact the Yafar had with a representative of the Australian colonial administration.

15. Habrif, for its part, also moved short distances without changing its constituents and is the present-day Yafar 2, the toponym of which is *Okufəgeeg-inaag kəbik* 'hamlet in the bamboo leaves', because of the vast surrounding stands of bamboo.

What do we learn from this list of twenty or so moves over slightly more than a century but highly circumscribed in space, since the furthest are no more than a few kilometres as the crow flies, and several can be measured in hundreds of metres? Such a scale hardly justifies the term migrations, especially since the lands traversed and occupied were already either under Yafar control, or (in the beginning) unoccupied territories, peripheral zones used for occasional hunting expeditions. There is little mention in this recent history of competing for land, of winning or losing territories, or of neighbouring groups fighting over access to resources. The only quarrels arise from accusations of sorcery from inside or outside the Yafar group, and these are determined by ideas about the causes of death and by the way various tribes view each other socially and psychologically. Economic reasons (sago-working or hunting) decide a very few moves, often temporary, which lead the Yafar to settle on the very edges of their territory, beyond which they would no longer be on home ground. During this entire period they were, therefore, in a manner of speaking, prisoners of the region they had – in conditions that must remain unknown – previously brought under their control, and the majority of their moves appear to have been successive readjustments which never brought full satisfaction. In point 8 we see a dispersal of the clans due to social tensions, followed once more by regrouping; the forest environment and the sparse population enable the society to get away from itself and individuals to appease their ill feelings without the group annihilating itself through dispersal or an irreversible break-up. The settlement pattern of the tribal group can be adapted to the social relations of the moment within a relatively fixed space. It is through such mobility that the Yafar seek to resolve their conflicts as well as to satisfy their economic needs. But this moblity is realized only within the framework provided by the territorial boundaries, which ensures economic security through the exclusive control of resources, just as it ensures a relative state of peace through territorial inviolability. This residential dynamic is governed by three factors:

1. natural resources, two categories of which (sago and game) confer privileged status on particular regions;
2. relations with neighbouring tribes, which develop against a backdrop of marriage exchanges and cognatic relations, of need for communication and wariness due to sorcery, entailing alternating closer or more distant contacts between residential units;
3. relations within the tribe, in which conflicts give rise to the final or temporary estrangement of the parties, in this case in the form of the splitting or fragmentation of the local group followed by new groupings.

Gradual population growth could also cause a group to split, but it happened too that the need for protection from neighbouring tribes, in times of strong internal cohesion, dictated the nucleation of hamlets. Recorded Yafar history contains only one such case, that of the first Sahya, which is not without similarity to the stability of clan hamlets in the Waina area already mentioned.

With regard to the fragility of village groups, in which residential solidarity rapidly meets with fragmentation, but where too any excessive or drawn-out dissemination triggers a new *rapprochement*, we may speak only of mobility or instability, in no case of nomadism. Sedentary living remains one of the basic structural features of Yafar economic and social organization:

physical space is not experienced as so many 'circuits' determined by economic needs.

The Confederation

The Yafar do not belong to a confederation, but this type of formation is attested for the Kumwaag[8] immediately to the south, who are made up of four tribes living in five (six as of 1980) hamlets as follows:

Confederation	Tribes	Hamlets*	Population	
			1970	1981
Kumwaag	Aynunkneri	Aynunkneri	119	128
	Muwagneri	Muwagneri	122	120
	Potayneri	Potayneri 1 Potayneri 2 (split in 1980)	245	216
	Gefayneri	Gefayneri	96	103
			582	567

* Through administrative usage, group names have become the names of hamlets. The Kumwaag used to employ toponyms, now infrequently used.

Table 3. Composition of the Kumwaag confederation

Each new tribe (and sometimes each hamlet) is divided into moieties, and each moiety into submoieties. Old clan segments engender independent lineages, which are renamed. The confederation is the outgrowth of a twofold phenomenon of expansion and segmentation, in the course of which the new local groups gain their autonomy. The choice of new names and the demarcation of separate territories give rise to new tribes within the confederation. This process entails a loss of cohesion, which in turn engenders subgroups, each of which has the same status as the original community. And yet at the same time something of this community subsists: the original name remains, as well as the feeling of belonging to a single unit. The Aynunkneri and the

8. There seemed to be a similar confederation south of the Amanab station by the name of Kubranag.

Muwagneri still share the same dual organization (see Ch. 2), whereas the Potayneri and the Gefayneri have each set up their own dual structure.

The confederation is the most encompassing form of organization that an Eri group can attain. Any larger, and one can only imagine the elements of cohesion and unity gradually weakening until no trace of them is left.

The limit of group expansion will obviously not be the same in other regions; it is kept low in this case not only by factors leading to fragmentation (conflicts or need for vacant land), but also by absence of the need for continual defense against invaders. Tuzin (1976) has shown that the Abelam threat to the Ilahita Arapesh territory was the reason for the complexification of the latter's dual system and their high population levels. The Yafar and their neighbours, on the other hand, evolved spatially on partially unexploited lands, often maintaining a respectable geographical distance between themselves and their neighbours or removing themselves from them, not turning over their lands with regret but leaving them due to conflicts or epidemics. The back-and-forth movement we have described, alternating between the loosening and tightening of social bonds, does nothing to promote the gradual construction of an ever more structured group. What the Yafar, or the other Border Mountains societies, have lacked in order to become less atomized are historical imperatives, threats of dispersal or destruction, demographic pressures from within or without.

Intertribal Identity and Mythology

The myth that opens this chapter tells of cutting down the original iron tree, *gungwe* (*Intsia palembanica*), in which Oög-angô, 'Melon-Woman', would take refuge when she was menstruating; she was fleeing the grotesque attentions of Abunung, the husband of her husband Wefroog. After one struggle, the cross cousin, a clever culture-hero and a bit of a rogue but vulnerable as well, 'dies' from blows received from Abunung, a strong but stupid man. With the aim of capturing Oög-angô (who always escapes in the end), Abunung calls upon the men of the region to chop down the tree. As it falls to the ground, it divides mankind into separate groups, into tribes that will take up residence in different territories. However, the secret exegesis of this myth adds that, besides containing blood in the wood, the *gungwe* tree also grew alongside other plants, primarily the coconut palm and the *Calamus* liana, forming a primordial set of plants, so to speak. It is the fall of the iron tree, a 'male' species, that serves as a discriminating agent for tribal identities, but it is the coconut palm, vegetal incarnation of the Great Mother, that provides the Waina and northern Eri tribes and villages with a unity sealed by matrilineal descent.

In effect, society or the village – sometimes fused into one – are shown in a distinctly feminine light and are linked by symbolic ties of consanguinity, in the sense that each tribe is assumed to have come from a part of the coconut palm, the flower or the petiolar fibre, and that the 'mother' palm herself or her *hoofuk* (reproductive principle: see Ch. 9) gave birth to the Umeda. Several nearby groups, including the Yafar, are called the 'daughters' of Umeda. Although our version of the myth does not mention the actual fall of the coconut palm, it would seem that, following an implicit episode, the flowers of the palm, scattered by the shock, each came to mark the site of a tribal group, or better still engendered it. The flowers are differentiated according to their place on the spadix (*wamuroog*). The names of certain societies are reminiscent of this totemic origin: Wamuru (*wamuroog*); Umeda or *umere*, which may refer to a Waina term for 'spadix'; Kumwaag, from *kumôg*: 'to hide or bury a seed', because the coconut flower from which this group stems is said to have lain hidden under the dead leaves before being 'discovered'; the same image also applies to the Yafar, even though the name does not reveal this. Certain names of Waina-speaking hamlets (at least the 'female' moieties,[9] see Ch. 2) make reference to the same representation; this is the case for the Sinai (Gell 1975), which the Yafar call *sig-aynaag*, that is to say 'at the tip' (of the spadix). We shall see elsewhere (Ch. 3) that a similar representation provides a link between certain Yafar clans.

The same tribes are also supposed to have 'received' or to have come from or to have been symbolically contained in the petiolar fibre of the coconut palm, *bǝsa* (a vegetal metaphor for the uterus): the Waina and Yafar are *hoofuk bǝsa*, fresh vegetal fibre,

---

9. 'Male'-moiety hamlets are affiliated with the totem of the mythic sago palm (Ch. 2).

pliable and next to the heart of the palm, while the Babuk are precisely *babuk bəsa*, 'old, hard fibre', perhaps because they are geographically more distant from the Umeda.

Lastly, another, even more secret version has the tribes of the northern Eri-Waina zone being born directly from the bones of the divided body of the Original Cosmic Mother (who died in the act of giving birth). The Umeda are said to come from her skull, the other groups from her long bones or from her backbone.

The dominant metaphorical reference to the coconut palm inflorescence makes it possible to unite into one identity the various identities of each tribal group. The inflorescence is the perfect image of both unification (but also dispersal) and reproduction or growth. Yet this unity, validated solely by the myth, does not afford grounds for the formation of what I have called a 'confederation'; the latter is the product of a historical process. However, it does foster a sentiment of cultural identity and a hierarchy of descent centred on the Umeda, the 'mother' group, guardians of the place where, in the beginning, the mythic coconut palm sprang up. This imaginary relationship takes on a concrete existence in the form of prohibitions linking the interested tribes; in the main, these rules concern relations between 'daughter' groups and the 'mother'. For instance, the Umeda on the one hand and several 'daughter' groups on the other are linked by sexual prohibitions (a man must never see a girl's sexual parts, which could happen when adolescent girls used to go naked until their first period) and by prohibitions on marriage and killing; nor could they exchange coconuts sprouted for planting, nor sago palm shoots (the totems of the two moieties; see Ch. 2), nor petiolar fibre from the coconut palm (used in constructing masks). A man from one group may not dig, sink a post (for construction, etc.) or plant either of the two species above on the land of another group. Lastly, conversing about sacred subjects is forbidden between these groups. These prohibitions make symbolic reference to reproduction and to blood (in the case of murder, people say that the blood spilled in the two groups would mix and set off torrential rains and epidemics). Some of these taboos apply between 'sister' groups (especially to marriage between certain Waina-speaking groups: Ch. 10). This is the case with the Sowanda, with whom the Yafar do not marry but with whom murder and exchange were allowed and were even intense, the Punda, with whom the Yafar marry and fight but where they may not dig the ground, and several neighbouring groups, with whom the Yafar may not exchange sprouted coconuts or sago shoots (see also Map 4).

The Yafar Village

The foregoing is already one definition of the residential group, the Yafar hamlet. But to this dynamic view must be added a description of the village space, first of all in its natural framework and then with respect to its social and cosmological organization.

Site

Topographically, the village or hamlet (*kəbik*) always stands on a rise. Unlike some southern Eri groups or the Anggor, whose land is more broken and who build their hamlets on steep ridges and therefore often far from waterways, the Yafar prefer a moderate elevation near a river and therefore also near stands of sago palms (Figure 3). The village area consists of a beaten-earth surface (*kəbik bəte*) on which the dwellings are constructed and at the centre of which a space (*mosuwaag*, from *mosuwô* 'navel') is cleared. Around this inhabited zone lies an orchard (*magigam*): at the foot of the houses and below the front porches facing outward from the village circle stands first of all a band of coconut palms, then areca palms (*Areca catechu*), together with some ornamental plants; further from the houses, the orchard is planted with breadfruit trees, pandanus and semi-cultivated species such as the *Ficus copiosa*. Grass is allowed to grow freely, care only being taken to prevent secondary spontaneous vegetation from taking hold. The orchard ends – at a distance of between several and twenty metres from the houses – with a narrow band of secondary vegetation or short bamboo, often already interspersed with sago palms, which form a transition to the forest proper. Since contact, some Yafar have begun making small gardens in the immediate vicinity of the village.

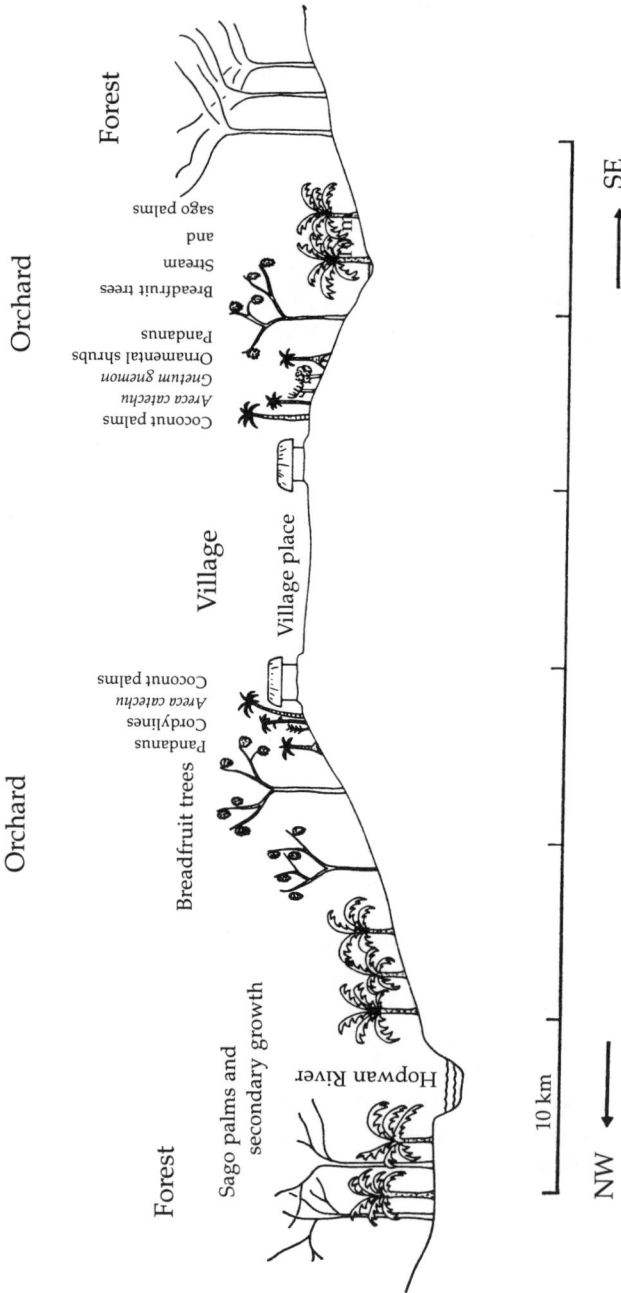

Figure 3. Cross-section of Yafar 1, Hopwan kəbik

The Village: Local Group

The homogeneity of the village comes from sharing a single space which is the site of social life and exceptional activities such as the public rites which, depending on their importance, involve only the local community or bring together the inhabitants of neighbouring hamlets, both Yafar and, less frequently, non-Yafar. In the latter case, they are always related to at least one of the host group's lineages. It does not often happen that visitors from other Yafar villages – and even less those from neighbouring tribes – spend the night with their hosts, something that is only imaginable between kin. The village group thus presents a high degree of social stability.

Mildly collective forms of daily communication take place in the morning before each family sets off into the forest, and more particularly in the evening, after the main meal, when the men gather at the foot of one of the houses and the women somewhere else. Between these two times, the hamlet is simply a place that is orderly (houses shut, stair-poles pulled up), but empty. The community disperses into family groups or lone individuals; moreover, visual communication between individuals is impossible because of the thick vegetation. The village thus appears as the centre of a twofold movement, centrifugal in the morning and centripetal in the evening, alternately pushing its members out to the periphery, only to pull them in again afterwards. For them, the forest is above all a daytime place of production but it also ensures the intimacy of couples and sometimes rest at night (under the garden shelter), while the village is a place of consumption, of sociality and of mainly nighttime rest.

Aside from the fact that it is obviously a residential group and stands at the centre of a tract of land exploited for the most part by the residents, the Yafar village (and Eri villages in general) is of no sociological significance unless it constitutes a tribe on its own. We have seen that the village can move, split or join with another unit, and its members can freely decide to take up residence in another Yafar hamlet. Social unity persists in spite of these modifications. The clans themselves are often divided between two or even three hamlets. During the time I spent in the field, each of the three Yafar villages had representatives of both moieties and thus each reproduced the unity of the dual organization, but this had not always been the case. In fact, residence and cultivating rights go hand in hand: a man lives in a

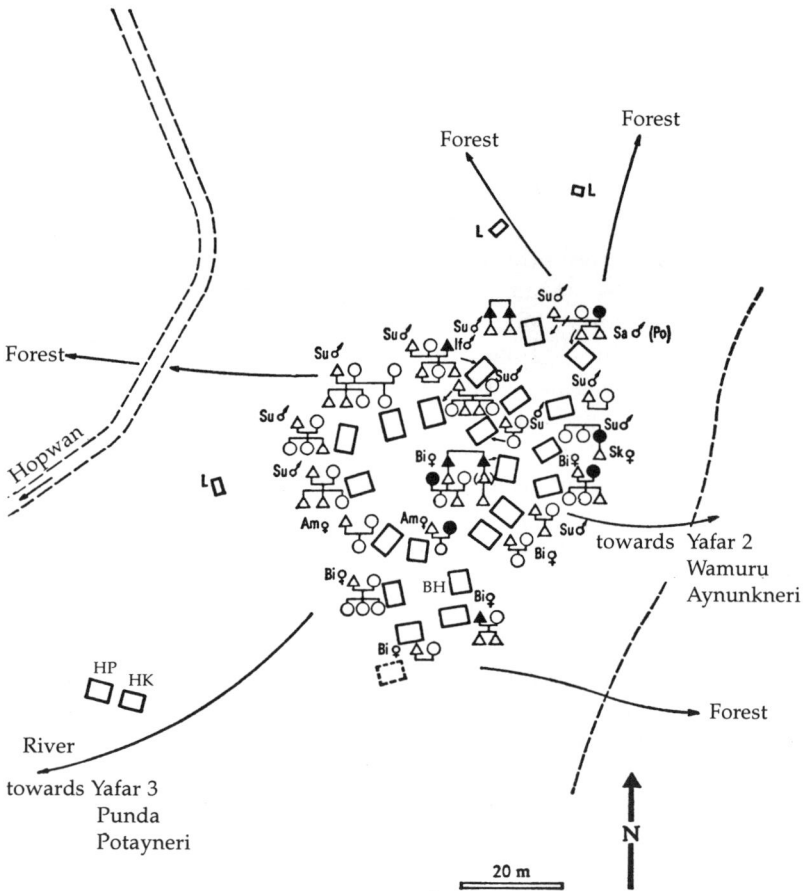

Figure 4. Ground plan of Yafar 1, Hopwan kəbik

Plate 1. Yafar 3 (Sangwer-inaag kəbik) in the 1970s (Photo Juillerat, Musée de l'Homme collection)

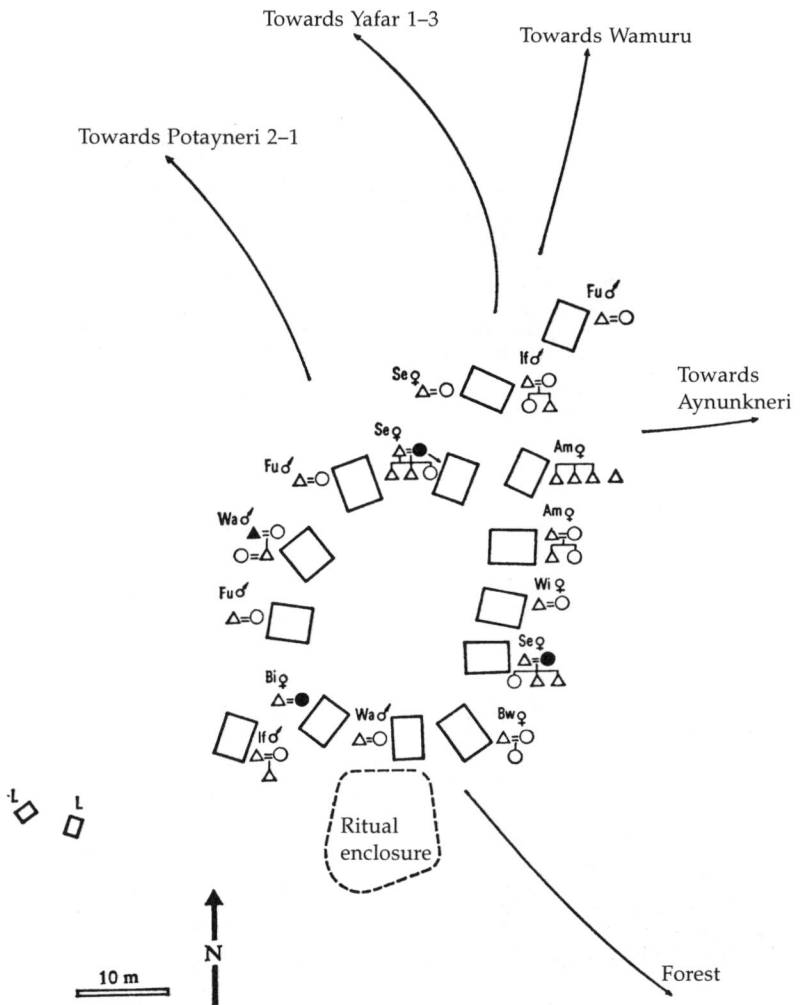

Figure 5. Ground plan of Yafar 2, Okufəge-inaag kəbik

certain village because he was born there, because he came there as a child with his widowed mother or because he had been orphaned and was adopted by a kinsman. At the same time he received rights to the land, and once these rights were realized and materialized in the form of trees and gardens, his residence became stable.

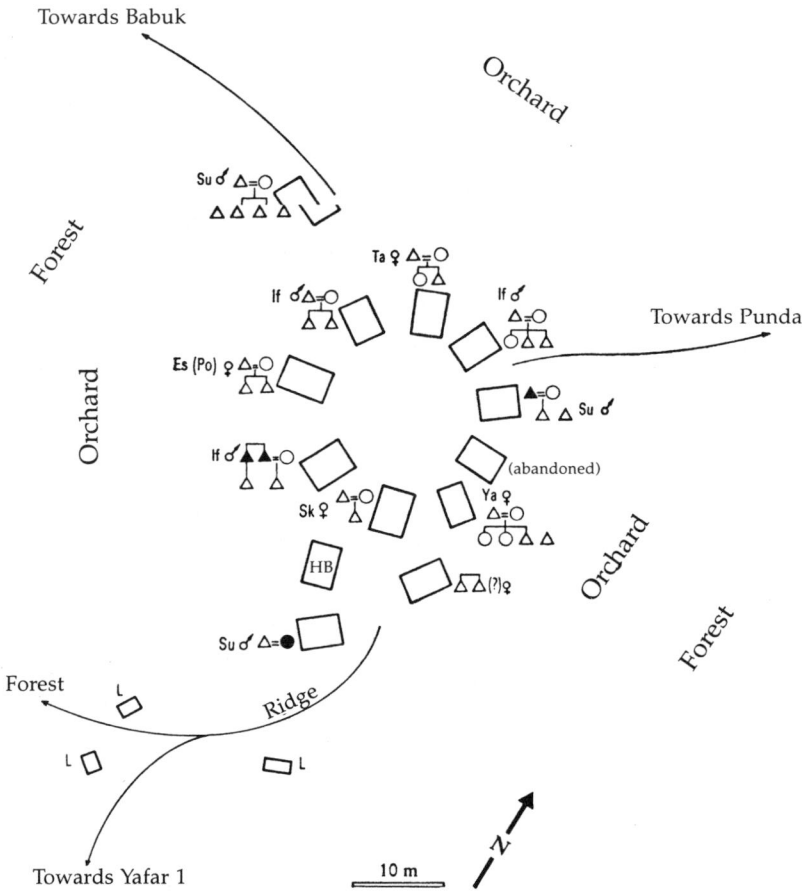

Figure 6. Ground plan of Yafar 3, Sangweri-wa-inaag kəbik

In principle each dwelling houses a nuclear family or a numerically equivalent household (Ch. 4). The fifteen to twenty-five houses in a village are not grouped by clan or submoiety, and only roughly by moiety. By performing the Yangis ritual – founded on the expression of an exoteric knowledge shared for the most part between the local Master of the Sky and the Master of the Earth and on ritual cooperation between the men of the two moieties – the village restores a form of socialized cosmic unity, conceived as the meeting and fusion of the male and female principles (Ch. 2).

The Sociocosmology of the Village

One myth uses the two primordial trees, the iron tree, *gungwe*, and the coconut palm, *sa*, to explain how the village is seen as the union of the two sexual principles: the male iron tree is central, in the sense that it provides the stilts that underpin the houses, while with its flowers, its fruits and especially its petiolar fibres, the coconut tree is the metaphor of the female principle and of the Great Mother, of whom it is the totemic incarnation. But both trees are in turn made up of a male part, the trunk, and a female part, the leaves and fruit. This myth posits first of all the incompatibility of the sexes, wherein the female principle, which engenders decay, degrades and contaminates the male principle; whence the failure of this first attempt at coresidence, followed by a second initiative, in which the iron tree divests itself of its female characteristics, and each of the two plants assumes a specific place and function in the hamlet. The first recipe, in which every species was both male and female, was doomed to failure, whereas the second is tantamount to a sexual differentiation which inaugurates a residential order that cuts across the natural order.

> On the site where the village of Sahya was to stand (see above), before there were any trees at all, there stood the penis of the primordial god, W. . ., which had sprung from the earth. Later, when the different species of primordial trees had appeared, the iron tree found the spot good, and established himself there. He sent for the coconut palm, who lived in the bush, to come and join him. Next came a few other species, including the *bêêbi* liana (*Calamus* sp.). But one long night a storm blew all the leaves from the trees. The iron tree decided that the site was spoiled by the leaves decaying on the ground, and he returned to the bush, followed by the other trees. Later he came back, first alone and without his leaves (*gungwe kêg* 'bones of the iron tree'), and then he sent for the coconut palm. This time the iron tree became the stilts of the house and he commanded the coconut palm to stay outside, in front of the doorway to the dwelling and around the edges of the village. The coconut palm

(comprised of its male trunk, *sa kêg*, and female petiolar tissue, *bəsa*) gave the forest iron tree some of its *bəsa* (i.e. the female part he was lacking). And so, later, the children of the iron tree married the children of the coconut palm.

The inscription of the village within a wider cosmic space can be seen even more clearly in the myth and ritual for the founding of a new hamlet. The village grounds need to be cleared, wrested from the forest, before any construction can begin. This first phase in the founding of a village corresponds to the symbolic register of the Mother Earth (forest), the womb from which one day all the game came forth (see p. 183).

Before the clearing begins, the men and women shave the sides of their head and bathe one last time. As they uproot the first shrub, the men sing to encourage the game to come and to favour its capture, and they evoke encounters with forest spirits. Then they clear and burn off the selected area. During the burning, other spells are pronounced to prevent the smoke and ash obscuring the hunters' vision, which would keep them from finding game (Ch. 7). The whole zone is cleared and levelled, except for a small mound left in the middle of what will become the village square.

During the construction of the houses, the men leave for a day to hunt wild pig, but the kill is left in the bush. Everyone then washes and shaves for the first time since beginning work, then the men (with the exception of the two village founders, *reeg* and *awaag*; see below) go into the bush, taking with them their ornaments, to butcher the animal. When they return, the decorated hunters, their portion of the meat slung over their shoulder, remove the rest of the earth in the centre of the village using ritual tools (areca or sago sticks, pig-bone spatulas); more hunting spells are chanted. Last of all the wooden trumpets and the drums are played before cooking and consuming part of the meat.

The rites of clearing and the prohibitions on cutting any plant, on shaving or washing, refer to the notion of fertility, which for the Yafar is associated with the sub-soil or maternal *hoofuk* (fertility principle): to clear or clean ('peal', *roof*, in the words of the magic spells) the ground is to accede to the growth principle or to enable it to reach the surface. To abstain from shaving or pulling even a blade of grass is to place a taboo on the fertility of the cosmos. To turn the soil, to penetrate it with digging sticks, is to fertilize the earth or open up passages where the sleepers' 'self' may stray. The reproduction of game and hunting are closely linked with this autochthonous fertility, and several rites, besides the myth cited above, attest to this. The entire period during which the new village is being established bears the stamp of this idea of fertility associated with hunting and is closed by the resumption of hunting. The collective act of the male community performed at this time, the removal of the mound, the last vestige of the natural world replaced by a social world, may be seen as an act of separation from nature, that is from the Mother; let us not forget that the place is called the 'village navel' and that the mound, called *kəbik bêwuk*, 'pointed end' or 'top of the village', seems to symbolize the umbilical cord that attaches the productive earth to the local community it receives. The return to the Mother supposed by any new village foundation (clearing, working the ground, thus access to the maternal *hoofuk*) must be followed by a rite of separation. Thus the community is reborn each time from the new village soil, from which it then breaks away through a ritual hunt in which the game is seen as a gift from the Mother Earth.

Once the ground has been prepared, the houses are constructed in a prescribed order and in accordance with both cosmological and social references. Let us look first of all at the cosmological aspect.

> Until then people lived in makeshift shelters in the bush. One day Wam, son of Tapi, decided to build a village. He tried to drive an ironwood (*gungwe kêg*) post into the ground, but it would not stand up and kept falling over. Wam's mother asked her husband to help their son. And so Tapi dug a trench under the ironwood post, crawled in and offered his back (*Tapi na rumuri-kêg*, 'Tapi's backbone') to the stake point. The father's back hurt; Wam took a dried coconut-palm rib (*sa gingêk*) and slipped it along the top of his father's backbone. The post now stands firm.[10]

The tip of this palm rib, called *say efreeg*[11] ('tail of the coconut tree'), comes up out of the ground at Hubwiy (the westernmost village of Yafar affines, in Irian Jaya), and its base, called *say mesoog* or *say kawuk* ('head' or 'jaw of the coconut tree'), is located in

10. This myth is analyzed in its complete version in Juillerat 1991: Ch. 1.

11. *Say* is the ritual name of the *sa* coconut palm. The pointed posts of Wam's house are imagined as coming back out of the earth in the west ('tail of the coconut palm') and as being surrounded by primordial magic plants.

Befan village, the easternmost group of affines (Figures 7 and 8, Map 2). The Yafar are 'in the middle' (*öruk-inaag*, 'at the heart') or 'in the middle of the backbone' (*rumuri-kêĝ na öruk-ya*). The underground pathway constituted in this manner is used by the sun and the moon to return to the east (*wos-ii akba-ii na məna*, 'the path of the moon and the sun') in their heavenly course from east to west, they follow a parallel pathway marked by the *bêêbi* liana. In the morning the sun climbs in the east along its young prickly leafy branches, in the evening sliding in the west down along its smooth stalk. On either side of the *bêêbi* run two more slender vines, *fag-we*[12] and *ogafəfa*, which form the path of the moon.

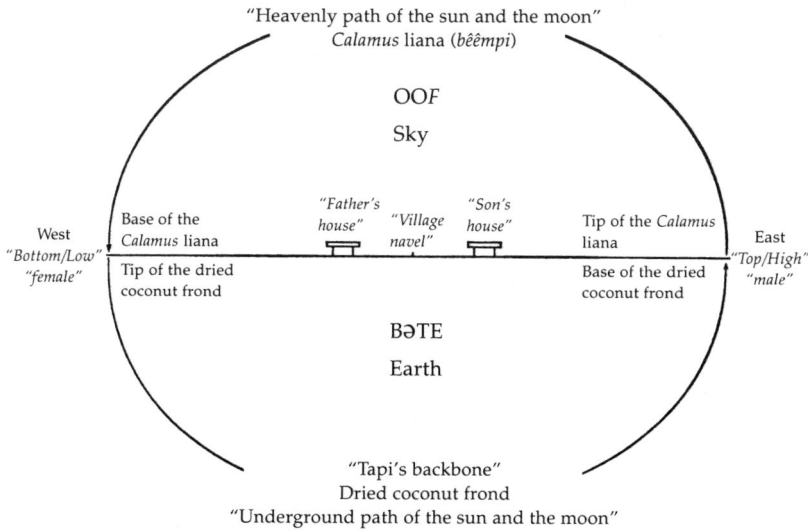

"Heavenly path of the sun and the moon"
Calamus liana (*bêêmpi*)

OOF

Sky

	"Father's house"	"Village navel"	"Son's house"	
West "Bottom/Low" "female"	Base of the *Calamus* liana			Tip of the *Calamus* liana
	Tip of the dried coconut frond			Base of the dried coconut frond

East "Top/High" "male"

BƏTE

Earth

"Tapi's backbone"
Dried coconut frond
"Underground path of the sun and the moon"

Figure 7. Cross-section of the village and territorial space in its cosmological representation

Thus the village is inscribed on an east-west axis, which constitutes its 'backbone', itself part of a much vaster cosmic body in which the rib of the coconut frond given to the father by the son structures and, as it were, solidifies the Mother Earth's body,

12. Rattan, which is used for bowstrings, literally 'arrow tie'.

while at the same time marking the renewal of male vitality through patriliny. The mother's role in the myth is also a sign of her function as mediator between father and son: it is through her, in effect, that male descent is ensured. But the east is also associated with the top, *ga-gam* or *mesoa-gam* (*mesoog* 'head'), and with the Son, *reeg*, whereas the west represents the bottom, *moa-gam* or *mwig-gam* (*moog* 'base'), and the Father, *awaag*; it is also the son, Wam, who sets the posts in the east, while his father makes his way underground by way of the west to go and solidify the maternal earth, which is too soft (*bəte eyuwawk* 'weak earth'). But this body also needs flanks, designated by the term *efêfêy* (or *efêfêyik*), corresponding in terms of human anatomy to either side of the waist, below the ribs, that soft part made of flesh alone, which needs to be consolidated by a bony framework; that is why the north and south flanks of a village, or more precisely the iron-wood posts of the two houses that stand there, are called, by metaphor, 'coconut ribs' *say na angmang-kêg*. In the words of a saying: 'Flesh without bones is bound to rot'.

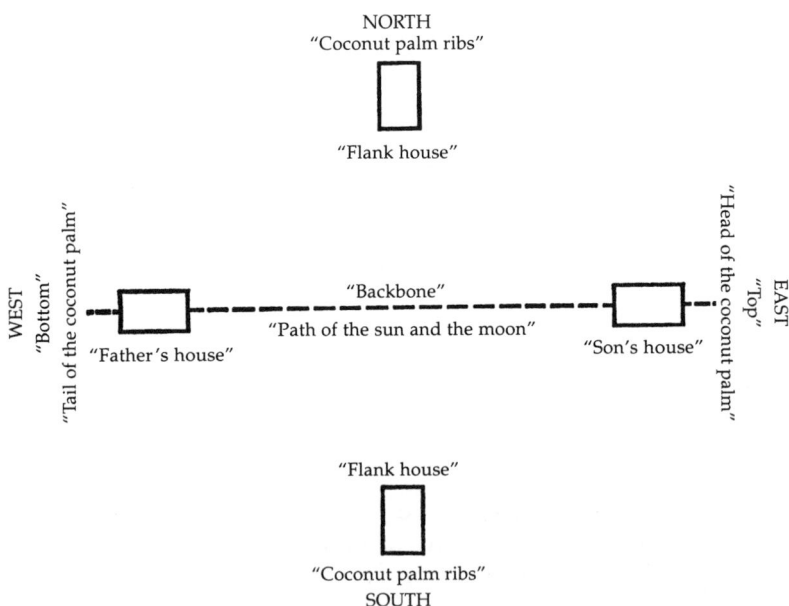

Figure 8. Ground plan of the village in its cosmological representation

Sexual differentiation, filiation and the succession of generations, key ideas found on numerous levels of Yafar culture,[13] are symbolically projected not only on to the universe, but also on to the social organization of the village space. Later we shall see that the clans are distributed between the 'male' and 'female' moieties and between the 'elder' and 'younger' submoieties. The disposition of the houses in the hamlet follows the same order, with certain lineages playing specific symbolic roles in the construction of the founding houses (those built at the cardinal points and on the parts of the village 'body' just discussed).

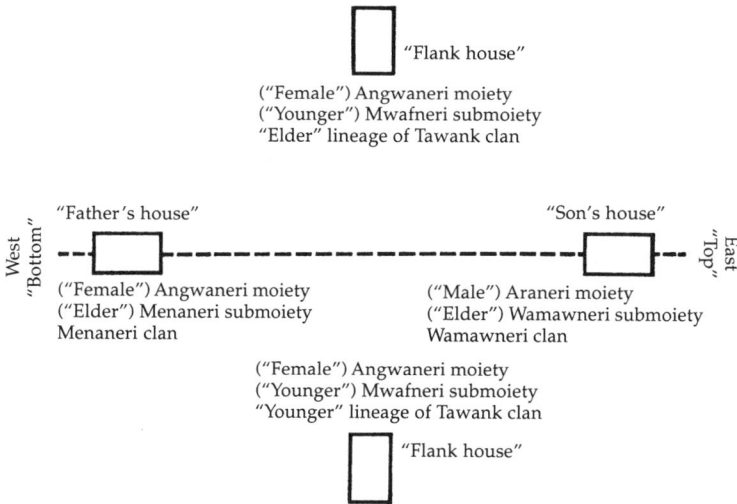

"Flank house"

("Female") Angwaneri moiety
("Younger") Mwafneri submoiety
"Elder" lineage of Tawank clan

West "Bottom"

"Father's house"

("Female") Angwaneri moiety
("Elder") Menaneri submoiety
Menaneri clan

"Son's house"

East "Top"

("Male") Araneri moiety
("Elder") Wamawneri submoiety
Wamawneri clan

("Female") Angwaneri moiety
("Younger") Mwafneri submoiety
"Younger" lineage of Tawank clan

"Flank house"

Figure 9. Ground plan of the village in its sociological representation

Accordingly, the first dwelling of a new village should be built to the east, by a man from Wamawneri lineage ('male' moiety, 'elder' submoiety; see Table 4, p. 77) – also regarded as the founding lineage of Yafar society; this man stands for the Son. When this 'Son's house' (*reeg na raara*) has been lived in (ideally when the inside has become blackened with soot), a man from Menaneri lineage ('female, elder') builds his own house, called the 'Father's house' (*awaag na raara*), at the other end of the cleared grounds. Then the other families and clans proceed to build their houses beside and behind the first two, leaving the centre of the

13. See, for example, Ch. 9, 'The social modalities of female pollution'.

grounds free. Finally the two lineages of the 'female, younger' Tawank clan build the last two founding houses, called *efêfêyik* (the 'flank houses'), one to the north (the 'elder' lineage), the other to the south (the 'younger' lineage) (Figure 9), aided in this by the other men of the female moiety. For each lineage involved, it is the heir to the office who inherits the role of founder; in Chapters 3 and 13 we shall see that these responsibilities can be taken over by a line from another patrilineal group if the elected line is not represented in the village or has died out. In the latter case, the office passes to a sister's son or to the son of a woman of a lineage of the same moiety.

As we saw in the myth cited above, the symbolic Father/Son relationship (which the Yafar term inversely *reeg/awaag* ('son/ father') expresses the continuity of male descent, illustrated by patrivirilocality, in which a married son first lives with his father and mother for a few years, even if he already has a child, and then builds his own house, where he will later take in his widowed father (or mother). It is also this taking over that is expressed by the symbolic placing of the Son on the side of the rising sun, the 'top' and the male moiety, while the father retires from the familial and social scene by identifying himself with the setting sun, the 'bottom', femaleness, and by renouncing his role as head of the family. While the orbit of the sun is the spatial mediator of the Son/Father relationship, the sun appears in the following myth as a precious good which an isolated son fears he will lose, but which father and son together can keep safe. When we come to examine solar symbolism in the context of religious offices (Ch. 13), the interpretation of this text will be further enriched, for it is meant to do more than simply legitimize the place of the two founding clans in Yafar cosmology.

> Kuwô, the 'father' (ancestor of Menaneri clan, 'female' moiety), lives in Sahya. His 'son' Wamaw[14] (ancestor and founder of Wamawneri clan, 'male' moiety) goes to live in a house at the foot of Hayif Hill, on the Mwasya River. He is the guardian of the 'net bag of the sun' (trophy of the Master of the Sun, see Ch. 13), but he is afraid that Aynunk, Gefay, Muwaag and Botay (founding ancestors of the Kumwaag tribes) will make off with it. He talks the matter over with

---

14. Kuwô and Wamaw appear as a replication of Tapi and Wam in the earlier myth. The fact that they are the founders of two different patriclans endows their relationship with a dimension that is more symbolic than genealogical.

Kuwô, who offers to found a village with him and to help him guard the Sun's netbag. They sink the ironwood posts, the son to the east, the father to the west.

The iron tree, especially in the form of a post (*gungwe kêg*), is a symbol of the Son (house), the Father being represented meta-phorically by the primordial *afwêêg* sago palm (forest) and the Mother by the coconut palm (village): 'Our Father is far away in the forest, but our Mother stays in the village.' The black sap, *sibi*, of the iron tree is seen to be its blood or *hoofuk*, its vital repro-ductive principle, and when the first ironwood post is set up at the founding of a new hamlet, the men of Wamawneri clan all take hold of it and shout first the name of the mythic hero – 'Wam *sibi hoofuk!*' – and then the Father's *hoofuk*, and finally that of the *efêfêyik*, which will be called upon for the corresponding houses when the other end and the flanks of the village space are closed. In setting the posts, the men are implanting the skeleton of the prostrate maternal body which is the village, but they are also stopping up the invisible holes in the earth that correspond to the entrances to the underground passage opened up by Tapi; this is why the men of the respective lineages shout as they work 'Close the jaws of the coconut palm' for the Son's house, and 'Close the tail of the coconut palm' for the Father's house. This is a magical operation that belongs to the *Gungwan* ritual (Ch. 12), the function of which is to keep the sleepers' self from wandering off into the underground world, a world of ghosts but especially the place where the original Mother's *hoofuk* is kept. Within the boundaries of the village grounds, between these poles of the cosmic skeleton, lies the village with its belly of bare ground, which indeed seems to evoke the maternal womb, where the father is changed into the son.

Thus the Yafar village is at the same time the locus and object of the sociopolitical and economic vicissitudes, to which it adapts itself through strategies of mobility and restructuring, and the reflection of a cosmic order, of which it is the socialized mini-aturization. Even when fragmented, the tribe recreates the same configuration in each of its settlements, where the limits of the universe correspond to the limits of the surrounding social space and where the oedipal triangle is inscribed non-conflictually in the succession of generations represented by the path of the

Plate 2. Hunter wearing chest and nose decorations made from wild boar tusks; he is carrying some *Salaginella* branches in his left hand and magic rhizomes in his right.

sun. This is not a purely poetic representation; its full meaning becomes clear only when one realizes that Yafar mental representations reduce the social on the one hand (the Wam myth) to a complicity on the part of the parental couple, which enables the Son to take over from the Father, and on the other hand (the village foundation) to the continuity of male filiation (east-Son→west-Father) through the mediation of the Mother Earth (see also Juillerat 1992b). The foundation of a Yafar village reproduces the moment when Wam, the Son, attempted to create culture, represented by the original house (*reeg na raara*), on the body of the Earth, which to begin with was still too soft; he succeeded only because of the Father's[15] 'sacrifice' or, to put it another way, because of the Son's recognition of his twofold filiation. This is in all likelihood the meaning of the myth: that society is a male invention but is still founded on this triangular relation, that the social is inscribed in nature, like a solidification of the cosmic female body, by cooperation between Son and Father.

But the Yafar village and society are also the deployment of the two natural principles which preside over this representation of social production: the male and the female, free of any ties of descent, but captured in their complementary function. This is more particularly what is expressed by their dual organization.

---

15. The rib of the fallen coconut frond in fact represents the failing Father. The continuously renewed frond is the manifestation of a regenerated male principle (vertical growth).

2

Dual Organization

To perform a rite is to recall the myth that goes with it. Without the rite, the myth is lost, it's forgotten.

(Conversation with May Promp, 1981)

Dual structures are one of the recurring features of Melanesian societies. Their totemic character can be obvious or not clearly attested, the complexity of their structure is variable, and their social function in the systems of marriage, exchanges and initiation more or less dominant. Lowie has already remarked on the diversity of the areas in which dual organization is found, but Lévi-Strauss refuses to see so many institutions. For him dual organization is 'above all, a principle of organization capable of varying widely and, in particular admitting of more or less elaborated applications' (1967: 87); but the basic nature of the principle remains unchanged and has to do with 'certain fundamental structures of the human mind, rather than [with] some privileged region of the world or [with] a certain period in the history of civilization' (ibid.). Tuzin (1976) takes the opposite view and, on the basis of a study of a Lower Sepik society, sees dual organization as the product of local history, in this case society's defensive and unifying reaction to the threat of dislocation emanating from neighbouring societies. Somewhere between formalism and historical determinism, however, there is room in the theoretical field for a determination that is both empirical and conceptual, in which symbolized experience is reproduced in the social structure. It is in the very least to this order of causality, in which the sociological sphere and the elaboration of reciprocity are posterior, that the Yafar lead us.

The Yafar are subdivided into two moieties marked respectively as 'male' and 'female'. Each of these moieties – which have no generic designation in the vernacular – contains a number of patriclans, as shown in Table 4 (Ch. 3). An individual thus belongs to one moiety or the other by the intermediary of his clan or lineage, but this does not make the moieties descent groups. Furthermore, a clan cannot be divided between the two moieties nor can it change moieties. If one moiety is much smaller, a redistribution not of clans but of men takes place, and only on the occasion of the Yangis festival, the chief and almost unique circumstance in which the moieties enter into effective cooperation. This redistribution of members is accomplished by dividing the brothers of a family between the two moieties, large families being able to give every other son to the moiety to which they originally belonged. Such redistribution is purely pragmatic (not structural) and only temporary.

Within each moiety, the constituent clans are further broken down into two submoieties, marked respectively as 'elder' and 'younger' sibling. This second-level subdivision is less evident than the first, and the Yafar never volunteer its existence. Moreover they regard submoieties as what we would call phratries, or even clans,[1] and their names are patronyms or matronyms which sometimes correspond to the name of the submoiety's founding clan. My investigation has shown that these units were nevertheless the product of a formal bipartite division of the moieties which, working together with the dualism of the first level, reflect on the whole a cross-cutting dual system in which the two axes of bipartition intersect at right angles. We shall see, when we come to the subject of marriage, to what extent the four submoieties can be considered exogamous groups and perhaps even marriage classes that have lost their function.[2]

1. Another way of classifying Yafar social units would be to call the submoieties 'clans' and the clans 'subclans'. The original exogamy of the submoieties, as posited by the Yafar, would support this. Nevertheless, I have opted for the term 'submoiety', given the bipartition of the gendered moieties according to their symbolic age-rank (elder/younger submoieties) which, like the criterion of gender, practically dictates dualism.

2. See also Juillerat 1981. Social structures based on four groups are frequent in Melanesia, but they may be determined by a variety of social or representational factors. As in this instance, they often seem to be the outcome of a twofold dualism; see, for example, Sahlins 1976.

The First Level of Yafar Dualism: Reproduction and Moieties

The moiety system I am about to describe is not restricted to the Yafar. With certain variants, it appears in all Eri groups, with the exception, it seems, of the southern villages, where a short stay in 1971 turned up nothing of this kind. Moieties having the same names are found among the Waina (Gell 1975). Dual structures also seem to exist further north, no doubt among the Walsa (Imonda area) and further to the east among the Bembi (Fas) and perhaps in the Sepik drainage plain at the foot of the Bewani Range. On the other hand, no mention is made of moieties in the Torricellis. Nor do Huber (1973) or Peter (1990) say anything about moieties in the areas they studied south of the Border Mountains.

Elsewhere in Melanesia, the moieties that do exist are often designated by the names of natural species or by proper names. Eschewing ambiguity, the Yafar and their neighbours call their moieties respectively 'of the Men' and 'of the Women'. In effect, Araneri breaks down into *ara na êri* or (according to other informants) *ara na ruwar*, respectively 'people of the Man' or 'children of the Man', and Angwaneri into *angô na êri* or *angô na ruwar*, 'people' or 'children of the Woman'.[3] For the sake of convenience, however, I will call these two units the 'male moiety' and the 'female moiety'.

The subdivision of society into two symbolically gendered units is grounded in cosmogonic mythology, which also determines a similar distribution of certain cosmic elements and natural species. The world was born from the activation of the sexual principles, which were the starting point, the *primum mobile* of the organization of the universe and of life. The mythic tale begins by presenting male and female as primordial beings and their coupling as the primal act. Versions vary, however, contradicting each other on certain points and all the more in that each is conserved in the secret lore of a small male elite. This knowledge is identical for the two moieties, but Araneri seems to emphasize the anthropomorphic divine couple, or even the anteriority of the

---

3. We also find the forms Aratuwar and Angwatuwar, derived from the terms used by Waina-speaking groups, who call their moieties Ertôr and Angwatôr (Edtodna and Angwatodna according to Gell's transcriptions [1975]; the *–na* suffix marks the genitive form). *Ara* is not attested on its own and appears as a segment related to *êri*.

god with respect to his companion (version *a*), while the Ang-waneri experts underscore the prime importance of the Mother Coconut as the first entity. The two versions below were provided by the same Araneri man at an interval of three years. The first presents the male as primordial, anterior to the female who proceeds from him, while the second stresses the parallel existence from the outset of the two divinities and emphasizes their couplings and 'labours'.

a) In the beginning, in the void and the darkness, there was only the god W. . . .[4] With his semen, with which he coated the top of his head, he raised the celestial vault above him, then, with the same substance, he created a semblance of earth beneath his feet. Next he circumcised himself; his foreskin became two coconut petiolar fibres, *bəsa*, sewn together (today these are the painted part of the ceremonial Yangis masks), which he painted (in all likelihood with body substances) and inside of which he copulated. From this copulation was born the mother goddess B. . ., also represented as a coconut palm.[5] A piece cut from W's. . . penis later changed into an *afwêêg* sago palm.

b) At first, W. . . and B. . . were separate. They drifted about in the void and the winds (*fufwêyik*, from *fufwêy* 'wind'). There were no earth or stars. W. . . caught sight of B. . . and called to her. They coupled for the first time. With a bit of his thick black semen (*hwis kêfutuk*, 'thick semen'), W. . . made a fragile frame. This was beginning of the Earth.[6] This first framework was called 'spider web' (*abwamsow raara*, '*abwamsow* 'spider's house'). It shook in the wind and tilted first to one side, then to the other. W. . . and B. . . coupled again and the spider web became hard. W. . . smeared his skull with his semen and raised the celestial vault above his head. He coupled several more times with B. . . and each time the Earth and the Sky became stronger. W. . . tested the solidity of the ground by shaking it: he did not find it firm enough. And so he took some semen and

4. His name is derived from the word meaning 'white hair' or 'white beard'. As the names of the original divine pair are a secret, I will denote them by their initials: W. . . and B. . .
5. When I asked where W. . . and B. . . came from, my informant first professed ignorance, then suggested that each came from a minute thread of white *hoofuk* (Ch. 9), which invites the hypothesis that their reproductive substances existed before they themselves came into being.
6. This first model of the earth corresponds to the Yafar's ancestral territory at the former site of Sahya, where a sacred cordyline represents W. . .'s penis, which sprang from the ground.

some of B. . .'s secretions (in this case called W. . .'s *sibi* and B. . .'s
sibi, from the name of the black sap of the iron tree, metaphor for
the original 'thick blood', *taf-kêfutuk*) and mixed them together: fire,
suwê[7] sprang up and spread to the ends of the Earth and the Sky and
hardened them further. Once again W. . . tried to shake the ground:
it still moved slightly. Another coupling and more fire: now everything was solid and dry.[8] From a hardened packet of W. . .'s semen,
the wood adze *maar* and the *hôn-hus* stone were born; a hardened piece of B. . .'s secretions became the sago scraper *hwagi* and
the *prisri*[9] stone. (According to this version, the sun also results from
the mixing of the divine couple's secretions and menstrual blood.)

The creation of the cosmos from the fusion of the sexual substances of an anthropomorphic divine couple is followed by a
time when the primordial beings are mainly of a vegetal nature
and, although they have a dominant gender, each contains both
the male and the female principles. The first two species, the
male sago palm[10] of the *afwêêg* variety and the female coconut
palm, *sa*, comprise another original couple, a duplication of the
divine pair W. . . and B. . .; because of this they are the totems of
the Araneri and Angwaneri moieties.[11] It is these palms – rather
than the two divinities themselves, whose names are never pronounced and are supposed to be unknown to the women – that
the Yafar evoke to explain the origin of their moieties, which have
the status of totemic units. More specifically (as indicated in the
epigraph to this volume), these totems are 'the blood of the
coconut palm (flowers)', *sa* (*səsêg*) *taf*, for the female moiety, and
'the blood of the *afwêêg* sago palm', *afwêêg taf*, for the male
moiety. But one can also say, respectively, *emwêêg taf na ruwar* 'the

7. This original fire, *ifêêg suwê*, is mentioned in the magic spells for firing garden clearings. In former times, producing fire by rubbing a liana back and forth under a piece of soft
wood was symbolically regarded as a representation of the divine couple's primordial act.

8. *Kôgôm egeh-na, suwê egeh-na*, 'shaking of the earth / he tries / fire / he tries'; *oof-ii
bəte-ii sabaga eyuwawêk*, 'sky – and / earth – and / two / (remain) soft'; *ogownyar pe fe-na
êrik aga-gêm*, 'big penis / he plants / body / to set', *bəte oof kêfutuk o-fe-na-ba*, 'earth / sky /
solid / he makes / therefore'. These attempts are accompanied by an increase in the god's
virility, expressed in these terms: *uguk ogos-na, ogownyar sum*, 'young sprout (weak penis) /
first / big penis / afterwards'.

9. Stone used for the blades of sago scrapers (Juillerat 1984a).

10. One of the thirty varieties grown by Yafar horticulturalists [or] cultivators. The sago
palm, *Metroxylon* sp., grows in marshes and is native to New Guinea.

11. The same two dominant totems are used to identify the moieties of the Marind-
Amind in the southern part of western New Guinea (van Baal 1966, Ch. 2) where, as among
the Yafar, the cassowary is associated with the coconut palm, and the pig with the sago
palm.

children of the vagina blood', and *hwig taf na ruwar* 'the children of the penis blood'. As far as I know, no myth tells of human beings emerging from these complementary bloods; rather, this is a double metaphor in which the coconut palm represents the Original Mother[12] and the *afwêêg* sago palm, the Father or the divine phallus full of semen (for the male moiety, 'blood' is a euphemism for 'semen', and the sago starch can become a magical ingredient representing the male seed).

Parallel to the anthropomorphic divine couple, or emanating from them, the two totemic palms are a vegetalized representation of the parental couple. Each pole of the pair is both complementary and antagonistic to the other; their nutritious substances (starch and coconut meat), for example, must not be mixed. The fact that the coconut palm can be planted only in the village suggests the static image of the mother, immobilized by her reproductive and feeding functions; while the sago palm, cultivated or proliferating throughout the forest, evokes the mobility or even the ubiquity of the father, unencumbered by the constraints of procreation. This spatial opposition suggests the natural roles of the sexes in reproduction; it reverses the sociological representation in which the man is tied to a stable residence, unlike the woman, who is the object of marriage exchanges and changes residence. Mythology also frequently alludes to the attributes of the totemic palms which make them gendered figures: the white sago starch, congealing and swelling when boiling water is added (sago jelly), lends itself to a metaphorical representation of semen, while coconuts hang on the tree like milk-swollen breasts, and the sprouting coconut is the image of the maternal womb in gestation. The petiolar fibre (*bəsa*) that envelops the new coconut fronds provides the image of the uterus and thus becomes the most sacred part of this palm's 'anatomy' (see version *a* of the above myth and p. 55). In addition, the sago palm provides the mainstay of the Yafar diet, its starch appearing as the symbolic food *par excellence*, while the coconut palm, of little economic importance, is unique in its scarcity and its absence from gardens (where it would be choked out by secondary growth before it got started).

But let us return to the myth. The way the primal couple came to be represented by these vegetable entities differs from version

12. The theme of the Mother Coconut is recurrent in New Guinea and the Moluccas.

to version. One variant tells of B. . . giving birth a number of times to fertility spirits or directly to the original coconut palm and the original cassowary, the sago palm having been formed from a piece of W. . .'s penis; another presents B. . . and the coconut palm as one and the same; yet another denies the primal couple any descendants without explaining how the natural species came into being. As a rule, W. . . is identified with the *afwêêg* sago palm and B. . . with the coconut palm. Sometimes the humanized and naturalized representations coexist on different exegetical levels within the same myth. While these two trees are in this sense primordial, all the other natural species, as well as the stars, were born directly or indirectly from them. One myth, perhaps not known or not acknowledged by all Yafar experts, makes a direct genealogical link between the maternal body and the cosmos: in this myth, the Great Mother died giving birth to the *ifəgê* (p. 53), who sprang from her spilled blood; she was dismembered by her divine companion, each of her organs and bones giving rise to a creature.[13] On the same occasion, the first earth, product of the repeated couplings of W. . . and B. . ., assumed its present-day dimension by integrating the flesh of the maternal body. As a rule, and despite sexual cooperation as practised by the divine couple, animals, plants and even minerals sprang spontaneously from reproductive substances spilled by one sex or the other. Yafar imaginary representations show a predilection for metaphors involving uterine blood, semen, umbilical cords, placentas, pubic hair or genital organs partially amputated by their owners because of their disproportionate size. Non-human nature is more inclined to spring from the intrinsic fertility of the reproductive materials than from the effect of sexuality itself. It is the result of a form of female or male parthenogenesis, which protects the eventual relative autonomy of each sex from the other. The ambivalence that founds sexuality as that which at the same time remains separate and must fuse appears more clearly in the next stage of the mythic chronology, in which total separation gives way to sudden symbiosis, but in which the symbolic power over reproduction (Yangis) can belong to only one of the sexes at a time (Juillerat 1988, 1991a). The problem confronting Yafar thinking in elaborating their dual structure is the incompatibility between the 'fundamental

---

13. Other species were born through the mediation of divinities or lower-level spirits.

partition' – to use Bourdieu's expression – imposed by differentiation of the sexes and the oneness of a power that cannot be divided between them. Mythology focuses alternately on the 'separation of reunified opposites' and the 'reunification of separate opposites'; and in the second case, at least, life is reinstated at the cost of a transgression, a 'sacrilege' (Bourdieu 1980: 366–7).

This mythic time, preceding man's appearance and dominated by the plant kingdom, is called *rəgaag angwaag* 'husbands wives'; it is founded on the idea of the couple, for the two sexes cooperate in, but also vie for, the reproduction of each natural species. It is mentioned in many profane myths, behind which are esoteric versions, which hint that most of the 'human' characters in these texts in fact represent the (anthropomorphized) principles of the sexual reproduction of plants. Distrust, lying, murder, abandonment between male and female characters or sometimes between elder and younger siblings often feature in mythic scenarios, and, once the secret allegorical meaning is known, they appear to a large extent to be the expression of rivalry between the sexes over the control of reproduction. Within each species there is a struggle between such principles as germination, growth, flowering, fruiting, etc., each of which is assigned a gender in Yafar thought. These constant differences led, so local specialists say, to a situation of violence and promiscuity which was abruptly replaced by a new era; the natural species were sent back to the bush and to the world of the wild, and two separate communities of 'humanoid' beings appeared: the *garbôangô*, female spirits or simply 'women', who, having retained control of the village, unbeknown to the men created the Yangis ritual and probably the dual organization indispensable to its performance; and the *suwomp*, male spirits or 'men', who lived alone in the forest, where they could hear the mysterious sound of the trumpets, or would sometimes come to admire the supernatural figures dancing in the public square of the women's village. But one day admiration gave way to espionage, and a young boy surprised the women constructing the Yangis masks and making colours for the body paints; once informed, all the men copulated with all the women (thus reestablishing interrupted sexuality) before killing them – with the exception of the children – and seizing possession of the masks and the control of fertility, thus initiating the present-day social order and male dominion. The beginning of mankind proper[14] and the founding of the social order coincide with this event.

This mythic history of sexuality can be summed up as follows:

1. The original anthropomorphic divine couple. Cooperation between the sexes.
2. Androgynous natural species and gendered principles of reproduction. Rivalry between the sexes for reproduction; violence and promiscuity.
3. The two sexual communities are separated: the women control reproduction. No exchanges between the sexes.
4. Repression of the women by the men. Resumption of sexual relations. Murder of the women. The two sexual communities reunited under male control (male domination).

Let us now return to the problem of moieties, which is significantly illuminated by the transformations of the relation between the sexes in the cultural imagination. Whereas equality and cooperation between the sexual principles are held to be impracticable and to lead to anarchy, the solution adopted is total segregation into two natural 'halves', decided on the basis of the real sexes and in which the primacy of the female corresponds to the men's implicit acknowledgment of women's exclusive power (represented by the Yangis ritual) to conceive and bear children. The next stage could only be the reversal of the situation to the advantage of the men; unable to show the latter monopolizing such a power, again the myth can only proceed by metaphor: the *suwomp* seize the masks and the pigments, and perform the rite in place of the *garbôangô*, thus ensuring present-day male exclusivity to the celebration of this fertility cult.

What were the men supposed to be doing by their repression if not winning a cultural monopoly over women's natural power in order to control not only female fecundity (on both human and cosmic levels), but also the use of *both* sexual principles in reproduction. In other words, the two natural halves of society abolished by the mythic men are replaced by two *symbolically* 'male' and 'female' moieties, *both* of which are placed under the

14. For a detailed analysis of this myth, see Juillerat 1988, 1991a. Countless myths positing women's knowledge and ritual control of fertility are attested in New Guinea, Australia and South America: see, for example, Ballini 1983; Bamberger 1974; Godelier 1982; Herdt 1981; Héritier 1984–1985; Hiatt 1971; Hogbin 1970; Langness 1974.

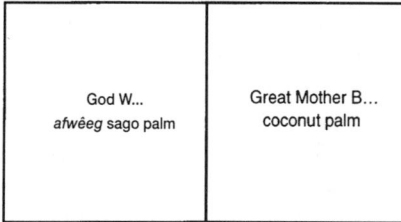

Divine primordial couple and their vegetable
incarnations (moiety totems).

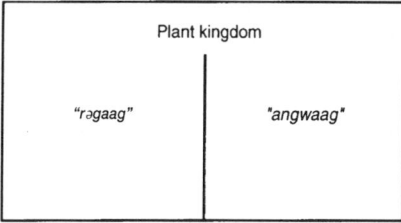

Mythic time of the original botanical species:
indistinction and rivalry between the sexual
principles.

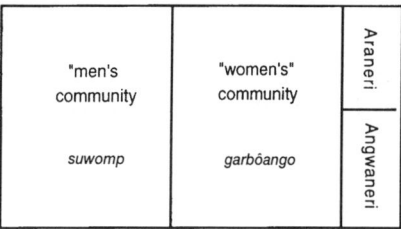

The mythic society of the *suwomp* and the
garbôangô: two separate communities.
The "women" perform the Yangis ceremony
(and are therefore subdivided into male
and female moieties).

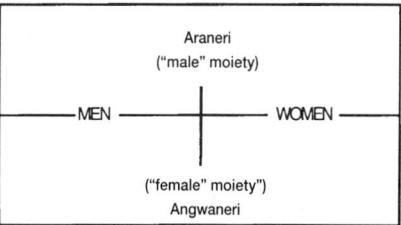

Present-day society subdivided into two
gendered moieties, men and women
together.

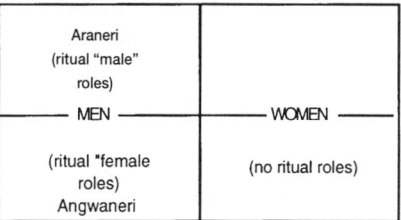

Dual divisions of society and the male
community in the celebration of the
Yangis ceremony.

Figure 10. Five Yafar mythic and sociological representations of sexual
duality

exclusive control of men. Today it is the men who, in the performance of the Yangis ritual, split into two groups according to their membership in one moiety or the other, one of which embodies the 'female' roles and handles the 'female' materials and ingredients in place of the women. Strictly forbidden access to the sacred enclosure where the masks are prepared, and restricted to a non-ritual role, today's women are supposed to believe that it is spirits who dance in the public square. Yafar men say: 'If the women happened to learn that we are the ones who dance and make the masks and pigments, all the men would die and only the women would be left alive', which means that power over reproduction would once again be in the hands of the women. The strategy of secrecy (secret knowledge of the meaning of the myths and rites) that men use against women functions implicitly on this level of analysis to prevent cultural regression to the time of the *garbôangô*.

Created out of the divinities or from gendered materials, the whole universe is theoretically divided into male and female. In reality, however, only the so-called original species or those used in ritual have a sexual identity, which the Yafar are often hard put to specify with any certainty. It is more often through a mythic episode or a ritual practice that a given species reveals itself as male or female. And often a doubt remains, or different mythic references give contradictory indications. Whereas the sky and the earth are clearly male and female, the sun is sometimes the product of a bit of W. . .'s semen (or a mixture of semen and menstrual blood) and sometimes B. . .'s amputated breast; nor is the gender status of the moon evident, as we shall see later (Ch. 13). If the *afwêêg* sago palm is said to be male-paternal, the *fэnaw* sago palm is female and it, instead of the coconut palm (whose scarcity prohibits its cutting), provides the fronds for certain masks. Gell (1975) presents the cassowary (a flightless solitary bird which lends itself readily to mythical thinking) as typically male, while a myth common to the Yafar, Punda and Umeda describes it as a hybrid, half bird, half coconut palm, assigns it a feeding role (egg = breast) and associates it with the sun (see below, Ch. 13). Species are symbolically assigned a gender according to their morphology, plants often as a function of the presence of sap or latex. The following very partial list gives only certain pairs.

The Sky/Earth opposition, product of the meeting of the original divine couple, is the expression of a separation (an Aust-

	Male	Female
Plants	*afwêêg* sago palm wild areca palm *sööbi* cultivated areca palm *Areca catechu* breadfruit tree liana *Calamus* sp. *Alstonia scholaris* sugar cane	coconut palm (*fðnaw* sago palm) wild pandanus *hoobi*
		cultivated pandanus (?) small bamboo *öku*
Animals	wild pig (?) pigeon *Ptilinopus rivoli* crocodile earthworm *maygo*	cassowary bird of paradise parrot *Domicella lory* *Paradisea minor*
		great flying fox the gallinaceous *abi* the night bird *suut* the spider *Atrax* sp. the frogs *Asterophrys* *robusta* and *Xenobatrachus* sp.
Minerals	the stone *hôn-bus*	the stone *prisri* red ochre kaolin
Objects	wood adze *maar* bow, arrows house stilts	sago scraper *hwagi* skirt *nay* netbag the container *sööbi* made from black palm sheaths fireplace
Cosmic elements	sky moon (?) thunder rain, dew boulders, cliffs	earth sun (?) lightning terrestrial water caves
Space	top east centre	bottom west periphery

ronesian mythic theme), but at the same time of a continuous coupling. If the celestial phallus planted in the Mother Earth is all that ensures her firmness, keeping her from both rotting and quaking (see Ch. 9, n. 29, the rite for preventing earthquakes), the sky can become angry at human faults and strike mankind with the *maar* adze;[15] the autochthonous maternal waters, product of the primordial blood and semen may reverse their flow, and the Ocean sweep up the waterways and flood the dry land. Between the threat of virile violence from on high and the danger of being swallowed up by the female principle below, mankind inhabits a middle region, where life goes on.

The most important ritual of the Yafar and Waina, briefly discussed above, is Yangis (or Ida for the Waina, where it originated). This celebration has the avowed function of promoting the growth of sago palms, but in fact it is the reactualization of the primal sexual principles, providing the symbolic conditions for the regeneration of the two totemic palms. On their continuity depends that of the two moieties, Araneri and Angwaneri. In this way, society ensures its own reproduction by miming the botanical and divine reproduction of their totems. Men are in exclusive control through the cooperation of their moieties in performing the ritual. In this sense, dual organization appears as an institution serving or instituted by male domination, within the framework of the management of natural and social reproduction.

Yangis: Ritual Complementarity of the Totemic Moieties in Symbolic Reproduction

As I have analysed this male cult common to the Yafar and Waina elsewhere (Juillerat 1992a, 1995),[16] my present effort will be restricted to showing the complementarity of the moieties in the preparation and performance of the ritual.

15. According to a slightly different tradition, the starry vault of heaven is also envisaged (without this corresponding to a belief) as a piece of land or a garden seen from below and inhabited by the *oof êri* 'sky people'. The stars are the plants they cultivate, among which are two totemic palm trees presenting themselves by the roots.

16. I also refer the reader to the two books mentioned above, to Gell's work (1975) for the description of the Umeda version of this rite, and to two films: *The Red Bowmen* by C. Owen and my own *Le Sang du sagou* (see list of films). For a discussion of the coherence of Yangis and Melanesian religions, see also Gell 1980, Juillerat 1980 and Wagner 1984. For the Anggor rituals, see Huber 1990.

The dual system is the social form of the sexual duality of the universe and mankind, and assumes its full meaning only at the time of this symbolic act of reproduction that is Yangis, in which the moieties must metaphorically assume the complementary roles played in procreation by the male and the female. Outside this ceremony, the moieties' existence is purely virtual. Yafar men are so imbued with this relationship with what they see as their primordial history, their 'prehistory', that it is only through it that they can think their dual organization. This no doubt explains why they define the function of their two moieties by Yangis alone. In an attempt to minimize, in the anthropologist's eyes, the importance this cult has for them, they always present their organization into moieties as the product of chance, something without importance, which simply plays an operative role in the ceremony and is not worth dwelling on. For a long time the Yafar successfully avoided talking to me about their social dualism, apparently uncomfortable with its enormous sacred background and consequently with the compromises this might entail for them – until the moment they began gradually revealing the secret mythology so profoundly permeated with dual or rather sexual representations.

It is as impossible to give a detailed description of every stage of Yangis as it is to list all the interpretations to which it gives rise. Let me say simply that the ceremony is: a) the ritual transposition of elements of the secret myth (primal divine coupling, the original divinity's pregnancy, parturition and loss of blood, the birth and socialization of a pair of primordial sons, etc.); b) the representation of the reproductive cycle of the sago palm, but also, and more secretly, that of the coconut palm as totemic species; c) the foundation of society.

The means of representation used are, for the public part of the ceremony, the succession of dancers painted from head to toe, wearing a mask over their head and carrying a bow and arrow, and for the most part wearing a ritual black penis sheath (*suhwagmô*), which they click against a bone belt by means of a vertical dance movement. The painted designs range from the black and white spots of the *êri* on the first night or on the *ogomô* (Ch. 3) the next morning, or the solid red, representing blood, of the two *ifəgê* (the young sago sprouts and totemic sons) or the *rawsuinaag*, to the complex and varied polychrome motifs of the two *yis* ('sago jelly') at dawn, the *sawôg* ('fish') at midday or the *amof* ('termites'), who follow them (see also Juillerat 1978a). The ritual begins one evening and ends two days later, as the sun is setting, with the *ifəgê* shooting their arrows at the sun. Unadorned men keep up an unbroken accompaniment on wooden trumpets,[17] except the second night, when the men of knowledge sing sacred songs until dawn. There are numerous *ogomô*, 'fish' and 'termite' masks which, in the case of the *ogomô* and fish masks, are worn by members of the clan whose emblem is painted on the mask (Ch. 3). The other ritual figures enter in pairs, and the masks are worn respectively by one man from each moiety, any one man wearing the masks in a prescribed order from one celebration to the next. The figures are:

Eri:	the 'persons', who dance through the first night and represent the original divine couple in the act of copulation; they are also called *afwêêg-ii fənaw-ii*, '*afwêêg* and *fənaw*', their masks being made respectively from *afwêêg* sago-palm fronds (male moiety, Sky) and *fənaw* sago-palm fronds (female moiety, Earth). As I pointed out earlier, the latter variety of sago palm in fact stands for the coconut palm, *sa*, whose fronds may not be cut. The *êri sabaga* couple, the 'two persons' (the couple), thus in fact represent the *afwêêg/sa* pair, but also, according to certain informants, W. . . and B. . .
Rawsu-inaag:	'in the fire of the *raw*'. *Raw* is probably the secret name of a 'part of the vagina' (the hymen?); *suwê* 'fire' is the metaphor for blood. These two figures are painted entirely in red and dance at the same time as the *êri*, but around the edges of the dancing ground. They represent the (virginal?) blood of the two divinities, the two bloods respectively 'of the penis and of the vagina' (*hwig taf, emwêêg taf*).
Yis:	'sago jelly'. These two figures come on after the exit of the two *êri* and the *rawsu-inaag*, at first light of day. They represent conception: parallel between the fusion of the male and female substances in the uterus and the confection of

17. See Fischer 1983; Juillerat 1992a and 1993; Sanger and Sorrell 1975.

sago jelly in the bark container, performed ritually at the same moment on the village square by the two Masters of the Sky and the Earth (Chs 3 and 13). The *yis* are also associated with femaleness and fertility and are sometimes designated by the name of the beautiful young mythic woman Oög-angô, 'Melon Woman'. The body of the dancers is painted with broad horizontal polychrome stripes.

Ware-inaag: 'in the wild (*pitpit*) canes'. These two figures come immediately after the *yis*, and their body paint and masks are similar. Their symbolic role is not clear (see however Juillerat 1995). In the Umeda rite they are called 'firewood' (Gell 1975).

Ifəgê: 1) 'original man'; 2) 'three-pronged arrow'. The appearance of these two figures entirely painted with red ochre marks at once the end and the high point of Yangis. They carry respectively a three-pronged arrow (female moiety) and a single-headed arrow (male moiety). They represent the young red shoots of the *afwêêg* and *fənaw* sago palms – the latter once again a substitute for the most sacred tree, the coconut palm – growing from the base of the parent palm or from the rotting sucker; but the *ifəgê* are also the 'new men' and the sons of the Primal Mother B. . ., born of her blood and, more specifically, according to one version, of a miscarriage from which she is said to have died. For this reason they are called *taf na ruwar* 'the children of the blood', a term that the Yafar use to define themselves in an almost totemic way, thus referring once again to the moieties. Each is led by a bare-headed man, symbolically said to be their 'mother's brother' and the incarnation of the social father. The Mother's dead body is dismembered and her single breast placed in the sky by the god W. . .. At the close of Yangis the *ifəge* shoot their arrow at the setting sun in order – according to one esoteric version – to capture the breast of their dead mother, which is nothing other than the sun.

Simplifying somewhat, the successive stages of Yangis can be said to take us from the two *êri*, the Sago palm and the Coconut palm, the procreators, the first generation, to the rebirth of the same species and the renewal of the same entities, founders of the world and symbols of life, with the appearance of the two *ifəgê*, by way of the different stages of pregnancy and socialization.

Through this public portion of Yangis, in which women and girls participate by dancing around the edges of the square, the pairing of the ritual figures is duplicated by the cooperation between the two halves of society, these two symbolic and social levels that always overlay the fundamental idea of sexual complementarity in reproduction. But it is also during the days preceding the public ceremony, while the men are collecting the materials in the forest and making the masks, that the two moieties express this idea.

On the eve of the day before the opening of the public rite – having sent the women and children into the forest to collect the fronds for wrapping the sago jelly and enough firewood – the men of both moieties gather in the village square, armed with their bows and arrows and discretely decorated. Tension runs high and it is good form for each man to show his virility by demonstrations of 'warlike' behaviour: bow drawn, charging about, shouting. . .. At a sign from the ritual masters, the men of the two moieties assemble face to face and, amidst war cries, 'threaten' each other by drawing their bows, arrows pointed skyward. Then the men from the female moiety run in pack formation around the square, their bows and arrows still raised, before descending to a hidden spot by the river. The men from the male moiety then do the same. As they set out, the men (or only the ritual masters) are all said to pronounce the words B. . .*wang*, 'the nape of B. . .'s neck', for the female moiety, and *Afwêêg wang*, 'the nape of the *afwêêg* sago palm's neck' (a euphemism for W. . .), for the male moiety. 'Nape of the neck' seems to refer to the idea of growth, verticality and power.

Down on the riverbank, a spot is ritually cleared and called 'the place of the fish' or 'the fish pond', since the fish are supposed to leave the water and embody themselves in the dancers: the Araneri men (male moiety) work upstream, the Angwaneri men downstream, and later, during the preparation of the pigments and the masks, the moieties will divide this space according to the same orientation. In the centre of the clearing, a hut is constructed – where the emblematic masks will be hung awaiting the ceremony and where they will be left to rot afterwards – which secretly represents the body of the primordial mother. This symbolic body is also divided between the two moieties, the Araneri taking the top and in particular the 'mouth', the Angwaneri the bottom and in particular the 'vagina'. The hut is constructed by representatives of the two moieties together, who first of all mark the respective ends with magical plants, while chanting and reciting spells for fertility and hunting: the marking of the maternal body corresponds to access to her *hoofuk*, her principle of fecundity, to the resources of the forest earth.

Then, unbeknown to the women, the men prepare the *bəsa* collected from the village coconut palms along with other materials to be painted, and they exchange foodstuffs between moieties. The colours are then prepared by Araneri and Angwaneri men indifferently. For the colour black, the Masters of the Sky and the Earth cooperate in mixing the ingredients (charcoal from a special wood, diluted sago and juice from *Schefflera* stems) representing the two sexual substances: when shaken up by the two masters, the mixture coagulates into 'black sago jelly' (*yis önguk*). They do this to the accompaniment of loud chanting, general excitement being essential, and a confrontation is again staged between the men of the two moieties. Behind this theatrical aggressiveness must again be seen the antagonism between but also the complementarity and fusion of the sexes. After this, the men of each clan paint their respective emblems on the *bəsa* (Ch. 3), which are then hung in the ritual hut for the night.

The next day, with the Angwaneri moiety once more in the lead, the men go into the bush and camp for the day at a spot off the trail. The tasks are divided between the two moieties (a symbolic sexual division). This division of labour applies to gathering the wood, foliage, the young petioles of black palms and the liana from which the masks will later be made at the 'fish pond'. Each plant is either 'male' or 'female' (associated with the Sky or the Earth) and must be found and brought back by the men of the corresponding moiety.

The main pairs of species are:

Araneri moiety	Angwaneri moiety
afwêêg sago palm fronds	*fənaw* sago palm fronds
young petioles of the black	young leaves of the pandanus
palm *söobi*	*hoobi*

Back at the 'fish pond', the Masters of the Earth and the Sky, with the help of other men of knowledge, split up into two groups and chop the *bêêbi* liana into sections of the right length for the masks; they hold it up to the East, shouting spells for erection and the growth of plants, while a group of young men plays the trumpets so that the women left behind in the village will not hear the sacred words. Then the masks are made. The ritual begins in the evening. As the two *êri* enter the dancing ground, two bundles tied up in leaves are hurled to the ground in the village square; they contain male and female *hoofuk* (see Ch. 9), that is sago (of both the *afwêêg* and *fənaw* varieties), taro (female), yam *Dioscorea alata* (male), etc., as well as sexual fluids furnished respectively for each bundle by the Masters of the Sky and the Earth and their wives. As this is done, the word *hoofuk* is shouted. This is supposed to set off an explosion that can be heard in the neighbouring villages.

These few details of the ritual should show the climate of dualistic cooperation – founded on the idea of complementarity of the sexes in the symbolic act of procreation – which reigns during Yangis and constantly focuses on the Araneri and Angwaneri men, or more precisely on the Master of the Sky and the Master of the Earth.

We have mentioned that the men of the female moiety precede those of the male moiety when going into the forest and when entering the enclosure; this is also the case at many points in the ritual. Men from other villages visiting during the ceremony descend first of all to the 'fish pond' in the same order, arrows poised to shoot skyward and shouting. This order gives the female sphere a primacy that it does not enjoy in social life; in effect, during the ritual the imaginary shakes off all social constraint and is free to express itself. We have already seen, in the case of the different representations of sexual dualism (Figure 10), how social order is the inverse of fantasy order. To acknowledge the importance of the female in the ritual is in a way implicitly to acknowledge that, on this level, men's power is artificial (cultural) and in the end 'rigged'. Men have symbolically confiscated the only indisputable superiority women, by their very nature, had over them, their biological femaleness, and they have turned it into the object of a cult, from which the women themselves are excluded. But there is also the spatial priority accorded to the Angwaneri moiety during Yangis, a representation of human copulation, and this is the aspect that certain Yafar specialists emphasize, for they do not like to acknowledge the superiority of women explicitly. One of these specialists told me that when they let the Angwaneri go first, they are following the way the woman stretches out on the ground first and the man lies down on top of her.

It is exclusively in its sexual symbolism that the relationship between the moieties is hierarchized. Top and bottom, centre and periphery, east and west are differentially integrated into dual organization only in so far as they are the poles of a spatial orientation of the sexes.[18]

The Second Level of Yafar Dualism: Age-Rank and Submoieties

The Araneri and Angwaneri moieties, their disposition in space and in the ritual, their integration into the social and mythological spheres, have enabled the Yafar to give tangible form to their representation of reproduction. The formal aspect and the fundamentally symbolic function of this social duality have appeared to us clearly. But what about the second level of Yafar dual organization, the one that causes each moiety to be in turn subdivided into two submoieties? As I have already mentioned, not all Yafar conceptualize clearly the internal duality of their Araneri and Angwaneri moieties; the younger ones seem unaware that these are dual units and sometimes even confuse the

18. Rubel and Rosman (1978: 339) have already pointed out the lack of social hierarchy in New Guinea dual organizations. Hierarchy in dual organizations, or what Dumont calls 'hierarchical opposition' (1978), is in fact determined by the social hierarchies (classes, castes, etc.) present at the time, and does not seem to me to be necessarily an intrinsic feature of dualism. For Oceania, see, for example, Hocart 1970; also Sahlins 1976 on dualism in Fiji society.

submoiety and the moiety's founding clan of the same name, or they designate the largest clan, Biyuneri, by the name of its sub-moiety, Mwafneri (see Table 4). I began calling the submoieties 'elder' and 'younger' siblings upon learning that those of the Angwaneri moiety were the mythic children of two sisters who were co-wives and those of the Araneri the children of two brothers, and upon establishing the parallel (see below) with the parental organization of the domestic space of the house and sibling kin terms. Moreover, my conclusion was enthusiastically accepted and confirmed by the informants I talked with.

The Amanab terms for (same-sex) 'elder' and 'younger' sib-lings are *eteeg* and *sumnik*, but we shall see, when comparing the neighbouring Potayneri society, that the terms *ifêêg* and *sumneri*[19] would be more appropriate were they not used by the Yafar for the two clans of the younger Araneri submoiety. In fact, not one of these four terms is used for the submoieties, which are des-ignated by two patronyms and two matronyms referring back to mythic figures:

Menaneri (matronym):   *Meni na êri* or *Meni na ruwar*, 'people —' or 'children of Meni' designates the members of the 'elder' submoiety of the female moiety (Angwaneri).

Mwafneri (matronym):   *Mwafo na êri* (— *ruwar*), 'people —' or 'children of Mwafo' designates the members of the 'younger' submoiety of the female moiety.

Wamawneri (patronym):   'people —' or 'children of Wamaw' des-ignates the members of the 'elder' submoiety of the male moiety (Araneri).

Aayneri (patronym?):   the legitimation of this name has not been clarified (a mythic ancestor named Hay is often cited). Hypothetically this would give us: 'people —' or 'children of Hay' for the members of the 'young-er' submoiety of the male moiety.

---

19. See, pp. 65–6 for the meaning of these words.

The inclusive relationship of the submoieties with the moieties poses a problem of form:[20] should the two-level articulation of Yafar dualism be regarded as cross-cutting moieties or, as the term 'submoieties' suggests, merely as a secondary bipartition of each moiety? Both ways of conceptualizing society can be argued, for the first corresponds to the underlying model reconstructed by analysing of the material (see below), while the second refers to the Yafar's own vision of the system: in effect, the Yafar never speak of elder and younger moieties (only male and female ones) and simply perceive, without attaching any importance to it (other than mythical for those who know about such matters), that the clans of each moiety are grouped into two ideal patrilineal units. As they see it, then, the principle of age-rank is minimized to the advantage of the principle of sexual differentiation. This can be explained 1) negatively by the absence of collective initiations requiring alternating interaction between so-called elder and younger groups (such as exist in societies along the lower Sepik, in particular the Iatmul and the Ilahita-Arapesh); 2) positively by the importance in the Yafar religion of the cosmogonic myth, which is organized from the outset according to the principle of antagonism and complementarity between the sexes. Inversely, the Sepik societies, which have initiation cycles and a dual mode of organization, have emphasized age-rank, relegating sexual differentiation to a minor symbolic role.[21]

The anthropologist's view on this point is somewhat different from that of the Yafar, for he feels himself impelled to reestablish the unity of the elder and younger moieties, despite their lack of any real social function. Three arguments, based on the ethnographic material, justify this endeavour: the mythic genealogy, sibling kin terms and the house plan.

Figure 11 gives two configurations of the same genealogical structure, these being two versions of the myth used to legitimize the existence of submoieties[22] within the moieties. The two male

20. The rest of this analysis is taken in part from a corrected version of Juillerat 1981.

21. See, for example, Bateson 1958, Ch. 15; Rubel and Rosman 1978, Ch. 3: summary of Bateson's material on the Iatmul; and Tuzin 1976, 1980.

22. Nevertheless, in the next chapter we will see that the differentiation of the 'elder' and 'younger' (*Eteeg/Sumnik*) groups appears in the subdivision of certain clans into two separate lineages or even in the fact that two clans now distinguished by different names are related. The case of the Punda hamlets and the Potayneri clans provide yet another example of dual differentiation by age-rank (see below).

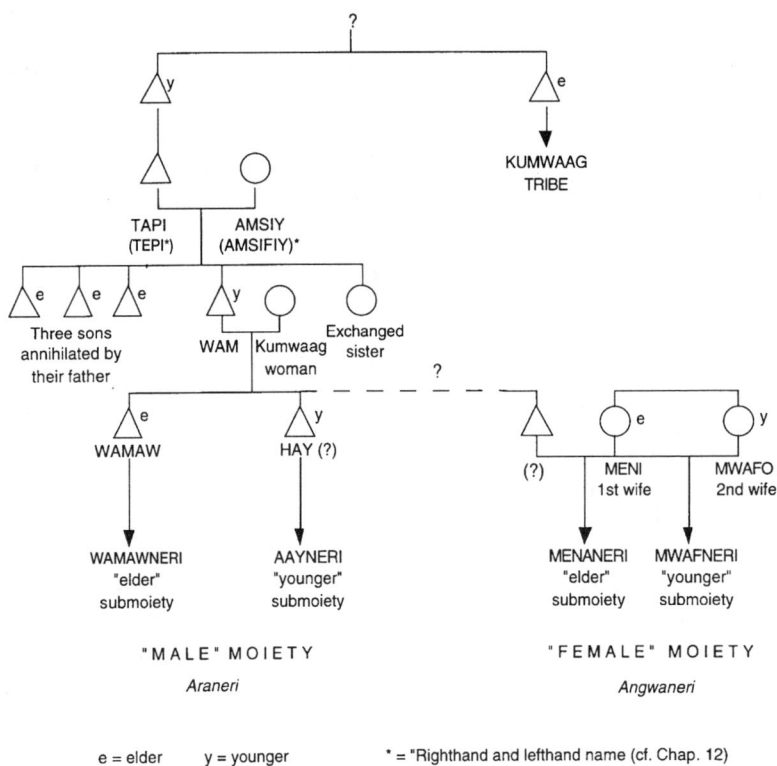

Figure 11 a and b. Two versions of the mythic genealogy legitimizing the twofold dual structure

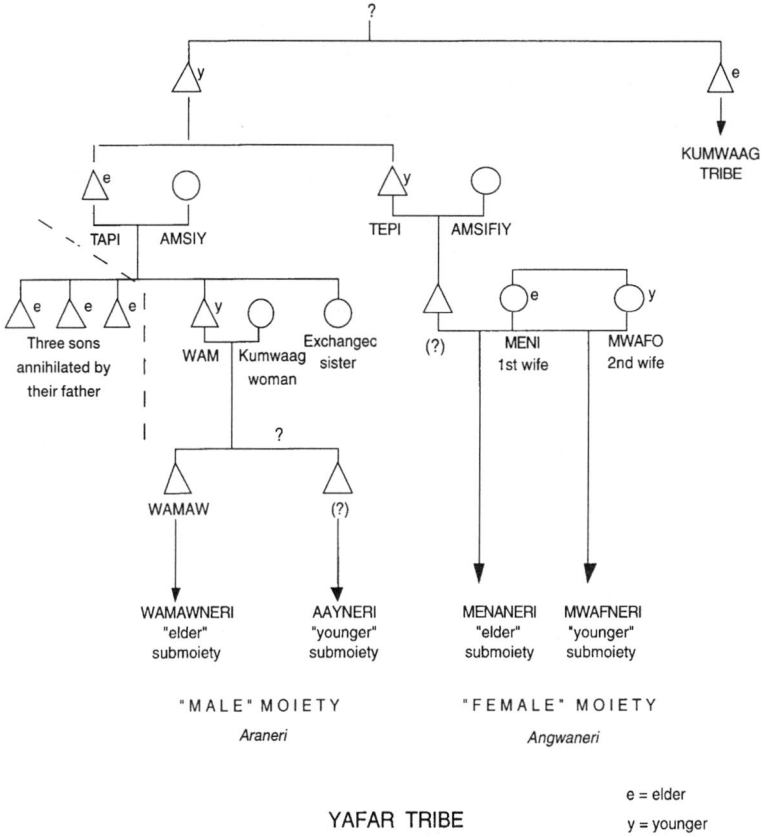

Figure 11 a and b. Two versions of the mythic genealogy legitimizing the twofold dual structure

submoieties are shown as having descended from a pair of brothers, while the two female submoieties are descended from a pair
of sisters married to the same man. Note in passing the 'stratagem' by which the pair of sisters is used to preserve patriliny and
yet are also ideologically necessary to represent both the femaleness of the Angwaneri moiety and the hierarchical age-rank
relation between the two submoieties. A fluctuating social reality,
changing over time at the whim of demographic evolution,
migrations and the assimilation of foreign clan segments, is thus
endowed with a formal structure legitimized by a mythic apical
genealogy whose articulations are organized by the twofold principle of differentiation by gender and by age, and whose stability
is ensured by the hiatus separating it from real clan genealogies.

Yafar sibling nomenclature, of the Polynesian type, faithfully
reproduces the schema of cross-cutting moieties: two non-
reciprocal terms designate opposite-sex siblings (*weerik*, 'sister',
for a male ego; *nisag*, 'brother', for a female ego); and two
terms designate the elder (*eteeg*) and younger (*sumnik*) sibling of
the same sex (Figure 12*b*). The architecture, and more specifically
the Yafar house plan, also reproduce this schema of cross-cutting
subdivisions, as shown in Figure 12*c* (for a detailed drawing, see
Figure 17). Figures 12 *a*, *b* and *c* thus reproduce the same dual
structure cutting across the specificity of each context.

At this stage of the analysis, it can be said that ideally the
dual model I have just given could, in the event of a need for
more complexity due to massive demographic growth of the
Yafar society coupled with a vital need to perpetuate the unity
of the group, reproduce itself on ever-more inclusive levels by
formalizing the principles of sex or age-rank. Parallel to the complexification of the social structures, the mythic genealogy would
develop vertically, adding pairs of figures bound into a relationship of gender or relative age with each new generation. Such a
vision – which would yield what might be called a system of
'nested moieties' – obviously remains in the realm of theory. In
effect, I have said that as far as the Border Mountains are concerned, it appears that large-scale demographic growth tends to
provoke subdivision into independent sociopolitical units which
reproduce variants of the same dual structure, rather than multiplying the levels of organization and maintaining the cohesion of
the expanded group.

The at least formal hierarchy which favours the 'elder' sub-

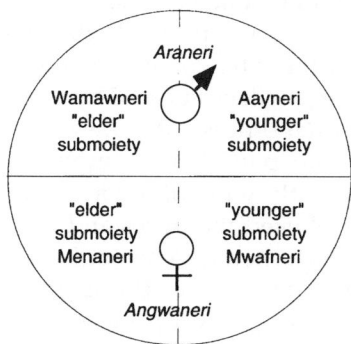

a) Abstract representation of overall
Yafar society (2 moieties and 4 submoieties))

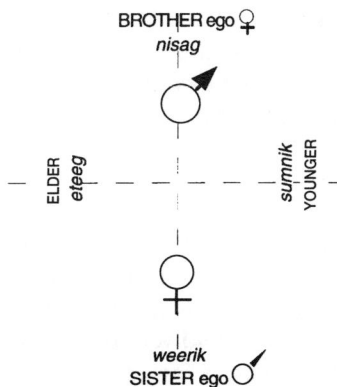

b) Sibling kin terms

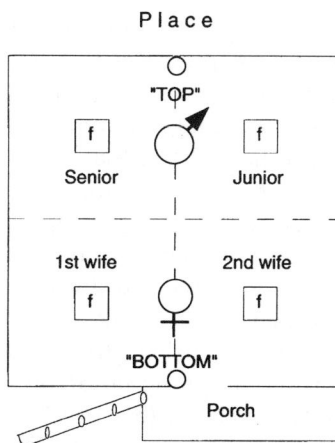

f = cooking fire

c) House plan

Figure 12. Three modes of cross-cutting moieties (from Juillerat 1981)

moieties is legitimized solely by the supposedly original occupation of the land by one particular clan of each submoiety, Wamawneri and Menaneri respectively, the founding groups that gave their name to the whole submoiety. It seems that to this should be added the privilege enjoyed by these two clans of controlling the main ritual offices (Ch. 3), even though transfers of these roles from one patriclan to another within the same moiety – but apparently without always respecting submoiety boundaries – have blurred the traces and made it impossible to draw up any kind of coherent schema. Finally – and this is no doubt the most interesting point – the submoieties, appearing as more or less exogamous groups, present a quaternary structure which takes on a meaning, if not a real function, in the system of alliances. This problem will be dealt with in Chapter 10.

Comparative Elements

The key principle of a social structure shows up most clearly when several societies from the same region, related by their history, by exchanges and often by intermarriage, are compared. It often becomes apparent that they have all used a common structural matrix, but that each society has arranged the parts as it sees fit and with more or less rigour. This is also what we see when looking at the types of dual organization set up by the Yafars' neighbours, the Waina-speaking Umeda and Punda to the north and the Kumwaag confederation groups to the south (Potayneri, Aynunkneri, Muwagneri and Gefayneri). I have already published the Umeda material elsewhere (Juillerat 1981), basing my presentation on Gell's work (1975), and will therefore only touch on this briefly in order to clarify a few points left unexplained at the time. The Punda have a dual system identical to that of the Umeda. The Kumwaag, on the other hand, present variants that bring them closer to the Yafar in so far as residence groups and the quaternary nature of the system are concerned, but which also throw light on Umeda and Punda 'hamlet dualism'.

   The latter two communities (as well as the other Waina-speaking groups) differ from the Yafar and other Eri first of all in the stability of their hamlets and in the social relevance of these, each of which is designated by a group name, whereas among

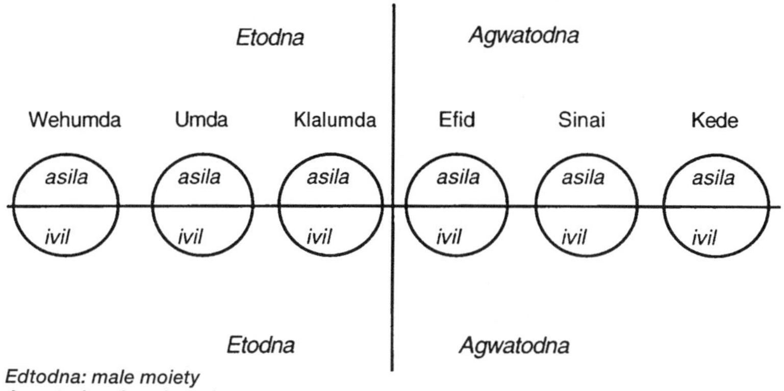

Etodna			Agwatodna		
Wehumda	Umda	Klalumda	Efid	Sinai	Kede

asila	asila	asila	asila	asila	asila
ivil	ivil	ivil	ivil	ivil	ivil

Etodna		Agwatodna

Edtodna: male moiety
Agwatodna: female moiety
Wehumdma, Umda, etc.: hamlet names

Figure 13. The two-level articulation of Umeda dualism (after Gell 1975: 85, Figure 10, 'Village and hamlet moieties')

the Eri it is only the society as a whole (which may comprise several hamlets) that bears a name, the hamlets having only a toponym. The Punda, like the Umeda, have six hamlets (the Sowanda eight and the Waina-Wiyara two), opposing each other as three for the male moiety and three for the female moiety (Figure 13).[23] The moieties names correspond to the Yafar terms.[24] The particularity of the Waina groups is that each hamlet is further divided into two moieties containing a few families, called respectively Ivil and Asila.[25] Gell (1975: 84–7) says that these two hamlet moieties may render each other services, particularly in healing rituals, and concludes that theoretically they must therefore be comprised of different agnatic groups so that interclan reciprocity is preserved. And yet he adds that, after he had left the field, he realized that the members of certain clans were divided between the two moieties of the hamlet. Here we will leave the ethnology of the Umeda and refer readers to Gell's interesting work for more information on this society's dual system.

23. Among the Punda, Gell had identified four hamlets for the male moiety and two for the female moiety, which the Punda denied when I questioned them in 1981, placing Ifêr hamlet (Evil in Gell's book) on the 'male' side (Gell 1975: 33).

24. See above, note 3.

25. Gell 1975. Ifêr and asôra according to my transcription, established when I visited the Punda in 1981. The Yafar (who are allies of the Punda but not the Umeda) say ifêêg and asəga.

Two more points need to be added to what I have said, plus
some comments on Yafar submoieties and Umeda and Punda
hamlets. First of all, on the subject of Ivil and Asila, the etymology given Gell by his Umeda informants – *ivil < iv* 'breadfruit
tree', connoting centrality and maleness, and *asila < asa* 'garden,
clearing', associated with the idea of marginality and femaleness
– was contested by two Punda informants I questioned
separately in 1981. They claimed Ifêr (Ivil) means 'elder, native,
anterior' (*ifêtuwar*, I was told, designates the first-born of a sibling
group, and *ifêrango*, the first wife in a polygynous household);
Asəra (Asila), on the other hand, was translated as 'younger, who
comes afterwards' (the two terms are not, however, used as
sibling kin terms). Nevertheless the relation with *if* (*iv*) 'breadfruit tree' (for which the more common word is *ruwô*, see
Amanab *guwô*) is not excluded, for the breadfruit tree is regarded
as one of the primordial trees in mythic chronology; the
etymology *asəra < asa* was categorically rejected in Punda. These
lexical clarifications run in the same sense as Gell's qualification
of Ifêr clans as 'original' and Asəra clans as 'immigrants' (1975:
88–9). However, when we come to the second dichotomy there is
a problem, which brings me to my other point. How are the
patriclans divided between the moieties of the same hamlet, and
how is it that certain clans are present in both? I put this question
to the Punda, who replied that when an Ifêr or an Asəra hamlet
moiety dies out, we wait until a man from the other moiety has
several sons and then we give one (or two) to the extinct moiety.
As an example, they cited the present-day case of Probonai, a
Punda hamlet where the Asəra are no longer represented and
where they hope that an as yet undesignated Ifêr man will be
able to provide a son (in the event, probably one of the younger
ones) to found a new Asəra line. This system is reminiscent of the
way the Yafar sometimes reapportion their sons (see above) – but
only temporarily and for the needs of Yangis – between male and
female moieties. This means of adjustment shows that Umeda
and Punda hamlet moieties are not based strictly on patrilineal
groups and that the important thing is to preserve duality for
reasons of socioritual reciprocity and symbolic order.[26]

---

26. Moreover, the Punda add that the Ifêr and Asəra moieties were not allowed to
exploit the same sago palms or fish in the same sections of river (even though they shared
the same land), but I did not have the time to develop this point.

At the level of the male and female moieties, Waina-speaking groups and the Eri share the same system, except that only the northern Eri have adopted the Yangis (Ida) ritual. It is at the second level that the dualism of these two regions differs. The Umeda and the Punda do not have submoieties, but hamlets and subhamlets.[27] As we shall see when we come to marriage alliances, the hamlets, although there are six of them, seem by their exogamic character to be in a way homologous to the Yafar submoieties. And yet Yafar submoieties are not in turn subdivided into two smaller units (the Ifêr and Asəra of the Punda and Umeda), or at least not systematically; in effect, as we will see in the next chapter, the elder male submoiety, Wamawneri, is composed of two clans also called 'elder' and 'younger', and the younger submoiety of the same moiety contains a clan named Ifêêg (the Ifêr of the Umeda and Punda) and a second named Sumneri (a term that means 'those who come afterwards' and therefore corresponds to the meaning given above for Asəra). It is not clear, however, that this is the case for the female moiety, where clans assimilated in the past have become indistinguishable from the rest.

But to make the parallel even clearer, Potayneri society exhibits a structure that partakes of both systems at once, since it has two moieties, Araneri/Angwaneri, each of which is subdivided into an 'elder' and a 'younger' unit called by patronyms or matronyms, as among the Yafar, and each of these four groups being again subdivided into two 'moieties' designated by the generic terms Ifêêg and Sumneri. The Potayneri lived in two hamlets until 1979, at which time, following a series of epidemics and a sharp drop in population, they split into three. Their local-group structure is therefore of the unstable or mobile type I described for the Yafar (Ch. 1); the hamlet is not a social unit clearly defined by criteria of descent or moiety. Society finds its coherence as a whole and independently of village fissions or recompositions. Figure 14 shows the three dual articulations of Potayneri society.

27. Unless one considers three regrouped semihamlets as submoieties, which would make four groups: male-Ifêr, male-Asəra, female-Ifêr and female-Asðra (Figure 13). But no such groups seem to exist in the minds of those interested, or in social reality, as a matter of fact; they are replaced by hamlets whose physical reality imposes itself as local groups and places of social relations.

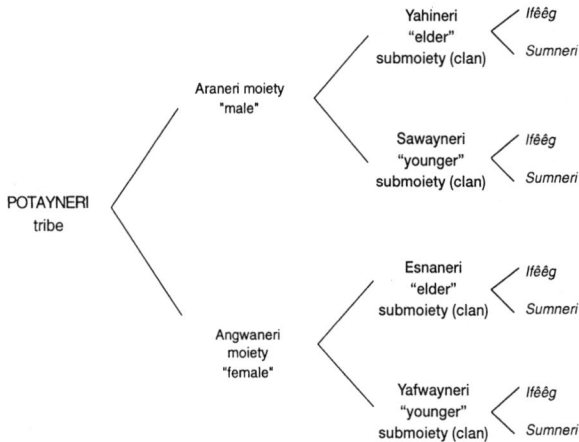

Figure 14. The three-level articulation of Potayneri dualism

Having spent only a few days with this group, I did not establish any genealogies and therefore cannot say if each submoiety constitutes a single patrilineal group and if the Ifêêg/Sumneri units are always a pair of distinct lineages or if, on the contrary, they are more patriclans than dual units. No one knew of a distribution of members from the same agnatic group between Ifêêg and Sumneri, as was the case among the Punda, and the Yafwayneri submoiety, which no longer had a Sumneri moiety, seems to have consented to this amputation without anyone envisaging a remedy for the moment. It may nevertheless be supposed that, from time to time in the past, the Potayneri also fell back on the system of redistribution through the splitting of a sibling group. This method respects the rule of solidarity, which says that he who is well provided for gives to him who is not (this also holds between kinsmen as regards plant cuttings for a new garden) and at the same time enables lineages to remain in the original dual unit. These societies do not like to transfer entire groups and prefer to perpetuate the same relationship between unilineal descent groups and dual units by moving, when necessary, individuals (males in this case, since this is a patrilineal descent system) whose role it will be to found a new branch somewhere else; I mentioned earlier the same process of implanting a new line from a foreign clan (Ch. 1) and the obvious parallel between this dispersal of lineages and the itinerant form of horticulture.

The other Kumwaag confederation societies also feature variants of dualism founded on symbolic gender on the one hand and presumed age-rank on the other. For example, besides immigrant lines from nearby groups, which they distinguish clearly from native-born clans, the Muwagneri have two founding clans corresponding to their Araneri and Angwaneri moieties, each of which is subdivided into two lineages ranked as elder and younger (in this case called Eteeg/Sumnik and not Ifêêg/Sumneri) (Figure 15).[28]

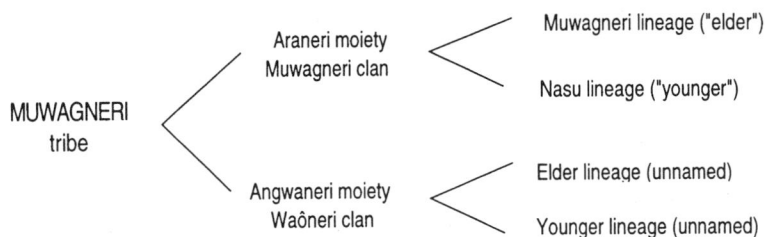

Figure 15. The twofold articulation of Mugwaneri dualism (immigrant segments from foreign clans not shown)

The Aynunkneri tribe has roughly the same two-level structure, except that the female moiety (Waôneri), which originally came from the Muwagneri, seems to have returned to them when the village last moved (1972). An 'elder' lineage (Eteeg or Ifêêg) of the Aynunkneri clan constitutes the male moiety (together with some immigrant foreign segments), while the 'younger' lineage, designated by the term Ametikneri, 'the people of the flank', or Efêfêyik (an allusion to their cosmological position when the hamlet was founded; see Ch. 1), were later assigned, it seems, to the female moiety. Moreover, the two communities, Muwagneri and Aynunkneri, who are neighbours, have a common myth in which their respective founding clans (the male moieties) are presented as two brothers, the elder – the Muwagneri clan ancestor – who 'grew slowly' and represents blood (game, hunting, killing), the younger – the Aynunkneri clan ancestor – who 'grew fast' and represents *hoofuk*, the life principle

---

28. Figure 15 provides a good example of the use of the same name (patronym) for the society as a whole, for the main clan of the male moiety (primacy of the male) and for the elder lineage of this clan (primacy of seniority).

associated particularly with plants and sago palms (Ch. 9). A fraternal bond ranked as elder/younger thus links the two societies, which also shared part of their female moiety (Waôneri clan) at some time in the past.

The Gefayneri, according to information gathered from Potayneri informants, have two principal clans that make up the Araneri and Angwaneri moieties: the Eftaneri (whose 'totem' or emblem is the wildfowl *efta*) as the female moiety, and the Ayberneri as the male moiety. Each is theoretically subdivided into two 'submoieties' (?) called Ifêêg and Sumneri, but there have been no Sumneri for a long time and no need has been felt to replace them.

Finally, the situation with the Wamuru, to the east of the Yafar, seems confused, but we do find the Araneri/Angwaneri moieties. No distinction appears to be made between elder and younger groups, or Ifêêg and Sumneri, but one of the clans, the Meso-me-inaag, is said to be divided between the male and female moieties. The Wamuru have recently thrown themselves into Christianity (at least the younger generation has), and no one now dares to talk about the Yangis festival, or ritual life in general; as a consequence, my informants seemed quite reticent in talking about moieties. In effect the abandoning of the traditional religious life with which the dual system is so closely tied may well lay these communities open to the destructuring of the system of symbolic exchanges and, more particularly, their dual organization.

Dual Reciprocity

Some readers may have found the approach and the materials presented in this chapter too formal and, if they are particularly interested in institutional repercussions on social practice, they will no doubt feel that the Yafar dual system has been analysed in a far too geometrical or symbolist fashion and that, aside from ritual, one sees little of the concrete relations that structures determine between individual members of the groups we have defined. This is in fact one of the striking aspects of dualism in this region. One would like to question the Yafar and Potayneri societies themselves on this subject and ask them, when you were constructing your society, why did you not seek to make these minor dual units, these clan moieties and submoieties, more of an institution? Why did you restrict the role of the Araneri and Angwaneri to the staging of Yangis? How is it that you were not interested in giving some of these dual units a function in such important social situations as funerals? Or inversely, how is it that the formal existence of these different dual levels did not lead to more complex systems of exchange (of goods or services)? This somewhat unorthodox way of putting the question at least has the advantage of bluntly posing the problem of the surprising formalism of these structures. The Yafar themselves are conscious of this and say that moieties and submoieties 'aren't for anything'. And in effect, it took me a long time to find any cases of reciprocity between moieties or submoieties.

The sexual symbolism that has been analysed so far *explains* the dualism of the Araneri and Angwaneri moieties, and all indications are that it is at its origin.[29] The few circumstances in which the men of the two moieties exchange goods or services, on the other hand, seem to be merely a contingent means of demonstrating social reciprocity.[30] These cases are as follows:

a) The gift by the hunter to a kinsman of the opposite moiety of the head and often the two forefeet of each wild pig killed (see Ch. 7).

b) The service of shooting (with bow and arrow) and butchering the domestic pig of a kinsman of the opposite moiety (see Ch. 7).

Therapeutic services (in healing ritual the patient is attended by men of the opposite moiety) of the type attested between Umeda 'hamlet moieties' (Gell 1975: 84) do not exist among the Eri,

---

29. I maintain here a staunchly conceptualist stance which I would nevertheless not want to generalize to all types of dualism or to other Melanesian societies. In contrast to Douglas' claim (1967: 4) that 'the two sexes can serve *as a model* for the collaboration and the distinctiveness of social units'; my emphasis), I would say of the Yafar that sexual differentiation *determines* a subdivision of the society into two symbolically gendered groups.

30. I oppose reciprocity and complementarity: dual complementarity relates two instances of different natures which, working together, ensure the unity of the whole (the society). Reciprocity relates two groups or individuals regarded, in the circumstances, as being on the same level and of the same nature. In Yafar dualism, complementarity and reciprocity bring into play the same units (Araneri and Angwaneri moieties), but their sexually complementary nature does not enter into their relations of reciprocity (the sexual symbolism of the moieties is cancelled out).

but they are said to have existed among the Yafar in the past. As we see, the two circumstances cited are not reciprocal exchanges between moieties as groups, but between kinsmen of opposite moieties. This would seem to indicate that the kinship dimension (and eventually, as we shall see, 'privileged kinship ties' called *segwaag*) is also borne in mind. Besides kinship, residence also comes into play, since the exchanges take place only at the level of each separate hamlet.

It seems, then, that in answer to the last 'question' posed above, the facts show small-scale systems of exchange which have grafted themselves on to the dual structure, although they already existed in the kinship network. As for matrimonial reciprocity, the moieties are not exogamous, even though informants sometimes present them as preferentially so; but as we shall see when looking at marriage alliances, the groups that enter into these exchanges are clans or submoieties.

These observations bring us back to the importance of the conceptual dimension in Yafar dualism, to its anchoring in the psychic and intellectual image of a sexual complementarity that is relatively egalitarian but stamped with female domination. It is the imaginary aspect of the relation between the sexes that is expressed here, in opposition to social relations, in which a certain male domination prevails. In this sense, dual representations in a way contradict ideology, which may explain the secrecy enveloping the symbolic meaning of the organization into moieties.

3

From Dualism to Patrilineal Units

> What did I come from? I didn't come from nothing:
> I came from my mother who suckled me.
>
> (Yafar saying)

Dualism of the first level became meaningful only when realized in ritual, where the symbolic unity of the gendered moieties was opposed to the separation of men and women in ceremonial practice and the control of knowledge. When the patriclans are taken into account, and even though each is definitively tied to one moiety or the other and thus figuratively marked with a gender, another aspect of the men/women relationship can be envisaged, this time from the standpoint of genealogical reality. And yet again, here, against a backdrop of sexual comple-mentarity, of undifferentiated cooperation corresponding to the recognition of all kinship ties in a global cognatic vision, the male sphere once more steps modifies the configuration, endowing itself with *de jure* and *de facto* primacy over the female. Links in the female line are given as much recognition as those in the male line, but those that are socially 'memorized' the best, to the extent of giving rise to constituted, named descent groups, are the lineal and collateral male links. In totemic dualism, men control female and male cosmic fertility. Through patriliny they dominate mastery of the management of the land (Ch. 5), of the fecundity of women (the exchanging groups are patriclans: Ch. 10) and of religious offices.

Moieties and submoieties on the one hand and clans and line-ages on the other are of different natures, then, even though a man is always a member of both categories by virtue of patri-lineal descent. Nor is clan affiliation optional: the individual has no choice but to be attached to the group of the man recognized as his father. He may be assimilated by a host clan as a lone individual coming from another tribe, but as soon as he has a son, he becomes the founder of a branch that breaks off from his original clan, thereby ensuring the permanence of his agnatic identity (Ch. 1).

Chapters 10 and 11 will show more clearly how the link with the mother (see the epigraph to this chapter) and the recognition of ephemeral uterine lines (which do not give rise to identifiable groups) are integrated into the alliance system or constitute a permanent theme of cultural imaginary representations.

Morphology and Rank

The genealogies collected show a set of named patrilineal groups, ranging from ten or so individuals to over one hundred (including the deceased), and extending over a total of from five to eight generations (three to five generations senior to a middle-aged informant). From the outset we notice a contrast between recent or present-day generations, in which the sibling groups are well stocked with both women and men, and the earlier generations (beyond the grandparents), in which there are only a few men per generation, usually without sisters, the apex of the patrilineage being occupied by one man or two brothers, whose identities often seem in doubt to even the best local specialists. One of the features of these remote generations is therefore that the names of the sisters given in marriage have usually been forgotten, while those of the wives received are still known (as are their origins).

Contrary to African-type lineages, which conceive of themselves as descending from an apical founding ancestor or from certain of his descendants who have founded lineages or segments of lineages, the Yafar lineage can only be thought of from the bottom up, not ending with a specific ancestor, but going as far back as possible towards the controversial frontiers of the group's memory. The most remote names represent nothing and are even totally unknown to most members of the lineage. And yet, as we have seen, the Yafar recognize founding ancestors, whom they place beyond genealogical memory; only a few mature men (*aynaag*) know these names, and sometimes even the origin myth of the clan in which they play a role. These ancestors are not worshipped, however, only the recently deceased or the primordial gods being included in religious practice: between the cult of the recent dead (*nabasa*) and the fertility ritual that calls upon the primal divinities, there is nothing reminiscent of an 'ancestor cult'.

Kinship terminology (Appendix C), of the Dakota-Iroquois type and therefore clearly respecting the criterion of generation, provides ascendants and their close collaterals of ascending generations with reciprocal pairs of gendered terms for ± 2 and ±3 generations, one neutral term for the ± 4 generation, and finally a neutral term unrelated to kinship proper (*asaag(a) bigik* or *mohna*[1]) for ascending generations beyond the fourth, which can be translated as 'ancestors' in the generic sense.

Some clans are subdivided into two lineages ranked as 'elder' and 'younger' (*eteeg/sumnik*). When this is not the case, the clan has a genealogical unity, and the term lineage should theoretically be used. For more clarity, however, I shall use the term 'clan' when speaking of a named patrilineal group and 'lineage' for minimal unnamed units and sometimes for clans comprised of a single lineage. The clan is the strictly exogamous unit (marriage is forbidden between the lineages of a same clan) and is the exchanging unit in marriage; but some clans do not intermarry, and ideally ('formerly', as the Yafar say), marriage was forbidden between clans of the same submoiety. Exogamy is thus inscribed on two levels: on the clan level and, with a few exceptions, on that of the submoiety, seen as a grouping of 'brother' clans (*nerete*). It is possible that in the past the opposition between exogamous groups (submoieties) and exchanging groups (clans) may have been more functional (Ch. 10).

The two-class ranking into elder and younger lineages also operates between certain clans of the same submoiety (Table 4). Clans thus linked may constitute an exogamous group midway between clan and submoiety. In the case of the submoieties of the Angwaneri ('female') moiety, the 'founding' clans (Menaneri and Biyuneri, respectively) are qualified as 'mother' clans (*afaag*) – symbolically associated with the Original Coconut palm – each being endowed with an elder and a younger 'daughter' (*röögunguk*) clan associated with the Coconut's flowers. This organization

---

1. Here *asaag* seems to have a broader meaning than its literal translation of 'great grandmother'; *bigik* means 'the remains, the bones' of a deceased person; *moh* alludes to bygone times.

Moieties	Submoieties	Clans	Number of lineages and status	Total number of members according to genealogy		Total number of living members in 1981	
				M	W	M	W
		Menaneri (Me)	1 (m?)	9	6	0	0
	Menaneri	Suwê enunguruk (Sk)	1(e) (d.e?)	16	9	2	2
		Mesew (Ms)	1 (y) (d.y.?)	10	1	1	0
	(elder)	Wiyneri (Wi)	1	23	14	5	2
		Sig-aynaag (Si)	1 *	18	13	7	4
		Yafwayneri (Ya)	1 *	9	4	3	2
Angwaneri (female)		Biyuneri (Bi)	1 (m)	53	33	25	14
	Mwafneri (younger)	Amisneri (Am)	2 (d.e.) (e)	17	8	1	3
			(y)	25	13	5	5
		Bwasneri (Bw)	1 (d.y.)	10	7	0	1
		Tawank (Ta)	1	8	6	3	2
		Esnaneri (Es)	1 *	4	5	3	3
		Wamawneri (Wa)	1 (e)	15	17	8	2

Total
Angwaneri
M 55
W 38
= 93

Araneri (male) / Wamawneri (elder)			25	8	6	4	
Fuwaneri (Fu) 1 (y)	fêêg (If) 2 (e)	(e)	21	13	5	1	
		(y)	19	17	8	5	
Aayneri (younger)	Ifêaroog (Ig) 1 (y)		36	19	13	2	Total Araneri M 68 W 36 = 104
	Sumneri (Su) 2 (y)	(e)	42	33	7	8	
		(y)	49	28	17	12	
	Sawayneri (Sa) 1 *		4	2	4	2	

Women married into other tribes are included in the above figures
e: elder clan or lineage; y: younger clan or lineage; m: 'mother' clan; d: 'daughter' clan
* recently immigrated branch of a non-Yafar lineage

Table 4. Breakdown of Yafar social units

gives rise to triangular 'uterine' structures; marriage prohibition links the mother clan with each of the daughter clans, but does not necessarily obtain between the two 'sister' clans (Ch. 10). No homologous male-termed structure appears for the submoieties of the Araneri moiety, where only elder/younger pairs are found. In the case of the Aayneri submoiety, the Ifêêg constitute the elder founding clan, while the Ifêaroog and the Sumneri are two so-called younger clans (only the Sumneri intermarry with the other two), with no difference of rank between them. The founding clan of the Wamawneri submoiety is Wamawneri, in the strict sense, Fuwaneri being 'younger'. The recognition of 'founding' or 'prior' clans determines an order of primacy which the Yafar sometimes express as successive settlements at Sahya, but which does not seem to be grounded in historical fact. Femaleness prevails over maleness and elder over younger, producing the following order:

Menaneri, first 'female' founding clan ('elder');
Biyuneri, second 'female' founding clan ('younger');
Wamawneri, first 'male' founding clan ('elder');
Ifêêg, second 'male' founding clan ('younger').

We shall see below that each of these groups possesses special status and responsibilities.

The elder/younger ranking of clans or lineages is sometimes disputed by those concerned. In the case of the Sumneri clan, for instance, the lineage now recognized as elder is purported in fact to be the younger, but the status of elder is supposed to have been demanded for the group by one of its members, an influential Yafar man, and the group is said to have acquiesced to please him. At least, that is the explanation advanced by a member of another lineage, which may obviously be suspected of harbouring a similar but inverse claim. And yet these ideological divergences do not result in quarrels, since lineages and their nominal hierarchy have no function in social reality. We are in the political arena here, but neither wealth, land nor marriage alliances are at stake, and the individual or group who already enjoys or manages to appropriate a higher status derives no practical advantage or special power from it. Nevertheless, as is the case between submoieties, the elder unit is supposed to have been the first to 'take possession' of the land (which land is not always clear) together with its fruit trees and sago palms. Quite simply, then, the elder group claims a status that is often validated by myth, unlike first arrival at a site, which is recognized without the need for legitimation.

Origin Myths

The elder/younger distinction is in several cases legitimized by a myth belonging to the clan concerned – or to a pair of clans – and kept secret. It seems that this is the clan origin myth, known only by a few *aynaag*, unknown to the members of other clans, and passed on in certain privileged lines. It is said that disclosing the origin myth of one's patrilineal group would weaken the group, causing its members to become ill or vulnerable. One of the ways of not revealing anything of one's clan's origins is to designate its members as the 'children of the dead leaves' (*sing na ruwar*) or the 'children of the *afe* ants', in other words the descendants of something insignificant and sterile (of a *roofuk* and not a *hoofuk*). The myth is an integral part of the agnatic group's identity; when it represents the validation of the hierarchical structure (elder/younger), as in the two following examples (the only ones that were revealed to me), it restores something of the clan's unity itself, of the underlying internal order. In the event, this order makes reference to the status of elder, and it is generally said that the elder group 'discovers' its younger sibling and then keeps the youngster by its side. But this opposition also refers to the two complementary categories of the Yafar vision of nature, plant *hoofuk* (sago palm) and animal blood (see myth *b* below).

a) The Origin of the Two Sumneri Lineages
A father (representing the large bamboo *wahuk*, but whose name and origin are not revealed) is sharpening an arrowhead made from the small bamboo *fako* (or *sama*). A bamboo shoot scratches the man's little finger. The next day the finger is swollen, but the swelling bursts and a great quantity of blood spills out. From this blood emerges Nafway. Nafway then marries a woman, Bweyfe, who bears two sons, Hawso, the elder and ancestor of the elder Sumneri lineage, and Tafnay, the younger and ancestor of the younger lineage (to which the narrator belongs).

b) The Origin of Wamawneri and Fuwaneri Clans

Wam[2] encounters Emwêy woman (from *emwêêg* 'vagina'). She is 'old' and foul smelling. She spends her time on the trail, for no one wants her and she is ashamed. Her belly is huge, but her sexual organ is closed and does not 'bleed'. Wam pricks her vulva with a sliver of sago: her sex remains closed. Wam does not want her. Yohwiy (an avatar of the Mwayfik sago palm's growth spirit) arrives on the scene and marries Emwêy. They work sago, he builds a shelter, she makes the jelly. Following Emwêy's counsel, Yohwiy couples with her by hanging on to an *ay* wood stick (*Canarium* sp.) driven into the ground and suspending himself from a hook stuck in the rafters. Bang! Emwêy's belly lets out a great gust of wind, then quantities of frogs, which go to live in the marshes among the sago palms (. . .). Come dawn, Emwêy gets up, her belly is flat. From her *hoofuk* (substance of fecundity) and her spilled blood a young woman is born, Manuay. Emwêy asks Yohwiy to marry her.

Now Wam is willing to have Emwêy. In the meantime he has married a young girl named Ahwar-fəge (*Curculigo* sp.), who has not yet given him a child (prenubile?). He therefore first has a son by Emwêy, who is Fuway, ancestor of the Fuwaneri, then another by Ahwar-fəge, who is Wamaw, ancestor of the Wamawneri.

In the second myth, the elder clan is descended from Wam's second-born son by his young first wife, while the younger clan descends from the first-born by the second[3] wife, a 'bad' woman because of her excessive fecundity. Moreover, Emwêy is 'on the side of *hoofuk*', that is to say, on the side of sago and horticulture, while Ahwar-fəge is 'on the side of blood', in other words game.

It was pointed out to me that the same opposition, associated with other symbolic categories, is found in neighbouring Eri groups. For instance, the origin myths of Aynunkneri and Muwagneri clans present them as the descendants of two brothers, opposed as follows: Muwagneri = elder, blood, game (hunting rites), slow growth / Aynunkneri = younger, vegetal (sago) *hoofuk*, rapid growth.

Some clan names contain allusions to their origin and, to my knowledge, have no attendant explanatory myth. The same is usually true of the eponymous ancestors. Here is the list of the Yafar clans and their corresponding etymologies:

2. Son of Tapi: see Figure 11.
3. This corresponds to the kin terms used between agnatic half-siblings, where the children of the first wife are terminologically the 'elders' of those of the second, whatever their ages (Juillerat 1977).

Menaneri	– Matronym: 'People of Meni' (see Ch. 2, Figure 13).
Suwê-enunguruk	– 'Without hearth or home, he who sleeps out in the cold'. A non-explicit allusion to an ancestor without fire.
Mêsêw	– ?
Wiyneri	– Wiy is a man's name, but the origin of the clan name is said to be different: the segment *wi(y)* can be found in *wi(y)kəga* 'torch'. Mythic element legitimizing this name: one night during a ritual, no one was able to rekindle the dying fire. A man appeared who met with success; his descendants were called *Wiy na ruwar* 'the children of the one who rekindled the fire' or *Wiy na êri* (Wiyneri). See the ritual office attached to this clan (below and Ch. 13).
Sig-aynaag	– (pronounced *səgeinaag*). From *sig* 'tip, end' and *inaag* 'in'. This Punda clan (in Waina: Sinay) is said to be descended from a coconut flower growing at the tip of the inflorescence.
Yafwayneri	– Patronym: 'people of Yafway' (originally Potayneri).
Biyuneri	– Patronym: 'people of Biyu' (no reference).
Mwafneri	– Matronym: 'people of Mwafô' (see Ch. 2, Figure 11).
Amisneri	– Patronym: 'people of Amis' (no reference).
Bwasneri	– Patronym: 'people of Bwas' (no reference).
Tawank	– literally 'stick of firewood' (*tawank kêg*). No reference. Clan descended from a coconut flower.
Esnaneri (or Esyaneri)?	– (a Potayneri submoiety or clan).
Wamawneri	– Patronym: see myth *b* above.
Fuwaneri	– Patronym: see myth *b* above. The actual name of the ancestor Fuway is said to come from the bird *fuwô*, because, when he was born, 'Fuway cried like this bird'.
Ifêêg (or Ifyêêg)	– literally 'original'. The name itself legitimizes the elder status of the clan. Clans or hamlets of the same name can be found

	throughout the Eri and Waina region (Ivieg, Ivil, Ifêr, etc.).
Ifêaroog	– Might be broken down into Ifêêg + *reeg* ('son'), or *röög*[*unguk*] ('daughter'), though this etymology is not recognized by the Yafar. See myth below concerning the office attaching to this clan.
Sumneri	– From *sum* 'to follow, to come after', therefore 'the people who came afterwards' or 'the younger' siblings (*sumnik*). See use of the pair Ifêêg/Sumneri among the Potayneri (Ch. 2, p. 68).
Sawayneri	– Patronym? (originally Potayneri).

Religious Responsibilities of Patrilineal Groups

The interesting question of the ritual specialization of groups or individuals and the power that goes with it will be discussed in more detail in Chapter 13. In the meantime, I would like to draw a general picture of the responsibilities attached to patrilineal units without, for the moment, going into the hierarchy that these offices may determine among persons or entering into detail on the symbolism of the subject.

All ritual roles and the exegetical elements that accompany them are strictly secret; in principle, women and children know nothing about them. Even I, on my earliest trips, was almost totally unaware of these inherited responsibilities, their symbolic function and how they fit into the social make-up. It was only during my fourth and especially fifth visits, in other words eleven years after I first began working among the Yafar, that I was surprised to learn of the existence, where I had previously seen only functionally undifferentiated patriclans, of specific responsibilities of a cosmological nature that were an integral part of these dual and patrilineal units.

Below is the general paradigm of ritual offices, presented in the sociological order of their presence in the groups rather than by order of symbolic function. I will begin with the female moiety to which the Yafar often accord precedence.

The distribution of masterships[4] throughout the social structure is organized by two principles, sameness of the symbolic gender of the cosmic or ecological element constituting the object of responsibility and that of the moiety that holds the title, and to a lesser extent priority of 'elder' submoieties or founding clans for the most important offices. Thus the Angwaneri moiety finds itself with a certain number of offices associated with the female elements of the universe: the Earth (i.e. the Primordial Mother, one of the permanent poles of Yafar symbolism), Water (control over the reproduction of fish and sago palms as well as the worship of the water spirits, *angor*) and the Moon (assimilated to the female reproductive cycle). Furthermore, the founding clan of this female moiety, the Menaneri, was responsible for the rite for purifying young novice killers contaminated by their victim's blood; this moiety occupies the position of 'bottom', of the setting sun, in village cosmology, as well as (together with another female lineage, this one from the younger submoiety) the north and south sides (Ch. 1).

The clans and lineages of the Araneri moiety hold offices complementary to those above, the mastership of the Sky and the Sun, while in the village space the founding clan (Wamawneri) occupies the rising sun and 'top' positions. Opposite this status of 'Master of the Village' (*kəbik na awaag*) stands that of the elder Ifêêg clan, from the younger submoiety, which is considered to be the first occupant of the Araneri lands and as a consequence bears the name of *nôô na awaag* 'Master of the Forest Lands'.[5] To this must be added responsibility for the opening rites of the ceremonial cycles dedicated respectively to the male forest spirits, *nabasa*, and the female spirits, *sawangô*, initially in the hands of the Ifêaroog (male moiety), who later transmitted the *sawangô* cult to a clan from the female moiety, the Amisneri. The cult of the *angor* river spirits was the responsibility of the Tawank (female moiety) who, through the Waw rite in particular (described below, pp. 133–134), ensured the reproduction of aquatic species. On the whole we note more offices in the female moiety than in the male, which corresponds to the predominant place of things female in the symbolic system.

---

4. I prefer the terms 'master' and 'mastership', for official religious responsibilities, my translation in this context of *awaag*, literally 'father'.

5. Today's members are also called *nôô na ruwar* 'children of the forest lands'.

Moieties	Submoieties	Clans	Offices
Angwaneri (female)	Menaneri 'elder'	Menaneri now extinct (founding) clan	1. Master of the Earth? (formerly) (bθte na awaag) 2. Master of homicide magic (fag seeg na awaag) 3. 'Father' role at the founding of the village
		Suwê-enunguruk	—
		Mêsêw	—
		Wiyneri	Master of Light-Fire (Wiy na awaag)
		Sig-aynaag	Master of the Earth for Yafar 2 (function received from the Menaneri)
	Mwafneri (younger)	Biyuneri (Mwafneri)	Master of the Earth for Yafar 1 (bθte na awaag)
		Amisneri	1. Master of the female sawangô spirits cult 2. 'Father' role at the founding of the village (after extinction of the Menaneri)
		Bwasneri	Master of the Moon (wos na awaag)
		Tawank	1. Master of fishing magic (sawôg seeg na awaag) and the angor water spirits cult 2. Role of 'flanks' at the founding of the village 3. Master of Murder Magic (collaborating with, then replacing the Menaneri)
		Yafwayneri	Master of the Earth for Yafar 3 (recently received from the Biyuneri)

Araneri (male)		Functions
Wamawneri (elder)	Wamawneri (founder)	1. Master of the Sun (*akba na awaag*)
		2. 'Son' role at the founding of the village (*kƏvik na awaag*)
		3. Only one to wear the 'Cassowary' mask in the Yangis rite
	Fuwaneri	Master of the Sky for Yafar 2 (*oof na awaag*)
Aayneri (younger)	Iféêg	1. First occupant of Araneri land (*nôô na awaag*)
		2. Master of the Sky for Yafar 3 (recent)
	Ifêaroog	Master of the male *nabasa* spirits cult
	Sumneri	Master of the Sky for Yafar 1 (*oof na awaag*)

Table 5. Distribution of religious offices among patrilineal groups and dual units

The vernacular terms in parentheses refer to the functions of the corresponding 'masters' (*awaag*) (see Ch. 13)

A responsibility is thus theoretically attached to each one of what we have qualified as the formal units (p. 3), even though it can be more easily transmitted from one clan to another or be shared by several clans of the same moiety. The semantic link and the symbolic function here are stronger than the sociological order. That the mastership of the Earth passes from one patriclan to another within the female moiety is not logically very important, since its connection with a particular lineage is only a matter of social convention; on the other hand, it would be absurd and unacceptable for this function to pass to the male moiety. Although the first type of transfer might give rise to objections of a political nature between the groups involved (though I never heard of any such rivalry), the second type would, from the very outset even before it developed into a political quarrel be rejected as inconsistent with the symbolic order. In this case it is the semantic identity between religious office and dual unity that weakens the functional coherence of the descent group. This is confirmed in concrete terms by the fact that the other clans of the moiety and especially of the submoiety play a helping role in ritual responsibilities. Through this sort of interclan fraternity, these groups can contribute to the ritual actions by assisting, or if necessary replacing, those officially in charge. A distinction must be made between patrilineal units of the same moiety or submoiety helping in the ritual and the definitive transfer of an office upon the extinction of the lineage responsible for it (Ch. 13). It should be noted that patriclans are not regarded as discrete units between which offices can pass back and forth; on the contrary, the only thing that enables such transfers to take place are non-agnatic affinal ties between individuals, just as maintaining a given mastership in the same line depends on the principle of unilineal descent. The transfer of ritual office thus depends above all on one man and his patriline and only secondarily on a group or lineage.

The same is true for a number of hunting rites each performed by a given lineage and attached to specific land. Founded on the use and custodianship of a magic clone that carries the name of the territory concerned, all these rites are supposed to 'make game appear' (Ch. 7). The members of such a lineage are designated as the 'men of such and such magical plant'; for example, the Amisneri are the Namhay-seeg êri, 'those of the magic plant (*seeg*) of Namhay's land', one lineage of Suwê-enunguruk clan is

Tubur-seeg êri, etc. Parallel to the hunting ritual, a specific magic spell for planting sago palms in the forest (as opposed to garden rites) depended on certain Biyuneri and Wiyneri lines, who were the custodians of the *Acorus calamus* clone used; one of those responsible would work the magic in secret. Recently, following interclan marriages, the clone was divided.

The coherence and paired organization (Sky/Earth, Sun/Moon, male/female spirits, east/west) of the principle offices being discussed here gives the overall appearance of a whole, the unity of which, on the symbolic level, lies in the functional complementarity of natural and cosmic elements whose conjunction is indispensable for the perpetuation of life.

Another complementarity, different from that of the patrilineal units, appears in certain ceremonial contexts, the most important of which is Yangis. In this ritual, described in the preceding chapter, the masks are made of two sheets of coconut petiolar fibre sewn together, both sides being painted with designs corresponding to what might be called clan emblems. In principle there are seven of these (four connected with the Angwaneri moiety and three with the Araneri moiety). One of the masks has a special status: the Cassowary mask worn exclusively by men of Wamawneri clan, the male moiety founding clan. To this must be added the pair of *ifɘge* masks (p. 53), worn by one man from each moiety, regardless of clan. Each painting, with the exception of those of the *ifɘge*, represents a species found in nature, which is, for the clan concerned, a taboo (in some cases a forbidden food) associated with an *ogomô*, a sago-palm fertility spirit; according to one exegesis, these are the twin sons of the Original Mother.

In principle a man may wear only the emblem of his own patrilineal group, but an exception is made for his sisters' sons (*rabiniga*) and his patrilateral cross cousins. Moreover, clans without an emblem join up with either their mother's brother's clan, or in some cases with their submoiety's brother clan. The Menaneri, a now-extinct lineage, do not have an emblematic mask, but they may have had one in the past, unless their role as premier clan of the female moiety provided them with a special status.

Another example of lineage groups cooperating in rituals to express an idea or a unified representation is provided by the Waw rite (no longer celebrated today and which, unlike Yangis, I have never observed), performed by the 'female' Tawank lineage and by its Master of the Multiplication of Fish (Table 5). The key

Moiety	Submoiety	Clan	Design	Name of ogomô
M	e.	Wamawneri	young cassowary (*kwoyrêmp*)	Kwoy ('cassowary')
F	y.	Bwasneri	insect *wank*	Bwampi
M	y.	Sumneri	grub *bwerinaag*	Urey
F	y.	Amisneri	python *ha*	Mwangwoy
M	y.	Ifêêg	screech owl *wêy*	Wêy
F	e.	Wiyneri	pigeon *yibus*	Waruwô
F	y.	Biyuneri	tree *sêhêf*	Bay
M/F	(var.)	(variable)	(non figurative)	(role of the *ifộge*)

Table 6. Clan emblems used in Yangis

ideas are duality, represented by the two species of tree used (opposed leaves on the *Gnetum gnemon*, associated flowers and fruit on the *bunwe* tree, *Endospermum* sp.); fertility, the phases of growth represented by the different parts of the trunk and the branches; and finally, the reproduction of the female fertility principle (*hoofuk*), represented in particular by the paired 'mothers' and 'daughters' masks, the latter having their head wrapped in nets, symbolizing the uterus. Here is a succinct description of this rite, which is organized without the women's knowledge:

> A large quantity of smoked fish and sago is taken down to the river. A young *Gnetum gnemon* is stripped of its bark and the trunk coated with red ochre and the blood of game (spells are said). The tree is then uprooted by a group of men who divide the task according to lineage: a) the Tawank, assisted by the other female moiety clans, grasp the base of the trunk; b) the Wamawneri and the Fuwaneri (male moiety) take hold of the middle; c) a special line of the Suwê-enunguruk (female moiety) takes the top. The tree is then replanted in the middle of the river, which is shallow. Another tree, *bunwe*, is then cut up according to the same lineages and painted. The base of the trunk is placed in the water downstream from the *G. gnemon*, and the upper part of the trunk upstream. Sticks of *ay* (*Canarium* sp.), also coated with ochre, are set into the river bed upstream and downstream, without distinction as to the clan membership of those officiating. The fish and the sago are eaten collectively.
> Next, two pairs of figures enter: a) two men from Tawank clan, their bodies painted with vertical polychrome stripes, their head

swathed in coconut petiolar fibre, (*bəsa*) position themselves face to face; b) two other men, a Suwê-enunguruk and an Ifêêg, bodies painted in many-coloured horizontal stripes evoking sago as the embodiment of *hoofuk* (Ch. 9), their head wrapped in a net, *wura*, come and go. The first two are called 'mothers', the other two 'daughters'. Another group of undecorated men plays wooden trumpets,*fuf*, the sound of which is associated with growth and reproduction. The old men of the group throw aromatic plants and coconut and sago meat, symbols of *hoofuk*, into the water, while calling out the names of fish and rivers. When the ceremony is over, the four masks are hung on the *G. gnemon*, which will be swept away by the next flood.

Suckers, seeds and tree stumps evoke, in the vegetal realm, the maternal role, whence the position of the female moiety Tawank clan in handling the *G. gnemon*. Vertical growth (as opposed to fruiting) as well as the trunk are the product of an active male principle, which is expressed by the presence of the two brother clans of the elder male submoiety at this level of the tree. Finally the tips of the flower- and fruit-bearing branches announce a return to the beginning of the cycle, which appears to be expressed by the presence of the 'female' Suwê-enunguruk clan, here apparently the bearer of this identification with rebirth. The roles of the 'mothers'' masks are once again played by Tawank, while the 'daughters'' masks are worn like the *ifəge* of Yangis by one man from each moiety. As the organizers of the Waw rite, the Tawank transmit life in a metaphorical manner, promoting new birth (of the aquatic species), while the Suwê-enunguruk and the Ifêêg represent the beneficiaries who, through the conjunction of the two 'sexes' (the moieties) will ensure the reproductive phase.[6] This rite is the enactment of a naturalized vision of the social units: the (intersubjective) inter-action between individuals expresses an intrasocial cooperation which finds its meaning in a figuration of vegetal growth, which in turn serves as a metaphor for the reproduction of fish. Even though it is now somewhat dated, it may be useful to conclude by trying to situate the Yafar descent system in the

6. In this correspondence between the symbolism of vegetal growth and that of social units, it is easy to recognize the gendered principles of the growth cycle as revealed in mythology, i.e. seeds = female-maternal; shoot = male (son); stem growth (trunk) = male (father); flowers and fruit = daughters; bursting of the seed by the violent action of the male principle (sexual act) = mother in childbirth.

problematic defined in the 1960s by various authors, principally
for New Guinea Highland societies.[7] The problem was to determine the place occupied in the social system by descent groups,
in this case by lineages or patriclans, and to situate these with
respect to a cognatic stratum or in opposition to a parallel matrilineal representation. Are these groups social actors in themselves
or are they merely the result of the projection of patrilineal ideology, permitting individuals to be affiliated with a lineage? The
Yafar answer is a compromise of sorts featuring named patriclans
and patrilineages (even though there is no generic term for them)
comprised of genealogically affiliated individuals. Such a group
therefore cannot recruit members from the outside to ward off
demographic extinction. We have seen, however, that an immigrant branch may choose to be called by the name of an extinct
founding clan (the case of the Menaneri), while at the same
time keeping its original name. Yafar clans come about, then, by
incorporating migrant segment founders, and they die a natural
death. Yet examination of land-holding (Ch. 5), marriage (Ch. 10)
and religious offices (further discussed in Ch. 13) will show
that most of the time, only part (one particular segment or line,
for instance) of a patriclan or patrilineage is taken into account
by the Yafar system in any particular situation, for example
when a piece of land is controlled by a single lineage segment, or
when the marriage of a woman into a collateral patriline of her
father's or mother's mother is tolerated (see prohibition 3, p. 300),
or when sacred knowledge is preferentially transmitted through
one agnatic line to the exclusion of all others. Here the principle
of individual patrilineal descent can be seen to prevail over the
consideration of agnatic groups as solidary operational units. The
fact that young, adolescent and even adult Yafar hesitate as to the
name of their clan or make mistakes and that they demonstrate a
very limited genealogical memory is symptomatic of the individual's weak identification with his descent group as such; this
group is perceived by ego uniquely through personal agnatic

7. Among others, Barnes, Brown, Kaberry, Langness, Lepervanche, Meggitt, Strathern
and Wagner, for the Highlands (see A. Strathern's critical review, 1968). For the 'Lowlands',
where the problem is just as crucial, the same period saw a debate between van der Leeden
(1960) and Pouwer (1960) on the Sarmi hinterlands in Irian Jaya and Mead's material on
the Arapesh (1970–1971). For more recent work, the reader can consult Kelly 1977, Stanek
1983, Tuzin 1976 and, for a comparative point of view, Rubel and Rosman 1978 (Ch. 12) and
Lévi-Strauss 1984.

relations. As a consequence the descent group is accorded little cultural value, which also explains the absence of an ancestor cult, as I have already pointed out. The primacy of interindividual relationships defined by bilateral kinship over the conceptualization of supra-individual genealogical entities explains the fragility of the latter as constituted social groups. When the life of a society is organized within the framework of agnation, it is bound by a recognized clan structure, but usually does not make full use of clans in the elaboration of social relationships. The patriclan provides a genealogical framework that is restricted by the unilineal principle, but it proves to be too vast to represent in any pragmatic way the ideology of patriliny, or too limited by the fact that it includes neither maternal kin nor affines. Thus Yafar society seems to correspond to the case in which the representation of paternal filiation has determined the formation of named, recognized groups, but where low numbers, high mortality and, as a consequence, the small size of these units has kept them from becoming effective elements in the global system.[8] This situation shows that the cultural symbolization of individual filiation is the basis of the constitution of unilineal descent groups.

---

8. I agree with Pouwer's arguments on this point (see Kaberry 1967: 111). In fact it is not only the small size of the tribal groups that is of concern, but the small size of the clans themselves and their demographic fragility.

4

Household and Family

— And what about you? Do you know how to build a car?
— Well no, that's not my job. Besides, you need a lot of people to make a car.
— Ah, I see, the father, the mother, the children. . .

(Conversation with Waya Warey, 1981)

The Yafar household is comprised of a small number of individuals living under one roof. This means constant economic cooperation, common management of goods despite individual ownership (Ch. 6) and the sharing of products at their consumption. As the smallest cell of society, the household is often synonymous with the nuclear or polygynous family, the morphology of which is in constant flux.

The sociodemographic dynamic is echoed by what might be called an intravillage settlement dynamic: when a lone couple begins to have children, they rebuild their house on a slightly larger scale. Soon the time comes for the married son to leave his parents and move into a new house, where he may eventually take in his widowed father or mother. Abandoned houses are quickly demolished and part of the material recovered; temporary breaches appear in the circle of dwellings. Some villagers have a garden house, where they prefer to live periodically with their family. Others, confirmed bachelors, young widowers or, more rarely, men who have chosen to live apart from their family, take up residence in a garden or in the midst of a bamboo grove, working sago on their own (normally the woman's job). One young lone wolf boasted of his independence by referring to himself as a 'wild pig'; having agreed to marry the widow of one of his clan brothers and decided to take her and her two young daughters to live with him in his bush retreat, he finally called off the marriage when his future wife gave him to understand that she was determined to stay in the village and live in society. These are exceptions, however, and the overall stability of marriages guarantees that of the household. The village house remains the principal residence, despite the occasional night-time use of garden shelters or of bush camps[1] established near stands of sago palms. The architectural uniformity of Eri hamlets points to a certain morphological homogeneity of the household. Moreover, the importance of the family as an indivisible unit tempers the now classic image of strong sexual discrimination in Melanesian societies. In effect, family cohesion in everyday activities contrasts with the ideological antagonism that opposes men and women in general (see Juillerat 1990).

The Yafar House

The Yafar house, *raara*, is a square building, four to five metres on a side, extended by a front porch and usually built on top of a low man-made mound of earth. Forked ironwood posts support the joists of the floor (*səme*), which is made of tight lathwork or flattened bark of the wild areca palm (100–180 cm off the ground) and into which are set four square clay fireplaces (*gemeso*). The walls, made from sago palm petioles (*tööf*), descend to the ground. A roof of sago-palm folioles (*rəba*) covers the single room, entered from the porch, which is accessible by means of a notched log (*ging*), which is removed when everyone is away. The solid balustrade gives the porch (*səmemôk*: literally 'bottom of the floor') a defensive air. A door (*mengêk tööf*, from *mengêk* 'mouth') enables the household to shut themselves in at night to keep the damp night air out and the heat from the cooking fires in, but they also believe this protects them from magical attacks by foreign sorcerers or from ghostly predations. The porch always faces on to the orchard and the slope, while the village side of the house has no windows, only two tiny apertures (*meeg səbeeg*) that have always been used more to keep an eye on the village square than to fire on assailants, as the Eri have never really practised warfare in the form of village attacks. The ridge pole, called 'the backbone' (*rumuri-kêg*), extending some distance

---

1. Waina groups take to family bush camps for long periods of time, leaving the village deserted, a custom much less widespread among the Eri.

beyond the ends of the house, is bound to the top of two tall iron-wood posts (*gungwe kêg*)[2] set deep in the ground. Slightly larger houses have a centre post called *yis bigik teteeg*, because that is where people wipe (*teteeg*) the remains (*bigik*) of sago jelly (*yis*) from their fingers.

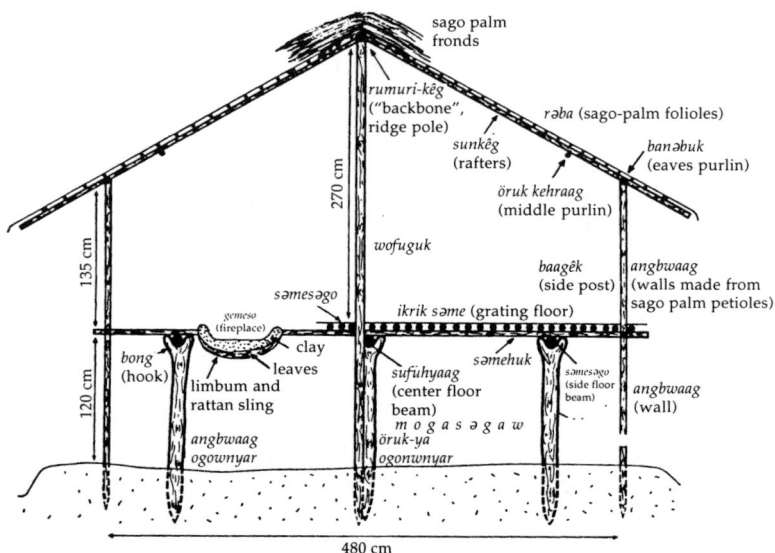

Figure 16. Cross-section of a Yafar house and architectural terms

Through its two opposing slopes, the rafters of which are sup-ported by a purlin midway between the ridge pole and the eaves (*öruk kehraag*), through an eaves purlin (*banəbuk*) set atop the outer wall, and finally through a thin purlin connecting the ends of the rafters under the eaves, the roof evokes the celestial vault. The Amanab language locates the position of the sun at points along the thatch: *rumuri-kêg-wa* ('at the zenith'), *öruk kehraag-wa* (around 10 a.m. and 3 p.m.), *banəbuk-wa* (around 9 a.m. and 4 p.m.) and *pupuk-ya* (around 7 a.m. and 6 p.m.).[3]

2. For the symbolic importance of this part of the house, see above, p. 30.
3. The positions of the sun in the afternoon can be expressed in terms of diminishing heat: 'the fire burns', 'the fire is dying down', 'the fire is out'. Other references closer to nature can be used to define times of day, such as *kwimpi-ya*, an allusion to the call of the *kwimpi* bird (*Centropus menbeki*), i.e. before dawn, or *kwekwe ate-o*, 'the *kwekwe* toads (*Platy-mantis papuensis*) are croaking' (early evening).

Building a new house is a collective undertaking in which the builder's female kin are charged with gathering and transporting the sago-palm folioles for the roof and collecting and sometimes working the clay for the fireplaces; the rest is men's work. Someone familiar with the ritual, the builder's father for instance, recites the charms and slips the leaves or roots of magical plants into certain parts of the house (ground, floor, roof, door, fireplaces); these rites are supposed to attract the forest guardian spirits of game, to associate them with the hunter's new dwelling in such a way that many trophies come to be lined up under the roof, etc. In particular, for the four founding houses (pp. 32–33), a magical rhizome representing 'Tapi's backbone' (see myth p. 30) is placed under the first post and spells are said to keep the self (*sungwaag*) of the household members from wandering about while they are asleep, retaining them, as it were, inside the dwelling, a symbolic process that comes under the heading of Gungwan ritual (analysed in Ch. 12). The inauguration of the wife's fireplace, where she will heat the stones for making sago jelly (*yis*), is done by the husband and wife together. Charms are used to evoke the smell of *yis*, which is compared to the odour of sweat and to that of the anal glands of small mammals that hunters sometimes rub on their bodies to make themselves pleasing to the forest spirits; a rhizome of a sago clone reserved for spells and a bit of powdered anal gland are placed on the first pieces of firewood. The husband performs a complementary ritual on his own fireplace, where he will braise the game he has caught, in the course of which he verbally associates the fire with various types of blood, menstrual blood or blood of childbirth as well as that of wild animals.

After a few years, the roof needs repairing; after ten or fifteen years, the whole house is replaced.

The furnishings of the Yafar house are comprised in the main of limbum containers (*sööbi*), most of which hang from the rafters, nets and bundles containing the men's ritual ornaments wrapped in pieces of bark cloth (*woom*), one or two hourglass drums and smoking baskets (*kaga*) hung over the fireplaces. Each individual's place near the fire is marked by a flattened limbum (*kəfe*), which serves as a sleeping mat. The walls are lined with supplies of firewood brought back by the women. Nowadays, one rarely sees the skulls of deceased relatives, but stuck into the soot-blackened thatch, one can see series of small mammal or

reptile skulls and jaws, and wildfowl egg shells, which attest to
the hunting activity of the head of the house. The larger trophies
are displayed on the outer wall, facing the village square, a row
or two of pig skulls or cassowary breastbones. At the rear of
the house, near the place of the head of the family, bows and
dozens of arrows, the height of a man, lean against the wall;
the arrows are of several types, some very old, with painted and
feathered tips formerly reserved for ceremonial use or murder.
Today there are also axes and bushknives. In a *sööbi* near the
wife's place stand some stone sago pounders (*hwagi*), together
with coconut petiolar fibres used for filtering and wrapping sago.
A pile of stones used to heat the water for making sago jelly or
for braising meat, as well as one or two pairs of wooden tongs
for plucking the stones out of the hot water stand near by. There
is no water storage in the house. When I made my first visit in
1970, manufactured objects were rare, with the exception of some
steel tools and a few items of European clothing carefully stored
in a wooden chest brought back from the plantations. Ten years
later, most of the young people wore clothes, and every house
had a flashlight plus a few covers and towels, while the village
occasionally shared a few aluminium pots, a radio or a shotgun
or two.

As a symbolic as well as a social structure, the Yafar house is
organized on two planes. On the vertical plane, first of all, it is
made up of an upper storey perched on stilts, where the household goes about its everyday life, and a ground floor room, entered
directly from the outside through a special door usually located
under the porch. The ground floor, called *mogasangaw*, is used
only by the women during menstruation or childbirth; in the latter case, they stay there with their child until the new moon (Ch.
9). In some non-Yafar villages, and then only in the houses
of widowers or elderly couples, the ground-floor room is sometimes used to keep the pigs at night. On the horizontal plane, the
domestic space is set up as a square in which the symbolic organization overlays the subdivision into four subspaces, allocated to
the members of the family according to sex and rank.[4] The back
of the house, which the Yafar call 'the head side' (*mesoa-gam*) and
which they associate with the 'top', has two fireplaces, one of
which belongs to the head of the house. The half of the house

---

4. See Juillerat 1981 and above, Ch. 2, Figure 12.

closest to the door, 'the loins side' (*emǝgo-gam*), or the 'bottom' contains the other two fireplaces, one of which (to the left upon entering) is occupied by the wife and her young children, the other (on the right) by the older daughters or by the second wife and her own children.[5] The *emǝgo-gam* is subdivided in its turn into the *mengê-gam* 'the mouth side', or the side next to the door and the porch, and the *ging furhya-gam*, the side where the log-ladder (*ging*) is stood (*furhyaag*) when drawn up. Ritual objects and weapons are kept in the 'top' part, while cooking utensils are arranged around the cooking fires in the 'bottom'. Associated with fire, with femaleness according to the myth and with women's work, stored firewood encloses the household space within its walls.

Household Composition

Table 7 shows that, of the total number of households[6] comprising the tribe in 1970 and 1981, half were nuclear families. The rest – not counting several regroupings of siblings or cousins and one boys' house per hamlet – were either couples who did not yet have children, families reduced by the death of a parent or the marriage of a daughter, or, conversely enriched by the arrival of a second wife or the recent marriage of a son, as the young couple lives for some time with the husband's parents; in a few cases there is reduction and augmentation at the same time. The category 'miscellaneous' contains households comprised of one pair of brothers, one pair of unmarried handicapped sisters living with a sister's son and a brother's daughter, and finally two agnatic cousins living with an old man separated from his wife. The unmarried boys' house is a constant of Eri hamlets; it should

5. These rules are not systematically respected in practice, where each family feels free to organize daily life as it sees fit, but they are formally recognized. Although each person has his or her allotted place, all are free to use the entire living space. However, women do not touch weapons or ritual objects and avoid stepping over the family head's *kǒfe*.

6. The average household had 3.70 persons in 1970 and 3.95 in 1981. Despite this momentary increase, the changes brought in by the Australian government in 1960, in particular greater security, have caused the household to move towards a reduction in size. Formerly, people say, dwellings were no bigger, but they were a bit fuller, and it was not rare to see two nuclear families under one roof. Allocation of space was nevertheless probably based on the same principles. This need for a denser household can be traced to the custom of several families working the same garden.

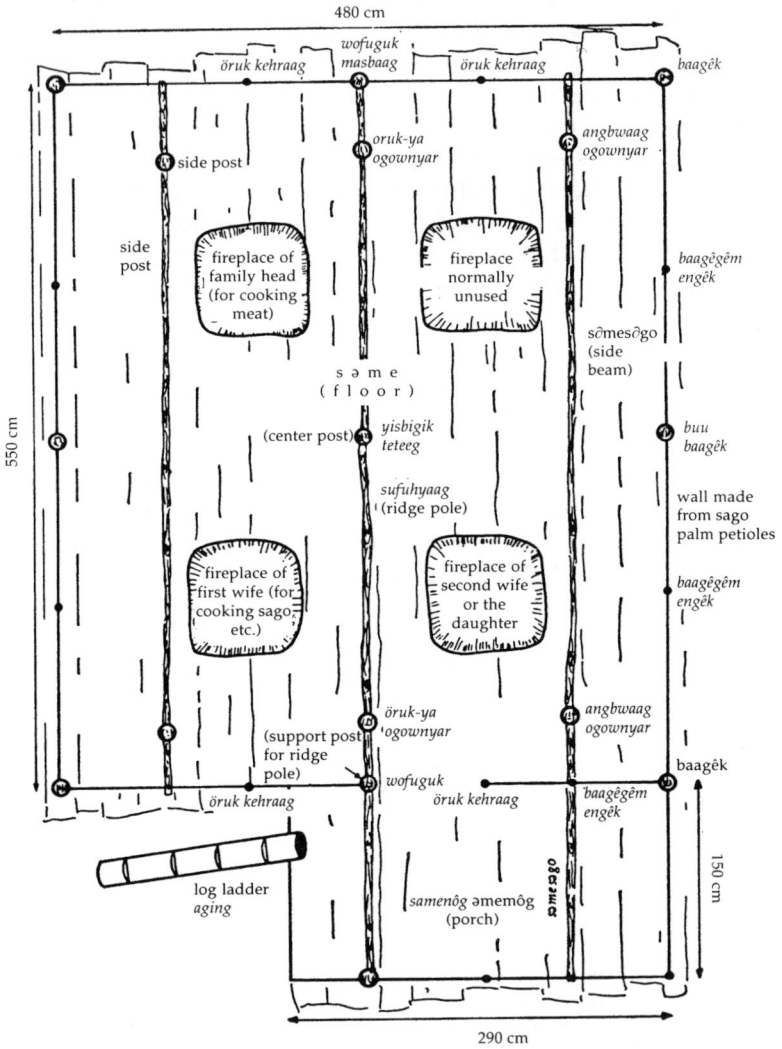

Figure 17. Floor plan of a Yafar house and architectural terms

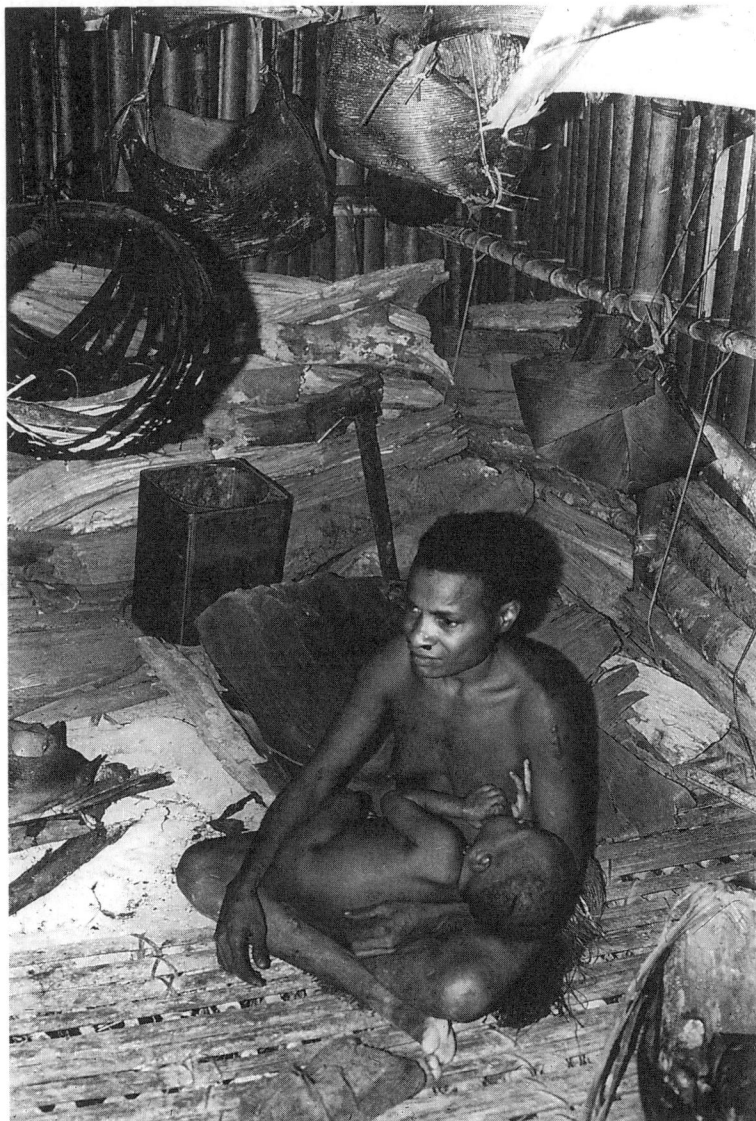

Plate 3. Inside a family dwelling: fireplace, smoking baskets hanging from the rafters, limbum, firewood.

be seen only as a way of relieving over-populated households and affording adolescent boys a partial escape from parental control while at the same time grouping together; this little household community has no economic autonomy, as each boy still joins his family for garden work or meals (he can, however, hunt small game, fish and do some light gathering for himself). The interior of a *mööf raara* ('bachelors' house') is easily recognized by the absence of cooking utensils. Furthermore, these household groups are particularly fluctuating. This reflects the high degree of residential mobility of adolescents, who, having gained some independence, like to come and go, and seek to assert their identity both through this mobility and through their increased hunting activity (see Gell 1975 and Oosterwal 1959). These households of unmarried adolescents, never comprising more than five or six individuals, are informal groups whose temporary homogeneity is not underpinned by any institutional rule (such as age-classes) or by any ties other than kinship and camaraderie.

Household composition	Number of houses	
	1970	1981
Childless couple	4	5
Childless couple + parent(s)	1	0
Nuclear family (with eventual adopted child)	21	23
Nuclear family + other relative(s)	2	3
Nuclear family + son's wife or 'fiancée'	0	1
Nuclear family + widowed father and unmarried children	0	1
Polygynous family (2 wives)	1	1
Polygynous family + parent(s)	0	1
Widower and child(ren)	7	2
Widower and child(ren) + other relative(s)	0	5
Widow and children	2	3
Widow and children + other relative(s)	2	0
Widower alone	1	1
Widow and children, including 2 childless married sons	0	1
Bachelor alone	0	2
Miscellaneous	5	3
Total houses for the 3 hamlets	46	52

Table 7. Household composition by house

Household composition	Number of houses	
	1970	1981
Unmarried men	14	17
Unmarried women	7	6
Married men	28	39
Married women	29	40
Widowers	9	10
Widows	5	6
Children	68	87
Total Yafar population	160	205

Table 8. Household composition by sex and social status

Typically in the nuclear family or half-family (one living parent) there is often a large age difference between parents and children.[7] The fact that a man's marriage is usually delayed by the lack of potential wives and low overall longevity means that all children rapidly lose their father and/or their mother. If the child has been weaned, the loss of its parents has no dramatic consequences, since it is taken in by a brother or cousin of one of the parents. But such losses do develop the system of adoption, so that every orphaned adolescent – i.e. the majority of children over 15 – can cite one or more adoptive fathers or mothers, always defined as the one who has 'fed' them.[8] Nevertheless, the terminology stresses the adoptive father, designated by the term *atôk*, rather than the adoptive mother, who is called simply 'mother'. If an infant or very young child loses its mother, the father will place it with a wet nurse, that is a relative already nursing a child. But this is not always possible, and a child still totally dependent on breast milk often dies shortly after its mother.[9] If the child loses its father, the mother will take it with her when, some months later, she goes to a new home (remarriage); we have seen that in this case a male child may become the founder of a new clan line outside his original tribe. An adolescent daughter remains with her widowed father and

7. The consequence of the protein-poor diet slowing the growth rate and delaying the onset of puberty for from three to five years is a longer period of dependence. For the neighbouring Torricelli Range regions, the average age at onset of menstruation is 17.8 years, and adolescents of both sexes go through their puberty rites at between 16 and 18 years of age (Lewis 1980: 107n).

8. See next chapter for the consequences of adoption on land-holding.

9. The precarious health of the population and in particular of women who are pregnant or have just given birth makes fosterage impracticable.

may replace her mother in the house and the garden. A widower who has no chance of remarrying may sometimes seek to retain his youngest daughter, even though she is of an age to marry. As available wives are scarce, he often comes under pressure to relinquish his paternal rights; sometimes the girl is abducted by her future husband. Lone widowers become dependants and, like orphans, may be taken in by a succession of different households. This shows the importance of sexual complementarity (even outside the couple) in the economic organization of the household. For a boy, the adoption system can foster a degree of independence during adolescence, as the child does not feel as strongly bound to his *atôk* as he would to his real father. The same is obviously not true for a girl, who, until her marriage, remains closely dependent upon her adoptive mother and has no side activities, like the boys' hunting, that would afford her some autonomy in conjunction with her age group.

The relative mobility of adolescent sons is a transitory, integrated stage (between childhood and marriage) which in no way threatens the truly remarkable stability of the parental couple. As we shall see in the discussion of marriage, while periods of instability do occur in marriages, these arise only during the first few months, while the couple is trying to find their economic as well as affective equilibrium. Once consolidated, the couple remain close, especially after the birth of the first child. Break-ups of the nuclear family and the household are therefore due to factors of a (illness, death) natural order rather than to social causes.

Later we will analyse the forms of exchange that enable a nuclear family to become a production unit in the context of shifting horticulture. The exact outlines of the economic unit are difficult to determine: it may be said that theoretically they coincide with the nuclear family, but to this must be added the occasional parent of the husband or wife. Conversely, a bachelor who shares a roof with a family can easily work his own land and sago, sharing his production with other kinsmen and maintaining a large degree of economic autonomy with respect to his host family. Households not based on the nuclear family are not generally close-knit economic units. Moreover, there is another type of product distribution that goes beyond the boundaries of the domestic group.[10] It is therefore simplistic and often false to equate household and production unit strictly (see Chs 6–7).

10. For further details, see below, Chs 6 and 7, as well as Juillerat 1983a.

Plate 4. The sago jelly (*yis*) is doled out in individual portions onto leaves.

Gathered at home for the morning and evening meals and their night's rest, the household tends to disperse during the day. In effect the distribution of daily chores tends to scatter the family, with the exception of a few tasks that require the couple to work together: felling a sago palm and preparing the filtering apparatus, gathering large quantities of shoots, the early stages of garden clearing. Some days, however, the whole family meets at midday in a garden for a meal of sago jelly, tubers or roasted plantain. In former times, when raids by neighbouring groups were a danger, women were rarely left alone away from the village, to work sago or in a garden, and the husband, father or a brother would stand watch nearby. Notwithstanding this day-time dispersal, the products are brought back to the village to be consumed in common.

The household can also be identified as a meaningful unit in the ritual sphere, even though other levels are also involved in delineating the social area addressed by the ceremony. In the horticultural context, ritual is inscribed within the cleared space, but when this ground is worked by a single family, ritual becomes a family affair as well. In the building rites already mentioned, the avowed goal of the magic is to confirm the alliance between the hunter and the guardian spirits of game within the walls of the dwelling and therefore of the household. Another example is one sequence from the Gungwan ritual (Ch. 12), the role of which is to curtail the wanderings of the 'self' (*sungwaag*) while the person sleeps: the *sungwaag* is successively confined to the different spaces to which it belongs, the individual, the household and the hamlet. The magical 'closure' of the exit from the house is performed at the foot of the *ging*, while the entire household remains inside, a symbolic way of defining the household as a localized social group. Finally the magical precautions taken by a young couple the first time they have sexual intercourse (Ch. 9) are already an expression of the family in the making, richly endowed with children and game.

Far from being a monad which simply reproduces itself by sending away its daughters in order to obtain wives for its sons, the family (or the household) is a highly permeable unit. But even more than the clan, the moiety or the local group, it is the depository, as the reproductive cell of society, of an essential function. And it is above all in this sense that it can at the same time be isolated and integrated.

Part II

Social Relations and Symbolic Function in Yafar Social Economy

Procure the tools and knowledge necessary for exploiting the natural resources, test the techniques and strategies for better control; then cut out a common tribal territory and defend it against neighbouring groups, divide it among one's own group in order to clarify individual rights better, mark off the good fishing rivers and allocate the sections; next plan the organization of work and the distribution or exchange of products, beginning with the garden patches before harvest (not the land now, but what is produced on it), implement systems for passing on the trees planted, for sharing game or domestic meat; finally render kinship relations more tangible by putting products and objects into circulation or, inversely, create partly fictive needs for barter capable of fostering social relations there where none existed: such is the stuff of the Yafars' socio-economic preoccupations.

But man needs more than simply to manage his natural environment well. For his psychic processes, enriched by culture he still needs to infiltrate his technical relationship with nature and enhance it with 'juridical' rules. Suddenly, the forest comes alive with spirits of the dead, the very earth harbours the primal cosmic blood, the hunter enters into exchange partnerships with his tutelary spirits, abolishing the notion of luck, the quavering voice of the medium conceals that of deceased relatives. Society invents prohibitions as much to say something about the transmission of life as to promote reciprocity, and it seizes upon pig-raising as a pretext to stage ancient family fantasies and to speak of purity.

It has long been observed that it is in the material area of food production that the imagination of societies is the most fertile. Rationality and dream, economy and spirituality, the two spheres can be analysed separately, but one can hardly do without the other. Both have the same goal: to find or produce abundant amounts of food, control the principles of natural reproduction, define one's own place – as an individual or a society – in the twofold filiation of family and universe.

5

Territory and Land

> The white cockatoos of my Hamyan land
> The white cockatoos of my Ugump land
> The white cockatoos of my Amaf land
> They tear apart the *koob* areca nuts!
> Waway! Humaw! (names of deceased relatives)
> The *kugwô* bird drinks at the Kurabôk river
> The *kugwô* and the *apurkow* drink at the river
> The bird of paradise of the Wayif river – Ruwô! (name of a deceased
> female relative)
> The bird of paradise of the Nubus River – Gawô! (name of a dec-
> eased male relative)
>
> (Wesko song)

A tribal territory is one of the vital conditions for the society's existence (Ch. 1). It is the group's vital space (in the full sense of the term), securing not only its subsistence, but also its inscription in a broader social zone. In this context, the territory has a political function and becomes the place of a collective identification 'in opposition to' the surrounding communities. Any outsider (non-kinsman) venturing to trespass is not only suspected of thievery or poaching, but of seeking to impair the group's wholeness by sorcery; in former times he risked being summarily killed. This first type of articulation gives tribal lands an indissoluble unity which is the spatial figure of the tribe's identity and its name; it is an affirmation of self in opposition to other.

But this unity masks a second type of articulation, that of the internal divisions: here a pattern of land-holding can be discerned which is the reflection of social groups, the highly fluctuating character of which we will be seeing. Self and other are much less clearly opposed in this articulation, for the stakes are purely economic, not political: here the other is merely a familiar kinsman, perhaps a member of the same local group who, even though he may have no rights to a given piece of land, is nonetheless on his own tribal territory. Tribal lands and their divisions mirror the different levels of group integration and interaction. Regardless of any topographical modifications these lands may undergo, they represent the most stable aspect of this relationship by reason of the relative permanence of the boundaries, whereas the groups inscribed in this space are fated, from one generation to the next, to be transformed in ways imposed not by demographic evolution alone.

External Boundaries

In Chapter One we saw that, three or four generations back, Yafar and Babuk on the one hand and Kumwaag on the other lived in the same vicinity on two territories on the edges of which they had built their villages. To the north, large tracts of land were only marginally exploited by the Yafar as far as the borders of Wamuru, Punda and Sowanda. In the wake of conflicts with the Kumwaag and constant suspicions of sorcery between the two groups, the Yafar finally moved, as we have seen, several kilometres to the north, after the Babuk had taken up definitive residence much further to the west. The fission of these local units and their spatial dispersal resulted in a more homogeneous occupation and exploitation of the land, and with it the need, where until then there had been merely zones of no man's land (*nôô ifêêg*, 'original forest lands'), to establish clearer territorial limits. Nevertheless, because nearly all these tribes intermarried, it was and still is the practice to tolerate a certain amount of movement back and forth across borders for the purposes of gathering and hunting, and sometimes for fishing; on the other hand, the clearing of land and the working of cultivated sago palms by outside groups, even when related, has never been tolerated. We were told, for instance, that on the northeast boundary of their territory, the Yafar sometimes used to work wild sago on Wamuru land with the tacit consent of the owners; or that the Yafar used to cross north on to Punda land to hunt or to collect wildfowl eggs; or again that conversely, the Sowanda and the Babuk used to feel free to hunt and gather along the limits of little-used Yafar land (even though Sowanda and Yafar have never intermarried). This trespassing was more likely to be accepted when the individuals surprised in the act turned out to be the affines or direct kin of the right-holders or 'fathers' of that piece of land. Today this toleration of hunting or gathering on another's land has become less usual for two reasons: first, people do not spend as much time in the bush as they used to and do not venture as far from their hamlets; and secondly, administrative controls encourage stricter respect of customary land rights.

But this relaxed situation prevailed only where land was plentiful. It was not and still is not the case in the southernmost part of the Yafar territory where, on the contrary, land disputes with the Potayneri were numerous and even today remain a bone of contention between particularly implicated clans. At an hour's walk from these two groups, another factor, of an ecological nature, enters the picture, and that is the Potayneri's limited supply of arable land, part of their territory being taken up by a relatively large rocky outcrop on which the shallow soil cannot be used to grow tubers or trees. In 1970, at the time of my first visit, the Yafar had agreed (after mediation by an Australian patrol officer from Amanab) to draw back their boundary a short distance in favour of the Potayneri and so put an end to the tensions and murders that had resulted from this problem: groups of Yafar not directly related to the victims had more than once ambushed and killed Potayneri making gardens or working sago on Yafar lands. In order to mark the new limit more clearly, the Yafar had sunk an ironwood post in the path connecting the two villages, but the Potayneri had torn it out, judging the Yafar concession inadequate. Since then, under the twofold effect of increased government control and intermarriage between the two tribes, the groups have come to accept official mediation and the new border. Nevertheless, when I was there in 1981, the Yafar were voicing their intention of taking back the lands they had relinquished.

Lastly, it must be noted that lands can be transferred between tribes through individual kinship ties, as is the case for 'clan' lands within the same society (see below). This type of land transfer is made possible by the many marriages with neighbouring tribes, though this is not, as we shall see, a built-in part of alliance structures, but a series of individual situations.

To sum up, present-day Yafar[1] territory is circumscribed by a boundary that the concerned clans can localize precisely at any point. The strictness with which intertribal rights are applied is roughly proportional to the geographical distance separating the zones inhabited by the Yafar from those of their neighbours. The greater proximity of the Potayneri hamlets, for instance, contrasts with the remoteness of the Sowanda and Babuk groups.

From a synchronic point of view, the territory remains a stable 'radiating space' with one or two central points – the hamlet(s) – nearby zones for short-cycle horticulture, more distant zones for long-cycle gardens, and finally peripheral zones for hunting and for the gathering of scarce products (eggs).

The Internal System

Land control within the tribal territory is based on static distribution among patrilineal units on the one hand, and a dynamic system of transfer between cognates or affines on the other. As Yafar clans are grouped into two moieties, the land-holding pattern is a fairly faithful reflection of this division: the southern part of the territory is exploited by the Angwaneri moiety clans, the northern part by those of the Araneri moiety.[2] We shall see, however, that this is only an approximation and that a statement of the type 'the tribal unit that controls the land is the patrilineal group' must be regarded as a basic tenet of customary law having juridical value, but not as a strictly observed or obligatory practice. This static rule is in effect rendered dynamic by the network of kinship and affinity, and by the individual ties organized within this network.

The Yafar themselves find it hard to say how the present-day pattern of internal land-holding came about, and in particular how land control worked around their former village of Sahya. They claim that the rules used to be more flexible than they are today, and some even say that 'everyone cultivated and hunted wherever he wanted'. Nonetheless, it does not seem likely that the system has changed much in only a few generations, and

---

1. Because of the inaccuracy and large scale of the available maps, it is impossible for the anthropologist to draw up a clear map of landholdings.
2. The midline thus falls roughly along the cosmological axis (Ch. 1).

I think that the difference lies more in the strictness with which the rights are applied than in the actual existence of such rights. What can be supposed, on the other hand, is that when Sahya was abandoned for the first extended period (Ch. 1), changes occurred in the disposition of internal boundaries and in the distribution of lineages or sibling groups. In the early stages of this northward expansion, Ifêêg clan was able to occupy the still vacant lands to the north, thus easing the strain on the present-day southern lands and allowing the other clans to spread out, closer to the boundaries under pressure from the Potayneri. In a second stage, when Nef (future Yafar 3) was founded, the Ifêêg ceded part of these lands to a Sumneri line to whom they had given a wife (Case 2 below). Today the Ifêêg still have rights on these Sumneri lands to the sago groves planted by their ancestors as well as their original fishing rights. We saw earlier that their role as first occupant in the area gives them the right to be called of 'masters of the forest land', *nôô na awaag* (p. 83), and other similar arrangements must have been made over the last few generations: visibly these involve redistribution among line-ages bound by tribal solidarity and kinship, necessitated by the new patterns of settlement within a space hitherto irregularly exploited.

Demographic growth does not seem to have been a highly determining factor in this case, as the population has actually shrunk since Sahya, while having, on the other hand, become more evenly distributed over the area. Demographic changes must therefore be examined at the level of the descent group as the basic land-holding unit for it is clear that, over time, the ratio of the size of a unit to the area of its land is going to change, and this change is not going to be the same for each clan. These variations are made even more palpable by the fact that Yafar clans are often very small, and high infant mortality can, in the space of a generation or two, reduce an already sparse group to nothing, while others will be fortunate enough to see their numbers grow in the same lapse of time. This makes for the fragility of the land-holding organization inasmuch as it is founded on patrilineal descent.

There are two theoretical remedies for such a situation: a) modify land-holdings as the population evolves; or b) keep the land-holding map as it is and modify the membership of the exploiting units accordingly by transferring some members of a prosperous

clan to land that has become too big for a unit on the wane.
The first formula would have the advantage of keeping the agnatic group together on the land, but this is not imperative for the Yafar, in the sense that it is not very important that patrilineal units actually work together as long as the *principle* of patrilineal descent is respected. Both formulas have the disadvantage, to my mind, of ensuring that some cultivators will keep (indefinitely for their descendants as far as sago palms are concerned) harvesting rights on lands they otherwise no longer have the right to work, even though such fragmentation of rights and work sites is not a problem as long as they are located in the vicinity of the same hamlet.

But rather than adapt to demographic fortunes by altering allotments, the Yafar prefer in fact to transfer individuals from one piece of land to another, with the new rights passing to the following generations. Thus some lineages find themselves subdivided into segments whose only reality is their land allotment; siblings are sometimes assigned to different lands, or single men may cultivate lands belonging to their mother's or their wife's clan, on which they establish their agnatic descendants. More than a redistribution of lands, then, we have a redistribution of individuals and groups (the inheritance of individual rights transforms individuals into groups) in the context of a relatively stable set of territories.

The modes of distribution are: occupation of newly vacated land by kin or affines, a man's inheritance of land from his dying maternal patriline, integration of a male immigrant who receives rights to the land held by his wife's lineage (uxorilocality), inclusion of a man from the same local group into his brothers-in-law's land (land-based uxorilocality), and transmission of rights to an adopted son and ultimately to his descendants. We shall illustrate these situations with a few typical cases.[3]

Case 1

'Land-based alliances' between two lines from different clans
Promp (Su 2) raised Nami (Am 1), an orphan. When he was grown, Nami continued to work the land with his adoptive father (*atôk*

---

3. For the abbreviations of clan names, see Ch. 3, Table 4.

awaag) instead of returning to his own lineage land; but Nami hunted, gathered and fished on his real father's land. This alliance applying only to horticulture and arboriculture was passed to the next generation, and Nami's son Bone now cultivates land from the Promp line with one of Promp's sons, along with his own lineage lands. Promp's invitation to Nami was partly motivated by threats of sorcery which at the time were thought to be directed in particular against the Amisneri.

Case 2 (Figure 18)

Land vacated due to occupation of new land. Extinction of a line and transfer of rights through a woman. Uxorilocality
When the Ifêêg (two major lineages) left Sahya, they first occupied what are now the lands of other Yafar clans, and then took over a vacant territory further west and founded Nef (Yafar 3) together with the Ifêaroog and the Suwê-enunguruk. Of the land left to the Sumneri, some was controlled by a particular branch of Ifêêg lineage 1 in its own right; this branch died out, leaving only one childless son and a daughter, Wawô, who received rights from her father and passed them on to some of her sons (Su 2). It is important to note that in such cases – and they are frequent – the land goes preferably to a daughter's or a sister's son rather than to a collateral line. The rest of the lineage occupied the new lands to the west. As for lineage 2, the present-day representatives (Awêr and Amis) of one of its branches live in Yafar 1, where they have kept part of the former Ifêêg lands, not without having worked as children with their mother's second husband, Woy (Su 1). Finally, Sey, lone representative of the other Ifêêg 2 branch, 'followed his sister' *(weerigim pahruku)* when, as a child, she went to live with her future husband in Yafar 2 (anticipated change of residence of non-nubile girls is frequent). And so Sey went to work on the land with his brother-in-law before marrying a woman from Yafar 2 and cultivating with her brother. A third Ifêêg lineage is no longer represented at Yafar, one of its members having left two generations ago to live uxorilocally with the Babuk (his two daughters came back to marry Yafar men).

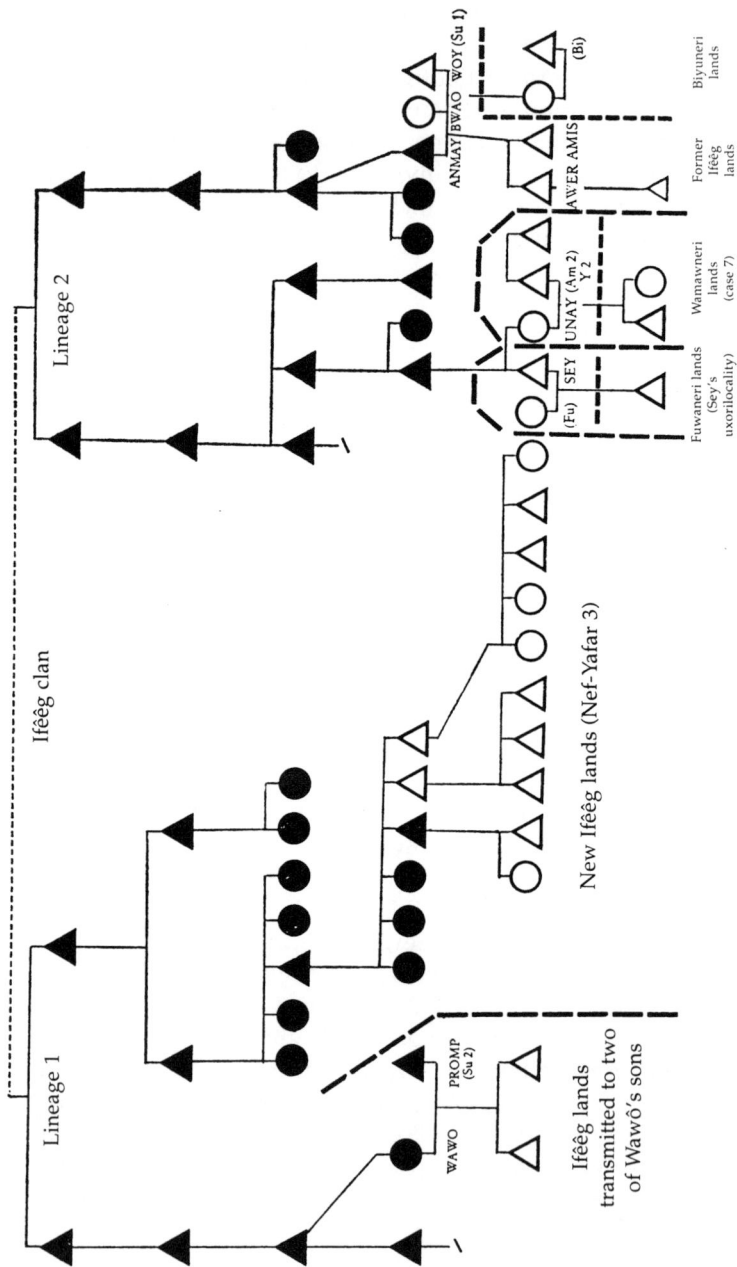

Figure 18. Land-holding: case 2

Case 3

Land transfer by adoption (mother remarries)
Awpiy (Bi) was a baby when his father Nahwey died. His mother remarried and he was raised by her new husband (Su 1) and worked the land with him while hunting, gathering and fishing on the lineage lands of his real father. His elder brother Kuray remained on Biyuneri lands. His sister Sotnê exploited her husband's lands. Awpiy's children worked the land with him, but his daughters married several years apart and cleared their own gardens with their husbands. A few years before his death, in 1977, Awpiy had decided to return to his father's lands and to clear new gardens; he urged his eldest son to come with him. But the latter, Awêy, preferred to remain on the Sumneri lands, where he now has sago palms and other trees planted by his father.

In this case, land transfer by remarriage of the mother, generally regarded by the Yafar as a temporary arrangement (pending the young man's marriage), became permanent in the following generation. It should also be noted that the Sumneri and Biyuneri belong to different moieties, which accentuates the importance of this line's split from Biyuneri clan.

Case 4 (Figure 19)

Land transfer by adoption (mother remarries) and implantation of an immigrant line
Very recently, a Potayneri clan segment, the Sawayneri, established itself among the Yafar by the second marriage, with Fewô (Su 1), of an Aynunkneri woman, Tuay, recently widowed by Yos, a Potayneri man. With her she took her three young children, her daughter Hwam and her two sons, Mafyaf and Kuray. Hwam came to marry May, a Sumneri man (Su 2). Tuay and her two sons worked on Fewô's lands. When Mafyaf and Kuray married Yafar girls, around 1970, they began clearing their gardens on the land of their fathers-in-law (Am 1 and Su 1, respectively). This situation, marked by an initial period of cultivation with the mother's husband, then a second on 'the wife's land', is frequent.

e

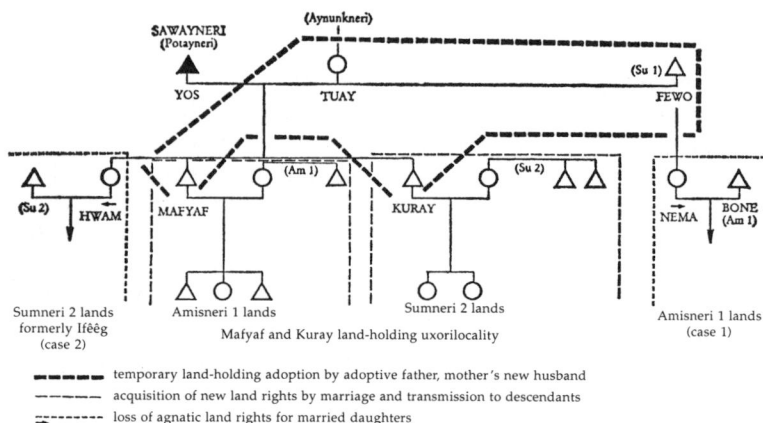

Sumneri 2 lands   Amisneri 1 lands   Sumneri 2 lands   Amisneri 1 lands
formerly Ifêêg   (case 1)
(case 2)   Mafyaf and Kuray land-holding uxorilocality

━━━━━ temporary land-holding adoption by adoptive father, mother's new husband
───── acquisition of new land rights by marriage and transmission to descendants
╤------ loss of agnatic land rights for married daughters

Figure 19. Land-holding: Case 4

Case 5 (Figure 20)

Extinction of a clan and land vacant. Uxorilocality. Implantation of an immigrant line

Menaneri clan has died out. Three generations ago, a Punda man from Sig-aynaag clan, Mway, married Yako, of the Yafar Menaneri clan; his affines invited him to come and live with the Yafar and work Menaneri land. In effect, his father-in-law had no sons, and Yako was his only heir (his other daughter Maran married a Punda of a different clan from Mway and took up residence there, thus forfeiting her rights to her father's lands). One other Menaneri branch had male descendants, but Yako's land did not go to them; once again affines prevail over kin.

Mway transmitted his rights to his two sons, Resay and Bwaynu. The second, upon marrying a Tawank (a Yafar clan) woman, cleared his gardens on his brothers-in-law's land, leaving his brother to pass on his own land rights to his children (including three sons living in 1981 and their children). At the same time, Menaneri clan died out two generations after Yako's clan, leaving Ahumwey the sole survivor; his only son did not inherit the Menaneri lands and, unless I am mistaken, the land went to the Sig-aynaag. Today the Yafar Sig-aynaag are commonly called Menaneri.

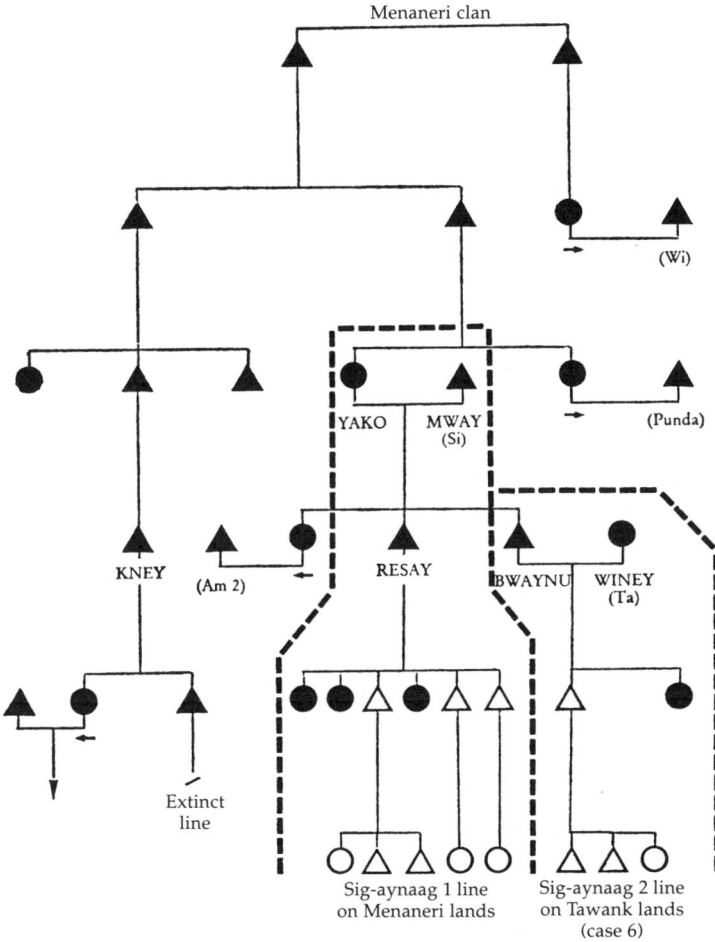

Figure 20. Land-holding: Cases 5 and 6

Case 6

Uxorilocality and vacant land. Sister's rights and transmission to sister's son

Aykwey, the only male heir to his clan's (Ta) land, preferred to reside in Yafar 3, where he had taken his two wives from the same clan (Ig). The Tawank land left vacant (near Yafar 2) was claimed by one of Aykwey's sisters, Hwabe, married at the time to Saphwaw, from Wamawneri clan at Yafar 2 (the other sister worked the land with her successive husbands). Thus the

Tawank lands passed to Saphwaw's line. Saphwaw died after having a son, who recently died unmarried: the land is therefore not cultivated by the Wamawneri. However, Aykwey's father's sister Winey had taken, in a second marriage, Bwaynu, a man from a recently immigrated Punda line, the Sig-aynaag (see Case 5 and Figure 21). Bwaynu found himself quite naturally working the Tawank lands and passed on his rights to his sons and grandsons.

Case 7 (Figure 21)

Adoption by a kinsman and transfer of rights. Extinction of the line and transmission of lands through a woman. Uxorilocality
The two Amisneri lineages found themselves working different pieces of land immediately after the initial split in the Sahya Yafar group. The first, so-called elder lineage acquired the land on the Hopwan between present-day Yafar 1 and Yafar 2, while the younger lineage, today residing at Yafar 2, inherited land several generations ago from the Potayneri Sawayneri clan. But as far as land rights are concerned, the latter split into two groups two generations ago, after the adoption of Ran, an orphan, by his mother's brother Nank (Wa). Ran's descendants continued to work the Wamawneri lands, while his two half-brothers kept the Amisneri plot. However, one of them, Poom, took up uxorilocal residence with the Befan tribe to the east; the other's branch, Manyow, died out after a generation. There remained the collateral branch of a great-uncle of Ran, Masuwô; this too died out a generation ago, leaving only two daughters, Yapo and Wasay. The second forfeited her rights by marrying into the Babuk, and only Yapo transmitted her lineage land to her two sons and her daughter (Su 2). The latter immediately lost them by cultivating with her husband (Bi); as for the two brothers, the elder, Wiy, took over his mother Yapo's land (contrary to the rule that the elder takes the father's land, the younger the vacant maternal land if there is any), while Gafnaw went on working his father Afas' land. This is a remarkable example because it presents the case of the 'lineage' plot of a non-extinct lineage which is no longer cultivated by the members of this group but by two other sublineages, in the first case after an earlier adoption, and in the second after the extinction of one of the two branches of the lineage.

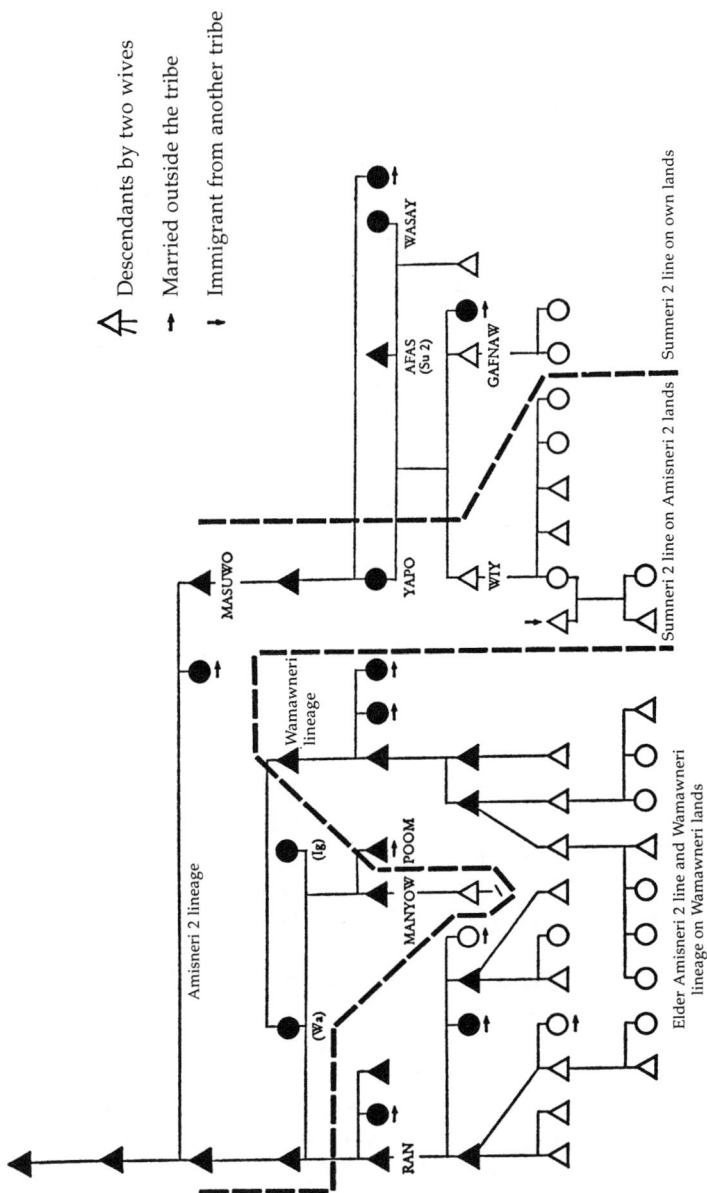

Descendants by two wives

† Married outside the tribe

→ Immigrant from another tribe

Figure 21. Land-holding: Case 7

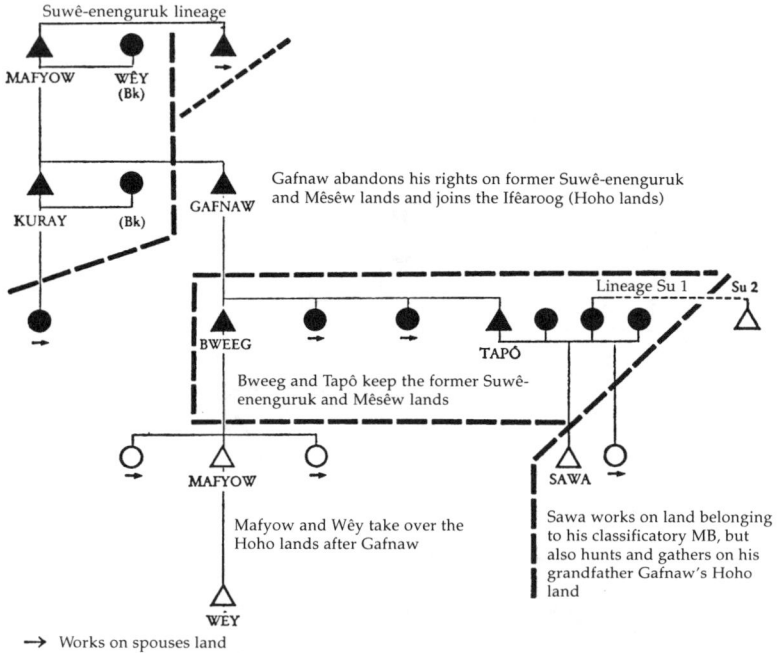

Figure 22. Land-holding: Case 8

Case 8

Uxorilocality. Adoption (Suwê-enunguruk and Mêsêw clans)
Three generations ago, these two collateral clans (the elder Suwê, the younger Mêsêw) exploited a piece of land near Sahya (still cultivated in part by one of the two last Suwê lines) together with another piece near the Wamuru boundary.

a) Suwê-enunguruk: Mafyow (+3 generation) married Wêy, a Babuk woman (shortly after the Babuk migrated from Sahya to their present-day land in the west). As Wêy's clan land was partially vacant, Mafyow took up residence with the Babuk and worked the land with his brothers-in-law. After a few years, he returned with his wife to Nef (later to become Yafar 3), which had just been founded. In this way he had access to his sago palms and fruit trees planted on his wife's land, situated on the Babuk/Yafar border. On the death of Mafyow, his wife returned to her people with one of her sons, Kuray,

who married there. The other son, Gafnaw, remained with the
Yafar, gave up his land near Sahya and on the Wamuru boundary, and took up cultivating land in the Hoho region, closer
to Nef, already under exploitation by Ifêaroog clan, who issu-
ed the invitation. His two sons, Bweeg and Tapô, preferred to
keep the ancestral land for themselves, sharing it with one of
the two Mêsêw lineage lines, also comprised of only a few
individuals. Tapô's son Sawa – one of the two Suwê men still
alive in the 1980s – hunted and gathered on Hoho land, but as
soon as his parents died he began working with two unmarried classificatory mothers (Su 1), who had no male help.
Since their death a few years later, the two Sumneri lineages
(his mother's clan) have been vying to adopt Sawa for their
own lands, each arguing that they were the ones who raised
and fed the orphan.

b) Mêsêw: while the men of one of the now-extinct Mêsêw lines
remained on the two ancestral plots with Tapô and Bweeg, the
other line found itself, two generations ago, cultivating with
the Wamawneri and the Amisneri 2: in effect, Abos (Mêsêw)
was invited on to their land by the brothers of his wife, who
was the daughter of Nank (Am 2) working with his mother's
brother (Wa), who had fed him (see Case 7). In the 1980s only
one representative of Mêsêw lineage was still living.

The ancestral plot on the Wamuru boundary line was then
vacant (hunting and gathering were open). The other piece of
land, near Sahya, was partially occupied by the Biyuneri.

A close look at these few cases shows even more clearly that,
in terms of land-holding, the patrilineage is not preserved as a
homogeneous unit. What does tend to be maintained is patrifili-
ation, the continuation of patriliny. Although breaks do occur in
this continuity, the modifications brought about are subsequently
passed on, which means that respect for filiation is reestablished
(in another lineage), usually for several generations. Reestablishing patriliny stabilizes the new land-holding pattern, which
becomes irreversible and cumulative over time. Thus together
with what we can gather from the genealogical record recalled
by the Yafar, but even more over a longer term, the social
space determined by land-holding appears, even in the absence
of migrations or the occupation of new vacant territories, to be in
perpetual motion.

Not only are the patrilineal groups not preserved as land-holding units, it seems that there is a tendency or even a need to provoke segmentation. As soon as there is a sibling group of any size, a split can be seen to occur, creating two lines which from then on will work different pieces of land. This phenomenon follows the principle that, that which is like must be differentiated, and therefore subdivided, whereas that which is different must unite, intermarry, whence the need to redistribute among agnates that which was previously held in common, and to place in common that which was separated (see also Ch. 11, pp. 344–5). Herein lies the dynamic principle of a social system that otherwise tends to value affinal relations over the more static kinship ties.

In the light of the above examples, these breaks in descent continuity can be reduced to three basic situations: adoption, transmission through a woman and uxorilocality.

a) Adoption. Setting aside adoption by a mother and adoption of orphan girls, two modalities that usually have no repercussions on land tenure (to be distinguished from the ownership of crops), a distinction must still be made between adoption of an orphan by a kinsman and adoption by the mother's husband. In both cases, the adoptive father – *atôk* or *atôk awaag* in the first case, *at* or *atôk* in the second – treats the child like his own son, nourishes him, raises him, leaves him planted trees, etc., and because of this makes the child work the land with him. When he is older, the adolescent can clear separate gardens with the bachelors of his generation and his adoptive lineage, or at least have his own patch in his new 'father's' garden. If the latter is a brother of the deceased father (*atôk* originally meant 'father's younger brother') or an adult agnatic cousin, this obviously may not entail a change in the rights inherited by the child; but the *atôk* is also frequently the mother's kinsman (Case 7 above). When the young man marries, he will take his wife and children to the land inherited through adoption, and later his sons will go on to work it, for there will already be fruit trees, sago palms and gardens recently planted for them there. The sons' return to their lineage land after adoption is cited as an alternative, sometimes even as the norm, but in the great majority of cases the newly inherited land is kept on in the following generations.

Adoption is regarded not as a burden but as a privilege, and arguments often arise between two men who have both helped raise a child (Case 8 above); this gives the right to organize his marriage (choose the wife), but also allows the adoptive father, in the case of a boy, to pass on his cultivating rights, later an inalienable proof of the bonds of adoption and authority that automatically result.

Adoption between non-agnatic kin is less common than adoption by a clan father or elder, or by the mother's husband.

According to the rule of pseudo-levirate (preferential marriage of the widow with an agnatic classificatory brother of the deceased), the last two situations may come down to one. But often the widow chooses to marry outside her husband's clan, or even his tribe, and if she has young children, she takes them with her (sometimes only temporarily); they are then taken in charge by their mother's new husband, their *at*, and will work the land with him and their mother. When daughters marry, they go to work their husband's land and forfeit their rights to that of their *at*, but – and this is the peculiarity – the same is true for sons: as soon as they are married, they stop clearing their gardens on their adopted land and begin working those of their wives, that is those of their brothers-in-law. Land-based adoption by the mother's husband is only a transitional phase which cannot be definitive, since the relationship between *at* and step-son is qualitatively supplanted, upon the latter's marriage, by the new relationship between *guweeg* (brothers-in-law). This rule is widely respected and is expressed by a stereotyped discourse:

Afaag wêsik obu-na	The mother (widow) brings her child,
Atôk meya wah-na ba	And so the adoptive father (MH) raises it,
Gwiyê bwehya-na ba	He grows with a will
Aso ih-na	He works the land (with his *at*)
Haf nungum ikag hwaynik	He does not go back home (to his own lineage),
Atôk na bəte: 'Ka na.'	(He says of) his adoptive father's land: 'It is mine.'
And when he marries:	
Angwafik nôô-a ogohôk,	He goes away to his wife's land,
Atôk na bəte wahag	He forsakes his adoptive father's land.

It indeed seems that forfeiture of the rights inherited from the mother's husband in favour of those brought by the wife works logically for the Yafar to terminate a relationship between father and adopted son that was not based on consanguinity and whose affinal aspect was distorted by the difference of generation. To bring the adopted son's wife into this relationship by way of land-sharing would be to set off on a false path, on an ambiguous kinship construction; whereas marriage and the relations between brothers-in-law offer a new, positive and valued basis, a coherent atom of kinship to which the coming generations will be tied by consanguinity. The pseudo-filiation determined by adoption by the foreign (non-consanguine) *at* is thus neutralized, at least in so far as control of lands is concerned.

b) Transmission through a woman. Transmission of land rights through the genealogical mediation of a woman occurs only in the absence of male heirs. Here again it is a single line that is concerned, while a collateral branch may continue in parallel; the land may remain at the disposal of the latter, but it often happens that despite the presence of a living collateral line, rights are handed on preferentially to the sons of a daughter or a sister, who then join the descendants of the other branch in cultivating without the land itself undergoing subdivision into two subterritories. In such a case it seems to me that a territorial partition could nevertheless take place at a later time, for instance if each of the two lines in question were to reach a certain population. What is valued here is the matrilateral relationship as opposed to agnation: the man inheriting a new piece of land from his mother willingly says: 'This is Mom's land' (*naya na bəte*), expressing a strong sentimental attachment to the mother's hand can be seen among the Yafar, as I. Hogbin, for example, observed among the Wogeo. As we saw in Cases 2 and 7, the mother's land is inherited by only some of the sons, while the others keep the father's land. My informants say that in principle, it is the younger son(s) who should benefit, no doubt because they are 'closer' to their mother (there is even a special name for the last born, *tot ne pothwaag*, which means 'taken from the breast'); but in the end the choice is probably made with other criteria in mind as well, since this rule does not seem to be respected in every case. Whether the mother received the rights she passes on to her sons from her father or from her brother is of no great importance, and it seems to depend on the availability for marriage and land-holding of the heiress, often the only legatee (if the daughter of the last male representative of the line is already married elsewhere or if this man has no children, the land will pass to his sister and therefore to her sons), but ideally the Yafar give preference to the daughter of the last man of the line.

c) Land-based uxorilocality. I will deal with the problem of matrimonial residence in a later chapter, but here we need to consider its effects on land tenure. The Yafar are patrilineal and virilocal, but a few cases of uxorilocality can be observed in which the man takes up residence in another tribe or in a Yafar hamlet other than his own. Most often this is at the invitation of his brothers-in-law; but sometimes it is his wife who makes the request, or her widowed father, who has not managed to marry his daughter to someone in the village and wants to keep her with him, especially for her economic contribution. Case 2 above showed the change of residence of a bachelor who had 'followed his sister', who was married very young, and who himself married with the help of his brothers-in-law. In such cases, the man begins to work the land of his wife's line with his affines; if his father's land is near his new home, he can continue to work this too, often in tandem with his brothers-in-law's land. Then, little by little, uxorilocal residence is confirmed as the couple comes to have fruit trees and sago palms. It seemed necessary to place under this same heading of 'uxorilocality' (land is a 'locality'), but with the added qualifier 'land-based', the situation in which a man marries a woman from his own hamlet (no change of residence) but abandons his father's land, except for hunting and fishing, in favour of that of his brothers-in-law. Extratribal uxorilocality is often only temporary or discontinuous (Case 8 above), while land-based uxorilocality with no change of residence is almost always permanent, as the land rights acquired by marriage are passed on in the male line to subsequent generations. The role of the wife's brothers is crucial in this case (her father is usually deceased), and this 'adoption' of the sister's husband as co-clearer is one outcome – albeit an exceptional one – of the high value placed on relations between direct affines of the same generation. It is even officialized by the expression *guweeg-na nôô-a ogohôk*, that is 'to take up residence "apart" (outside patrilineal descent and the land boundaries that go with it) with one's brothers-in-law'.

To sum up, the Yafar land-holding system is based on a contradictory twofold orientation: on paternal filiation with its particular tendency to determine descent groups (the size of which depends on the ratio of birth to death rates), but also on the implementation of mechanisms for breaking the unilineal continuity, which engender lineage segmentation and autonomous land rights for the lines that have broken away.

The plasticity (Kaberry 1967) of Melanesian land-holding systems has often been pointed out and defined as the result of individual choices and strategies within a social structure which may otherwise be founded on the principle of unilineal descent and the transmission of rights and property in the male line (Crocombe 1974; Hogbin and Lawrence 1967; Lawrence 1984). But the Yafar do not justify their individual choices (adoption, uxorilocality, etc.) on the grounds of land: a man will say that he cultivates other land, not because it gives him more space but, for example, because he gets along well with his brothers-in-law and wants to work with them. Equally absent from the Yafar land-tenure system are a) the rule in force elsewhere in Melanesia that the ground belongs to those who first brought it under cultivation and b) the wife's automatic contribution of new rights. The first situation cannot occur because every piece of land, even those not under cultivation, already belongs to a group. The second is not attested either (except for rare cases of uxorilocality) because in practice the woman forfeits her inherited rights for as long as she lives with her husband. There may be an option, then, but no cumulation.

Hierarchy of Holding Rights

The territorial units we have just examined and the rights exercised there by producing groups are associated with three types of economic activity: horticulture-arboriculture, gathering and hunting. The transfer of land outside the paternal lineage bears mainly, in the Yafar conception of things, on the right to clear new gardens, to fell trees, clear, burn and plant crops over a certain area of bush; it is especially for this reason that recognition of rights is necessary. To this must be added hunting and gathering rights, which are, so to speak, 'included' in cultivating rights. But often, when the place of residence permits, the land that has been forfeited for purposes of horticulture continues to be used for hunting and gathering as well as for harvesting the product of trees previously planted and passed on by the father, mother or other relative. The former piece of land is therefore not completely abandoned.

This ranking of rights clearly stems from the great difference in the span of time over which each of these economic activities takes place. While hunting and gathering draw on the environment for only a short time and are without long-term consequences, clearing a single garden determines the use of land cultivated for some twenty years (fruit trees) and even indefinitely for sago palms, as well as its unavailability until the end of the fallow period.

River Rights

Despite their modest flow, many Yafar streams harbour enough resources (fish, crabs, mussels) to come under social control and for fishing rights to be recognized. The system of rights governing rivers works differently from the control of the land through which they run; in other words, transferring the rights to a piece of land does not automatically entail a corresponding transfer of the right to fish on that land. Furthermore, the units held (the section of river covered by the rights) and the juridical production units (in the sense of the group sharing the rights but not necessarily working together) are smaller than for land-holding. The unit is a 150–300 metre section of stream together with its banks; the products that come under control are everything that lives in the water, the products gathered along the banks (as well as the standing timber and firewood) and even all game that might be killed there (except for game shot with a gun). By this definition, then, the rights cover more than the water course proper.

Rights are transmitted by the father to his children of both sexes. The girls enjoy them after marriage only if they reside in their home village; in this case they exploit their section with their husband. If not, the rights pass to her brothers (or other agnates). However, a widow may, recover her rights if she returns to her father's hamlet. If there are no male descendants, girls transmit their rights to their sons, who, as in the case of land rights, will hand them on in the male line. When there are no descendants at all, the river passes to male cousins or sister's sons. If several sons inherit, the section may be exploited by the set of brothers who, under the direction of the elder, divide up the stretch for the fishing season without this subdivision being permanent; or, if the section is long enough, the elder subdivides it definitely into shorter sections which he apportions between himself and his younger brothers. The number of river sections to which a man has rights (women have fewer, but fish with their husbands) varies from three to ten or so, most being located on the father's land. When, in accordance with one of the dynamic principles analysed above, a man acquires new land rights – especially when he has changed residence – he is also given new fishing rights, which he then shares with some of the kinsmen who have adopted him onto their land.

Symbolic Control of Land: The Forest Pantheon

Parallel to management of the land through the implementation of a flexible 'juridical' system, a 'symbolic space' can be discerned, principally in the form of local spirits. The map of divinities and spirits of the dead is congruent with the territory, but is broken up into different, more compact parcels, since each spirit is believed to control its own piece of forest, the boundaries of which are not always clearly drawn. The Yafar say there are countless numbers of these spirits, but only some of them (a few hundreds for the totality of Yafar lands) have names, separate personalities and a precise location and most of the time a social identity (spirits of the dead). Four main classes can be distinguished, which are related to ecological categories:[4]

> Male *nabasa* spirits. Principally spirits of the dead sprung from the deceased's blood (Ch. 12), but some of them are non-human. They live under large trees but are otherwise highly mobile. Guardians of game, occupants of tracts of bush, pathogenic, integrated into

4. For the eschatological function of these spirits, see Ch. 12.

society (dreams, possession, hunting and healing rites). *Nabasa* is
also a generic term for all socialized forest spirits.
   Female *sawangô* spirits. Female counterparts of the *nabasa*, the *sawangô* are either the spirits of women who have died (Ch.
12) or pre-
human genies. They live in stands of small bamboo and latex-
producing trees, but are less mobile than the *nabasa*. They summon
their 'husbands' with the call of the *abô* bird (*Cracticus cassicus* –
butcherbird) and have a 'younger brother', Rafuu, who is called
upon in healing and fertility rites. Pathogenic like the *nabasa*.
Through their mythical origins, associated mainly with the large
hairy spider *ifot* (*Atrax* sp.) that lives in holes in the ground, and
with the monitor lizard and flying fox, of whom they are the
guardians. The central and southern Eri ascribe to the *sawangô* a
cannibalistic aggressiveness towards humans, whom they attack in
the form of large flying foxes.
   Male *kê-ruur* spirits. 'Children of the bone', these are the spirits of
the dead sprung from the deceased's bones. Live in large rocks or
irontrees (Ch. 12). Member of the *nabasa* category and, like them,
bringers of game and pathogens.
   Male *angor* spirits. Local water spirits, non-human. Guardians of
fish and other aquatic species, bringers of game surprised near
streams. Pathogenic (now abandoned fertility and healing rites).

Non-human spirits are associated with cosmogonic myths that
tell of the circumstances in which they appeared and their first
contacts with humans. These spirits are believed to live in
families (people speak of X-*awanaag*, 'the kindred of spirit X') and
to reproduce in parallel with human society. In the vertical
division of space, they are located at what could be called the
shallow chthonian level (as opposed to the deeper world of
ghosts and the natural fertility principle), but they move through
the forest 'with the wind' and take possession of various animals,
mainly birds and insects.
   A large portion of religious life has to do with the relations
between humans (almost exclusively men) and the different
categories of spirits. Communicating is done through dreams or
medium trance, and the relations determine the outcome of hunting, to a lesser extent fishing (it is especially the *angor* that are the
guardians of fish), and health (all classes of spirits send sickness
to punish those who fell their trees or violate certain taboos).
Death, however, is not attributed to spirits and can only result
from sorcery. To win their favour, people offer them rituals as
well as food through the intermediary of mediums, in the form

of offerings left in the forest near their home trees, or fastened on to the masks during rites. A small group of agnates, in principle the close relatives of the deceased for the spirits of the dead, or those who work the land occupied by a non-human *nabasa*, ensure the worship and transmit the responsibility to the next generation. The person who makes regular offerings to a spirit is called *nabasa na awaag* 'forest spirit's father'.[5] But once again, the cult may be handed over to another clan through a daughter when her line dies out, and it happens that men worship the spirit of a maternal ancestor on maternal clan land in addition to (or instead of) the spirits of their own lineage. Only the direct kin of the deceased man or woman are concerned. Forest spirits therefore come with the land; their cult is passed on more with land-holding rights than through genealogical ties. Broadly speaking, *nabasa* are the mediators that link individuals and lines with lands and their exploitation. Here too, personal relations with the deceased relative yield to the bond with the land and its game.

Spirits of the dead are located during medium seances or in dreams. The new spirit possessing the medium[6] – who has suddenly entered a state of mental dissociation – may introduce itself and even indicate the place it has chosen to reside or where food offerings are to be left. This information may confirm what the dream of another member of the group had previously indicated. Non-human spirits have been in the area a long time, but seem to have been located using the same techniques of divination, even though the Yafar are unable to say for certain when or by whom.

As a rule, once located no spirit changes residence; the same is true for water spirits, even when land rights or boundaries are modified. When, exceptionally, they do move, it is to somewhere near by and because their first tree was felled; they then inform the human community of their new location. The sedentarization of spirits contrasts with the plasticity of land rights and the occasionally cognatic mode of transmission of the cult; this sometimes leads to discrepancies between the identity of the lineages of the spirit of the dead, that of the person ensuring its worship, and the group working the land. Often, though, there is coherence among the three levels and almost always between the first

---

5. *Awaag*: 'father, master, owner, one who has rights to, over'. There is no female equivalent of this term except in the restrictive sense of 'mother' (*afaag*), but a woman may be said to be *awaag* of a piece of land, a river or a spirit.
6. For Yafar and Eri mediumism, see Chs 7 and 13 and Juillerat 1975a.

two. Moving a boundary line may cause the cult to be divided between the two groups concerned: for instance, the northern boundary of the land controlled by the 'elder' lineage of Sumneri clan, which adjoins the neighbouring Punda territory, was shifted slightly two or three generations ago, to the advantage of the Yafar. The three *nabasa* residing on this strip of land are Punda spirits of the dead; these are still worshipped by their descendants, while the Sumneri who cultivate and hunt in the region have also begun bringing their own offerings (in propitiation for the trees felled during clearing).

One informant told me of a phenomenon confirmed by the mapping: there was a greater concentration of *nabasa* along certain land boundaries (i.e. a network of spirit subterritories which was denser in these places). The Yafar offer no explanation for this, and likewise they deny that the pantheon fulfils any function legitimizing land-holding. For them, these are spirits who, of their own free will, prefer to live along boundary lines. But it should not be forgotten that it is mediums who, in a more or less genuine state of trance, locate the spirits, even though they do this independently of any kinship ties with them. One wonders whether this might not be a semi-unconscious process of legitimation of land rights which, in the event of a boundary change, allows the holder to prove the existence of former rights that have been abandoned but which might one day be reasserted. Moreover, the attribution of spirits to a fixed place would serve the same purpose, and the case of the common boundary with the Punda is a good example. Territorial marking procedures have been observed in many societies (even though the phenomenon has certainly not received the attention it deserves), and the rooting of the dead in the ground, although at a non-material level (bones and graves quickly disappear), is not the least effective of these.

Angor spirits are found only in water courses of a certain size; smaller streams still have fish and are exploited by the technique of damming and bailing, but they do not contain *angor*. Where these spirits are attested, the Yafar identify one or two per river section (the holding unit for fishing rights). Given the non-human character of *angor*, it is more difficult to connect them with a given clan, although they were originally worshipped by specific agnatic groups. In the ritual context, the *angor* come into play either when a wild pig is brought down in the vicinity of their home, or when fish are poisoned, an exclusively male undertaking; the fishermen then place food offerings along the riverbanks and recite spells so that the *angor* will 'open the doors' and let the fish out. *Angor* enter into mediums more rarely than do *nabasa* or *kê-ruur*, but when they do speak it is mainly about hunting, rarely about fishing. Given the slight economic interest of fishing in this region, the water spirits seem to have been 'taken over' by hunting ideology.

Toponyms

Land is divided, inherited and sacralized; it is also named. Yafar toponymy is not directly related to the land-holding map or to that of the pantheon, in the sense that it is not determined by and does not determine these levels of relationship with the territory. Defined on the contrary by topographical and ecological factors, it is largely independent of the social.

The toponymic system operates on two levels: names of lands (*bǝte* 'land' or *nôô* 'remote forest land') and places (*kǝbik*, generic term for 'place, village'). In practice, all lands are named after rivers. The Yafar territory has few distinctive relief features, but it is crossed by numerous water courses, all of which, down to the smallest gully that runs only after a rain, bear a name. This name designates both the area around the stream and, by extension, the gardens cleared there. If the waterway is long, clarifications are added: 'headwaters of —' (— *mesoog* 'head'), 'middle of —' (*öruk-inaag*) or 'mouth of —' (— *moog* 'base, stump'); but it is the tributaries rather than the large rivers that serve as place names. The etymology of these names has usually been lost.

The toponymic system would remain vague were it not completed, when necessary, by more specific names corresponding to given places; these are 'anecdotal', that is they recall a particular incident that happened at that spot. Table 9 gives a series of illustrations. The presence of giant trees or particular species can also be used to name a place. On the other hand, the names of local spirits have no toponymic function.

Sensory References and Orientation

From their earliest years, Yafar children explore the forest, first of all perched on their mother's shoulders, then the little boy with his father, the little girl with her mother. Even before they reach adolescence children (especially boys) already know every detail of the territory they roam with kinsmen as well as a good part of the other village lands, where they often go with friends to hunt and gather. For a particularly close environment like the tropical rain forest, it may be useful to talk about the sensory references available to those who live and make their living there.[7]

In the vicinity of the place of residence (up to thirty minutes walk away) the Yafar man or woman circulates in a perfectly familiar space where it is not necessary consciously to check for references in order to orient oneself. The same goes for frequently travelled paths like those leading to gardens or stands of sago palms, even at some distance. On the other hand, the necessity for such references is greater when improvising itineraries for the needs of hunting. A distinction should be made between natural references and man-made ones. Among the first, there are also permanent references and those that are temporary. Permanent natural references can be features of the land or the river, but also particularities of the vegetation, which is highly diversified: giant trees, particular species, stands of bamboo, thickets of dry canes, etc. Temporary natural references can be fallen trees, species in flower or fruit, congregating places for birds that feed on a fruit tree or have made their home on a specific territory (birds of paradise, for example, which attract attention with their calls), or alterations to the environment by animals such as pigs' feeding grounds, bandicoot burrows or termite hills. References stemming from human action are all temporary, but some more than others. These are first of all the footpaths, which may change after a few years, except for the most important; next, all the old or new places where planting has been done, such as clearings (whose shape carved out of the thick forest remains perceptible for several decades) or stands of sago palms; trees in an old garden that but for them would go unnoticed, wild fruit

---

7. Beyond sensory references and a sense of direction, one can also speak of mental topographical representations (see Huber 1979).

Toponym	Translation	Event evoked
Rəhê Yay ate-səngoog	firewood – m.n. – finished action – to deposit	Yay (G + 4) deposited some firewood at this place and has never come back for it.
Kayfô kas hogohraag	m.n. – dagger – to place in crotch of a tree	Kayfô (G + 4–5) stuck his bone dagger in a tree.
Mwas sa-kêg hogohraag	m.n. – coconut palm wood – to place in crotch of a tree	Mwas (G + 5) put a piece of coconut wood in a tree and has left it there.
Nuey somse fefsaag	m.n. – tree sp. – to bend	Nuey (beyond genealogical record) bent a young *somse* tree to make an adze handle, but was unable to snap it.
Gafnaw Ahyas hôn hogohraag	m.n. – river name – to place in crotch of a tree	Gafnaw (G + 5) left some heating stones too heavy to carry back to the village in the crotch of a tree near the Ahyas river.
Ahmu tenenguk fakag	m.n. – tree sp. – to cut and lay flat	Ahmu cut a *tenenguk* tree but left it lying there without using it (usage unknown).
Nuf nay hugfu səngo-na	w.n. – skirt – tear off – deposit	Nuf (G + 4) tore off her fibre underskirt and threw it away (women replace their underskirts by putting new ones on over the top).
Yu koom səswaag	m.n. – (leaves of the) *koom* areca palm – to gather	Yu (beyond genealogical record) gathered these leaves for a ritual purpose (but probably in an unusual context or way).
Haye wos mesourag səngoog	m.n. – moon – drawings in the shape of chevrons – deposit	Haye (G + 2) carved chevrons into a tree to count the moons before the organization of a ceremony for the *sawangô* spirits.
Semay wamog-wa genofôk	m.n. – tree sp. – on-drew	Semay (G + 2) made drawings on a tree at this

Semayim rəbwame theg	m.n. – cuscus – attacked	place (no reasons). Semayim was attacked in this place by a cuscus (unusual behaviour for this animal).
San awye kwaag	w.n. – bird of paradise – shot with arrow	A woman, San, shot a bird here (with the bow of her husband who was away – women do not hunt).
Ihaw təta thek	m.n. – wild pig – attacked	A wild pig charged and killed Ihaw (recent).
Saman mumweri kwaag	w.n. – to trip – to throw forward (?)	Saman tripped and killed herself at this place.
Yey kahraag	m.n. – to hang	Yey was seriously injured in a battle with the Sowanda (cf. Ch. 14); his friends who brought him home on a carrying pole hung it between two branches during a rest stop.
Mwasa sengêg	m.n. – placed under a burial shelter	Place of Mwasa's burial shelter.
Awêr fakag	m.n. – to lay flat	Place of Awêr's grave.
Mwahas koom-wa gêhêk	m.n. – areca palm sp. – tried out	Mwahas (G + 2) was especially tall: his friends measured him against a tree and scored the bark.
Masiy bəme koog	m.n. – hole – dug	Masiy dug a hole there.
Umtafaag kseeg	old people – copulate	An old couple made love there.

Table 9. Some examples of place-names

m.n.: man's name; w.n.: woman's name

trees planted in a clearing and persisting after the forest has regrown, or old hamlet sites of which only the band of coconut palms remains in a zone of secondary growth. Among the even more temporary references are abandoned sago-working sites (gutted trunks, shelters, filtering apparatus), makeshift rain shelters in the forest, waterholes or platforms for storing packages of sago, finally the marks left by hunters: ground or tree blinds, stakes left from a fence or a pig trap or dug up bandicoot burrows.

Alongside the visual references can be found a series of social references inscribed by horticulture and arboriculture in nature itself: groves of breadfruit trees, areca palms, pandanus, stands of sago palms left over from old plantings, or (often slow-growing) semi-wild species which have been more or less planted by someone and which belong to them. Each tree that has been planted or propagated from an earlier planting has its own genealogical history, and any man or woman can name, for their own land, the original planters and the successive owners. This is the type of 'sociological' discourse a Yafar is fond of expounding when showing a stranger over his land. Genealogies, filiation or collateral relations, personal affinities are projected on to the land as the various plantings take place. Not only are the plants inscribed in a spatial setting, they also bear, as it were, the mark of time (the weeds and secondary growth in a clearing, the age of a tree, the size of a stand of sago palms).

In the following chapter, we will be examining crop ownership, harvesting rights and inheritance of individual rights, not to the land but to what has been planted there.

6

Horticulture–Arboriculture

> The next day Wabuminaag's old house had vanished: a big new house stood in its place. The old woman got up, put some wood on the fire and stirred it. Where yesterday the old man had been, she saw a handsome young man decked out in his pectoral ornaments and his elbow rings of boar's teeth, his bone dagger hanging down his back. There he sat. She went up and touched him with the tip of her finger and instantly he was drenched in sweat. Nearby stood his wife and children. Day broke, the *kwimpi* and the *athwe* birds sang, slowly the mists of the night began to lift.
>
> (From a myth)

In the preceding chapter I did not feel it necessary to distinguish between ownership and use of land, since in practice the two blend into a single apprehension of the space to be exploited. One may abstain from using a piece of land to which one has rights, but if one regularly works a piece of land, it is because one has acknowledged rights to it. To the Yafar way of thinking, the two situations do not differ in nature, and the language makes no distinction between them. On the other hand, in the case of a given piece of land to which one has rights (seen as cropping potential), the producing plot becomes, for a certain number of years, the personal property of the person, man or woman, who owns trees there. On this level, the land under cultivation is inseparable from the crops growing on it. A distinction must be made between rights to tracts of bush and rights to cultivated land. The latter, through the work done there, becomes the property of one or several persons. Once planting has begun, a distinction can no longer be made between ground and crops; they form a whole protected by family usage and harvesting rights and, within the family or the garden group, by private individual rights.

The cleared plot is called *aso*, as opposed to *sangweri* 'primary forest', *wanweri* 'secondary forest', *wamô* 'land covered with secondary forest', or *nôô* 'forest land far from the village'. There is no generic term for crops, but they may be described as *aso-na* 'from the garden', as opposed to spontaneous wild species, called *sangweri-na*. A man or woman will therefore say *ka na aso* 'my garden', and not *ka na bəte* 'my land', *bəte* being a term reserved for the territory as a whole.[1]

'Production Unit'[2] and Garden Group

In Chapter 4, I showed that the household was not necessarily identical to the production unit, even though this is usually the case with a nuclear family. The same may be said of the garden group (individuals working the same garden clearing). This unit is subject to slight modifications from year to year, and so the garden does not always bring together the same people each year. Thus the initially tempting equation between the three units turns out in practice to be an illusion. Like the house, a shared place for resting and eating, the garden is a closed space in which a cooperative undertaking is organized through the production and attribution or exchange of cultivated plants. And yet, just as products can circulate between households, trees may occasionally be attributed to close relatives working in different gardens. The custom of giving away each cultivated tree at the time of its planting or of exchanging annual garden patches creates a step midway between production and distribution (after harvest). Nevertheless we can venture a definition of the Yafar 'production group' as an economic unit whose nucleus is the limited family to which may temporarily be added a third party, or as a small group of close relatives, not necessarily sharing the

1. The opposition *wanweri/sangweri* corresponds to a differentiation between two types of garden: the *wanweri aso* is a clearing in secondary forest, usually close to the village, which can be reused after some thirty years; the *sangweri aso* is a clearing in primary forest, further away, which can be cleared again only after the complete regeneration of the forest, or in other words not before seventy to eighty years (see Juillerat 1983b).

2. This study was already well advanced when I realized that my attempts to define the Yafar 'production unit' were producing a growing list of individual situations. I had begun with the assumption (the real existence of a stable form of group called a 'production unit') only to bow to the evidence that I was unable to give this group a precise sociological definition. The Yafar 'production unit' is not a group, but a fluctuating configuration of relations.

same roof, whose membership may change over the years. Collaboration between the sexes is not indispensable to horticulture; or to put it more accurately a group of men (brothers or orphaned cousins, for instance) can constitute an independent garden group or production unit, while women cannot, since they need men for the clearing and later, for protection (see below). That being said, one can only have reservations about using a would-be universal theoretical concept which has no connection, in the society under study, with a stable reality. As the only recurring feature is the nuclear family, its disappearance with the death of the parents forces the garden group to reorganize along other lines, eventually through fusion with other horticultural units. What follows, then, is based on this dominance of the family and is meant to be only a general model or paradigm.

Every adult member of a household and every child having reached adolescence receives from the family head a patch (*abêsik*) in the same *aso*. The boundaries (also called *abêsik*) are roughed out before the trees are felled, then more clearly drawn using logs and stumps as markers, and then finalized by planting rows of cordylines and cane. The father usually keeps for himself a plot larger than those of his wife or wives and his children; this signifies that he is taking on more work, not that he is attributing to himself more of the product, since it is usually his wife who harvests his plot and vice versa. But there is no hard and fast rule, and all depends on individual needs and the likely number of future beneficiaries per planter (see below).

Family gardens are not laid out in any particular spatial order from one year to the next; as a rule they are from one to several kilometres apart. The same is true synchronically for the gardens of different members of a lineage. And yet in some years the Yafar cut larger clearings (*aso narik*) in which several families work side by side. Cleared land is shared on two levels, then: the big family plots and, within each of these, the smaller individual patches. The reason for multifamily clearings, which were made twice between 1970 and 1981, was the security they were thought to provide while the Sepik-Vanimo road was being opened. And indeed the big gardens did have the advantage of bringing the women together under the protection (from sorcery or seduction) of one man not working on the road. Formerly, when the fear of raids by neighbouring tribes was greater, these large gardens were more frequent. In 1973, each moiety (together with a few isolated horticulturalists and their families) cleared a big collective garden of similar size. In the Araneri group, for example, there were seven families and one married man whose wife had joined another production group. Family plots vary from 1500 to 3500m². The area under cultivation is not only proportional to the family's size, but also depends on other factors such as the yield of previous gardens, availability of cuttings, likely yield of the new garden or plans for distributing crops to children (see below).[3]

Elsewhere (Juillerat 1983b), I have indicated that part of Yafar horticultural production remains unharvested because there is no immediate need for it. This pseudo-surplus represents the indispensable security margin between estimated production and needs at time of planting, and real production and future needs. This margin is calculated against a background of systematic underproduction with respect to ecological potential and the availability of shoots and cuttings. Yet there would be no use in producing more because it would only increase the margin of security beyond the necessary threshold. Better programming of domestic consumption, however, would make such waste avoidable, although the underlying problem of malnutrition in this region is one of quality (lack of protein-rich foods). Underproduction is therefore due not, as Sahlins writes, to 'modest ideas of "satisfaction" locally prevailing' (1974: 41), but to the nonstorable nature of the products from the garden and the trees, and to the natural scarcity of meat for consumption. Furthermore, the notion of carrying capacity should be looked at separately, in conjunction with clearing on the one hand and hunting and gathering on the other.

Horticulturalists working together on multifamily gardens are not bound by any system of interfamily exchanges. Social relations are articulated at the individual family level (or some

---

3. In 1973 Waya had cleared 600m² for himself, 900m² for his eldest son, who was 17, and 450m² for his wife; he also had a ten-year-old son and a younger daughter without patches. Wagif and his wife, a young couple who had lost their first child, cleared 3500m². His elder brother Buwô and his wife (plus a son with no patch) cleared 2350m². Bone and his wife (with an infant daughter) cultivated 2120m², but six months earlier had cleared a complementary garden of 250m² in secondary forest. Finally, Wiy and his wife (with four children without patches, two of whom helped with the gardening) worked 1950m², plus a *wanweri* clearing of 250m² cut during the preceding cycle. It appears, nevertheless, that single-family clearings in primary forest, the most common case, are usually bigger than the family plots in a multifamily garden, with the largest attaining 4000m².

other form of production unit), independently of the other families. Sharing a 'big garden' entails no obligation between families; as far as the organization of work is concerned, one finds a coordination between groups (for clearing and burning) rather than cooperation.

As I said above, a family will often invite a close relative to help with the garden during the time needed to do the clearing. This can be one of the husband's agnates or – less frequently but at least once after they are married – one of the wife's brothers. These ties extend beyond the current year, thanks to the fruit from the trees planted and exchanged with the guest, which will go on for fifteen or twenty years. The guest thus acquires rights to the crops which have been allotted to him (see below), but this does not mean that he acquires new rights to the land. The inviter 'gives the cleared land' to work to the one he has invited (even though the latter has usually come to fell the trees), as indicated by the expression *ka nem aso ko feaka nam* 'I am clearing you a garden'.

Organization of Work[4]

Choice and Decision

The refusal to rank social relations other than in respect of gender, age and ritual specialization is especially striking in the organization of production, and horticultural production in particular. Ask a group of Yafar who decides where to clear, when to start one stage or another, whether or not to call on a working party, and the answer is always the same: each does as he sees fit, and no one can force his peers to do anything. There is indeed a hierarchy of production relations, but it is restricted to the family and articulated mainly by ties between husband and wife, between parents and children or between elder and younger siblings. This absence of coordination of clearing tasks, in the village or the tribal territory as a whole, is merely the corollary of the sparse population and the long fallow cycles which are therefore

4. The technical operations of Yafar gardening and the list of the plants cultivated are detailed in Juillerat 1983b and 1984b. For details of horticulture-arboriculture in another Border Mountains society, see Huber 1978.

Plate 5. Harvesting cuttings in a year-old garden.

possible; it is obvious that, in such a system and in the absence of demographic constraints, any attempt at authoritarian or central-ized control would make no sense. The head of the family is thus the sole deciding agent in horticultural matters. He alone chooses what piece of land to clear on his lineage territory and then in-forms his family and eventually the other gardeners working on the same territory. If he wishes to combine his efforts with those of other families, he seeks the consensus of his kinsmen to make up a garden group. He also gives sufficient advance notice to the man he wishes to invite as co-cultivator: in this matter promises have already been made, often a year in advance, and the invi-tation may be extended in the course of an alternating reciprocal exchange.

Working Groups

In view of such individualism, of this organization founded principally on the family, it is not surprising that the Yafar find few occasions for group work. In the area of horticulture I noted only two instances when people from outside the nuclear family came to the aid of a man or his wife: for clearing and for harvesting certain types of cutting. These groups are always limited to a few individuals bound by kinship or personal choice, but a person may also politely refuse to cooperate without incurring any social sanction other than a similar refusal when a reciprocal situation presents itself. Pressure is stronger when the aid is owed by a younger sibling or half-sibling to an elder; the converse is less frequent, as elder siblings rarely offer to help with their younger siblings' work. On such occasions (tree-felling mainly), the authority of elder siblings may be exercised if necessary by publicly expressed criticism of an uncooperative younger sibling. Obligations of mutual aid mark affinal relations too, and more particularly a son-in-law's duties towards his father-in-law (Ch. 10). Moreover, the time to be spent helping is limited with respect to the total duration of the work: a week for felling trees, two or three days for beginning planting. The wife, whose task it is to clear the undergrowth before the felling proper, may also be aided by one or two of her husband's female relatives. In the case of harvesting and transporting cuttings, the groups, based for the most part on the husband's kinship ties (classificatory daughters, nieces), are essentially female. In the middle of planting season (November), groups of young men and adolescents may come to help with the construction of the shelter which every gardener erects in the midst of his crops.

Formerly, when large multifamily gardens were cleared deep in the forest, and especially if the soil quality looked particularly promising, the first day of felling was marked by a communal meal taken by all the families: the previous day the women would have prepared quantities of sago jelly, and the men would bring smoked game (or fish) that they had been storing for the occasion. While felling the trees, the men would sing *popwamôk* songs evoking the mythic felling of a primordial irontree, which as it fell divided the human race into tribes (see epigraph to Ch. 1).

In general it can be said that the system of horticultural working parties is based primarily on a hierarchical relationship between elder and younger members of the same generation (especially siblings and half-siblings), or between (real or close classificatory) parents and children. With the exception of a few special cases in which the younger sibling may suffer from excessive authority, this dependence is not felt to be coercive, for it remains infrequent and, out of the whole annual cycle, represents in reality only a small investment of labour. In principal all work provided is paid in uncooked foodstuffs handed out at the end of the task or by a portion of the harvest.

Allocation of Cultivated Patches

Once each member of the family has worked to produce a cultivated patch, these are divided and redistributed within the garden group. This should be seen more as the implementation of intrafamily reciprocity than as a primarily economic mechanism, for this redistribution – at least in so far as annual crops are concerned – is neutralized by the pooling of production at consumption. We will first examine the case of annual crops, and then trees, whose production is deferred and covers a number of years.

Annual Crops

Unlike trees, annual crops (whose harvest spans from two to four years) are redistributed by whole individual patches or subpatches. Subpatches are the result of dividing an individual patch with a view to its allocation to two or more persons. The person who receives a cultivated patch or subpatch acquires the harvesting rights and usually gives in exchange a patch (or part of a patch) that he himself has planted. Such reciprocity is not an obligation, however, and cultivators sometimes prefer to keep their crops for themselves. When reciprocity occurs, it takes place within the garden group and uniquely between actual producers. As the harvest is imminent, children are considered to be too young to own crops or consume them independently, or even to manage the partial distribution of the product. The most obvious reciprocity takes place between husband and wife (only his first wife if he is polygamous), then between the husband and his invited co-worker (his younger brother in Figure 24). The quasi-obligation for the head of the family to exchange his standing crops with several relatives explains why he must plant a greater area. This system often makes more work for the head of the family, but his wife must herself take care of the production of the family's sago.

The harvesting rights acquired following the exchange of patches are clearly defined, but are less closely respected in practice. As the nuclear family usually comprises the consuming group and as the production of family members is pooled in

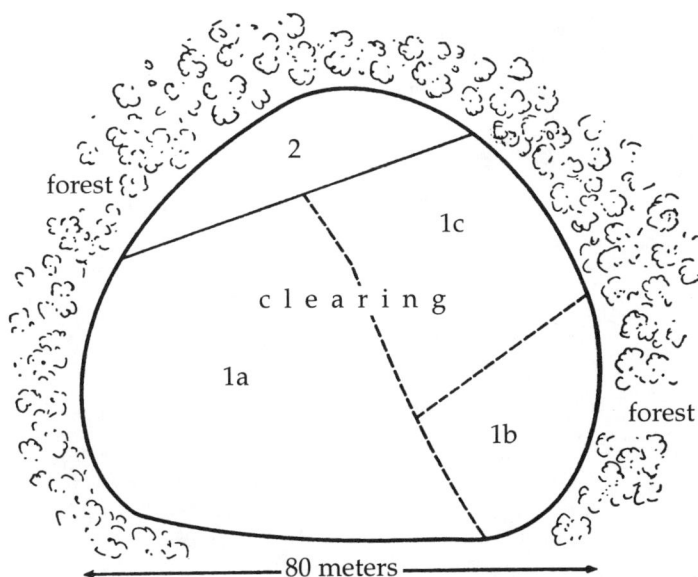

Figure 23. Distribution and allocation of individual patches in a family garden: Case 1

Plate 6. Carrying taro cuttings to be planted in a new garden.

preparing meals, the appropriation of annual crops still in the ground in no way gives rise to inequalities in the later sharing of food and appears essentially to be a mechanism for ensuring the unity of the garden group which, on this level, is the production unit (see above). This coherence is disrupted, however, by the allocation of trees to relatives outside the garden group.

Trees

Once the annual crops are harvested and, especially after a few years, when secondary vegetation is already reclaiming the cultivated land, the Yafar garden begins to look like an untended

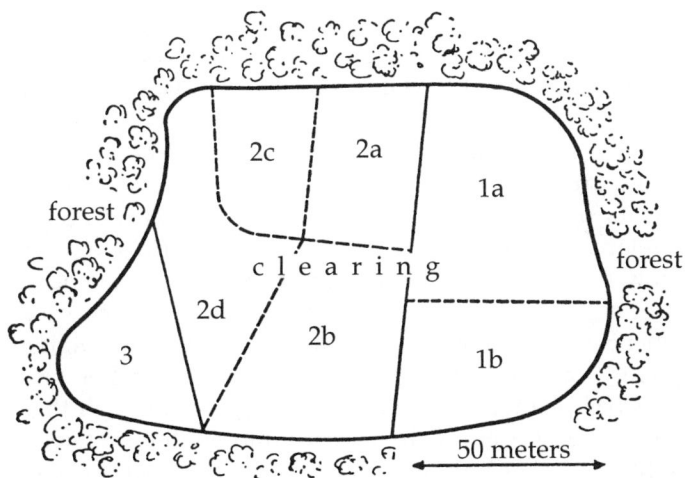

Figure 24. Distribution and allocation of individual patches in a family garden: Case 2

orchard. Clumps of breadfruit trees grow next to stands of *Areca catechu*, pandanus, and here and there little bunches of trees with edible leaves (*Gnetum gnemon, Hibiscus manihot*), not counting a few isolated semi-wild subjects and especially the sago palms at the bottom of the clearing with their huge fronds.

On average, fruit trees or those with edible leaves begin to produce after five or six years and go on until they are fifteen or twenty. The only tree grown *in situ* from seed or shoots is the sago palm. The years separating planting and the time when trees can be harvested annually allows them to be attributed to different relatives, including young children, and to engage these in a long-term relation with the planter. Trees are thus allocated as soon as they are planted, by clumps or individually. Taken together, the orchards correspond to the patches set out for the annual crops, but the latter must often be re-subdivided for the benefit of the planter's non-producing children. As for annual crops, trees with edible leaves, semi-wild trees and possibly breadfruit trees, an individual may eat what he has himself planted; but the taboo on consuming personal production is strictly respected for pandanus, areca and coconut palms (see the parallel with the taboo on the product of one's own hunting). The product of any one of the latter species will always be harvested and eaten by someone other than the planter, either from his or her own generation, or from the following generation – never from the preceding one.[5] This means that whoever plants a tree is not its owner; he or she gives exclusive harvesting rights to a relative, spouse, brother, sister (or cousin), son, daughter, nephew, niece. These relatives are not necessarily members of the planter's garden group, although this is often the case. The beneficiary must in any case have easy access, by residence, to the trees received. Thus a daughter for whom her father or mother has planted trees forfeits her rights, although they may always be reasserted, if she marries into another hamlet; in the meantime, it is her brothers who have the usufruct of the trees. If the owner of a tree has no use for the fruit, he makes it available to a close relative, according to a secondary, more informal level of redistribution.

---

5. Here is a parallel with the taboos surrounding menstrual blood (Ch. 9): the produce cannot go up the generation ladder, just as menstrual blood is polluting for kin of ascending generations.

Whereas for annual crops as well as for cloned trees, the shoots are usually taken from former gardens, in the case of trees which reproduce sexually (*Areca catechu*, breadfruit, coconuts) an individual sometimes tries also to obtain seeds from a co-villager of the opposite moiety, or from another hamlet or even a neighbouring tribe; this supposes generalized reciprocity between kinsmen or affines, but such exchanges remain informal and fairly rare. Moreover, they are strictly forbidden with certain tribes in the case of coconut palms and sago shoots, the two moiety totemic trees (pp. 20–1 and Map 4). Only men engage in these exchanges (even if the gift must go through a wife): women do not exchange seeds or shoots with each other. An ethnobotanical approach could explain this tendency by pointing out the need to disperse varieties, but is seems that the sociological and even symbolic factor is more decisive: desire for reciprocity between moieties or hamlets and between affines, and also the need to bring seeds for germination in from the outside, for the seed symbolizes the fertile young woman (*angômêg*) from another group (clan, submoiety, village or tribe) who, when fecundated by her acquirer, will give him a son (represented by the sprout) to ensure his posterity. The symbolic fertilization of the seeds by the planter is suggested by the technique of first leaving them in a layer of mulch (place of gestation) to germinate in the forest, before transplanting them to the garden. Wives also often bring their husbands seeds from their home group. More often the planter takes the shoots and seeds from the patches and the trees allocated to him by a male or female relative and which he has therefore not planted himself; the social transfer of a standing plant is thus ensured immediately after its planting and does not have to be renewed later by the gift of a shoot.

Human and plant reproduction; the mobility of women through marriage associated with patrilineal descent and the occasional exchange of seeds between men; the maternal place of gestation for the 'son' and earth-mother place of germination for the seed, both under the control of men – these form a coherent set of biological, social and symbolic facts characteristic of horticultural societies.

Trees are planted around a new hamlet when it is founded (Ch. 1), and are later replaced. Usually planted by men, but also by a few women, each tree is attributed to a close male or female relative, usually a child. Coconut palms, the only species planted exclusively in the vicinity of the village, are attributed to younger siblings or children only. As a rule, a woman who has helped her sister in giving birth plants a coconut palm for the child, which will grow along with him or her. In this way, coconuts often accompany the growth and life of their owners and have a symbolic function of identification and protection (see the Gungwan ritual, Ch. 12). But the life of a coconut palm is considered to be longer than that of a human; as the saying goes: 'Man dies, the coconut remains, [for] man's bones are soft [while] the coconut's wood is hard.'

The system for distributing trees does not end with their attribution at the time of planting: over the years, the planter has received trees planted by others which he has not yet (or not sufficiently) redistributed, for his posterity was not yet fully assured. These trees will later be redistributed[6] to the less-favoured younger children. The father generally waits until his children are past the critical threshold of infant mortality (the Yafar say they wait about five gardens) to make them the beneficiaries of trees planted before their birth. These trees can come either from gardens controlled by the father or the mother, or from patches already attributed to a son or elder daughter who turns out to be favoured with respect to the younger siblings. This redistribution for the benefit of younger children does not prevent the father and mother continuing to give all their children part of the trees planted each year. At the parents' death, the elder siblings will themselves continue this redistribution to the younger children. The attribution of trees at the time of planting and deferred redistribution are complementary processes.

Both spouses harvest the trees inherited by the husband, and eventually those received by the wife if the couple does not live too far from her father's lands; this is not redistribution, however, but sharing during the lifetime of those concerned. In effect, if the husband should die without children, his trees go to his agnates (or eventually to other kin), and the widow must return to her own lands to reassert her rights or must remarry. On the other

6. The term 'redistribution' is used here in the sense of secondary attribution, and not, as it is usually employed by economic anthropologists, to mean the redistribution of a product previously amassed by a high-ranking person. In the latter case, a centrifugal movement follows an initial centripetal movement of the merchandise, whereas in the Yafar case (where such a process is unthinkable), the image is one of a two-phase distribution by 'ricochet', something like 'generalized reciprocity' and 'pooling' (see Sahlins 1974, Ch. 5).

hand, if she has a child, it inherits from its father, and the mother can exploit the deceased's trees with their child. While the child is small, its mother will control the production and distribution; afterwards she must yield to the inalienable rights of her son or daughter.

Inheriting Trees

This leads us to distinguish redistribution (of which we have been speaking), which is done during the giver's lifetime, from inheritance, which is the obligatory transmission of goods after death.

When a person dies, the annual crops are harvested and consumed by the nuclear family, which does not constitute inheritance in the true sense of the word; when the planter dies during the planting season, his close relatives may, as a token of mourning, pull up or at least not harvest what he has just planted. Inheritance properly speaking concerns mainly the trees. As in the case of redistribution, what is inherited may be an isolated tree or a whole grove. The beneficiary can be a relative of the same generation or the following generation, but never of the elder generation: goods cannot flow against the stream of social time. The basic principle of inheritance rests on the key role of the elder son or daughter; but with the process of continuous redistribution, the elder child is ultimately not or only slightly favoured, for his or her role is to see that the younger siblings receive their share. The elder daughter may be excluded from this role if she is already married, and certainly will be if she is married into another local group. The elder in fact stands in for the father (or the mother) and carries on the task of redistribution, which – depending on the parties – can be done more or less even-handedly. When an elder sibling dies unmarried, the trees he or she has received from one of the parents often go directly to the last-born of the sibling group (this is also true for annual crops), for it is felt that the youngest is always disadvantaged, and this is one way of making the distribution more equitable. If a man or woman has no children, the trees pass preferably to a brother, but may also go to a sister if she has not married out, who will then hand them on to his or her own children. If the sister lives at some distance, the inheritance can go directly to her son or daughter (*rabik,* child of the deceased's sister); trees can also go to cousins. The same is true for the trees of the village orchard which, as a rule, are inherited by a direct descendant. When the heir is too young, the other parent or uncles ensure the intervening period; this is the only case in which kinsmen from the preceding generation may harvest fruit belonging to a classificatory child or a nephew of the deceased. In principle affines do not inherit; a man may be given the usufruct of the trees inherited by his wife, but he does not own them.

It should be noted that there is apparently no sexual discrimination in the inheritance system. The exclusion of a married daughter or sister in another village can hardly be seen as spoliation – it is merely a mechanism whose aim is not to favour a woman twice who already disposes of her husbands crops and works his land. Moreover, she does not lose her rights, which she can reclaim from her brothers if she returns to her village after the death of her husband; and even if she does not return, her children can inherit or assert their claim if they take up residence in their mother's hamlet (with their mother's brother, for example). It is only the geographical and social distance which temporarily or definitely suspends rights. And yet a slight inequality between the sexes does appear, as I have already said, in the quantity of trees planted and the size of the plots; the result is that the mother transmits less than the father.

The cognatic transmission of inherited trees is valid only from one generation to the next, however, for if a woman can pass on to her children trees planted by herself, by her husband (if she is his first wife) or by a relative of her generation, she cannot hand on the inheritance from her own parents, mother's brother or other kinsmen from ascending generations unless she has no brothers (or other male relatives capable of inheriting in her stead), in which case her children are effectively the only legitimate heirs. Here again is the principle, which we have already seen in the case of the transmission of land, of patrilineal dominance (in practice, uterine descent is recognized over one generation only). Adopted children (orphans of both sexes) inherit trees from both their true and their adoptive parents. The Yafar stipulate that a child adopted as a youngster receives as much as one's own child.

The above applies to all trees, including sago palms, which can be inherited one by one as they are planted, and then go on to constitute groves (because of vegetative propagation and transplanting shoots) which are inherited as a block or may be divided among several heirs. After a few decades, the sago stand is still there and goes on growing indefinitely, but the original clearing is no longer visible in the reconstituted forest, even though its past existence is recognized and it is known who did the planting (which can go back four generations). On the other hand, if the planting dates back too far, the Yafar can no longer identify the original planter. Palm trees are then inherited through a different system (lateral inheritance), which consists in transmitting the rights first collaterally, to the siblings of both sexes down to the death of the youngest. Only after that can the eldest child of the eldest deceased sibling inherit, before transmitting this exclusive right, upon his or her own death, to the younger sibling, etc.

Finally, the Yafar go on to distinguish stands of sago far from the village which may have been planted by men or by forest spirits, they say they do not know which. These 'wild' sagos, rarely worked because of the distance, are regarded as products to be gathered and as being at the disposal of all members of the group controlling the land. These remote territories are said to be *ofu bəte awtinaag* 'old land from ancestral (mythic) times', and the sago palms growing there, *ofu yis awtinaag, ifêêg yis* or *fut yis*, expressions which translate as 'original sago jelly'.

Redistribution and Inheritance in a Polygynous Family

Differentiation of the status of co-wives takes the form of greater economic and jural autonomy for second or third wives. We observed no relations of authority between co-wives, merely a greater identification on the part of the first wife (*ifya-minaag*) with her husband in matters of harvesting and consumption rights, which can give rise to dominance of the *ifya-minaag* over the second wife, *sum-inaag*[7] (Juillerat 1977) when it comes to exploiting and sharing a product belonging to the husband. The hierarchy is one of rights to the husband's production.

Secondary wives are just as concerned as the first wife in the context of reciprocity and the redistribution of the patches

---

7. *Ifya < ifêêg* 'that which is at the origin'; *sum* 'that which follows'; *minaag < me-inaag*, literally 'in the hole', i.e. 'inside'.

worked by the husband: they receive garden patches and trees planted by their husband. The reverse is not always true, however, and sometimes the second wife plants her patch, cleared with the help of her spouse, and then allots the products to herself and her children, as shown in Figure 24. It is in the system for transmitting the trees received or inherited by the husband that the status of these wives diverges, for only the *ifya-minaag* has access to trees that her husband has received from a third party. The Yafar stress that the *ifya-minaag* can say *ka na*, 'it's mine', when speaking of a tree that her husband has come into by inheritance or redistribution; with his consent she may organize the harvest and distribute the produce. The first wife's privilege extends to consumption: often the second wife shares the produce of her own gardens with her children, while the husband, together with his first wife and their children, make up a separate consumption unit; nevertheless partial pooling by the whole polygynous family is frequent.

In the next generation, the children of all co-wives inherit from their father, but none will inherit from a 'mother' other than his or her own. Upon the death of the husband, it is once again the first wife who will have the enjoyment of his trees until the eldest child has grown up, while the second wife, not having the management of the crops inherited by the deceased, finds herself suddenly economically on her own, but retains the trees that her husband planted for her.

Distribution of Products and Consumption[8]

Attribution, redistribution and inheritance also apply to standing crops. Distribution concerns all harvested products, usually before they are cooked. With distribution and consumption, we enter a much less formal type of network than for land-holding, redistribution or inheritance. In principle, the distribution – or more strictly speaking, pooling – of products goes without saying within the nuclear family, where it leads to consumption in common (nevertheless see the case of the polygynous family, above) and often overflows the boundaries of the nuclear family to take in close relatives or needy co-residents (elderly widowers or

8. For food taboos and horticulture, see pp. 150, and 357–8.

Plate 7. Working sago with a stone sago-pounder (*hwagi*).

widows, unmarried adolescents) or privileged kin and affines, in particular *segwaag* (Ch. 11).

Sago deserves special mention, for there are two separate modes of distribution or sharing (before or after the tree is worked): a) giving a male or female relative of a bit of sago, most often in the form of portions of cooked sago jelly (*yis*) wrapped in leaves and ready to eat, more rarely of uncooked sago starch (*aba*); b) inviting a female relative (of the wife or a sister of a kinsman) to work a sago trunk with the official male or female owner, or giving a whole sago trunk ready to work. This gives rise to little groups of two to four women (no more than two per sago trunk). Each woman has her own apparatus where she filters what she has extracted from the section of palm trunk that has been given her. It is the relatively elaborate technique of sago working which occasions these groups, which must be distinguished both from mutual aid groups (where aid is lent without prior division of the product, but a small portion may later be given in payment) and from redistribution of sago palms, in which the beneficiary works his own trees as he sees fit. In Chapter 8, I will analyse the extra-tribal systems of exchange by which foodstuffs or other products can leave the local group and the tribe to enter wider circuits.

The importance of arboriculture[9] and the jural system it determines has given us some idea of the way Yafar society conceives of the social management of goods in general. The system for transmitting individual rights reveals more a male dominant than male domination. As with exchanges, the social control of the transmission of goods is first and foremost the concern of men. Despite the fact that women have a recognized right to own trees and to pass on non-inherited trees to their children, patriliny requires that the continuity of the social control of crops be ensured exclusively in the male line. It is in this sense only that there is a male monopoly on production in this area.

---

9. In fact trees are the only valuables governed by a formal system of private property. Their value comes from their productivity spread over ten or twenty years and from their reproductivity.

Plate 8. Washing sago pith on the *bwêr*; the filtered sago is left to settle in the trough below.

The Symbolic Order

The Yafar's symbolic vision of the living world likens production to reproduction: to produce a garden is to create a unique link in the uninterrupted reproductive chain that ensures the permanence of life. Clearing, burning, making cuttings and weeding form the technical, material level; boundaries, attribution, inheritance and distribution are the forms of social control; and cosmological representation and ritual provide the imaginary framework and guarantee symbolic efficacy.

To cultivate the land is to perform a purposive act on untamed nature, on Mother Nature, and at the outset this is an act of violence (clearing and burning): before production, there must be destruction. Yafar religious behaviour would seem to confirm the psychoanalytical thesis that taking from nature (as a maternalized place) induces guilt (see, for example Mendel 1972). The Yafar clearer begins by politely sending the forest spirits out of the area to be cleared, leaving them a day to seek another home; moreover, *nabasa, sawangô*, etc. (Ch. 5) are pathogenic spirits that visit sickness on anyone who has cut their trees or cleared their undergrowth without warning or offering. The area of nature on which one wishes to act must therefore first be desocialized, but one must also have the tacit authorization of the masters of the place or pay them a price (a food offering) before striking the first blow. Another element of this preliminary rite is symbolically to close, by reciting the Gungwan magic spells (Ch. 12), the underground 'paths' of the earth (which will be bared by the clearing), so that the clearers' self (*sungwaag*) will not wander while they sleep and go to 'ripen' (*abuk feg*) like a fruit upon contact with the maternal depths. Without going into the details of a psychoanalytical interpretation, I think we can see here a twofold symbolic mechanism, preliminary to the act of cultivating, of deculpibalization and protection against regression to the Mother, an eventuality experienced as producing anxiety and represented by the notion of *abuk* 'ripe', in other words close to putrefaction and death (see Ch. 12).

Once these precautions have been taken, the trees can be felled without further ritual intervention. Before the burning, spells are said and eventually a chant may be sung while the clearer(s) light and then fan the first fire in the centre of the clearing. They symbolically burn the 'house of the *sawangô*', those female spirits scattered throughout the territorial pantheon and here taken as an anonymous whole, but they also reinvent W. . . and B. . .'s Primordial Fire (*ifêêg suwê*)[10] (Ch. 2). Shortly before the end of the burning, the digging sticks for the garden are ritually cut and shaped in the forest.

Once the ground has been completely cleared, the planting rite[11] – called Wabuminaag, the name of the garden spirit in its elderly stage, in other words fallow – enacts the phases of the process of fertilizing the ground and the plants:[12]

1. The garden is 'opened' by introducing the specimens to be planted and by chanting a call to all the gardens of the region, whose principles of fertility are summoned to converge on this new clearing.
2. The ritual ground is cleared of all sticks and twigs (*roof* 'to peel').
3. Then it is struck and anointed with red ochre and magical rhizomes (an analogical act calling to the surface the terrestrial-maternal fertility principle *hoofuk*, represented by the ochre 'blood').
4. Specimens of each species to be planted are prepared and laid out around the planter to a chant evoking 'Wabi's garden' (a rejuvenated figure of Wabuminaag).
5. A fecundating bisexual ingredient (*suhêêg* 'mature, fertile and black') is prepared from charred taro (female) and the juice of sugar cane (male), with which the clearer then coats the tip of his digging sticks, which, according to mythology, represent Wabi's penis (and, on a more secret level, that of W. . .).
6. A long spell with stick(s) over the shoulder and an evocation of erection.

---

10. People also say *mwig suwê* 'original fire', or *kêfutuk suwê* 'solid (sacred) fire'. These terms are not pronounced during the rite or the fire might spread to the surrounding forest and villages.

11. This rite concerns only annual crops. Simpler rites are performed as the first tree of each species is planted. Wambuminaag comes from *wabi* (that which becomes bigger: tubers, rivers in flood, etc.; see also Ch. 7, n. 31) and *meeg* 'hole', + *inaag* 'in'. This crop spirit, also called Wabi, appears in mythology as sometimes old and alone, sometimes rejuvenated and surrounded by his family, an allegorical vision of the horticultural cycle and the alternation between clearing and fallow (see epigraph to this chapter).

12. Two species of fish (probably symbolically gendered) are magically used (perhaps buried) and also eaten during this rite – *ningɔgaw* and *bana*, both from the *Eleotridae* family.

7. First a taro cutting is planted: the ground is thoroughly worked with the digging stick, the planter pronouncing spells suggestive of shattering a woman's pelvis and the roots in the ground, as well as the room the future tuber will make for itself in the earth.

8. The other species are planted to the accompaniment of the appropriate spells and chants, the yam (*Dioscorea alata*) directly after the taro, with magical plants to ensure the garden's cosmic equilibrium.

9. Again spells from the Gungwan rite to close the invisible paths of the ground that were opened by the Wabuminaag rite and to protect the cultivators' self (*sungwaag*) as they sleep.

10. Finally the Wabuminaag rite ends with digging sticks held upright, spells associated with the mythic character Riyu, the symbol of stem growth. Now no one except the planter himself is allowed in the garden for 24 hours to avoid 'frightening the garden's *hoofuk*', presently at the surface of the ground, at this critical onset of gestation.

In a secret variant of this rite – called *aso seeg* 'magic garden plants' – the sexual principles set in motion are overtly the original divine pair W. . . and B. . . (Ch. 2). The cultivated land is the place where the celestial male meets the chthonian female in cosmic confrontation; this may explain the near-obsessive care with which the Yafar clear the ground in their gardens. The opposition between top and bottom is also rethought in terms of the topography of the clearing, the top of the slope of the ritual ground being planted with a magic clone which in the event bears the name *bêêb(i)*, the great celestial liana (Figure 7), 'path of the sun and the moon' and bringer of rain (this liana, *Calamus* sp., is gorged with water), and the bottom of the slope, planted complementarily with a clone bearing the name 'wedge' (*nihraag*) because it is used to 'raise' the bottom of the garden so that the rain does not wash away the plants or their life principle. In addition mythic entities are set about the ritual grounds in the form of aromatic magic plants or cordylines.

A projection on to the cultivated space of an imaginary cosmic equilibrium, the planting rite thus expresses the concern to maintain a naturalized sexual complementarity and a cyclical alternation of ageing and renewal of the species and the soil. It sets in motion the active principles of this reproduction and

Plate 9. Planting rite (Wabuminaag) and breaking ground with a digging stick in a new clearing.

ensures the physical conditions for successful gestation. After protecting themselves – prior to the transgression represented by this necessary violence perpetrated on nature – from the guilt and stigma of too sudden a return to nature, men are now better equipped to manipulate the reproductive principles and substances, and thus procure the illusion of controlling the fertility of nature and the production of gardens, as well as the power to do so.

Having progressed from the jural domain to the threshold of symbolic (and psychic) structures, we now find ourselves projected beyond the social sphere. But at the same time, we are brought back to this realm as soon as we ask ourselves the question, who, among the Yafar, possesses this control? The answer can easily be imagined: the man, not the woman, the adult or elderly (*aynaag*) man, not the adolescent or the bachelor, nor even a young married man with as yet no children, who does not know all the spells and does not dare pronounce the most sacred names. Now on the scales of the cosmic complementarity of the sexes, femaleness (the earth, the forest, maternal *hoofuk*) outweighs maleness (the digging stick, rain [?], the sky). It is therefore always by a stratagem of inversion, which we have seen portrayed in myth (p. 48), that men gain their power over natural reproduction.

7

Foraging and Husbandry

> A man went hunting. He spotted a red wild pig and shot it in the thigh with an arrow. The animal ran away. The hunter followed the trail of blood. He wondered to himself: 'Did I really shoot a pig?' He arrived and saw a young woman wiping away blood running down her thigh.
>
> 'What's this? I thought I shot a wild pig. . ..'
> 'I came here to gather grubs; you shot me and I ran away.'
> 'Alright, I'll leave you alone.'
> 'No, you shot me, now come to my village.'
>
> (From a myth)

In this chapter we will look at how natural resources not requiring a long-term investment of labour nor the control of domesticated botanical species are exploited, distributed and consumed as a function of the quantity of what is produced, land-holding rights, participation in capturing or gathering, gender, age and kinship.

Whether the produce comes from gathering, hunting or fishing, the amount to be distributed is always limited, except in the case of two large game animals (the pig and the cassowary) and the product gathered from certain types of tree (*Canarium* spp. and *Pometia pinnata*). Even in these instances, the quantity is relatively modest, as there is never more than one animal or tree at a time. The same is not true of raising pigs, where ten or fifteen animals may be slaughtered on the same day. Nor do the ecological and technical conditions of fishing allow great quantities of fish to be taken. Apart from this quantitative caveat, two types of distribution can be distinguished, one restricted to the 'production group' (more or less fluctuating – gatherers or hunters who have worked together on occasion but who also share certain land rights) and to the nuclear family or household, the other, much broader than these units, which involves the entire local community and some of the surrounding villages.

This differentiation in the quantity of what is produced and the social area over which it is distributed is reflected in the use of secrecy. Information about foraging activities is kept to a minimum, even totally blocked, by quasi-institutional taboos. It is reestablished, however, as soon as a large quantity of something is definitively acquired and is about to be distributed, whereas for small amounts (especially meat of any kind), secrecy pertains to production *and* distribution. This applies primarily to hunting and fishing, but extends to a certain degree to gathering sago grubs or certain species of 'almond trees'. Such behaviour has causes of a symbolic order – for example, women must learn nothing of the outcome of a hunt before the animal has been butchered and brought back to the village – and in the case of scarce items, motives of a socio-economic character, aimed at keeping unwelcome visitors away and thus avoiding over-distribution of a rare product.

Gathering

In principle each person gathers only within the boundaries of the territory to which they have rights, unless they have been personally authorized to use another piece of land. Since many wild trees are planted in gardens and later go on producing under the regenerated forest cover, it follows that gathering rights to these semi-wild specimens often belong to individuals and that the product is collected and distributed under the supervision of the man, or more rarely the woman, who holds the rights, in other words, the person to whom the planter attributed the tree. This system of rights, then, is the same as for domesticated trees (Ch. 6). In the case of wild species having no known owner, the produce is gathered and shared by a few men from the group that works the land, then distributed among all members of the group. Each member may subsequently redistribute his share among his kindred.

Both men and women gather forest products irrespective of the species. In the case of unowned wild trees, it seems that it is always men who organize the distribution if the fruit is to be picked from the tree; however, women may help collect the fruit off the ground or pick branches that have previously been cut. For *Canarium* and *Pometia pinnata*, small gathering parties are put together at the request of the owner or the person who has spotted the tree. As a rule, the women gather produce on the ground (fallen fruits, almonds,[1] leaves from the liana or semi-wild *Gnetum gnemon*, bamboo shoots, mushrooms) and distribute their own production, usually within the nuclear family. Fruit-picking (the category *fôk*) seems to be a particularly esteemed activity and therefore organized by men because these species fruit at a specific time but in fairly great quantities, unlike species which provide a regular food supply throughout the year, or nearly, but little at a time (the category *ohoof*: leaves, bamboo, mushrooms). However I am also tempted to see, in this spatio-economic hierarchy that appears in the picking of wild trees, the, influence of the spatial gender hierarchy, already widely attested in other contexts (habitat, sexuality, cosmology, etc.), which ranks the place of men and women in vertical space and implicitly, there-fore, in this occasional situation, namely gathering from big trees.

Animal products can theoretically be gathered as freely by wo-men as by men, or even by children, and they belong to whoever takes them. Grubs (*nibik*) of the *fut* beetle (*Rhynchophorus* sp.) found by chance beneath the bark of a log belong to whoever discovers them, but grubs that have matured in a tree felled for that purpose belong to the person who took the initiative and announced his rights. For the *wiy* tree (*Lithocarpus lauterbachii*), which often harbours large quantities of grubs, bands of gath-erers form around the man who felled the tree. When it is a sago palm (which is usually the case), the gathering rights belong to the owner; but the one who planted the sago palm abstains from eating the grubs as well as the sago from his or her tree.[2] Bird nests (particularly those of the wildfowl *Talegalla* or *Megapodius* spp., which lay their eggs in fallen leaves) may be reserved by the man or woman who has found them by depositing a leafy branch (*egih*) as a sign of ownership. A dozen types of frog are captured, especially by women and children, but two of these (*ahgo* and *ow*[3]),

1. In the case of the *Terminalia impediens* (*aw*) and one species of *Canarium* (*bogwa*), the kernels are cracked on the spot against the butresses of the tree. The other species of nut are opened in the village.
2. The same tree can produce both, since the top of the sago log is left for the *Rhycho-phorus* to lay their eggs in.
3. Respectively *Asterophrys robusta* and *Xenobatrachus* sp. (identified by Professor Menzies, University of PNG). The men will catch only these two species, which have a place in mythology, whereas frog 'hunting' is generally looked down on; the economic value of the product is enhanced by the symbolic representation culture gives it.

Plate 10. Gathered products: the fruits of the *Semecarpus papuanus* must be cooked to make them edible.

which have precise, antinomic (female) roles in mythology, are also caught and eaten by men.[4]

Lastly, firewood in the form of fallen logs, as well as black-palm petiolar sheaths (*sööbi*; for making containers or sleeping mats), can be reserved by means of an *egih*; the same holds for a tree that has been purposely ringbarked by an individual, who thus signals his ownership until the tree is dry enough to fell and be broken up by his wife.

Trespassing on hunting or gathering rights used to be discouraged by the use of *eney*, arrowheads stuck in the ground on which the thief would wound himself and thus be easily identifiable.

As a rule, men are more likely than women to happen upon rare products because they have more time to roam the forest. Women spend a great deal of their time working sago or gathering wood. Their mobility is also hampered by children or heavy loads and they must be home earlier to make the evening meal. Having more free time, the men go out looking for a product, often to return only at nightfall.

Hunting

Yafar Hunting Strategies[5]

While gathering does not require varied or complex techniques, hunting is a different matter. Before analysing the social relations which make it a privileged site of confrontation and exchange, something must therefore be said about the techniques used.

Wild pig, *təta* (*Sus scrofa papuensis*),[6] the most desirable game animal and one still found in abundance, is no doubt the object of the widest technical diversity. Let us look first of all at the individual devices or those possibly requiring the participation of another person. The first technique consists of lying in wait near bait, usually a split sago log. A straight fence or screen of sago fronds (*na pəpak*, 'sago pen') with 'windows' in it separates the bait from a carefully cleared zone beyond which – at a

---

4. Other species, such as the *ragwe* red ant, which live in large nests made of leaves and are eaten raw with water, or the *ifot* spider (*Atrax* sp.?), or the eggs of the *abumsow* spider, are minor products gathered by men and women.

5. For a typology of New Guinea hunting 'strategies' and a succinct inventory of the fauna, see Bulmer 1968.

6. See Bulmer 1968; Groves 1983; Laurie and Hill 1954.

distance of some 15m – a blind (*iyaha*) has been erected. When he hears the animal eating the sago pulp, the hunter steals up and shoots an arrow through one of the openings in the screen. As this type of hunting is done essentially at night, moonlight is useful, otherwise the hunter may take aim by ear. Nowadays a friend often goes along and, when the time comes to shoot, switches on a flashlight. The hunter does not lie in ambush every night, but only when the owner of the bait has noticed an animal's spoor in the course of his daytime rounds. But the hunter may also lie in wait (*nis awô*) at night at an unprepared spot but where tracks show that a pig has come to feed on previous nights, usually on windfall fruit.[7] In this case the hunter uses neither screen nor blind. A pig may also be surprised during the day, asleep in his lair, which he makes when it rains heavily. In almost all cases the wounded animal escapes and must then be tracked down by a band of hunters.

True traps, which do not require waiting, are of two kinds. One is the pit fall (*sês bǝme* 'game hole'), which also catches game smaller than pigs, such as wallabies and other ground-dwelling animals, including bandicoots. This technique is not often used (the southern Eri use it more). The other trap, called *awra*, is a wooden structure with a run, at the end of which is a platform holding a piece of sago bait; when touched, the platform tilts and trips a bundle of posts which falls and immobilizes the animal. When the hunter discovers his quarry he shoots it inside the trap. This technique is used only when preparing a big ceremony requiring a large quantity of smoked meat (see below).

Wild pigs are normally hunted by ambush or encircling drives (to use Bulmer's terminology), or by tracking: one morning a man spots the fresh spoor of a pig that has laid up for the day in a stand of bamboo or canes. The man first circles (*magfyêg*) the stand to make sure the tracks do not come out the other side. If they do not, the rest of the village is alerted, the area encircled (*kagwôg*) and the animal roused by a drive in which the dogs play the role of trackers and spotters. The animal still often manages

---

7. The Yafar are perfectly acquainted with the eating habits of animals, which is essential for stalking. For instance, the pig eats a lot of windfall fruit from wild areca palms and the *rabaf* tree; the cassowary feeds on certain varieties of areca nuts, but also on the fruit of the *Caryota* (*nöngô*) palm, of the *Semecarpus papuensis* (*wêên*), on pits of the *Terminalia impediens* (*aw*) and different varieties of *Canarium* (*sawô-sǝgo, buwof, hêgwa, nuray*), which are swallowed whole; and the wallaby eats wild taro (*rumo*) leaves, the leaves of certain *Aracea*, of the liana *Stenochlaena* (*nahmô*), etc.

to get away, wounded or not, the men posted around the thicket being too far apart or not having had time to draw their bows; the surrounding dense undergrowth is an additional handicap. No form of screen or net is used. If the animal is wounded, the hunters track it, sometimes for kilometres and all day long (often in vain). It is while being tracked that the furious pig may charge a hunter who often has just enough time to drop his bow and scramble up the nearest tree. It even happens that all he can do is to come to grips with the animal and try to neutralize it, calling for help while trying to protect himself from the thrusting snout and tusks with his carrying bag. A lone hunter wounded by an enraged pig runs a serious risk of being killed and partially devoured.[8]

A hunter, or more likely his dog,[9] may also simply come across a wild pig or fresh spoor. The hunt then turns into a chase, man and dog running with extreme agility on the heels of the animal already out of sight, the man calling encouragements to the dog, quite often only to end up calling him off when the animal has too long a lead. In effect, coursing game in this way is rarely successful, even if the hunter has a gun.

The hunting of cassowary or *kwoy*,[10] a large, solitary, monogamous, flightless bird with atrophied wings, is not organized or characterized by any particular technique except waiting in a blind near a stream where tracks have been spotted (the bird is a water lover and takes its chicks to bathe), or under a tree where it comes to feed on windfalls. If a wounded animal gets away, the tracking is done as for pigs.

In the varied category of small mammals, a distinction must be made between ground-dwellers and tree-dwellers. Wallabies or *ifwawi* (*Dorcopsis* or *Thylogale* sp.), little bush kangaroos, can fall into a pit trap, be shot by moonlight or flashlight, or more rarely be surprised during the day while asleep or be flushed out by a dog. Bandicoots or *hosigi* (*Echymipera rufescens*), small burrowing mammals, are no doubt the most common and most often killed species. The burrow is partially destroyed and then smoked. A hunter may also lie in wait for bandicoots at the foot of certain species of *Ficus* on whose windfalls they feed. Tree-

8. Three have been killed and several wounded in ten years.
9. The dog barks to tell the hunter the size and location of the game to be stalked or coursed. It guides the hunter and, for small animals up to the size of a wallaby, can seize the quarry in its mouth (see below, dog-raising).
10. *Casuarius unappendiculatus* Bly. This is the species found in this area.

Plate 11. Hunter performing a multiplication rite on a wild pig using a magic rhizome and spells.

dwelling mammals, such as opossums, cuscus (*Phalanger* spp.) and tree rodents like the *Uromys caudimaculatus* (*sawôh*), are sometimes spotted during the day asleep in the fork of a branch (Yafar hunters often walk with their heads back, looking up at the foliage); but they are usually located at night, by moonlight or flashlight, as they move through the trees in search of food, calling back and forth. If the game is too high, it cannot be shot from the ground, and the hunter must climb the tree, holding bow and arrows in the crook of his neck; a partner remains on the ground to catch the animal when it falls. Small animals can also be smoked out of hollow trees and caught with bare hands.

Fruit-eating 'flying foxes' (*Dabsonia moluccensis* and probably *Rousettus* spp.) and bats are either ambushed at night from near a papaya or banana tree or nowadays shot with a gun during the day as they roost in trees (*webô*) or caves (*agmasa*).[11] All reptiles are eaten, either beaten to death or shot with bow and arrow; snakes and lizards (of which the most prized is the monitor, whose skin is also used for the head of hourglass drums) are roasted whole.

For birds other than the cassowary or the crowned pigeon (*Goura victoria*) (Rand and Gilliard 1967), the most common technique is to build an *iyaha* blind in certain trees, often quite high up, when they are in fruit: the Yafar are thoroughly familiar with the feeding habits of each type of bird. The seeds of a wild *Ficus* (*anof*) are often planted in gardens, since the fruit serves as bait for *wos* pigeons (*Ducula rufigaster*). These seeds are collected from the gizzard of a pigeon killed in the tree and rapidly planted in another spot, an example of the alternating cyclical interweaving of wild-species arboriculture and hunting. Another species of bird hunted by the same technique is the white cockatoo, which feeds in particular on the fruit of one species of *Prunus* (*hogampi*) as well as on wild areca nuts. All species of birds can also be lured by whistling their call (no mechanical call is used), but this usually goes together with the strategy of the blind in the fruiting tree. A hunter may also surprise a bird on its nest or conceal himself near the nest and wait. Birds sought more particularly for their plumage are hunted using the same techniques, but are shot using bird bolts or three-pronged arrows in order to stun the bird without soiling its feathers with blood.

Sometimes, instead of being hunted, a bird may help the hunter: the warning cry of a certain number of species (notably *Pitohui kirhocephalus senex*, or *athwe*) signals the presence of a small mammal or reptile.[12]

11. On the Potayneri's land, where there are big caves with hundreds of *agmasa* flying foxes, these are often struck down as they fly out at dusk with a pole wielded from a wooden tower built at the cave entrance, while one or two men finish them off on the ground. The *agmasa* have a slightly shorter wingspread than the *webô*.

12. The hunter's weapon is still almost exclusively the bow (*fango*) and arrow (*fag*). The bow is cut from the hard wood of the wild areca palm, the string being of rattan (*we*). The arrow consists of a shaft about 150 cm long taken from a kind of cane (*wog*), to the tip of which strips of liana (*Tetrastigma* sp.) are used delicately to bind a point whose material and form vary with the type of game to be hunted: a sharpened half-section of large bamboo for pigs and cassowary; areca wood or small bamboo carved into single or double prongs or a single point with a circular section for small game; multiple heads, called *ifəgê* (two to four points), of areca wood for very small game. A small stone inserted at the base of the head of certain arrows acts as a weight, and white clay is used to hold the bindings in place. The flightless arrow is simple rested on the 'string', and the bowman pinches the arrow and

Social Relations in Hunting

Capturing Game
The hunting strategies we have just examined will have shown the reader that hunting is primarily the affair of one or two persons, and that only a few special operations require the cooperation of a large number of participants. All the actions preceding the shooting of the first arrow demand that as little noise as possible be made. The most frequent setup, then, is a lone hunter or possibly hunter and friend. In the second case, as mentioned above, cooperation is organized according to technical complementarity: holding the light/firing; climbing the tree and firing/ waiting at the foot of the tree and catching the animal when it falls; watching two burrow exits; watching in opposite directions (birds from a blind); both stalking the game (bows drawn); blocking different exits from a thicket, etc. But it is also often the pleasure of hunting together that incites men to this dual undertaking, hunting providing the occasion for a male complicity enhanced as much by the enjoyment of stalking the game as that of a meal shared in secret.

Small game can be dismembered as soon as it has been killed and then shared by the hunters without the necessity of sharing with others, although the distribution continues discretely in the village among certain close relatives. For wild pig and cassowary, as the animal is not killed outright, tracking must be organized. The bands of trackers are usually made up of ten or so men, mainly from the lineages which hold rights to the land where the animal was shot, but they may be joined by any other villager who so desires. There is no hierarchical structure to the group, although the eventual *sut boi* (the owner of a gun and a hunting license), who is necessarily a participant, has not authority over the others, but a paramount role, for he considerably betters the chances of success. Excitement runs through the hunters, even though they know how little chance they have of finding the animal and

---

the string together. He must take aim (rarely from more than 10 m) quickly and surely, as the bow can be bent for no more than two or three seconds. Arrows are lost or broken; when they can be recovered, the points are changed, and new arrows are constantly being made by every hunter. The bow remains flexible for a long time, but the rattan must be replaced periodically. The spear is unknown in the Border Mountains. Guns are still rare, and in 1980 there was one gun for twelve to fifteen bowmen; later they were banned by the government and today the only hunting done is with bow and arrow.

how tiring the chase can be. This is the same type of mutual aid group that springs up when one man has detected the presence of a pig in a thicket. But in the latter case, the tasks are split up in a complementary fashion between the lookouts encircling the thicket and the small band of beaters scouring the underbrush with their dogs.

If the animal is finally killed, a rite of plenty is performed, after which the 'hunter' (i.e. the one who fired first, who asked the group's help) carries the animal literally 'piggyback' to the nearest stream, where it will be butchered. One of the men, not the 'hunter', volunteers to direct these operations. At this point, some of the men go ahead to the village, the others remaining to transport the animal, thus preparing the first stage of the distribution; these same men are often among the main recipients of the first level of distribution (see below).[13]

The use of *awra* traps, described above, represents a special case of hunting organization. The traps are built only in conjunction with the preparation of an important ritual such as Yangis or Sawangô-raara. Three months before the feast, small groups of from three to five men are formed (these may come from several 'lineage' territories, but all belong to the same land unit); they are the only ones who are involved in making the trap, allowed to approach it while it is in use or even to know where it is. Each of these small groups coordinates its work with the others throughout Yafar territory. A large part of this task is of a ritual nature, and there is always at least one *aynaag*[14] per group. When a pig has been caught in one of the *awra*, the news goes out in the village; only the hunters of that particular group go to retrieve the animal, which has been shot to death while still in the trap. The trap is not reset (except possibly once, and then only after all traps on the tribal territory have caught an animal), and the whole undertaking has the character of a single event. We see here production and work groups with a strong ritual orientation, each sworn to secrecy, but all associated through the synchronization of their operations.

---

13. The above holds for the cassowary as well, but not for smaller game.
14. A mature man who knows the rites and possesses the knowledge behind them.

Plate 12. The hunter carries the slain animal back to the outskirts of the village, where it will be butchered (Wamuru group).

Distribution: Large Game

It is the size of the game rather than the collective or individual nature of the hunt that decides whether the meat will be distributed publicly to the whole community, or secretly and only to the hunters and their family. In effect, the pig and the cassowary are the only animals which are shared with all members of the hamlet as well as with certain relatives in other villages. The extent of the distribution has nothing to do with how the animal was caught. Distribution is carried out temporally and socially on three levels:

a) Fairly large portions of raw meat are distributed to the main recipients during or immediately after butchering.
b) The receiving families cook their share, then distribute it within the family and, quantity permitting, to a wider circle of relatives.
c) Each person may then make gifts of meat, usually after smoking it, to whomever they like.

Let us take the by far most frequent case of the wild pig. At the time of butchering, it is the main hunter's brother (elder or younger, and reciprocally) who presides over the distribution of the quarters. The organization of this first level of distribution takes place among agnates (siblings if possible); it is not lodged in a hierarchy based on primogeniture, but in reciprocity (the roles are interchangeable from one occasion to the next). The main hunter does not consume the product of his own hunt, however. Hunting large game is a gift to the community, though it brings social gratification to the hunter.

Since the animal was killed by a band of hunters mostly belonging to the same village moiety, it is expected that the head and forelegs will be given to the other moiety, who will organize their distribution. This gift is based on reciprocal alternation and must never take place in the same direction twice in a row. The hunter's brother reserves a choice piece for the owner of the dog which first picked up the pig's trail, and similar pieces for the *aynaag* of the group which holds the rights to the land where the pig was killed; naturally, the men who took part in the hunt must also be compensated for their cooperation. After that, the man in charge of the distribution parcels out the quarters according to kinship with the hunter. The most favoured relatives should be the brother(s)-in-law, *guweeg* (WB or ZH), the mother's brother, *nonoog*, and the sister's son, *rabik*. As far as possible – and bearing in mind the systems of reciprocity between *segwaag* (see below) – these relatives receive the choice pieces, namely the hind legs (the heart also goes to the brother-in-law). A newly married man gives one hind leg of the pig from his first hunt to his parents-in-law rather than only his wife's brother;[15] the latter do not eat it but instead redistribute the meat in their own family. If there are no *guweeg* or *nonoog*, a full brother can also receive a hind leg, or it can go to the father's younger brother, *atôk awaag*, but the portion that normally goes to agnatic 'brothers' (*nerete*) in particular is the brisket (*baharik*).

The first operation of the second level of distribution is cooking, done separately in each household over the fire of the head of the house. The man, with the help of his son or wife, cuts up the meat, places it on banana leaves, and adds some edible leaves together with the hot stones his wife has previously heated on her own fire; he or she then sprinkles a bit of sago over the whole – conjugal and familial cooperation, no doubt, but in which only the man handles the meat, choosing and dividing it. After the meat has been braised for an hour, the bundle is removed from the coals and unwrapped. Once again it is the man who will officiate in cutting the hot pieces of cooked meat into individual portions, which, as he cuts them, will be distributed into little *sööbi*, each of which corresponds to an individual or a family.

Domestic pigs are cooked and shared out in the same way. In both cases the distribution requires a mastery of the kinship networks: no one must be left out, for it is believed that anyone who is neglected or displeased may remain silent but later take revenge by sorcery. One also needs to know if a person is going to receive something indirectly from another household where another piece of the animal is being distributed. Being obtained through an exclusively male activity, game circulates through a network which again is entirely controlled by men in order ultimately to reach consumers (third level of distribution) among whom are to be found women and children. The wife acts as mediator between her husband and her own brothers, making sure that the hunter does not forget his in-laws and does not stint

---

15. See pp. 333–4, the rite marking the first time a son-in-law gives his parents-in-law the hind leg of a pig.

them; she may personally take the hind leg to her brothers, but may not keep a piece for herself. The woman takes the portion that the man – husband, brother or father – gives her.

The third level of distribution is carried out by individuals, beginning the same day or the day after the meat is cooked and continuing for a variable period of time, since the meat is smoked. If a ceremony is in preparation, and especially if the hunt (see use of *awra* traps, for example) was conducted in that perspective, part or all of the smoked meat is stored for distribution to visitors from other villages on the day of the celebration; in this case, several weeks may elapse between hunting and distribution.

We see, then, that the three levels of big-game distribution correspond roughly to the three stages of the product's transformation: raw meat (*beh-na nihik*), cooked meat (*tuhru-na nihik*) and smoked meat (*foog nihik*). It would nevertheless be rash to indulge in a structuralist partition in which each state of the product corresponded to a class of kin; it is impossible on this level to distinguish between kin and affines or between agnates and cognates (see also Huber 1980). Rather the hierarchy is organized in terms of degrees of kinship and *segwaag* relation, the wife's brother or the sister's husband, the mother's brother and the privileged partners being the first served with raw meat.[16] The other two levels (cooked meat and smoked meat) differ in that the first is carefully organized and involves a greater number of relatives, whereas the last is carried out much more informally according to chance encounters (small quantities of smoked meat are often carried around in the netbag and distributed to relatives or friends).

Privileged Reciprocity in the Distribution of Meat:
The Segwaag *Relationship*

The privileged *segwaag* relationship of reciprocity between kin will be analysed in Chapter 11. Nevertheless it is important to situate this relationship here in the context of hunting, as it is through the exchange of meat (*nihik səfôg*) that it is more particularly realized. Within a given kinship relation, *segwaag* practice

---

16. Further research needs to be done in this area and in relation to sexuality. For example, an unmarried younger brother may never distribute raw meat to his married older brothers.

a more formalized and frequent reciprocity than non-*segwaag* kin in the sense that they reciprocate particular pieces of meat, always the same from one hunt to the next – this being done at the first level of distribution (raw meat). Furthermore – a feature also found between non-related exchange partners, *sêh* (Ch. 8) – this reciprocity is passed on from father to son, with the necessary arrangements being made when there are several sons, and independently of changes in kinship terminology. While old reciprocal relations die out for want of descendants, new filiative chains of reciprocity can be formed from ordinary (non-privileged) exchanges between two brothers-in-law (Figure 25) or between two non-*segwaag* brothers, or from a brother's occasional gift of a particular piece of meat to his non-*segwaag* sister (Figure 26). Thus an initial gift or exchange of meat between two non-*segwaag* relatives can determine a regular *segwaag* relationship in the following generations. The male monopoly on hunting engenders these pairs of lines linked by reciprocal exchanges of game just as uterine lines are founded on balanced exchanges of sago. Meat, as a scarce product, increases the worth of male reciprocity, whereas sago, an abundant staple, weakens (at least in the mens' eyes) female reciprocity. *Segwaag* also exchange other goods besides meat, and giving meat to a female *segwaag* generates a countergift of sago.

Small Game

For the hunting of small game, the cooperation described above entails sharing the product among the hunters, but the hunters usually go on to share with their own close relatives: siblings, wife, children. As a rule the elder brother receives a choice piece from his younger brother or half-brother, which demonstrates his allegiance. Often the elder brother (or the brother in general) receives an even bigger portion than the wife and the children. The taboo on the product of one's own hunt can be respected as one wishes (p. 199). Pelts or plumes are kept by one of the hunters or handed over to a male or female relative for adornment. In the case of small game, then, there are at most two levels of distribution. The cooking may take place in the bush or at home, in both cases before any distribution.

The Yafar feel morally obliged to give a portion, however small, to anyone having seen or heard about the outcome of a small-game hunt. But reciprocally, etiquette dictates that one does not

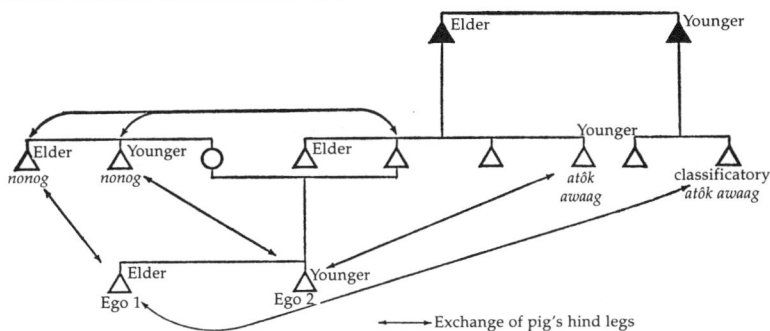

Figure 25. *Segwaag* partnership by exchange of pig's hind legs

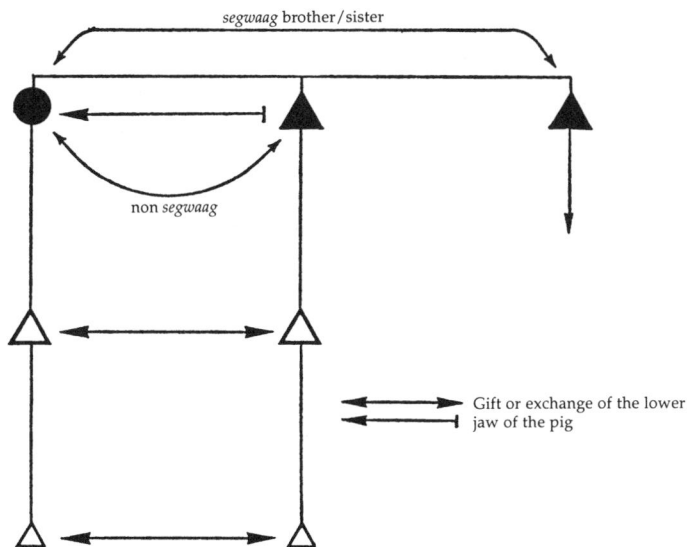

Figure 26. Example of a *segwaag* relation by exchange of the lower jaw of the pig, initiated by brother's gift to his non-*segwaag* sister

call on the hunter, which he would consider an improper request for a share. If several individuals committed such an impropriety for the same animal in effect it would result in *overdistribution*, cancelling the effect of the hunt through too great a fragmentation of the food supply. In a sense, then, the hunting of small game is what some have called 'selfish hunting'. If 'selfishness' or 'generosity' can, to various degrees, orient the way an individual manages the product, we would do well to seek sociological criteria for defining the behaviours proper to this type of hunting. As I said in the introduction to this chapter, the products of foraging, especially meat of any kind, are often the object of restrictions on information. Secrecy is proportional to the scarcity and nutritive and symbolic value ascribed to the product. Its function is to regulate and limit the scope of the distribution, but it is also the inevitable reverse side of the standard of 'obligatory generosity' which characterizes the ways the Yafar behave towards food. If someone has seen the game or lets it be known that he knows about it, there is an obligation to give him some. This is particularly true for men. Cooking the animal in the bush avoids this type of compulsion, which is often provoked by the agreeable aroma floating around certain houses in the evening, even though one would have to be fairly rude in such a case to call on the hunter at such a time.

But it is not only the product of the hunt that is concealed, it is the entire undertaking. One of the first rules of good breeding one learns when living with the Yafar is never to question or even speak to a man or men leaving the village with a bow, or returning. A hunter will never say: 'I'm going hunting' or 'I'm off to see if I can find some game on such and such land.' If questioned, he may eventually reply: 'I'm going roaming', or 'I'm going to search'.[17] But to ask him a direct question would be understood as an expression of jealousy or even an intention to impede the hunter in his endeavour (see below). The same attitude is also required in collective pig hunts, but in this case the prospect of public distribution unlocks the information once the animal has been killed, and the obligatory silence in front of a group of men trotting off bows in hand becomes a mere social convention of a ritual nature. Small-game hunting thus appears as a socially 'closed' activity, while 'big-game hunting' shatters, as it were, its own social boundaries under the very weight of the meat to be distributed.

Hunting with a Gun

With one or two rifles per hamlet – and even though the monetary economy is relatively undeveloped and makes it hard for

---

17. The same attitude has been observed among Amazonian groups, such as the Achuar of Ecuador (Descola 1986). On the 'hunting secret', see also Jamin 1977.

the Yafar to procure cartridges[18] – a certain transformation in the social relations found in hunting is underway. The fact that the number of firearms is severely restricted by the administration engenders a sort of specialization. The *sut boi* finds himself surrounded by an aura of prestige emanating from the use of an object that comes from the white man's world. In the case of big game, this benefit remains purely symbolic, since the hunter does not eat the animals he shoots.

A second point is the social use to which the cartridges are put. Villagers without a hunting license buy cartridges (called *supia* 'arrows' in Pidgin) and give them to a *sut boi* who will hunt for them; in this case the whole animal belongs to the owner of the cartridge, who will give part of the take back to the hunter if the animal is small, and for big game, will retain control over the distribution, even if he did not take part in the hunt. Cartridges are individualized by the hunter, who marks them with an identifying sign. Women are now beginning to procure their own bird shot.[19]

Hunting Symbolism: Representation and Ritual

The Forest, the Spirits of the Dead and the Hunter

A man and a woman had four sons and a daughter. Every day the father brought home a pig or a cassowary he had killed. The three elder sons, on the other hand, did not find any game (for at this time the forest contained no animals). They asked their youngest brother to spy on their father. The child discovered, and reported to his brothers, that their father found his pigs and cassowaries in an underground passage which he entered by a secret door located between the roots of the *ahômp Ficus*. This place was full of all kinds of game. The next day, while their parents were working sago far from the house, the three elder sons went to shoot several animals in the father's cave and forgot to close the door behind them: all the animals ran into the forest. The father heard the animals and saw them go by; he guessed his son's treachery. When he got home he said nothing; but each night he dug a tunnel deeper and deeper into

---

18. A cartridge at the Amanab missionary shop, in 1978, cost 0.40 kina (.50 US$).

19. From the mid 1980s, weapons and cartridges were prohibited first of all along the border (because of OPM resistance in Irian Jaya) and then throughout Papua New Guinea (due to the rise in crime).

the ground of the village; then he lured his three sons into the hole by playing trumpets and drums and making them believe there was a celebration. The sons walked into the trap, decorating themselves, taking their drums, and without realizing what was happening entered the hole, which the father walled up. Meanwhile the mother had protected the youngest who soon went to another group to exchange his sister for a wife, after refusing his father's suggestion that he marry his own sister.[20]

The esoteric version of the above myth says that the father does not get his game from the ground but directly from the womb of his wife, the Coconut divinity,[21] who thus appears as a maternal figure of cosmic dimensions; and it is to the same place that, in his anger, he sends his three 'incestuous' sons. Illuminated by its exegesis, this myth clearly states the principles of the maternal (re)production of animals, paternal legitimacy, transgression and punishment. The object of oedipal desire is expressed in terms of fecundity, and sexuality, be it legitimate or incestuous, in terms of hunting. The hunting ritual reproduces this twofold representation, since its two differentiated functions are on the one hand to promote the (re)production of game and on the other to facilitate the encounter with the animal through mediation by the spirits of the dead (*nabasa*), the game's guardians; to fill the forest with animals good to hunt and then to render the hunt fruitful are the two symbolic registers of cynegetic production (Figure 27).

The first register is fulfilled in the course of secret rites performed by officiants from a certain number of clans; I was unable to learn the details, except that they are supposed to make 'the game appear' (*sês pugug*) on an ancestral land, or more particularly mountain,[22] belonging to this clan. It is said that the verbal part of the rite evokes the *ahômp Ficus* of the myth and the population of the forest by the animals set free. The non-verbal portion is based on the manipulation of a magic plant clone (*Acorus calamus* or *Homalomena* sp.), which is cultivated in secret and bears a proper name also used to designate the officiating lineage. Chapter 3 showed that these ritual responsibilities are part

20. This myth is analyzed in *Oedipe chasseur* (Juillerat 1991a).
21. The *Ficus ahômp* is replaced in one of the versions by the coconut palm. Here the Mother is also the original goddess B. . . (Ch. 2).
22. Mountains, because of their topographical form, are particularly evocative of pregnancy, and mountain caves are associated with the womb.

of a set of religious offices and that although they are connected with specific lineages, they serve the entire tribe. These rituals are performed in principle at the onset of the rainy season, when the gardens are already growing.[23]

The second register is ritually more diversified and less secret. The rituals are performed either individually, by an isolated hunter, or collectively in the form of public rituals. The encounter with game, although it may eventually be due to chance, is in principle brought about by a *nabasa*, most often the spirit of someone recently deceased who 'puts the pig or cassowary in the hunter's path'. The hunter must be visually pleasing to the *nabasa*, appearing to him as 'fire coloured' and therefore marked with the sign of blood (see below, p. 401 and Juillerat 1978b): this is the purpose of the rites of passage and is re-enacted notably in the public Gêpôk ritual. But the link with forest spirits – and more particularly with one's tutelary spirit, *nabasa segwaag*, to whom the hunter is personally bound by a tacit exchange contract (Ch. 12) – also takes the form of personal encounters, in a dream or a trance, and gifts of food from the hunter in exchange for game received.

Gêpôk are the most common public rituals,[24] and are part of a several-year-long cycle (called Nabasa raara 'house of the *nabasa*', from the term used to designate the shelter constructed in the village inside a ritual enclosure forbidden to women), which appears as a well-defined period of reciprocity between men and spirits. The cult is celebrated at the village level, but each rite draws visitors from outside. If the hunt is productive, the cycle is extended. In the opposite case, or if an epidemic strikes the population, it is interrupted and a more propitious time awaited.

23. The importance in hunting of the symbolic filiation with the mythic Mother is shown by the ritual petition for game addressed to the maternal Coconut Palm during the preparatory period preceding the *Yangis* festival (above p. 50–7 and Juillerat 1992a and 1995): the inflorescences are shaken over the heads of the assembled men from the top of one of the hamlet coconut trees. Those who receive a flower regard themselves as having been elected by the Mother; those who do not regard themselves as 'abandoned by the Mother'. The flowers symbolize the mother's milk. The spells pronounced during these operations are requests for game. This rite is followed by a month or two of intensive hunting during which the men build up stocks of smoked meat for the ceremony. Then a closing rite is performed on the same coconut palm.

24. See Introduction above. The Anggor have the same rite, designated by the term *tupuri* (Huber 1975: 633–5). The Yafar and the Wamuru are the northernmost groups practising this cult, although the Waina-speaking Punda are in the process of adopting it.

Figure 27. Triangular structure of symbolic relations with game

The Nabasa Raara Cycle

1. Opening of the cycle:
   a) A new sacred enclosure (*pəpak*) is built in the village and a new *nabasa raara* erected in the middle. Individual offerings are hung inside the shelter.
   b) Nabasa hugufa obô ritual, 'seize and bring the *nabasa*'. The mediums (and often one or more young novice mediums) are possessed by the *nabasa* and so transport them to the *nabasa raara*.
   c) Communion meal with the *nabasa* in the *pəpak*. Then a nocturnal Gêpôk ritual: a line of men, their faces unmasked and painted, wearing a crown of white feathers with a cassowary quill in the middle, which they wave, backs adorned with a large netbag overflowing with yellow- and red-leafed crotons,[25] hourglass drums, two trumpets and *wesko* songs.
   d) Daytime ritual with masks, resounding *suh-wagmô* penis sheathes, two trumpets and two whistles.

25. One myth introduces a giant python, which the men finally kill and whose sloughed skin changes into crotons. The line of men in the Gêpôk represents this snake, which is secretly associated with hunting rutuals and whose name is muttered during the spells. The colours of the crotons (*segtag* or *aw*) are reminders of fertility, *hoofuk* and also of the 'ripening' of game (see below).

2.
   a) Periodic repetition (about twice a year) of the Gêpôk rite for from two to six years.
   b) From time to time, following a Gêpôk, a daytime ritual with masks, called Sing-raara ('house of dead leaves'?).

3. Closure of the cycle:
   a) Nocturnal Gêpôk as before.
   b) Daytime Sing-raara closing ceremony.
   c) Ritual shelter abandoned.

A new cycle with a new enclosure will be opened a few years later.

Outside the Nabasa raara cycle, the Gêpôk element can be found in other ritual contexts, such as the Rii-buu healing rite for the pathogenic *nabasa* whose forest residence dwelling has been damaged by clearing, or the Gungwan ritual, which will be dealt with in Chapter 12. In the past, the effectiveness of the rite was also supposed to favour successful killing raids: the dancers used to wear their *metiy* pig-teeth ornaments (Ch. 14, n. 18) and their bone daggers.

Body and face paintings mark the participant, particularly the novice, with 'blood', which will make him acceptable to the game's guardian spirits, while the use of coloured leaves is a reminder that the Gêpôk is associated with a major concept of Yafar symbolism, namely 'ripening',[26] which is the vegetal metaphor for the weakening of a person's or an animal's self (*sungwaag*). In the hunting context, the initiation ritual for the novice who is taking part in his first Gêpôk casts him as a substitute for 'ripe game' (*sês abuk*), in other words vulnerable to the hunter's arrows. The Yafar think that only game whose *sungwaag* is 'ripe' die from the arrow they receive, much like the man whose 'ripe ego' becomes vulnerable to sorcery.

Formerly, Gêpôk participants would go hunting at dawn following a night of ritual. They kept their paint and their ornaments until the vegetal components dried, and thus appeared painted and decorated before the *nabasa*. It is said that the spirits would then think to themselves: 'Here is a handsome man, I'm going to

---

26. For this notion, see Chs 12 (p. 372ff.) and 14 (p. 464), and Juillerat 1978b.

Plate 13. Gépök: Rite devoted to the forest spirits: brightly colored crotons in the netbag, ginger lives in the armbands, cockatoo feathers, cassowary quills waving on top of the headdress, face and body paint, hour-glass drums.

give him some game' (see excerpt from the initiation song used as epigraph to Ch. 12).[27]

The beating of the hourglass drums (Juillerat 1993b) accompanying the *wesko* songs can also be heard at the purely musical celebration that goes on all night after the killing of a pig or a cassowary. At times a tune played on the two wooden trumpets (*fufuk*) is interspersed between two series of songs. The *wesko* singers participate in three's or four's (sometimes in two alternating groups), standing motionless in the village square. The nostalgic words evoke places, hunting grounds, the growth of cultivated plants and the birds in which the spirits of the dead are embodied (the *wesko* was originally a funeral dirge).

Mediumism[28]

Our study of landholding showed the localized character of *nabasa* as well as that of their worship, in particular the leaving of food offerings. The spirit for which an *angaag*, a gift of food (p. 132), is hung in the forest is not necessarily the exchange partner of the hunter, who often remains anonymous. The offering – which is recovered before it rots and once the spirit is supposed to have eaten its fill – can be a compensation for trees felled to make a garden, although its most frequent purpose is to perpetuate the hunting alliance.[29] But the gift of food may also be made in the village, through a medium.

Medium possession is in effect closely linked with hunting and *nabasa* worship (see pp. 132–4 and 454–5). Seances are often sparked by the killing of a wild pig or a cassowary, but at the same time they stimulate hunts to come: the embodied spirit comes to eat his 'compensation' (which he receives particularly from the hands of the hunter) for the game given and simultaneously promises more animals, incites the villagers to hunt on such and such land and expresses surprise at seeing them so passive, sitting around too often in the village or in their gardens. The hunters

27. The idea of overhunting, noted for example among Amazon groups, does not exist for the Yafar. Paradoxically, the scarcity of game seems to explain the fact that the hunter can hunt all he wants without incurring the sanction of the guardian spirits, as the 'risk' of a truly abundant take is almost nil. In the preceding chapter, we saw that the same did not hold for the plant world, since thoughtless clearing or failure to perform the required rituals could unleash the anger of pathogenic spirits.

28. See Ch. 13 and Juillerat 1975a.

29. The *nabasa* can demand a gift of food through the call of the *ero* bird (an unidentified ground warbler or babbler; see note 33).

explain, make excuses (they had to work on the Government road, the next census was approaching, the visit of a local patrol officer), they promise to make amends or talk about the gifts (areca, pandanus, tobacco, grubs) they are going to let ripen or reserve for the *nabasa* when it sends a new animal in their path. Hunting and possession are thus intertwined, the one engendering the other and vice versa. It is certain that the decline in the number of mediums, linked to the gradual abandonment of the Nabasa raara cycles which characterizes the present evolution of Eri societies, will provoke and is already provoking a certain withdrawal of the energies invested in hunting. Weakened relations with the spirits sap the hunters' confidence. In this area no one believes in luck or the intensification of traditional techniques (traps); they do, however, believe in guns, which is in no way incompatible with representations of hunting. Nevertheless, the withdrawal is relative, for meat remains a much-coveted product, and there are also moments when interest seems to rally: in 1981, at a time when the Yafar were recovering from the heavy blow of an epidemic in 1979-1980 and putting the bulk of their energy into a Cargo Cult (Ch. 15), I saw one of the two Yafar mediums (hamlet 1), also Master of the Earth and number two leader of the new cult, fall into several self-induced trances in which, through the supposed voice of a *nabasa*, he called for the resumption of hunting. This can be seen as a deliberate strategy for enhancing his own prestige, but it contained something of a call to return to the somewhat neglected hunting economy and to the ancestral spirits.

Reciprocity between the dead and the living may be voluntarily suspended in exceptional cases (at least for part of the community). In effect, the Yafar *aynaag* may decide temporarily to banish the spirits from tribal land if they feel that the exchange is no longer equal, that the *nabasa* are no longer respecting their commitments. To this end, clones of magic plants associated with *nabasa* are burned at the base of their trees: the hunting contract is thereby broken, and the dead flee to foreign lands until their masters' (*awaag*, 'fathers') anger has cooled. Their return is announced by dreams or medium revelations. Breaking off the symbolic exchange in this way results in a reduction in hunting activities, which can henceforth be only the result of luck.

Plate 14. Medium seance on the evening of a successful hunt. Standing, from left to right: the hunter and three mediums possessed by *nabasa* spirits.

Dreams[30]
In parallel with possession, the places and days for hunting are often determined by dream revelations made by forest spirits.

30. When considering the question of dreams in any society, it is obviously important to make a clear distinction between the system of interpretation proposed by the culture in question and the 'scientific' (psychological, psychoanalytic, Freudian, Jungian) interpretation that certain individuals may make of these dreams. We shall be dealing with the first aspect here, but Freud's key work (1900) is nevertheless helpful for 'interpreting' the local 'cultural interpretation'. On the relation between dreams on the one hand and myth and ritual on the other, see Bastide 1972b; Juillerat 1991a, 1995; on dreams and hunting, see among others Wagner 1972 and Descola 1986; an already dated work, but one that can be consulted with a critical eye, is Lincoln, reissued in 1970.

Whereas mediumism works more on a collective level, dreams are a much more individual mode of deciphering the *nabasas'* moods and supposed intentions regarding the hunter. The dream (*ite-wabi*, the segment *wabi* suggesting the growth of a fruit or a tuber)[31] announces, in coded discourse, the forest spirits' intention to provide or not to provide the hunter with game. Any gift, for instance, made by a figure in a dream – identified as a *nabasa*, a *kê-ruur*, or as the duplicate forest self (*segwaag* as opposed to *sungwaag*, Ch. 12) if it is a man known to the dreamer, all of whom are encountered in the course of the excursions of the dreamer's *sungwaag* – is interpreted as a promise of game. On the other hand, the absence of a gift or the loss of any object in a dream is seen as a refusal of game. The places seen in the dream and associated with any kind of gift can also be identified, and the dreamer will go there at first light.

In particular, promises of a pig are deduced from dreams of a good catch of fish, a river in flood, a stone or a big stump floating in the river (the pig will be given by an *angor* water spirit), a large bundle of sago received, a great number of men gathered together (if they are talkative, it indicates that the hunter will encounter a flock of birds in a tree whose warning calls signal the presence of game), the murder of someone by the dreamer (a child victim = the promise of a young pig), a man building a house (the pig makes its lair, where the hunter surprises it), a man sitting motionless at home, the father or another of the hunter's relatives dying (a pig will die), any valuable object received (especially Western goods), and a plane, helicopter or vehicle approaching the village (the incoming direction of the craft or vehicle indicates the direction of the next day's hunt).[32] Erotic dreams are interpreted not for their obvious meaning but again as a promise of game. The intensity of the carnal relation is proportional to the size of the animal.

---

31. *wabi*: 1) the yam *Dioscorea alata*; 2) a giant latex-rich tree (*Alstonia scholaris*); 3) the clone of various cultivated plants used in seduction magic; 4) the name of the garden growth spirit (for tubers in particular); *wab-we*: liana (*we*) that overruns fallow gardens (*Parabaena tuberculata*).

32. For game other than pig, we have noted the following analogical equations, in which each type of object received announces the killing of a corresponding category of animal: small dog = small game; big dog = big game; old net or newspaper = monitor lizard; tree leaves for rolling cigars = lizard; areca nut or tobacco = all small game; stones, breadfruit or crotons = cassowary (?), etc. Receiving a gift from a *sawangô* female spirit also promises a monitor lizard, of which this class of spirit are the guardians.

The interpretation of dreams is an individual matter; one does not tell or discuss dreams, except when their meaning involves someone else (the person concerned is then informed) or when it concerns the community as a whole (these are no longer about hunting but about collective therapeutic rites). Women's dreams are interpreted in the same way, for the benefit of their husband, or their brother or father if they are unmarried. A woman who has had a significant dream tells the household hunter as soon as she wakes so that he can set out immediately if he thinks it advisable. Below, in conclusion, are five men's dreams which illustrate the dialectic of 'receiving', 'not receiving or losing', which is the key to Yafar interpretation of dreams in a hunting context (see also Ch. 15, pp. 535–6).

Woy – 'A helicopter landed in the village and unloaded "cargo" for May [a man in the process of acquiring a certain status at the time]. The white man from the helicopter called May. The latter asked everyone in the village to help him carry the "cargo" back home.'

Interpretation: The white man was a *nabasa* who was promising May a wild pig. When May's dog scents the animal, all the villagers will be able to track and kill it at May's request. May must therefore go hunting that very morning, and Woy tells him of the dream at dawn.

Wagif – 'I saw my elder brother, Kofay. He told me that he had made a dam in the Hopwan River and that I could go and take some fish.'

Interpretation: Early on the morning after the dream, Wagif went to the river but caught no fish or game. 'The *nabasa* lied to me', he concluded.

Wagif – 'I set off towards Wamuru and encountered some of their men on the way. They told me they needed to talk. "Talk about what", I asked them (we talked about sago, betel, tobacco...). They said they wanted to give me something, but in the end they didn't give me anything.'

Interpretation: Faced with the ambiguity of the dream, Wagif still set off at dawn towards Wamuru in the hope of finding game, even though he knew he had little chance, for 'the people in the dream did not give him anything'. In the event, he heard a pig in some bamboo, but the animal ran away at his approach.

Now – 'I went to my garden to pick an *Acorus calamus* (magic plant). On my way back, I stopped and I forgot it on the trail. Then I noticed and went back: the plant was gone. Another man had stolen it.'

Interpretation: 'The other man' in the dream is more specifically the forest self of another sleeper (who may have had a complementary dream), even though he is not identified. Conclusion: 'If I had gone hunting following this dream, I would have seen some game, but it would have got away.'

Now – 'I went to see a married couple in Yafar 2. They pulled a package of sago out of a water hole where they kept it and went away without giving me any. I saw the trail of water from the sago dripping along the path.'

Interpretation: If Now had gone hunting when he woke up he would not have caught anything, and the hunters from Yafar 2 would have been the ones to benefit from the game that got away, 'for that was what the *nabasa* had decided'.

Personal Magic

We have just seen that the hunting ritual is based on secret rites performed by specialists on behalf of the group, on the one hand, and on public ceremonial cycles, on the other, and that the two main modes of communicating with game's guardian spirits are possession and dreams.[33] These institutions are easy for the anthropologist to define, but it is altogether another matter for more individual hunting rites founded on analogical magic.

These rites break down into two categories: a) propitiatory rites for promoting encounters with game; b) rites performed on the animal killed, so that the meat will be plentiful and the hunter's luck will continue. In the first case, the hunter puts the ingredients into his netbag, ties plants on to his bow, carries out secret operations alone in the bush using magic rhizomes, red ochre, animal (or menstrual) blood, sexual secretions, inviting the participation of his young wife during their first sexual relations (Ch. 9), or he rubs his body all over with a violently smelly ointment made from the anal glands of opossums,[34] magic rhizomes and the aromatic leaves of the *Evodia hortense* (*fəni*). He also shares

33. There are other minor forms of communication, such as revelations by the *ero* bird, which answers questions put by the person who hears its repeated song; it may be asked about the presence of game.
34. These glands, usually located in the area of the anus, produce foul-smelling secretions which have a defensive function in certain small mammals of New Guinea and Australia.

the benefits of his magic with his dog (see below). In the second procedure, the hunter often calls upon an *aynaag*, and the rite is performed at the spot where the animal was killed. The body orifices of the pig or the cassowary, including the wound, which are believed to close up at the moment of death, are magically 'reopened', and a special rhizome, called *mosuwô* or 'umbilical cord' is passed under the feet and other anatomical zones to 'bind' all animals of the species to be killed in the future, to retain them, to bring them under the hunter's control. Then, with both men seated astride the animal, the *aynaag* recites spells for promoting good hunting in the future. When an adolescent kills his first wild pig, it is his father who performs this rite: alone with his son, he touches his own penis, marked with masticated magic rhizomes, to the animal's orifices. The explanation I was given was that 'with this he engendered his son'. In this instance, the animal has a mediating role in male filiation: the father passes on to his son something of his own confirmed relation with game and with nature's *hoofuk* he hands on to him his own access to fertility.[35]

The establishment of filiation in the individual hunting ritual reveals the extent to which Yafar production magic is an integral part of a broader representation of the mastery of nature's fecundity and the social transmission of this control. The magical act works on both the coveted object and the father-son relationship, which alone makes it possible for the realization of this desire to be socially reproduced. A magic of production, in the strict sense, which is not inscribed in social time would have very little meaning. Parallel representational paradigms are also attested between mother and daughter or between mother's brother and nephew (Ch. 11). If one receives power over nature from an elder and makes the necessary effort to exercise and develop it through one's own productive work and personal magic, it is ultimately in order to transmit the power, enriched, to one's descendants. This process of symbolic reproduction corresponds to a fundamental idea in Yafar thinking which has to do not only with hunting, but also with the fertility of the earth and of women.

35. As in the other fields of magic, all these procedures are accompanied by ritual formulas (which are implicitly validated only by the knowledge that explains them). Undertaking any operation while magically enhancing its effectiveness is termed *mô-na* 'with words'.

The expression which formulates the performance and transmission of the hunting ritual is literally 'to follow the trail of blood' (*taf pahrukug*), which means both to track a wounded animal and to entertain (individually and from one generation to the next) a fruitful relationship with the animal world.

Hunting Failures

There are no prohibitions on the individual hunter's activities. Nevertheless he sees his relationship with game and their guardians as being subject to fluctuation. The irregularity of his success will be experienced as periods of fortune or misfortune, which he will seek to interpret.

If, in spite of favourable dreams, a man ceases to kill game, he defines this state of affairs through the concept of *mabiyik* (*kam mabiyik feg* 'to-me unsuccess-in-hunting it-does'. He decides that he or his lands and the animals on them are 'covered with fog' (*rangôk kagwôg*) and that he has therefore become blind to the game and invisible to the *nabasa*. This state may be the result of an evil spell, called *mwaywey*, cast by some relative angered by an inequitable distribution of meat. The rite is a simple formula to be muttered ('let fog cover the pig, the opossum, etc.') while discretely brushing the head of the victim, who does not take any notice but can later identify in a dream the person who has cast the spell. This 'fog' can also accidentally cover someone who has chanced to see another man's magic hunting plants (in this case the 'fog' is called *awus na suweegik* 'emanation from magic plants') or someone who has broken a taboo, such as revealing religious secrets to women and children,[36] using a close affine's proper name or eating one's own game, or the cultivator who has worked intensely burning slash and finds himself 'covered' with smoke and ash.[37] The Yafar see repeated hunting failures as the result of the hunter's symbolic 'blindness', like the effect of a breakdown of visual communication within the *nabasa*-hunter-game triangle. Thus the hunter is not punished for excessive hunting (see above, n. 27), but for excessive talk about fertility, excessive identification with the quarry (which is similar) or again, conversely, a physical separation from fertility through excess of

36. The information secretly given me concerning religious exegesis almost always ended with the expression of fear of never again finding game (or fear of seeing one's gardens fail or one's children die).
37. For the same reason people avoid stepping over a smoking fire.

smoke, in other words *roofuk*, to use the generic term (see below).

Whatever the case, rites of reparation can always be tried, either on the hunter by a third party, or by the hunter himself at the scene of the hunt. In the first case, the hunter seems to identify with the game, for the formula says that the pig, cassowary, etc. is 'peeled' (*roof*)[38] to get rid of the 'fog', while in the second instance, it is more particularly the trees (the varieties are named) which are rid of the *rangôk*. If the *mabiyik* state is due to the hunter unfortunately seeing someone else's *awus*, the owner of the plants is the only one who can perform the rite, by chewing the rhizomes, which he then spits on to the victim. Ridding the clearer of slash smoke that has turned into 'hunter's fog' is usually an individual process accompanied by such formulas as 'rend the cassowary's fog, etc.'. On occasion, at the start of the monsoons, it can also be a collective rite (called *aso roofuk* 'the garden's skin'), in the course of which are renewed, among others, alliances with the *nabasa*, which may manifest themselves at that time through possession.[39]

Vengeance by means of *mwaywey* is attributed only to the victim's maternal relatives or his affines and can in no way come from agnates. The opposition between the two kinship categories reflects the distribution of game described earlier. Whereas ego's brothers share his identity, as it were, and are bound to him more through solidarity than through differentiated reciprocity, maternal kin and affines are rather partners in formal exchange, the conflictual reverse of which is the *mwaywey* or other forms of sorcery (Ch. 14). They are also linked to the subject through a woman – mother, sister or wife – who becomes the more or less unconscious stake in the mandatory gift of meat. Of the affines, the father-in-law, *kowaag*, is even more readily suspected than the brother-in-law, *guweeg*, with whom ties are seen as being symmetrical. The same goes for the mother's brother, *nonoog*, who has more right to a share of game than his son, the hunter's cross-cousin. The generation gap seems relevant across the board: one fears an evil spell from an elder more than from a peer, especially if the elder is a wife-giver (*kowaag*) or 'mother-giver' (*nonoog*). Women, on the other hand, have no access to any form of sorcery

---

38. See below and p. 241ff., the opposition *roofuk* (skin) / *hoofuk* (fertility principle) beneath the notion of 'fog' and the 'peeling' rite.

39. The men all go down to the river, bathe and smear themselves with chewed rhizomes, applying the symbolic 'peeling' (*roof*) to their own bodies.

and, in the strictly male context of hunting, thus seem all the more innocent. As we shall see later, however, they can turn to a 'brother' to order or perform a *mwaywey* rite.

The etiology of hunting failures also attributes occasional lack of success to the *aftur* of people (women and children included) who might accidentally have seen the hunter setting out. In this case we are no longer talking about evil spells (and the *nabasa* are not involved), but about the unintentional action of a person's secondary self (to be distinguished from the *sungwaag*, Ch. 12), which, harbouring feelings of covetousness or 'food jealousy', can temporarily detach itself. The *aftur* is supposed to go out of the individual unbeknown to him, to outpace the hunter and startle the game by making a racket, or 'to tug the elbow' of someone taking aim at his quarry. It is also believed that asking questions of a man as he sets out to hunt is a manifestation of the *aftur*'s malicious desire. This belief has to do with the discretion and secrecy surrounding hunting in general, of which the problem of possible overdistribution of the product is only one aspect.

In effect, economic control combines with the sacred dimension of capturing game, a product that comes from the depths of the entrails of the forest and is parsimoniously dealt out by the forest spirits. It is as much this relationship with a sort of 'supernature' as the obvious need to control the distribution of the product that sets hunting apart for the Yafar. We will conclude with a last and this time negative relation with fertility.

Just as the Nabasa raara cycles described above cease and hunting activities are reduced in consequence when the community feels its productivity and strength diminished, so the alliance with the *nabasa* (rites, offerings, the motivation to go hunting) is suspended during the mourning period for an adult and until the bones are removed (Ch. 12). The same used to be true when a climate of insecurity reigned for political reasons, or when death – the sorcery of neighbouring tribes – struck the group. Feeling itself in danger, the community spontaneously shuts down its relationship with the primordial powers, as though forbidding itself access to this domain. Death or the threat of death and illness are seen as anticipated punishment, whence the need for some form of sacrifice.

Consumption

The symbolic order of hunting does not stop with distribution, but extends to consumption, which is governed by a number of negative rules, the main one being the taboo on one's own kill.

This prohibition, observed in many societies around the world, should be seen here in the broader context of taboos surrounding acts performed for the first time and the individual's corresponding status of *asagyam* or 'novice' (see Ch. 12). The prohibition boundaries depend on the sacredness of the species: the cassowary, particularly loaded with symbols, remains taboo to the hunter without restriction as to time or the number of animals killed, whereas only the first ten or fifteen pigs, marsupials, birds, pythons, eels or monitor lizards are forbidden. In other words, a mature male no longer has to respect this taboo except for cassowaries.[40] The punishment for transgression is the end of the hunting contract with the forest spirits. One often hears: 'If I eat my own hunt, I will never again kill any game', or '—, I will go blind [to game]', or — 'fog will cover me (or will cover my land)'.

To be *asagyam* in an activity is to come into proximity, to make contact for the first time with a symbolically significant or dangerous body. What are these substances? They are the materialized principles of procreation: blood and *hoofuk* (Ch. 9). The danger incurred from this new contact corresponds to a return, to a regression to the primordial essence of life from which we all come ('we all come from blood'), and from which man and the other species have gradually become removed, but of which they have retained enough to be able to reproduce. The taboo on one's own game – to be catalogued with the prohibition on eating the fruit or starch of a coconut, sago or pandanus tree one has planted (pp. 357–8) as well as the red eggs of the *abi* wildfowl – should be seen as part of the overall arrangement with the active principles of reproduction and the original wellsprings of life. With respect to game, whose value is enhanced by its scarcity and the technical difficulties of its capture, this compromise takes the form of a taboo followed by its cancellation. The prohibition limits the hunter's identification with his kill and the mixing of their two 'bloods' occasioned by

40. Sometimes hunters keep a tally of their successes by notching a tree in the forest with distinctive marks for each kind of game.

the animal's 'murder'.[41] There is prescription after a certain number of animals have been killed, when the reiteration of the act has finally 'immunized' the hunter, who has in the meantime become a married man, in other words has secured himself against that other contact with fecundity which sexuality imposes.

The punishment for transgression (being covered with 'fog', going 'blind') is founded on the already familiar opposition between *hoofuk* and *roofuk* (the life-giving essence or fecundity versus skin, external sheath). Between the hunter and his game, there is the *nabasa*, who legitimizes the appropriation of the animal and at the same time acts as a barrier against too direct a contact with 'blood'. Is it not logical, then, for the transgressor who, by eating his own game, is, as it were, guilty of overstepping normal relations with natural fecundity, to find himself penalized by the 'fog' that, like a *roofuk*, comes between the *nabasa*, himself and the game? Suddenly symbolic communication within the triangular relationship jams and forces the hunter, now both invisible and blind, into sterile solitude.

But why is the hunter's 'immunization' not effective in the case of cassowaries? Initially it is a matter of classification which makes this species (*Casuarius* sp.) unique among the fauna of New Guinea. This animal's physical and ethological peculiarities make it a sort of hybrid (see Bulmer 1967 and Douglas 1967), even though taxonomically it clearly fits into the Yafar category of *tuwafik* 'birds'. As a flightless, ambulatory bird, incapable of using its atrophied wings, living unseen in the depths of the forest, leaving occasional tracks on muddy paths or riverbanks, it has been ascribed quasi-human traits, whence its role in cosmogonic mythology, in which it appears as a maternal, nurturing entity (p. 430). Its meat as well as its eggs are eaten by everyone, but women and children abstain from eating the heart and the leg joints; moreover, only 'thin' men can eat the leg joint without danger. Ingesting the heart is supposed to have aphrodisiac effects leading to rape and adultery. In case of violation of these prohibitions, a body 'cooling' rite, called *səmofuk-nam*, can be performed using ashes (*səmof*) placed on the big toe which is then cracked (a sign that the evil has left the body) once the parts of

---

41. An even clearer identification between hunter and game can be observed among the Gnau of the Torricelli Range (Lewis 1980: 174). It should be noted that in their seduction magic the Yafar also speak of 'mixing' the bloods of the man and the woman.

the body to be cooled have all been designated. Eating leg joints causes pain in the knees by analogy between the bipedaism of humans and cassowaries. Moreover, after eating the meat of this bird, one abstains from working the land for a day or from entering the *nabasa raara*. Breaking the first taboo would cause the sugar cane (which is said originally to have come from the feet of the primordial cassowary) and the banana trees to topple over, for the terrestrial *hoofuk* would return to the depths of the earth following the 'trampling' of the growing plants by the ghost of the cassowary. The second transgression is said to incite the cassowary to take revenge on children by crushing their soul (*sungwaag*) as they sleep.[42] Whether it results in falling sugar cane (the juice of which stands for semen in agrarian rites) as an evocation of castration or, conversely, exacerbated and asocial sexuality or the massacre of progeny (the annihilation of posterity), breaking taboos on consuming cassowary always brings about disorder leading to the disruption of socialized reproduction. It can be postulated that the cassowary, when hunted and eaten according to the rules, represents the incarnation of a principle of equilibrium that needs to be preserved (see p. 430 on the homologies which can be drawn with respect to solar symbolism).

The secrecy surrounding cynegetic production made it impossible to gather any statistics which would have allowed us to rank hunting with respect to horticulture and collecting. The overall situation of diet and health in the region nevertheless suggests that the proportion of meat in the global food mass remains very low. If increased monetary income and easier access to guns (also in terms of administrative authorizations) seem the only remedy, taking care not to overstep the threshold at which the fauna reproduces itself, it remains the case that the primary cause of this protein deficiency resides in the natural features of the New Guinea island biosphere.[43]

The scarcity of game, the difficulty of locating it and the inadequacy of the techniques used (the short range of the highly rigid areca-wood bows, flightless arrows, unfamiliarity with blowguns[44]

42. Chapter 9 gives the more general food taboos for parturients; products of hunting are listed together with those of gardening and gathering.

43. To be convinced, it suffices to compare the list of species killed by Amazon populations (of the same demographic importance) reported by certain anthropologists.

44. The blowgun is however known in western New Guinea and the Bismarck Archipelago (Bulmer 1968).

and arrow poisons, absence of spears, limited use of traps) certainly have something to do with the elaboration of the representational system just examined. But many societies have taught us that the abundance of a product is not inversely proportional to the importance of the magical process by which it is procured. The configuration structuring the symbolic relations the Yafar man entertains with the animals and spirits of the forest is, as we have seen, the outcome of a projection on to nature of parental images and filiative links. It is this psychic experience that allows the male Yafar to situate himself in his environment with respect to the foraging he does there.

Fishing

Techniques

The moderate hydrographics of the Border Mountains region and the very small number of ichthyological species[45] make fishing the least profitable productive activity over the year, and the Yafar attach little importance to it. Whereas gardening, gathering and hunting are productive all year round, the Yafar fish only when the streams are low,[46] mainly at the peak of the dry season (from July to September). This seasonal restriction can be explained by technological factors, as the methods call for shallow water, but it also ensures the reproduction of the species. Some years no fishing using ichthyotoxic plants is done in a given hamlet, whereas it is said that, in the past, people fished the same river sections every year. However any one holding unit of river (Ch. 5) was worked only once a year.

The simplest and most common technique is damming and bailing, *wafêg*, practised by women and children as well as men; but it is said that several generations back, only women fished that way. There is no rite associated with this technique, which consists in bailing the water out of a stretch of river that has been dammed at either end. These dams (*pepaw*) are made from logs, branches and mud. The resulting pool takes up the width of the

45. A few were identified at the Biology Department at the University of Papua New Guinea using slides: *Melanotaeniidae, Eleotridae, Plotosidae, Theraponidae* (including ? *Pelates quadrilineatus*), *Apogonidae* (of which *Glossimia wichmanni*).

46. The Yafar consider the lowest level of their rivers to have been lower several decades ago.

stream bed (2 to 5 m) and averages 4 to 6 metres in length. Once the dams are in place, the water is thrown over one of them using a scoop (*koobru*) made from a sago palm petiole.[47] As this scoop is not watertight, the movement must be brisk. This task, generally performed by two or three people, takes about an hour, depending on the amount of water, after which the fish are gathered up by hand, pulled out of the nooks and crannies and thrown up on to the bank. Today only one or two pools are usually fished by a given group along any one holding unit. In the past, however, the entire river section could be fished, making a series of pools, starting upstream and working down. The whole operation for one pool takes between one and a half and two and a half hours, depending on the current, the quantity of fish and the number of people. Small streams can be worked by a single man or woman.

Fishing with the aid of vegetal poisons,[48] called simply *waher-na* ('with *Derris* sp.'), is surrounded by male rites and secrecy; more rarely, it can be carried out by women on small streams and without ritual. When using fish poison, no dam is built upstream, only a weir made from branches and bamboo is set up downstream to hold back the stunned fish. A man using *Derris* sp. can fish alone, without a weir, on a small, slow stream. Individual fishing is done during the day using only *Derris*, but as soon as a larger group gets together, the fishing is done preferably at night, and then several fish poisons are combined. The torches used for light do not serve specifically to attract the fish.[49]

47. The flaired part of the petiole which curves slightly inward is the active part, while the thin end makes a handle; a stick placed horizontally halfway down serves as a grip for the other hand. Total length: 130 cm.

48. The most frequently used species is *Derris* sp. (*waher*), cultivated or wild (the cultivated clone is the most effective). The following species may also be used together: *Maesa* sp. (*ey-we-koog*), the bark of which is used; *Embelia* sp. (*buwe*), bark used; *Ternstroemia* sp. (*kekeso*), bark used; *Bubbia* sp. (*gêfèn*), a species cultivated in fallow gardens after its introduction by Dutch patrols around 1950; fruit used. These various species, often used together, are mixed in a container made from the bark of the *Sterculia* sp. (*uwô*).

49. Other secondary techniques are to be noted. One is bow-and-arrow fishing either alone or combined with bait. Termite nests are shaken out over the water while one or several teammates waiting along the bank shoot the fish with multi-pronged arrows. The Yafar make fish traps, long rattan tubes 2 m in length and 20 cm in diameter at the mouth, closed at the other end, which are set against the current. The fish do not stay trapped but are found when the fisherman makes his rounds. Sunken trunks of certain small palm trees or wild pandanus, once the rotted heart has been taken out, make natural 'traps' where fish like to hide. It seems that the Yafar used these as a model for their traps. Bait (red ants' nests) can be placed inside the trunk of palm trees or in the trap. The fish is grilled or wrapped in leaves and cooked on top of the coals. When smoked, it can occasionally be conserved.

From Social Relations to Representations

Fishing is of such little importance that it does not give rise to any social system of production or complex distribution network. The organization of the task and the distribution is controlled by the small group of agnates (men or women) who have inherited the rights to a section of water. These 'fathers of the river' (*buu na awaag*) sometimes send relatives to fish their 'waters' (*buu*), mature men sending especially their younger siblings to bail for them, after which a portion of the produce is given back. This delegation of rights to younger siblings stems in part from the physically demanding nature of the *wafêg* technique. Married women living in another village also have their brothers fish their river, receiving part of the dried fish in return. When production is modest, the catch is often divided up on the bank; but when, exceptionally, there is a large quantity of fish (especially when plant poisons have been used), the distribution continues in the village and involves a broader social field. In such cases, the small, almost fleshless flat fish (called *ksik*) are often thrown back.

But let us return to the sexual division of labour with respect to the techniques of bailing and poisoning. We have said that today bailing is practised by both men and women, but that it is said that in the past only women used this method, while only men used fish poisons (today available to women with severe restrictions, and then only for individual or family use). When, for example, large quantities of fish and meat need to be stored up for a ceremonial feast, the men do most of the work, secretly organizing a working group under the direction of a few *aynaag* (men of knowledge) which will fish at night using all available fish poisons and no end of rituals.[50] In these circumstances, women are unwelcome (at best a few will be allowed to watch, well back from the stream): their presence (as well as that of outsiders), is supposed to 'cool' the 'warm' active principles of the poisons through the agency of that 'envious' part of their personality called *aftur* (see above).

In myth, it is always the women who do the fishing, and they make exclusive use of the bailing technique, as a rule working in

---

50. Fishing magic is based on the mastery of ichthyotoxic substances, on the one hand, and on control of the *angor* spirits, on the other, who are asked to free the fish and are left gifts of fish on the riverbank while spells are recited.

pairs. Is it for this ideological reason that the Yafar maintain that it used to be only women who fished this way, or can this fact be seen as a historical confirmation of the female exclusivity that appears in myths? Whatever the case, the myth represents the ideological view of a technique and its social dimension, that which the unconscious and culture project on to it, in the present instance, the association of femaleness with water (procreation, pregnancy) and fish (embryo). Furthermore, mythology makes no mention (at least not in the corpus we have collected) of men fishing or of the use of vegetal fish poisons: while women fish, we see men hunting. The opposition game/fish, moreover, corresponds to another opposition, blood/no blood (Western science would say warm blood/cold blood). When one is aware of the importance of this concept in Yafar representations and the danger that blood evokes (notably for women themselves), one comes to see that the economic monopoly of game by men goes hand in hand with the symbolic control of blood: this could only relegate women to the bloodless flesh of fish (see Testart 1986).

If now we set the real present-day relations of production against this ideological backdrop, we may say that the men are 'trespassing' on the female domain, while the reverse is not true (women do not hunt). But this 'excess' necessitates the controlling of powerful substances, whence the twofold dichotomy between the two techniques and the two genders, relegating women to the purely mechanical, non-ritualized method and granting men control over the 'warm' powers of poison as well as the ritual developments that are determined secondarily by them (Table 10). As for the 'competition' between men and women over bailing,[51] which is supposed to have arisen gradually (?), this seems to be determined not by an implicit rivalry engendered by a technical feature and from which the men emerge victorious, but (at least in this case) by a better distribution of work and a lightening of the women's burden of labour already made heavy enough throughout the year by the working of sago.

---

51. Although couples can be seen fishing together, men and women rarely cooperate, preferring to work separately in small groups of one gender or the other.

		Men	Women
Today	Bailing	+++	+++
	Poison	+++	+
Formerly	Bailing	–	+++
	Poison	+++	–
Myth	Bailing	–	+++
	Poison	–	–

Table 10. Sexual division of fishing with respect to the two techniques of bailing and poisoning.

Animal Husbandry[52]

Pigs

Techno-Economic Behaviours
The northern Eri make a clear lexical distinction between wild pigs, *təta*, and domestic pigs, *wahmuh*. But the semi-domesticated pig is in fact nothing but a wild pig caught young and raised in the village by one of the hunter's female relatives, who becomes its 'mother' (*afaag*).[53] It is not only the same species of animal, but one which was wild for the first few months or weeks of its life, or at best was born in the bush of an already semi-domesticated sow and a wild boar. It is rare that this semi-rearing is pursued for more than two generations. Husbandry is cyclical and the cycles short, and as a consequence the animals are never completely domesticated.

The young *təta* (called *mahure*, whose coat still has stripes), ordinarily caught after its mother has been killed, is carried around in a string bag for the first few weeks by the woman in charge of raising it 'so that it will get used to the smell of humans'. Then its 'mother' cautiously lets it run free under surveillance, and it sometimes seizes this opportunity to run away for good. This is why the string-bag period is generally followed by a fairly short phase (a week or two) during which the piglet, which has already grown and is now called *noog*, is kept on a 'leash' of

52. Information on the modern forms of husbandry and pisciculture tried by the Yafar will be found in Chapter 15.

53. Wild pigs and domestic New Guinea pigs come from the same stock (*Sus scrofa papuensis*) believed to have been introduced by humans some 10,000 years ago (S. Bulmer 1975).

braided rope. Its timidity and attachment to its keeper are tested by frightening it. When it is finally felt to be tame enough, it is turned loose. Depending on the pig, the domestication period can last from three weeks to two months. During the time it is still under constant control, the *mahure* sleeps indoors with its masters, together with one or more dogs, who learn to leave it alone. During the day, however, its 'mother' takes it along in her carrying bag. Like puppies and sometimes children, the piglet is fed on premasticated sago jelly.

When still young, its 'ears are docked' (*angôk hegefatik*), but this is not always done; the purpose of this operation is to enable the hunter to tell domestic and wild pigs apart. Somewhat later the animal undergoes a ritual (see below) and receives a definitive name. Finally, when a young male is several months old and its testicles begin to show, it is castrated: two slits are made in the skin with a bamboo blade and the testicles extracted, a simple operation which takes no more than a couple of minutes, but requires the aid of several men to hold the animal down on its back. All males are castrated, as reproduction is ensured by wild boar during the sow's daily foraging sessions in the bush. Castration is essential not to control reproduction, but in order to lessen the males' natural aggressiveness.

Once tame, the *wahmuh* follows its human 'mother' around all day, into the bush, to the gardens and sago-working sites, rooting for food and sometimes ravaging part of the taro or sweet potato crop (sweet potatoes, introduced recently into the region, have been abandoned for this reason). Morning and night its mistress gives it a portion of sago jelly at the foot of the house; in effect, pigs and dogs are fed the inferior quality jelly found at the bottom of the bucket.

Because of the incomplete domestication process, pigs are truly tame only with their adoptive family (household) and often show fear of other villagers. Despite being castrated, adult males retain a good part of their natural aggressiveness. Wild boars will often follow domestic sows back to the village. I observed some, in the Wamuru and Muwagneri territories, that entered the village in the middle of day following a domestic sow coming home with her mistress. A sow always returns to the bush to farrow, and her 'mother', acquainted with her habits and haunts, searches until she finds the nest. The woman then merely keeps a discrete eye on the sow's movements and brings her sago jelly;

Plate 15. A Muwagneri women with her hand-raised pigs.

after a time, she tries to coax her back to the village with her litter by calling her; often the sow takes the initiative and comes back to the hamlet followed by her offspring. Without the watchful eye of the mistress, there is a danger that the sow will return to the wild at this time.

From the moment a hunter brings home a young *mahure,* after a pause in the husbandry cycles, other hunters are encouraged to do the same, and gradually a new herd is built up. For the hamlet of Yafar 1 (85 inhabitants), there were eight pigs in 1970 (all slaughtered at the same time that year); at the end of 1973 normal husbandry had not yet reappeared; in 1976 there were eight pigs; in 1978 there were nineteen, spanning two generations; and in 1981 only one animal, quickly sold to the schoolteachers at Yafar 2. While a village herd is constituted only gradually, since this depends on the fortunes of the hunt, it meets its end as a result of a collective decision. But only the adult animals are killed, and the young, if there are any, are kept for the next slaughter. In July 1970, the killing of the eight village pigs put an end to a period of husbandry lasting several years. In 1978, seven pigs were killed, another got away (when it came back a month later, it was decided to spare it), and eleven piglets were held over.[54]

Started during a hunting party in the forest, the pig herd ended with a hunting party which had begun in the village, and in which the men manifestly took pleasure. It sometimes happens that a pig escapes and is never found, but that is exceptional. The Yafar do not formulate their motives for raising pigs primarily in economic terms but in terms of the group and more specifically kinship: it is the desire to give a piglet to a sister, mother or daughter. Nor are all the reasons given for putting an end to the herd primarily alimentary; generally mention is made of the animals' depredations in the gardens, the filth and smell in the village and the ensuing lassitude.

Social Relations

We have just seen the extent to which semi-rearing is a voluntary extension of hunting, a sort of suspended sentence for the wild piglet before it is ultimately put to death. The maximum husbandry cycle of two, rarely three generations of domesticated

54. For comparative elements on the same type of pig husbandry in New Guinea, see for example Iteanu 1983; Kelm and Kelm 1980; Rappaport 1968; Schwimmer 1973; also Oliver 1967 for the Siuai of Bougainville; Cooper *et al.* 1981.

pigs illustrates the fragility of this hold on nature. And yet, in terms of social relations, the transition from hunting to husbandry is a radical change. From the moment a hunter decides to bring home a wild piglet, not only is the pig's status altered, going from a state of *tata* to that of *wahmuh*, but new socio-economic roles and relations are brought into play. The most obvious change is the role women have in raising *wahmuh*, whereas they have almost nothing to do with hunting and distributing meat. But this properly maternal function of taming (rearing) and feeding is opposed on the one hand, to the transient role of the hunter and on the other, to the jural status of the head of household (most often the pig-raiser's husband). It is the hunter who gives the *tata* to the relative of his choice (she can also ask for one), but it is the head of the household who becomes the pig's owner (*awaag* 'father'). While the hunter plays only a momentary role, and following the extraction performed on nature seems to need to 'get rid' of the captured game by engaging it in the social network, the pig's 'father' acquires this role only in his capacity as close relative of the woman raising it, and exclusively through her. His role will become effective above all when the meat is distributed.

If we add to these roles that of the official bowman and butcher (see below), chosen from the moiety opposite that of the owner, Yafar pig husbandry can be seen to be articulated formally around three male roles and one female role.

1. Hunter-capturer   ⎫
2. Raiser, pig's 'mother'   ⎬ close relatives
3. Pig's owner or 'father' and   ⎭
   distributor of the meat
4. Main bowman and butcher   relatives from the other
                                  moiety

Because of its economic importance and duration, it is nevertheless the female role that is considered the most crucial, and when one asks who a pig belongs to, the name of the woman raising it is almost always given. In effect, the woman is the socializing agent by which the *tata* will become a *wahmuh*. However, the process itself is set in motion and ended by men. There seems to be an obvious parallel with rearing children, raised and fed by the mother but engendered by the father and jurally placed under his control by the rule of patrilineal descent. In this respect, raising a pig is an adoption.

Other men intervene more freely or help the animal's owner on the three occasions mentioned above and, against the background of the ongoing female role, contribute to the process of the pig's socialization: ear docking, naming and castration. Each clan has its own repertory of pig names (unlike dogs, which are given names common to the whole tribe), often the names of rivers located on ancestral clan lands. But until it becomes a *noog* (p. 206), the piglet bears the mythical name of the *sawangô* female spirits' pigs, Utfe. It is not until it is completely tame that the pig receives its definitive name, chosen by its owner and its mistress. When a piglet is born of a domestic sow, it is first given its mother's name, and later another name. The naming ceremony (called *wahmuh buu-a fatik* 'to throw the pig in the water') is organized by a few men in the absence of women; the animal is taken down to the river, where it is struck with a piece of *ganguk* (a mineral concretion) and with the pith from a stem of wild banana palm, the first representing quantity, the second *hoofuk* (the growth principle). The pig's name is repeated using the formulas 'go into its flesh, go into its head, go into its leg', etc.). This is thus a naming rite, but above all a rite of growth and abundance, the purpose of which is to fatten the animal. Ear-docking and castrating are done by any man in the village handy at these jobs; no rite accompanies them. It is not without significance that it is the men who control the body-marking associated with the pig's 'social' identity (name), just as it is they who organize children's rites of passage.

The redistribution of piglets born of a domestic sow (Table 11) is done under the supervision of the mistress or the owner. A new 'mother' and, optionally, a new 'father' are chosen for each of the litter. Here again the owner seems to be designated secondarily as a function of the identity of the new mistress, transmission taking place from woman to woman. But the contrary is apparently sometimes the case, the connection then being made between the keeper or owner of the sow and a male relative, whose wife or mother is charged with raising the animal. Nevertheless, the nurturing function always prevails over the jural. Local-group solidarity extends this distribution beyond the kindred proper to the local community as a whole, but rarely further (Table 11 shows no animals given outside the hamlet).

Source of the sow	Sows' mistress	New mistresses of the piglets
Kuray's hunt	Tuay, Kuray's mother	1. Hwata, Hwam's co-wife, Tuay's daughter 2. Nêma, Tuay's daughter 3. Wêy, Tuay's DHyBW 4. Tuay herself
Buwô's hunt	Angwawaw, Buwô's classificatory sister-in-law	1. Aywa, Angwawaw's MZ 2. Hwafii, Buwô's wife
Kabyo's hunt	Anu, Kabyo's classificatory mother	1. Samow, Anu's classificatory daughter 2. Awan, classificatory affine 3. Afwêy, classificatory affine 4. Abi, wife of one of Anu's classificatory sons 5. Wêy, Anu's classificatory daughter 6. Sefwi, Kabyo's mother
Kabyo's hunt	Wêy, Kabyo's agnatic classificatory sister	1. Awan, wife of Kabyo's adoptive father 2. Mangwoy, Kabyo's classificatory sister 3. Amô, Afwêy's daughter

Table 11. Example of redistribution of domestic piglets (Yafar 1, 1978)

When a *wahmuh* vanishes into the forest for several days and there is a risk of it returning to the wild, it is the mistress who actively searches for it, calling its name from the village or the bush. Spells can be said by the pig's owner to make the *nabasa* set it free from the 'underbrush', the 'fogs' the 'mists' that keep it captive. If a medium enters into a trance, the visiting *nabasa* is asked to pass on a request for the liberation of the vanished pig, and the spirit may give the reasons for the animal's abduction (offering prematurely removed, etc.). Often it is a hunter who comes upon the lost pig; its mistress then personally goes to the site, for 'a pig will answer only its "mother's" voice'.

Hunting Domestic Pigs: Staging the Slaughter

All the adult pigs are killed the same day, at the crack of dawn, following a consensual decision taken a few weeks earlier. To kill the pig they have raised and fed, the owner (the raiser's husband) calls in a relative of the opposite moiety (a kinsman or close affine). This man usually volunteers his services. He asks the help of two or three other villagers in killing the animal, but it his arrow that must be shot first. After the pig has run off and been tracked down (a search that can last a day or more but usually succeeds after a few hours), it is carried back to the village and laid out on a door placed flat on the ground in front of the raiser's house.[55] In principle, the chief bowman directs the butchering, assisted by his helpers. But let us first look at how the animal is shot.

Its 'mother', who, together with her husband, respects the consumption taboo, nevertheless participates in the slaughter of her pig by luring it before the line of hunters with sago jelly, which she sprinkles along in front of the animal. This procedure may seem odd, given that the simplest way would be to come up on the animal and shoot it where it stood, for instance while it was waiting at the foot of the house to be fed in the morning, or even tying its leg to the house. Instead, small groups of men post themselves at various spots around the village, passive lines waiting for the raiser to coax the animal, often with difficulty, until it is directly in front of them. At the moment the arrows are loosed, it becomes obvious that the flight of the wounded pig is part of the plan, even symbolically necessary. I wondered about these two behaviours that might, from an essentially technical point of view, be described as needlessly complicated, even illogical. It was then that the woman's role appeared to me as decisive; first of all in the social order, and more specifically in the framework of the complementary relation between hunting and husbandry, where, in response to the hunter's initial gift, the keeper must return the animal, now a *wahmuh*, to the hunters, so

---

55. There is an opposition here between the wild pig, which is always butchered in the forest, and the domestic pig, brought back to its owner's house. Also, the pig killed in the forest is taken to the place where it is to be butchered (usually by a stream) by the hunter, who carries it unaided on his back, while the runaway domestic pig is borne back to the village tied hanging from a pole carried between two men. It seems that this expresses the dichotomy (see below) between the wild world, free of stain, and the village ground polluted by menstrual blood. Only the village pig, already partialy 'immunized', can be cut up in the village, while the wild pig goes directly from the forest to the inside of the house in the form of quarters of meat.

Plate 16. Killing a domestic pig lured into the line of fire by its "mother's" food.

that they may once again treat it as game. In effect, at the outset a man, bow and arrows in hand, presents a woman with a wild piglet; at the end, she returns the adult, through the mediation of food, for it is not only the woman who presents the pig to the hunters, but the foster mother. The *wahmuh* must receive the three or four fatal arrows while it is eating from the hands of its human mother: it is brutally torn from its status as protected 'child' and thrust back into its original state of game good for killing. The bond between the pig and its mother is here represented by the food strewn on the ground, a sort of umbilical cord severed at the moment when, pierced by the arrows, the pig-child runs off into the forest to die.[56]

Another level of interpretation brings in the notion of *heyfu*, the pollution of menstrual blood. The ground of the village as well as that of the forest trails is considered to be contaminated by the passage of women and, in the case of the village, by the contact of their genitals with the ground when they sit down, or by their blood, which is spilled when menstruating women or new mothers are isolated under the house. Any animals discovered in the village square (notably snakes) are for this reason regarded as unfit to eat and declared *heyfu-inaag*. Now the same should hold for the pigs which feed on village refuse and are in physical contact with women. But to recognize this state of pollution would be tantamount to making husbandry economically useless. A symbolic device had to be found that would emancipate pigs from polluting factors and restore their original purity. By ritually separating them from their 'mother' and by sending them back to their native forest before their death – in other words by reinstating their nature as game – they are rid of female pollution and their flesh is made edible once more. The staging of the pigs' slaughter is, on this level, nothing other than a rite of purification and even of separation from the mother like those performed on boys.

The two explanations are complementary, since separation from the mother allows the child to enter the world of adult men while

---

56. In one myth, a man is pierced by an arrow while dancing at a public ceremony. As he flees, he breaks the string headband he is wearing, the other end of which is still being braided by his mother (the local gloss explicitly identifies this strip, *rabing*, with the umbilical cord). Having hidden in the wild rushes (where wild pigs sleep), the man is discovered by a mother and her daughter out hunting wild pig and 'adopted' by them (see Juillerat 1991a, Ch. 3).

cleansing him of maternal 'impurity'. For the pig, death and the gift of its flesh as food bring to a close this cultural detour, this sociosymbolic parenthesis introduced into the hunting process through husbandry.

Distribution and Consumption
When the principal bowman and his helpers have butchered the pig, its 'father' presents them with the first gift, consisting of pieces of rib and meat with leaves and especially blood, which they will eat with sago jelly. This portion is called *taf-yis* 'blood sago-jelly'. The other pieces of the animal are distributed following the same principles as for wild-pig meat, that is, on three levels: raw, cooked and smoked. However, no one may cook his own portion before the bowmen have cooked and eaten the *taf-yis*. Children or adolescents of both genders can also receive pieces of raw meat for their participation in raising the pig or because the animal was attributed to them at the distribution of a second-generation litter. As a rule, pig meat is distributed primarily among the kindred of the hunter who captured the animal or its mother, and among the relatives of the raiser and her husband.

The taboo on eating a pig one has raised is fairly well respected, but this is better explained by sentimental arguments (the women's fondness for their pigs). It seems too that the hunter who originally captured the animal prefers to abstain from eating it, but his relation to its blood is weaker, since the only blood he has let is that of the mother of the captured piglet. On the other hand, as we have just seen, the men who kill the *wahmuh* in the village ritually consume a portion of the animal but receive no further pieces: in effect, the *taf-yis* appears as a sort of 'hyperconsumption'. Whereas the hunter abstains from butchering the *tǝta* and eating its flesh, the bowman who kills a *wahmuh* is appointed official butcher and consumes its blood. The only symbolic opposition which might suggest an explanation for this difference is that the *tǝta* is taken in or from the forest (from mother nature), while in the case of the *wahmuh* this responsibility falls solely on the one who captured it, as the bowman not only did not tear the animal from its natural environment, he was the one who sent it back. Perhaps we could say that by momentarily returning the *wahmuh* to nature and to the *nabasa*, the bowman avoids incurring guilt with respect to the first or the anger of the second: he can thus fully assume his 'relation to blood' by becoming an official butcher and consumer. From the standpoint of consumption as well, Yafar pig husbandry becomes a hunt whose outcome is deferred. In the New Guinea Highlands and in other parts of Melanesia, domestic pigs (husbandry is often a continuous process) are used in ceremonial exchanges (A. Strathern 1971), barter (Oliver 1967), as blood price (Koch 1974), in marriages (Glasse and Meggitt eds 1969), or in sacrifice to spirits (Rappaport 1968). They are used as 'substitutes for a life', as living fertility symbols (Lemonnier 1993). Pigs may also be exchanged, either alive or freshly killed, in the form of raw meat or as a meal (Oliver 1967). The Orokaiva (Iteanu 1983; Schwimmer 1973), whose mode of domestication closely resembles that of the Yafar, use pig-meat feasts to neutralize conflicts and give new impetus to exchanges. Characteristically, the Yafar keep their pigs out of any exchange other than the attribution or distribution of the young or the distribution of meat described above. Husbandry does not serve any other social function than the relationship analysed above.

Dogs

The opposite of the domestic pig, the dog, *mawank*, is entirely on the side of culture, and its relation to the wild replicates that of the hunter. The dog neither comes from nor returns to the world of the forest, it belongs to society, where it is born and dies. Its primary role is to go hunting with its master. Whereas the domestic pig is on the women's side, the adult dog is on the men's. And yet it is most often fed by women. Like piglets, puppies are fed with pre-chewed sago jelly and are watched over by women, who carry them around in string bags or bark containers as they go about their work. But as soon as they are able to hunt, they usually follow their master. The hunter sets out on the forest trails and without looking back, calls his dog repeatedly, using the same intonation. This call is then reiterated for the duration of the hunting, while the dog casts around in the undergrowth trying to pick up a scent. Thus constant sound contact is maintained between a man and his dog(s). When a man goes to his gardens and does not want to take his dog, he can hobble it by tying one leg to its neck. The daily sago ration is not enough for the dogs and they complete their intake by hunting on their own. They are almost always healthy, slender without being thin, usually with a tan coat but sometimes black and white. At night, if they are not roaming the bush, each dog sleeps shut up in the house with its master, seeking out the heat of a fireplace or settling down in the warm ashes. They are treated well and from time to time act as playmates; they are struck only when they get too close to meat being butchered or distributed. When a dog dies, it is buried in the forest. Its flesh is never eaten. Each litter is distributed by the owner as he pleases. Puppies can be given to relatives in other villages, but they are never traded.

Parallel to the treatment of pigs, men see to the dog's socialization by giving it a name, training it to hunt and subjecting it to a rite for finding game, and finally by castrating some of the males. The reason given for this last operation is to keep the males from fighting all the time; the argument of canine birth control is not advanced, even though it is certainly a deciding criterion.

When a young dog begins to hunt, its master performs a rite (called *mawank seeg* 'dog's magic hunting plants'), which, like the rites consecrating young hunters, is an introduction to and identification with blood (fertility) as well as a presentation to the guardian spirits of game. The dog is taken into the bush to a small stream where the man has made a pool. He plants stems of the *sesa* liana in the stream, having coated them with red ochre while reciting the ritual spells for game. Magic rhizomes (each of which has a specific function) are chewed with betel and spit on to the dog's joints,[57] into its mouth and on its nose, heart, tail and genitals as well as into the pool, which gradually takes on a reddish tint. This means that the dog will have to run fast after its quarry, smell the scent and carry game in its mouth, its heart will have to beat hard (*öruk konkoneg*) and get 'hot' and it will have to wag its tail when it finds game. The names and the meaning of the magic clones evoke other types of relations between dogs and game and the forest, in particular 'seeing' the quarry clearly, having sharp eyesight even in the dark. The owner also names all the spots the dog will have to pass through, stands of bamboo and thickets of *ware* cane (where pigs lie up during the day) into which the dog will go 'to meet game while breaking the stalks',

57. It seems that only the males (or at least above all the males) undergo this rite.

and he names the trees to the foot of which the dog will track its prey, he calls out the names of the lands and the water courses, etc. One chant also evokes 'Ban's dog' (the mythical man found in the reeds by the dog who belonged to two women; see n. 56), and then the 'dog belonging to the coconut palm, the penis, the vagina, the umbilical cord...' It is said that dogs would eat placentas if one were not careful, and that they lick the ground where a birth has taken place. There is an analogy between the 'smell of fertile substances' (*hoofuk funguk*) and the scent of game, and the purpose of these spells is to sharpen the dog's sense of smell, to set it on the trail of wild pig.

But above all – as is also the case for young adolescent hunters – through this rite, the dog must be presented to the forest spirits, the *nabasa*. By spitting the red betel juice on the dog, its self (*sungwaag*) is made luminous; thus adorned with 'blood', the dog will appear 'perfectly visible', 'red as fire' to the *nabasa*, and will receive game from them. The dog is bespat with magic clones of *Curcuma*, normally used for seduction rites, to make it pleasing to the spirits. The purpose is to establish the visual contact mentioned earlier: the dog will not be 'covered with fog' but will be seen by the spirits and will see the game given by them. Also brought into play are the usual Yafar themes of *hoofuk* (in this instance *sês taf* 'the game's blood'), made accessible by 'peeling' (*roof*) the forest animals, and that of the intervention of the dead – not the *nabasa* and *kê-ruur* spirits of the dead (who only put game in the hunter's path), but ghosts, *ifaaf* – and corpses, which are requested to open their mouths and let out the ritual words. The word transmitted in this way is also the renewal of life, from the depths of the earth where the *ifaaf* dwell. From the putrefaction of the body to which they are eternally bound, ghosts transmit the means of fertility, in other words the magic words, to the living. Lastly, in the *mawank seeg* rite, the dog is reborn by being dunked into the red water of the pool from which it immediately leaps and runs off into the bush, perhaps already on the scent of something. When he throws the dog into the water, the man shouts '*Say taf buu*' ('Coconut-blood water'), explicitly alluding to the uterine waters of the Primordial Mother (the Coconut Palm). During these operations the dog's name is pronounced repeatedly after the names of mythic dogs to which it is thus linked by an imaginary genealogy.

This rite is performed only once for a dog, but the animal will later be subjected to minor rites: periodically bits of rhizome from certain magic clones are mixed into its food and at times a small amount of dried menstrual blood. When the dog is old, it once again becomes 'black' (invisible) to the *nabasa*, the rites are abandoned and for the rest of its days it only rarely hunts.

This chapter has shown the central position occupied by hunting in a diversified economy based primarily on horticulture and sago. The latter two types of production represent food security, while hunting is the epitome of uncertainty. In this sense there is something worrying about hunting, and one might detect a system of defense against this anxiety in the richly developed rites and representations.

Through the dominant character of male ideology, expressed in the men's monopoly of hunting, collective fish-poisoning and certain aspects of gathering and their control of distribution circuits and ritual, one perceives in effect the continual concern not to be excluded from the fragile relationship with maternalized cosmic fertility or *hoofuk*. All social relations surrounding hunting seem to be organized for a large part as a function of this quest or fear, which ascribes a spiritual dimension to every production or exchange activity. Through this not only techno-economic but more specifically alimentary relationship with nature, man constructs a number of symbolic and social systems. The two go hand in hand: the material procedures, socially organized, are developed or inhibited by the way man feels 'accepted' or not by the powers of nature or the spirits of the dead. Conversely, communication through the exchange of products, performance of rituals or the sentiment of a transcendent relationship with fertility are linked to the vagaries of production. It is somewhere amid these various orientations that the community seems to be seeking its point of equilibrium.

8

Exchange and Circulation of Goods Among the Eri

Three o'clock this afternoon, commotion in the village: fourteen Sowanda visitors have arrived laden with coconuts, yams and arrows which they have brought to exchange for manufactured products: matches, razor blades, glass beads, mirrors, etc. The exchange took place slowly, without hurry, the Sowanda clinging together and visibly uneasy against a house, the Yafar walking around making fun of their visitors, going away and then trickling back with their products for exchange.

(Field journal: 14 June 1973)

In the foregoing chapters I have already said a fair amount about the circulation of products in discussing modes of distribution. I will now step back from these immediate and for the most part internal exchanges and look at how they fit into a broader socio-geographic context, which is the Amanab linguistic group (Eri) and part of the Waina group, and then look beyond this sector to the exchange routes.[1] First of all, however, it might be useful to propose a classification of exchange goods as a function of their availability before going on to define the different modes of exchange or circulation.

Categories of Goods

Goods of generalized production include all foodstuffs, for there is, to my knowledge, in the region outlined above, not a single food item that is not produced by all of the groups. Some communities, however, are more or less favoured with coconuts (soil

1. This chapter is an augmented and revised version of a paper given in 1980 at Professor Lerou-Gourhan's seminar on settlement structures.

221

quality), game or fish. Moreover, some groups can find themselves temporarily (between the old and the new crop) short of certain products (yams, coconuts) compared with their neighbours. Such inequalities are in principle of a nature to spark exchanges or gifts, but in practice they have very little importance and never constitute the primary motive for a transaction. The amount of game and the importance of hunting also create an inequality in the availability of ornaments made from possum fur, feathers, teeth or bone. The same holds for tooth or bone tools, but these are rarely exchanged.

As for certain types of stone, much sought until 1950 for making adzes (and still important for sago-scrapers), production is confined to certain regions, namely northeastern Eri and groups from the eastern foothills for *maar* black stone (adzes), the Nayneri tribe of the southern Eri for red *baha* stone and the Hugumon group for a certain quality of *prisri* stone (flakes for sago-scrapers), to which can be added certain river-shell products from the Anggor group. These stones, whose origin is relatively well known and sometimes unique, create trade routes radiating out from production centres; shellrings, netbags, arrows and, in exchange for *baha*, magical plants and their rites travel in the opposite direction.

Another category of locally produced items takes in goods from remote sources (a category unknown among the Eri before the region was colonized), in particular from the sea: shellrings, cowries, and also white and blue beads from Indonesia. These are particularly prized valuables, but have never been used for 'money' by the Eri, with the exception of the big shellrings (*kir* or *agfô*), used in marriage payments by the eastern Eri of the Bapi plain. The Yafar, central Eri and Waina were not involved in these large-scale networks and received only a few cowries and the occasional small ring, called *sês nofuk* 'game's eye', from western New Guinea, and then used them only as jewellry.

The Eri distinguish two categories of goods, *teh* and *ag* (*agi*). *Teh* means 'food' and includes all food products. *Ag* designates all locally manufactured goods, such as ornaments, arrows, musical instruments, tools, etc. The approximate English equivalent is 'valuables'. In the context of marriage, the term also covers the entire set of gifts of this type which the young groom presents to his wife's brothers.

Finally, there are a few objects which are produced throughout the region but which never circulate. These are the wooden trumpets (*fuf*), particularly sacred musical instruments, and certain objects which, on the contrary, are regarded as too ordinary to be used in exchanges or as gifts, for instance, material made from pounded *Ficus* bark[2] (used for wrapping feather ornaments and formerly as blankets), or small bone tools, such as awls and spatulas.

Modes of Exchange

Three modes of exchange can be distinguished:

a) 'Generalized exchange' (Sahlins 1974) between kin, in which goods circulate freely and informally, with no immediate reciprocity or accounting for the future;
b) 'Immediate exchange', or barter between unrelated exchange partners (more rarely between relatives from different tribes);
c) Formalized matrimonial exchanges and gifts.

The degree of diversity of the goods exchanged in these three modes of circulation decreases from a) to c).

Generalized exchange

In this mode of 'diffuse reciprocity',[3] all categories of goods circulate: horticultural products, gathered fruit, and meat (*teh* 'food'), as well as objects manufactured locally or far away (*ag*). Its characteristics are:

1) Gifts between kin or affines exclusively, motivated primarily by bonds of kinship and affection;
2) The private character of the relation: gifts often exchanged between two individuals unnoticed by outsiders;
3) Usually informal occasions for exchange.

2. Beaten barks are not used here in intertribal exchanges (see Lemonnier 1981).
3. I will not deal with 'pooling' (Sahlins 1974) here, which I differentiate from generalized reciprocity and which concerns only food. Sharing among the Yafar is apparent essentially within the nuclear family, starting with the individual 'producer' (gatherer, hunter, etc.).

Most of the time the economic motive is weaker than the social and affective functions, but it can become decisive when it comes to locally produced goods such as adze blades, shellrings, etc. In the latter case, a given object seems to be 'aspirated' by the economic shortage in a certain direction and away from its place of origin. The object then follows a path which is unpredictable in its detail and which is based on kinship ties between individual members of neighbouring villages and tribes. Each leg of this path is represented by an individual who has received the object from a kinsman or an affine, and who may in turn pass it on to another kinsman or affine, in principle from a community other than the one from which he received it. When the object (in the case of generalized production) is not attracted by an economic need and only socio-affective motives intervene, no linear path is created, and the item is in principle given only once; unlike demand, which 'attracts' the object away, the affective bond 'retains' it in the possession of the receiver who, through it, feels linked to the giver. This is more of a one-time transaction, and the object rarely goes out of the circle of close kin; even if it were to be given a second time, it would not necessarily follow a linear path away from its point of departure. In other words, the geographical dimension is decisive only when there is a localized economic demand which to some extent modifies the 'path of kinship'.

This hand-to-hand mode of circulation is directly engendered by the sociocentric structure of marriage alliance: wherever women have been exchanged, the principle of generalized exchange is adopted for the circulation of goods.

The *sêh* exchange partnership

The term *sêh* also exists in Waina, as *sehe* (Gell 1975: 25–6). In Amanab, the *s* at the beginning of a word sometimes indicates the notion of otherness in a relationship between two persons; it seems that this is the same segment that we find in *segwaag* (privileged partnership between kin: Ch. 11). The segment (*a*)*h* refers to duality (and therefore exchange) and, prefixed to a verb, signals a dual subject.

This institution originated with the Waina, and more particularly in the Sowanda tribe (*suara* in Amanab). Gell (1975), however, mentions *sehe* alliances between certain Umeda and Walsa hamlets (Map 3) in addition to those occurring between Waina groups, and the Yafar used to organize expeditions to barter with these same Walsa (Waris: see Map 1). The northern Eri (Potayneri and Yafar) entertained *sêh* alliances only with the Sowanda, and it seems that it was the latter in particular who established such relations with the Punda, Umeda and Waina-Wiyara. This points to a relationship between this non-kin partnership and the fact that the Sowanda and the Waina are largely endogamous groups (Ch. 10 and Map 4). This in fact seems to be the origin of the *sêh* exchange system, which thus serves to establish reliable and peaceful relations by means of a friendship contract founded on exchange with non-related but neighbouring groups. As Eri groups were not organized into endogamous connubia but into concentric zones of close exchange, and as there was already a tightly woven network of kinship bonds among neighbouring tribes, they did not need to create a partnership of this type. The *sêh* system thus appears to have been initiated by the absolute necessity for a group isolated by endogamy to ensure itself of some other form of (non-marriage) alliance with its neighbours. In the context that concerns us, the need for security seems more compelling than the need for reciprocity, which can be arranged between internal units (the Sowanda, for instance, are split into ten clan hamlets). On the other hand, it seems difficult to imagine, especially in precolonial times, such an atomized society will-ingly remaining confined within its territorial boundaries and surrounded by 'strangers' (*angôruwaag*), who were seen as sor-cerers or potential murderers. In this region no form of positive transaction was conceivable if the way had not previously been smoothed by institutionalized ties. Now the only two such ties were marriage and kinship on the one hand and *sêh* partnership on the other.

Like the *segwaag* relationship (pp. 179–81), the *sêh* partnership is passed on from father to son, another indication that the *sêh* is the non-kinship alternative of the *segwaag* partnership. Moreover, we saw that exchanges between *segwaag* are more formalized than those between relatives who are not partners, especially where exchanges of meat are concerned. This indicates that the passage from informal generalized exchanges between kin to a dual form of exchange (*segwaag*) is realized at both the level of position in the kinship network and that of the goods exchanged.

The *segwaag* relationship, which I have chosen to analyse in Chapters 7 and 11, would have its place here as the homology of the *sêh* system. But the two modes are also differentiated by the circumstances in which the exchanges take place.

Exchanges between *sêh* took place on the occasion of an expedition of one of the groups to visit the other and vice versa, the only purpose of the visits being to exchange products, strengthen already established ties between the two communities – more particularly, between pairs of exchange partners – and possibly to contract new *sêh* partnerships. The Yafar and the Sowanda made these trips once or twice a garden (annual cycle), which is not very often given the short distance (four hours' walk), but is significant, for it shows that the encounters were thought of symbolically as being part of the annual horticultural production: each person needed to give yams from each of his gardens to his *sêh*.[4] Everyone would bring along what he wanted to exchange with his *sêh* or with other members of the host community. But the first exchanges were always made with the official partner, and only afterwards with other members of the group; there might be a little friendly bargaining, often expressed jokingly. The visitors usually spent the night at their host's home, each being housed and fed exclusively by his partner, for generalized trust was still quite limited. No rite marked a new alliance: the new partners squeezed each others' arms and said, 'You are my *sêh*', before going on to their first transaction. The women did not enter into exchanges, for – according to male testimonies – they never went with the men for reasons of security. Although entirely admissible, this argument also enabled the men to keep for themselves the pleasures of bartering and mobility, as well as that of insecurity itself and the potential violence contained in the situation. Nevertheless the women of the host group could ask their husband, father, brother or son to exchange a string bag for them, or a yam or a sprouted coconut. Goods manufactured by women, mainly string bags or flying-fox-bone belts, entered the circuit in this way, but the women – even if they received the return – were not present at the exchange.

Once grown up, the sons of two *sêh* partners would take their father's place in the exchange relationship, which remained a

4. Following serious conflicts (murders) between the two communities, exchanges were temporarily suspended.

stable fixture between given lines through this renewal of generations; exchanges also took place between groups of brothers,
usually full siblings. As a rule, the partners came from the same
age class. A man might also have two *sêh* with whom he carried
on separate exchanges; alternatively, some Yafar had no partner
at all. A *sêh* relationship between two men was never formally
broken off, but it could be more or less active depending on the
moment.

The various categories of goods defined above all entered
into these exchanges, but the Yafar claim that from the Sowanda
they used to receive more especially coconuts, blades for sago-
pounders (*hwagi*) – which the Sowanda made from the broken
stub of wood adzes blades (*maar*) –, woven bands decorated with
Coix lachryma jobi (*sawe*) seeds, as well as Indonesian glass beads
(*wara na kêg*), small shellrings, and, beginning in 1950, steel axes
through western New Guinea exchange routes. In the 1950s, following the northward expansion of the Gêpôk rite (p. 185) and
the arrival of metal axes from Holland, the Yafar and other northern Eri groups also gave the Sowanda (in the Dutch enclave of
Waris; see Ch. 15), who did not know how to make them, hour-
glass drums in exchange for axes. Bows and arrows circulated in
both directions, mainly in symmetrical exchanges (a bow for a
bow, an arrow for an arrow). The same system was used between
Sowanda and Potayneri and, unless I am mistaken, Babuk.

In principle, each transaction took the form of barter,[5] in which
the worth of the objects was supposed to be equivalent, but *sêh*
often gave each other gifts without expecting immediate repay-
ment. Here are a few examples of relative values:

1 *hwagi* sago-pounder	= 1 *hogof* belt, or 1 small netbag, or 1 dog-tooth necklace
1 sprouted coconut or 1 big netbag	= 1 large yam
1 European axe (formerly 1 *maar* adze)	= 1 big netbag or 1 hourglass drum

For the Yafar, the notion of exchange value is in principle attached only to transactions between *sêh*. But we found that occasional

5. The word for 'to exchange, to barter' is *ah-sfaôgôk* (*ah*: the dual prefix + the root *sfô* + *ôgôk* marking reciprocity) or *məmanga ah-feg*.

barter went on between certain intermarried Eri groups, for instance between Gefayneri and Babuk, who did not have *sêh*
partnerships. The relative value of the goods was the same in
these cases.

Today the Yafar claim that *sêh* still exist but that no more transactions occur, or that the rare exchanges there happen at the
request of the Sowanda and do not involve exchange partners.
The last trading between Yafar and Sowanda took place in 1973
and then again in 1978–1979. During my second stay in
particular, a group of some dozen Sowanda men and boys turned
up one day in Yafar 1; all the men were armed with bows and
arrows, and were loaded down with yams and coconuts as well
as with extra arrows for exchange. They appeared extremely
anxious and wary of their hosts, and stood lined up against two
houses, apparently afraid of being attacked. A few Yafar men
proceeded unenthusiastically with the exchange, during which
the visitors did not let go of their goods before they were sure
that what they were receiving was equivalent. The Sowanda then
set up camp for the night in the village *haus kiap* (the cabin used
by government patrol officers), where, after much hemming and
hawing, the Yafar finally brought them some food. It was
explained to me that these Sowanda were not their real former
sêh and that in any case today exchanges were made with
anyone; as a consequence they felt in no way obliged to offer
them hospitality, but had simply felt sorry for them because they
were hungry. In effect, the Sowanda had brought nothing to eat,
which leads one to think that they were counting on a better
reception. But they had a special purpose for organizing this visit
to their former partners: to procure Western goods, of which the
Yafar had more, particularly small knives, razor blades, matches
and shorts. The Yafar were unable to comply with the request,
being at that time very short of European items.

A month later, another group of Sowanda called on the Yafar,
who were even less inclined than the first time to play along;
frankly exasperated, they regarded this return of the Sowanda
after so short a time as excessive and decided to let them go hungry. The next day the Sowanda left before daybreak and did
not return for several years. Thus the *sêh* relationship between
these two communities ended because of the abandonment of
individual alliances, the refusal of hospitality and the appearance
of a new need, that of European articles. Conversely, the Yafar

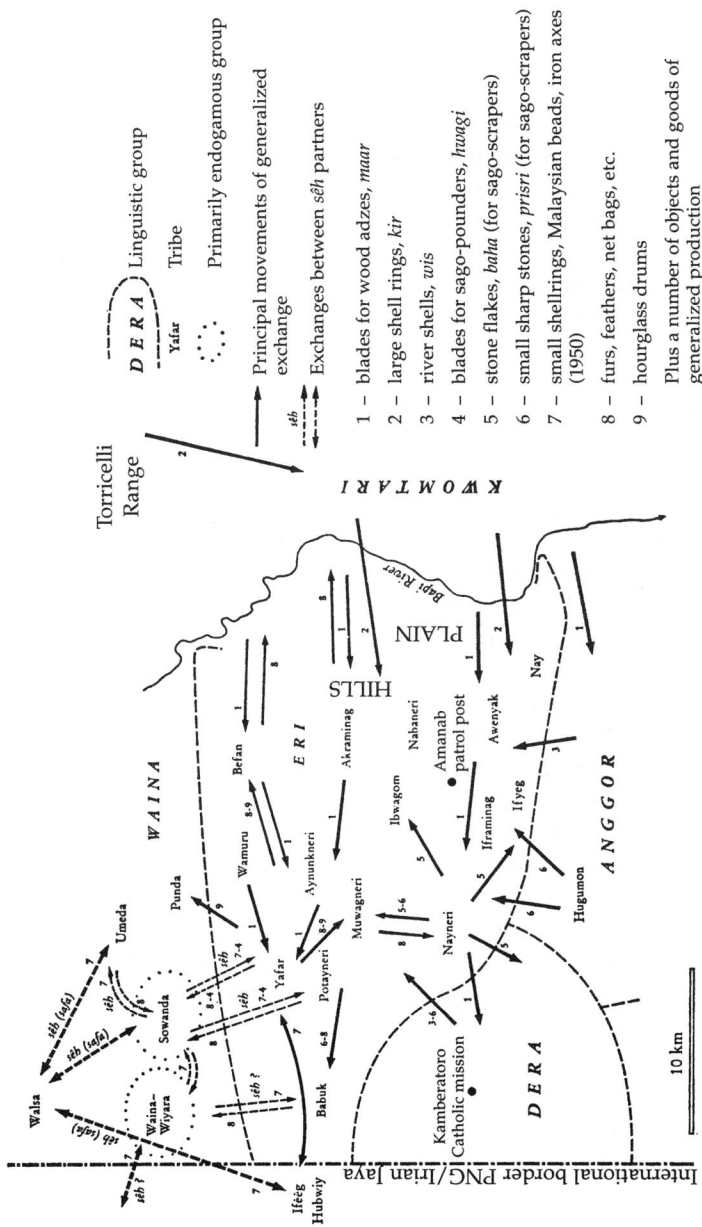

Map 3. Principal exchanges in the Eri zone

DERA Linguistic group

Yafar Tribe

Primarily endogamous group

Principal movements of generalized exchange

sêh Exchanges between *sêh* partners

1 – blades for wood adzes, *maar*

2 – large shell rings, *kir*

3 – river shells, *wis*

4 – blades for sago-pounders, *hwagi*

5 – stone flakes, *baha* (for sago-scrapers)

6 – small sharp stones, *prisri* (for sago-scrapers)

7 – small shellrings, Malaysian beads, iron axes (1950)

8 – furs, feathers, net bags, etc.

9 – hourglass drums

Plus a number of objects and goods of generalized production

Torricelli Range

KWOMTARI

Bapi River

HILLS

PLAIN

ERI

Akraminag

Nabaneri

Amanab patrol post

Befan

Wamuru

Aynunkneri

Ibwagom

Muwagneri

Nayneri

Iframinag

Awenyak

Ifyeg

Nay

ANGGOR

Hugumon

WAINA

Umeda

Punda

Yafar

Potayneri

Babuk

Sowanda

sêh (safa)

Walsa

Waina-Wiyara

sêh (safa)

Ifêêg
Hubwiy

Kamberatoro Catholic mission

DERA

10 km

appreciated their Sowanda partners in the years the first steel tools began arriving from Dutch New Guinea; but from the moment they had sufficient stocks of their own (after working on plantations in the Bismarck Archipelago), there was no more need to continue relations with the Sowanda, a need felt all the less as the growing attraction of the modern world was contributing at the same time to the final loss of interest in traditional forms of exchange, which were not economically stimulating. The social function of *sêh* alliances was further weakened by pacification, since administrative control assuaged the uneasiness between two groups not linked by marriage alliances. This rapid decline of the *sêh* institution at the first signs of Western impact on the region also shows the fragility and relatively artificial character of an institution not legitimized by kinship or genuine economic need.

At the time the first Dutch axes were coming into the Walsa region (Waris linguistic group: Map 1), the Yafar had momentarily distanced themselves from the Sowanda, following a number of homicides. They therefore turned to the Walsa in order to obtain their first steel axes, without having to cross Sowanda territory, thanks to the mediation of the Hubwiy and the Ifêêg, two villages across the Irian Jaya border which had intermarried with certain Yafar clans. Hubwiy and Ifêêg already bartered with the Walsa, but they did not undertake matrimonial exchanges until more recently. It was through this geographical and social detour that the Yafar obtained their first axes in exchange for yam cuttings.[6] Although they had no official partners among the Walsa, except through the intermediary of their allies on the other side of the border, they nevertheless used the term *safa* to designate those with whom they bartered, probably the Waris equivalent of *sêh*. Their last expedition took place in 1960, at the time the Amanab patrol post was being built.

---

6. Following a series of clashes with Dutch patrols, many Walsa had been jailed in Waris or Hollandia. They had now returned to their villages and did not have any yam cuttings after this several-year break in their horticulture; it was at this time that the Yafar were seeking to procure axes.

Bridewealth and Shellrings

In a later chapter, we shall see that Yafar marriage is not validated by bridewealth but simply by limited exchanges of food and *ag* between the father-in-law and his son-in-law, and especially between brothers-in-law. There never was, then, a special category of goods, a 'money' used specifically for acquiring a wife; the same holds for all central, northern and western Eri. In these regions, the young groom's gifts and the countergifts from his wife's family are made in the course of generalized exchanges within the kinship network (the new in-laws are usually already related) or inaugurate the new relations that will bind the two families.

On the other hand, before the advent of colonial control, the eastern Eri (Akraminaag, Nabaneri, Yumor, Nay) used among themselves and with the Kwomtari-speaking villages in the plain bridewealth consisting of large shellrings (*kir*) brought in from the Torricelli Range. These rings – which could be worn as ornaments, but were above all accumulated with a view to future marriages – were presented to the woman's father or brother strung on a stick the same height as the bride. This might indicate a preference for tall women, but it is also a way of preventing bridewealth inflation, always a possibility with the new supplies of *kir* arriving along the exchange routes.[7]

Exchange Routes

In the discussion of generalized exchange among kin, I showed how economic need 'aspirated' an object in one or more directions in a radiating pattern. Logically one may deduce from this observation that if there is large-scale production, the goods can go further than if production is limited, for the village receiving a certain category of objects passes them on only if it has a sufficient supply, and it is the surplus that permits the extension of the exchange route. Now it appears that no item is produced in large quantities in the part of the Border Mountains that concerns

---

7. I do not have much information on this subject. Today the eastern Eri have very few *kir* and use them only for personal adornment. First steel tools and then money replaced the rings in marriage transactions.

us here. The only objects transported over long distances are sea-shells and glass beads, but as we have said, the Eri and the Waina are geographically marginal to these networks.

Whether these are small local routes taken by *baha* flakes, *maar* and *prisri* stones, river shells or netbags and drums, or major routes from the coast, what makes it possible to speak of a 'route', that is a chain of people transmitting the same objects over a certain distance, concerns only one direction of exchange. It is only the *baha* flake or the *kir* ring that is going to determine the route, whereas what circulates in the opposite direction is made up of various one-time gifts used to pay for one leg of the flake or the ring.

Objects transmitted over long distances can be involved indifferently in generalized exchange, barter between *sêh* partners or between occasional partners, or even at a given moment be part of a marriage payment. Their progress is relatively independent of the mode of exchange. Moreover, societies in which the form of marriage calls for the accumulation of great quantities of rings are an obstacle to the extension of exchange routes beyond their own geographical position, for the influx of more rings threatens to produce regional inflation; this surplus would then enter the local circuit instead of being passed on.

The varying importance (in length but also in the quantity of goods) of the exchange routes further shows that there is no difference in nature between occasional exchanges and the transactions or gifts that make up a 'route'. As soon as one type of object has a tendency to go beyond the immediate gift and its recipient seeks to pass it along, there is the beginning of an exchange route. On the other hand, an object which 'creates the route' by being passed on several times in a given direction does not have the same function as an object which is given only once, or even several times but with no fixed orientation and which is merely part of a local kinship or marriage network. As we have said, it is most often this second category of objects which, through exchanges, enables the first type of goods to be passed along.

What seems to characterize Eri exchange is the fact that the object is never consciously intended for a group or even an individual situated geographically or socially beyond the immediate receiver. Or if the giver suspects that the object will be passed along, he does not care, because he sees the transmission of the item as a personal transaction. Whether it is a free gift to a relative, a marriage payment or an exchange between *sêh*, the operation is always situated in a specific interpersonal social context and is part of the history of the individuals involved, and only secondarily of that of the groups. But – and herein lies the paradox of the existence of long pathways of objects crossing a country made up of microsocieties with no other form of communication between them – this personalization of exchanges, stemming from the principle of transmission chains, in no way hampers the supplying of remote regions with 'foreign' products.

In the end, the whole dialectic of exchange in this region reflects the opposition between economic and social functions, between use-value and exchange-value. We see that exchange between individuals or between links of a 'route' arise more from the need to obey social (kinship) and affective imperatives, but that it is precisely the dominance of social considerations which enables the basic economic function to be fully realized between remote or terminal links in the chain. The man at the end of the road who receives an adze blade and hafts it for his own use thus becomes economically linked with the man at the opposite end of the chain who extracted the stone and set out to shape it. However, this economically crucial and humanly non-existent link was made possible by the mediation of a certain number of highly socialized interpersonal exchanges which had no immediate techno-economic function of their own.

Part III

Sexuality, Symbolic Reproduction and Social Continuity

One element is missing from this part of our study and that is the analysis of Yafar dual organization, which I preferred to place at the beginning of the book (Ch. 2). This is because it was necessary to circumscribe the group structures I would be dealing with as early as possible in the study, and as dualism is one of the keys to the Yafar conceptual system, I did not want to wait until now to discuss its importance. In the pages that follow, I will therefore ask the reader to keep in mind that the society as a whole is often the expression of reproductive sexuality through the indivisible unity guaranteed by its 'male' and 'female' moieties, and that while the exchange of women, the stability of marriage and the organization of power ensure the social 'reproduction' or continuity of the community, dualism assures its symbolic reproduction.

Yet this last expression of social continuity is a static one. Inscribed in synchrony, even though originating in mythology, it states that the living social unit is based on the pairing of the sexual principles. This is not the case with the apparatus of marriage and social ontogeny. The first lays out simultaneously, in both social space and social time, its exchange strategy, which is a prisoner of the system of kinship compatibilities; the second places milestones along the linear lifetime of the individual, marking off the steps in his or her socialization against the less-differentiated backdrop of inborn identity. But silently, behind these ongoing attempts at social construction, outside the bounds of ll social communication, another principle is at work: the occult control of the powers of nature. Socially repressed, these hidden powers seek to ensure that the society holds its place in the universe as well as maintaining its relationship with primordial fertility. Since these powers operate deep within the culture, all that appears on the surface is their profane manifestation, that of the mundane dialogue between the medium and the spirits of the dead. But social continuity implies biological reproduction, and therefore this part of the book opens with an attempt to apprehend Yafar sexuality on both sociological and symbolic levels.

9

Sexuality, Procreation and Powers

A young man, Pêpi, came to the women's village. He surprised them
in the act of preparing the [Yangis] festival; he watched them making
the masks, preparing the colours, painting their bodies. He climbed
a breadfruit tree and hid there. Oög-angô arrived and entered the
river to wash off her paint. She noticed Pêpi's reflection in the water
and raised her head. He came down and the two copulated. . .

(From a myth)

Sexuality and Fertility

To devote an entire chapter to sexuality is something of a wager
when, in the society under study, sexual notions and practices are
governed by rigorous taboos, a strict moral code and tight control
of language. Despite my many stays with the Yafar, I was never
able to broach the subject openly, and any attempt at an interview, even non-personal, had to be broken off after a short time.

This restraint applies both to sexuality itself and to the individual social situations in which it appears. Social control proper
is obviously maintained through the control of communication;
yet we shall see later that, beyond a certain threshold of no
return, information may break into the open and sometimes
exceed the reality of the facts. Another type of restriction, this
time linguistic, continuously blocks the use of words to different
degrees, depending on context. It is from this angle that we can
grasp something of the 'sacred' aura surrounding sexuality when
it is thought of as the means of reproduction. In effect, while the
basically anatomic terms designating the genitalia (as well as the
general verb for 'to copulate') are tolerated as simple signs of
the morphological differentiation of the sexes or their relationship, words alluding more directly to procreation are prohibited
and replaced by euphemisms. At best they can be whispered,
in a spirit of complicity, out of both discretion and a taste for
transgression: 'semen, vaginal fluid, menstrual blood, uterus,
umbilical cord, placenta, amniotic sac', but also 'clitoris' (that

female phallic element that blurs categories), 'foreskin' (for symmetrical and inverse reasons) and 'glans' (because of its analogy with the sprout or the young plant shoot emerging from its sheath). On the other hand, these same terms show up regularly in spells associated with fertility. I have also heard a Yafar man (married and a ritual master), in good spirits and far from all women and the village, suddenly and repeatedly shout the word 'semen', as a challenge, this time fully assumed, to the whole forest. The same term can be used by a woman gravely to insult a man, something that formerly could have met with reprisals, perhaps a way of underlining the derisory part man has in the act of procreation. Generally speaking – as is the case for revealing religious exegeses which deal with cosmic sexuality and the reproduction of the primordial species – too much talk about sexuality spoils the hunter's luck (Ch. 7) or makes a man's garden unproductive: talk about fertility causes sterility.

Emotional restraint, the avoidance of words, the uncomfortable relationship of individuals and society as a whole with sexuality appear here as nothing other than a reflection of the sacredness that permeates the phenomena of reproduction, fertility or growth. Through the weight of words, sexuality, in the strict sense, is subordinated to procreation, from which it can be separated only with difficulty in the perceptions of the individual and society. Sexual intercourse, if only because of the reciprocal contact of sexual substances highly charged by their very nature and ill-defined origin with its intrinsic force, is too intimately bound up with fecundity to be able to break free and be regarded as an innocuous activity, a simple shared pleasure or a game.[1] Far from being the result of a moralistic sublimation which inhibits behaviours and language 'from above', this restraint seems to come 'from below', as the result of a more 'archaic' (in the psychoanalytic sense) fear of pollution, the effect of anxiety about too direct a contact with life-giving substances and its ill-assumed projection on to the social domain. It is therefore more than a question of 'puritanism': there is a permanent need for regulation and avoidance of nature's reproductive forces. It is primarily on this representation that Yafar sexual 'morals' are founded.

---

1. Here I am talking about the ideology of sexuality, as distinguished from its practice and from relations between the couple (see Juillerat 1990).

Let us now take a more sociological approach to the question. It is publicly recognized that sexuality is in a sense the monopoly of married adults. Premarital relations, if they occur, must be concealed, for they are often the occasion for rivalries. Society contrives to turn a blind eye to these internal disorders and to preserve its own cohesion. Through implicit consensus, talk of sexuality is also avoided because such conversation could lead to social conflict. Later we shall see that the sexual partners open to a man are very few. Despite the existence of more or less recognized furtive extramarital relations, a bachelor's sexual experiences remain limited and sporadic, and marriage sometimes brings together a man and a woman who, although they have been thrown together over a long period, have spent this time avoiding each other.

Hoofuk

It has become a truism to point out the importance of the plant kingdom and the reproductive processes found in nature in the symbolic representations of traditional agricultural societies. When a human group lives deep in the tropical rain forest and when its members spend much of their time manipulating cultigens, making cuttings, transplanting, weeding, harvesting and keeping a close eye on plant growth, fruiting, seed-germination and tuber-formation, it becomes even more obvious that this ecological framework and these technical interventions are going to form the permanent stock on which the imagination will draw to reconstruct a symbolically coherent cosmic and human order.

At the heart of this naturalized vision of reproduction, the Yafar place a key concept, which needs to be defined on several levels: *hoofuk* (< *hoof*). In its most common acceptation, *hoofuk* is the inside, the matter at the heart of an object, the inner stuff, that which cannot be seen from the outside; in this, the term is opposed, by simple substitution of the initial phoneme, to *roofuk* (< *roof*), meaning 'bark, envelope, skin'.[2] *Hoofuk* and *roofuk* both suppose a relatively soft material which decomposes easily. In this,

2. This conception of living matter recalls what Bachelard (1975: 98–102) terms 'the substantialist obstacle' which engenders a 'myth of the interior': the 'true' substance is within.

the pair of terms is opposed to another: *kêg/keeg*, the first meaning 'pit, bone' (as well as any hard, solid object associated with a place at the core of the whole) and conveying the idea of resistance to rotting (for example very hard wood), the second being translatable as 'shell (egg, coconut, etc.), palm sheath' and designating also any hard envelope to be discarded once it is empty (the hull of a sago palm, an empty tin can, an empty paper envelope). One last term is needed to complete this structural vision of living matter: *nihik*, 'flesh (of a fruit), meat (animal, fish, grubs, etc.)'. Yet the flesh of a (pitless) tuber is not *nihik* but *hoofuk*, like the heart of a palm tree. Fruit (*fôk*) is not *hoofuk*, but both its pit and its flesh are *nihik*.

In its botanical sense, *hoofuk* designates first of all the pith of palm trees, the sago palm in particular, and the flesh of taros and yams. In these cases, the *hoofuk* is white, or possibly yellow or very light pink when it has just been cut open. It is not insignificant that sago pith and tubers are the staples of the Yafar diet. But *hoofuk* is not associated with food alone, since there is *hoofuk* at the heart of all tree trunks, at the centre of the concentric growth rings, and a banana tree's *hoofuk* (as for palm trees) is found at the core of its stem and not in its fruit. The common point that can be gathered from these examples is that *hoofuk* is associated with the central and often vertical element of plants (whether or not they are edible) and is present in or designates the material which fills this part of the plant. Now the volume of this material increases as the plant grows, and that is where the living matter is made, at least in so far as quantity is concerned. Seen from this perspective, *hoofuk* also takes on a more abstract meaning and becomes the very principle of this growth, or the invisible substance which, at the outset (in the seed or the shoot), will enable future development to take place.

Animal and human *hoofuk* exists on two registers that need to be distinguished. The first corresponds to the image of plant *hoofuk*, filling and animating the central vertical axis. This *hoofuk* is associated with the digestive tract, with the idea of its renewal by food and its loss by the evacuation of faeces (diarrhoea carries away a great deal of *hoofuk* at one time and weakens the subject). The second register of human (and animal) *hoofuk* is that of sexual reproduction: in men as well as in women – but more emphatically in the latter – *hoofuk* is present in the sexual and reproductive substances. Semen, secretions and menstrual blood are not themselves *hoofuk*, but they contain it (it is hard to say whether the Yafar see it as a material essence or merely a principle). On the other hand, women from puberty to menopause have in their uterus a substance which is female *hoofuk*.[3] It seems that the Yafar see this as *hoofuk par excellence*, the source of life but also of the pollution men must fear from sexual intercourse or 'contact' with menstrual blood. A woman's *hoofuk* may be more or less fertile. The best *hoofuk* is white (*busuk*), and women with this *hoofuk* get pregnant easily and often; red *hoofuk* (*abuk*) is less effective, and many sexual acts are needed to make a woman with this sort of *hoofuk* pregnant (comparison is often drawn with the fertility of a garden). Lastly, women who are sterile or have reached menopause have black *hoofuk* (*önguk*). It is also said that their *hoofuk* is 'hard(ened)' (*kêfutuk*), whereas young *hoofuk* is 'soft' (*mêsik*). Menstrual flow also depends on the fluidity of the *hoofuk*, and the woman who loses a lot of blood in childbirth is thought to have runny *hoofuk*, which is compared with 'fire' (*suwê*); the parturient who loses little blood has, conversely, 'firmer' *hoofuk*; she is said to 'keep her *hoofuk*'.

The relation between *hoofuk* and blood (*taf*) appears to be at once complementary and antagonistic. The word *taf* is often used as a generic euphemism for menstrual flow, female *hoofuk* and semen. It is also in this sense that the Yafar say of themselves that they 'come from the blood' or that they are the 'children of the blood'. Yet in the framework of the categories into which nature is divided, *taf* is connected with game, while *hoofuk* is associated with sago and garden products. It is also said, however, that both *taf* and *hoofuk* are present and complementary in all living beings, including plants: certain pink-fleshed yams, sago that turns red on contact with the air, varieties of red banana and especially pandanus fruit are proof of the presence of 'blood'. In humans, a balance must be struck between the two elements: 'Blood goes first, *hoofuk* follows.' Old age occasions the slowing and thickening of the blood, causing the *hoofuk* to become too 'heavy' (*hoofuk kinim*). In this case, there is too much *hoofuk*, which brings on such symptoms as shortness of breath and a feeling of oppression in

---

3. When I presented the scientific theory of the subject to my best informant, he immediately identified the ovum with *hoofuk*, concluding that the Western and Yafar theories were the same.

the chest.[4] The temperature of an individual's *hoofuk* also determines his or her health: it should be warm, for 'hot *hoofuk*' (*nöruk-
na hoofuk*) causes illness and 'cold *hoofuk*' (*hoofuk təgehraag*)
means death. In the plant kingdom a tuber with 'cold' *hoofuk* has
lost its nutritive substance.

The notion of *hoofuk* is also used in defining primordiality. The
earth, first of all, as the original maternal *materia*, contains the
primeval *hoofuk*, which is the condition, enhanced in planting
rites, for the growth of plants. The ocean (attested in mythology)
is believed to have come forth from the *hoofuk* (blood, semen, etc.)
of the primordial divine couplings (Ch. 2) and is for this reason
called *kêfutuk buu*, 'firm (but also 'sacred') water'.

Next the mythic places, particularly those located underground
(galleries, etc.), contain original cosmic maternal or paternal *hoofuk*, which can be found in the form respectively of large deposits
of kaolin or whitish seepage. Red ochre comes from the blood of
the first female divinities. A recent Cargo Cult from western New
Guinea promises access to an underground place where the dead
of the Yafar live as guardians of the 'cargo'; this location is also
described as the 'original place' (*mwig kəbik*, or *as ples* in pidgin),
or as the 'place of the original kaolinic *hoofuk*' (*mwig rabô hoofuk
kəbik*). *Rabô* means 'kaolin' or 'white paint', and in Yafar paintings
– on masks or on the bodies of the dancers in fertility rituals – the
colour white represents *hoofuk* as the source of life. More generally, the ritual or profane personal decorations worn by men (and
to a lesser extent women) to enhance their appearance (paint, pig
fat, ornamentation) are referred to as *hoofuk*, and a man decorated
in this manner is 'like fire' (fire = blood), 'he is *hoofuk*' (*hoofuk ehe*),
whereas a man whose skin is dry and dull is 'like ashes' (also
seen as the *roofuk* of fire). In this instance, cosmetics act as metaphors for life-giving body substances, and it is through these that
men both communicate with the gods and seek to please women.

The word *hoofuk* is also pronounced over and over in the fertility spells with a sometimes male, sometimes female connotation,
the two often being paired, in association with the names of cosmogonic divinities, parts of the body, sexual fluids, sweat, blood
and mythic places. Lastly, this same concept is used to define the
sources of the esoteric knowledge handed down through certain

---

4. See also below, the symptoms of the man polluted by menstrual blood and, in Ch.
12, the signs of approaching death and its immediate causes.

lines as well as the exegetical versions of myths. In this case it carries the sense of first cause, true origin, metaphysical truth. Like the Waina-speaking groups (of whom the Umeda are the 'mother' group), the Yafar speak of themselves as being 'in *hoofuk*' (*hoofuk-wa-inaag*), in other words in contact, by means of religious knowledge, with life and its origins.[5] Their sago palms are held to be more productive, while the other tribes 'on the periphery' (*magig-aynaag*) are judged to be less favoured.

From its most concrete acceptations to its most figurative meaning, by way of the designation of imaginary substances, this notion is an integral part of a structured substantialist view of living matter in which the centre contains and retains the source of life, while the exterior – the *roofuk* – is only an outer protection which must be shed (materially or magically) in order to reach the *hoofuk* and enable its reproduction.[6] This sense of the *hoofuk–roofuk* opposition can be found in the metaphor used by Yafar experts to distinguish the many profane versions of esoteric knowledge myths, which are both the source and the explanation of this opposition. They say that the first are like the intertwined runners of the yam (*roofuk*), the second like the yam's flesh (*hoofuk*) which remains buried and which one must dig down to in order to understand (see Juillerat 1991a: Introduction). The two semantic categories to which the term refers – i.e. a (partially imaginary) physical structure of matter on the one hand, and the (more or less materialized) principles of sexual reproduction on the other – coincide only very approximately. For the plant kingdom, in particular, misinterpretation of the processes of sexual reproduction in plants locates the *hoofuk* restrictively in the vertical axis of the plant, by confusing the sap or the water absorbed from the ground with the life-giving reproductive substance. The status of the flower and the fruit are ill defined but are sometimes (in the case of coconuts at any rate) related to milk-filled breasts, and seeds germinate only when acted on by a *hoofuk* belatedly acquired who knows how. For clones, the Yafar vision is much more consistent, since it is from the tuber or the base of the stem – and therefore from the material *hoofuk* itself – that the young shoot emerges. In the case of humans (and mammals), the idea

5. By extension, access to the wealth of industrial production ('cargo') is defined by the same phrase, which comes close to our concept of (material) wealth.
6. Similar substantialist notions are attested in pre-scientific Western thought (Bachelard 1975).

of *hoofuk* acquires its full semantic weight only in the complementarity of the sexes, even if its female dimension is dominant: to the intrinsic sacredness of male or female *hoofuk* is added that of their conjoining in the act of procreation.

The Female Cycle

Conception

Like most Melanesian peoples, the Yafar consider that a certain number of sexual acts are needed to start a pregnancy. The frequency of a woman's pregnancies therefore depends not only on the quality of her *hoofuk*, but on her husband's assiduity as well. Moreover, Yafar men do not always agree among themselves on the responsibility that should be imputed to the man or the woman in the event of sterility. But the *quality* of the man's semen is never questioned.[7]

The embryo is made from the coagulation of the mother's *hoofuk* with the father's semen. Through his repeated interventions, the father is thought not only to cause the embryo to attach itself but later to help the foetus as it begins to take shape. I did not, however, find the idea that the father 'nourished' the foetus with his semen (Gell 1975). Nevertheless, as soon as the pregnancy becomes noticeable, sexual intercourse ceases and will not be resumed until the child is able to 'walk and play' and has therefore acquired the beginnings of autonomy from its mother. The interruption of menstruation is not divulged, except perhaps to a few other women; in principle the husband is not told right away, but he may notice that his wife no longer isolates herself periodically.

Let us pause a moment over the problem of the legitimacy of paternity that can arise, but rarely does, when a woman who has just been recognized to be pregnant loses her husband and remarries immediately. Only one case was brought to my attention, and the Yafar, aware of the problem this posed, maintained that it was the new husband who, having had numerous relations with the woman, was therefore the 'father', *awaag*, of the baby, whereas the deceased had just had time to start the pregnancy. The son that was born therefore belonged to the lineage of his

---

7. For a comparative discussion of these notions, see Héritier 1984.

adoptive father, *at*, whom he called *aya* (dad). It is obvious in such a case that the determination of filiation by the theory of conception is overlaid with socio-economic motives, in the first place the urgent need to remarry the pregnant widow (who will need a husband to provide for her while she carries the child and nurses it), and in the second place the preference for attributing social paternity to the one who is going to raise the child rather than to a dead genitor. The second argument assumes particular importance if the woman changes residence with the new marriage and if, as a consequence, her son will receive land-holding rights through his mother's husband (Ch. 5). Nevertheless social advantage does not *explain* the Yafar theory of biological paternity, it merely advances it. To my mind it is not the social function, in this case, which explains the cultural theory: this is directly determined by a representation constructed from the experience and its symbolization. Nevertheless it could be said that the sexual diligence of the new husband also appears as a claim to the paternity of the child (see Douglas 1975).

Yafar ideas about foetal growth do not seem to result in a complex, or even a very confident theory. Furthermore the fact that this kind of knowledge, closely related to the religious, is kept secret by *aynaag* and the masters of fertility (Ch. 13) tends considerably to limit the anthropologist's access. Nevertheless, everyone seems more or less to adhere to the idea that first the blood, *taf*, is formed (it is not clear if *taf* is to be taken here in the metaphorical sense of *hoofuk*) and then the eyes and the head. Next comes the trunk and last of all the limbs. Generally speaking, the bones are believed to be formed first, then the mother 'adds' the flesh (*nihik*) and finally the skin (*roofuk*) 'to protect her child'. The umbilicus closes the finished body; in the sacred *sangêk* songs of the Yangis fertility ritual, one series opens with an evocation of the 'eyes' (*nofuk*) and closes with a representation of the navel (*mosuwô*), the whole apparently recreating, by means of animal and plant metaphors, the formation of the embryo. The now classic opposition between mother's blood (and flesh) and father's bones remains implicit and is not incorporated into the theory of procreation. In a general way, the Yafar associate hard, rot-resistant materials with maleness (hard woods, bones) and blood and materials subject to putrefaction with femaleness, but they do not claim that it is the father alone who gives the child its bones and the mother alone its blood or its flesh, even though people sometimes speak of the 'father's bones' (*aya na kêg*). Here, as in other areas, the Yafar view seems concerned to play down the antagonism between the genders and to dilute it in a more subtle acceptation: *hoofuk* is female *and* male, and so are blood and bones. These few notions that I was able to gather must be set against a backdrop of marked agnosticism, especially in the young men. The Yafar first claim ignorance, then curiosity to know more. 'How can we find out. . .', they ask, but they also add that they have sometimes seen the foetuses of animals killed by hunters, and it is from this experience that they try to imagine how it is with humans. Nevertheless despite their observations of nature, the mystery of procreation remains whole, as it was for the Western world before the discoveries of modern genetics in the second half of the nineteenth century.

Childbirth

Only the last weeks of pregnancy are marked by food taboos,[8] which are maintained throughout the breast-feeding period and until the child begins to chatter. The woman continues all her household activities until the start of labour. When the time comes, she isolates herself in the *mogasəgaw*, the space under the house, or the ground floor (Ch. 4). Sitting on a *kəfe*, an areca sheath normally used as a sleeping mat, she keeps a fire going by her side. In the daytime, only one woman usually keeps her company, to help with the birth if necessary. If the birth takes place in the evening or at night, one or two other women may be present. No man enters the *mogasəgaw* or even speaks of the parturient or the child. The situation is voluntarily concealed by the men, and the father himself does not mention it or acts embarrassed if he is questioned.

The woman gives birth in a squatting position and, if she is able, receives her child in her own hands. The other woman or women present – relatives or neighbours who have already had children – intervene only if needed (for instance to press on the

---

8. Coconut, pandanus and other red foods, turtle meat, flesh of the hornbill: besides the dangers of too much blood, of haemorrhages, punishment for violating these taboos might take the form of an illness that will strike the child with an affliction reminiscent of the morphological features of the animal.

Plate 17. A mother and her newborn child in isolation under the floor of her house.

woman's abdomen while squatting behind her[9] or to attempt to manipulate an infant which is in a bad position). When the child is born, one of the women takes it from the mother's hands and cleans it off with rough leaves.[10] Informants always mention the notion of 'sloughing' in this operation, since the 'filth' (*nǝfweh*) that coats the newborn is also called *arfêêg* 'outer skin, sloughed skin of a reptile'. In principle it is the mother who cuts the umbilical cord with a bamboo knife, about eight centimetres from the body. If the afterbirth does not descend easily, the parturient

9. The Yafar claim that in doing this they are copying the behaviour of frogs, in which the male bestrides the female and helps her lay her eggs. They seem unaware, however, that the male fertilizes the eggs at the same time.

10. No one botanical species is particularly recommended; they use rough-leaved plants found widely in secondary growth, such as *Ageratum conyzoides* and *Coleus scutellarioides* (*ahnam-bǝgo*).

herself pulls it out with her foot after wrapping the end of the cord around her big toe. Her abdomen may be massaged, as described above, to help the delivery. The placenta is placed in a *sööbi* (a container made from sheaths of the areca palm) and buried in the forest on the outskirts of the village. It is thought that if the child is not born when the waters are lost (*kwakerebuk*) it may die; on the other hand, if it comes right after the waters it will be strong. If it cries as soon as it is born it is a sign that it will die later in its village; if the child takes long to cry it is doused with cold water to make it react. The Yafar say that if the placenta does not come within two days, it will make the woman die; this situation is attributed to sorcery (*agi* or *aysiri*), or more rarely to the *nabasa* and *sawangô* forest spirits. In this case the parturient is treated by the application of hot leaf compresses (*bosif*), by washing with hot water and, to ease the pain, by friction (very common in native therapies) with stinging leaves of the *kwiy* (*Laportea* sp.). Similarly to encourage the descent of the child or the afterbirth (*mosuwamp*), magic interventions may be undertaken by a man (usually the woman's father or brother rather than her husband); the parturient is made to drink water collected from a waterfall (an analogy with the idea of evacuation) while spells are recited evoking a sequence from a myth.[11] The afterbirth and the *kɔfe* are buried in the forest. One of the women present at the birth will become something like the child's godmother and will entertain *segwaag* exchange relations with him or her (see Ch. 11). A coconut tree is planted near the house for the child.

Following the birth, mother and child remain isolated in the *mogasɔgaw* until the new moon (when the birth occurs at the end of a cycle, the seclusion covers the whole of the next moon); the isolation period thus lasts from two to four weeks. During this time, the mother receives few visits and those exclusively from women bringing her food. Nevertheless she is able to talk with her husband and the other members of the household through the floor. These also pass her food, tobacco, areca nuts, etc. through a hole made for this purpose. She occupies her time

11. Someone lists the names of rivers and imitates the sound of pouring water. *Nabasa* can also be held responsible for a difficult delivery; these spirits of the dead are suspected of wanting to hold on to the food (sago palms, etc.) that the child to come will one day take from them. And so water is fetched from a hole dug in the river bank near the *nabasa*'s (father or grandfather of the wife or her husband) home and given to the parturient to drink. The corresponding myth is analysed in Juillerat 1991a, Ch. 2.

by making net objects; she eats a normal diet, but consumes more sago salt, *sake*, than usual; the aim of this seems to be to warm up her body, which 'cooled down' with the birth. The mother keeps the child on her lap and nurses it on demand (the child is put to the breast as soon as it is born).

The long isolation of the new mother and her baby protects the husband, the other men and the whole village group from contamination (*heyfu*) by the *hoofuk* or the *mosuwô taf* ('umbilical cord blood') which have been spilled and with which the child is still coated. It is said of the infant that it is *taf-na*, 'with blood', and its father can under no circumstances touch it until the mother and child have emerged from seclusion, bathed in the river and rejoined the family group. As during her periods, the woman cannot cook for her husband or other male relatives (see below). She is still highly charged with *hoofuk* and is therefore 'polluting'.[12] As she is dangerous, she must be physically isolated for a time, placed outside the social circuit, sexually prohibited. Because of its identification with the mother, the child undergoes the same treatment and enters life by way of this sort of rite of passage which, by extending the child's symbiosis with its mother beyond birth, begins by making it an outcast. No one comes to see the child, much less touch it; it has not yet been named, and people pretend to ignore its existence and even its sex (Ch. 12). Its father – the reverse of the *couvade* – goes about his daily affairs and continues to live in the village without a word about his wife or child, and no one asks about them. The husband's 'disidentification' with the new mother and her child enables him to keep his masculine identity intact and protect it from the female–maternal principle, whose contact, even in a figurative sense, would cause his self (*sungwaag*) to 'ripen' (see Chs 7, 12 and 14) and make him vulnerable to sorcery. This is also a way society has of separating the sexes and their respective roles at these intrinsically female times: the man relinquishes to his wife that which is hers by nature, postponing his own socializing intervention of appropriating the child by filiation.

---

12. The expression *amtaag-wa-inaag* 'in [that which is] bad' is also applied to a menstruating woman or a new mother, to a couple who have just had sexual intercourse and to the protagonists of an *agi* rite for undoing an evil spell of the same name (Ch. 14). All are implicitly connected with 'cold', hence their exclusion from 'hot' activities: fishing with toxic plants, hunting, making musical instruments, etc.

Women's Fertility, Men's Magic

The Social Modalities of Female Pollution

Because they contain within their body the most powerful part of *hoofuk*, which not only enables them to conceive the embryo but also to make the whole child, give birth to it and then nurse it, women undeniably possess a natural force that men lack. In men's eyes – and in those of the culture as a whole, founded primarily on a viricentric view of the world – women therefore carry a power that is held in awe because it is not shared and not controlled cognitively. It should be remembered that even women are obliged to protect themselves from an excess of 'blood' by forgoing certain red foods. I am not saying that Yafar men 'envy' the women's procreative power, nor that they seek to reproduce upon their own bodies something resembling menstruation or pregnancy (Bettleheim 1954; Hogbin 1970). On the contrary, while they show their recognition of women's power by not talking about it (the paradox here is only apparent, and the taboos surrounding female fertility only confirm this recognition), they hotly defend their own virility; but they press their claim in an indirect (sublimated) manner through violent action (hunting, formerly homicide, stick fights, more or less stereotyped expressions of anger, etc.) and by a conventional misogynistic discourse. Threatened with immanent danger from female *hoofuk*, the man reacts in two ways: he protects himself by distance, and he tries to control and turn it to his advantage through magic. Let us take these two strategies in turn.

There are three circumstances in which a man may come into (direct or mediated) contact with female *hoofuk* and consequently be contaminated by pollution, *heyfu*: sexual intercourse, those times when *hoofuk* (or blood) flows from the woman's body, in other words menstrual periods and childbirth. The distance maintained with respect to intercourse takes the shape of adolescents' and bachelors' fears of sexuality and the non-valorization of the sexual act in favour of a narcissistic male image.

The material conditions of the distance established by a man in order to protect himself from a menstruating woman or a parturient consist, as we have seen, in temporarily desocializing the woman by isolating her from the household and the village community under the house, or in a bush shelter if the family is camped far from the village at the time. There is no question of a menstruating woman or a new mother taking up quarters in the cultivated portion of a clearing that is still producing: the blood spilled would 'attract wild pigs', which would lay waste to the crops. To the spatial and corporal distance is added a culinary separation, since the woman no longer cooks for her husband and, as she cannot go to the gardens, no longer brings him raw food either. Furthermore she cannot do any harvesting. The man cooks his own meals or is given food by a relative. In effect, raw food can carry *heyfu*, as can, to a lesser extent, water drawn by a woman who is menstruating or has just given birth. Firewood gathered by a woman in one of these states and used for cooking is another good mediator of pollution, but it is especially the fire itself, lit by a woman in a state of impurity, that is a conductor (even if the food is actually cooked by someone else), for fire is associated with female blood; fire was created during sexual intercourse between the divine couple W. . . and B. . . (Ch. 2) or, according to other versions, from B. . .'s menstrual blood. Food cooked on the fire of a menstruating woman is therefore said to be *heyfu-suwê-inaag* 'in the fire of female pollution'. A *heyfu-inaag* woman cannot look on the masks if a ritual is held during her isolation, nor peek inside a drum being made (it would not have a good sound), nor touch a bow (it would not shoot true), nor be present at the preparation and use of fish poisons (they would lose their 'heat'). Taboos on objects or male techniques also apply to couples who have just had sexual intercourse, pregnant women and sometimes women in general (it is considered unlucky for these categories of people to step over these objects).

The taboo on cooking for her husband remains in effect for a day after the end of a woman's period (or the parturient's purification). The wife's reintegration into the household at the end of her period is marked by washing (she washes her hands before cooking food again) and discarding in the forest the mat, *kəfe*, on which she sat.

It is said of the victim contaminated by female *heyfu* that the '*heyfu* acts' (*heyfu o-fe*) on him and that his 'body' becomes 'ill' (*êrik abôgêk*). The symptoms of *heyfu* are a chronic cough and difficulty in breathing.[13] Old men's bronchitis is often regarded

---

13. This symptom, often associated in Melanesia with menstrual pollution, refers implicitly to the idea of inhaling polluting emanations (*suweegik*).

as the inevitable mark of the contamination of all married men. Women are more generally supposed to weaken men by sexual intercourse, but they do not cause his *sungwaag* to 'ripen' (Ch. 12). Unlike their Umeda neighbours, however, who maintain that 'women kill men and men kill women' (Gell 1975: 115), the Yafar do not recognize the reverse. Theoretically there is no cure for *heyfu*. Sometimes a rite is tried, but with little hope of success. The subject goes down to the river and drinks water drawn by women (unspecified relatives); as the sick man runs back to the village, the children follow him mimicking his cough and shouting 'Here he comes, here he comes!' The children's voices are a bit like the pure deriding the impure, while the water that has been drunk appears as a purification, the effectiveness of which is believed to be ensured by the fact that it was given by the only ones who could perhaps control the impurity or remove it.

But the transmission of *heyfu* has its modalities, in which, it seems to me, lies the originality of the Yafar system of female pollution. These modalities are three in number: a) men are not the only ones vulnerable to *heyfu*; b) vulnerability depends on the kinship relation between the subject (man or woman) and the impure woman; c) there are varying degrees of vulnerability.

Table 12 places a few women among those individuals susceptible to contamination by food prepared by a woman who is menstruating or has just given birth: the woman's mother and grandmother, her aunts, her mother-in-law, her daughter-in-law. These female relatives cannot eat food prepared or given by a woman during her period or immediately after the birth of a child, but they may approach her and enter the *mogasəgaw*, something men cannot do. Conversely, the (real or classificatory) sons, nephew, grandsons, brothers and first cousins need not fear eating food prepared by a *heyfu-inaag* woman. To explain the absence of a taboo for the latter categories of kin, the Yafar call upon the notion of 'one blood' (*mungwô taf*, or *wan blut* in pidgin): the son or the brother is not afraid of *heyfu* because both come from the same blood as *heyfu-inaag* woman. This sameness renders him invulnerable (*kêfutuk* 'strong') because he cannot be contaminated by his own blood. The same isomorphism connects him with his grandmothers, aunts, uncles and first cousins. But the contagion is not neutralized reciprocally, which is why, in order to understand the system, one more parameter is needed, that of generation. The contagion is not passed from one gene-

Not vulnerable to *heyfu*	Vulnerable to *heyfu*
	female ego
Siblings of both sexes	Father and father's brother
(*eteeg/sumnik; nisak*)	(*awaag*)
First cross cousins	Mother and mother's sister
(*magawô*)	(*afaag*)
First parallel cousin	Mother's brother
(*nisak, haneruk*)	(*nonoog*)
Son, daughter	Father's sister
(*reeg, röögunguk*)	(*amagunguk*)
Brother's son/daughter	Grandparents
(*amagunguk*)	(*abiniga*)
Sister's son/daughter	Husband, husband's brother
(*reeg/röögunguk*)	(*rôgaag, riyagunguk*)
Grandsons/granddaughters	Husbands parents and grandparents
(*abiniga*)	(*kowaag*)
Sisters-in-law	Son- and daughter-in-law
(*maminiga*)	(*kowaag*)
	Any male outsider

For the vernacular terms, see Appendix C.

Table 12. Modalities of vulnerability to female pollution

ration to the following or between consanguines of the same generation; on the other hand, *heyfu* can be caught in the opposite direction, from a daughter by her mother, father, grandparents and their collaterals, despite having the same blood. Affines are, by definition, of 'another blood' (*ming taf*) and therefore the most susceptible to being stricken with *heyfu*. The husband heads this hierarchy of vulnerability, and it is no doubt his sexual and spatial closeness that requires him to take special precautions. Repeated sexual intercourse does not give him immunity to his wife's *hoofuk*. The only exception among the affines is the sister-in-law (*maminiga*, HZ or BW); as a woman of the same generation, she appears to be assimilated to a sister and can without risk accept *heyfu*-carrying food. It is no doubt the institution of sister exchange that makes these two women 'symbolic consanguines', since they regard each other as 'classificatory sisters', *haneruk*, and feel united by a privileged tie.

The materials to which anthropology has accustomed us when dealing with the taboo on female blood are founded primarily on gender opposition. The Yafar model does not neglect this antagonism, quite the contrary, but it is placed exclusively on a general level. The *generalized* fear men have of menstruating women or parturients is an ideological backdrop, based on the collective representations of reproduction, against which are silhouetted particular kinship relations that modify the structure of this representation and attenuate its dichotomy. The Yafar strategy for protection from female blood must therefore be read on two registers, the first, more biological, built on the physiological difference between the sexes, the second, more integrated with society, constructed simultaneously on the principle of consanguinity and on a temporal vision of reproduction, that of the irreversible flow of generations. Let us pause for a closer look at the last two principles.

The notion of 'one blood' refers to the transmission of blood according to symbolic uterine descent; but practice does not seem to respect *stricto sensu* transmission uniquely through women (patrilateral cousins, for example, are also resistant to *heyfu*, but here the classification is modified by the criterion of generation). The same principle is used to define the social and kin-related rules of shame: modest behaviour is required in front of strangers and affines of the opposite sex, but not (or much less) between close consanguineal relatives. The sharing of 'one blood' removes the obligation of modesty, and a man may go naked in front of his sister, mother or daughter (and inversely), whereas he cannot in front of his sister-in-law, daughter-in-law or mother-in-law, nor even theoretically in front of his wife. This is something like the principle at work in the sociosymbolic management of female blood, since in both situations avoidance applies to distant relatives (remote consanguines or affines), whereas proximity stemming from sameness of blood dedramatizes the relationship and, setting aside the fear of incest, abolishes the risks of both sexuality and pollution.

The second principle in the social management of female pollution is based on empirical view of the transmission of life from one generation to the next, of *descent*. This temporal order of reproduction is an irreversible one-way street, and the disorder suggested by even the symbolic implementation of a reverse filiation, in which life-giving substances and principles pass from the 'children' to the 'parents', is avoided by the establishment of taboos not only on female blood, which, in the category of close consanguines, contaminates only when it flows back up the generations, but also on the eating of foods when two generations are involved. Chapter 11 provides a more detailed analysis of the rules governing the filtering and consumption of red pandanus, but the parallel with female blood needs to be mentioned here: in effect, pandanus can be consumed only among members of the same generation. Furthermore, a man or woman may not consume the pandanus, coconuts or sago of one of their children; they cannot receive a tree planted by one of their children, nephews, etc. The punishment for violating this taboo would fall on the person of the ascending generation (weight loss) just as, in the case of menstrual blood and in the order of generations, only the relative from the ascending generation is vulnerable to *heyfu*. The notion of immunization – or mithridatization (Héritier 1984) – can also help understand the non-reversibility of the transmission of pollution, but to me the concepts of descent and the transgenerational flow of life appear crucial.[14]

The woman's power of procreation is thus the object of representation and of ambivalent social experience: it is the keystone of the fundamental antagonism between the sexes, of their irreconcilable natures. At the same time, however, the mother's *hoofuk* and blood are the bond between generations and between consanguines; *hoofuk* 'flows', as it were, down through social time and ensures that descent takes place where and in the direction in which contamination is not to be feared. *Hoofuk*, as the transmittable power of fecundity, circulates in the opposite direction from pollution. It is the improper social use of menstrual blood that makes these materials dangerous. But to my mind, if the society used reproductive substances in constructing a socialized order, it must be because these substances, by their very nature, possess special symbolic weight. The social order does not explain why female blood is so charged with meaning; on the contrary, it is because the processes of reproduction, and particularly the female cycle, are experienced as major events, repetitive and rationally irreducible, that men feel the need to bring them under their own control and to socialize them.[15]

14. F. Héritier tells me that very similar conceptions (danger of the daughter contaminating the mother, sexual taboo for parents when their daughter reaches puberty) have been described by M. Wilson for an African society (1957: 115–16). See also Héritier 1984: 143–6.
15. This remark suggests reservations about Douglas' sociologically oriented theses (see also Sahlins 1976, Vos 1975).

Now that we have seen how the community protects itself
against contamination from female blood, we will look at how it
turns the *hoofuk* contained in this blood to its own advantage.
Once again it is no longer consanguinity or descent that intervenes but the basic antagonism between the sexes. The ambivalence
does not now lie in the social domain, but in the value or power –
good or bad – attributed to women's *hoofuk*: (supposedly) unbeknown to women, men recover as much as they can of their
wife's menstrual flow and use it in fertility magic, in particular
hunting ritual. It is not without significance that it is usually the
husband (i.e. the man with the most to fear from pollution) who
goes directly into the *mogasəgaw*, shortly after his wife has left, to
gather his provision of magic substance. This apparent contradiction can be explained by metonymy. All that remains of the
menstruating woman's presence are a few dark spots in the
dust; a good part of the blood was discarded with the *kəfe*, the
emanations surrounding the woman are gone, she has been reintegrated into society, and the *hoofuk* is so powerful that only
a minute amount is needed for the ritual to be effective.[16] Yet
it is the particularly dangerous character of the wife's menstrual blood that enhances the performance of the magic, to the
husband's benefit. The very effectiveness of the magic seems to
depend on the degree of potential pollution, and this, like the
latter, is determined by kinship.

Mixed with red ochre, animal blood and extracts of strong-
smelling rhizomes, and thus associated with the mythic blood
of the Primordial Mother and with her cosmic *hoofuk*, human
menstrual blood is used to redden the ground in planting rites
(Wabuminaag, Ch. 6), and the middle of the adolescents' sternum
in rites consecrating the young hunter. It is fed to hunting dogs in
their sago, mixed with the red paint used on masks or in the Yangis dancers' body paint and, in the ritual, is smeared on the tip of
a blunt arrow which is shot at the sun. In these magic mixtures,
the female blood is always the most secret ingredient, the one
that is not talked about, it is real blood that is copied by the red
colour of the ochre. All married men are acquainted with these
uses for their own hunting or their horticultural rites and may

---

16. That is why the placenta and the mother's blood cannot be used in magic. In particular the loss of a large amount of blood, called *yis bogo* 'sago-jelly marsh', is especially
dangerous for the husband and the rest of the woman's affines.

therefore carry around in their net bags, wrapped in leaves, a bit of earth darkened by their wife's last period; but only men of knowledge, *aynaag*, make use of menstrual blood in rituals.

In the same order of magic by the appropriate use of *hoofuk*, a piece of a son's umbilical cord is kept and dried, a minute amount of which will be given him to chew (as the Original Mother's *hoofuk*) together with betel and a sweet-smelling rhizome during a puberty rite. The apparent paradox consisting in ingesting a part of that which tied the young man to his mother in the course of a 'puberty rite', in other words a rite of separation from the mother, is illuminated by the idea that access to game supposes a link with the productive maternal forest land and that it is the real mother's *hoofuk* (the umbilical cord) which acts as mediator.

In order to include the social dialectic of the genders through the mediation of *hoofuk* and blood, one last issue needs to be raised, the classic question of Melanesian specialists: if men both fear and admire women's power of procreation, what about women's attitudes toward male *hoofuk*, semen? The neighbouring Umeda's outlook (Gell 1975), as we have already said, resembles that of the mountain Arapesh (Mead 1970–71) in that they see sexual pollution as reciprocal. The Yafar, on the other hand, regard male semen as harmless for women, and even beneficial: it makes them strong. If a woman's strength ebbs away, it is more likely due to the loss and gradual desiccation of her own *hoofuk*. Semen does not carry the ambivalence of menstrual blood, and its correlation with the latter lies in its positive ritual use by women: after intercourse, the wife takes a bit of her husband's semen and rubs it on her own chest, her stomach and her hands. This male *hoofuk* will act by analogy on the sago – of which, as every Yafar knows, semen is the human equivalent[17] –, which the woman, bending over her *bwêr*, will wash in the coming days, and will make it more abundant. Sago multiplied by male semen is thus the counterpart of game magically summoned by menstrual blood. It should be remembered that *taf* 'blood' and *hoofuk* are opposing terms associated respectively with hunting and horticulture-arboriculture. But in the sexual division of labour (male hunting/female sago-working), the roles are deliberately reversed for the needs of reciprocity and, as it were, of 'dialogue'

17. In the myth, the original sago palm comes from W. . .'s penis and the starch of this palm was divine semen. See also the sago-jelly rite in the Yangis ritual (pp. 52–3).

between the sexes. Each gender lends the other its *hoofuk*, its natural part, for the success of each side's specific economic production.[18]

Two Dance Steps

I will now pause for a short choreographic interlude which will provide a more visual illustration of the interplay between the sexes. In the section on Yafar dual structures, I have already shown how the men base their claim to the control of fertility on the myth of separate male and female communities followed by the resumption of sexual relations and the men's theft of the masks (p. 46 and Juillerat 1988 and 1991a). One of the characteristic postures of the dancers at Yafar ceremonies is a particular straddling step, enabling them to swing a ritual phallocrypt made of a blackened gourd, *suh-wagmô*, upwards, *vertically*, so that with each step it strikes against a bone belt worn around the abdomen and makes a typical clacking sound which sets the rhythm of the dance. The women dance around the edges of the village square with a swaying movement of the hips that makes the back of their skirt swing from side to side, *laterally* (the *ira* dance). The male choreographic style, called *ogohyaag*,[19] can be seen as a form of phallic exhibition in which the men show off their virility, their exclusive endowment with the male attribute, in front of the women, or as an evocation of erection and the sexual act. In fact however, although this interpretation should be taken into account, it does not restore the crux of the hidden meaning of these dance styles, of which the myth says that formerly the fertility ritual was performed only by *garbôangô* women who attached the *suh-wagmô* to their outsized clitoris. The Yafar men of knowledge themselves say that the *ogohyaag* does not represent the sexual act but the *'hoofuk* at work' and growth. So what we are dealing with is once again procreation, not simply sexuality. This 'phallic' dance mimics the fashioning of the foetus in the womb, 'work' (*gafungô*) that is symbolically taken over by the men and exhibited ritually. For two days and a night the different Yangis masks

---

18. The unmarried hunter may, however, use his own semen for his hunting magic. On the other hand, I do not know whether or not women use their own menstrual blood for purely female 'sorcery' or fertility spells, as is the case in other New Guinea societies.

19. *Ogo*: 'to stand' + — *hyaag*: verb suffix indicating repetition.

succeed each other, but all dance in this way until the close of the celebration, when new masked characters (*amof* 'termites') enter and walk around without doing the *ogohyaag*, letting their phallocrypt hang down (they often even wear an everyday gourd), unleashing the joy the audience had been holding back until now. Their 'passive' dance style shows that the totemic gestation is finished and immediately after the *amof*, *the* two *ifəge* come on stage, the mythic children born of this long labour of *hoofuk*. The male and female roles are doubly ambivalent, since the mythic women with their enormous clitoris in a sense robbed the men of what was properly theirs, the penis (and not only the phallus), and used it to 'make the *hoofuk* work' by means of dancing and the use of body paint (which the Yafar themselves, as we have seen, recognize as representing *hoofuk*); but conversely, the men steal the women's power to procreate by dancing in their stead and 'making the *hoofuk* work' by performing the *ogohyaag*. There is therefore a certain ambivalence in the sexual roles representing a reciprocal claim (in the myth) to the features characteristic of the opposite gender on the one hand, and in the necessary intervention of a *phallic process* in the 'work' of gestation, on the other. While the men lay claim symbolically to the work of female *hoofuk*, the women have been forced to give up their former phallic attribute and, by tying white feathers (*hoofuk* is white) to the strings of their best skirt – which, in many sequences of rites of passage, represent the umbilical cord which is cut – seem modestly to indicate that they still have the exclusive privilege of gestation and the bond with the child.

These two bodily movements, male and female, clearly symbolize gender complementarity in the growth process: the men's vertical movement for the 'upwards' growth of humans and plants, the women's lateral movement for the 'outward' growth in the volume of the foetus, tuber or fruit. And that is how the Yafar symbolic system divides this twofold natural process between the sexualized principles (allegorized in named mythic characters).

The Hunter's Wife

We saw above that female fertility is materially recovered for men's magic. This section will show that the same holds for the blood of defloration, sexual fluids and on the whole for sexual intercourse, at least in the case of the married couple's first relations. All sexual magic is restricted to the legitimate couple, as one of the symbolic functions of the couple in the service not only of the production of the household, but in that of the entire village community when it comes to procuring meat by hunting.

Here it is imperative to refer back to the oedipal myth of The Stolen Game, related in Chapter 7 (p. 183–4), because its exegesis clearly states the relation between the hunter and sexuality. The fantasized womb as the place where game is produced is the equivalent of the equation game = child, and, as we shall see when we examine sexual rites, this is more than a metaphor. The sociological context of marriage will be analysed in the next chapter, but here it should be remembered that sexual intercourse takes place for the first time, in principle, some weeks or months after the marriage, in other words after the wife's change of residence and the couple's acquisition of their economic autonomy. In the interim, the young husband is instructed by his father or another mature relative in the rites that will accompany his first relations with his wife. This ritual is performed only with women married for the first time; virginity, which seems to be the rule, is important to the success of the rite, but this is not only a rite of defloration. It seems that there is, in this ritual, a concern to capture the plentiful new *hoofuk* of the 'young fertile woman' (*angômêg*) and not to let it 'get away'. Like all Yafar magic, this rite is based on the use of strong-smelling rhizomes chewed with betel and spells characterized by repetition and occasional analogies with mythology. The main sequences of the rite, as described to me by a Yafar man already the father of several children and partially confirmed by two other informants, are as follows:

> The couple go into the forest to a lonely place they have chosen and first of all stand in the bed of a stream. The man begins by ritually clearing away all the debris left by floods. This is the *roof* rite ('to peel, bark, skin, uncover', p. 241), found in many different contexts. The spells pronounced are of the type 'Peal Nip, peal Amôp [two mythic places, respectively celestial and chthonian, male and female], rend the ants' fog, rend the *ifot* spiders' fog, rend the *abw-amsow* spiders' fog, etc.' 'Fog' (*rangôk*), a notion that we encountered in discussing hunting (see p. 196), is associated with small creatures that live on top of the ground and, like a skin, prevent access to the earth itself. However, according to one informant, *rangôk* is used

euphemistically here for the *suweegik* ('polluting female emanation')[20] which coats her body and which her husband washes off, using the same spells. Then the man touches his wife's vulva and she touches her husband's penis, while he recites another spell: 'Clean (*roof*) the vagina, clean the penis. . .'.

The couple then choose another spot in the nearby forest, making sure it is dry. The area is again ritually cleared: 'Clear away the dead *ahômp Ficus* leaves (see myth p. 183), clear away the dead *Intsia palembanica* leaves, etc.' Then the husband makes a bed of foliage from the *səsa* vine (not with branches of *Selaginella*, as he would do in a non-ritualized context); it is said that in doing this he is imitating the behaviour of the wild pig who, when it rains, makes himself a bed out of the same materials. Then, slowly removing his wife's string skirt, he says: 'Take off the *afwêêg* sago skirt,[21] take off the *fənaw* sago skirt'; then other sago palm clones are mentioned. The woman lies down on the bed; the man touches her clitoris and the woman grasps her husband's penis as he pronounces spells evoking the appearance of game (when he will go hunting) and chews betel with a rhizome of *Acorus calamus* from a clone called 'uvula of the *afwêêg* sago palm' (the uvula is a phallic symbol for the new sprout, the young shoot emerging from deep in the 'throat' of the plant): 'Let the cassowary blood appear, let the wild pig blood appear, let the wallaby blood appear, etc.', then good hunters from the village are named so that they will find game. Next, at each moment of the sexual act, the husband pronounces spells alluding to either the plant kingdom, the primordial species and germination, or especially to hunting. Each gesture of the act is slow or well separated from the next so that the incantations may be repeated enough times. To begin with he says: 'Open the vagina of the coconut palm (Mother-goddess), open the vagina of the *afwêêg* sago palm, open the vagina of the *fənaw* sago palm, etc.' As he penetrates her, the man says: 'Penis of the *bêêbi konkonkonkon* vine, glans of the *bêêbi konkonkonkon* vine. . .' (this onomatopoeia is also pronounced when using the digging stick in the planting rite and evokes an erection; it comes from the verb *koneg* 'to pulsate', which is also the origin of the name of a mythical character). If there is blood, the husband collects it and deposits it on a leaf made ready for the purpose. After intercourse, he says: 'Withdraw the penis of the *bêêbi* liana. . ..' Then he

---

20. Cf. *suweeg* 'smoke', from *suwê* 'fire'.

21. It will be recalled that this clone corresponds to the 'male' primordial sago palm, the totem of the Araneri moiety. My information comes from a man from this moiety; an Angwaneri would have cited his own totem, the coconut, or its euphemized form, the *fənaw* sago palm. But, as is the case here, both are often mentioned, whatever the officiant's moiety.

rubs around his wife's clitoris a mixture of the blood of game, red ochre, leaves from the *Evodia hortense* (a sweet-smelling plant grown in gardens) and a certain magic clone of the *Kaempferia* sp. while pronouncing the spells: 'Let it go to the female possum (*mêy*) blood, let it go to the male possum (*erof*) blood, let it go to the cuscus blood, etc.' (The mixture of sexual fluids and ingredients is supposed to 'seek out game' by identifying by analogy with the blood of the animals of the forest.)

At this point there is a mutual exchange of sexual substances, which, to my knowledge, is the only ritual operation repeated periodically throughout the couple's life. As I have already said, the woman takes a bit of semen and rubs it on her chest (sternum = 'heart', *öruk*), stomach and genitals, in order to increase her production of sago in the following days; her husband lends his help by chewing an appropriate magic clone while invoking the 'semen sago, the vagina sago and the penis sago'. In turn he takes a bit of vaginal fluid from his wife as she stands before him and rubs it on his own sternum, saying: 'meat of the back of the neck *sererere*, meat of the hind legs *sererere*, meat of the head *sererere*. . .'; the onomatopoeia evokes going hunting after an erotic dream (?), interpreted as the promise of a fruitful hunt (p. 192). He repeats the gesture on his wife's sternum while evoking game appearing in front of the hunter: 'Shoot a cassowary and a pig comes out, shoot a bandicoot and a *sawôh* (rodent sp.) comes out, shoot a cuscus and a wallaby comes out.'

After that, the blood which was set aside from the defloration is mixed with premasticated magic hunting rhizomes (*seeg*); as he prepares this mixture, the man says 'fire of the cassowary blood (*taf suwê*), fire of the wild pig blood, fire of the possum blood. . ..' Then he rubs the mixture on his forehead: 'Fire of the vagina blood, fire of the penis blood, etc.', then on his sternum: 'Let the vagina fire go to the game, let the vagina fire go to a boar's heart, let the vagina fire go to a wild sow's heart, etc., let the vagina fire go to the heartbeat.' Then he opens an areca nut, places some lime in it and says: 'Make the cassowary's heart burst,[22] make the wild pig's heart burst, make the boar's heart burst, etc.' He places it on his wife's pubis, then takes it in his teeth and chews it, saying: 'Eat the vagina blood, eat the penis blood, eat the wild pig blood, eat the tree kangaroo blood. . ..'

After that the man goes hunting. Back home, the next morning at dawn, he once more removes his wife's skirt very slowly, saying: 'Take off the dead *ahômp Ficus* leaves, take off the dead coconut leaves, take off the dead *afwêêg* sago leaves, take off the grass (*pos*) skirt (skirt = grass; woman/wife = bare land, without *roofuk*), take

---

22. *Təkya* 'to burst, to split', evokes the germinated seed and pregnancy.

off the dry palm fronds, take off the dead *Crinum asiaticum* leaves (plant grown for rituals), etc.' Then, as he removes the last piece of the skirt: 'Take off!' Then he introduces the tip of a magic hunting rhizome into his wife's vagina, saying: 'Vagina blood fire!' Then he advances it: '*Rur!*' ('advance slowly, go forward'), then he 'withdraws' it: '*Rəga!*' While this is being done, his wife closes her eyes and then opens them suddenly when the rhizome is withdrawn. At that point her husband recites spells about 'opening the cassowary's eyes, the wild pig's eyes, etc.' This sequence is unclear, but it seems to represent the formation of the 'game's' embryo in the woman's uterus (see myth, p. 183). Moreover, we have seen that life begins with the eyes: the woman opening her eyes is identified with the 'game' (child) conceived within her. The fact that the rite takes place at dawn, the day after first sexual intercourse, is highly significant: dawn is symbolically connected with whiteness and sago, the colour white recalling female *hoofuk* and the emergence of life (Juillerat 1978b, 1993b) and therefore conception.

We could cite variants of these rites, all grounded in homology with hunting. For instance, if the hunter does not kill any game in the weeks following the couple's first relations, he will perform a slightly different magic rite with his wife, the purpose of which is to 'tie up' the wounded game, in other words to keep it from getting away. That is why the plant used is a clone of true ginger, called *mosuwô-we* 'umbilical-cord (*mosuwô*) tie (*we*)':

The man ties a leaf of ginger to his little finger and little toe, then grasps his wife's foot as he stands behind her (she is the 'game' here) and ties ginger leaves to her hand and foot as well, saying: 'Tie the umbilical cord, tie the cassowary's umbilical cord, tie the female possum's umbilical cord, etc.' Then the man couples with her *a tergo*. As he withdraws, he evokes plentiful game: 'Many cassowaries appear, many wallabies appear. . ..' After that (if he is from the Araneri moiety, like my informant), he 'cleans up' the immediate surroundings and the base of an *afwêêg* sago palm (a *fənaw* sago palm if he is from the Angwaneri moiety), speaking the *roof* spells; then he picks the tip of a young palm frond while chewing a *Curcuma* clone, used against lack of success in hunting. Next he breaks the petiole of the frond, saying: 'Break the cassowary bone, break the pig bone, etc.', and takes the white latex (*yisêk*) which gathers and which he names as he does so: 'In the cassowary blood sago jelly (*yis*), in the pig blood sago jelly, in the possum blood sago jelly, in the vagina blood sago jelly, in the penis blood sago jelly etc.' He then rubs the latex up and down on his forehead: 'Go, *afwêêg* sago fire, go [to the blood of the game, find the game]! *Afwêêg* latex fire, go! *Afwêêg* vaginal secretions, go!, etc.' Then the man places a piece of ginger root from a clone called 'in the umbilical cord' under his wife's knee or binds her legs with a *we-fəge* vine, saying, 'Tie up the possum, tie up the wallaby, etc.' And chewing a bit of this clone with betel, he adds: 'Eat the umbilical-cord tie, eat the wild boar's umbilical cord, eat the wild sow's umbilical cord, etc.' Finally, his wife turns on to her back and lies on a monitor lizard scale (?) which her husband has placed under her (I still do not understand this symbol).

The next morning at dawn, her husband goes hunting. He takes along the *we-fəge* vines he used to bind his wife's legs and will use them to tie the legs of the first pig he kills. He also takes along some of the sexual fluids wrapped in leaves in his net bag.

Bachelors have similar hunting rites in which blood from an incision in the penis replaces the female substances:

The bachelor performs this rite alone in the bush. With the blood he has obtained by incising his glans, he mixes a bit of white from an *abi* wildfowl egg (which has a reddish shell), some blood from a game animal, red ochre and extracts of hunting-magic plants (*seeg*). The spells he pronounces compare the glans with the game animal's 'head'. As he incises himself, he says 'Burst the cassowary's head, burst the pig's head, burst the wild boar's penis, burst the wild sow's glans (*sic*). Penis blood! My penis blood! etc.' He then eats the egg, which he has cooked over the fire with some sago jelly (egg = female element; sago jelly = semen). His own blood, egg white and some root of a ginger clone are made up into two packets wrapped in leaves, one of which is carried in his netbag and the other tied on to his bow. As he mixes these ingredients, he calls up images of hunting: 'Let me see cassowary, let me see wild pig, etc.' And as he is tying the bundle on to his bow, he adds: 'tie the penis' female blood (*angô taf*), tie the groin's female blood, tie the pubis' female blood, etc.'

It is tempting to see the conjugal rites marking the couple's first sexual relations as a male attempt at 'recovering' female fertility for use in hunting. This is at least what comes through in the magical discourse, which does not speak of children and pregnancy but of cassowaries and pigs. The *mosuwô-we* rite, however, clearly showed that game was also a metaphor for the child and vice versa; that tying a magical plant called 'umbilical-cord tie' onto the man and the woman was tantamount to making the game fall under the hunter's arrows but also to 'binding a child to its mother', making her conceive a 'game-child' whose animal double would simultaneously be surprised by the hunter in the forest. This also recalls the myth of the Three Oedipal Sons or the Theft of Game (p. 183), in which we see the Original Mother 'give birth', as it were, to pigs and cassowaries, which are promptly felled by her husband's arrows. That is why the interpretation of 'male domination' simply using the woman's passive body for purposes that, in the end, do not directly concern her must be carefully shaded, for it is through his wife's potential pregnancy that the hunter will find game; the conception of a child appears, at the end of the *mosuwô we* rite, as the condition for this encounter. The appearance of game and the conception of the child are fused into a single representation of the man's relationship with natural fecundity. In the myth, the woman had two dimensions: a human dimension as a mother protecting her young son (whom she tied to her skirt with one of its strings = umbilical cord) and a cosmic dimension as the place where game is produced. That being said, it is true that, in Yafar society, it is the man who kills the animal and controls the distribution of its meat, and it is through him that the child's filiation is ensured.

But there is one more link missing between the wife's blood and that of game: this is where the *nabasa* come in, the spirits (often of the deceased which come from their blood, pp. 387–9) who are the providers of game. Now – as we shall see later in dealing with the rites used in contracting alliances with the spirits – it is the colour red (female blood or paint made from ochre or roucou) that the hunter dabs on his forehead or in the middle of his sternum ('heart'), in other words the metaphorical blood of the Original Mother, which makes him 'pleasing' to the *nabasa*, makes them 'like' him and makes them give him the animal he is seeking (p. 185).

Are there then no pregnancy rites that do not involve hunting and no hunting rites that do not involve women and sexuality? Chapter 7 has already answered the second question in the affirmative. As for the first, and to keep to male discourse, I found several elements, but it was difficult for me to question women on this point.

Sterility in a couple is not often attributed to the woman. It is said that any woman can have children, has *hoofuk*; it is the

Plate 18. With her child in a netbag on her back, this woman is netting another object.

quality of this *hoofuk* (see above) that determines the frequency of her pregnancies. It is said of a woman who has many children that she is *təta-gêm* 'like a wild sow', of another who is not often pregnant that she is *kwoy-gêm* 'like a cassowary'. The man, on the other hand, may be held responsible for sterility because he is lacking in assiduity. But a woman who never becomes pregnant is said to be *ruwar mööfuk*[23] 'barren of children'. Let us look at the ritual measures my male informants indicated for such cases.

During the first process, which is reminiscent of the rites described above, the couple desirous of a child rub their genitals before having intercourse with a chewed *Curcuma* clone, called *mwaywêy wahwe*. *Mwaywêy* is a term we have already encountered (p. 196), which qualifies the spell cast on the hunter to make him unsuccessful and which is neutralized by using this *Curcuma*; once again we find ourselves back at the parallel between pregnancy and hunting, and to what might be called the hunter's 'sterility'.

In another rite, performed before intercourse, the childless couple consume some betel mixed with a bit of latex from the breadfruit tree (*uguwô ninimp*, symbolizing semen) and stirred into juice from the (female) *toto* plant. The man then says: 'Breadfruit latex children, *toto* children, the belly will provoke cries of pain [birth], the entrails will provoke cries of pain, the pelvic bones will spread. . ..' Then, during coitus, the man will evoke the living child, not without some allusions to the animal kingdom: 'With the *ksê* rat children, with the *sawye* rat children, etc., *wanmon* [untranslatable reference to the moon], full moon children,[24] they crowd together [in the uterus], one child on her shoulders, another in front [the way mothers carry two small children], my penis' children, the vagina's children, etc.'

Better known and less secret is a rite that uses a *Saccharum edule* (*pitpit*) clone called *koob*, which is fed to the woman in reference to a myth: a man shot a bandicoot [with an arrow], and it ran off; when he got home, the hunter found his wife (named Kan Ken) dying from an arrow in the abdomen. The parallel between the act of releasing the arrow which penetrates the animal and the fecundating sexual act is once more obvious, as is the image of death by which the mother gives life (a metaphor from the plant kingdom where the shoot emerges from the seed or the rotting cutting). This rite is called Kan Ken kini awô ('Kan Ken is pregnant'), and the spells pronounced by the husband as his wife eats the *pitpit* no

---

23. *Mööfuk* (*mööf*) also means 'bachelor' and designates new coconuts just beginning to form.
24. On lunar symbolism, see pp. 433–7.

longer evoke hunting, but pregnancy and parent-child relations: 'Kan is pregnant, Ken is pregnant, the *pahgo* frog is pregnant, the *agro* frog is pregnant, my pregnant Kan, my pregnant *agro*, my pregnant *pahgo*, my round-bellied *agro* . . . my words will bear their fruit, my mouth will bear its fruit, in the time it takes a garden [she] will bear her fruit, in the time it takes two of my gardens [she] will bear her fruit, sit it [the child] on my thigh, lift it in my hands, carry it sitting on my neck, I will have two children [one after the other], I lift the little sister in my hands, carry the brother on my shoulders, etc.'

We will end here with a rite which facilitates conception but is used primarily for divination.

The couple go to a river, the woman sits down in shallow water with her legs apart, and her husband places in front of her pubis an *asurangro* insect, whose typical means of locomotion is to scoot upstream on the surface of the water using its long legs. More than the actual sexual act, this jerky movement again evokes for the Yafar the 'work of the *hoofuk*', in other words the 'fashioning of the embryo', a movement similar to that of the ceremonial penis gourd, *suh-wagmô*, described above. The husband asks the *asurangro* 'Do you want to do the work (*gafungô*)?. . . Don't you?. . .' This divinatory questioning is done preferably after intercourse, and the 'work' is therefore that of 'starting the pregnancy'. If the insect reacts, the woman has a chance of being pregnant. If her child is 'strong and handsome', the couple will repeat the rite at the same place the next time they want a child. The Yafar do not seem to believe that the *asurangro* has anything to do with conception, however, and this must not in any way be seen as an explanatory element of a theory of reproduction. We are somewhere between belief and simple metaphor, as though the mind were acting by analogy at one level, while at another reason refused to recognize a causal relation.

To this already long set of descriptions, let me add a few negative rites used when no more children are wanted. The magic clones used and the words spoken are different – allusions to hunting have disappeared, but the technique remains the same.

In one rite I recorded, the words spoken during intercourse evoke the breaking of the umbilical cord and the ceasing of the flow of sexual fluids: 'Break the umbilical cord, break the penis' umbilical cord, break the vagina's umbilical cord, break the amniotic sac's umbilical cord. . .the uterus', the penis' pubic hair's, the vulva's pubic hair's. . .reduce the semen to ashes, stop up the coconut water [*hoo-fuk* or amniotic fluid], etc.' When the act is finished, the man again says 'Let the penis water have no effect! Let the vagina water have no effect!' While he is chanting this spell, he chews the root of a special *Acorus calamus* clone, called *gungwan*, whose function in other ceremonial contexts is to 'block the road' to keep the person's dangerous double from returning (especially during sleep) to the Primordial Mother and the netherworld (Ch. 12). Here it is mother-hood itself that is being blocked: the chewed rhizome is spit on to the woman's abdomen.

In order to encourage barrenness, another rite is performed to put a premature stop to the woman's periods. The husband places ashes (to 'cool' the body, the opposite of 'fire', which we saw was the metaphor for blood and *hoofuk*) on his wife's big toe,[25] which here symbolizes the umbilical cord, and recites spells: 'Belly ashes, vag-ina ashes, uterus ashes, clitoris-blood ashes, penis-blood ashes, iron tree sap-blood ashes, pandanus-blood ashes, python-blood ashes, etc.'

In all the fertility rites described above, and despite the benefit the woman wanting a child may derive from the mediation of the game coveted by her husband, it is always the man who knows and performs the magic, who grows, harvests and manipulates the plants and who pronounces the ritual words. Yet the man is not considered to be endowed with any particular power, and there are no specialists in this type of magic, which remains a private matter. Plants and sacred words (behind which myths are often to be found) are the two inseparable means by which a hus-band controls his wife's fertility. The fact that these rites usually take place before, during or right after intercourse indicates that it is the meeting of the genders, the mixing of the two sexual substances that are the object of the magic – and not only the woman. Although the man is the acting subject, he includes himself in the object of his magic, for it is the couple in its com-plementarity that provides the materials.

Yafar reproductive ideology is based primarily on this co-operation between the genders as found in the interaction of the Araneri and Angwaneri moieties in the Yangis ritual (Ch. 2). The man is only the keeper of the necessary knowledge and the one who acts, by his magic, on the couple, of which he is himself one

25. It will be recalled that, if necessary, the parturient brings down the placenta by pulling on the cord, which she has wrapped around her big toe (p. 250).

of the poles. Because of his intervention a child will be born of his wife, just as from the forest game will appear. Sexuality and hunting are in a way symbolically interchangeable and lend each other their potentialities. Each of these two allied domains is an operative metaphor for the other. The child and the game will belong to the man (patriliny, control of meat distribution or owner-ship of the domestic pig), but the woman will rear and feed the child and will perhaps raise a wild piglet and become its 'mother' (Ch. 7).[26]

Women's Rights

What do women have to say about this attempt at birth control by male magic within each couple, about these chancy under-takings which men nevertheless still claim to be effective? And what do women do to enhance or, on the contrary, restrain their own fecundity? These are questions that will naturally spring to the reader's mind; unfortunately I am afraid I must confess ignorance. It is nearly impossible for a male anthropologist to question Yafar women on these matters: the embarrassment of discussing problems of reproduction is aggravated by sexual and linguistic barriers; in addition a man will arrange to be present if someone has caught wind of the interview. Men find asking women questions ridiculous because 'they are ignorant', and the minor magic that they might 'perhaps' use among themselves seems laughable to the men. They prefer not to hear about it, even if their virility is at stake: 'Women's affairs should be left to women, we men don't want to know about them.' I can only say, then, that women surely practise magic. But it seems unlikely that they are acquainted with the medicinal plants that induce abortion, for instance, as the pharmacopeia is not highly developed on the whole and the known plants are little used in comparison

26. These comparisons show that the parallel between sexuality and hunting is not based on the simple sexual metaphor of shooting the arrow and on the expression of male dominance and hostility between the sexes. Yafar symbolics go beyond Honigmann's def-inition, later adopted by Roheim (1950), in which the slain game represents the woman, and develop the theme of procreation rather than that of the sexual act in the strict sense; a correspondence is established between cynegetic production and pregnancy, game and the child. Nevertheless, the Freudian explanation remains relevant: this is demonstrated by the myth excerpt that opens Chapter 7 as well as what is said later about the role of visual perception in sexuality and hunting (p. 287).

Plate 19. Mother and child. The cord is normally passed around the mother's neck so the child will not fall.

to magic therapies. Furthermore, the virtually non-existent role of Yafar woman in ritual suggests that there is little diversity in female fecundity or sterility rites, which, if they do exist, are kept a close secret among women.

In particular, abortion is never put forward as a technically feasible or socially acceptable solution. If a couple has enough children and the woman is pregnant again, this child is supposed to be accepted like the others. For an unmarried girl, abortion would be a way of avoiding the reprimand she is going to receive, the questions she will be asked about her lover or the 'shotgun' wedding that is going to be forced on her, perhaps against her will. She can call upon a more experienced female relative, but the method attempted will be of a magical order (make the child 'fall like a ripe fruit' – a metaphor found in sorcery aimed at making a woman abort: see Ch. 14) rather than medicinal or mechanical.

However, societies unequipped to practise abortion can and do resort to infanticide, a sort of deferred abortion. I was able to gather a little information on this subject from both Yafar men and women as well as from one Nayneri woman (southern Eri). In the first place, infanticide is not only accepted, it is encouraged when the child is malformed (deformed limbs, blindness, monstrosities, etc.) or in twin births. In the last case, it is the weakest or homeliest twin that is killed. The only reason given for refusing to raise twins is of a socio-economic order: 'A woman can't breast-feed or carry two babies at once, how could she work?' In principle, when a child is born to an unmarried girl who could not be married while she was pregnant, it too is killed: it would be a social aberration to keep a child with no known father. If the father is identified, he is subjected to so much pressure that he will feel forced to agree to the marriage. But if the man is married or if the girl does not want him for a husband, she can refuse to divulge his identity, thus running the risk of being herself subjected to group pressure to kill her child at birth. Another cause for infanticide used to be the birth of a child too soon after the marriage, when the parents were still very young. The Eri feel that a child born too early in the life of a couple will grow to the detriment of its parents and will make them age prematurely. This practice must have been fairly exceptional among the Yafar, more frequent among the southern Eri.

In all these situations it appears that the mother has a right to decide and this right is recognized by the father and the community. Above and beyond the restrictions that may be imposed on her when it comes to preserving the social order, the mother has the final say, and it is also she (more rarely one of the women who assisted the parturient) who kills the child, usually shortly after birth. Two techniques may be used: striking the child on the sternum with a stick (where the heartbeat can be seen) or smothering it by stuffing its foot in its mouth. As for stillborn infants, the body is wrapped in an areca palm sheath and suspended without ritual in the forest.

In conclusion, these choices and constraints must be placed in the demographic context of infant mortality, which is sharply increased by ecological and dietary conditions. Malaria, tuber-culosis, various parasitic infestations and protein deficiencies in the mothers and children comprise a set of factors of which the child is the first victim. Traditional or modern birth control[27] makes little sense in such a sparse population (disposing of more than enough land) in which half of the children die in the first years of life. According to figures I recorded in 1973, 42 married Yafar women had given birth to 173 children of whom 80 had died before they were (approximately) five years old; of the 93 surviving children, 37 were still under five, which is to say that some 15 would not survive. That brings to around 55% the rate of infant mortality in the first five years. This situation has prob-ably improved slightly since a small first aid post was set up at Yafar 2 in 1974. To this must be added mortality in older children and adults which, especially during 'influenza' epidemics, is dra-matic.

In these conditions, given the risk of death, the Yafar cannot help wanting children (as many as possible, even). It was only when they had more than six (including one or two under five years of age) that I heard men and women express the desire not to have any more. But these cases are exceptional (only two fam-ilies out of the whole society, one of which was polygynous).

Concealed Sexuality and Social Order

The Fiancée under the Bushel

I will begin this section by reviewing a few facts already con-sidered in Chapter 4. The childhood and adolescence of Yafar boys is marked by increasing autonomy from their family and by a search for new solidarities with other boys of the same age group and with kinsmen in particular. This social and psychological process leads to the intensification and valorization of hunting. Girls of the same age, on the other hand, find themselves tied down to domestic production, especially by their participation

---

27. The post-partum taboo does not exceed twelve to eighteen months, but breast-feeding continues until the child is three or four. The spacing of births fluctuates between these extremes; as exact birth dates are not given in the annual census, it is impossible to be more precise as to frequency.

in sago-working, which is a predominantly female enterprise but also involves the family. When the adolescent girl leaves her home for a time, it can only be to join another family (there are no groups of unmarried girls). This other family is most often that of her future father-in-law (or brother-in-law) and where her future husband lives, where she takes part in the women's work and helps her future mother-in-law as she does her own mother at home. After intermittent visits lasting a few weeks, she returns to her village, where she stays until the marriage. Young people promised to each other by their parents' engagement to exchange their children are relatively numerous.

What interests us in this chapter, however, is not the system of child marriage in itself, but sexuality during the prematrimonial period, and in the present case the sexual taboo that characterizes the young couple's relationship, the embarrassment and even 'shame' (*afwane feg*, 'to shame/make ashamed') that marks their mutual presence. When they share the same roof (that of the boy's father), the young 'fiancés' not only never speak to each other, they pay no attention whatsoever to each other. The boy in particular seems not to notice the girl meant for him, who in the evening, for example, works, eats or talks with her future mother-in-law or sisters-in-law only a few metres away. The virtual subdivision of the single room of the house (Ch. 4) and the way the group members are distributed around their assigned fireplaces and between the gendered zones of the living area introduce a spatial order into this non-relation. Often the young man spends his nights in the *mööf raara*, the (adolescent) bachelors' house, coming home only to eat. In the daytime, he goes to his garden alone or with his father or his 'brothers', leaving his fiancée to accompany her mother-in-law to a sago log being worked or to another patch in the garden. The boy spends as much time as possible hunting or going with friends to take part in rituals in neighbouring villages. If exceptionally the whole family does go to work in the garden or on a sago palm, the young people arrange never to be alone together; the prohibition does not need to be enforced by a third party, it is 'self-induced', as it were, by the young people themselves. Thus the girl does not stay with her future household (these visits do not take place when both are from the same hamlet) in order to see her fiancé, but to get used to her parents-in-law and gradually to confirm the engagement previously entered into by the two families.

Far from promoting adolescent sexual life, then, the institution of child marriage tends to paralyze it. 'Shame' has come between them and will only gradually lift when they are obliged to organize their work together without the parents, as an independent married couple. The assumption of their sexuality follows their economic autonomy. This discomfort is expressed in front of outsiders (members of another group or the anthropologist) by denying the 'fiancé(e)'s' existence. In the course of my inquiries, no adolescent boy would ever freely admit that a woman had been promised to him, being even less willing to name her. The young Yafar bachelor always maintains that he is alone, without a wife, and is going to stay that way for a long time to come; he explains this alleged imposed celibacy by the (very real) lack of women in the area. His companions deny knowing anything about him, unless it happens that they want to play a dirty trick and so reveal the name of the young girl chosen. When I would tell the boy what I had learned, he would deny that the girl in question was promised to him or claim that he did not want her anyhow and that she could stay at home for all he cared. This denial of entry into married life lasts until the marriage is concluded and everyone can see the couple (often still living with the father) constituted as an economic unit, striking out in the morning into the forest for the work sites, which are also places of sexual activity.

These behaviours are systematically adopted by all young people, from which it can be deduced that the sexual taboo between the betrothed is total in most cases and that the culture determines a social inhibition which takes on a psychological dimension in the individual. To what can we attribute this extreme distance between the man and the woman, the very ones who are to live together for the rest of their lives and to have children according to a socially recognized covenant? Two types of interpretation can be advanced: the first concerns the 'spectre' of reproduction, which from the outset creates a distance, an attitude of avoidance in the young couple; the second, related to the first, has to do with the autonomy of the young bachelor, who exercises his claim to independence and solidarity with his age-group comrades. These two aspects are in fact one and the same thing, expressed in general terms of sexual antagonism and 'fear' of procreation on the one hand, and personal flight on the boy's part in the face of an irrevocable social commitment (see the high stability

of Yafar marriages) and loss of a status characterized by autonomy and comradeship, with perhaps a hint of homosexuality,
on the other hand. Once marriage is accepted, this loss will
be partially compensated by over-investment in the new relationship with the brother-in-law (Ch. 10). In this way the initial
distance that paradoxically founds the Yafar couple's ties is set
within the overall representation of the disjunction of the sexes
in their reproductive encounter itself (taboo on menstrual blood,
nudity: see above) and of the neutralization of their difference within the circle of consanguinity (non-avoidance between
brothers and sisters in particular). More generally, the embarrassment with which bachelors approach marriage is related to a certain
incompatibility, on the representational level, between libidinal
and social sexuality (see below).

'Disorderly' Sexuality

Once the fiancée has been evacuated from the avowed preoccupations of the male adolescent or bachelor, what can one say
(when one is a non-integrated outsider and held to be indiscreet
by the nature of one's work) about 'seduction' and pre- or extramarital sexuality?

Publicly seductive behaviours are noticeably missing from the
picture of Yafar society. In daily village life or during festivals,
never is there a perceptible sign (glances, approaches, conversations, smiles, etc.) of the attraction that a man or woman may
feel for someone of the opposite sex. The men and women who
speak to each other in public are close kin between whom sexual
relations are forbidden or spouses whose sexuality is socially ratified. Between these two extremes, there is a set of relations
in which sexuality is only potential and which therefore form a
taxonomically ambiguous category; here not only are statuses ill
defined, but rivalries raise their head.

Above and beyond the symbolic barrier of reproduction, already
discussed, which is a cultural factor socially inhibiting sexuality,
there is the sociodemographic situation, which seems to me to be
of prime importance in trying to understand why seduction and
extramarital sexuality are concealed. It should first of all be remembered that there are barely eight women for ten men in the Eri
population (p. xxviii), to which must be added the small size of

the society (200 inhabitants) as well as that of the surrounding social space (approx. 600 persons) in which the Yafar contract their marriage alliances; these facts determine an especially dense network of consanguinity that severely restricts the choice of non-prohibited partners. Another sociological factor apt to limit the number of available women is – independently of the 'engagement' of children, which does not irrevocably bind the intended – the early marriage of girls (shortly after puberty), whereas boys often remain unmarried until the age of 25 or 30. It can be said, then, that the combination of demographic conditions (themselves determined by bad health conditions) and the social system make it practically impossible for a young man to find a sexual partner who is not prohibited in one way or another: kin, married, promised or prenubile. In any case, even assuming that he wants to disregard taboos, he runs the risk of colliding with social reprobation which can and especially in the past could be violent. It is therefore not surprising that Yafar ideological discourse preaches complete sexual abstinence before marriage and confirms conjugal sexuality as the only legitimate form, whereas when the point is pursued, it is acknowledged that secret and unpreventable meetings take place in the anonymity of the bush. When sexuality tends to produce clashes and therefore threatens to disrupt the community's cohesiveness, and when the social group or the society as a whole, because of its small size, cannot entertain conflict without the risk of breaking apart, constraint sets in: prohibitions, moral code or violence. It is to such a constraint that the concealment of seductive behaviour and sexual strategies seems to correspond.

But just what do these behaviours consist of? For the man, essentially meeting the woman he desires without being seen, in other words in the forest, to propose a later rendezvous or sexual intercourse on the spot. Usually the woman is sought out while she is alone working sago in some isolated place. The man sneaks up to make sure she is indeed alone and 'whistles' to signal his presence, which is in itself a direct invitation to have sex. From what several men told me, the use of language in the early stages of seduction is minimal. If the woman refuses his invitation, the man can withdraw and ask her not to say anything, especially if she is married; and if he does not trust her, he may eventually threaten her with *aysiri* (sorcery) if she were to talk. He can also bring pressure to bear, using the same means of intimidation, so that she will submit to him; he even sometimes shows her an evil plant root and his weapons (arrows, dagger) to impress her. It is also said that inexperienced adolescents are more shy and rarely use force, whereas a mature man is determined and sometimes resorts to rape. These furtive meetings, fraught with a certain violence directed towards the woman, can sometimes develop into more regular, better balanced relations. But a long-term adulterous relationship seems hard for the Yafar to conceive, and they feel that in such an event the man should abduct the woman and settle her in his own village, or if she is from the same local group, hide out with her in the forest. While avoiding immediate confrontation and the murderous violence that used to follow, this act is tantamount to a public confession of their relationship: by fleeing, the couple annuls the concealment and decides to live out the conflict to its resolution, with all the risks that entails.

The prematrimonial or extramarital strategy of the young bachelor is the same, then, as that of the married man or widower. In all cases, sexual activity outside marriage is experienced as a social disorder which must be hidden; but when a new couple emerges from such a crisis, it is to be reintegrated into the social order, even if this causes momentary alarm: that which was hidden is suddenly made public, the community is confronted with a *fait accompli*. For the lover, this is also a way to solicit social recognition and to forestall secret reprisals, sorcery or murder, on the part of the husband aided by a relative or two, or on the part of the woman's brothers if she is not yet married.

For bachelors, what began as an 'adventure' may lead to marriage, but such cases are rare. It seems that marriage or the steps leading up to it are antithetical to sexuality, as order is the antithesis of disorder. This opposition would explain why the 'fiancée' chosen by the father is kept 'under the bushel', whereas the young man can secretly carry on sexual adventures with the women of his own choice, married or not. The fiancée is the one who is kept and fed with care (in part by her future in-laws) and who is allowed to grow up so that she will give the agnatic line of her husband and father-in-law a posterity. From the start, she belongs to the order of social reproduction because she must be integrated in one fell swoop into her multifaceted role of legitimate sexual partner, prolific wife, mother, worker-producer and companion. The occasional sexual partner, on the other hand, remains outside the sexual order and belongs to the family of another (husband or father). After the encounter, her lover fur-tively leaves her in the bush, he does not spend the night with her in a house by the fire, does not eat her sago jelly; at best he shares a piece of fruit or game with her, but on the run.

Staying with the idea of 'concealed seduction', the modes of physical approach must be completed by magical procedures used to ensure success in seduction or sometimes the acceptance of the husband by an unwilling young wife (see Ch. 10). These individual rites are based on the use of a set of ritual clones given the general name of *wêên*, and on the mental repetition of ana-logical spells evoking the woman's desire or love. The man casts this spell while chewing a rhizome of the clone in question with some betel and contriving to fix his gaze on the woman he desires without her noticing. Another technique consists in giving her, by way of an accomplice she cannot suspect, a cigarette made from native tobacco which has been mixed with some magical plant over which appropriate spells were spoken. The action of these rites is supposed to produce the 'mixing' of the man's and woman's blood through the intermediary of their selves (*sungwaag*): *awaag na taf, angwafik na taf ehuwa ah-feg*, 'the man's blood and the woman's blood mingle'. It is very likely that women have similar rites for arousing a man's desire.

The Order of Repression

I said above that the concealment of asocial sexual behaviour was determined by various types of constraint, some of them violent. In fact, violence is a response to the disorder created by an adul-terous sexual act or to the violence of the seducer himself. The extreme case is where rape has been committed or attempted, especially if the woman was also threatened with sorcery by the man. In this case, she can try to cry out, which may drive off her aggressor, or she can submit to his desire for fear that he may cast an evil spell there and then, or formerly – if the man was from an outside group – for fear that he might shoot her. In most cases she will report the facts to her father, brother or husband. Formerly the men would then get up a group in secret to surprise the aggres-sor and execute him before he had time to perform his sorcery (Ch. 14). If the man is from the same village and provided no threats of sorcery were made, the matter can be settled, formerly by a stick fight, today by violent public reprimands. The reprimand is addressed not only to the guilty party, but to his whole lineage; the women also join in and express their anger among themselves. This public denunciation is an attempt to 'shame' the aggressor's agnatic group. Less serious is a simple invitation to have intercourse: if the woman refuses and the man withdraws with no threats of reprisal, the matter can be totally ignored or still be revealed by the victim. This type of situation has never come to anything more than reprimands and collective expressions of anger, fighting stick in hand.

If an adulterous relationship is discovered, first the woman is beaten, then the lover, who has often fled into the bush, is tracked down and brought back to the village, where the conflict is settled by a collective stick fight or, when the lover is still young or a bachelor, simply by reprimands shouted by the *aynaag*. As a rule, the adulterous woman is held to bear the most responsibility unless she can prove that she cried for help or she denounces her partner without delay. If the woman is beaten, she can be defended by her brothers, which used to give rise to new confrontations with sticks between brothers-in-law.

Another type of offence is to chance upon a couple having intercourse. As sexual activity takes place for the most part in the daytime and in the forest, it can happen that a lone hunter noiselessly comes upon them. However legitimate the couple may be, they consider the matter a serious offence and feel so ashamed that the only compensation used to be a spell cast on the importunate visitor or to kill him. Today the discomfort would no doubt be partially dispelled by a public expression of anger or a stick fight.

According to our informants, sexual offences against non-nubile girls or against boys are non-existent. On the other hand, homosexual games between young boys consisting of touching each other's genitals and a little masturbation are regarded as innocent and, in the case of children, often go on in the village. Women are said to have equivalent pastimes. It is on the Bismark Archipelago plantations that the Yafar were introduced to real homosexual aggressions and the sodomization of the youngest workers, and it is there too that they were first introduced to female prostitution.

The important fact in this diversity of situations is that concealment is often followed by a momentary crisis (ranging from murder to simple stereotyped public anger), which paves the way for either neutralizing the public disorder and forgetting about it or eventually making it legal. Total secrecy suddenly gives way to public divulgence, not only by word of mouth, but by the public staging of collective anger and the verbal reprimands of the elders. I will return to this problem in Chapter 14.

Sexuality in Nature

This heading has two meanings, as it refers on the one hand to the *loci* of human sexuality and on the other to the sexualization of nature and the cosmos.

The territorial space occupied by the Yafar can be defined by various types of binary opposition, and I will use these to talk about the places allocated to sexual activity. First of all, of the village (*kəbik*) and the forest (*sangweri*), only the latter lends itself to the sexual act, and for several reasons. The most basic is the need for a private place, which, paradoxically for us, is afforded by nature itself and not by the dwelling or the village. The single-room Yafar house provides no privacy and, even for couples without children, the proximity of the neighbours and the silence of the night would make discretion impossible. The Yafar sense of 'shame' would find such situations intolerable. Moreover, there is a myth that tells how the first couple, of which the woman with no sexual organ had just had her vagina opened by her father-in-law (Wefroog, one of the two culture heroes), was also obliged to ask him to create the forest to hide their first relations:

At that time there was only a grassy plain and no forest. An old man (Wefroog) lived with his son and daughter. He said to the boy, 'Marry your sister.' The son refused: 'I'm not a possum.' 'All right', said his father, 'go away and exchange your sister for a wife.' The son went away to the Kumwaag, exchanged his sister and came back with his wife. The couple went into the bush but could not mate because the woman had no vagina. Wefroog in turn complained that his daughter-in-law did not give him anything to eat. He asked her to gather him some areca nuts: 'Climb the tree, throw me down some nuts, then slide down the trunk.' While the woman was up in the areca palm, he planted a stick equipped with a sharp *prisri* stone at the foot of the tree. As she slid down, the woman impaled herself and the stone opened her vagina. Before his daughter-in-law could get up from her fall, Wefroog (who was already chewing the areca nuts she had thrown him) spit his red saliva into her vagina and then tossed in a *Piper betel* fruit (clitoris).[28]

After that, the couple went into the bush a second time. The man and woman looked back but were still in sight of Wefroog's house; they walked some more, looked back and could still see Wefroog's house. They did not dare make love because Wefroog might see them. They returned home. Discontented, the woman complained to her father-in-law. And so, during the night, Wefroog sowed the hairs of his beard and then caused a strong wind to blow which carried them about. The woman was afraid and took refuge beside her father-in-law. He made the wind stop. In the morning there was forest everywhere. The couple set out once more. When they had gone a certain distance the man and woman looked around; they could no longer see Wefroog's house and so they made love. The woman returned pleased and made her father-in-law a good meal.

The second reason is that the Yafar see sexual intercourse as something impossible to socialize; it belongs to nature and therefore should never take place in the village. The only possible setting for the physical meeting of the sexes, the only receptacle for the fusion of the reproductive substances and their contaminating power, is the earth and the forest, far from any socialized place.

On a second level of opposition, where the cultivated garden (*aso*) is opposed to the wild forest (*sangweri*), a further distinction must be made between the new garden not yet harvested (*awik aso*), where all sexual relations are prohibited, and the garden already being picked or the old garden (overrun with weeds), *nôhôk aso*, where sexual activity is allowed, though the forest is preferred because it affords more privacy. The Yafar explanation for prohibiting recent gardens is that the sexual fluids 'would attract wild pigs', which would destroy the crops. That is obviously not where the real reason lies, but rather – indirectly – in the relation between the 'smell' of human *hoofuk* and food (remember that *hoofuk* also designates the flesh of tubers), the pig being merely a mediator that makes it possible to rationalize the unconscious representation linking the domains of sexuality and

28. The secret version adds that Wefroog poured coconut water (*sa buu*) into his daughter-in-law's vagina, a metaphor for amniotic fluid and uterine *hoofuk*.

eating. This relationship is attested lexically by the metaphorical use of the word *neg* 'to eat', for copulation (at least when the subject is masculine) or in the expression that states that 'a wife is a man's sago', but it is also found in the myth just cited, in which sexual satisfaction is the counterpart of alimentary satisfaction, and where the female organs are necessary for reproduction, just as the forest is necessary for horticultural production. The growing garden planted by the man and woman is a '*hoofuk*' whose growth must not be hindered. The idea that animals are drawn by the smell of the sexual fluids, by *hoofuk* (earlier we saw that dogs would try to eat the afterbirth), also corresponds to a classification in which sexuality is placed on the side of nature.

The couple may meet anywhere in the forest. The man cuts some foliage to make a bed, if possible branches of *Selaginella* sp. (*rǝge*), a bush that grows abundantly, especially in secondary forest. The woman lies down on her back and raises her legs; the man sees her sexual parts, desires her and couples with her. This schematic description of the awakening of desire is how the few Yafar willing to talk about it spoke of sexual intercourse. The purported absence of preliminaries or foreplay should certainly not be taken literally, but corresponds rather to an ideological view of sexual relations. Nevertheless, two constants run through these accounts: the posture of the couple, in which the woman is beneath the man, next to the ground, and the central role of sight, which triggers the man's desire. Let us pause and examine each of these two particularities.

The posture corresponds to a cosmological vision and to the divine couplings. To the sexualization of the cosmos and its subdivision into a male Sky, the god W. . ., and a female Earth, the divinity B. . . (see Ch. 2), must be added the idea of a male power poised to strike down mankind from above, to which is opposed the more passive power of the netherworld, equally disposed nevertheless to overflow its bounds, to let the divine primordial maternal *hoofuk* rise to the surface (waters, cosmic blood, ocean). These threats appear as potential punishments for human failings, in particular in the area of esoteric knowledge and its divulgence to 'non-initiates'. Thus the cosmic order imposes a spatial hierarchy on the sexes which according to the Yafar themselves is also expressed in the Wabuminaag rite, in the course of which a gardener's digging stick is thrust into the newly cleared ground for the first time (Ch. 6). The phallic penetration can be realized only from top to bottom, and I have already said that the sky is sometimes seen as being connected to the earth by a phallus 'anchored' in the ground, thereby ensuring its solidity.[29] The myths are often careful to make it clear that the divine matings[30] are performed in this position, and we have seen, when dealing with the domestic space, that the wife occupies the 'bottom' or the 'loins' of the house (the part near the door), the man the 'top', that is to say the back of the room. Or during the maskmaking for Yangis, the men of the Araneri moiety occupy the top of the grounds, those of the Angwaneri, the bottom. Lastly, in the context of present-day acculturation, more and more young men sleep on beds which they have built on legs and fixed to the wall of the house, while their wives still sleep on the floor close to their fire: this, too, is a material use of vertical space that cannot be reversed. One mythical sequence, however, shows, with the necessary comic relief attendant upon such a transgression, the figure of the beautiful young fertile woman Oög-angô (Melon-Woman) having taken refuge in a tree and letting her long clitoris hang down to the ground, through this provocative behaviour inciting the man pursuing her with his favours to take hold and climb up, as though it were a liana. But each time he tries, he falls grotesquely to the ground and ends up copulating (from top to bottom this time) with the crab holes in the earth (Juillerat 1991a: Ch. 4). One more word needs to be said about coupling *a tergo*, which, as we have seen, is used ritually when, if I understood rightly, the couple is supposed to be identified with game. Another myth also shows a couple having intercourse in this position, setting off an explosion of the mixed male and female *hoofuk* and a sudden rise in the stretch of river where the act takes place. The feeling of transgression associated with this posture (closer to nature and the origin of things) seems associated in Yafar imaginary representations with a redoubling (but perhaps also a deflection) of reproductive efficiency.

29. To calm the earthquakes caused by the earth's softening, the Master of the Sky performs a brief metonymic rite in the middle of the village square, in the course of which he touches his penis vertically to the ground while pronouncing spells to solidify the earth by the perpetuation of the celestial erection.

30. The cosmogonic myth summarized in Chapter 2 relating the first divine couplings specifies that when they first came together, B. . . was *on top of* W. . .; that did not produce the expected result (to create the beginnings of an earth), so the position was reversed.

The gaze (*nof*, *nofuk* 'view, gaze, eye') in the sexual act is not simply an erotic detail nor merely a corollary of the fact that sexual activity is supposed to take place in the daytime ('otherwise', a Yafar friend asked me, 'how could we see?'). It has above all to do with the relationship that we have already seen between hunter and game, and between the *nabasa* forest spirits and the hunter. Now our discussion of sexual rites for couples has already shown how closely hunting and sexuality are associated through the ideas of *hoofuk*, blood, childbirth and reproduction, penetration, quarry and food. Hunting and sexuality work on the same principles: the man has to see the object of his desire before seizing it and, to do this, the new husband is instructed ('authorized') by an older man, who teaches him the cynegetic rites which are to mark the couple's first intercourse. The parallel between seeing the game, drawing one's bow and shooting, dismembering and consuming on the one hand, and seeing the woman's vagina, having an erection, copulating (making something bleed) or consuming (*neg*) on the other might perhaps seem forced if countless Yafar incantations and the myths were not there to provide constant confirmation. Furthermore, on a negative note, male impotence is semantically linked to the impotence of the hunter, who, 'covered with fog' and 'sightless', has forfeited the *nabasa*'s confidence as well as his own control over 'blood'.

The integration of sexuality into nature brings us back, in conclusion to this chapter, to the idea of control, of subject and object (man/woman-game-earth), and therefore to the idea of power and symbolic domination. The reader may consult Chapters 3 and 13, recalling that with the gendered poles of the cosmos are associated ritual masters, always male, whose responsibilities are more or less directly connected with the notion of *hoofuk*, blood, reproduction. Their role is to rank within society the cosmic functions which the men then apportion among the lineages and moieties in order better to control their force. On the side of power we find men as a group (against or without women), social control and secrecy. On the side of nature we find opposition but also ambivalence between male and female, but as a general rule a surplus of femaleness, an 'overflow' of maternal *hoofuk*.

In this chapter I have leaned more towards the structures of symbolic representations than towards social practice, so inclined by the asocial character the Yafar attribute to sexuality.

Closely associated with nature, the libido and its exercise lie outside the social realm and do not lend themselves to direct socialization. This is why marriage and the beginnings of domestic cooperation precede marital sexuality, and why extramarital desire is satisfied outside the bounds of social control or in spite of it. As Roger Bastide has said: 'The social sphere and the libido are two different domains, they have neither the same nature nor the same origin. But the two are linked by a whole series of relations, fusions, conflicts, complementarities' (1972a: 260; 1972b: 222, n. 30). In the next chapter, we will leave sexuality in itself and move on to the analysis of that central pillar of the social edifice, marriage: the system of exchanges tailored to ensuring the reproduction of families, as reproductive social cells whose biological sexuality is both the heart of the institution and the pretext.

10

Alliance Structures and Matrimonial Behaviours

Father: 'Marry your sister.'
Son: 'I'm not a possum.'
Then he took his sister to the Kumwaag and came back with a wife.

(From a myth)

With marriage, we now turn from non-socialized sexuality, which we dealt with in the preceding chapter, to sexuality integrated not only into the family, but into society as a whole, which implicitly sanctions its lawfulness. At one level, each individual marriage brings sexuality into domestic life and restores its reproductive function in accordance with the rules of patrilineal descent; at another level, all marriages taken together are part of a broader and more complex system of alliances, which is governed no longer by biological reproduction, but primarily by the search for social equilibrium through the exchange of women, or in other words through the management of the potential fertility that each group (lineages, clans, dual units, Yafar society, neighbouring societies) has at its disposal. The marriage system is a strategy for continually manufacturing new families whose children will in turn be separated and used in new exchanges in the same network of alliances. Although the dynamics of Yafar marriage are not repeated from one generation to the next, for they depend on the (limited) availability of women, they do follow certain recognized prescriptions and prohibitions. I will begin by exposing the dynamics of groups as exchanging or exogamous units and then go on to analyze the system of rules and prohibitions. Last of all marriage as the birth of a new couple will be described in its chronology.

Exogamy and Neighbouring Groups

Demography and Dualism

Demography is a decisive factor in contracting marriages. The population of the societies, villages, clans and exchanging groups together with the sex ratio determine whether or not a system is viable, whether or not the rules are applied and whether or not the whole evolves and changes. The table below shows the demographic situation in the Yafar marriage zone for 1970.[1]

Tribes	Age groups					
	11–15 yrs		16–45 yrs		Total 11–45 yrs	
	M	W	M	W	M	W
Yafar 1–3	12	13	58	34	70	47
Aynunkneri	10	3	33	22	43	25
Potayneri 1–2	18	21	57	45	75	66
Wamuru	20	10	61	49	81	59
Totals	60	47	209	150	269	197
Percentages	100	78.33	100	71.78	100	73.23

(No figures exist for Babuk and Punda; *Government Census*, Amanab, 1970.)

Table 13. Sex ratio for the Yafar marriage zone

The lack of available women in the region is obvious at a glance, not to mention that a certain proportion of even these women are forbidden to a Yafar man because of marriage prohibitions. The result is that some Eri bachelors between 25 and 30 years of age maintain that they may never marry 'because there aren't any women' and they do not have a 'sister' to exchange in more distant groups. This situation has obliged the Yafar to build the widest possible network of marriage exchanges, that is to seek wives in all neighbouring tribes, including the Punda, who do not even speak the same language. It also seems to have encouraged marriage by exchange. The policy of widening the marriage

---

1. We do not have recent figures for the same age groups. However, in 1981 there were 60.37 girls for 100 boys under the age of 18, and 75 women for 100 men over 18 (*Government Census*, Amanab).

network, imposed by demographics but also by the needs of reciprocity and ensuring the safety of the immediate social periphery, is in contradiction with an opposite but never realized[2] tendency towards tribal endogamy, a not only economic but social 'self-sufficiency' by which the group seeks to keep its daughters for itself and exchange women 'at home'. At one level it is in terms of this inside/outside alternative that the Yafar conceive of their marriage system.

I will begin by examining the intratribal marriage network before going on to look at how alliances are organized with neighbouring groups. The subdivision of Yafar society into two moieties and four submoieties gives it an internal structural coherence, the hypothetical functional value of which needs to be tested in the endogamous marriage exchanges. Tables 14 and 15 provide the statistics for this. We see that[3] of 166 marriages between Yafar, 63% took place between the two moieties,[4] 21% within the Araneri moiety and 16% within the Angwaneri moiety. Of the marriages between moieties, 60% transferred a woman from Angwaneri to Araneri moiety and 40% in the other direction. Moiety exogamy is not particularly obvious, then (see also Gell 1975), and it would probably be more advisable to speak of 'agamy' (Lowie 1948).

What about the submoieties? Only Aayneri submoiety features a large number of internal marriages (although none between two of the three constituent clans), while the other three show none or almost none. This fact raises the question of the former function of submoieties as exchanging groups; for the moment, however, I can only say that submoieties are more clearly exogamous than moieties and less so than clans. Keeping in mind the difference in submoiety populations (Table 4), I do not see any preference for marriages between some submoieties rather than others. Nor does the situation seem any simpler at the level of interclan marriage. The Yafar do not pair their clans or lineages

2. The endogamy of the Sowanda or Waina-Wiyara tribes to the north of the Yafar always includes an opening, however slight, to the outside.
3. The statistics contained in this chapter are taken from genealogies established for all Yafar clans. The 361 marriages recorded are spread over five generations, but are concentrated for the most part in the last three; most therefore do not go back more than eighty years.
4. These figures do not include local groups as relevant units.

Table 14. 166 marriages between Yafar clans

Women in the moieties, submoieties, clans

Men in the moieties, submoieties, clans			Araneri						Angwaneri									
			Wamawneri		Aayneri				Menaneri						Mwafneri			
			Wa (32)	Fu (33)	If (70)	Ig (55)	Su (152)	Sa (6)	Me (15)	Sk (25)	Ms (11)	Wi (37)	Si (31)	Ya (13)	Bi (86)	Am (63)	Bw (17)	Ta (14)
Araneri	Wamawneri	Wa			1		1								1			1
		Fu		1	1		2					1	2			2		1
	Aayneri	If	2			3	4					3			3	2	1	
		Ig	4	1	6		6			1	1	1			5	9	3	2
		Su				1	1	1		2	2	4	2	2	8	1		2
		Sa					1		1					2				
Angwaneri	Menaneri	Me	1		1	1	2		1							1		1
		Sk																
		Ms																
		Wi		1			1		1			1				1	1	
		Si					2									1	1	1
		Ya			1		3											1
	Mwafneri	Bi	1		1	2	5		1	3		3	1		3	1		1
		Am	1	2	4	1	4			2		1					1	
		Bw	1		1	2	2						1					1
		Ta					1					1						

Circled (moiety-level) totals: Araneri men × Araneri women = 35; Araneri men × Angwaneri women = 63; Angwaneri men × Araneri women = 42; Angwaneri men × Angwaneri women = 26.

Total clan populations are shown in parentheses under each clan abbreviation (for full names, see Table 4, Chap. 3); circled numbers correspond to total number of marriages at the moiety level.

into marriage partners as do the Southern Highlands Etory, for instance (Kelly 1977), but certain clans do not intermarry either because they are regarded as submoiety 'brothers' or because they are bound by a *rangwarik* taboo, which will be analysed later.

Exogamic Solidarities

The clan exogamy I have just indicated should be taken only as a basic principle of the system as it operates today. Two other types of phenomena intervene and modify the model. The first leads us to see clan exogamy as the outcome of the gradual evolution of a situation originally based on submoiety exogamy (see Ch. 2). This hypothesis is based on the statistical scarcity of effective marriages between clans from the same submoiety and on the comments of my best informant, May Promp, who regarded these submoieties as groups of 'brother' clans (*nerete* 'classificatory brothers'), all hypothetically born of the *same mother* and, because of this, forbidden to intermarry; he maintained that marriage between such clans was a relatively recent practice.

The second type of phenomenon contradicting the clan exogamy model is comprised of what I call the 'exogamic solidarities' linking certain clans. This process can also sometimes show how the clans of one submoiety legitimize an ideological line of descent or collateral relationship. The resulting purported 'consanguinity' can be due to real marriage alliances in which two ancestors (one from each clan) married two sisters (from a third clan) or to a collateral link or a line of descent symbolically legitimized by a myth. The first situation is related to the sixth prohibition below, and will be analysed when we come to it. The second is illustrated by the clans of the younger submoiety of the female moiety (and probably other submoieties for whom we do not have mythic references), in which descent lines linking them to the 'Great Mother', represented by the Coconut, dictate a marriage taboo largely respected by the facts: Biyuneri (a clan connected with the Mother and the Coconut) do not marry with Amisneri or Bwasneri, 'daughter' clans which emerged from the Coconut Flower, but their symbolic collateral ties ('sister clans') do not forbid their own intermarriage (Figure 28).

Table 15. 159 marriages between Yafar moieties and submoieties

| | | Women in the moieties, submoieties | | |
| | | Male *Araneri* | | Female *Angwaneri* | |
Men in the moieties, submoieties		Elder Wamawneri	Younger Aayneri	Elder Menaneri	Younger Mwafneri
Male *Araneri*	Elder Wamawneri	–	5 / 3.1%	3 / 1.9%	5 / 3.1%
	Younger Aayneri	8 / 5%	22 / 13.8%	17 / 10.7%	36 / 22.6%
Female *Angwaneri*	Elder Menaneri	2 / 1.3%	8 / 5%	3 / 1.9%	6 / 3.8%
	Younger Mwafneri	5 / 3.1%	23 / 14.5%	13 / 8.2%	3 / 1.9%

Another example is provided by the exogamic solidarity of the Ifêêg and Ifêaroog clans. It is said that once upon a time the Ifêaroog were *nabasa* spirits and were 'discovered' by the clans of the female moiety, who tried to kill them. The Ifêêg intervened and took the Ifêaroog, who later became human, under their wing (whence perhaps the etymology of *Ifêêg na reeg*, 'sons of the Ifêêg' [?]). One last case is that of the only two clans of the 'male' elder submoiety, Wamawneri and Fuwaneri, already mentioned in the discussion of elder and younger rankings, who, according to the myth, were the children of the two sisters of their ancestor Wam (p. 80).

Chapter 1 described similar mythic bonds of kinship between tribes, and Chapter 2 (Figure 11) provided the reconstructed genealogical validation of the collateral relationship between moieties and submoieties. At every level of the social structure the same need is expressed: to adduce blood ties between the constituent units of society in order to ensure its ideological unity.

Intertribal Alliances

The Yafar territory is surrounded by that of six contiguous tribes, two of which speak the Waina language (Map 2). One of these, Sowanda, lies further away than the others and is separated from the Yafar hamlets by a little-exploited territory; moreover, the Sowanda maintain almost total tribal endogamy among their ten hamlets. There has never been a direct marriage between Yafar and Sowanda, but in Chapter 8, we saw that they engage in economic exchanges based on institutionalized partnership. The Yafar have contracted marriage ties with the five other tribes along their borders, which they renew at varying intervals. Beyond this belt of allied tribes, a Yafar clan may find itself allied with one of the clans of a more remote tribe (which in turn belongs to the 'connubial belt' of one of the other contiguous tribes) through the remarriage of a Yafar woman initially married into one of the adjacent societies or through the marriage of her daughter. Those involved are themselves often unfamiliar with this type of relationship as they do not entertain relations with these peripheral allies. Up to a certain point, geographical distance is a deciding factor,[5] for it is above all the social isolation of these 'sisters' or 'sisters'' daughters and their affines in the midst of otherwise foreign communities that prevents sustained communication. The security circle constituted by adjacent related groups appears as a sort of barrier to individual mobility and to exchanges between groups. It seems that as a rule (Table 16), the rate of

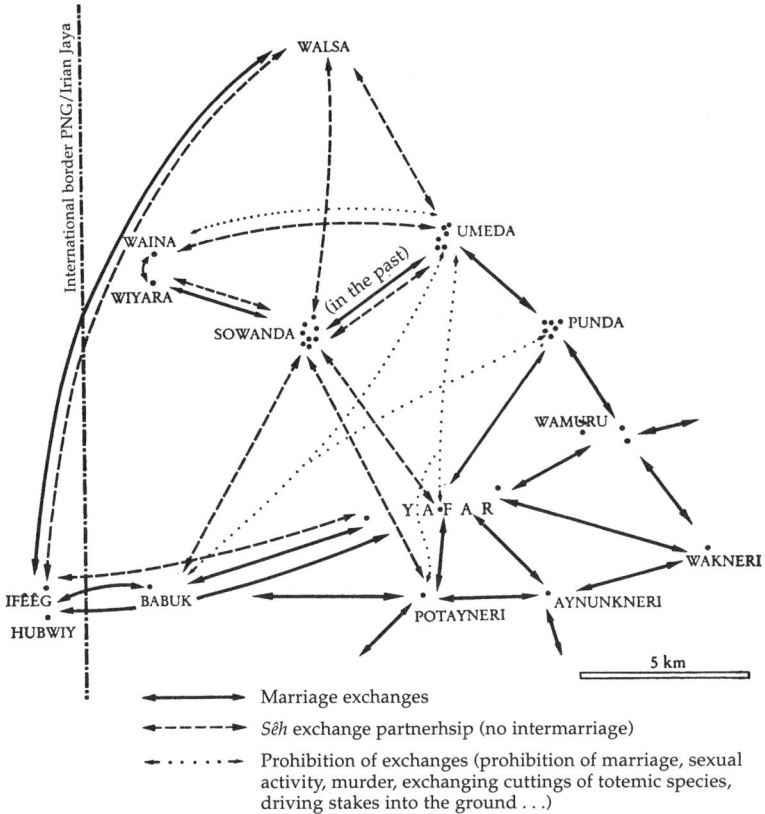

Map 4. Three modalities of intertribal relations in the Northern Eri and Waina regions

5. Certain adjacent tribes, like the Babuk, are no less distant (up to three and a half hours' walk) than an outside group located on the other side of a bordering tribe (an hour away, for instance). The Muwagneri and the Wakneri, some two and a half hours from the central Yafar hamlet and on the other side of Aynunkneri territory, once entertained marriage and ceremonial relations with the Yafar, which, even if they remained rather limited, existed nonetheless; for the Muwagneri, these relations were probably determined by the fact that this group, part of the Kumwaag federation, used to form a single residential unit with the Aynunkneri.

marriage between Yafar and their neighbours is inversely proportionate to geographical distance, in accordance with the concentric or sociocentric structure of the intertribal marriage network.

Marriages between Yafar and other tribes	Yafar women given	'Foreign' women received	Total	Number of clans involved		Distance in minutes
				Non-Yafar	Yafar	
Wamuru	5	6	11	3	3	150
Wakneri (Wogineri)	0	3	3	2	3	170
Muwagneri	1	7	8	2	4	150
Aynunkneri	2	16	18	5	7	120
Potayneri	15	38	53	4 *	12	60
Babuk	6	12	18	6	9	210
Punda	23	28	51	6 **	9	150
Misc.	7	11	18	–	–	–
Totals	59	121	180			

* The four Potayneri 'clans' are also submoieties.
** These are exogamous hamlets which may correspond to a single clan.

Table 16. Marriages recorded between Yafar and other tribes

Marriages between				
Yafar, Araneri	/	other tribe, Araneri	42	63 Yafar Araneri marriages with another tribe
Yafar, Araneri	/	other tribe, Angwaneri	21	
Yafar, Angwaneri	/	other tribe, Angwaneri	29	91 Yafar Angwaneri marriages with another tribe
Yafar, Angwaneri	/	other tribe, Araneri	62	
Totals	71 parallel marriages (same moiety):		46.1%	
	83 cross-marriages (opposite moieties):		53.9%	
for a total of 154 marriages for which the moieties were known				

Table 17. Marriages recorded between Yafar and other tribes according to membership in Araneri and Angwaneri moieties

Looking at the frequency of interclan marriages, one is struck by the disparity in the figures; the apparent concentration of marriages between certain clans is due only to their relatively large membership (see Table 4, Ch. 3). I see three reasons for this. The first is the scarcity of women, already mentioned, which obliges men or clans to take wives where they find them, without regard to matrimonial debts or credits. The second reason is that women are exchanged in a social context of solidarity among clans of the same tribe and among clans of different but already allied tribes, which gives rise to a form of generalized reciprocity in which women are not 'paid for' (unless it is with another woman), but are given. The only security backing this 'generosity', with the exception of the less frequent 'sister' exchanges and rarely practiced deferred exchanges (see below), is kinship in the broad sense. In effect, the majority of marriages take place between *heheeg* (kin and affines); and when a man is forced to seek a wife among *angôruwaag*, non-allied strangers, it means he has a 'sister' to exchange. The third reason is because any further marriages between two patriclans are forbidden for the next two generations (see below).

Between different tribes, trust tends to extend beyond the boundaries of kinship to the whole local group and, to a certain degree, even the whole allied tribe. For instance, a Yafar man with affines in clan X of a neighbouring tribe can circulate freely in the local group of this clan and even, to some extent, in the other hamlets of the tribe without having to fear the hostility of the clans to which he is not related. On the other hand, a man whose clan has never contracted a marriage in a given nearby tribe will never pay them a visit, for his presence would be regarded as suspicious. The co-residence of clans in the same village or the sharing of a common territory alters the level of the 'feeling of being allies'. The rigorously defined bonds of alliance between two clans (and implicitly between the two corresponding submoieties) are thus enriched by ties of solidarity between broader groups defined by residence or tribal identity.

As already mentioned when discussing Sowanda endogamy, the spatial organization of alliance in Waina-speaking groups is different from that of the Eri, being connected with a settlement pattern of stable hamlets. No concentric structure is evident, and the tribes intermarry or not, depending on ties that go back to their origins, legitimized by mythology which attributes anteriority to the Umeda 'mother' group. I do not have much information on this region (see Gell 1975 and above, pp. 79–81), however, and it is not absolutely obvious that the logic of marriage exchanges today corresponds to the logic of the myths of origin. For example, Yafar and Punda are designated as 'daughters' of Umeda, but while Umeda and Punda on the one hand and Punda and Yafar on the other intermarry, marriage is prohibited between Yafar and Umeda. The last two groups are also linked by other taboos, including homicide and the exchange of shoots of the totemic species, whereas Yafar and Sowanda used to fight each other and carry on privileged exchanges of sprouted coconuts (p. 232).

Abutting on Waina, entertaining relations with Sowanda and Punda, and with Umeda by way of Punda relatives, and sharing with them the same mythology and the same totemic cult, Yafar is partially implicated in the Waina system of intertribal relations, even though they are governed for the most part by the concentric model of exchange proper to the Eri.

Rules and Strategies

Prohibitions and Preferences

Although Yafar kinship terminology is of the Dakota-Iroquois type (Juillerat 1977), the marriage system, because of its negative rules (prohibitions) for choosing a spouse, is related to the Crow-Omaha type (Lévi-Strauss 1967: Preface) and therefore comes under the heading of semi-complex systems (Héritier 1981). We shall see, in effect, that the rules governing prohibited marriages resemble those of societies using Crow-Omaha terminology, but the Yafar system is further complicated by the introduction of dualism, since – as we have just seen – the four submoieties constitute (and according to our best informants, used to constitute even more strictly) exogamous units between which the clans, as the smallest exchange groups, exchanged their sisters symmetrically (isolated direct exchanges) or asymmetrically (cyclical exchanges over four generations). But the past or theoretical exogamy of the submoieties raises questions (for which there are no sure answers) about the hypothetical status of marriage classes which might have accrued to the submoieties had they engendered a four-group exchange circuit. We can see outlines of generalized exchange appearing here with the emergence of exchange founded on prohibitions. Nothing, however, authorizes the assumption that each of the four exchange units had a permanent status of wife-giver or wife-taker with respect to another given unit; moreover, marriage was certainly never prescriptive (with the matrilateral cross cousin), as in true generalized exchange (Héritier 1981; Lévi-Strauss 1967).

Let us begin by examining the prohibitions, of which there are six:

1) A man (or a woman) may not marry within his own patriclan, not even with a lineage distinct from his own, nor in a clan of his own submoiety regarded as a 'brother' (*nerete*) which is linked to his own through exogamic solidarity (see above).

2) A man (or a woman) may not marry in his mother's clan (maternal kin termed *nonanənga*, from *nonoog*, MB), or even in a collateral lineage of this clan. Marriage in a 'brother' clan from the same submoiety as the mother's may be prohibited or 'tolerated', depending on the case. The Yafar express this rule by saying that 'a daughter must not retrace her mother's footsteps'.[6]

3) A man (or a woman) may not marry in his father's mother's clan or in his mother's mother's clan (*rangwarik*[7] kinship category). This rule is more strictly observed for a female ego (all lineages of both clans are prohibited) than for a male ego, who may be allowed to take a wife in a lineage collateral to that of his mother's mother.

4) A man (or a woman) may not marry in the patriclan of his real maternal uncle's wife or his real paternal aunt's husband (collateral lines are allowed).

5) A man (or a woman) may not marry any cousin up to and including those of the second degree (third degree as defined

---

6. Certain groups, like the Koiari from the Port Moresby region, reverse the rule ('the daughter must follow the path by which her mother came'), thus making reciprocity of the alliance from one generation to the next the basis of their marriage system (Williams 1976: 151–3); in this case, the rule determines a dual exchange by two marriage groups. The point shared with the Yafar is that the two groups state the rule in terms of uterine descent and the woman's mobility between stable male 'places' (kinship and sometimes local groups).

7. This term is used to define this category only in so far as it is prohibited; it is not used as a kin term for 'grandmother' (*asanənga*).

by Canon Law; Héritier 1981: 181), even if they do not belong to any of the prohibited clans (*nonanəŋga* and *rangwarik*).[8]
6) The two spouses may not belong to patrilines of which two ascendants in the male line married two sisters (Figure 31).

A few remarks are needed to complete these statements. Regarding the first prohibition, the rule is always respected at the lineage level (where genealogical ties are known), and almost always at the clan level, that is between two lineages. Out of all the recorded marriages contracted by Yafar men or women, I found two cases in which the spouses belonged respectively to two unnamed lineages regarded as collaterals of the same named clan. The Yafar judged these marriages to be irregular and to unite a 'brother' and a 'sister' (*nisag/weerik*) in the broadest classificatory sense. On both occasions, quarrels and even stick fights broke out, but the marriages went ahead nevertheless because the young people involved were decided.

At the submoiety level, marriage prohibitions between clans bearing different names but regarded as 'brothers' (*nerete*) are respected to varying degrees, depending on the types of exogamic solidarity defined above. The Wamawneri elder male submoiety is strictly exogamous, as the two constituent clans are mythically linked by a common male ancestor; they share an agnatic identity, then and their differentiation is founded on links to two separate mothers (pp. 96–7). The Aayneri younger male submoiety is comprised of one strictly exogamous bloc, Ifêêf + Ifêaroog, two clans symbolically linked (p. 298) as father and son, against which stands Sumneri clan. In the female moiety, Menaneri elder submoiety is comprised of five clans (one of which, Menaneri proper, is now extinct), which are not bound by a marriage prohibition, even though they are all supposed to have descended from the same mother, Mena (Figure 11), and two of them, Suwê and Mêsêw, have never intermarried. I counted a total of only two marriages between the other clans of this submoiety, excluding the earlier Me/Si[9] marriage which founded the implantation of the Sig-aynaag segment that broke

8. It seems this prohibition should be explained by the notion of degree of consanguinity, not by an opposition between 'making kin into affines' and vice versa, according to whether the system is asymmetrical or semi-complex (Crow-Omaha); see Héritier 1981: 76; Lévi-Strauss 1967: xxvii). Closure of the cycle, as described below, by marriage with the third-degree *taway* cross cousin always partakes of the transformation of kin into allies.
9. For the list of clans in the submoieties and their abbreviations, see Ch. 3, Table 4.

away from Punda three generations ago. Lastly Mwafneri younger female submoiety – called 'Mwafo's children' for their mythic female ancestor – respects the prohibition within the Bi/ Am/Bw trio, except for one marriage between the last two clans (see Figure 28); but two other marriages link one of the three to the fourth clan, Tawank, with whom they do not share a mythical origin. The recently immigrated Yafwayneri segment does not enter the picture.

Regarding the second prohibition (marriage in the mother's clan or one of her 'brother' clans), no case of transgression appeared in the 180 intertribal marriages recorded. On the other hand, of the 166 marriages between Yafar, there were eight exceptions in which the spouse belonged to a 'brother' clan (same submoiety) of ego's mother's clan (five between Bi and Am, and three between If and Ig), as well as four exceptions in which ego married in his or her mother's own clan. Of these last cases, only one involves two different lineages of the same clan (If); in the three others, the lineage of ego's mother and that of his wife are the same, and we were able to reconstruct the genealogical link between the two (Figures 29 and 30). In all three situations (two of which involve, in fact, the same lines of Bi) the tolerance stems from the fact that the lines descend from two different wives of the same ancestor.

There is no need to count up the transgressions of the third prohibition, against marrying *rangwarik*, since the Yafar already agree that a man may possibly marry in one of his grandmother's collateral patrilines. In a way, we are alerted to the fact that this is not true for a female ego by the way the Yafar state the prohi-

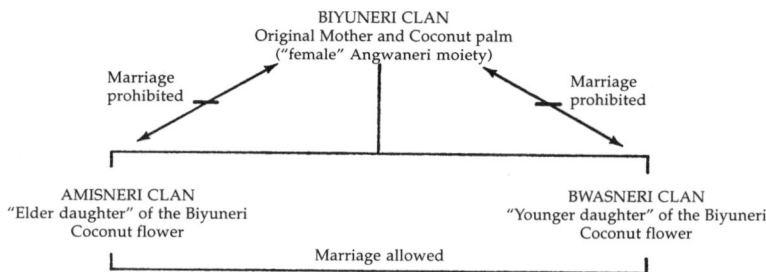

BIYUNERI CLAN
Original Mother and Coconut palm
("female" Angwaneri moiety)

Marriage prohibited

Marriage prohibited

AMISNERI CLAN
"Elder daughter" of the Biyuneri
Coconut flower

BWASNERI CLAN
"Younger daughter" of the Biyuneri
Coconut flower

Marriage allowed

Figure 28. Symbolic uterine descent and collateral relations between three clans of the 'younger' submoiety of the 'female' Angwaneri moiety

bitions on *nonanəŋa*, and by extension, on matrilateral *rangwarik*: 'A daughter must not retrace her mother's [or her mother's mother's] footsteps'. This makes it easier to understand the differentiation according to ego's gender as well as the distinction made between mother's and father's mothers. Héritier (1981: 93) has shown that only the reiteration of a marriage in the father's mother's line (FM) constitutes a repetition of the alliance. The mother's mother's (MM) lineage, however, has not given a wife to ego's lineage and is therefore not necessarily prohibited. The Yafar forbid FM's and MM's lineage and use the same term for both, *rangwarik*. The criterion taking into account MM's lineage seems determined by the matrilineal ideology that appears in the Yafar statement mentioned above: a female ego must not 'retrace' her uterine line. Later we will have occasion to confirm this interpretation when we draw up the model for 'closing the consanguineal cycle' (Héritier 1981) in the four-generation cycle of exchanges (*kəgaag*).[10]

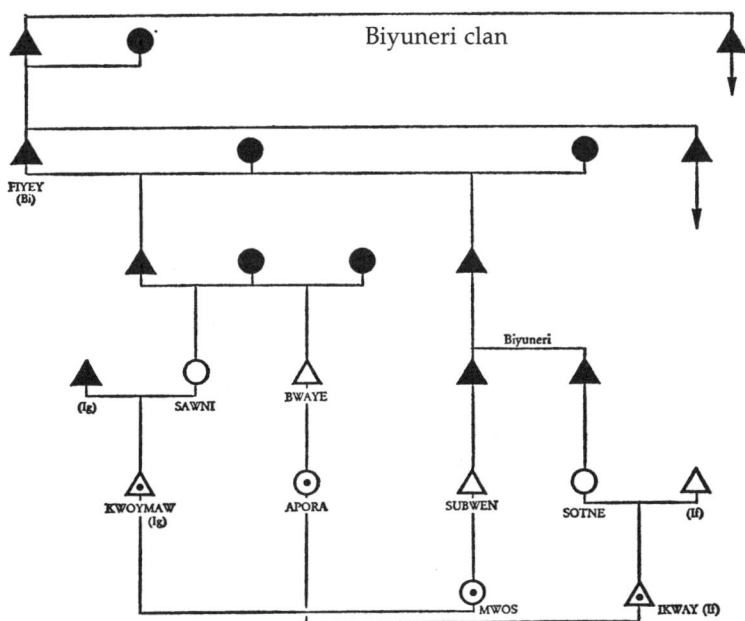

Figure 29. Transgression of marriage prohibition 2: Case 1

10. See the symbolic aspect of the *kəgaag* cycle, pp. 346–7.

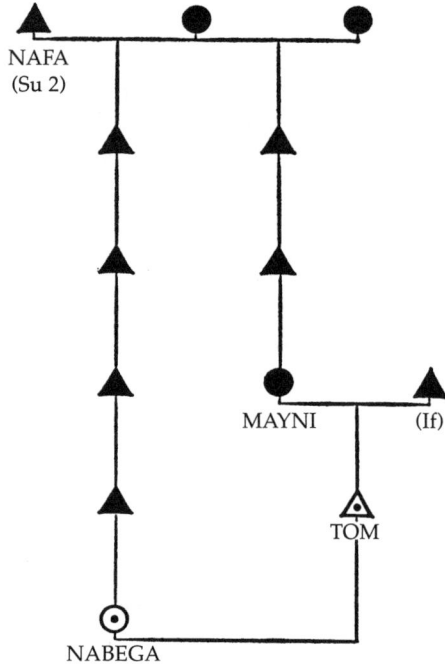

Figure 30. Transgression of marriage prohibition 2: Case 2

The fifth prohibition, dealing with all second (Canon law third-degree) male or female cousins refers to the prohibition on *non-ananga* and *rangwarik*, as well as to what Héritier terms '*the sharing of the same maternal* (in the broad sense) *lineages*' (*ibid.*: 100, my emphasis). This is the Yafar idea of a 'common mother' (*mungwô afaag* 'a single mother').

The same criterion appears in the sixth prohibition forbidding marriage between two lines descending patrilineally from two full sisters married to two men of different clans. A typical case often cited by the Yafar is that concerning the exogamic solidarity of two lines of Sumneri and Amisneri clans (Figure 31). The genealogies show that thirteen marriages have actually been contracted between these two clans (each comprised of two un-named lines) over the last three generations, but only two of them between direct descendants of Nafa and Agwe, which highlights the restrictive choice of the patriline as the unit affected by the prohibition. A secondary function of this type of exogamic

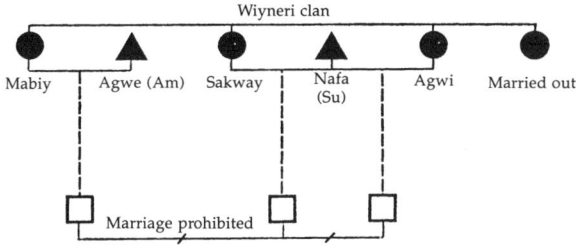

Figure 31. Case of exogamic solidarity through the earlier marriage of several sisters

solidarity is to create ties within the community, to develop a history of the society, laying a trail of social or ideological experiences. Moreover, the scarcity of women and the demographic fragility of the society make it impossible to respect this type of matrimonial prohibition for any length of time.

The rules governing *nonanǝnga* and *rangwarik*, which apply to both a male and a female ego, show that the marriage may not be repeated in either direction. Symmetrical exchange can be carried out only in the same generation and therefore may not be deferred until the next generation. Similarly, a marriage may be duplicated in the same generation, in other words, two men from the same lineage may marry two sisters[11] or the same man may practise (polygynous or successive) sororate, but a son may not repeat his father's or grandfather's marriage.

A symbolic point of order must be added here concerning the prohibition of the mother's and grandmothers' clans. The Yafar associate the lifting of this prohibition with the disappearance (decomposition) of the mother's or grandmothers' remains (*bigik*).[12] For example, to express the prohibition on taking a wife among his *nonanǝnga*, a man will say: *'Ka na afaag ka fakak, ka na bigik mahri igi'*, 'My mother/ I buried (or placed under a funerary shelter), /mine/ [her] remains (bones)/not finished/lie.' The interdiction is even more strongly felt if ego's mother or grandmother is still living (which is rare, even in the case of the mother) or only recently deceased. Conversely, if the grandmother's bones have already been scattered or have disappeared, ego's marriage

---

11. Only one case was found of two brothers marrying two sisters.
12. This temporal reference has to do with the idea of mourning (cf. Ch. 12).

with a male or female *rangwarik* (lineage of this FM or MM) of a collateral patriline can be tolerated.

The negative rules for *rangwarik* as well as those for male or female cousins up to the second degree set a limit on consanguinity, beyond which it becomes possible to marry: non-agnatic cousins of the third degree or more are potential wives providing they are not *nonanənga* or *rangwarik*. This notion of threshold seems to be important because, while all women situated beyond this limit of kinship are allowed without restriction other than clan prohibitions, attention is naturally directed to the closest, in the sense that third cousins enjoy a special status, that of being ego's closest non-forbidden consanguines. These non-prohibited male or female third cousins call each other *taway*. The Yafar see them as a special class of cross cousin, *magawô*, because their defining criterion, here at least, is the ancestral brother/sister couple which determines the male (*fango-inaag* 'in the bow') and female (*nay-inaag* 'in the skirt') lines (see below pp. 343–44 and Juillerat 1977). The outer boundary of incest becomes a privileged tie, a preferential site in which to look for a spouse (Héritier 1981; Juillerat 1981). I should add that a Yafar will never be heard to say that it is good to marry such and such a cousin. At least he will not say it in so many words, but he will state it indirectly by describing a 'cycle' of successive marriages which logically, according to the *rangwarik* rule, should take place between four exchanging groups over four generations. These groups are patriclans which today can be distributed unequally between the four submoieties, but one wonders if they did not once obligatorily correspond, in cases where demographic conditions permitted, to different submoieties. I presented my suppositions to the best Yafar experts, who promptly agreed, adding that they thought that was indeed the old system, but it has now been abandoned 'because there are not enough available women'. Despite the caution demanded by such an affirmation, it is possible to suggest that the cyclical system with closure in the fourth generation as determined by the prohibition on *rangwarik* may have been part of the four-part structure of crosscutting moieties. It is only with difficulty that one can push beyond this simple hypothesis and ask, for example, whether there was a set order for the transmission of women between the four groups. Each matrimonial 'cycle' is in fact unique and is closed by the return of the woman from group D to group A

(Figure 32): the cycle is 'closed' as soon as enough generations have passed for a marriage to be authorized once again. My informant, May Promp, commenting on this discussion one day, correctly said that this was all the result of the prohibition on *rangwarik* and that the whole system was based on this rule.

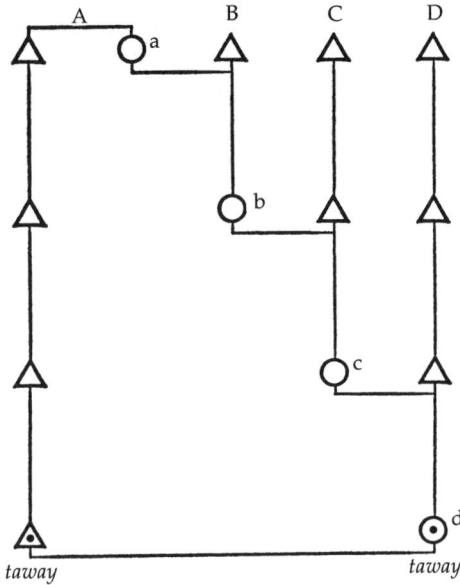

Figure 32. Model of the ideal *kƏgaag* cycle based on the prohibition on *rangwarik* and taking into account four patrilineages and uterine descent between the women

Sometimes the Yafar call the system (or simply marriage between *taway*) *kƏgaag*, 'branch(es) of a tree'. It seems that this metaphor should be interpreted to mean that ego's generation is like the branches growing out from, and still bound by prohibition to, the 'base/stump' (*moog*) of the tree, the first giver in the cycle, but to which the allowed cousin (*taway*) of the last clan 'returns'. It is also said that this cousin (d in Figure 32) 'returns to the source' (*mwig-gam ika*) or to the 'mother stump' (*afaramoog*); such a marriage in accordance with the rule is called *taway-taway*. Once again it is tempting to see a parallel here with the reproductive cycle of plants inspired by the idea of (the fruit-bearing) 'branch': the woman returning to the 'mother' plant is like a fruit that falls at the foot of the tree so that its seeds will produce a new tree there (a new marriage cycle).

One last important point needs clarification: as Figure 32 shows, the Yafar define the *kɜgaag* system by linking the four women given successively by direct uterine descent; in other words the daughter of the woman received should theoretically be given to the next exchange group. This means that a male ego will marry FFFZDDD, a female ego MMMBSSS. A matrilineal dominant surfaces here within a system otherwise governed by patriliny. This appears, among other places, in the Yafar's gynocentric explanation of how the cycle operates, eschewing any specific social reference (like the Umeda, where Gell noted evidence of a similar system, and the Punda, where I confirmed the same; both groups use Omaha terminology) when speaking of women and their daughters given successively to different clans until the uterine great-granddaughter returns to her great-grandmother's patriclan. Matrilineal descent is directly established as the founding principle, against a background of agnatic exchanging groups.[13] Yet no spontaneous connection is usually made between this structure and the prohibition on *rangwarik*. In effect for all practical purposes, ideal matriliny is scarcely possible at every point along the way, and often an agnatic classificatory daughter of the husband of the woman received is given in the following stage. This determines, for a male ego, the chain FFFZD*H*B*DD. It also happens that the cycle is closed not by the 'return' of the *taway* cousin to the original giver clan, but once again by the giving of a *taway* by this clan, in other words in the same direction. In fact the difficulties of respecting male and uterine lines of descent (Figure 32) are so great that the actual cases usually 'deviate' on more than one score (Figures 33–35).[14]

---

13. Here we have the same 'opposition between male discontinuity and female continuity' (Bourdieu 1980: 360) which characterizes the process of biological reproduction (fertilization/gestation-breast feeding) so often evoked in Yafar myths.

14. There is a case altogether similar to the *kɜgaag* in the groups studied by van der Leeden (see Pouwer 1960, van der Leeden 1960 for a discussion of the problem). For non-Melanesian examples, the reader may consult Héritier 1981, particularly the Samo system of Burkina Faso (p. 115); the different realizations are defined in Figure 39 of Héritier's study and in the Inca model (p. 144), which also stresses the ideal matrilineal link between the women given in the course of the same cycle (with, however, one justification in the inheritance system).

Figure 33 shows, for example, a case already closed in the third generation by a marriage in which the younger brother (Saifer) of the first woman given at the beginning of the cycle is himself the beneficiary of the return of Mur (non-equivalence of age and generation are allowed, Saifer, Wagif and Mur being roughly the same age). Furthermore, whereas the AWPIY=Suwi marriage was concluded without exchange, Saifer exchanged his sister's daughter Wey with Wagif for the daughter of Wagif's elder brother. This exchange caused some people to say that in this instance, one could not speak of either *kəgaag* or *taway*. Moreover, Suwi is not Mur's direct ascendant, which is no doubt what authorized her marriage in Wiyneri clan. Saifer and Mur are not called *taway* because the cycle is a generation short and they are not related as (parallel or cross) 'cousins'. It is already planned that Mur's daughter will be exchanged in a new clan by her maternal uncle, although the identity of the exchange partner has not yet been decided or at least not been divulged.

Figure 34 shows a case in which the position (or the genders) of ego and alter are reversed. The marriage alliance is repeated in the same direction in the third generation (and therefore at the correct generational level), but only two clans (instead of four) and three lineages are involved in the cycle, first of all in the wake of the 'incestuous' marriage between the two Sumneri lineages (WAREY=Ebe) and secondly because it is this couple's son (Waya) and not their daughter who enters the chain. Besides the marriage between a clan 'brother' and 'sister', which caused a scandal at the time, the *taway-taway* marriage between Ufwan and Samow is regarded as barely within the norm; but this marriage was facilitated by the fact that their great-grandparents' remains 'had finished rotting' (*ate nöngêk*) a long time ago and because they were already inscribed in a deferred exchange (completed some ten years later) of agnatic sisters with Saw, Samow's agnatic cousin.

The last example, Figure 35, shows a more complicated case in which a double marriage by exchange (YOW=Yay and UW=San) is considered to close a cycle. First of all, though, an irregularity appears in the Bi/Su2a (WAMPI=Hetay) marriage, which does not respect the *rangwarik* prohibition (Ahnay, Su2b); but Hetay and Ahnay belong to different patrilines (a and b) of Sumneri 2 lineage. Next, Yow marries in his mother's clan (Su) (but in the other lineage). Yay's death, at the birth of her first child, was interpreted by some as punishment for this marriage. Finally, San is married to a man from her paternal grandmother Hetay's clan (but again from a different lineage). This diagram reveals a

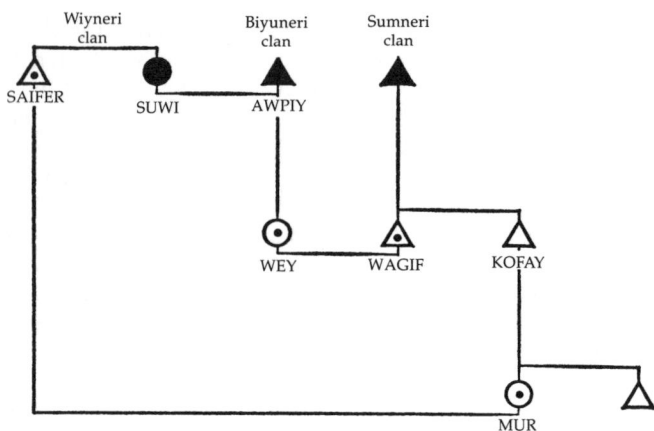

Figure 33. Case of closure in the third generation

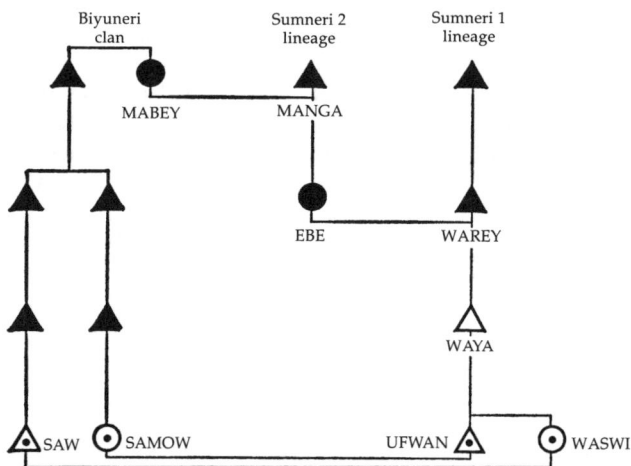

Figure 34. Closure in the third generation through 'sister' exchange

number of 'transgressions', but always partially attenuated by the collateral distances between the lineages or lines involved. Only the WAMPI=Hetay marriage created a real problem (the *rangwarik* are from the same lineage), degenerating into a stick fight in which Wampi was attacked by his half-brother and his agnatic half-sister as well as by one of Hetay's agnatic class-ificatory brothers.

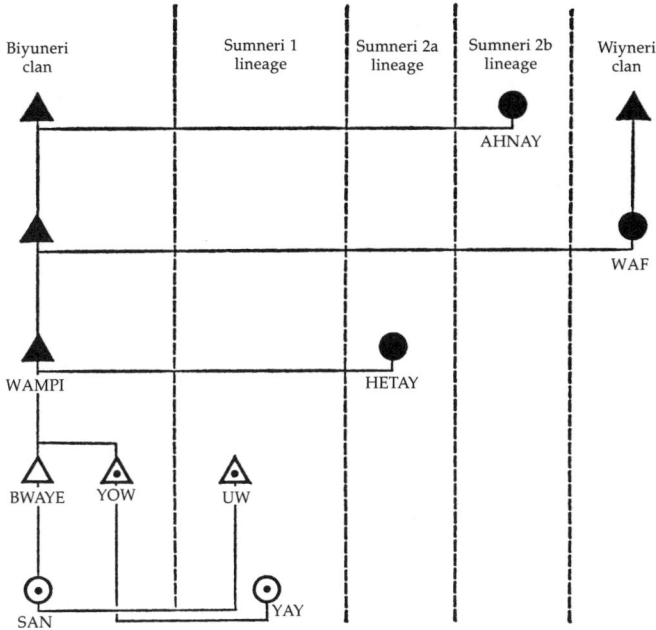

Figure 35. Closure through 'sister' exchange

The above illustrations are all drawn from Yafar society, but the *kǝgaag* system and the prohibitions also apply to the inter-tribal marriages which often enter into these cycles.[15]

Marriage Strategies

For the sake of convenience, I will make a distinction between strategies and rules. The latter, which have just been described, are stable dispositions and apply to every marriage contracted. Strategies, on the other hand, are more or less spontaneous, positive and contingent initiatives for making the system work. The

15. I have used the word 'cycle', but the validity of this concept for defining the *kǝgaag* system might be questioned, even though the Yafar speak of marriage between *taway* as closing a cycle that has a genealogically identifiable starting point. In point of fact, the cycle really takes shape only at the moment of its closure, but it cannot be predicted from the outset. Each time a marriage is arranged, the adults supervising its legitimacy see if they cannot make it into a marriage between *taway*, thus closing a cycle that did not exist as such until then; such plans can be made at best a generation in advance.

rule defines the kinship and social fields of spouses which are allowed and prohibited for a given group or individual. The strategy is an individual dynamic plan – which may be recognized as following or countering the norms – the aim of which is to allow a group or individual to appropriate a particular woman from another group.[16] Among the Eri, for whom, as we have seen, the demographic context severely restricts the choice of spouses, the aim of any matrimonial strategy is on the one hand to obtain a wife who is not prohibited and on the other to achieve maximum coherence of the system. By this I mean that the operation does not have a political or economic goal located outside the marriage alliance itself. The absence of social hierarchies and of a region-wide system of military alliances, as well as the lack of any form of dowry (land in particular), means that the matrimonial policy of the tribes of this area has no other function than to supply the group with wives and to enable it to reproduce itself in accordance with the ideology of marriage alliances.

Five strategies can be identified: 'sister' exchange, 'child marriage', requesting a wife without compensation, marriage with bridewealth and abduction.

'Sister' Exchange[17]

Direct exchange seems to be a long-standing practice in the region, even though the Yafar and their neighbours tend to see the alleged increase in the number of 'sister' exchanges over the last generation as resulting from the influence of the first Australian administrators (in the early 1960s). The administrators from Amanab are said to have encouraged the Eri to intensify their use of this form of marriage, which they claim rarely to have practised previously. There may actually have been similar government

16. This opposition can nevertheless be relativized. The prohibitions just analysed in fact open on to strategies (how to close a 'cycle'). The strategy consists precisely in knowing how to use the rules; as these cannot be respected absolutely, matrimonial praxis has more to do with strategy than with the statement of norms (see Bourdieu 1980).

17. The Yafar seem to encourage the repetition of marriages in the same generation through 'sister' exchange (opposite direction) or sororate and levirate (same direction), whereas they forbid it between generations. This apparent contradiction shows that 'strategy' is inscribed on another level of apprehension of the social than that of 'rules': rules are mandatory whereas strategy is optional. However, the lapse of time between the gift of a 'sister' and the equivalent countergift which lends direct exchange a character of deferment is never very long. Here a distinction must be made between temporal duration and social time (the passage from one generation to the next); the two are not necessarily identical. See also Héritier 1981: 99–100.

encouragement to avoid clashes over 'debts' of women, although this was not a frequent occurrence in the Eri social system. Actually, Yafar genealogists indicate very few exchanges in earlier generations (+3 and above), but this may be because the circumstances of these old marriages have been forgotten (similarly we see omission of women given in marriage to outside groups). Yet the antiquity of marriage by exchange is attested in mythology; certain texts even attribute the origin of sister exchange to the rejection of incest (see epigraph to this chapter and p. 283). Lastly, the language attests 'sister' exchange in the different ways it has of designating this form of marriage: *haneruk ah-səfa-ôgôg* 'exchanged woman/(dual)-to exchange-(reciprocity)', *weerigim ah-səfa-ôgôg*,[18] again *haneruk məmanga ah-feg* 'exchanged women/ exchange/(dual)-to do', or simply *mungwaag fayig mungwaag fayig* 'one [woman]/to give/one/to give'.

Table 18 gives the figures for marriage by direct exchange. In most cases (two thirds), the woman exchanged is a full or classificatory agnatic sister; the Yafar attach great importance to the role of the patriclan as the group controlling its 'sisters', that is it is important that the giver clan also be the beneficiary. In this case, the identity of the unilineal descent group takes precedence over individual kinship ties. Nevertheless, they are careful to exchange their younger 'sister'; the exchange of an elder 'sister' is not prohibited in itself, but occasions are few and far between, as girls marry earlier than boys – when there are two brothers and two sisters, the elder is given by the elder and the younger by the younger.

Variations from one society to another are revealing: whereas the Yafar and the Kumwaag avoid exchanging a matrilateral or a cross cousin (a few cases are attested nonetheless), which would be tantamount to an exchange between two men and not between two clans, the Wamuru and the Babuk as well as Waina groups (according to Yafar informants) frequently practice this type of exchange. Alternatively, like the other groups, the Yafar tolerate a man exchanging his uterine niece (*rabik*), providing the age difference is not too great; in this case, it is said *nonog rabugungum ah-səfaôgôg* 'maternal uncle/uterine niece (obj. case)

---

18. *Haneruk* is a reciprocal term used between classificatory sisters which, by extension in this case, designates the two women exchanged. *Weerik* means 'sister' when the speaker is male.

/(dual)/to exchange'. However, this form of exchange is said to be more frequent among the Wamuru and the Waina. Nowhere in the region does it seem to be acceptable for a father to exchange his own daughter in order to obtain a wife (but a father may give his daughter for his direct or classificatory son or nephew), and when the Yafar mention the only case of this, among the Wamuru, they express shock at such behaviour. It is said that a man who exchanged his own daughter for himself would be stricken with a sickness called *akuk* (acute loss of weight and strength resulting in death due to the 'ripening' (p. 374) of the soul, *sungwaag*), and that this is exactly what happened to the Wamuru man a few years after he had given his daughter for a wife. On the other hand, for a man with no available sister to exchange, his elder brother's daughter is not only acceptable but normal and sanctioned by the expression *eteeg na röögungugum sumnik-awaag məmanga ah-feg* 'elder/of/daughter (obj. case)/younger-father [=father's younger brother]/to exchange/(dual)-(auxiliary)', or 'the younger brother exchanges his elder brother's daughter'. This choice is based on the privileged relationship between the father's younger brother and the elder brother's child, marked by the term *atôk*, which in a broader sense also means 'adoptive father' or 'adopted child'.

From these few cases, we see that there is an ethical dimension to the choice of the woman to exchange (a choice which often precedes that of the wife), and that culture determines, though in a more flexible way than for the choice of the wife, the kinship categories allowed or prohibited within the framework of agnation, descent, generation and age groups. A direct exchange is perfectly balanced only when each giver patrilineage is at the same time a taker. When this is not the case, some sort of compensation must be made (in the form of gifts and vegetable foodstuffs, or more regularly, game) to the brother or the agnatic male relative of the 'sister' given and regarded as wronged. Consider the exchange of the uterine niece. This may obviously be regarded as one of the rights of the maternal uncle, who gave his sister to his niece's father in the preceding generation, but this reciprocity is not the only reason, for the exchange of a sister's daughter might just as well take place if sisters were exchanged between this girl's father and maternal uncle, in other words if the reciprocal exchange were already closed. In any case, if the

Woman exchanged	Marriages by exchange between Yafar*	Marriages by exchange between Yafar and non-Yafar**	Total	%	Woman's status	
					unmarried	widow
True sister or agnatic half-sister	16	9	25	46.2	2	3
Sister's daughter	8	1	9	16.6	8	1
Elder brother's daughter	3	3	6	11.1	5	1
Agnatic cousin	5	0	5	9.3	5	0
Uterine half-sister	3	0	3	5.6	3	0
Cross cousin	1	2	3	5.6	2	1
Unknown	2	1	3	5.6	3	0
Total	38	16	54	100.0	28	6

* Each figure indicates the number of marriages, not exchanges (double marriages).
** Only the Yafar woman given is counted in this column (i.e. 16 marriages for 16 exchanges).

Table 18. Yafar marriages by exchange from all genealogies, or 361 marriages

mother's brother has taken his niece in order to exchange her on his own behalf, thus leaving his uterine nephew a bachelor with no sister to exchange, it is the latter who will be compensated in the future by receiving the hind legs of pigs that his brother-in-law, his maternal uncle's exchange partner, would normally have given to the latter: the loss of a sister as a woman to exchange for a wife is compensated by the game that the maternal uncle will not get. In other words, the husband of the sister and uterine niece uses this way of paying his brother-in-law for having taken the latter's sister through another exchange partner (his WMB) (see Ch. 9 on the parallel between women and game). Similar compensations are made when the lineage providing a woman to exchange does not benefit directly from this exchange. But the maternal uncle's right also points up the more general right of maternal kin to make use of a girl born of the 'blood' of an agnatic sister in order to procure a new wife.

As exchange is not only the concern of two men but that of two or several patrilineages as well, the two individuals engaging in the exchange are expected to consult the others involved. No objection arises when a man exchanges his own younger sister, since his rights are held to prevail over those of any of the woman's other relatives; rivalry between brothers is hardly an issue either, as the younger usually respects his elder brother's advantage in their common sister. When the exchanger is not the woman's full brother, he must ask her father, or if this is not possible her brother(s). A father cannot refuse his own son or his younger brother (exchange of the *atôk* agnatic niece). The mother and her brother also have their say and can influence the father's decision when differences arise.

In principle the two marriages resulting from an exchange are closely linked and if one ends, the other should as well. The Yafar claim that if one of the two women exchanged happens to die before having children, the other marriage should be dissolved. Nevertheless I was unable to find a case in which a couple wanting to remain together were forced to separate following the end of the other marriage in the exchange. Widows are not exchanged unless they are young and have no children, but a young widower may acquire an unmarried girl through exchange.

Marriage by exchange obviously appears to be a strategy for procuring wives more easily, not a rule that must be applied, failing which the marriage will be considered improper.[19] One question arises concerning the compatibility or incompatibility of direct exchange with the *kəgaag* cycle. One day, I was told that a *kəgaag* cycle should in principle end with a 'sister' exchange, that is between lineages A and D (Figure 32). My informant added that this was a closure, and that this exchange did not open a new cycle with the gift of a woman from A to D. Figures 34 and 35 above attest just such a 'closure' of the cycle founded on the prohibition of *rangwarik*, but in the cases I collected I was assured that the girls of the next generation would be given in marriage 'to other groups' not yet chosen. In view of the doubts expressed above as to the validity of the notion of cycle as an element separable from the system, however, it seems that in recommending the exchange of 'sisters' when the *rangwarik* prohibition is lifted, the Yafar want not only to return a woman to the giver group of the third ascending generation, but at the same time to renew reciprocal marriage relations between the lines. This problem needs further investigation; for example, it seems to me highly unlikely that such a 'sister' exchange would be recommended when the ideal model of the cycle (with ties of uterine descent between the women given, Figure 32) had been successfully applied, for the reciprocity of the direct exchange would cancel out that of the deferred transaction.

When 'sister' exchange occurs in the course of a *kəgaag* cycle or when this exchange does not respect the succession of generations, as in the case of Wagif and Saifer (Figure 33), it seems that the validity of the *kəgaag* system is called into doubt by the Yafar themselves. In the case of Wagif and Saifer, the direct exchange between the two caused Wagif to deny the very existence of an ongoing cycle, while his elder brother saw no contradiction. But this case is too atypical to be a good test. It seems, in effect, that a special combination of circumstances enabled the symmetrical exchange to take place within the cycle while at the same time precipitating its closure. Having taken Wêy for his wife, Wagif could have waited for a daughter and then have returned her to a collateral line of the first giver clan or have handed her on to a fourth group. Instead, by giving a girl from his own agnatic group, indeed his elder brother's daughter, back

---

19. In the Tor region (northern part of western New Guinea) marriage is practically impossible without direct exchange (Oosterwal 1961).

to clan A at the time of his own marriage, he respected the one-generation distance in closing the cycle without actually waiting out the time, and simultaneously realized the perfectly legitimate exchange of his *atôk* niece, Mur, of marriageable age, while Saifer was himself seeking a wife. But by giving his uterine niece in exchange, Saifer cancelled, as it were, the wife-giver role that the Wiyneri clan would otherwise have acquired to the advantage of Biyuneri. Wêy was given both by her agnates, in the framework of the *kəgaag* cycle, and by her maternal uncle, in a direct exchange. It was because of these coincidences and the staggering of the age groups that a premature closure of the cycle could be tolerated under normally unacceptable conditions.

'Child Marriage'
What commonly goes by this term does not appear so much as an institution in itself but rather as a measure to be expected in a society when sociodemographic conditions make it necessary to calculate the best formulas for marriage alliances. When marriages are 'arranged' by adults, who are the only ones who know the alliance networks and the marriages contracted in preceding generations and are therefore able to make the best use of the possibilities open at a given moment, it is only normal to think ahead and project possible marriages into the future. The strategy here is of a temporal order, which takes the form of locking up future matrimonial potentialities. But this is not done when the children are born and rarely in early childhood (perhaps because of the risk of infant mortality), or if it is done, only the preliminary plans are laid. Such arrangements are obviously not possible for all children, and many boys and girls reach adolescence – and even beyond for men – before a spouse is found for them or they find one themselves.

When I tried to learn what the Yafar called this anticipated arrangement of marriages, I was given expressions that provided only metaphorical and not specific definitions: *korko feg*, which can be translated as 'to pretend to' (give one's daughter or son in marriage); *waskwes* 'dissimulation, lie'; *wahôgô*, which alludes to a reciprocal gift of food but may designate by metaphor the arrangement of a marriage between two children; *hwatiy sohwatinag* 'to take out an areca nut' (from one's netbag and give it to one's future son-in-law; or simply *fayig* 'to give' (in marriage). The dominant idea in these strategies is of an arrangement that is both fragile and secret: what does it mean to promise if not 'to pretend to give', and so in a sense 'to lie' (also the meaning in Pidgin of the term *giaman*)? This uncertainty created by the time that must elapse before the plan is realized is determined by the necessity of obtaining the prior agreement of the interested parties. As for the secrecy surrounding any matrimonial arrangement of this type, it is the natural preamble to the avoidance that will characterize relations between the two 'fiancés', as described in the preceding chapter. Bit by bit these pre-marriage ties between the two families are confirmed by the young girl's increasingly frequent or prolonged stays with her future in-laws and by the work the adolescent boy does for his future father-in-law. The food the parents-in-law (or the 'fiancé's' elder brother) give their future daughter-in-law is compensated by the girl's economic help, and sometimes by non-compulsory gifts of sago or firewood from her agnates.

The agents responsible for the older generations taking in hand the younger ones the better to bring them into the alliance networks are not only the parents (including the mother), but also the close maternal relatives. As a rule this strategy is more a sign that the society as such takes charge of its own reproduction policy than a symptom of the elders' repressive domination of younger members.

In many cases 'child marriages' are 'sister' exchanges.

Marriage without Reciprocity
Esmunam means 'without reciprocity' (without compensation, for free, for nothing) and is used in various contexts, homicide when the murder is not followed by reprisals as well as marriage when a man receives a wife without giving a 'sister' in exchange: *Esmunam ka fwa (fay)* 'Without reciprocity I take (give) [wife].'

Notwithstanding a few gifts made to the woman's father, the Yafar say that she has been given 'for nothing'.[20] They explain the absence of demand for compensation by the fact that the marriage takes place within the kinship network, between *awan-ənga* (members of the same social community) or *heheeg* (kin and affines), and one cannot ask a 'brother' (*nerete*) for a 'price'. Women circulate within a framework of generalized reciprocity

---

20. *Esmunam* translates in Pidgin as *givim* – or *kisim nating* 'to give – or to take for nothing'.

in which an equilibrium is eventually attained. But a wife received *esmunam* can also become a link in a *kəgaag* cycle which is not always perceived as such until the final stage (marriage between *taway*). This solidarity or generosity is due to the small size of the local groups and tribes and to the resulting close-knit network of exchanges reproduced there; but the strategies of symmetrical exchange and the calculation of cycle closures have shown that such solidarity is only relative.

The strategy adopted by an unmarried man who has no 'sister' to exchange but has identified a possible wife (who may still be prenubile) in his own tribe or in a neighbouring group consists in making his request known to the young woman's father (or to a substitute or to the mother if the father is deceased) through a go-between. The reply may be sent straight back by the same mediator or the man may be kept waiting. The woman's father begins by consulting his entourage: his wife, his eldest son if he is adult, his wife's brother (the girl's maternal uncle) and the girl herself. The outcome may be a categorical refusal for reasons of distance (they do not want to marry their daughter into a different group) or because another marriage has been planned for her; the suitor can press his case via the same go-between, and the parents may reverse their decision. If the request is accepted – and it may be against the girl's will – the father sends the young man some areca nuts and tobacco. The future son-in-law distributes this pledge to those around him, as he would be ashamed to consume it himself. The 'shame' felt here is the same as that marking the non-relations between future spouses (Ch. 9): the father-in-law's areca nuts represent the handing over to another lineage of the uterine blood (betel juice) necessary for the beneficiary's reproduction and his agnatic descent. The whole representation of social and biological reproduction is contained in this gift of areca nuts, whence the receiver's embarrassment and his haste to be rid of everything, but while accepting the message. This transaction validates the father's acceptance but not the daughter's.

A few weeks later, the young woman's father (her mother or elder brother if her father is dead) presents the future son-in-law with some sago jelly (*yis*), after ascertaining (once again through the go-between) that the areca nuts were indeed accepted. While areca mixed with lime and betel represent blood, *yis* already symbolizes conception, the jelly – as we saw in Chapter 2 – standing for the coagulation of female *hoofuk* and male semen. This gift seems, then, to prefigure the offspring that will result from the marriage. A countergift follows shortly, with the son-in-law giving some of his own sago jelly to the family of his future wife. Gift and countergift may be seen as reciprocal participation in the twofold, agnatic and uterine, descent. At this time the young woman, who has sometimes scarcely been consulted, can reject the marriage by refusing to eat her suitor's *yis*. By this passive act, she makes public her dissent and avoids a verbal confrontation with her father. Discussions and arguments will follow in which the parents may rapidly bow to their daughter's wishes or, on the contrary, if the marriage is important to the group's matrimonial policy, bring pressure to bear on her, as I will show later.

The gifts of areca and *yis* can also be made after a 'child marriage' when the moment for the actual marriage approaches, and similarly after an 'abduction', once the conflict has died down. When 'sisters' are exchanged, gifts and countergifts of sago jelly are made, but it is not clear that the fathers' agreement falls under the sign of areca, as the arrangement is made between the exchanging parties (who are not necessarily the beneficiaries).

Marriage with Bridewealth
Since about 1975, the affines of the Yafar belonging mainly to the Kumwaag and Wamuru groups have begun demanding money (5, 10, then 20 kinas[21]) for giving a woman in marriage without an exchange of 'sisters'. The immediate consequence was, first of all, a marked tendency to look for endogamous marriages or 'sisters' to exchange and, secondly, for some bachelors unable to find a wife in better conditions, a tendency to save up bridewealth from money earned selling small red peppers or doing maintenance on the government road under construction. The money is paid along with the usual exchanges of items described elsewhere in this chapter. The Yafar feel this demand to be a barrier to the development of extratribal alliances with certain groups because of their lack of income, but they do not reject the principle of adding a few kinas to the presents made by the future son-in-law. A transition is in progress, then, between marriage *esmunam* and marriage by 'payment'

---

21. In 1975 the kina was worth about 1 Australian dollar (= US $ 1.00 in 1984).

Marriage by 'Abduction'
Marriage by abduction without the woman's consent does not appear to have existed, as in any case it could never lead to a definitive arrangement between groups that were moreover geographically and socially too close for a complete break to occur. 'Abduction' (*hugufa kuk*, 'to seize/gone away') must therefore be understood as a concerted act on the part of a couple (see also Ch. 9, 'The disorders of sexuality'). This strategy is used only when the parents are opposed or the woman is already married. The woman herself may take the initiative, in this form of marriage imposed on society, by deciding to move in with the man of her choice (in another village or tribe) with the complicity of some of his agnates; it is said that the man himself is not always warned or even consulted. The woman is not abducted in this case but runs away. This type of female strategy, which may require some daring, depending on the social tensions reigning at the time, will also be discussed in dealing with marriage failures. It consists in running away from one's domestic group (the family) in secret and imposing oneself on another, in other words acting as a free individual in the face of social strategies and transactions. This *coup de force* provokes temporary conflicts or stick fights, but if both the man and woman are determined, it ends with the exchanges of goods that legitimize the union.

The main sociological feature of this type of marriage is that it is not part of a plan, of a controlled policy of alliances, but arises from a personal relationship in which the psychological (affective) dimension in a way forces the hand of society.

Forms of Secondary Marriage

Levirate and Sororate
Widowhood is a state that should last as little time as possible after the mourning period (the time it takes the flesh of the deceased to decompose completely, a few months), as the couple is a prime economic necessity. And yet – for men in any case – widowhood often stretches to several years; a post-menopausal widow will also remain alone longer than a young woman, or even definitively. As in drawn-out male celibacy, the lack of women is the main cause of protracted male widowhood. The metaphor for the couple is a tree trunk (the man) wound round

with a betel vine (the woman); thus it is said of a widower (*awaag esik*) that he is a bare trunk whose vine has died: *Nunung uhaag, rii sabam ogo* 'Betel/has died/tree alone/stands.' Any widow (*afaag esik*) who is still young will be courted as though she were unmarried by bachelors, married men or widowers from inside or outside the tribe. The local community, in the person of its elders in particular, will try to find her a new husband. An older widow nearing menopause can be married by a widower from her own age group.[22] Marriages between different age groups are rare, and no form of monopoly on young women by elderly widowers is found.

Levirate and sororate are two forms of marriage implicitly confirmed by kinship terms, even though the latter is less frequent than the former. The potentiality of levirate is indicated terminologically by the reciprocity of the term *riyangunguk* 'husband's brother/brother's wife (male ego)', and that of sororate by the reciprocity of the term *abwari* 'wife's sister/sister's husband (female ego)' (Juillerat 1977 and Appendix C), whereas the system generally does not use reciprocal terms between male and female kinship positions. In most cases levirate takes the form of remarriage with an agnatic classificatory brother of the deceased. The Yafar say that remarriage with the full brother is not 'good', though I noted a few cases of remarriage with the younger brother; remarriage with one of the husband's agnatic half-brothers, on the other hand, is 'correct', though I found no examples. Table 19 shows that out of 52 widow remarriages, only eleven came under the heading of 'levirate', five of which were with the younger full brother (none with the elder brother).[23]

These figures show that a woman is free to remarry elsewhere: those who do usually go outside the tribe, and the woman may even take her small children with her. Levirate has a place only inasmuch as it enables the already established interclan alliance to be maintained; but this alliance may be opposed by the individual desires of the 'brothers', who may not want a second wife or widow, by those of the widow herself, and by the possibility of other strategies for her remarriage. Nevertheless the tribe or local group tries to retain her, especially if she has or is still

22. There was one exception in 1981: a young man under thirty unable to find a wife 'married' a widow of over fifty. This was a sterile marriage, the function of which was basically economic.

23. On levirate in other New Guinea societies, see in particular Kelly 1977.

Remarriage of widow with	Number of cases	
Younger full brother of the deceased husband	5	(or 11 cases of leviritic type)
A 'brother' from the deceased's patrilineage (first- or second-degree agnatic cousin)	3	
A 'brother' from the deceased's patriclan (no known genealogical link)	3	
A man from another clan of the same submoiety	7	
A man from another submoiety	16	
A man from another tribe (the widow leaves the Yafar)	18	
Total remarriages of Yafar widows	52*	

* I have not included five cases in which widows remarried outside the Yafar tribe contracted a third marriage, again outside the Yafar group (four cases in the same clan hamlet with the Punda, one case between two tribes of the Kumwaag federation).

Table 19. Modalities of secondary marriages of Yafar widows and leviratic marriages

capable of having children. If she can no longer bear children or has had none, however, she will be sent back to her natal group.

The Yafar claim that true sororate, whether successive or simultaneous (sororal polygyny) is possible only if the younger sister is still available and if the son- and father-in-law enjoy good relations. A man is not considered to have any special rights to his sister-in-law. Some Yafar maintain that marriage should be avoided with the full sister of the deceased wife (nonetheless, six cases were recorded) and that it is better to chose a half-sister or an agnatic (or even non-agnatic) cousin. Once again we see the need to observe a consanguineal distance between one spouse and the next. Sororal polygyny (a single case recorded with a full sister, three cases with an agnatic parallel cousin) cannot be achieved by a single double marriage. The younger sister may be requested only later, assuming that she is still free. On the other hand, sororate can be facilitated if the sisters themselves wish to remain close and to go on living in the same domestic group. It is often because of their solidarity, their identification with each other, that two sisters go on to become co-wives. My attention was drawn to one case, among others, of an elder sister who herself suggested to her younger sister that she should join her as a co-wife, pointing out her husband's qualities as a hunter. Without actually offering to share her spouse, the elder sister usually sees to it that the younger finds a husband, possibly from the same clan as her own. This creates pairs of parallel marriages. The unmarried younger sister is also supposed to replace her deceased elder; she will be told *Rii sabam ne na ogohôm* 'The tree/ alone [without its vine]/for you/stands', and speaking of the practice of sororate in general (even in the classificatory sense where the replacement wife is an agnatic or non-agnatic cousin of the deceased), the Yafar say that 'the younger sister follows in her elder sister's footsteps (*noor*)' (*eteeg na noorum bwes*), in contrast to the statement that 'a daughter must not retrace her mother's footsteps', which sanctions the non-renewal of an alliance from one generation to the next. This type of solidarity also exists between brothers, the elder often periodically helping to 'raise' (feed, house) his younger brother's 'fiancée'.

Polygyny

Polygyny remains fairly rare (Table 20), and I recorded no cases of more than three wives at one time out of the 288 marriages of Yafar men recorded in the genealogies, although some men had had up to six wives in succession. Second and especially third wives are often widows, but they do not make up the majority of the 26 cases of bigamy on record. The first wife may just as well be a widow and the second never before married.

Polygyny probably underlines a man's status, but the Yafar do not say so and prefer to explain the desire for several wives by personality traits and individual tastes. Nor is the argument of economic security to be excluded for the middle-aged or older man in fear of one day finding himself a widower with no daughter to work his sago. From this point of view, polygyny can be seen as an anticipated security mechanism.

The hierarchy between co-wives admits of two ranks, *ifya-minaag* (*ifêêg* 'original, first' and *me-inaag*, 'inside') designating the first wife and *sum-inaag* (*sum* 'who follows') for all others. In principle it is the first woman firmly promised by her father who will become *ifya-minaag*, even if, while waiting for her to become nubile, the future husband takes an older woman or a widow (who will be *sum-inaag*). Chapter 6 discusses the rights attaching to the status of first wife.

Number of bigamous families	26	or 52 marriages
Number of trigamous families	7	or 21 marriages
Total	33	or 73 marriages

Table 20. Number of polygynous families in all Yafar genealogies (288 marriages contracted by Yafar men over five generations)

	1st wife	2nd wife	3rd wife
Unmarried women	23	18	1
Widows	10	13	6
Separated women		2	
Total	33	33	7

Table 21. Marital status of wives in polygynous families

Marriage, The Couple and Exchange

The pre-marital period is marked by the young man's relations with his future father-in-law (or his substitute if the girl's father is deceased); we have already seen, when discussing marriage without compensation, the symbolic exchanges used to seal the alliance. But once the interested parties, including the girl, have agreed, frequent visits will be made in both directions, longer ones by the girl, shorter ones by the future son-in-law; in particular the young man comes at the request of his 'fiancée's' father to help with certain horticultural tasks such as clearing, burning, certain harvests, felling sago palms, building a new house or shelter. The young man begins helping as soon as his *yis* has been accepted by the girl's family. On each visit, the son-in-law works a few days, up to a week, and sleeps at his father-in-law's (if he lives in a different hamlet), after which he goes back home and waits for the next request. Each time, he arrives with gifts of food (meat, grubs, gathered fruit, tobacco, betel or simply some sago) and departs with similar presents.

Depending on the age of the future wife at the time of the agreement between the two families, the period separating the father's acceptance and the marriage varies, from three months if the girl is already nubile, to several years if she is still a child. The father can draw this out as he wishes, for example according to the future tasks with which he needs help. In this case the son-in-law's gifts of food continue until the marriage. In the first months after the *yis*, the future father- and son-in-law (*kowaag*, a reciprocal term used between parents-in-law and son- or daughter-in-law) each intensifies his own hunting in order to offer his partner smoked meat. As we saw in the discussion of premarital sexuality, the 'fiancée' will periodically take up residence at her father-in-law's, where she is fed in exchange for her help with the domestic economy; it is said of this practice that the future daughter-in-law should not be fed for free. It should be remembered that during these bilateral visits a strict taboo separates the 'fiancés', who do not communicate with each other, thus expressing their 'shame' (Ch. 9).

When the young woman's father gives his consent for the couple to live together, the event is not marked by any ritual[24] or celebration and goes almost unnoticed. The rights to the woman are simply handed over to the husband, and the bride moves in definitely with his domestic group. From this moment too, ties between the son- and father-in-law will relax (in the early stages the young man will still help his father-in-law on occasion), while relations between brothers-in-law (*guweeg*), until then very discrete, will intensify.

The couple itself experience this time as a period of gradual transition towards the stable state of marriage and not as a distinct event (whence the absence of a 'wedding'). First of all the shame that had until then marked their relations lasts another few months, and the marriage will be consummated only after that period, during which, as the Yafar men say, the wife must get used to her husband. Accepting to share a meal face to face from the same banana leaf is the sign that she has overcome her shame. In the already familiar context of the relation between eating and sexuality, sharing the same dish precedes and heralds the first sexual relations (Ch. 9).

---

24. When a symmetrical exchange takes place between two tribes or two villages, the two families meet at a halfway point in the forest and share a meal, then the exchanged women leave with their respective affines.

But these few months of transition are also a trial period for mutual acceptance. It is a time when the woman can still refuse the marriage, which may have been forced on her, when she can still go back to her father or her brothers, and a time when the husband can send his wife away for economic reasons: 'laziness', 'non-obedience', etc. The interruption of a marriage by the woman's departure is nevertheless much more frequent than termination by the husband, for it is more often the woman who is forced into marriage than the man, and often she does not dare openly oppose the men before the marriage. Running away in the first weeks after moving to the new home appears, then, to be a female strategy well adapted to the social context. During this time, relations between the two families are just idling, almost suspended in the case of the bride's father, not yet confident between brothers-in-laws. The fact is that while the ties between the two families and the male protagonists have had months and even years to develop, relations between the spouses are still fresh, and they too need a trial period, for it was not only sexual activity that was forbidden them up to this point, but any expression of affection and even free verbal communication. They will be brought together primarily by their work, by the daily acts of economic cooperation (gardening, sago working, cooking), but starting up a new domestic production group takes a little time. At first the new wife still tends to work with her mother-in-law, and as far as horticulture is concerned, the young couple must wait for the new annual clearings to be made to have their own garden. In the end, residential autonomy is achieved as a rule only some years later, after the death of the parents; the son becomes the active man of the household, while his ageing father gradually becomes his son's responsibility (Ch. 4). But it must be kept in mind that the short life expectancy, the often late marriage of men and infant mortality mean that one or both of the parents are often deceased by the time their son marries. If both have died, the couple builds a new house.

Depending on how the union was arranged and if the woman was not consulted and is opposed, marriage can be a trying time for her. According to her personality, she will try to overcome the difficulties or will rebel by running away to her parents, by hiding in a garden shelter or by moving in with another man of her choice. Since the agents who arranged the marriage – especially if 'sisters' were exchanged – are not fond of seeing their plans thwarted, they will often seek to change the runaway's mind, first by reasoning and, failing that, by force. Her own agnates (father, brothers, father's brother), as well as her maternal uncle or, in the event, adoptive father, are the ones who attempt to persuade her to return to her husband: they seek her out at her father's house, or in her natal hamlet (where she is usually no longer to be found), then in the forest in her clearings, and they bring her back, lecturing and sometimes beating her. I was told of one case in which the woman was retrieved several times and was finally beaten and tied up for a few hours in her husband's house. The husband then took her away to a remote garden for some time, and when the couple returned to the village, the wife had become submissive. In most cases, there is no need for such measures because the bride's 'discomfort' dissipates as the couple's relations improve, or because she has long since accepted her spouse, or because the legitimacy of her refusal has been accepted by her husband, who gives her up and asks that she be left alone. The last situation is fairly common, providing the bride leaves her husband's house within a short time, set theoretically at one moon, but which may be slightly longer. In this case, the marriage is not consummated, the couple have not cleared a garden together and may not even have worked a single sago palm. This is why it is said that the woman only stayed 'long enough to gather two loads of firewood'. There are a few, altogether exceptional cases of women who have run away from as many as five husbands before finally settling down.

Magic, already present in the establishment of a new couple (sexual rites, building a house), has a place here as well, particularly when the bride seems undecided. Mature men from her own clan use clones of ritual plants and charms to 'settle' (*aga-bahra*) the woman into her husband's home so that she will 'cling' fast there or even so that she will 'stick': 'Settle the skin (these spells are said over the *kəfe*, the bark mat that the bride brings with her and which will mark her place in the house), settle the thigh, settle the head, settle the heart, etc.', then 'Attach with *amo* lizard claws, attach with *botot* lizard claws, attach with *wabogwe* lizard claws, etc.', or 'Stick with wild breadfruit tree latex, stick with *rohwe* vine latex, stick with *yuwe* vine latex, etc.'

When the bride's 'instability' is attributed to her beauty and to attempts to seduce her, her father may perform another analogical rite to make his daughter 'ugly' in men's eyes. It is said that with the exception of her husband, 'men will no longer find her attractive'; but when she has settled down with her husband and had a child, her father will perform the cancellation rite which will restore her natural charm. At least that is the idealized way the Yafar define the rite called *roofuk kahra-na* 'to seize hold of the skin'. But a recent case cited below shows that *a posteriori* it can enable a man or a group to lay claim to a woman's matrimonial fate.

A Yafar man from Wamawneri clan (Yafar 2) lived uxorilocally with the Aynunkneri and raised his adopted daughter, N, there. In agreement with a man from Yafar 2, WO, he wanted to marry N to Y, WO's younger brother, of the Sig-aynaag clan. But it turned out that N was pregnant and refused to identify her lover. Y rejected this wife, who was subsequently 'married' to two young bachelors in succession, from Yafar 1 and 3 respectively, who involuntarily served as 'temporary spouses' during her pregnancy, but in the end refused the marriage (after several months of waiting and tergiversation). In the end, N returned to Yafar 2 and gave birth in secret: the child died shortly afterwards, and some think that she killed it, the only acceptable solution in the absence of a social father. Y then married N.

I was present at the time of these events: P, N's first 'temporary husband', had nonetheless agreed to give his full sister in exchange to WA, a Wamawneri man (this marriage was not annulled when P persisted in rejecting N), who thus became N's brother in the exchange. Ten years later, the incident was once again related to me, but in the following terms:

WO wanted to marry N to Y. But Y did not have a 'sister' to exchange for Wamawneri clan, and it was P who gave his sister to WA. But WO, who hoped to make N return later, performed the *roofuk kahra-nag* rite on her, which is why P, as well as the second man to whom she was 'married', wanted nothing to do with her: they saw her skin covered with a rash. In the end N returned to Yafar 2, but then WO performed the counter-rite, and Y, seeing that she was beautiful, married her.

As we see, N's true 'ugliness', that is her pregnancy, is completely mystified in the second version and, thanks to the unpremeditated system of temporary marriages, Wamawneri clan, which received a wife in the course of an aborted exchange, agreed to give N, having recovered her 'beauty' (without a bastard child) to Sig-aynaag clan, and Y no longer had any reason to be reticent.

Unstable couples seem to be extremely rare, even though separations are attested which result in partial mutual independence in the economic sphere or in one of the spouses joining another domestic group. According to whether or not a couple is stable, the children are defined as being 'in clear water' (*ugufob-wainaag*) or 'in muddy water' (*bubwes-inaag*). This is a metaphorical way of pointing up the wife's infidelity, which 'soils' the agnatic descent of her husband by casting doubt on his biological paternity.

Despite this eventuality – and that of the husband's adultery, which does not affect his group in the same way – once the Yafar couple is established, it is to all appearances remarkably stable. This may be linked to the atomization of local groups having strong internal solidarity, the existence of consanguineal ties between affines, a little-developed social life, the residential unity of the family, economic ties between families stemming from the division of labour, and the system of exchange and ownership of planted trees.[25] Alongside the couple's growing stability, relations between affines of the same generation grow stronger. Essentially these are the eminently privileged relations between brothers-in-law (*guweeg*), in contrast to relations between son-in-law and parents-in-law (*kowaag*), now reduced to a minimum. The *guweeg* strengthen their ties by reciprocal gifts, frequent visits and joining in the same activities (hunting, rituals). A man going to spend a few days in his wife's brother's hamlet often takes her along, which maintains contact with her kin. The most common gifts are food or arrows and ornaments (marsupial pelts, plumes, pigs teeth, etc.), or more recently, manufactured items purchased at the local administrative post or missionary station. All these presents may be solicited[26] or given spontaneously. Before the marriage, at the start of affinal relations, more prestigious gifts used to be made, such as pig-tusk ornaments for the chest (*wamero*), face (*anəngu*) or forehead (*metiy*), which the beneficiary

---

25. On the sociology of marital stability in New Guinea and some examples for comparison, see Glasse and Meggitt 1969: 6–7.

26. Unlike the gifts given by the father-in-law, which at best may be solicited only through a third party.

was not allowed to wear before having achieved a certain status; stone adzes were also given. When the wife has no brothers, her husband makes a few modest presents to his sisters-in-law and gives masculine objects to his wife's maternal uncle or, if he is deceased, to the latter's sons (his wife's matrilateral cross cousins).

The opposition of relations between son-in-law and parents-in-law (especially father-in-law) corresponds, according to our informants, to an opposition between gifts of food (*teh*) and gifts of objects (*ag*). It is said that the father-in-law asks his son-in-law for food and work, while *ag* circulate primarily between brothers-in-law. Furthermore, the relations between *kowaag prepare* the marriage, while the exchanges between *guweeg* are the *result* of the established marriage and unfold around the life of the young couple. Once the marriage is finalized, the wife's kin find themselves marginalized, their role in the marriage process at an end. On the other hand, the young wife and sister become the mediating point of the developing relations between the *guweeg*, marked by reciprocity and comradeship. This is more apparent when the exchange is symmetrical, but even in the case of a unilateral marriage, the groom's embarrassment *vis-à-vis* his brothers-in-law in the early days of the marriage gives way to a relationship in which the feeling of 'indebtedness' between taker and giver rapidly disappears. The Yafar explain this by the same factors mentioned above: preexisting consanguineal ties between the two clans and solidarity of the *awanənga*. Nevertheless, at least at the outset, a unilateral marriage calls for more gifts on the husband's part. It is these initial *ag* given to initiate reciprocity with the *guweeg*, but also to 'compensate' for the sister received, which must be returned in part if the woman dies without having borne a child.[27]

The husband must also be the first to present – and thereafter more often than he receives in return – the hind leg of a wild pig to his wife's brother. In this context, occasions for which will recur throughout the lifetime of a married man, the wife's parents

---

27. It is evident that this type of unilateral *esmunam* marriage still involves a certain form of compensation, since there is a provision for returning the *ag* if the husband is widowed before becoming a father. It is more because of the slight value attributed to the *ag* (arrows, ornaments, adzes, etc.) on the one hand, and because there is no brideprice involved on the other, as well as a climate of reciprocity which soon erases the hierarchy between taker and giver, that marriage without 'sister' exchange is described as a free gift.

(the hunter's *kowaag*) respect a food taboo and may not eat game killed by their son-in-law; the taboo is also observed by the brothers and sisters of the father-in-law, who may accept only boneless meat. The real parents-in-law must be content with offal. Violation of the taboo would result in severe weight loss, which can be interpreted as excessive consumption of bone. This prohibition once more calls upon the criterion of generation (see pp. 256–7): bones, as a symbolic part of the body, cannot move up the generational ladder on the side of either the affines or the mother's kin. In effect, the compulsory gifts of hind quarters presented to the wife's brother will later gradually be duplicated, and then replaced by ones given by ego's son to his maternal uncle, who must also respect the bone taboo for game presented by his uterine nephew; the beneficiary remains the same but the giver changes. One sees here that the services to the wife's brother and those to the mother's brother are part of the same compensatory system. The father's affines are the son's maternal kin, both categories being associated with the flesh and the blood (as opposed to the bones) in their function as givers of the means (wife and mother) of reproduction. This is no doubt why the heart of the animal, the organ physiologically associated with blood and the equivalent of blood in eschatological representations (Ch. 12), is reserved for the *kowaag* (father-in-law). The prestations made to the brother-in-law are not eliminated if the woman dies, even if she has left no children.

Here is the rite used when the young groom presents his first hind quarter to his in-laws:

> When the young husband has killed his first pig (or cassowary) following his marriage, he makes a ritual presentation of a haunch or a leg to the family of his *guweeg*. The rite is designated by the expression *angaag fe awô wabu-bo feg* 'to make a handle/sling, *angaag* (out of rattan for carrying the hind quarter over the shoulder), (and) to bring (it)'. The young couple calls at the home of the wife's parents, where her brothers and sisters have gathered for the occasion. The hunter comes with his bows and arrows, and it is important that it is the wife who carries the leg. At the house, it is the classificatory agnatic brother of the *guweeg* who directs the ritual, in the course of which the bride's mother 'grabs' the leg that her daughter has brought in a big net bag, while one of the bride's sisters also takes hold of it with a pair of wooden tongs (*rank*). They are symbolically 'capturing' the pig, I was told. While the two hold on to the pig,

spells are spoken and roots chewed by the master of the rite: 'Go shoot [the game] downstream, go shoot upstream, go shoot in the bamboo thickets, go shoot in the wild-pig wallows, go shoot under the fallen tree trunks [where pigs like to sleep], go shoot in the vines between the trees [where possums climb at night], etc. Gather up and bring! Bring on your shoulder like the flying fox [flying foxes carry the food gathered for their young under their wing].' This rite is also performed, and reciprocally, when there has been a direct exchange of 'sisters'.

In Chapter 9, I showed the symbolic relationship between killing game and the act of procreation. Here is yet another representation: the young wife who is expected to bear a child in the near future is the one who is supposed to carry the leg of meat, while the man comes with the attributes (bow and arrows) of his two-fold role as hunter and future father. The meat is 'captured' in a netbag, *wura*, symbolizing the uterus, *wuraag*, held by the mother of the bride. For this rite represents the mother's transmission to her daughter of the power to bear children, a theme whose importance will be seen again in Chapter 11. The spell spoken over the hunter can also be interpreted as an incitement to procreate; the wet and dry places in the forest, upstream and downstream, the vine reminiscent of the umbilical cord carrying the child-possum, the hiding places where game sleeps, all these places where the husband is sent to shoot his arrows are also sites on the woman's body suggesting the potentiality of motherhood. At the level of kinship and alliance, this rite appears as a claim on descendants by the group of the future mother: the child to come will be born from the womb (netbag) of the uterine line but will belong to the patriclan (represented by the bow) of the husband, who, in exchange, will provide his in-laws with legs of game and other kinds of meat.

In conclusion, let us look at the place occupied here by *segwaag* relations (Chs 7 and 11), those privileged exchange partnerships linking pairs of consanguineal relatives. Although in principle *segwaag* relations do not exist between affines, when the young wife has several brothers, her husband finds himself more closely linked with his wife's *segwaag* brother. When there are two brothers and two sisters in the same family, the two elder and the two younger form parallel *segwaag* pairs, so that the husbands of the two sisters each have privileged relations with one of the brothers, with the elder for the man married with the elder wife, with the younger for the other (Figure 36).

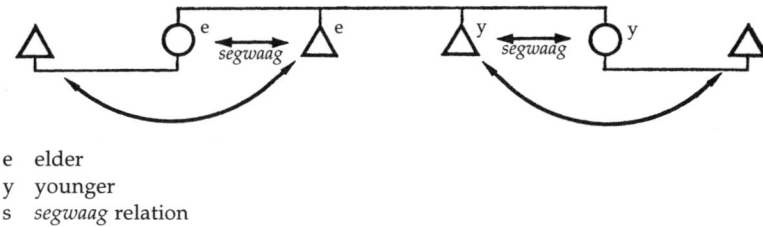

e elder
y younger
s *segwaag* relation

Figure 36. Partnership between brothers-in-law with respect to *segwaag* relations between brothers and sisters

And yet these ritualized exchanges, which give meaning to affinal relations, come under a lifelong interdiction on the use of proper names. This prohibition, widespread in Melanesia, applies to all close affines, regardless of generation. Violation would make the transgressor 'blind' to game, in other words cynegetically sterile, a punishment which refers to the principal mediating object (the woman), who by definition provides the link between affines.

A (Crow-Omaha type) semi-complex marriage system combined with a quadripartite social structure and the practice of 'sister' exchange constitutes the organizing principle of Yafar marriage. Matrimonial policy lies in the hands of the 'elders', who do not acquire through it a coercive power over young people, but contribute their knowledge and know-how to the optimal functioning of society. In this way society ensures its reproduction with the help of strategies complying as much with the rules imposed by the system as with the tolerances authorized by it. In every case and in the framework of this institution, the individual actors engage in partially ritualized interactions in which dual reciprocity and the expression of the transmission of reproductive powers through lines of descent play a central role.

It is these motifs of social symbolism that we will discover in more detail in the discussion of kinship that follows.

11

Kinship and its Representations

We all come from the blood.

The maternal uncle is the breast.

(Yafar sayings)

We have touched on kinship in most of the preceding chapters, whether in its representations, in the rules of 'common law' or in social practice. Named, discrete descent groups were the first sign of a patrilineal system; these appeared again in the land-holding system, this time exhibiting a dynamic of rupture within unilineal continuity (Ch. 5). We will see another aspect of this ambivalence in the transmission of ritual offices (Ch. 13). Inheritance (of trees), we saw, operates bilaterally, whereas marriage brings out – ideally at least – a tendency to constitute fragments of uterine lines serving the idea of a transmission of female fertility parallel to the ongoing patriclan. In every instance, kinship has appeared as the pre-established field (by its genealogical reality) in which social relations are organized. As it has often been said, kinship is the dominant feature, but it is not because it fulfills this or that function, or because it provides the framework for a type of privileged social relations, like those organizing economic life, that it is so omnipresent; it is because of the 'infrasocial' nature of kinship which, even when its biological bases are reorganized by culture and language, makes it the compulsory site, so to speak, or at least the privileged site of any true social elaboration.[1]

1. A certain misunderstanding seems to have grown up in anthropology over the extent to which a biological nature (genealogical lines and consanguinity) of kinship should be recognized beneath the various transformations that every social system imposes on this basic structure. The rejection of a persistent biological substratum along with the implicit recognition of biological ties in spite of the development of classificatory terms, genealogical manipulations and sometimes modes of recruiting not validated by blood ties has made people forget that while ego, for example, calls classificatory kin or even outsiders 'mother', it is always because that is what he calls his real mother. The biological *reference* persists, even if it is not always confirmed in reality.

Kinship dominates the entire social field; and if it takes up more room in relations of production this is only because these demand a more complex and better regulated social investment. I have already proposed a formal analysis of kinship terms (Juillerat 1977 and this volume, Appendix C), which include, among other characteristic features, cousin terminology of the Iroquois type (distinction between cross and parallel kin), respect for the criterion of generation with reciprocal terms between ego and kin of ±2 and ±3 generations, and lastly – we shall return to this later – sibling terms distinguishing between same-sex elder/ younger and specific terms for siblings of the opposite sex. Despite the terminological diversification, however, there is little differentiation in attitudes between consanguines.

To avoid repeating myself, I will therefore not review the terminology and will dwell only briefly on the social mode of production. Instead I will attempt to bring to the definition of the main kinship relations elements that are more properly cultural, by referring to mythology and to certain aspects of ritual. These areas provide an idealized view of social relations, filtered, as always, through the ever-present ideology of reproduction. The chapter will examine successively collaterality, descent and filiation, and – combining the two – oblique relations.

Collateral Relations

Brothers and Sisters

The terminology is very clear about the different types of sibling relations Yafar culture distinguishes. These are organized on the same model as the cross-cutting dual system, in other words as a function of sex and age on perpendicular axes (see Ch. 2, Figure 12, and Juillerat 1977 and 1981). This produces the paired terms *eteeg/sumnik* ('elder/younger' of the same sex) and *nisag/ weerik* ('brother/sister', regardless of age, for ego of opposite sex), often used as they stand, in conversation, to define the corresponding *relation* and in opposition, for instance, to *awaag/afaag* ('father/mother', parents), *nonoog/rabik* (MB/ZCh) or *rəgaag/ angwaag* ('husband/wife', couple). *Nerete* designates all classificatory brothers (and by extension all male, even cross cousins) for a male ego; *haneruk* designates all classificatory sisters for a female ego, as well as two women married by direct exchange.

For moieties and submoieties, gender prevails over age, since siblings differentiated by sex do not need to be distinguished by age though the converse does not hold (otherwise distinction by age would exist whatever the relative sex). Gender opposition between siblings determines first of all a *complementarity* and secondly an identity (consanguinity, the notion of 'one blood'), whereas a mere age difference between siblings of the same sex engenders only secondarily a complementarity masked by a feeling of *identity*.

Let us look first at the second situation, *same-sex siblings*. The myth summarized below is particularly significant, for, by casting two brothers and two sisters in a relationship dominated by the elder brother, it posits first of all that seniority operates less between sisters than between brothers, and secondly, that parallel marriages correspond to a bad combination of relations between the sexes on the one hand and between siblings on the other.

Two brothers and two sisters lived together. The elder brother married both sisters. The younger brother had a secret liaison with the younger sister. When the elder brother realized this, he drew his younger brother into the forest and killed him by causing him to fall on some arrowheads that had been stuck in the ground and camouflaged. He hid the body in a nest of dead leaves, where there were also some *abi* wildfowl eggs. The next day he asked the younger sister to go with him to gather the eggs. The younger girl found her lover's body. The older brother told her that he knew all about their relationship and made her swallow the younger brother, head first. The young woman did this and was then unable to move, as her lover's feet protruded from her mouth. The man left her there and told his wife that her younger sister had gone to their brother's in another village. The younger sister finally called upon two birds to help her remove the younger brother's body, which was rotting inside her. The bones she removed (or to which she 'gave birth') changed into *ogomô*, sago-palm growth spirits; these promptly left to take part in a ritual (Yangis: Ch. 2) in the neighbouring village, where they played the *fuf* trumpets. The younger sister – their 'mother' – soon followed and fed them wildfowl eggs. At that point dawn broke, after a very long night.[2]

2. This myth is analysed in a more extensive version in Juillerat 1991a, Ch. 2.

What this story seems to be saying in particular is that non-reciprocity is socially sterile and leads to the world of untamed nature. The legitimate couple (the elder pair) is presented as childless, and the younger couple's relationship appears as illegitimate from the very fact that they are younger. It takes the elder pair's excessive behaviour and revenge, the mediation of the fratricide and the younger sister's forced cannibalism (a sort of digestive gestation) to make the younger siblings' union fertile: *ogomô*, maternal role, dawn. *Awaag eteeg sumnik, angwafik eteeg sumnik* '(two) men elder/younger, (two) women elder/younger': these are posited from the start as the ingredients of an inevitable failure. They do not lead to *social* reproduction because no exchange is possible: this is the reverse of sister exchange. As death (putrefaction) in the Yafar system of symbols is the condition for reproduction in nature, social disorder and murder become the only way out of a blind alley imposed at the outset. It is male-gendered seniority that will function as the operative principle, since the elder abusively exercises his twofold authority, as a man over the women and as an elder brother over his younger brother. The brothers are separated by rivalry, expressed unilaterally (the younger brother appears as an innocent victim: killed, eaten, but finally restored to the wild), while, in a sequence that I did not include in the summary, we see the two sisters helping each other in opposing the elder brother after the younger brother's murder. Female seniority implies a hierarchy that is merely formal and therefore without consequence. In other words, the pair of brothers are internally split over an external stake: the woman, or more precisely her reproductive potentiality. The pair of sisters, on the contrary, solidary and united, are separated only by the man's external action.

Of course in real society the opposition between male and female pairs is not as clearcut. Solidarity between brothers exists and takes different forms, such as the taboo on physical aggression – homicide, but also stick fights in which brothers are supposed to avoid each other if they are on opposite sides – or the reciprocity which serves to control the distribution of the product of a hunt. But there is also a visible tendency for brothers to split, particularly over the inheritance of land-holding rights or in stick fights where solidarity is not obligatory and mutual assistance between brothers-in-law takes precedence. Another type of distance is created, which takes the appearance of a sort of 'incest of the second kind' (Héritier 1994), by the avoidance of remarriage with the deceased husband's full brother or the prohibition on an elder full brother participating in his younger brother's 'initiation' rites (Ch. 12). The last rule is not restricted to siblings, however, since it also applies to the father and even the mother's real brother. Sisters, for their part, are often doomed to residential scission by the fact of virilocal marriage, and that is perhaps what is being referred to in the divergent reproductive destinies of the mythic sisters, Penef and Konof. One narrative sequence, for example, shows the younger sister being raped by the spirits of the wild breadfruit tree (p. 350); it is said that the girl 'bursts and no longer moves' (*təkya səngo-na*), a recurring expression in oral literature designating fecundation transposed to the plant kingdom, the woman split open and immobilized like a germinating seed. Marriage is this too, the socioresidential immobilization of the young fertile woman who will provide her husband and his lineage with descendants.

Sororal polygyny, rare but corresponding to a sort of polygamous ideal, can be seen as a way of getting around the separation of sisters. 'The younger follows her sister's footsteps',[3] as the Yafar saying goes, either to take her place at the side of her widowed husband, or to share the same hearth with her and give their respective children the same father, in other words to make the children agnates. The sororate/polygyny relationship may also be inverted: two co-wives have no term for each other, but their respective children, if they are of the same sex, will call each other *eteeg/sumnik*, according to their mother's rank (*ifya-minaag/ sum-inaag*; see Ch. 10) and not their own age. This makes the co-wives elder and younger sisters of sorts, at the origin of two agnatic lines, an 'elder' and a 'younger'. As a member of a patrilineage, the man thus sometimes becomes responsible for strengthening a pre-existing sororal tie or for creating a new one.

The fact that true levirate (remarriage with the full brother of the deceased man) is held to be undesirable, while (at least successive) sororal polygyny is encouraged by a popular saying allows us to grasp something of the fundamental difference

---

3. As already mentioned, this saying should be compared with the one forbidding repetition of a marriage, cited in the preceding chapter: 'A girl must not retrace her mother's footsteps'.

between what makes brothers or what makes sisters the same. Patriliny is the unifying principle which dictates that whether it is one or two women who give children to a man, it all amounts to the same thing. There must be only one father for all of his children to be both siblings and agnates, while the different mothers merge in the same reproductive function. This might be seen as a plausible explanation for the Yafar tendency to separate brothers and to unite sisters, whereas residence rules stipulate just the contrary.

From the sameness of same-sex siblings, let us now turn to the complementarity of opposite-sex siblings. Complementarity could be defined as a difference that leads to reciprocity and unity, a difference that is socially (and symbolically) profitable.[4] Let us first recall that the Yafar regard brother-sister incest as impossible and in no way feel it necessary to guard against it, whereas they consider that sexual relations between adolescents promised in marriage need to be prohibited. Whence an attitude of avoidance between the latter and, on the contrary, dedramatized – literally fraternal – relations between brother and sister. I have already shown that the notion of *mungwô taf* ('one blood') determined, with a few generational reservations but irrespective of gender, the absence of certain taboos, for instance regarding shame, the pollution of menstrual blood (Ch. 9) and consuming red pandanus juice together (pp. 357–8). The *nisag/weerik* relationship falls into this category, which tends to neutralize the opposition between the sexes. To this must be added a relationship of economic complementarity present, in particular, between a brother and sister associated in a *segwaag* exchange partnership (see below), which takes the form of gifts of game, bird of paradise or cockatoo plumes by the brother and sago or netbags and other netted ornamental objects by the sister. Such exchanges may also link a married couple as well as other relatives. They are an expression of sexual complementarity in general, based on division of labour, but they also strengthen the ties between brothers and sisters and sanction the existence of *segwaag* brother-sister *pairs*.

---

4. The structural and symbolic importance of the brother/sister pair, combining 'siblingship' with opposition of the sexes, both of which are inscribed in descent reckoning, has been pointed out by several authors, including Burridge 1959; Moore 1964; and Goodale, Rubinstein and Schneider (in Marshall ed. 1981).

The pivotal point of brother-sister complementarity, however, is marriage by exchange as the ideal form of matrimony. We have seen that if a woman is given in marriage 'for nothing' (*esmunam*), at a later time her brother may exchange his niece for a wife. Indirectly the man relies on his sister's mediation to ensure his posterity. It seems fairly obvious that the potential exchange of the *weerik* puts a stop to any fear of incest. There is no myth telling of incest between brother and sister, but two stories end with the father ordering his son to 'marry his sister', proposition rejected by the son, who goes to another group to exchange her for a wife. This dialogue (see epigraph to Ch. 10) is meant to show the origin of sister exchange in the rejection of incest, but also the socialization of marriage and the passage from a state of nature to one of society (allusion to the animal kingdom, where they marry their sister). The sister's destiny (or destination) and her social function constitute the prime sociological factor guaranteeing the absence of internalized conflict over the taboo on incest between siblings of the opposite sex.

Being a means of transforming a sister (*weerik*) into a wife (*angwaag*), direct exchange also determines a new set of relations, those already examined (Ch. 10) between brothers-in-law (*guweeg*), and those less prestigious and socially less integrated between the two women exchanged, who will thenceforth call each other *haneruk* ('classificatory sisters'), regardless of their respective ages. The exchange thus results in the constitution of two new pairs of 'false siblings' in which sameness of sex is mediated by the true sibling of the opposite sex (exchanging brother and exchanged sister). The freedom and prestige of relations between *guweeg* in particular seems, in terms of sexual symbolism, possible only through the mediation of sisters and wives. When there is no exchange of sisters, only a single marriage, the relationship between the *gugweeg*, although asymmetrical, is similar due to the neutralization of the giver-taker hierarchy (Ch. 10); nevertheless, it is obvious that the pleasure of the exchange attains its perfection only in absolute symmetry. On this point, the Yafar count among those societies for whom direct and simultaneous reciprocity is the ideal form of exchange.[5]

---

5. On the opposition between societies preferring direct exchange and those choosing deferred exchange, see Godelier 1986.

Examination of these few cases shows that in order to be fully assumed or socially consolidated, dual relationships always need a third party: the bigamous husband reinforces or creates the feeling of sorority between his wives, the sister (for a male ego) and the brother (for a female ego) mediate the couple, the given or exchanged sister enables the *guweeg* to form the most positive male relationship in the kinship network, etc. The mediating kin position is of the opposite sex to that of the poles of the same-sex dual relationship. In triangular relationships of this type, there is always functional complementarity in accordance with the opposition non-reproductive/reproductive function or asexuality/sexuality. In this sense, the *guweeg* relationship can be said to be 'sexualized' (even if no real homosexual relation occurs between the brothers-in-law),[6] for it stems from the transformation of the asexualized brother/sister pair (*nisag/weerik*) into a reproductive husband/wife (*rəgaag/angwaag*) pair.

Cousins

The sibling relationships I have just described are handed down to their descendants and determine whether or not the initial relationship continues over generations. The same-sex children of two brothers or two sisters (parallel cousins) call each other *eteeg* and *sumnik*, in accordance with the relative age of their fathers or mothers, their own ages being of no consequence for terminology. This will carry over into the following generation and so on down through the two lines between cousins of the same sex. If in any one of these later generations there are two parallel cousins of opposite sex, they will call each other *nisag/weerik*, and their children of both sexes will call each other *magawô* (cross cousin). The children (regardless of sex) of a brother and a sister will be *magawô*, and their children will use sibling terms if their respective parents are of the same sex, or the term *magawô* if of opposite sex.

For as long as the sex of the descendants in each generation allows the term to be transmitted according to the rules I have just outlined, this determines elder and younger (*eteeg-inaag/ sumnik-inaag*; *-inaag*: 'in') lines and line segments if the ancestral

---

6. Among the Etoro, the ideal homosexual partner is the brother-in-law (Kelly 1977).

pair is of the same sex, and 'brother' and 'sister' lines (*nisag-inaag/weerik-inaag*, or *fango-inaag/nay-inaag* 'in the bow/in the skirt'[7]) if the ancestral siblings are of opposite sex.[8]

The representations associated with these collateral positions are ill defined and seem to be based more on the respective gender of the interested parties than on their cousin status. A female parallel or cross cousin is always 'good to exchange' unless she is a *taway* (Ch. 10, pp. 306–7), who cannot be exchanged but should be married. Yet the *magawô/magawô* relationship seems to be associated with 'joking', which is no doubt why the licentious rivalry-cum-friendship linking the two civilizing heroes comes under this cross relationship rather than the hierarchy between brothers. But in this case, the hierarchy of inherited age rank is replaced, symbolically speaking, by that of 'inherited sex' (*fango-inaag/nay-inaag*). The latter hierarchy is cancelled, however, if sisters have been exchanged, as the father of one of the male cousins is the maternal uncle of the other and vice versa. The cross-cousin relationship is therefore at the same time the logical outcome of the maternal uncle/uterine nephew and the paternal aunt/agnatic nephew relationship, and of the alliance maintained by their respective fathers. Might not, then, the Yafars' joking relationship – although not strongly marked – stem precisely from this reshuffling of relationships between their parents and from the ensuing blurring of categories?

In contrast to the *magawô* relationship, there is a noticeable absence of features distinguishing the relationship between parallel cousins. As for siblings, these relations are marked by strong solidarity, but it is a solidarity of blood, which is difficult to socialize. In this case, homology is the dominant factor, homology that is in the end too strong to give rise to a dynamic, significant relationship. For it would seem that (non-agnatic,

---

7. See Goodale *in* Marshall 1981, where the same terms are used by the Kaulong of New Britain.

8. In Juillerat 1977, I postulated that the terminology used by cousins of the second degree and more was determined by that used in the preceding generation and not by the sex of the cousins of that generation. A later discussion with the Yafar revealed that the criterion could be retained as an option. Furthermore, today's young Yafar tend increasingly to simplify the system by keeping the same pairs of terms (*eteeg/sumnik*, *magawô/magawô*) from one generation to the next, beginning with the ancestral sibling pair; this classification of cousins determines, in the case of cross cousins, *fango-inaag* (or *nisag-inaag*) and *nay-inaag* (or *weerik-inaag*) lines descending from an ancestral pair of opposite-sex siblings. This simplified cousin classification is criticized by older Yafar.

cross, affinal, etc.) difference is what instigates the establishment of a specifically defined relationship: between maternal and uterine kin, or rather between cross kin, and above all between affines, there is a gap to be bridged and therefore to socialize, whereas between agnates or parallel kin, the feeling of sameness prevails, blocking exchange and neutralizing differentiation. It is indeed in accordance with this criterion, among others, that the hierarchy of relationships is fixed: absence of hierarchy (other than between generations) between 'different' relatives; hierarchy, on the other hand (elder/younger) between 'same' relatives.

Descents

It is not only the fact that elements of a matrilineal ideology appear in the Yafar patrilineal descent system that leads me to use the plural in speaking of Yafar descent reckoning in general, but also the necessary distinction between unilineal descent considered over several generations and descent as the filiation between a man or a woman and his or her father and mother or his or her son and daughter. My purpose is not to go into individual cases or to take a psychological stance, but to seek an understanding of how Yafar culture represents to itself these relations between parents and children which are polarized according to the respective genders involved. This dimension will make it easier to grasp the meaning to be given to unilineal representations in the social system. Such an orientation could have used a much more thorough investigation into socialization and parent-child relations in daily life; I did not explore these in depth, however, because I was not equipped to do so, and now I will again attempt to identify only some of the models used in representing descent and filiation in myth and ritual. As in the case of collaterality, these areas allow us to grasp something of the unconscious paradigms operating in parallel with and forming a background for the social sphere. Whereas the social structure imposes patrilineal descent reckoning and includes only a few sketchy matrilineal features, Yafar imaginary representations produce systems in which maternal ties and femaleness are centre stage.[9] Apprehension of the principles structuring these

9. See also Green 1977, 1992; Juillerat 1991a, 1992a.

mental models may, thanks to their very disproportion, enable us to discover the meaning of these matrilineal descent structures where they are visible in real life.

A close look at types of individual filiation leads us to reconstruct a succession, as we did for siblings, of parent/child pairs of the same or opposite sex. Let us begin with the 'daughter/ mother' (*röögunguk/afaag*) relationship, whose formulation in myth or ritual signifies the transmission of *hoofuk* (Ch. 9), or female fertility. The female principle is represented simultaneously or successively over two generations in the chronology of an account or a rite; what is represented in this case is the *transfer* itself from one generation to the next of the capacity to procreate. Ritual, for example, often features opposing masked figures said to be 'mother' and 'daughter', facing each other as in the Waw rite (pp. 88–9) or following each other as in Yangis (*êri* and *yis*, p. 52). In myth, as a general rule, the following features, sometimes contradictory but complementary, can be found:

a) mother/daughter solidarity against the father;
b) mother/daughter rivalry over a man and defeat of the mother;
c) transmission of the *hoofuk* from mother to daughter by an act of violence on the mother's part and male intervention on behalf of the daughter to 'liberate' her *hoofuk* (enable her to give birth);
d) sometimes greater continuity of the female characters in the story than of the male ones, who tend to pop up only to disappear again.

Points a) and b) are opposed and complementary. The first also explains why the father/daughter relationship in mythology is usually negative (either ignored or characterized by hostility: daughters killing their father to avenge their mother, for example) and absent from ritual. It seems that c) constitutes the idea central to all forms of matriliny; as such, the tendency to form a chain of uterine descent through the successive women given in the *kəgaag* marriage cycle (Ch. 10) corresponds to the need to signify, in this asymmetric exchange structure, the continuity of female fecundity, whereas the male side is revitalized at every stage by the intervention of a new patriclan (Figure 32). This is the familiar pattern we saw in representations of reproductive sexuality (Ch. 9), which included a view of female reproduction as a form of parthenogenesis in which the male principle interceded only to deliver the woman when her time had come by enabling her not to conceive, but simply to give birth. In its ideal form, asymmetric exchange can be seen as a series of operations performed by the men on behalf of their patriclan by which they draw off some of the flow of fecundity (*hoofuk*) from the female line. This four-generation flow produces children for different patrilineal groups at each stage. The *kǝgaag* cycle thus partakes of the order of continuous female filiation and of interrupted male descent (re-established only at the close of a cycle), whereas 'sister' exchange operates in a collateral mode. The transmission of female *hoofuk* and its differential distribution over social time correspond to a generational order which must not be violated: this is why positive descent through the transfer of female fertility is also comprised of a series of ruptures expressed in myth by rivalry or hostility between mother and daughter. The following myth neatly summarizes these contradictions:

> The severed penis of Wefroog[10] (the culture hero) changed into a *bihik* lizard. This lizard sought out a woman and made love to her by 'sucking' on her clitoris. The woman could not hold still. Her husband wondered to himself 'What is making her move like that?' While his wife was away getting some firewood, he told his daughter, Afwêy, to go and look on her mother's bed. She looked and found the lizard. Father and daughter killed and ate it. They promptly grew fat (the *hoofuk* from Wefroog's penis).
>
> When the woman returned, another lizard, a *hwabrink* (an ugly lizard with a rough skin), took the place of the *bihik*. It began nibbling on the woman's clitoris, and she wiggled and squirmed. Suddenly the lizard bit it right off. She gave a jump. Pretending to make her bed, she took a peek at what had bitten her. Her blood flowed freely. She caught the *hwabrink* lizard and killed it.
>
> The next day she went fishing with her daughter. Having bailed out the pool, she kicked up the mud in the hollow of a rock to cloud the water, then she told her daughter to go and catch the big fish which – she claimed – was hiding there. The daughter went in head first; her mother plugged up the hole and went back home, leaving her daughter trapped. The father asked her 'What has become of our child?' – 'She went down river looking for fish.'

10. This figure does not castrate himself: he cuts his penis down to a more modest size when he is about to get married. This is the anatomical expression of what might be called a socialization of sexuality.

A man named Knonk (secret name Nönk, from *nönguk* 'rotten')
came down to the river. He cut a *fənaw* sago palm (symbolically female as opposed to the male *afwêêg* sago palm; see p.
52) and left it
there for edible grubs to develop. He tossed a piece of the palm's
hoofuk (pith) into the hole in the rock where Afwêy was trapped.
Then he went away for two moons and came back to harvest the
grubs. He opened them up and threw the innards (also called *hoofuk*)
into the hole. 'Boow!' He heard a big noise, then a cry, 'Yaa!' He ran
away, came back and threw the innards of another grub into the
hole. 'Boow!' – 'Yaa!' He ran away, came back and asked: 'who's
shouting in there?' – 'It's me.' Knonk set Afwêy free. In her arms she
was holding the son she had borne (named *fənaw hoofuk na ruwar*
'*fənaw hoofuk* child'). She gave off a strong odour (*mosuwô funk*
'placenta smell'). The man made a skirt of young *fənaw* fronds and
put it on Afwêy. He left with her and the child as well as with a dog
he had found there eating the afterbirth. The lost amniotic fluid
became a river which was rich in fish when it flooded (also called
Knonk and located on Umeda land).

The Yafar exegesis tells us that Knonk represents the 'male'
afwêêg sago palm and Afwêy the 'female' *fənaw*, and that the
father corresponds to the recurring figure of the 'bad (old) father'
(*Awarəhak*). Knonk is also designated as the man-in-the-middle
(*öruk-aynaag*), because he lives in the area lying between the
Umeda-Punda lands and those of the Yafar, in other words between
the 'mother' group (Umeda) and the 'daughter' group (Yafar)
(Ch. 1), and he 'listens to what is said on both sides'. This role
shows once again that female *hoofuk* is reproduced by the (one-
time) intervention of the man from the outside as mediator of the
mother/daughter relationship. The mother, having undergone
the amputation of her reproductive phallic power, can only retire,
but not before she has put her daughter in a condition to carry
on.[11] Stuck in an aquatic and ichthyological environment favourable to gestation, the daughter waits for the maternal fecundity
(represented by the *fənaw hoofuk*), which comes to her through
Knonk's mediation, and then her delivery, by the throwing of the
grubs, a metaphor for Knonk's semen which opens up Afwêy's
pregnancy and allows her '*fənaw hoofuk* child' – and herself as

11. Mother and daughter cannot be represented as being fertile at the same time: the
former must first lose her reproductive power in order for the latter to realize hers. Here
we clearly have the idea of the transmission of an indivisible capacity and of the need for a
clearcut differentiation between generations.

mother – to be born. The role of the (hunting) dog announces a frequent theme of Yafar mythology: the passage from plant *hoofuk* (the woman-sago palm's *hoofuk*) to animal blood (*taf*), in other words to hunting (pp. 243 and 446), while at the same time it puts the finishing touches to a complete domestic group based on sago-working and hunting.

The episode of the *bihik* lizard gives us an exceptional glimpse of father/daughter filiation. The short-lived complicity between Afwêy and her father, at the expense of the mother, enables them to recover the (phallic) *hoofuk* for themselves while castrating the mother, who is too old to have any right to sexuality and procreation. The daughter therefore inherits this right through her father's mediation, while, thanks to the daughter, the father is rejuvenated and reappears as the character Knonk. Once again we find another aspect of the triangular relationship already noted in the case of siblings.

In another myth, too long to be told in full,[12] the representations of descent are organized even more strikingly in terms of rivalry between the sexes:

1) A mother and her two daughters surprise her husband and their father hiding sprouted coconuts in the bush (control of coconut palm reproduction).
2) They kill him and wrap him in coconut petiolar fibres (representing the uterus).
3) Gradually he emerges (the new frond growing) and comes back to the three women.
4) He invites his wife to go gathering coconuts with him and throws a coconut out of the tree and on to her genitals, killing her.
5) He returns to his daughters, hiding his crime.
6) They are distrustful and shut him up in the house, setting it on fire.
7) They find their mother's corpse, which has given birth to a son *post mortem*. The boy is exploring his environment in the vicinity of his mother, bow in hand, looking for small lizards (the Yafar exegesis says he is looking for his mother's breast).

---

12. This myth is analysed in its complete version in Juillerat 1991a.

8) The three siblings leave. Turning a deaf ear to her sister's advice, the younger sister is raped and impregnated by the spirits of the wild breadfruit tree and remains behind, unconscious (pregnant).
9) The elder sister comes upon a python, which turns into a man.
10) The couple raise the little brother, then one day abandons him and vanish.
11) The boy lives alone and works sago until he meets two sisters, whom he marries.
12) The elder sister steals a baby possum from the pouch of its mother, killed by her husband, and adopts it.
13) The husband looks for his possum 'son', finds him and gets him to 'initiate' him ritually into the animal kingdom (hunting).
14) The father turns into a parrot (*Domicella lorius*) and flees his wife by perching in the top of a latex tree (*Alstonia scholaris*).
15) The younger sister, disobeying the elder, drinks water from between the roots of this tree and becomes pregnant.

This myth, secretly dealing with competition between the sexual principles in the reproduction of the coconut palm and other species as well as with the passage from *hoofuk* to *taf* (see above), provides some interesting information on representations of descent relations, collaterality and reproductive sexuality. It is constructed around a series of filiative relations intersected by those of the couple. In each generation, there are branches reaching out to different species of plant, finally ending with game. Local specialists explain that the python-man is a reincarnation of the father, killed in and saved from the fire (the growth principle is not destroyed when the clearing is burned), while the posthumous son is the sprout growing from the rotting coconut. Once again, reminiscent of the asymmetric *kəgaag* cycle, we have a reincarnation of the male principle from one generation to the next with no visible continuity, while one after the other, the female characters leave the scene after coupling with a man. The young women appear by sister pairs; the younger son, on the other hand, stands alone and remains dependent for some time, first on his mother (even though she is dead), then on his elder sister. Thus the elder sister takes her mother's place, whereas the younger is destined for a special procreative fate (see also the Abi myth, above, p. 338): she is to be integrated into the reproductive cycle of the wild breadfruit tree or to be made pregnant by the parrot-man.

These mythic references may seem somewhat obscure in regard the father-daughter tie, which is expressed only with respect to the mother, as is, moreover, the case in the relations within the family: if the mother dies prematurely, the unmarried daughter takes over her economic activities. We have also seen that a widower may seek to retain his youngest daughter to work his sago palms and prepare his jelly.

The 'son/father' (*reeg/awaag*) tie represents the permanence of the masculine principle, not in the transmission of the power of men's biological reproduction, but in their social control over female fertility (patriliny), the land and game. In Chapter 9 we saw the parallels between human procreation and hunting; in Chapter 13 the forms of transmission of ritual powers will be examined. While the transfer of female fertility from one generation to the next is often expressed in myth, the permanence of the male principle as a representation appears especially in the cosmological organization of the territory and the village (Ch. 1), the eastern and western poles of which represent the son and the father and are linked by the path of the sun: father to son by way of the sun's underground passage from west to east, son to father by its heavenly pathway. In other words, the father engenders the son by his passage through the earth (see the myth of Tapi and Wam, p. 30), which for the Yafar is always a site of gestation, while over time the son will age and become a father, just as the rising sun will ultimately go down in the west. But Wam sinking his iron-wood stake in the ground made firm by the presence of his father is also the acknowledgement of a double filiation through which the young man ensures his identity.[13]

The same need for mediation is found in the last filiative relationship, not yet examined, 'son/mother' (*reeg/afaag*). Although this relationship is also mediated, it seems to enjoy a privileged status in the culture and imagination of the Yafar which in part runs counter to the unity of the male descent rule. In the discussion of the dynamics of (local and clan) social units, we saw the mother's role as a vehicle, bringing her young son into a new group (pp. 9–10); we also evoked the parallel between this

13. See also Juillerat 1992b.

process of a woman implanting a new agnatic line with the technique of making cuttings in shifting horticulture. Looked at
through the plant kingdom, the mother is seen as giving life (germination) by dying (rotting). It is her death that is the condition
of the son's emergence. This image is totally different from that
of the transmission of the mother's *hoofuk* to her daughter.
The daughter is the replica of the mother, whereas the son is of
another nature. The mother-son tie is defined by what might be
called non-reciprocal complementarity. The Yangis ritual (Ch. 2)
takes this very relationship as its subject, the conception, gestation and birth of the son (in two copies) emerging from the blood
of his mother, who dies giving him birth or, in ethnobotanical
terms, the emergence of the two new sago and coconut shoots,
the totemic trees of the two moieties. We saw earlier how the son,
standing for the young coconut shoot, is born from his 'rotted'
mother and sets out in search of her missing breast.

Alternatively, in the story of the Stolen Game (pp. 183–4), the
triangulation of the mother-son relationship through intervention
by the father takes the form of a typically oedipal scenario. It
is the only allusion to incest in Yafar mythology (I have found
no suggestion of father-daughter or brother-sister incest). An
even more subtle version is found in Yangis, where the son's
relationship to his mother's body (the arrow pointed at the
ground by the *ifəgê*) is inverted with respect to the breast (arrow
shot towards the sun). In the myth, the same differentiation
opposes the elder sons, already separated from the mother and
having become the father's rivals, to the younger son, who still
has a right to his mother and is therefore spared the father's
wrath.

Certainly unilineal descent cannot be taken alone and can only
point to the importance of the absent parent, who becomes a
mediator. This third element is indispensable in reconstructing
the bilateral reality of descent, for this bilaterality forms the basis
of all representations of descent. Moreover, this seems to be what
is signified by the Yafar institution, described below, of assign-
ing children alternately to the mother and the father, as they are
born.

This rejection, by Yafar culture, of unilateral descent reckoning
or of the institutionalization of a strictly unilineal system can
also be found not only in the transmission of land rights (Ch. 5),
but in the relations people have with a certain category of spirits

which have not yet been discussed and with the food taboos associated with them. *Uguwak* spirits are a category of the Yafar (and Eri) pantheon unto themselves in the sense that they do not control game, do not punish cultivators for excessive clearing by sending illness, do not live in specific trees or known sites and are not spirits of the dead; it is said simply that they live in the white cliffs and their houses can be recognized from the ridge that turns up at the front end. These signs, together with the forbidden food, recognized in a dream by an individual, indicate danger from his or her *uguwak*(s). In effect, each *uguwak* is connected with a particular food by means of which the spirit visits young children (and sometimes adults as well) with illness or upsets, or even causes accidents. Moreover, with each food is associated a particular ill related by analogy to the prohibited species, for example:

> The breadfruit tree *uguwak* 'throws babies into the fire' (an allusion to the fruits roasted over the flames), or causes sores (due to lice) on the child's head, as the fruit of this tree is sometimes infested with larva that the *uguwak* is thought to put on its victim's head.
> The *pas* bird *uguwak* retards the child's growth, and it remains small and weak (like this bird).
> The *binik* rat *uguwak* makes the child listless and drowsy, as this rat spends all day asleep in its hole.
> The *uguwak* of butterfly larvae makes stone adze handles break, as the larvae bore funnels in wood, etc.

It is also said that an *uguwak* likes to be beside a cultivator when he plants a tree; if the man plants without the spirit, it may keep the tree from growing normally and bearing fruit. We see, then, that *uguwak* are also guardians of human growth and health. A healing rite can be performed for a sick child. But it can also happen that an *uguwak* enters an individual without being asked and takes frenzied possession of him or her.

The food taboos corresponding to the inherited *uguwak* are not usually observed unless the spirit has shown itself in a dream or a couple has lost one or more children in infancy. In order to pacify the *uguwak* in question, the child can be given the name of the prohibited food, either as a first or second name (Ch. 12).

Every man and woman thus has a certain number of *uguwak* foods that are in theory personally taboo; the number ranges from two or three up to a dozen. These are received from the father, the mother and sometimes the spouse. The number of *uguwak* an individual mentions depends partly on whether he or she chooses to count only patriclan taboos or some or all of the mother's, grandmother's or spouse's as well. The general rule is that one *respects* one's own agnatic *uguwak*, one's mother's agnatic *uguwak*, sometimes one's father's and mother's uterine *uguwak* and the agnatic and uterine *uguwak* of one's spouse. Individual choice in this matter is as broad as the strictness with which a person chooses to observe the taboos, and depends on the circumstances and the seriousness of the child's illness. All *uguwak* taboos are inherited through descent, but new *uguwak* can join the pool. In this case, their inclusion in the stock to be transmitted is triggered either by a dream or the strange behaviour of a small animal.

These food taboos are passed down indefinitely in the male line and over one or two generations in both lines, with optional transmission to a spouse. The boundaries of these prohibitions resemble those for *rangwarik* in the marriage system (Ch. 10).

Oblique Relations

The terminology separating parallel and cross kin and distinguishing in particular maternal uncle from paternal uncle, and paternal aunt from maternal aunt does not explain the special status of collaterals in the +1 generation; this is instead one of the results of the symbolization of filiative relationships combined with relations between siblings and affines (brother-in-law). The rite examined earlier (p. 333), performed the first time the sister's husband makes a kill, clearly showed that this meat is the counterpart of the future child given to the young groom through the transfer of a woman. Through this act, the husband compensates his wife's family for his future descendants and will subsequently repeat the gift. I have already pointed out that the identical gift presented by the uterine nephew (*rabik*) to his maternal uncle (*nonoog*) has nearly the same significance: the *rabik* symbolically 'pays' for his own maternal descent, that is to say he compensates the same transfer of a sister (his own mother) by his *nonoog* to his own father. The Yafar define the maternal uncle metaphorically as the mother's 'breast' (*tot*), and so it might be said that the nephew repays his mother's milk (*totom*) in meat.[14] Between brothers-in-law it is a woman and her fertility that are owed by the taker, who will appropriate the product by virtue of the patrilineal descent rule; between uncle and nephew, it is rather the mother's feeding function that calls for compensation. The transition from gift to the wife's brother to gift to the mother's brother is part of father-son filiation. In both cases the gifts of hindquarters travel in one direction, from the sister's husband to the wife's brother and from the sister's son to the mother's brother; nevertheless smaller gifts of meat also go in the opposite direction, in accordance with the reciprocity rule, which overlays, as it were, the unilateral relationship. It is therefore necessary, in this relative reciprocity linking brothers-in-law and the uterine nephew with his uncle, to distinguish the direction of the gift which gives the relationship its meaning from the direction of the countergift which merely serves to balance the exchange.

Nonoog ba tot ogwa 'the mother's brother is the breast': this proposition – of which adolescents are reminded so that they will honour their uncle – brings us back to the relations between brothers-in-law, but in their roles as ego's father and his maternal uncle; we are enlightened by the high point of the Yangis ritual, especially if it is compared with the myth of the Three Incestuous Sons discussed above (pp. 183–4). In effect, we have seen that mother-son descent relations were conceived in two stages: an allowed relationship between the younger son (child) and the mother, in the feeding-protecting relationship, and a prohibited relationship with the mother, expressed in the elder son's identification and rivalry with the father. Yangis closes with a scene in which the two 'children of the blood' (*ifəgê*), born from the blood of their dead mother, are led around by a figure representing their *nonoog*, who shows them the sun – the mother's breast, according to the secret Yangis myth – at which

14. The inhabitants of the village of Teloute, near Lumi (Torricelli Range, West Sepik), express themselves clearly on this point when they remind the nephew of his duties to his maternal uncle: 'You weren't born from a hole in the ground [. . .] You came from the womb of our sister. And since her marriage she has worked hard. She suffered a lot at your birth and produced a lot of milk for you, and it is only because you drank our sister's milk and because we worked hard on the rites necessary to make you grow that today you are a healthy adult [. . .] Now that you are married and have children of your own, it is high time you paid us for all she has done. Even though your clan paid the bridewealth for your mother, she is still our sister and, since her marriage, she has worked hard [for you]' (McGregor 1975: 65–6).

they shoot their arrows. The maternal uncle has a twofold function here: to direct his nephews away from their mother's body, in other words from incest (the *ifəgê*'s penis, pointed at the ground like his arrow, is supposed to be 'looking for the mother', *afaagêm isəgê*), and to show them that part of the mother which they are allowed: the breast (sun). The *nonoog* thus visibly stands in opposition to the biological father. Identified with the mother in her strictly feeding role, the uncle also embodies the socializing father, while the real father can only draw the son into desire for the mother. And so the function of the father is here divided between an oedipal father vying with the son and a social father who is the model for identification and separation, and personified by the uncle. On this level, the *nonoog* is the agent who neutralizes the oedipal conflict – he asexualizes and socializes the mother-son relation, perhaps because he himself is the asexualized pole of his sister's twofold orientation, both mediatrix between her brother and her husband, and given by the former to the latter. For a male ego, at least, the two relationships are mediated by the mother, who is central to both. There is only one alternative. The myth of the Stolen Game stages the incest punished by the father in the absence of the mother's brother, while the culmination of Yangis shows incest being avoided thanks to the maternal uncle and in the absence of the biological father from the ritual stage.

For a female ego, the relationship with the *nonoog* is less marked (notwithstanding the gifts of sago by the *rabik* niece), for although the 'milk debt' is unchanged, the daughter is continuous with her mother (transfer of *hoofuk*), but she will not transmit her paternal filiation to her children. According to this model based on the principle of mediation, father-daughter incest could come about only through the daughter's desire for the father by identification with the mother, not the reverse (the father's desire for the daughter cannot be mediated). Apparently Yafar culture rejects the paradigm of the woman taking the initiative in incest; in the event, the relationship between *amagunguk* (father's sister/brother's child) becomes indifferent for the nephew as well as the niece and can never be the symmetrical counterpart of the *nonoog/rabik* relationship. Even the reciprocity of the term seems intended to cancel any specificity in the relationship between paternal aunt and brother's child.

To sum up, the Yafar conceptualization of their principal kinship relations is more differentiated than the actual practice. The symbolic oppositions I have just defined are masked by a great uniformity of real relations to which it would be difficult to assign a plus or a minus.[15] To be sure, authority lies with the father, while the *nonoog* appears as more of an exchange partner: he receives meat from his *rabik* and allows him to wear his clan emblem (p. 87). In some cases (although we have seen that this is rare), he may take his *rabik*'s sister to exchange for a wife, renouncing his quarters of wild pig, which the nephew will give to his brother-in-law instead; nevertheless, unlike the practice of other societies in the area (see, for example, Lewis 1980, McGregor 1975), the mother's brother is not duty bound to be his nephew's 'initiator' (see following chapter). Moreover, these ties are stronger between a *segwaag* uncle and nephew (see below), and the *segwaag* uncle is the mother's *segwaag* brother. The same symmetry is found between *amagunguk*, even though there is no obligation to exchange.

Kinship and Food: Consuming 'Blood'

The taboos surrounding menstrual blood have already shown the importance of the combination of the two notions of consanguinity and generation (pp. 254–5). In the present chapter we find another aspect of this demand for social order, more particularly within the kinship structure, in relations touching upon red foods, and pandanus in particular.[16] Because of its deep red colour and its symbolic associations with blood, pandanus is the food most strictly regulated in terms of planting, preparation and consumption.

15. Lévi-Strauss was the first to show the irreducible character of the 'atom of kinship', of which he writes that 'it is the building block of the more complex systems' (1958a: 59; see also 1973). Rather than adopt the opposing interplay of positive and negative relationships within this family cell, I prefer to consider these dual relationships with respect to their mediating pole, which leads to a more psychoanalytically oriented view of descent reckoning and, secondarily, of collateral and cross relationships (see also Green 1977).

16. The pandanus tree (*Pandanus conoïdeus* Lamk), *kway*, is widely cultivated in New Guinea, producing long, sterile bunches of fruit from 30 to 60 cm in length; the hundreds of tiny bright red (24 clones) or yellow (2 clones) berries are braised once the edible pulp of the fruit cluster has been removed. The berries are then filtered through the hands (*raw feg*, which can be translated as 'to make bleed') and water is added. The condiment is eaten mixed with a starchy foodstuffs such as mashed bananas or taro, or with sago jelly. See Juillerat 1984b and the film *Un jardin à Yafar*.

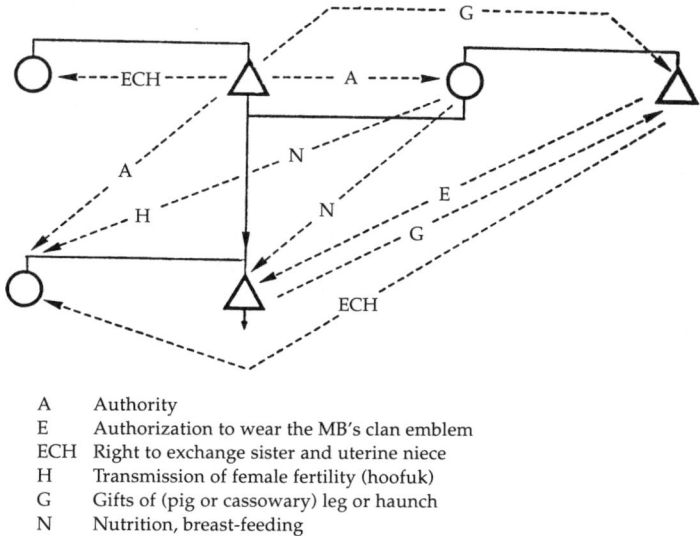

A	Authority
E	Authorization to wear the MB's clan emblem
ECH	Right to exchange sister and uterine niece
H	Transmission of female fertility (hoofuk)
G	Gifts of (pig or cassowary) leg or haunch
N	Nutrition, breast-feeding

Figure 37. Some conventional exchanges and representations within the atom of kinship

The first rule, reminiscent of the taboo on consuming the quarry one has killed (p. 199), strictly forbids preparing or consuming the fruits of a pandanus one has planted: one does not consume one's own blood.[17] This does not apply to the owner of the tree, only to the person who planted it (see Ch. 6). The planter's spouse (who is often the owner), however, is free to filter and consume the berries, as are their children. But the direct ascendants or collateral kin of senior generations may not prepare or consume pandanus planted by their sons, daughters, nephews, etc. Planting, then, is a determining operation (as opposed to preparation-consumption), which makes the man and the food of one blood.

The prohibition on 'self-consumption' applies to all pandanus clones grown by the Yafar. Alternatively, the following rules about common consumption apply only to the traditional clones, recently

17. The most common spells pronounced when planting a pandanus cutting are: 'Let the blood of the back of my neck work! Let my thigh blood work! . . .' On the connection with one's own blood, see also Gell 1979.

introduced varieties being exempt. It is forbidden for both consanguines and affines to filter or consume pandanus in common with kinsmen one generation removed: parents-children, maternal uncle-uterine nephew (niece), paternal aunt-brother's child, parents-in-law-son- or daughter-in-law, etc. These relationships are to be understood in their classificatory dimension extending to approximately the third generation. Exception can be made for young children, non-nubile girls, and boys who have not yet been ritually blooded (anointed with animal blood and ochre on the sternum; see p. 399) or who do not yet have their own adult bow. On the other hand, grandparents and grandchildren (who call each other by a reciprocal term) do not come under this restriction. The action prohibited in this case consists as much in consuming pandanus filtered by a member of the other kin category as consuming with them pandanus prepared by a third party. The taboo extends to simply looking: a married son and his wife may not see pandanus berries (even if still on the tree) from a tree planted by their father and father-in-law; a uterine nephew, even if unmarried (but having been ritually blooded), may not look on the fruit of a pandanus tree planted by his uncle, nor a son-in-law on that of his father-in-law, etc. To avoid violating this taboo, a man (or a woman) does not enter the cultivations of these kin. The man or woman who filters the pandanus goes on to consume it with kinsmen of the same generation. The others present (± 1 generation) move apart or look away. Sometimes the 'shame' is so strong that the persons involved prepare and consume the fruit in a clearing away from the others. For the two clones bearing yellow fruit, the taboo on looking is not observed, but the prohibition on consumption is identical.

Similar though less strict prohibitions apply to other red-coloured foods, notably the reddish-shelled eggs of the *abi* wildfowl. Nor is it allowed, between the same kin categories, to share a partially smoked cigar or an areca nut (red betel juice) by biting it in two. The notion of blood extends to the bow as well, and a boy or a man may under no circumstances use (or even draw in play) the bow belonging to his father, maternal uncle or father-in-law: the weapon would lose its strength. The sanction falls on the member(s) of the ascending generation only in the form of loss of strength and weight; here we find the same principle as in the case of menstrual blood.

The consanguineal distance – third degree – mentioned above was curiously associated by my informant, May Promp, with the prohibition on marriage between *rangwarik* (Ch. 10). Yet the two types of prohibition do not overlap, since it is not forbidden to share pandanus with a real sister or a matrimonially forbidden female cousin; the common point has to do with the kinship boundaries assigned to these taboos, with the one restriction that symbolic 'incest' through consumption of pandanus can be said to occur only when the kinsmen involved are a generation apart. The three areas, marriage, rules surrounding menstrual blood and the consumption of red-coloured foods, present for our analysis three modalities of what may be called the social management of blood.[18]

Privileged Reciprocity Among Kin: The *segwaag* Relationship

Simply within the Yafar group itself, an individual can apply some term of kinship to nearly eighty percent of the community; and if he goes beyond the tribal boundaries he has a certain number of maternal kin as well. For each category, then, this individual will have a few direct kinsmen and a great number of classificatory relatives. In order to set some limits on relations, society applies a system of selection, defining privileged ties among certain relatives within each category: brothers, sisters, maternal uncles, paternal aunts, cross cousins, etc., and even between parents and children. These privileged pairs of kin are called *segwaag* (or *segwôg*), and an individual may sometimes call these kinsmen by the term *ka na segwaag* 'my *segwaag*', or even address them as '*Segwaag!*'

When the pairs are taken from two different categories (the most frequent case), they are usually made by placing elder with elder, younger with younger, and possibly those occupying an intermediate rank (*öruk-inaag*) together; for instance, in the case of three maternal uncles and their three uterine nephews, the elder nephew will establish *segwaag* relations with the elder of his uncles, the next younger with the next, and the youngest

---

18. We have also seen a similar system of prohibitions between 'mother' and 'daughter' tribes or clans; p. 20 and Figure 28.

with the youngest uncle. But if there is only one nephew and three maternal uncles, he will be paired with his mother's own *segwaag* brother. The same principle operates for the other classes of uncles and aunts. When the pairs are formed from the same category, between siblings, for example, the members will be taken by age and alternate order of birth, the first-born being paired with the third, the second with the fourth, etc., while another arrangement will pair off brothers and sisters. Sibling pairs will give rise to pairs of first-degree affines (of the same generation) of either sex, a woman's husband becoming her *segwaag* brother's privileged brother-in-law; the term *segwaag* is not used between brothers-in-law, however, as this relationship stems only from a pair of consanguineal *segwaag*. This may also lead to the constitution of maternal uncle-uterine nephew or cross-cousin pairs (Figures 25 and 26). Lastly, a woman will assist the wife of her husband's *segwaag* brother in giving birth and will subsequently establish a *segwaag* relationship with the child (classificatory son or daughter).

In the parent-child relationship, the children are attributed alternately,[19] with the first-born usually being placed in *segwaag* relationship with the mother (in accordance with the primacy of female over male which is also found in ritual: p. 54); but some permutations also take the sex of the child into account, with each parent being careful to come out with children of both sexes. Yet a deviation from this bipartition of children between their parents can be detected, for it is sometimes said that the children go 'to their father' (*awaag-gam*) and to 'their maternal uncle' (*nonoog-gam*), and not to their mother (*afaag-gam*). Loosely speaking, however, the Yafar speak of dividing the children between 'father' and 'mother'. This would seem, therefore, to be a semantic displacement from a relation between individuals (which is what the *segwaag* relationship is supposed to be) to an opposition between paternal and maternal kin.

One other important point, which brings us back to descent, is that a *segwaag* relationship is passed on to the following generation in both lines, along with the prestations that go with it; for example, two *segwaag* brothers who exchange certain cuts of game (Ch. 7) hand on the same exchange to their respective sons

19. Birth order takes precedence over gender. J.A. Hecht (*in* Marshall 1981) reports a similar system on the Rukapuka atoll (Cook Islands).

(parallel cousins), just as they transmit their respective age ranks. We have seen that the same system prevails in dyadic exchange relationships not involving kin (*sêh*, Ch. 8).

What is exchanged between *segwaag* varies in quality and frequency according to the kinship categories and the relative sex or age of the partners. In a given relationship, a pair of *segwaag* will channel the better part of the prestations they customarily owe each other into this relationship. For instance, a man exchanges game and work (clearing) or help in ritual tasks (mask-making, etc.) primarily but not exclusively with his *segwaag* maternal uncle, uterine nephew, brother or cross cousin; he will give meat mainly to his *segwaag* 'sister' or female cross cousin, or will help clear her garden plot, and he will receive from her sago or other cultivated foods as well as netbags she has made. The *segwaag* relationship between brother and sister is especially strong and takes precedence over solidarity between brothers-in-law, highly valued though this may be: for example, in the case of marital conflict, the woman's *segwaag* brother cannot side with his brother-in-law against her, whereas he can in the case of a non-*segwaag* sister. A man will also officiate as 'initiator' for his younger *segwaag* brother; he will plant trees for all his children, *segwaag* or not, but will also plant for *segwaag* classificatory nephews or children. Between parents and children, the *segwaag* relationship above all strengthens affective bonds and attenuates dominant-submissive relations; for instance, a child will go for consolation preferably to his or her *segwaag* parent (regardless of whether or not they are of the same sex), which alters the authoritarian father/appeasing mother paradigm. But the priority of this relationship can, in certain cases, be cancelled by the interplay of complementarity, which dictates that a child who disobeys one parent should be punished by the other, a way of presenting a non-contradictory image of the parental couple.

As a rule, wherever men give their *segwaag* meat, women give sago; wherever they provide help in clearing trees, women lend a hand in extracting pith from sago palms; and while male *segwaag* hunt together or help each other in rituals, women *segwaag* work sago together or fish and assist each other in giving birth. The organization of these services is thus clearly divided according to sex into equivalent or complementary reciprocity. *Segwaag* solidarity is particularly effective in clashes and shoot-outs or stick fights.

The *segwaag* institution makes it easier to control kinship relations, to channel exchanges into them and to reorganize them into a multitude of dyadic relationships, thus helping to satisfy dualism's need for reciprocity and complementarity. By choosing to analyse kinship with reference to the primary relationships within an 'atom of kinship' (which may be defined by the interplay of collateral, descent and affinal ties within the restricted circle of first-degree kin) and by attempting to identify what culture projects on to these various relationships, we find ourselves looking at three main operating principles: 1) the generational order based on the idea of the non-reversibility of the flow of life and social time, which is inscribed in descent reckoning; 2) the dual order, which calls upon ranked complementarity (elder/younger distinction between individuals, lines or entire agnatic groups) and/or upon egalitarian reciprocity (*segwaag* relations), which is inscribed primarily on the axis of collateral relations; and 3) the distinction between same and different (kin/non-kin, consanguines/affines, male/female, parallel/cross) (see also Héritier 1979), which overlays and extends beyond the other two orders. The dual order is inserted in the time flow of the descent axis by the transmission of elder/younger or *segwaag* relationships in particular. The material exchanges marking these relationships serve either an idea – that of compensation for the procreative power of the woman received or for her maternal services – or a need for sociability (exchanges between *segwaag* of the same generation). We are not dealing here with the mode of production as such and the distribution of these products in the kinship network at large (Chs 5–7), even though the circle of first-degree kin is included in the latter. The meaning the Yafar ascribe to kinship (and not the way they use it) stems from the way they symbolize, and inscribe in their culture, the cross-dialectic of relations of filiation, collaterality and marriage, no single one of which can be said to prevail. It is this dialectic, reduced to the combination of a few seemingly simple parameters, which seems to provide the basic principle behind such practical rules or thought patterns as patrilineal descent as an institution for controlling land, cosmic fertility and the circulation of women, but also behind uterine descent as a representation, the parallel/cross terminology, sister exchange and the prohibition on marriage between *rangwarik,* together with the *kəgaag* exchange cycle it determines.

12

Individual Identity and Social Ontogeny

Whose is this child I see coming?
It is my beloved handsome butterfly-child
He's coming along the big trail.
He's my child of the blood.

(From a hunting 'initiation' song)

Chapter 2 showed how the Yafar implicitly justify their present-day view of society and the figurative construction of the world they have developed, from the genesis of sexuality and reproduction, and through its 'evolution' to the dual organization of today. To this imaginary sociocultural 'phylogeny' corresponds an 'ontogeny', a reconstitution of the person, the social individual, inscribed on two levels: a) the invention of an inborn identity proper to every individual without distinction from birth and persisting after death; b) the gradual construction over an individual lifetime of a differentiated social identity, secured by the successive acquisition of ever more marked statuses, ranging from near non-being (the newborn infant) to the more or less accomplished prestige of the *aynaag* or holder of a 'hidden power' (Ch. 13). The innate identity is based on a conception of the individual as made up of both physical components and his or her relationship with the natural environment, the forest. The social identity is linked to the process of socialization, to the acquisition of certain statuses inherited at birth (responsibilities stemming from a patriline, but which must later be confirmed by apprenticeship) and to access to other age-linked statuses acquired through ritual. I will analyse each form of identity in turn, which will bring me to address the Yafar's view of death.

364

Innate Identity

This is what anthropologists have grown accustomed to calling the 'person', corresponding to a body of ethnopsychological knowledge about the human being and to a cultural representation of the person in general, independent of specific individual traits. As far as the Yafar are concerned, any attempt at an ethnographic definition of such a cultural fact must take into account the bodily and ecological space and materials on the one hand, and tangible/non-tangible (material/immaterial) duality on the other. Death is equated with integration of the bodily elements into the ecological elements, with a restructuring of duality and with a sort of dispersal of the person. This dynamic view defines the human being in his sociosymbolic dimension and – with the exception of a few subtleties presented below – applies to men, women and children alike.

The Body, Trees, Forest Land

The Amanab language is relatively rich in anatomical terms, despite the inevitable limitations of their physiological knowledge. As far as its general structure is concerned, the body (*êrik*, from *êri* 'person, human being') is made of bone(s) (*kêg*), flesh (*nihik*), blood (*taf*) and a skin (*roofuk*); the latter is in turn covered with a thin epidermis (*arfêêg*) resembling the slough of reptiles. The skin is covered with body- and head-hair (*raag*), the ritual shaving or abstention from shaving of which is equated with access to or, on the contrary, shutting in of the *hoofuk* (Ch. 9), the reproductive principle. The axis of the bony structure is the backbone (*rumuri-kêg*), whose anthropomorphic projections on to house structure and the organization of village space we have seen. The ribs (*angmang-kêg*), 'side bones', are also found in village and house structure as well as in the *wamero* pectoral ornament. The head (*mesoog*) is also the treetop, which is evoked in growth magic. The headbone, or skull, (*mesoog-kêg*) serves as a mortuary relic; it is distinguished from the lower jaw (*kawuk*), which corresponds to another clearly differentiated symbolic entity and, even more than the tongue, is seen as the organ of speech. The blood (*taf*) radiates out to each limb and part of the body from the heart (*öruk*), which is the centre of both its diffusion and convergence. Over the span of an individual life the quality of the blood changes: from being 'clear and fast-running' (*taf ugufoog*), it gradually becomes 'thick' (*taf mwerik*) and in the end, for the elderly, 'hard' and slow (*taf kêfutuk*). The heart is centred on the midline of the body and corresponds, on the outside, to the bottom of the sternum (*bweyfôk*), where the heartbeat can often be seen; this is where the boy undergoing initiation to the masks and the guardian spirits of game is anointed with red ochre and animal blood. The heart is the centre of the body and the person; it is also the site of thought, the brain being considered as mere *nihik* and without a function. 'To think about something' is *öruk gingêg*, 'to open the path to the heart, to clear (in the sense of to clear undergrowth) the heart'. The air we breathe 'lifts up the heart', and most informants do not associate the lungs (*susuk*) with respiration. Digestion is seen as a process of food 'rotting' (*nönguk feg*) in the stomach (*ehnog*) and being transformed into faecal matter (*ata*) – the final stage of rotting – as it passes through the intestine (*ataag*). The liver (*uguhaag*) and the kidneys (*ôgôg*, generic term for anything shaped like a kidney or a gland) have no known function. Water or the liquid part of food passes directly from the stomach into the bladder (*tôrôk*), where it becomes urine (*tôr*). Apart from the bones, the body is riddled with *bəgaag* 'roots', a general term for tendons, nerves, muscles, arteries and veins. The pulse (*pinpin*), wherever visible on the body, is thought to be vibrations of the *bəgaag*, suggesting body tone and quickness of reaction. The reproductive function is explained by the notion of *hoofuk* (analysed in Ch. 9), which is at once the white substance in the uterus, semen and the life force renewed by eating; the origin of the male seed or the female *hoofuk* is not, to my knowledge, clear.

The body as a whole, together with the face, have a form and appearance that are found in a person's 'duplicate selves' (the 'self' and the 'forest self') both during life and after death. We shall see later that the three elements that persist after death are spiritual emanations from the blood, the bones and the rotting body.

The parallel between *êri* and *êrik*, and *rii* 'tree' is not only based on lexical evidence. Analogies can be seen in many myths, in ritual representations and in the perception of trees as the home and personification of spirits of the dead. The tree stands upright (*ogo*) like a human being and, after it dies, the same term, *bigik*, can be used for its rotting trunk as for the remains of a human body. When the wood is hard, the tree trunk is also termed *kêg*, and the black sap, notably in the case of the red-wooded iron tree, is associated with blood, *taf*, whereas conversely, the same-coloured resin of the *Intsia palembanica* (*sibi*), also called *taf*, symbolizes by this sacralized term the original 'blood' shed by the mythic Great Mother, B. . .. The latex of the breadfruit tree or the *Alstonia scholaris*, on the other hand, represents semen in mythical accounts and in ritual, while the coconut flowers represent mother's milk. Fruit is structured like the body, with a *kêg*, *nihik* and *roofuk* (pit, flesh and skin), and seeds swell and germinate just as a woman conceives and bears a son.

The forest land (*sangweri* 'forest' or *nôô* 'distant forest land') is also globally anthropomorphized, since the earth (*bəte*) is like flesh made firm by the underlying rocks and roots (bones) and is a site of gestation (agriculture and various mythic representations), traversed by waterways as the body is by blood. These correspondences will take shape more clearly when the time comes to discuss eschatological representations.

The Forest Self

Somewhere in the forest, in the invisible world of the *nabasa* spirits, every individual – man, woman and child – has a duplicate *nabasa* self. This *nabasa* is born at the same time as ego to his or her mother's duplicate self, previously fertilized by his or her father's duplicate self. This self is the exact replica of ego, has the same names and undergoes identical parallel rites of passage. It is born into a *nabasa* society, the totality of which is the collective duplicate of the local visible society. Throughout its life, this alter ego maintains a constant relationship of identification with the individual, particularly for a man, whom it accompanies from around the age of ten on all his forays into the bush and in his economic activities: it fishes, cultivates, eats and hunts with him. A woman's duplicate self is more of a loner, and some say that only the parturient has her own alter ego with her in the same act of giving birth. As is the case for the other categories of forest spirits, the human equivalent or person in charge of the cult is called the *awaag*, 'father, master, owner'. The human being and the duplicate self are said to be 'the two together', a free rendering of the expression *ah* (dual prefix)-*ogohôk* ('to be on their own'). One may meet other selves in dreams, but obviously not one's own. Each duplicate self lives on the land exploited by ego, but in no particular spot; it does not enter into mediums in a trance in the village, but stays in the forest, spending the night in its own hamlet, identical to that of its human double and located – as for all *nabasa* – in a world just below the surface of the ground.

Certain contradictions emerge when, beginning with the category *nabasa*, one tries to learn the specific term used to define the forest self. The word that first springs to a Yafar's lips is *segwaag*. But this concept contradicts the definition of a forest self. We saw in Chapter 11 that the *segwaag*, in kinship terms, is the privileged exchange partner and that the resulting relationship is founded on the exchange of goods and thus on the differentiation of identities. Now the Yafar are unanimous in saying that one does not exchange anything with one's forest self and that not being localized and not speaking through mediums, it is incapable of receiving offerings (food hung in the house tree or given to the medium to eat): it only eats *with* ego, in other words, feeds on the invisible duplicate of ego's meal. Reciprocally, it is often implied that the duplicate self does not put game in the hunter's line of vision – this is the role of the spirits of the dead and of other forest spirits (Ch. 7). In these conditions, it is hard to see how the duplicate self could be a *segwaag*. The use of the term seems to stem from a confusion with the *nabasa*, which favours one hunter over another and enters into exchange with him (game for garden produce); it will be remembered that this purveyor of game may or may not be identified, but that in most cases it remains anonymous. The importance of hunting and of the cynegetic relationship with the forest spirits would explain the semantic shift in this term. Men also say that women do not have a *nabasa segwaag* because they do not hunt, but they do recognize that women have a forest self.

My best informants, however, made a clear distinction between the forest self and the *segwaag*, reserving for the latter the role of giver of animals and taker of offerings. One informant in this case designated a man's duplicate self by the expression *ah-ogohôk*, explained above, using it as a noun (but this lexical use was contested by others). The *ah-ogohôk* was in this case clearly differentiated from the *nabasa segwaag* according to the opposition same/other, non-reciprocity/reciprocity, or sharing/exchange: the *ah-ogohôk* neither gave nor received, but merely 'duplicated' its *awaag* in every action (e.g., shooting the game *with* him), while the *segwaag* led a separate life from his *awaag*, but encountered him to solicit a gift of food or to shove a wild pig into his path, danced beside him in rituals and watched over his sleep. This comes down to saying that there is no specific term for the forest self, *segwaag* appearing as an erroneous semantic usage leading to a confusion of categories, and *ah-ogohôk* as a grammatical error.

But whatever terminology is used, our information confirms a differentiation between the forest self and the *nabasa* as privileged purveyor of game. The latter, which I will call (*nabasa*) *segwaag*, is not a constituent element of the person but a tutelary spirit and an exchange partner from the spirit world. (For more on this subject, the reader is referred to Chapter 7 and later parts of the present chapter.) The notion of tutelary or guardian spirit fits both the forest self and the *segwaag*, but only in part. The first accompanies ego and is present at crucial moments of his life; the second is generous to him and watches over his sleep. Nevertheless in either case the relationship develops according to one of the two models I have already defined: sameness or otherness.

Sungwaag: The Personification of the Self

While the forest self is a faithful replica of the person in the unseen world and the *segwaag* an exchange partner in the same world, the *sungwaag* is an integral part of the individual: it *is* the individual. Yet it is neither localized in one part of the body[1] nor necessarily present in the body at every waking moment. It is thought of as escaping from or returning to the body through the feet, but also as accompanying or mirroring ego, or as walking with him or her. Although it may withdraw momentarily, the duration of a fright or a faint (*uhaag bwehyaag* 'to die to get up'), and longer if the subject has been bespelled, it is more normal and expected for the *sungwaag* to leave the body during sleep. It

---

1. It is occasionally associated with an elongated organ next to the stomach (the duodenum?).

is, then, that which may be lost and then found again by a man or a woman, which may temporarily and partially be estranged (illness) and which, after death, goes its own way as an *ifaaf* ('ghost'). It is also the 'hot' part of the person, whose sleeping body grows 'cold'.

Concretely, *sungwaag* designates both shadow and reflection.[2] These two kinds of replica accompanying all individuals are here – unlike in many other cultures, which make a distinction – merged under the same term, even though some neighbouring groups consider them to be two distinct eschatological entities (see below, note 13). The term *sungwaag* (sometimes only the root, *sungo*,[3] is used) therefore refers to the shadow and reflection of a living being or an object as well as to what I will call, not the 'soul' or the 'duplicate self', but simply the 'self'. Both shadow and reflection belong to the realm of appearance, of form and physical resemblance, therefore to the realm of the body. It is with this aspect of the individual that the *sungwaag* is connected, and the *ifaaf* into which it is transformed after death will remain attached to the corpse for a short time before descending into the netherworld, taking along part of its odour. This definitive separation imposed by the destruction of the body is already present in the *segwaag*'s propensity to slip its bonds. The life of an individual is made up of this fragility of the self, of the alternation between presence and absence, waking and sleeping, with the risks of loss and injury that this entails.

For the Yafar, sleep (*nono*) does not *determine* the *sungwaag*'s departure; rather, it is the sign that it *wants* to leave. Waking signals its return, and having difficulty waking someone indicates that the *sungwaag* is far away (one does not suddenly wake a sleeping person, one calls him or her to give the *sungwaag* time to come back); consequently, merely dozing indicates its nearness. A dream is simply the part of the *sungwaag*'s action that one recalls, but it spends the entire duration of the sleeping time wandering. The territories visited vary in distance, but also in terms of the levels of vertical space and the categories of spirits that inhabit them.

Normal nighttime behaviour for a *sungwaag* is going 'to see

---

2. Or the silhouette and the physiognomy: during the individual's life, the *sungwaag* reflection is realized primarily in the pupil of other people's eyes.

3. *Sungo* is also the root of a verb meaning 'to put down, to deposit (an object)'.

the *nabasa'*, in other words it visits the forest spirits' world just beneath the surface of the ground (without delving deeper into the world of ghosts) and entertains socialized relations consisting of conversations, exchanges and consumption of betel and food (see Ch. 7, on the interpretation of dreams in terms of gifts). Still, it is not good to dream too much, and while there is a ritual plant clone (in particular *Curcuma* sp.) called *itê-angô* (*itê*[4] 'dream', plus *angô*, idea of femaleness and fertility), which can be eaten to promote dreaming, there is another clone used to curtail it. To reduce the frequency of dreaming, one can also sleep in a garden for several nights to 'cool off' the *sungwaag* or, more simply, change eating habits in the evening and roll one's cigars in other types of leaves. The Yafar think it good to dream every other night. This dream contact with the forest spirits is necessary for maintaining the cynegetic exchange between *nabasa* and hunters (Ch. 7); it is the opportunity for a man to receive the *nabasa's* gift, which represents the game he will shoot the next day, or more rarely the sign that will provide the community with information pointing to the diagnosis of the illness of one of its members and the healing methods to be used.

More specific classes of spirits which the *sungwaag* can encounter without risk are the *kê-ruur*, the spirits of the bones of the dead, which can be recognized by their skeleton-like appearance and by the fact that they keep their fleshless backs turned to the dreamer; the *uguwak* (Ch. 11), with their hairy bodies and faces, who dwell in the white cliffs and whose houses are recognizable by their up-turned ridge; or Wabuminaag, the crop spirit, who can appear as ego's father working the garden or simply as smoke rising from a clearing. Women seen in dreams are the wives of *nabasa* or spirits of the blood of the dead, while the true prehuman *sawangô* appear wearing long nose sticks through the sides of the nostrils. In principle ghosts (*ifaaf*) do not appear in dreams, but it is possible that the dream figures who do not give the dreamer anything or who give the dreamer an item of food that he or she does not eat may be ghosts, for they have a habit of eating inedible substances and are the epitome of the impossible exchange partner. Recurrent dreams of ghosts can only presage the approaching death of the dreamer or a relative. Other types

---

4. 'I dreamed' is more frequently expressed as *ka na sungwaag ate nangôk. . . .* 'my *sungwaag* saw. . .'.

of inauspicious sign can appear in dreams. For example, a dreamer seeing a male acquaintance dancing the *ogohyaag* with the ritual penis gourd – which means that this person's *sungwaag* has identified itself with the primordial growth spirits, like the *ogomô* (Table 6), and is therefore in danger of 'ripening' – will warn the person concerned so that he can perform an *agi-wahwe* rite (see Ch. 14). As a rule, dreaming of rituals is a bad sign for the same reasons and may foreshadow a death. Any dream of a man or an animal committing an aggression may announce an *aysiri* sorcerer's attack, for which there is no prophylactic rite.

These premonitory features of dreams are not determined only by the identity or behaviour of the spiritual entities encountered by the *sungwaag*, regarded as a mere witness or passive subject, but by the very actions of the *sungwaag* as an acting subject. The disembodied self is endowed with a free will not controlled by the individual, who can only recall at some later time the action executed, which by then is irrevocable. In both cases, there is a principle of determinism at work, whether in the form of a sign to be decoded or an action performed initially by the *sungwaag*, but which predicts the accomplishment of the same act in the waking reality of the following day. For instance, to dream of working in the garden, hunting or visiting relatives in another village announces that in principle, the dreamer will be doing these things the next day. In fact the dream decides the waking agenda only in so far as it promises something (hunting, cultivating, gathering, calling on relatives). But in most cases the action undertaken in waking reality is only supposed to have been previously experienced by the *sungwaag* during sleep. This determinism, reasoned and a posteriori, is based on the idea that the *sungwaag* 'precedes' the individual. These considerations lead us to take a closer look at the 'risks' incurred by the *sungwaag*. In effect this notion is at the heart of the very definition of the self in Yafar culture and is, as we shall see, an integral part of their system of eschatological representations.

Estrangement and Loss: The 'Ripe' *Sungwaag*

The idea of a self (what anthropologists used to call the 'soul') being estranged, lost, found or detained is nothing new, and countless examples have been cited by authors like Tylor, Frazer,

Lévy-Bruhl and Roheim. But such lists do nothing more than confirm the existence of universal features in cultural conceptions of the human person. Granted this universality, it is more interesting to look at how such a representation is specifically shaped by other sociocultural features and by regional material and historical facts.

Estrangement, injury to or loss of the self (*sungwaag*) can be caused by three distinct factors: a) spontaneous behaviour on the part of the *sungwaag* as a subject acting in accordance with its own nature; b) harm done to the self by human agents (sorcery) and the repercussions of this on the individual's health; c) harm done to the self by forest spirits and the repercussions of this on the subject. To these three categories of threat, the Yafar respond with ritual procedures which will be analysed below, the principal rite being Gungwan.

The first type of danger is inherent in the mortal nature of the self: the *sungwaag* spontaneously behaves like an *ifaaf*. This can be seen in its irrepressible tendency to eat ghost food and to descend into their underground world. One can deduce the probability of such behaviour from the morbid symptoms exhibited, or one may 'surprise' one's *sungwaag* during a dream ingesting non-edible foodstuffs (certain *Ficus* fruits, coconut flowers, raw eggs, earthworms, etc.) or approaching dangerous plant species (*Cycas circinalis* palm, *Schefflera* sp.) too closely. The identification with *ifaaf* in this case is made through the food item and belongs to the register of orality: the *sungwaag* contaminates the individual (the sleeper) and hastens his metamorphosis into a ghost by incorporating as food that which is not. The other death-inducing mode of identification is of a spatial order: not only does the *sungwaag* 'go to see the *nabasa*', it tends to descend into the deeper world of the dead, which is also the maternal world of primal fertility, of the primordial *hoofuk* or 'blood'. The cosmological association of death and rotting (*ifaaf*) with the original *hoofuk* takes on an additional meaning through the mediation of the *sungwaag*, which, now contaminated, returns to its owner with a double-edged promise of death and rebirth. In effect, like a fruit, the *sungwaag* can 'ripen' (*abuk feg*).[5]

---

5. This notion was introduced earlier, in the discussion of hunting (Ch. 7).

Here we broach only one of the many aspects – one of the most significant, however – of the continual metaphorization of human beings in terms of the plant kingdom, whether in their morphology or in their growth and reproduction. The idea of ripening or maturity (*abuk*: 1) red; 2) ripe) is associated with that of falling, dropping (to the ground). To be 'ripe' is to be about to fall and to rot, therefore about to die; it is to be vulnerable and to arouse aggression. The opposition between a 'strong' self (*kêf-utuk*) and a 'ripe' self (*abuk*) is also expressed in terms of colour: the first is black (*sungwaag önguk*), the second orangish-yellow (*sawik*). *Ate sawik* (*fatik*), 'he turned orangish-yellow (he fell, dropped)', is said both of a contaminated self and of a fruit or edible grubs ready for harvest. It is also said of the *sungwaag* that it is *boof abuk*, ripe like *boof* (*Rejoua aurantiaca*)[6] fruits. The intermediate state between the hard, green fruit or the 'black' self, and their complete maturity is designated by the term *heweheg*, 'half-ripe'. The semi-stricken or recently contaminated *sungwaag* is *heweheg*: a rite will make it *kêfutuk* again, without which it will gradually evolve into the state of *boof abuk* and bring on its owner's death. The same applies to game, which can magically be made *abuk* so that the quarry will fall under the hunter's arrows. A wounded pig that manages to escape had a *sungwaag önguk*; only the quarry whose *sungwaag* is ripe falls and dies (Ch. 7 and below). The state of the self commands its relationship to the individual in his waking state. It is said that the black *sungwaag* walks in front of the subject, the ripe *sungwaag*, behind. In the latter case the order is reversed between the physical person and his self: the self no longer clears the way, but, in its weakened state, trails behind. In this case, during sleep it can do nothing but accentuate its ghostly behaviour, until it is ultimately pierced by the arrows of a sorcerer's *sungwaag* who has noticed its victim's 'colour'.

But how does a *sungwaag* become *abuk*? By eating the 'ghost foods' cited above and in particular fruits that fall from the tree as soon as they are ripe (notably several species of wild *Ficus*); by visiting, once the individual is under an *agi* spell (Ch. 14), the same places and in particular the *sasa* palm (*Cycas circinalis*)

6. These dark orange inedible fruits are also used in making ritual ornaments to express the same idea of ripeness-caducity: in particular for hunting rites and by the 'termite' masks in the Yangis ceremony, who announce the imminent birth of the 'children of the blood' (p. 53).

where the leavings were deposited by evil-doers to attract the victim's *sungwaag*; by encountering ghosts which are in fact the *sungwaag* of deceased persons, in other words *sungwaag* that have gone beyond the ripe state, rotted *sungwaag*; by being contaminated by the primal *hoofuk* or maternal 'blood' concealed in the chthonian depths. The same relationship with blood can be found in the idea that a woman who has had several miscarriages is left with a *sungwaag abuk*, which makes her vulnerable to attacks by sorcerers.

The symptoms of premature ripening of the self are extreme weakness and gradual loss of weight, which is called simply 'sick body' (*êrik abôgêk*). The individual rite that can be performed by anyone who fears that his *sungwaag* is *heweheg* consists of bathing and rubbing oneself with the root of a particular *Curcuma* clone.

Of the two kinds of sorcerer identified by the Yafar and analysed in Chapter 14, only certain *agi* practices result in the ripening of the victim's self. Alternatively, an *aysiri* sorcerer is capable of killing a victim who is already ripe. It is above all with the parallel sorcery between disembodied *sungwaag* that we are dealing here, for the 'black' *sungwaag* of the *aysiri* sorcerer goes unnoticed by his victim, whereas at night the sorcerer's *sungwaag* easily detects the brighter hue of a ripe *sungwaag*. He will release his arrow, and the wounded *sungwaag* will return to the body of the sleeper, who will die a short time later. As we shall see, one of the functions of the Gungwan ritual is to prompt the sleeper's self to hide from the *aysiri* sorcerer's *sungwaag*. Another scenario is said to begin with a 'real' attack by an *aysiri* man in a waking state (shooting an 'invisible' arrow) and to continue with his using spells to order the enthralled victim to have an accident (fall out of a tree, drown, etc.). The *sungwaag* of the attacked individual is then supposed, one night in the near future, to become the victim of the accident, thus enabling the real event actually to take place. If a man having experienced a similar piece of bad luck had perchance visited Punda relatives or Sowanda exchange partners shortly before, it would be concluded that he was the victim of an *agi sêh* spell (Ch. 14) and that his *sungwaag* had been ordered to fall or drown, thus deciding the same fate for its owner.

The last category of risks encountered by the disembodied self is less irrevocable and does not result in ripening. Nevertheless, it provides matter for a rich nosological taxonomy, and it is to a great extent on the analogies between classes of spirits, vegetal elements associated with this class and nosographical features that a theory of Yafar illness should be based. It is not my intention, however, to set out on this path, and the few examples given below have their legitimate place in the context of the matter of this chapter: the conception of an autonomy of the self which, in its relationship with the physical subject on the one hand and with the spirit world on the other, allows both society and the individual to think their relationship with sickness and death in a dynamic mode.

The *sungwaag* carries on veritable social relations with the *nabasa* spirits (as different from the forest self): it eats with them and receives presents, which are promises of game. The Yafar place great value on these relations: the *nabasa* are good, useful, for many Yafar they are their dead ancestors, 'fathers' or 'mothers', some are their *segwaag*; in return for dream visits from the *sungwaag*, they come to converse and chew betel with the villagers via mediums. But as in any social relation, reciprocity can go awry, conflict can momentarily take the place of balanced exchange. In this process of destabilization of the relationship between humans and *nabasa*, through the intermediary of the *sungwaag*, three elements can be identified, which can occur in different orders: 1) the human 'offense', 2) the *nabasa's* punishment (sickness), 3) atonement or prevention (rite). For the Yafar, the offence comes first, but a propitiatory rite can enable someone to 'offend' the spirit without incurring a sanction, or the healing rite offered the *nabasa* on behalf of someone who is sick can serve as anticipated protection for the rest of the village. Sometimes, however, the offence is conceived as the omission of the preliminary rite, for example when a sago palm is cut down without prior appeasement of the *nabasa* who had rights in the tree during his lifetime. Indeed the inheritance of planted trees often lies behind the differences that arise between humans and their dead. In most cases, however, the offence attributed to the appearance of symptoms is the felling of wild trees – homes of the *nabasa* – in the course of clearing, or the premature retrieval of an offering hung in the forest by the spirit's 'father'. The *nabasa* do not interfere in such social conflicts as adultery or murder; they defend their own interests and do not assume the role of censors or guardians of the group's morality that is played by the spirits of the dead in other Melanesian societies. Among the

Yafar, relations between humans and spirits hinge essentially on the continuous renewal of reciprocity.

Nabasa sanctions vary: the *nabasa* may refuse to give the hunter any game for a time – although hunting failures are more often attributed to human deeds (Ch. 7) – but in the case of the *sungwaag*, they can hamper its freedom or damage its health. In the first instance, the self is seen as being estranged by a *nabasa* who holds it in its sway night after night. The *sungwaag* is powerless to resist the *nabasa*'s lure when it ventures forth. It loses its autonomy and its sociability with regard to the other spirits. The most frequent punishments meted out by the *nabasa*, however, are pathogenic attacks on the *sungwaag*'s 'body'. The means employed depend, as we have already said, on the sex and class of the spirit and on the vegetal elements or objects it has at its disposal; the victim's symptoms are believed to be determined by analogy with these causes. In other words, the type of illness orients the search for a diagnosis on the one hand, towards a class of spirits (symbolic analogy) and on the other, towards something that may have offended them (factual correlation). The *nabasa*, in the strict sense of spirits of the blood of deceased persons, shoot 'arrow heads' (*sosoog*, or *fag* 'arrows') into the *sungwaag*'s 'body', which then cause the individual to experience pain in breathing and fever. If the patient gets worse, the deterioration is attributed to an attack by an *aysiri* sorcerer, and the illness, called *af*, is considered fatal (lung disease). Swellings, running sores and abscesses are caused by *sawangô* spirits, who burn the *sungwaag* with firebrands, rub it with the stinging hairs of the *öku* bamboo, which is their favourite home, prick it with thorns, smear it with or force it to drink latex, which causes sore throat and hoarseness accompanied or not by fever.[7] Sometimes they beat the *sungwaag* with their bone belts or other female objects, which causes muscle ache and extreme fatigue. The non-human *angor* water sprites also cause sores and swellings. The growth spirits, like Wabuminaag (horticulture) or Mwayfik (sago palm), through their control of the reproduction of plant *hoofuk*, send swellings caused by too much *hoofuk* in the patient's body (*hoofuk sahô*, '*hoofuk* inside'); Mwayfik uses sago thorns for this purpose. An excess of *hoofuk* is accumulated during times of intense work in growing gardens and contrasts with the danger of being covered with smoke and

---

7. The ideas of secretions and swelling obviously refer to the female domain.

ashes when burning slash, which comes back to the idea of *roofuk* (pp. 241–6). Too much *hoofuk* or too much *roofuk* are transmitted by the *sungwaag* to the body of its owner. The *kê-ruur* (spirits of the bones of the dead) work preferably by striking the disembodied self with their bones or introducing into it insects (ants, etc.) which are often found on bones exposed in the bush. As far as ghosts (*ifaaf*) are concerned, assuming that the *sungwaag* gets as far as their dwelling place, these communicate something of their putrefaction and strike it with their bones or drive them into its 'body':[8] the victim will suffer from extreme weakness and persistent diarrhoea, with or without fever, entailing a loss of *hoofuk*. As a rule, it is thought that the *ifaaf* inflict these ills mainly on their own orphaned child whom they want to take with them (in this case the infant can die without being attacked by a sorcerer), and female ghosts on their husband because they are jealous of his new wife. Miscarriage can also be the result of action taken on the *sungwaag* by a *nabasa* who is jealous of the birth of a grandson who will inherit from his father or mother the trees that belonged to the *nabasa* in life. For the same reason, the *kê-ruur* can hinder a birth by barring the child's passage with his bones. In all of these cases, with the exception of the *ifaaf*, the pathogenic action is mechanical and does not cause the *sungwaag* to 'ripen'. Transmission occurs in accordance with the principle of analogy between the agent (spirit + weapon) and the symptom, and with the principle of sameness between the subject and his or her *sungwaag*.

There are many rites for stopping *nabasa* attacks or for healing the ailments that have been inflicted, from simple spells spoken while twirling a leaf over the patient's head and spitting the root of certain cultivated clones chewed with betel, to complex collective rites using ornaments, masks, body paint and music. The first procedure is individual and can be undertaken at the patient's request by any man (never a woman), usually a kinsman, who knows the spells. There are no specialized 'healers' except for the rite recently imported from eastern Eri groups, which consists in extracting 'arrowheads' shot into the body by a forest spirit. But this function is not restricted to any one line; around 1980, it was known by a single Yafar who had

8. Hence the curing process consisting in 'removing the bones'.

learned it only recently. Because of its special nature, this technique seems nevertheless to require secrecy, for it is based on sleight of hand, the *soosog* 'extracted' from the patient's chest being then exhibited by the healer in the form of broken arrowheads or an old rusty blade.[9] The other techniques, on the other hand, do not seek to hide anything from the patient or the onlookers: whether the patient is smeared with mud brought back from the spot where he recently cleared trees and which is the home of the suspected *nabasa*, or whether he is brushed with an arrow by a masked man in the healing ceremony dedicated to the *sawangô*, it is always the attendant spirit who is supposed to carry the ailment back to the forest, and sometimes to return what he or she has taken from the victim's *sungwaag*, thereby 'dis-estranging' it. Arrows, mud or water collected from the forest, leaves, netbags, sago jelly, areca nuts (food is used to attract the spirit), etc. are the mediating objects with which the *nabasa* identifies; once the ritual is over, these are charged with the ailment and discarded far from the patient. But the cure is realized through the combined actions of the magical plants and the right words only: it in no way depends on a personal gift or a body of knowledge amassed by the officiant.

These examples should suffice to demonstrate that the disembodied self (*sungwaag*) is used, in Yafar thinking, as a channel for bad omens as well as for promises of life. In particular it is vulnerable to human or non-human pathogenic agents and appears as a mediator between the invisible world of the spirits and society. Above and beyond the rites which have just been evoked, the Yafar have invented, as protection against the external dangers threatening their *sungwaag* and against the self's own mortiferous character and its regressive tendencies, a symbolic ritual complex whose declared function is to keep the *sungwaag* in the village, to dissuade it from leaving the house, and even the body, to hide it from the eyes of sorcerers and to close to it the galleries leading to the ghosts as well as to the original maternal *hoofuk*.

---

9. Several of these practitioners saw their reputation destroyed when the sleight of hand was discovered. But confidence seems to be based more on the kinship ties between healer and patient than on the former's skill in producing the 'arrowheads'.

Gungwan: Closing the Way Back

The word *gungwan* designates a wild-growing shrub, of which the Yafar recognize two 'varieties', one 'for men' (*Antiaropsis decipiens*), the other 'for women' (*A. toxicaria*). The same name is also given to an *Acorus calamus* (*gaf*) clone, whose rhizomes are chewed with betel while chanting spells. The particular feature of the *gungwan* bush is that its fruits do not drop off when ripe ('its fruits only rot when the tree does'). This tenacious character contrasts with the *boof* fruits and those of the *Ficus* mentioned above as 'ghost foods'. This is why one of the key words in Gungwan spells is *kêfutuk* 'strong, firm, hard, resistant, invulnerable, brave' (see p. 374). To ward off the risks of 'ripening' and caducity incurred by *sungwaag* during sleep, Gungwan proposes a botanical species with which the self is supposed to identify, while respecting a segregation of the sexes also found in the spells pronounced at the foot of coconut palms. The two sexes of *sungwaag* are not supposed to mix: the social order of sexuality also holds for the spirit world. *Abuk* (*sawik*)/*kêfutuk* (*önguk*) are the two incompatible poles of the self's destiny; Gungwan is the ritual implementation of the second, a bulwark against the natural process that leads to the first. Firmly rooted in this dialectic, the rite does not deal with attacks on the self perpetrated by forest spirits, as described above.

Gungwan takes a variety of more or less complex and public forms ranging from a simple verbal rite performed by one or several men (non-specialized, but sometimes divided into moieties) to a ceremony comprised of several parts, among which the Gungwan phases properly speaking can be distinguished from other symbolic complexes. In the narrow sense, the rite consists of figuratively hardening the earth, closing off the underground pathways used by *sungwaag* or barring the exits from the village and the house. In its ceremonial aspect, the same principles, repeated on various levels, are worked into the mask dance or procession dedicated to the *nabasa* spirits (male hunting cult). This is a way of countering the excess of female *hoofuk* that has contaminated the *sungwaag*. Whether in simplified form or as a complex ceremony, Gungwan is performed each time it is felt that the *sungwaag* of the village are in danger, in a weakened state (*heweheg* 'almost or half ripe') and therefore particularly vulnerable to sorcery. These circumstances may be exceptional or, on the contrary, predictable and cyclical, for example when they result from clearing. A rite is organized:

a) when the founding houses are constructed at the creation of a new village (stakes breaking the ground);
b) whenever the ground of the village or the forest has been worked: clearing (see p. 160), harvesting the first tubers, levelling an eroded village place, etc.;
c) whenever the ground has been symbolically 'opened': fertility rite when planting is begun in a new garden site (pp. 161–2), after the celebration of rituals having to do with the original maternal force (Yangis, Sawangô raara);
d) whenever an increase in the vulnerability of the *sungwaag* makes its effects felt: too many ('bad') dreams in the community, numerous deaths.

Gungwan is a collective undertaking (except in the case of the isolated cultivator) conducted by men (*aynaag*) with sufficient instruction in the details of the ritual. The officiants operate separately according to their moiety. Women have a passive role: they do not dance, but they and their children are regarded more particularly as the beneficiaries of the rite, since they are considered to be more susceptible to sorcery attacks.

The following summary of the successive sequences is taken from the Gungwan ritual performed in April 1971, following the levelling of the village place, which had been eroded by rains. The Yafar had not organized a Gungwan for a number of years and also felt the need to reinforce this safeguard against the *aysiri* sorcerers in nearby groups. They claimed that this protected them from ghosts and ailments of the *agi* category (non-lethal sorcery) by prompting their *sungwaag* to stay in the village during sleep or to conceal themselves in the trunks of palm trees. The danger of contamination from the primal *hoofuk* was not explicitly mentioned because of the secrecy surrounding the notion, but the fear was expressed that the *sungwaag* would delve too deep into the invisible subterranean galleries or natural caves. Gungwan is always celebrated for a single hamlet; this time it was Hopwan Kəbik (Yafar 1), and no one was allowed to leave or enter the hamlet from the eve of the ritual until two or three days after its close, with the exception of the group responsible for collecting the materials for the masks. The 'confinement' of the community reproduces its social and ontological unity even as it prefigures the *sungwaag's* sedentarization.

Afternoon of the first day. A ritual enclosure (*pəpak*) is built on the edge of the village square; the young men bring the plant materials, the ornaments made from animal products and the pigments needed for preparing the body paints and the *ra* headdresses for the Gêpôk night ritual (Ch. 7). Sago jelly is distributed to the different houses for those visiting from other hamlets.

Towards five p.m., while the young men are getting ready in the *pəpak*, the men of knowledge (*aynaag*) assemble the rest of the men and the women into two groups at the foot of two different coconut palms. The men gather around a coconut with 'black' nuts from the Araneri ('male') moiety of the hamlet, the women at the foot of a coconut palm with 'red' coconuts, from the Angwaneri ('female') moiety. A few *aynaag* (only one or two in the women's group) chant spells while placing their feet (the *sungwaag* leaves the body through the feet) on the base of the palm tree. After shouting '*Gungwan kêf-utuk!*. . .', they name the *hoofuk* of various species of black palm and other palms. This is meant to incite the *sungwaag* to spend the night in the safety of these trees, where, if they are high enough, they will be protected from the sorcerers' *sungwaag* prowling around on the ground. The different parts of the coconut palm are named for the Angwaneri, then the parts of the sago palm for the Araneri (Ch. 2). Then other hiding places are suggested to the *sungwaag*: treetops in the forest, mist, drizzle, fog, rising dew, etc. white clouds, black clouds, the blue of the sky. The very voice of the *sungwaag* needs to change into the cry of an owl to throw the sorcerers off the trail. Lastly, sorcerers from the other tribes named are enjoined to 'forego' their deadly plans, and then the *hoofuk* and the hardiness of the *gungwan* bush is evoked once more.

5:30 p.m. One man per house (in principle the head of the family or one of his clan brothers) symbolically bars the *sungwaag's* exit from the dwelling by burying a stone or planting a cordyline plant (from a clone called *hoogof*) at the foot of the pole ladder, or by simply placing his foot on the bottom of the notched pole. Betel and *Acorus calamus* (from a clone called *gungwan*) are chewed as these spells are recited, while the rest of the household remains inside the house. The *sungwaag* are exhorted to 'stay in the house, under the floor, under the *kəfe* mat, in the thatch, etc.' Then once more fog, cries of night birds and the foreign sorcerers' 'renunciation' are evoked.

6:15 p.m. A similar rite is performed at the door of the ritual enclosure where the Gêpôk participants are getting ready. They declare that they are 'barring' (*pawêg*) the path with the *gungwan* bush, with

Plate 20. Gungwan: Once the stones have been set into the ground to "close off the underground passages", women and children gather around the masks to enjoy their protection.

the stone, with the coconut palm fibres, with its inflorescence. Then various spells are chanted inside the *pəpak*: betel and '*gungwan*' root are spat on to the feet of the costumed participants, who first circle while beating their drums and then make their appearance on the dancing ground. At this point the spells name the undulating back of different kinds of snake. The line of Gêpôk dancers will then wind around the grounds all night, like the mythic serpent (pp. 185–7); some images in the spells are reminiscent of old age and therefore longevity, and no doubt also of the resistance of a solid, flexible spine, and (or) perhaps of the immortality associated with the phenomenon of sloughing old skin.

The Gêpôk dance goes on all night. Special *mwaage* songs are sung during this rite, in which the Araneri men call themselves the '*afwêêg* sago palm *hoofuk* children' and the Angwaneri, the 'coconut palm *hoofuk* children': in other words they articulate their totemic origins (Ch. 2).

The next morning, an *aynaag* accompanied by a group of young men goes into the bush to gather the materials for the masks, in particular the long stalks of the *uguf* tree (*Dysoxyluum* sp.), which will be used as centre poles for the several metres tall masks. When they return, they remain on the outskirts of the hamlet for a few minutes, holding the *uguf* poles upright, and the *aynaag* shouts spells while another group of *aynaag* replies from the village. The spells allude to the biological reproduction of the community, naming the '*gungwan* children' and the children of several prolific species of animals (rats, frogs). Then the *sungwaag* are reminded of their hiding places, and the sorcerers are once more commanded to lay down their arms. Then the group enters the ritual enclosure to make the masks.

Beginning at 1:00 p.m., two *waray* (dragonfly) masks perform a hopping dance and flick switches at the women who follow them around jeering.

Inside the enclosure, during the mask-making, adolescents who are to wear a given category of masks for the first time are 'initiated'.

A medium may be seized by a *nabasa* and fall into a trance. The spirit possessing him gives information on the *nabasa* present and sometimes on certain details of the ritual.

5:00 p.m. The women bring sago jelly to the entrance of the *pǝpak* and distribute it among the men, who eat it after the procession of the masks, each of which is in communion with a *nabasa* whose name is kept secret by the participants. Then the enclosure gate is opened, and the procession slowly emerges. In the lead is the tallest mask, *ogosôk*, 'the one who goes in front', followed by a slightly shorter mask, *engêk*, 'the second'. Next come various masks, 'dragonfly', '*Ptilinopus* sp. pigeon', 'butterfly', etc., worn by young adolescents. The procession is brought up by two men walking side by side and playing bamboo whistles (*fefero*) followed by two *fuf* players. The procession circles the dancing ground for a few minutes.[10]

Then the masks gather in the middle of the ground with *ogosôk* at the centre, and the whole village presses around, women and young children on one side, men on the other. The *aynaag* repeat their magic Gungwan spells, spitting their betel and *Acorus* root on the feet of the *ogosôk* mask. Then all the masks return to the *pǝpak* and the participants eat their sago. Later the masks will be taken into the forest and tied upright to a *gungwan* bush 'for men' (in 1971 this operation

10. The minor masks go by the name of *agig*; this is the same procession and the same sequence, used in a number of rituals (Gungwan, Gêpôk, Waray, Agig), as that performed in 1976 following Yangis (Juillerat 1992a, 1995 and my film *Le Sang du sagou*). What follows, on the other hand, is an optional development of the Gungwan theme that I observed only in 1971.

was omitted, and some children played with the masks; this set off a collective demonstration of anger, and people were heard to say 'Now we are all going to die', p. 500).

At 6:00 p.m., two groups of two or three *aynaag*, from the Araneri and Angwaneri moieties respectively, circle the hamlet and perform the Gungwan rite on each path leading out, burying a stone using an unstrung bow (made of hardwood from the black palm) and planting a *hoogof* cordyline: this bars the path to *sungwaag* and hardens the ground, closing the underground pathways. The spells name these passages with a number of metaphorical images alluding more particularly to rotted matter, the cold, the underground gallery where Tapi made his three sons disappear (pp. 183–4), the body orifices and ghosts, each image being followed by the word *pawêg* 'to bar'.

Although the word *sungwaag* is never pronounced, Gungwan has every appearance of a prescription, or even an order addressed to all members of the village. However, the direct object of the action is not the villagers but the environment they frequent and the sorcerers and ghosts they might encounter. This space is circumscribed (body, house, village, plant species, underground territories) by the words of the *aynaag*, who assign the *sungwaag* to remain there. By naming the refuges, by showing them the *gungwan* bush and helping them rediscover the original tie with the *hoofuk* of the totemic trees, by enjoining them to pay their visits to the *nabasa* spirits of the dead and not to ghosts, the *aynaag* binds them to their original source, to the cosmic parent couple, to the recently deceased, in other words to life (we will see that the *nabasa* represent the 'life' side of the other world).

But that is not enough. This individual self must be given a social dimension, which is clearly expressed in the public and ceremonial aspects of Gungwan. The *uguf* poles held upright to the chanting of spells about the multiplication of prolific species of animals and against sorcery represent the community on its feet and united. The adolescents wearing the 'dragonfly' masks probably stand for the 'sons' of the women they try to strike with their switches, a gesture marking the breakaway of the new male generation from the ascendancy of their mothers. The mask procession would seem to be the staging of a social order, a hierarchy, since the role of the *ogosôk* is played by a young bachelor already 'initiated' into the other types of masks, wearing an *uguf* mask five metres tall and followed by his 'younger' *engêk*, who might be seen as his younger or female counterpart. At the tail end of the procession, the two pairs of musicians (older mar-

ried men), unmasked but wearing the *ra* Gêpôk headdress and
decorated with foliage and red and yellow body paint (idea of
ripening), represent bi-gendered fathers on the decline driving
the new generation before them.

Gathered together and surrounded by all the villagers of both
sexes, the masks assembled around *ogosôk* once more show the
group at full strength, already represented by the bare *uguf* poles
before they were finally left, but still upright, next to the 'male'
gungwan bush: 'If we were to lay the masks down, we would all
die', meaning that the individual *sungwaag* would make their way
downwards and 'ripen' on contact with the *ifaaf* and the maternal
'blood', and would allow themselves be attacked by sorcerers.

Then the paths of the Primal Mother and of death are closed
once more, prohibiting any return to them. In order to highlight
this break, nothing could be more fitting than the reiteration
of the cynegetic tie with the *nabasa*, that is the 'good' dead who
have, as it were, stayed in the group. The essentially female cosmic powers of reproduction are thus replaced by exchange relations
between hunters and those recently deceased. It is difficult not
to see in this effort to control individual *sungwaag* a renewed investment in the social sphere (reciprocity, food, speech) and
more particularly in its male dimension. The only tie with mythic
origins which is encouraged, and even recommended, concerns
the two ancestral palm trees, protectors and sources of new life,
image of the totemic parent couple. On a more material level, the
complete Gungwan ritual is also an incitement to cynegetic production through the perpetuation of social ties with the guardian
spirits of game.

The Person after Death

Death is an accident which breaks into the apparent stability of
life and nothing can explain it. That is why death is systematically attributed to *aysiri* sorcery, except in the case of babies and
elderly people, who can 'die of nothing'. As there are practically
no very old people, death by 'murder', with or without the help
of magic, is considered to be the inescapable fate of everyone.
But this immediate cause is conditioned by other human acts of
aggression (*agi*: Ch. 14) or by 'errors' on the part of the *sungwaag*
which favour death's intervention. As we have seen, the notion

of the self's 'ripening' is crucial to the dying process. This is also characterized by longer and longer absences and 'abnormal' behaviour on the part of the *sungwaag*. An individual struck down by an *aysiri*, or a pregnant woman – two dangerous situations – have a *sungwaag* which is disturbed and which attracts attention at night by the 'noise' it makes in the forest. When the subject is in a coma, his or her *sungwaag* (consciousness) has already left, taking with it the faculty of speech and the peripheral body heat. All the blood has withdrawn from the limbs (whence the weakness and the chill) toward the heart (chest still warm), which is believed to 'turn white' (*öruk ate bus o-fe*). Meanwhile, the person's *nabasa segwaag* is at his or her bedside as previously during the *sungwaag's* other absences (sleep). Physical death is defined as the *hoofuk* rising up (Ch. 9) into the throat and cutting off the subject's breath. At this point, the heart's blood is collected by the *segwaag* (it is also said that the *segwaag* carries off the heart, *taf* and *öruk* being equivalent in this context) and 'hangs it up at home'. The blood will dry and the *nabasa* (*stricto sensu*) will emerge: this will be the deceased's principal spirit, the one that usually speaks through the medium and which will later be worshipped in its own right (Ch. 5).

When it emerges in the hereafter – the first level of the underground forest world – the new *nabasa* falls asleep and sloughs its skin. The old skin (*arfêêg*) (p. 365) comes away, starting with the forehead, while the *nabasa* is shaken with convulsions like a medium in a trance (or a snake sloughing its skin); when it awakes, it is rejuvenated and begins its existence as the spirit of the deceased. Gradually, however, it will age, but will have the possibility, some say, of changing skins several more times. The *nabasa's* old age or 'death' seems to correspond to the moment when the society ceases to recall its name. The old *nabasa, nabasa awtinaag*, is then 'driven to the periphery' by the young ones, where it enters the firewood (*tawank kêg* 'branches of hardened dead wood'). Some Yafar experts contend that the change of skin has already taken place in the heart of the person dying, and that the *nabasa's arfêêg* is nothing but the cadaver, 'which is like a snake's slough: the skin is there but the reptile has gone'.[11] Once

---

11. If the body is the *arfêêg* or the *roofuk* ('skin'), the *nabasa* that emerges from the blood represents the *hoofuk*, the life principle and the source of food production: in effect, the *nabasa's* main function, as we have seen, is to provide the hunter with game.

the *nabasa* has grown old and become *tawank kêg, it* will slough its skin one last time, and its *arfêêg* will then become the firewood that the women gather for their hearth. The definitively 'dead' *nabasa*, whose names are no longer recalled, are pictured with wild eyes sitting motionless in their village in the hereafter, a situation that contrasts with the mobility typical of the active spirits of the dead.

The blood of women who have died also becomes a separate spirit, but is not taken away by a *nabasa segwaag*. Yafar eschatology remains vague about the female hereafter. Some say that a

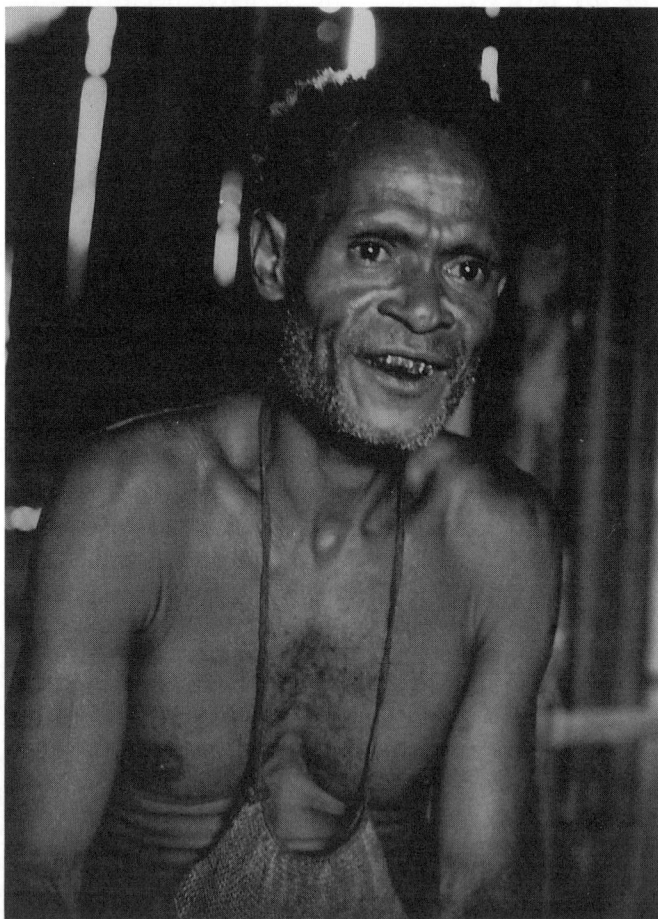

Plate 21. May Promp, one of the authors most faithful interlocutors.

woman's heart turns into a *sawangô* (p. 131), but others prefer to speak of *nabasa* wives or even women *nabasa*; according to them, a woman's *nabasa*, having grown old, could only become a *sawangô*, a sort of dehumanized forest sprite. And yet many women of the last three generations are localized on Yafar lands under the name of *sawangô*.

This masculine note dominating the spirit world can be explained for the most part by the importance of the spirits of the dead for hunting. The same holds for the *kê-ruur*, exclusively human spirits that claim their autonomy after the mourning period, when there is no flesh left on the cadaver (see below). The *kê-ruur* 'bone child' (*kêg-ruwar*) can take up residence in a skull preserved by a relative, or in an iron tree in the vicinity of the grave. Like the *nabasa* or the *sawangô*, the *kê-ruur* sloughs its skin and ultimately 'dies'. Generically speaking, it is a *nabasa*, and the relations society entertains with it are identical to those carried on with the *nabasa* that spring from the blood. For the Yafar, the *angor* river sprites are not spirits of the dead. But for the southern Eri, the deceased person splits into three spiritual entities: blood + heart = water spirits; speech = tree spirits, corresponding to the Yafar *nabasa*, who speak through the mouth of mediums; bones = bone spirits. The correlation blood (body) = water (territory) renders this ternary classification more coherent.[12]

But what becomes of the 'forest self', the deceased's alter ego? Nothing: it dies with ego, vanishes, or perhaps flees to other lands.

As for the *sungwaag*, whereas it had a tendency to anticipate its ghostly destiny during the subject's lifetime, now that it is an *ifaaf*,[13] it will do just the opposite and remain near the corpse and

12. I found other eschatological variants in the Eri region. In the eastern part, the *ungor* water spirit collects the deceased's blood (heart), the *kêruwar* bone spirit collects the small bones and Ufroog, the culture hero, carries off the large bones. When a woman dies, the *ungor* takes the blood, and the *sawangô*, female spirits, the bones. As a rule, women's bones undergo a separate fate, becoming *fifi* and appearing as a fleshless version of the deceased, living among the boulders or the bamboos, or in the form of giant man-eating flying foxes. In certain groups, the sternum of old women becomes a separate entity.

13. Among the Anggor (Map 1), *ifiaf* designates the living person's self, and *yif* means 'corpse, cadaver'; this concept is opposed to *hohoanim*, which seems to correspond to the Yafar *nabasa* (blood, heart), but exists before death. P. Huber defined these notions respectively as the 'dynamic and the rational components' of the person (1975: 628).

Variants of the *ifaaf* also appear among the Eri. The Muwagneri see the person's shadow and reflection as two distinct eschatological entities: only the latter becomes a chthonian *ifaaf*, while the shadow remains on the surface and helps identify the sorcerer responsible for the death (Ch. 14). This being done, the *ginge* changes into a particularly meaty bandicoot (for the distinction between shadow and reflection, see also Malinowski 1948).

the grave for a while. Just before death, it is believed to rise up to the Milky Way (*gwos na mɘna* 'pathway of the shooting stars') and traverse it in the form of a shooting star (*gwos*), which makes the Yafar who see one of these say that someone is dying in the vicinity. Immediately after death, it descends for the first time into the land of the ghosts (*ifaaf na kɘbik*), but comes back up to settle at the grave site for the duration of the mourning period. In former times, it would finally leave the body only after the death had been avenged, often with its help, since the victim is the only one able to identify his *aysiri* murderer (Ch. 14). From then on, the *ifaaf* lives in an overcrowded world far below ground, where night and day are reversed; it does not age, it does not grow younger (no change of skin), it does not fall ill and, during its nighttime visits above ground, it cannot be caught or harmed by the living, as it has the ability to change into all kinds of animal or to appear in the guise of living persons. It is heard in particular shortly after the death, in the hooting of a black bird called the *kwimpi* (*Centropus menbeki*) or great coucal, at first light of day; this species, which darts about in the underbrush and whose meat is said to taste like a cadaver, is not eaten. Unlike *nabasa*, ghosts can be encountered in real life, almost always at night, in the forest or the village. In the latter case, a hullabaloo breaks out in the hamlet as the witness rouses the local population with his shouts: everyone comes running with his weapon and beats the bush into which the shadow seems to have vanished. Once in a while, a man or woman awakes with a start at the touch of a cold hand slipped up through the floorboards. Or come dusk, some man spots the *ifaaf* of a person recently deceased hovering near a forest trail. Physical concealment, theft, dirty tricks, pleasure in frightening women and children, a blurred appearance and running away are all features of *ifaaf* behaviour. One genre of Yafar oral literature is comprised of ghost stories in which the human antagonists try desperately, but in a comic vein, to avoid the treachery and threats of *ifaaf*, which can even resort to cannibalism (human flesh is the epitome of ghosts' 'bad food'). Oral tradition casts ghosts as tricksters *par excellence*, but in a narrative tone which at the same times leaves them open to derision.[14]

14. This last aspect seems to be due to the fact that the *ifaaf* comes from something that has rotted (the cadaver); from there we can go on to think of an unconscious association with anality.

There is an obvious contrast between these ghosts and the class of *nabasa* sought out for exchanges. The ghost is desocialized, immoral, perverse. It is the negative and irredeemable principle of the deceased, the part that rots down and returns to the *hoofuk* of Mother Earth. It is irredeemable only in social terms, however, for the *ifaaf* are the guardians of cultivated plants: in the planting rite, the dead that are named and requested to return the *hoofuk* of the domestic plants which they have kept during the period of fallow are ghosts, not *nabasa*. Once again we find the opposition seen earlier between plant *hoofuk* and blood: the rotting body is the condition for the regeneration of the plant, whereas it is mainly from the deceased's blood that *nabasa* game guardians emerge. And yet the game animals themselves originated, as we saw (pp. 183–4), in the belly of the earth: the religious exegesis says *Aso na mǝna, sês na mǝna, ba mungwô mǝna hug* ('The path of the cultivated species and the path of the game are one great path'), thus signifying that the maternal depths produce *both* plant *and* animal species. The *ifaaf* are on the side of the female origins of the world, of chthonian fertility, of all that putrefies (they have soft bones), on the side of death, but also of regeneration, whereas the *nabasa* (including *kê-ruur* and *sawangô*) are on the male side, the side of hunting and society. This duality brings us back to sexual antagonism, to reproduction, top and bottom, the concepts of 'ripe' and 'strong', maternal and paternal. This hierarchically ordered landscape can sometimes be seen in dreams, where *ifaaf* villages appear ensconced in the valley floor, the *nabasa* villages perch on hilltops (called *sesi-ya kǝbik* 'the villages at the top'). In turn the latter are divided into two groups situated at slightly different altitudes, depending on their moiety membership, Araneri (higher) or Angwaneri (lower).

The same duality is attested by the belief in a path of the dead. There is first of all a 'broad path' (*mǝna hug*) leading, if one is not careful, straight down to the world of the *ifaaf*, where the deceased would find bad ghost food. In the middle of the path stands a big *boof* tree (p. 374) indicating that one is already under the sign of 'ripeness' and caducity; moreover, the *mǝna hug* is guarded by a sort of 'bad father' (*awarǝhak*, from *awaag*, 'father') of mythological inspiration, named Wanghora, who smashes the nose of the deceased with a stick.[15] His attention is drawn by the sound of the deceased inadvertently stepping on an unsteady flat rock. It is important not to go that far, but to locate the 'small path' (*məna wêsik*), off to one side, which leads up to the *nabasa* villages; two barely discernible crossed grasses mark the fork. There among the *nabasa* one finds one's dead relatives and the *hoofuk* of 'good' foods. This tradition, in which the individual's mortal fate is presented as an alternative, is difficult to reconcile with the simultaneous dualism of the eschatological representations analysed above, in which the deceased, come what may, is destined to become both *ifaaf* and *nabasa*. The only way to integrate the two conceptions would be to consider that it is indeed the *sungwaag* that seeks the 'small path' in order to go up not to the world of the *nabasa*, but to the 'good' *ifaaf*, guardians of food *hoofuk*; whoever misses the fork will descend immediately to the lower regions of the nether world, thus definitely regressing to the *hoofuk* of the Primordial Mother. Clearly the tellurian space of the hereafter is divided into three levels:

1) *nabasa*: socialized mediators, guardians of game;
2) *ifaaf*: asocial ghosts, guardians of cultigen *hoofuk*;
3) maternal *hoofuk*: the chthonian womb.

We have tried to circumscribe the main features of the innate identity of the person as seen by the Yafar; now it is time to turn back to the social domain and see how the individual's life unfolds, showing the successive stages that ratify his or her integration into the group. Indeed it seems indispensable to associate these conceptual and sociological aspects of the personality before attempting to synthesize how the Yafar define the human being.

---

15. Those who are punished in this way are definitely marked by a sort of castration. They are *bosuk fəte kareg*, the 'smashed noses'. Aside from the phallic symbolism of the nose, a flat nose evokes difficulty in breathing.

Social Identity

Childhood and Adolescence

When a child is born, boy or girl, the mother's sister plants a coconut palm for it in front of the house. This tree will grow along with the child, something like its plant self, and will perhaps outlive him or her, for the wood (*sa kêg*) of this palm is considered to be harder than human bones (*êr kêg*).

As the primary form of an individual's personal identity, the anatomical sex is initially mystified, in the sense that it is not openly announced to the group until the end of the postpartum isolation period, or even later, and is socially recognized only by means of its name, which indicates gender. As long as the name is kept secret (or rather not spoken, even though more or less everyone knows it), the child's sex is also unnamed. This analogy was brought home to me one day by the spontaneous response of a man I had been questioning on the sex of a child born a few days earlier (a question which, I realized later, was completely out of place): 'I don't know, the child doesn't have a name yet.' This refusal to recognize sexual identity on a purely biological level also shows in the metaphorical terms by which the Amanab language designates a child's sex: a boy is *fango-na* 'of the bow', a girl, *nay-na* 'of the skirt'. There is a mythic episode in which an identical mystification of the anatomical sex is practised. Two sisters, coming upon the child their mother has just brought into the world, administer a test to determine its sex: the child furiously rejects the skirt they present first, but gleefully accepts the toy bow they have made for him and promptly sets about hunting lizards.[16] Here it is not only the cultural attribute but also the economic function that 'creates an individual's sex'.

The mandatory isolation of mother and child, both 'impure' (*heyfu-inaag*), in a way determines the newborn's lack of sexual differentiation. The new baby, still 'with the blood' (p. 251), bar-

---

16. As I have already said, the Yafar exegesis of this episode specifies that hunting lizards is an expression of the search for the mother's breast (see the *ifõge* shooting their arrows at the end of the Yangis ritual), which underlines the fact that appropriation of the breast is idealized as the first 'capture' of food and that the little boy's first 'hunt' already announces the gifts of meat he will make to his maternal uncle to 'pay for' his mother's milk.

ely free of its mother's *hoofuk*, ignored by its father, can in fact partake only of the female sphere. Come the new moon and the end of claustration, it emerges from this non-identity, from this social anonymity, and its mother performs two acts: she cuts the child's hair and she herself bathes. First she shaves a portion of the infant's head, leaving some hair front and back, over the fontanels; for this she uses a bamboo knife, *fako*, cut from the top of the stalk (*sama*), symbolizing growth. Then she takes her first bath since the birth; if she is still feeling weak or feverish, she merely washes her hands. She also washes her child by sprinkling it with water and rubbing it with her hands, then she dries it with leaves. Approximately a week after the mother-child couple has rejoined the family group, the mother goes into the forest to collect some of the castings thrown up by certain large earthworms (*maygo*) and rubs them into the child's forelock, 'to strengthen the fontanel'. It is not insignificant that this ossification treatment takes place precisely when the father begins to exert his rights over the child, which partially confirms the validity of the notion of *aya na kêg* ('the father's bones') mentioned in Chapter 9. It is also from this time that the child's name may be spoken freely. Washing – as we shall see in the treatment of the cadaver – has a regenerative function and corresponds to the sloughing of old skin, while shaving the head both frees and strengthens the skull and facilitates growth, which will from then on be closely watched by the parents.

The father maintains a physical distance, even when the new mother's isolation is over, and waits still longer before touching his child; this lapse of time ranges from a week or two to several months, depending on the person. Some fathers prefer not to take their children in their arms before they start walking. Nevertheless, if it is a boy, shortly after the mother's return to the group, the father performs a little rite – the first in a long series – starting the boy out on his career as a hunter. He first of all 'cleans off' his son with rough leaves, once more the idea of 'removing (*rəbe*) his *arfêêg*' while reciting spells which identify the child with wild animals (*rəbwame rəbe* 'make the cuscus slough his skin'; *mêy rəbe* 'make the possum slough his skin', etc.), then he touches the child's forehead, nose and eyes with the root of a special magic clone; this is already a rite to 'open the eyes' of the future hunter. Marking the face in this way seems to be an anticipation of the facial paintings the adolescent will receive the first time he takes part in the Gêpôk rite (see below and pp. 187-9). Thus the child begins life by undergoing several symbolic transformations: a first cleansing right after birth physically to rub off the sebaceous secretions, then, at the end of the isolation period, a bath from its mother, and finally, in the case of a boy, a change of skin, this time performed by the father, who, by magically instilling the qualities of the hunter he will one day become, endows him with his definitive sexual status and at the same time inscribes him in his own line of descent. There is no equivalent rite for girls. This precocious orientation partakes of the path already opened by the couple's first sexual relations (Ch. 9), where female fertility was assimilated to successful hunting. From this moment on, the boy's childhood and adolescence will be punctuated by similar rites, the last of which will be performed when he takes on the most distinguished ritual roles, but they will 'close' with the ritual performed the first time the young man and his wife have intercourse. Going from the status of 'game-child' to that of great hunter, the cycle of 'cynegetic fecundity' is closed and ready to begin anew with the next generation.

While the father's ascendancy applies more particularly to the son, both the son and the daughter are (equally) concerned by the effects of a prolonged period of breast-feeding followed by an abrupt weaning. This notion is attested by the nosological interpretation of 'black diarrhoea' in children as the continued presence in the child's system of a certain amount of 'thick milk' (*totom kêfutuk*), called *afôr*; this term is used to define both the symptoms and the substance causing them. The imaginary non-eliminated milk seems to come from a representation of excessive breast-feeding, as the 'hardened' milk can also be the kind the mother produces shortly before weaning, as opposed to the fluidity of the early milk. The appropriate healing spells, said by the father, make mention of 'coconut milk' (maternal totem) and other botanical species, which must be 'eliminated'.

There seems to be no naming rite as such. At some later time a ritual is performed, once only, to promote growth, during which the father – it used to be the mother – washes the child in a stream using the stem of a young wild banana palm, *kos*, which has a particularly firm *hoofuk*, and an *Acorus calamus* root called *nihik gaf* ('flesh *A. calamus*'); the spells recited 'make the flesh penetrate the different parts of the body'[17] and list the names of fast-growing trees. Then, gently pulling up on the child's hair and raising and lowering its body in a vertical rocking motion (*əgim*),[18] the father names the 'crown' of tall trees and vines as well as the birds that live in the treetops. The child's names are uttered and they enter its body along with its 'flesh'.[19]

Yafar personal names (*unehraag*, from *uneg* 'to call' and *hraag* 'performing a fully accomplished action') are clearly masculine or feminine; in principle every individual receives two names (rarely one or three), the 'right-hand' name, *nihigam unehraag*, and the 'left-hand' name, *sahagam unehraag*.[20] The right-hand name is the one commonly used, even though sometimes the left-hand name is used to hail someone from a distance. Nevertheless, a child who does not grow may, in the course of the growth rite described above, have the right-hand name replaced by the left-hand one for the rest of his or her life. The name thus indeed seems to be linked with the physical person and his or her growth and health.

The father and mother pick the names of their children in secret, sometimes in consultation with their close kin; they choose them from the names of the child's ancestors in the third and fourth generations (more rarely the second), from either side and preferably from non-agnatic kin. Both names may be taken from the same forebear, but this is unusual. For boys a new name may also be revealed by a forest spirit during a medium trance or in a dream; this is generally the *nabasa's* own name. Between 1920 and 1925, masculine names were also borrowed from Dutch New Guinea bird-of-paradise hunters and then incorporated into the Yafar's onomastic pool.

17. See the parallel with the rite performed on domestic pigs (Ch. 7). There is also a similar healing rite for curing chronic weight loss.
18. A movement already mentioned in discussing the *ogohyaag* dance (p. 260) and representing growth.
19. Another growth rite, performed only in the case of characteristic infantile weight loss, consists of the father using his penis sheath to pour over the child rainwater that has been collected in the exploited trunk of an *afwêêg* sago palm. Like the starch of the *Metroxylon* clone, the water represents the god W. . .'s semen, as suggested by the spells recited. Then the mother dunks her skirt in the same water and sprinkles her child, while her husband recites spells over its 'long limbs' and imitates the cassowary's call (this bird has long legs and bathes its chicks in the river).
20. Compare *nihik* 'flesh', but more particularly *nihig* 'to show, present, to extend the arm'; *sahêg* 'to ask for (something)'. This semantic association with the right hand (giving) and the left hand (receiving) remains hypothetical.

Before continuing with the ritual for socializing the young Ya-far boy, I would like to pause briefly for a few remarks of a more general order. The Yafar child lives with its nuclear family, which, as we have seen, shares a single room. This supposes the prox-imity of the father as soon as the mother has joined the group after her postpartum isolation, in other words from the time the child is three or four weeks old. This fact is worth emphasizing for a region – Sepik Province or New Guinea as a whole – where the men frequently stay together in a men's house or live apart from their wives and leave the mother and her infant relatively on their own. Even if he avoids physical contact with his son or daughter for the first few months, the Yafar father takes part in his child's education around the village and often in the garden or at the sago-working site. The mother sleeps with her child, feeds it, carries it with her into the forest, first on her back or in a netbag or in her arms, then astride her shoulders, if need be perched atop a load of garden produce or firewood. But the father keeps an eye on the child when his wife is busy with household chores or working sago, advises on its diet,[21] and also begins thinking about the child's future marriage. No restrictions are placed on the very young child: it is not forced to eat food it does not like,[22] and there is no punishment for making a mess or, when it is older, for throwing tantrums. Weaning takes place in the third or fourth year, when the child begins to bite too hard on the breast. The mother may resort to a technique of gustatory or psychological dissuasion, in the first case by coating her nipples with *Curcuma*, in the second by touching a skull to her breasts in front of the child (forebears' skulls used to be kept in the house). The cultural choice of the second technique associates weaning with the idea of death, which is conjured up by separation from the mother; its effectiveness cannot be guaranteed if the child is too young. When the child becomes more independent, it is liable to be shouted at by one of its parents and often slapped if it hap-pens to break an object or overturn a container. Later it will be

21. From the second or third month, breast-feeding is supplemented by pieces of soft food, such as ripe bananas, the tip of cooked yams or taro, fresh sago jelly or papayas. When the child's incisors appear, it is also given a bit of fish, deheaded grubs, liver or pre-chewed food transferred directly from mouth to mouth (*tehwage fayig*). The death of the mother supposes premature weaning, and the child usually dies if it is under two.

22. This often happens with sago jelly, and there are some adults who continue not to like it but eat their sago roasted or braised.

scolded for being too noisy, for repeated laziness or vanishing into the forest just when it is needed, but also for spending too much time playing with children of the opposite sex (after the age of five or thereabouts) or for talking about sexual matters in public. Good conduct, on the other hand, will also be rewarded with a small gift of food or a toy. Boys run a greater risk of sanction than girls, particularly corporal punishment, due to the fact that they tend rapidly (from the age of five or six) to become relatively independent from the family group, first of all playing with friends, often beyond the village limits, then foraging in company or alone, hunting lizards, edible insects, frogs and birds, catching fish with their hands or shooting them with bow and arrow, gathering, looking for grubs or pilfering from gardens. Boys no doubt spend the best moments of their childhood playing (games: *uguwagi*) together, from shooting at moving targets to making traditional patterns on the ground, and imitating every possible scene suggested by nature or man: bird fights, countless scenes of hunting and capture, the fury of the wind in a tree, etc. Apart from the small child's bow, tops made from *Ficus* seeds and a few musical instruments discarded as easily as they are made, most games involve only the body, movement and interaction between individuals by means of physical contact, sight and speech. Girls, on the other hand, play very little or enjoy more solitary games, like a Yafar version of 'cat's cradle' (*wahiye*). One never sees bands of little girls running around; instead they spend their spare time learning from older girls and women how to make netted objects (netbags, men's ornaments) that they will then be able to give to a 'brother'. The rest of their time is – as we have already said – much more taken up by helping their mother in her economic activities than boys their father.

With this rapid portrait in mind, I would now like to isolate the articulations. Since childhood is thought of as the time for learning certain tasks reserved for one sex or the other and as a series of new experiences, it follows that *the first time* these are performed by the child, or even the adult, is of special importance and may even call for a rite, however discrete. Two complementary statuses flow from this notion: *asagyam* (novice, neophyte) for the person who is still ignorant or is going through the experience for the first time, and *anuwanam*, for the person who has acquired the knowledge and has succeeded in putting it into practice at least once. These two terms are used widely and apply to every new experience – seeing a rare animal, building a house, clearing a garden plot, having sexual intercourse, killing, etc. – whether or not it is ratified by a rite of passage. It is only in the life of a boy, however, that these rites are numerous, for they mark on the one hand, the steps through which he advances in hunting (and formerly homicide) and on the other hand, his access to several categories of masks or ritual roles, both spheres of activity closed to women. For the boy, this begins, after the ritual performed in the first few months of life and already described above, when his father (or his father's stand-in) gives him a child's bow and some darts,[23] which the little boy will use to pierce pieces of fruit that he rolls down a slope or to shoot small lizards. Before actually giving the bow to his son, the father holds it out to him several times while reciting the spells 'possum bow, wild-pig bow, etc.', then 'shoot a male, shoot a female. . .'. At the age of four or five, a boy has already started on his hunting 'career', endowed through his father's line with the attribute of his potential virility of which he now needs only to learn to make use. For the first lizard, bird, small mammal or snake, monitor lizard and eel, the father or another male relative merely recites a few spells evoking bigger game. For the small mammals and then for his first wild pig or cassowary (during adolescence), the rite is completed by a modest feather decoration and by marking the novice's body (shoulders and centre of the sternum) with red betel juice (= blood) chewed with magic roots that will make the hunter more motivated and effective. The first five murders, as the continuation of hunting exploits, used to be rewarded by similar rites, which I will describe in Chapter 14, culminating in the honour, for an accomplished man, of wearing pig-tusk ornaments. Parallel to hunting, horticulture, although less prestigious, also has its 'firsts', such as felling trees and planting a sago palm, most of which are not marked by a rite but by food taboos. The fruit of the first banana and breadfruit trees planted by a girl or boy *asagyam* cannot be eaten by their parents or parents' siblings, but may be consumed by the planter and his or her siblings. There is an obvious continuity between these prohibitions and those, already discussed (Chs 7 and 11) concerning hunting and applying to the first ten or fifteen animals only. The notions of *asagyam* and *anuwanam* are implicit in these prohibitions, with variations in the

---

23. These are splinters some 60 cm in length split off from the sago petiole, *nays*.

time needed for the status of *asagyam* to be reduced, the extreme case of the cassowary, whose meat is forbidden the hunter for life suggesting that with respect to this animal the latter never becomes fully *anuwanam*. Immediately after marriage, like restrictions must be observed, which implies that the hunter is once more *asagyam*, this time exclusively in his relations with his affines, for the first pig he kills, of which his parents-in-law do not consume the hind quarter they receive, and for his first bird, the thighs of which may not be eaten by his wife.

For a small girl, the only *asagyam* experience marked by a ritual is sago-filtering, the techniques of which she learns from her mother or other female kin, but which is ratified by a fertility rite performed by her father. A piece of *Pometia pinnata (baf)* wood – suggesting rapid growth and profusion (of fruits) – is placed under the filtering apparatus (*bwêr*), while the man utters fertility spells; other incantations are chanted for abundant production when he grasps his small daughter's hands and goes through the preliminary motions of filtering the pith.

During a boy's adolescence, his various hunting successes are completed through his step-by-step access to the different categories of ritual roles in fertility or healing rites. The number of steps is not set, but if one counts up the types of roles and questions the men about the stages they have gone through, it is possible to identify between three and five hierarchical levels for the ceremonies dedicated to the *nabasa* (hunting and healing) or *sawangô* (fertility and healing) spirits, plus three or four levels for Yangis, also arranged hierarchically and partially ranked with respect to the rites of the first category. As a general rule, the *asagyam* for a specific ritual role goes through a rite, divided into several sequences, which here too comes mainly under the sign of hunting. The real father, or sometimes even the mother's real brother, in principle avoids acting as the novice's initiator (called simply *anuwanam* here); this role is usually taken by one of the father's brothers, a classificatory maternal uncle, an older male sibling or cousin having already gone through all the principal stages. I will not go into the rituals of these 'partial initiations', which are each time more or less complete and involve variations. The phases comprising each of these steps towards full access to the sphere of the sacred are as follows:

a) *Suwê* 'fire': some blood from the animal killed by the novice is mixed with red ochre and magic hunting rhizomes (*seeg*). The centre of the *asagyam's* sternum is then marked with the red substance, while spells are pronounced along the lines of *abi suwê pah, rəbwame suwê pah, soone suwê pah*, etc., that is the name of an animal followed by the formula 'to burst into flame' (*pahêg*). The ochre and the blood smeared on the young hunter's chest are 'like fire'; the novice's *sungwaag* is believed to turn entirely red and will consequently be noticed and loved by the *nabasa*, who will place animals in his path. His eyes are often outlined using an *Acorus calamus* rhizome (*seeg noofuk* 'hunting-magic plant [for the] eyes') so that the young hunter will see the animals clearly. Sometimes he is also made to chew an areca nut with some rhizomes to which has been added, unbeknown to him, a piece of his own umbilical cord that his mother has been saving (the idea of a continued link with the Mother Earth).

b) *Mosuwô* (to cut the) 'umbilical cord'. The first ritual role played by a boy is often that of a *sawangô* (female spirit). The *asagyam* is dressed up in a thick skirt of young black palm leaves. The bottom of the skirt is cut off by his *anuwanam* before the ritual begins, or a few snippets are cut during the procession by the novice's mother, who walks beside him: the gesture represents breaking away from the mother's sphere.

c) *Gingêg* 'to paint'. This ritual is performed above all for initiation into the Gêpôk rite (Rii-buu, in its therapeutic version): the protagonists walk with their faces painted but uncovered, wearing a *ra* feather headdress topped by the waving *ra-bwaraag* cassowary quill (see pp. 187–9) and beating their drum. The ritual is subdivided into a succession of songs sung by the initiator(s), while painting the initiate with white, red and black stripes and decorating him with coloured leaves from *Crinum asiaticum* and crotons. The songs allude in particular to the hunter's encounter with the *nabasa*, to blood and to the 'ripening' of animals' *sungwaag*.[24] The adolescent's painted face is called 'game head' or 'possum head' (Juillerat 1978b).

d) *Ahômp-me-inaag* 'in the *ahômp Ficus* hole'. This 'hole' is the mythic underground gallery where the primordial game animals were concealed by Tapi (see summary of myth, pp. 183–4). The incantations evoke the hunter's behaviour and state of mind: leave at dawn, stay alert (for a charging pig), be ready to spring, see clearly, eat the quarry, etc. At the same time, the *asagyam* is made to 'bob' up and

---

24. See epigraph to this chapter and Juillerat 1978b.

down, the *əgim* movement, while he nods his head: this teaches him
the dance step used in the Gêpôk rite during which he will nod his
head to make his *ra-bwaraag* wave. This is the way the three sons in
the Tapi myth entered the gallery dug by their father and, by means
of this transgression, came to the maternal *hoofuk*.

e) *Fango wabwayêg* 'to give the bow'. When the ritual role involves
carrying a bow (which is usually the case), the initiator ritually
bestows the bow on the *asagyam* (the initiate's own, in reality). This
gesture recalls the father's gift of a toy bow to his little boy. The bow
is presented either during the mask procession or while still in the
enclosure, before the public ceremony. Spells evoke the capture of
different kinds of game.

Aside from the discreet allusion to separation from the mother,
all these rites marking the repeated passages from the status of
asagyam to that of *anuwanam* work to make the neophyte capable
of controlling fertility and production. To this is added, in the
case of hunting and even more in that of homicide, the mark of
courage and of a valued violence that serve as an outlet for the
young man's virile qualities and highlight his social role as producer of meat and protector of his group. In the field of hunting,
the *anuwanam* (who are not necessarily the same from one rite to
the next for the same adolescent) repeatedly present the young
hunter to the *nabasa* spirits by figuratively placing him under the
sign of blood. It is because he bears this mark of 'fire' on his heart
that the neophyte – who may already be a good hunter – will be
'recognized' by the forest spirits as their 'child of the blood', in
other words as worthy to receive their presents of wild animals.
But the reminder the myth of the theft of game (from the father)
in the maternal depths of the earth also brings the novice into
contact with the cosmic *hoofuk* and inscribes him in an oedipal
structure. The red ochre used here is not only a metaphor for
animal blood, it also represents the mother's 'blood'. The initiation to the Gêpôk rite adds to this the already familiar idea of
'ripe game' (*sês abuk*) expressed notably in one of the *anuwanam*'s
songs. Having been covered with coloured leaves (*sawik*: see
Juillerat 1978b) by his *anuwanam*, the *asagyam* dons a ripe 'skin',
an *arfêêg*, beneath which he appears to be made 'of blood' and
shining 'like fire'. His disguise suggests on the one hand, the
ripening of game and therefore its vulnerability and the hunter's
success, and on the other hand, the change undergone by the

hunter, regenerated by the original fertile blood[25] and then reintegrated into the male community by receiving the bow, the sign of the accomplished hunter and adult male. These phases of the ritual can be divided into the three stages of the rite of passage as defined by van Gennep (1981) and developed by Turner (1969), namely separation, margin, aggregation.

Young men's rites go on into maturity, with the man's progressive acquisition of the status of *aynaag* (old man,[26] man of knowledge). The definition of this term, translated into Pidgin as 'big man', remains vague in the sense that it is often applied to mature men devoid of any noteworthy status or knowledge, even though in principle it is supposed to confer a certain prestige on the person addressed in this way, who is never simply an elderly man. Although the term rarely qualifies a female, an elderly woman may be called *aynaag afaag*, 'great mother'. Besides his cynegetic exploits, and in past times his murders, an adult male completes his status by taking on, when the opportunity presents itself, the ritual roles open to him, mainly at the time of Gêpôk or especially Yangis rituals. In the first case, at the beginning and end of the Nabasa-raara cycle, he takes the role of one of the two *fuf* or whistle players bringing up the procession and, while waiting for his call, stays shut up with his three other companions in the *nabasa*'s enclosure, his body painted red from head to toe. The four men are compared to 'marsh game' (an ecological category associated with procreation and the notion of *hoofuk*). For Yangis, the mature male roles are principally the *êri*, representing the old generation, and the *anuwanam* conducting the 'children of the blood' (*ifəgê*) at the end of the ceremony, together with a few secondary characters.

These few key ideas found in the rites of passage show the emphasis Yafar culture places on man's relations with nature and her reproduction, rather than on the acquisition of a status of 'initiate' that would fit somewhere into a hierarchy of power. While men keep the control of 'blood' to themselves and relegate the women to sago, the different degrees of this control do not determine any relationship of authority between age grades. The Yafar believe that progressive access to this privileged relationship

---

25. See note 24. The reader may also find it helpful to consult Lewis (1980) regarding the Gnau of the Torricelli Range, where the neophyte is rubbed with blood from an incision made in the penis of his maternal uncle.

26. Given the short life expectancy, 'elderly' here must be understood as around 50.

with nature through the mediation of the forest spirits makes for better production. In this light, the violation of a taboo will be experienced as a loss of productive potential and fertility (game, gardens, children) corresponding to abandonment by the *nabasa*. While a woman acquires adult status – if we stick to these passages from *asagyam* to *anuwanam* – through her ability to produce sago and children, a man accedes to his by killing ever bigger game and by taking on ever more important ritual roles. Hunting gives access to the world of the *nabasa*, and conversely, the initiations into the ritual roles create the reciprocal ties indispensable for productive hunting. We have already pointed out (Chs 7 and 9) the analogies drawn by the Yafar between hunting and pig-raising on the one hand, and procreation and patrilineal descent on the other.

Puberty Rites

Under this heading I include all rites more directly connected with sexual maturity. These are the attribution of the penis gourd or the skirt on the one hand, and the piercing of the nose and the ears on the other.

Yafar boys and girls go naked until puberty and sometimes slightly later. It is on the occasion of the preparation of some public ceremony, and inside the ritual enclosure, that the young man receives his first *wagmô*, an oval penis sheath made from a yellow gourd (grown around the edges of gardens) and engraved with designs, mainly spirals (*fəga gweeg*) inspired by the tail feathers (*gweeg*) of the *fəga* bird, herring-bone patterns (*meso-wura* 'forehead wrinkles') and 'eyes' (*noofuk*), the last two elements referring to the hunter's visual concentration. The *wagmô* is made and placed on the *asagyam*'s penis by a kinsman, preferably a cross cousin or the elder sister's husband, never by the real father, uncle or elder brother (this would make the boy die). The preference for the male cross cousin recalls, in this context, the permissiveness and note of humour that go with this relationship (Ch. 11). In any case, the giver of the *wagmô* must be a mature man and have killed at least one wild pig. A helper grabs the adolescent from behind, shouting '*Awaag arampi!. . .*', while the sheath is rapidly put in place. *Awaag*, 'father, male', here designates a boar; *arampi* (*Artocarpus* sp.) is an extremely painful stinging plant. The association of the two words suggests, according to my informants, the 'heat' (itching) that the young man will feel when hunting pig. The *anuwanam* and his helper next spit betel and magic rhizomes on to the boy's shoulders and breastbone while enumerating all the types of game. The *asagyam* then runs to the edge of the village and flings away his *wagmô*; this conventional gesture expresses his shame and his rejection of adult status. When he returns, his kinsman puts another sheath on him, identical to the first; for a few days the adolescent hides himself and does not venture into public. Although expressed by conventional behaviour, the new *wagmô*-wearer's shame is no less real, for through the metaphor of hunting, stinging *arampi* and the impatience to shoot game, it is indirectly the sex drive that is alluded to. The *awaag*, the accomplished male, is also the *asagyam* himself. It has been shown, however (Ch. 9), that sexuality is socially inhibited before marriage, which will not take place until several years later; it can therefore only be rechannelled (sublimated), as it were, into cynegetic activity which thereby becomes the bachelor's main preoccupation. The *wagmô* – as opposed to nudity, but also to the ritual penis sheath, *suh-wagmô* – becomes, in this context, both the sign of sexual maturity, of its potential realization and, because of its yellow colour (*sawik*, colour of 'ripe-deciduous' things as opposed to the black *suh-wagmô*, the symbol of growth), of sterility and impotence. The *wagmô* bearing designs evoking the sun cancels out reproductive sexuality properly speaking, whereas the black *suh-wagmô* exacerbates it in the *ogohyaag* dance.[27] This is why the penis sheath given to the adolescent can be seen as the attribute of his intermediate status of unmarried adult able to fulfil his libidinal drive only through hunting.

The girl receives her skirt (*nay*)[28] at the time of her first period (see Ch. 4, n. 7). The *nay* is a string skirt which comes down to the knees. Yafar women wear several, one on top of the other, replacing the underskirts as they wear out with new ones on top. As I have only incomplete information on the female rites, I cannot guarantee that the presentation of the girl's first *nay* takes

27. But see above, p. 260, for the meaning of this dance and the *suh-wagmô* movement. Cf. also Gell 1971.
28. *Na* 'sago palm'. *Nay* 'outer layer of young sago fronds', which is twisted and the resulting strips plaited into thin ropes for the skirts. *Nay* also designates the tail feathers of the male bird of paradise *Paradisea minor*, which the Yafar take for the female.

place without a ritual, as the men claim. The woman who fastens the skirt around the girl's waist cannot be her mother nor, in principle, any of her sisters. This role is usually taken by the paternal aunt or a brother's wife, who have preferably reached menopause. For the girl as for the boy, the distance imposed on kinship ties seems to signify the avoidance of an incestuous gesture, but perhaps also a need for the change in sexual status to be taken in charge by a cross kinsman or kinswoman or affine situated clearly outside the subject's sphere of identity.

Like wearing the penis gourd and traditional skirts, interventions on the face are falling out of practice: young people today prefer the coquetry afforded by European clothes to nose and ear ornaments. Apart from the allusions to game mentioned below, there is no explicit symbolism attached to the holes in the nose and ears, whose function is to hold ornaments. These are made after puberty in the following order and by an older kinsman (real fathers and mothers excepted) of the same sex, individually, in private, and outside the village:

1) The septum is pierced with a pig-bone awl (*rakis*), more recently with a sharpened hardwood stick. The hole is made from one side and then the other, and the awl is left in place until the flesh has healed. Afterwards it is replaced by a thin *öku* bamboo stick, then by a larger bamboo. Adults also cut pieces of areca wood (today replaced by the central axis of flashlight batteries). This type of decoration, called a *wagbone*, is worn by both men and women. High-ranking men sometimes replace the *wagbone* by a pair of pig's tusks whittled down (*anəngu*) and tied together.
2) a) Two holes are pierced at the tip of the nose with a splinter of wood from a sago petiole or a sago thorn. The instrument is left in place until the flesh heals. The decoration that will take its place, called *busunk-ra*, consists of a pair of short, thin sticks made from *öku* bamboo or *busunk* liana. Boys only.
   b) When these holes have healed, a similar hole is made in the side of either nostril with the same type of instrument. These too will hold short sticks or a small carved flying-fox bone, also called *busunk-ra*. Boys only.

The installation of a complete *busunk-ra* decoration is the only operation of this series that is ritualized. A bundle of *busunk* sticks, flying-fox bones and a cowry placed on the tip of the nose and topped off by a cockatoo crest or the tail of a *boof* rat is attached by a kinsman other than the father, uncle or full brother. A spell chanted simultaneously – 'On the cuscus' nose, on the possum's nose, on the kangaroo's nose, etc.' – again compares the young man to a forest animal. Facial embellishments often refer to the animal kingdom, which is admired for the variety of its pelts and plumages.

3) Some time later, the earlobe(s) of the boy or girl are pierced with a thorn from the *rohwe* vine (*Cudrania javanica*), always by a relative of the same sex. When the flesh has healed, the thorn is replaced by sticks of *öku* bamboo, called *angbone* (*angôk* 'ear'). Women sometimes hang a bundle of light fibres, the bark of a variety of rattan (*bursya*), from one ear.

4) Lastly, for boys only, the upper rim of the ear is pierced with a sago thorn. This enables them to insert an ornament (*angsəso*), usually made from a honed flying-fox bone, that hangs down over the ear and on which is impaled the orange-coloured fruit of the *Rejoua aurantiaca* (*boof*) or a bundle of bird-of-paradise feathers.[29]

The wearing of ornaments, apart from ceremonial occasions, is concomitant with the annual horticultural cycle. Periods of clearing, burning and planting seem to a certain extent incompatible with personal ornamentation. Ornaments used to start appearing – formerly when the men in particular took pride in their appearance – towards the end of the planting season, when the gardens were growing well and the hunters were stepping up their activities. The Yafar say that the ornaments made the hunt more productive, especially the strands of cowries wrapped around the head and from which a larger cowry dangled on to the forehead. It seems again that this was in order to please to the *nabasa*,

---

29. No operation is performed on the body. Circumcision is attested only in myths (p. 55) and symbolically in the Yangis ritual, where the *ifəge* (p. 41) have their foreskin pulled back and the glans decorated with feathers, representing the new shoots of the totemic sago and coconut palms. The partial self-castration of certain mythic heros corresponds to what I have called a socialization of sexuality: the character desirous of marrying or procreating shortens his 'overlong penis', the amputated portion of which changes into a snake or some other creature (myth of The Origin of the Species). Among the heroines, amputation of the clitoris is more of an accident, but it also gives rise to a new animal species (worm, leach, etc.). The most spectacular mutilation, however, is the dismembering of the dead body of the great Original Mother, every bone and organ of whom is transmuted into a new natural species.

Men	Women
Rites for the newborn	
Newborn child is cleaned with leaves.	Newborn child is cleaned with leaves.
Mother bathes baby in water.	Mother bathes baby in water.
Mother treats baby's head.	Mother treats baby's head.
Rites for hunting and murder	
Father ritually marks baby's face: says hunting spells.	–
Father gives child (3–4 yrs old) a toy bow: says hunting spells.	
First lizard killed: father says spells.	
First bird killed: *idem*.	
First small mammal killed: *idem*.	
First snake (monitor lizard or eel killed: *idem*).	
First pig (or cassowary) killed: father gives feather ornament, says spells, spits betel and magic rhizome on to boy's body.	
First murder: rite by the *Faq-seeg na awaag* (Chs 3, 13, 14).	
First four murders: feather decorations, spells, betel and magic rhizome spit on to body.	
Fifth murder: *idem* and right to wear pig-tusk ornaments.	
Horticultural rites	
First trees planted (no rite).	First trees planted (no rite).
First sago palm felled (no rite).	First sago filtered: fertility rite performed by father.
Sexual rites	
Presentation of penis sheath.	Presentation of first skirt (at menarche).
First legitimate intercourse.	First legitimate intercourse.

Facial mutilations

Septum pierced (no rite).	Septum pierced (no rite).
Other nasal perforations (no rite).	–
Earlobe pierced (no rite).	Earlobe pierced (no rite).
Upper rim of ear pierced (no rite).	–

First ritual roles

(for each role, a special rite is performed on novice in the ritual enclosure)

1. Ritual dedicated to the forest spirits.
   a) plays *sawangô* (healing rite) or wears minor masks in the *nabasa* (hunting or healing) or the *uguwak* (healing) rituals
   b) plays role in Gêpôk rite (hunting) or Rii-buu rite (healing): wears *ra* head-dress.
   c) plays more important roles and wears masks like *ogosôk* (Gungwan, or Singraraag rite for *nabasa*), 'Cassowary' (Singraraag rite), *ïfəgê* (healing rite for *sawangô*), etc.
   d) plays whistle or trumpet at end of *agïg* mask procession: Singraraag and Gungwan.

2. Yangis festival (see Ch. 2): a man takes on only one role at each festival.
   a) plays the 'Fish', *ogomô* and 'Termite', *rawsu-inaag* roles
   b) *êri* role (first night)
   c) *yis* role (dawn)
   d) *ïfəgê* role ('child of the blood')
   e) *anuwanam* role (guides the *ïfəgê*).

Table 22. Recapitulation of rites of passage

although good looks, a clean skin rubbed down with pig fat or a strong-smelling musk (extracted from the anal glands of marsupials) were already the condition for access to abundance.

Having killed his first pig, the Yafar hunter would put his manliness to work in the service of social justice, defense of the community against sorcery emanating from neighbouring groups or, more simply, to satisfy his taste for tracking and a certain valued violence by showing his courage during murder raids. The reward for the first man killed and up to the fifth was a direct continuation of his hunting exploits. It was such a strategy of retributive murder, more rarely gratuitous killing, which a man desirous of acquiring a higher status would adopt, even as he sought more responsibilities in the religious field and in the social arena. For women, adulthood holds no noteworthy events aside from a succession of births and the tacit status these confer. Depending on the individual, the elderly Yafar man becomes an either diminished but still prestigious person or someone who is slightly ridiculous and looked down on, although never openly rejected, even when, as a miserable hunter, a fearful warrior and a bad orator, he appears in his lack of sociality as merely waiting for death. And indeed, death usually intervenes before such situations go on too long.

Funeral Rites

Two types of funeral are practised without distinction and were already the custom before government and missionary control came into effect: a) suspension of the body under a shelter; b) burial. In both cases, the corpse is wrapped in areca sheaths which have been removed from their domestic use as containers and placed in a growing garden. I was never given an explanation, either of a sociological or a symbolic order, of these two opposing techniques; there has never been, in living memory, any correlation whatsoever with the dual organization of society nor with the sex or status of the deceased. The decision is made by the subject before his or her death, or by close relatives. Formerly both formulas led, a few months later, to the gathering of the bones (*kêg totump*). The shelter, *sengêri*, under which the body is suspended looks like a garden shelter, only narrower; the body is tied on to a carrying pole attached to the shelter at either end so that the head is slightly higher than the feet and pointing uphill. A roof, made of unsplit sago fronds, is then laid just above the cadaver, which is some 1.60 m off the ground. The bodies of infants are placed on a post, the top of which has been split and tied open in the shape of a basket by rigid rattan. The grave, *fakag* (literally 'to lay flat'), is a rectangular pit some 1.20 m deep. A platform is constructed slightly off the ground by setting sticks transversely into the walls of the grave, and is overlaid with leaves. The body is placed on the bed, wrapped in its sheaths and oriented as under the *sengêri*. A second platform is then built over the body with a new bed of leaves. The rest of the grave can then be filled in without the earth touching the body. Lastly, a roof is built over the grave to shelter the mourners as well as the deceased. Both the government and the missionaries have discouraged the use of *sengêri* for reasons of hygiene; nevertheless, this technique was still in use in the early 1980s.

The Yafar's mortuary apparatus is striking in its discretion and lack of social potentiality. Death is not an occasion for exchanging goods between families, nor do the sex of the deceased or the circumstances of death make a difference. Only the funerals of children still at the breast or not yet able to walk are performed without wailing or ritual; the mother places the baby on the funeral post set in the ground by her husband.

Wailing and weeping (*we*), primarily by close kin, announces the death. Soon, and usually over a period of two or three days,[30] relatives from other hamlets arrive to view the deceased and express their grief by wailing and touching the corpse. The deceased is laid out in the house, supine, the arms alongside the body and the feet together. The deceased's young children are sent away to sleep at a neighbour's for fear that they might be made ill by the ghost (*ifaaf*) of their father or mother wanting to carry them off to the other world. The rest of the household goes on living, cooking and eating in the single room. Close kin may fast for the first meal. The lamentations (*wesko*),[31] beginning on the day of the death

---

30. A close relative may request to keep the body longer; this is the case with mothers as regards their children. As a rule, the dead were kept longer before the advent of government control.

31. From *we* 'weeping' and *sungo* 'to put (down)'. *Wesko* also designates the men's songs accompanied by hour-glass drums which mark the Gêpôk rite or a successful pig or cassowary hunt.

and continuing until the end of the first part of the mourning period, evoke the ties of economic dependency between the mourner and the deceased. The widower laments that he will no longer have anyone to work his sago or make his jelly, the widow that she will no longer have a husband to clear her garden plot or bring her meat from the hunt. Between two brothers or brothers-in-law it is their activities in common that are evoked: hunting, participation in public festivals, etc. For the loss of a son, the parents will lament the fact that he will never enjoy the trees they planted for him.

On the day of the burial or the exposition of the body, the penis sheath[32] or the skirts (except for the old underskirts) are removed, and a few close relatives, mainly women, bring young banana stems full of water, which they wring out over the corpse and with which they wash the body thoroughly. The washing seems to have various functions: simply to wash the body, to rid it of the 'filth' (*nəfweh*) that covers it. This notion, however, conceals a representation that goes back to the already familiar idea of sloughing the old skin: when the body has lain more than three or four days, the washing removes the epidermis, *arfêêg*, which is then discarded in the forest. Secondly, the moisture from the heart of the banana stalk, *fôô hoofuk*, seems to have a purifying power which also acts on those polluted by the cadaver's fluids. Lastly, the washing brings out 'scars', regarded as those left by the invisible arrows of the *aysiri* sorcerer and evidence of the foul act; in the past, these legitimized the organization of retaliatory action (Ch. 14). The body is dried with leaves from the *ahnam-bəga* (*Coleus scutellarioides*), a plant growing abundantly on the outskirts of villages), then wrapped in areca sheaths, in front of the house; at that time the hands are folded over the pubes. A few objects belonging to the deceased – axe, knife, netbag, modern glass-bead ornaments, money – are often placed on the body. This task is done mainly by the man or the two men (first-degree consanguines or affines excepted) who have volunteered to carry the body. The sheaths are taken from the old *sööbi* containers in the deceased's house and are renamed *koom-ke* (*koob* 'a variety of black palm', *keeg* 'sheath'). Unless the deceased is to be buried and is light enough to be carried by a single man, the body is

---

32. A sick man will already have removed it. One can see in this gesture the need to mark the desocialization pre-supposed by sickness and death.

lashed to a carrying pole (*tawari*) and borne by two men. In the garden, the *sengêri* is erected by other kinsmen (men only, as for all constructions); the grave is dug by both men (work with the digging stick and construction of the shelter) and women (earth removal, leaf-gathering). The digging is done by two kinsmen of at least the second degree, working with a digging stick, one at each end of the grave (a son may do this work, however, if the parent being buried was elderly). The lamentations continue while the body is being installed.

The first mourning period and, if the deceased was suspended, the smoking of the body, now begin. Each morning and for at least the first five days, a new fire is kindled and kept burning under the body, and the nuclear family sings lamentations for part of the time. Second-degree consanguines or relatives further removed mourn on the day of the funeral and then do not return. Only garden produce is eaten (no sago jelly). On the day of the funeral, a meal may be shared by all those who accompanied the body to the garden. Every day an offering of bananas, *Saccharum edule*, sugar cane, etc. is hung on the burial shelter for the ghost (*ifaaf*), whose return to the village the night after the funeral is avoided by going to sleep at the neighbours', since the ghost is believed to come back for its personal possessions, tobacco, as well as fire for its 'torch' (*gwos*: see above, p. 390 and Ch. 14). In principle, this first stage of mourning – which might be called the active mourning – lasts until the odour of the cadaver has disappeared. The corpse is then said to be *êrik foogêk* 'smoked cadaver'.

Before going any farther with the chronological description of this ritual, let us pause for a moment to look at a few points, beginning with those who wrap and bear the corpse. Whereas a very close relative is not afraid to touch the body, even several days after death, and a mourner, in order to express his or her grief, will sometimes smear him- or herself with liquid from the cadaver (*biyimp*), non-kin or more distant relatives fear pollution. This is why it is said that the mourner must be 'strong' (*kêfutuk*); after the funeral ceremony, he or she washes off the *biyimp* with moisture from a banana stem, as the use of water is forbidden. The correlation with washing the corpse as described above seems once again to be grounded in the notion of sloughing old skin: *nəfweh* ('filth') and *biyimp* are like *arfêêg* (sloughed skins) which one rubs off. This is a surface purification, but it draws on the idea of regeneration, expressed by the use of banana sprouts:

the outer waste is cleaned off by the *hoofuk* of the young plant. The risks of contamination incurred by the bearers are compensated by gifts of food presented by the brother, father or son of the deceased; in the case of serious pollution, the bearers may be given a section of river to fish or a clump of sago palms, inalienable rights passed on to the following generations.

The choice of the garden as a funeral site[33] also requires some comment. This must be first of all a clearing in which the planting is finished and where the tobacco, *Setaria palmifolia*, beans and *Amaranthus hybridus* have been harvested. The clearing may belong to the deceased (or to the husband of the deceased), or to a first-degree consanguine or affine. When the garden does not belong to the deceased but to one of the mourners, this presents the advantage, the Yafar claim, of being able to mourn where one works. A man may have expressed the wish during his lifetime to be buried in a given garden, or close to the remains of his spouse or a sibling; the body of a married woman, however, is always placed in her husband's garden, unless her father asks for her remains, a request that can be honoured only if one of his gardens has never held a dead relative.

The deceased's crops are often abandoned or even torn up if they were not attributed previously (Ch. 6). However, the new shoots will be collected when the time comes to make a new clearing. In former times, only the man who had avenged the death by killing the presumed sorcerer was allowed to consume the victim's production. The trees attributed to the deceased from which he had not yet eaten fruit are killed by ring-barking. The deceased's personal belongings are distributed among close relatives without any strict rule; it is said that the owner's odour clings to the possessions: to lay claim to an object is therefore expressed metaphorically by the desire 'to keep the odour of the deceased'.

Now, after these clarifications, let us return to the mourning process. Once the body is dry and the grass has grown back under the funeral shelter, lamenting ceases and people can once more shave their hair and their beards, which had been allowed to grow since the death. There are almost no other signs of mourning: a widow simply carries her husband's empty netbag on her back until it wears out. Besides the partial uprooting of the deceased's crops, close relatives sometimes destroy some of their own posses-

---

33. For another Melanesian example, see de Coppet 1976.

Plate 22. Funeral shelter (*sengêri*) in an abandoned garden. The corpse is wrapped in old limbum food containers and hung by the carrying pole (Photo Juillerat, Musée de l'Homme collection).

sions, notably by burning ornaments they used to wear in public festivals celebrated with the deceased brother or brother-in-law. Some stop gardening for a time. At the outset of the mourning period, but only for mature men and sometimes also for women having attained a certain status (mothers of several children or elderly women), a rite is performed by an *aynaag* to suspend temporarily the hunters' tacit compact with the *nabasa*. This procedure, called *nabasam mwaywey* (see p. 197), resembles a sort of sacrifice or a collective renunciation characteristic of mourning, the effect of which is to keep the forest spirits outside of society, to deprive them of their potentiality as purveyors of game by 'covering' the animals and the forest 'with fog' (*rangôk kagwôg*)

(Ch. 7). Hunting itself is not forbidden, and any quarry encountered by chance may be shot and tracked; but we have already seen that this results in a loss of motivation to hunt and in a sharp drop in cynegetic production.

The end of the second stage of mourning (passive mourning) is marked by the removal of the bones and the renewal of the hunting 'contract' with the *nabasa*. This rite is performed on the (re-opened) grave as well as on the *sengêri*; it used to take place when the state of the remains allowed and after the deceased had been avenged, or, if identification of the sorcerer's village or reprisals were too long in coming, when the rotted *sengêri* collapsed of its own accord. Today the rite is performed after the collapse of the funeral shelter and not always for graves, which suggests a gradual abandonment of secondary funeral rites. The 'separation of the bones', *kêg totump*, is done by a group of *aynaag* under the direction of the person who performed the *nabasam mwaywey*, at the beginning of the mourning period: the one who closed hunting is responsible for reopening it. The reactualization of the alliance with the *nabasa* is once again placed under the sign of 'blood', which in this instance takes the form of daubing the bones with red ochre; the incantations accompanying this gesture speak of 'ripe game', of the removal of the different forms of *rangôk* ('fog') that covered the fauna and the trees, and of the blood (*suwê* 'fire') of the different species of animal. It is also at this point that the *kê-ruur* 'bone child' (p. 131) is thought to leave the remains and take up residence in an iron tree, where it becomes a new *nabasa* capable of providing hunters with pigs, but also the guardian of the garden, which it protects from thieves (in particular the owner's relatives) by afflicting them with a passing illness characterized by vomiting. Every two or three years, the owner of the crops leaves a food offering for the *kê-ruur*, the first being made the day of the *kêg totump*. The large bones (skull, jaw, long bones) are separated from the small ones; the latter are buried on the spot. The skull used to be kept in the village house or in a garden shelter by a close male or female relative; when this person died, the skull was placed in a tree growing in the garden. The jawbone and the bones of the limbs (and most often today the skull) are wedged by the father, brother or son in the fork of a tree in the garden, usually a *Gnetum gnemon*.

The counter-sorcery murder used to be followed by a rite at the funeral shelter: the ground was bared and the posts painted red (anatto, formerly ochre), *boof* fruits (p. 374) and red croton leaves decorated the shelter, and spells were recited by the *aynaag* as their betel juice reddened the ground.

A Tentative Interpretation of Yafar Individual Identity

The cultural elaboration of the person in Yafar society is founded on the two paradigms examined above, which are articulated by that moment in which the identity is shattered and which we call death. During life, the person is conceived of according to three basic orientations, which are organized in both space and time. First of all, there is the 'mirror self', represented by the mirrored life of the forest self which, contrary to an exchange partner, restricts its role to 'being two' (*ah-ogohôk*) with the subject. As a simple alter ego, the unseen forest self merely duplicates the subject, eschewing any form of communication. In these circumstances, the forest self is of no real dialectic interest.

Opposite the forest self *nabasa* stands the *nabasa segwaag* – and behind it, the entire set of forest spirits – which simultaneously becomes the object of a sublimated libidinal investment from which the forest self is excluded. This is the living person's second basic orientation, represented not by some element of the self, but by this idealized, anonymous Other with whom the hunter's *sungwaag* can and must communicate. In effect we have seen just how much Yafar culture values this relationship, experienced as producer of food and bounty (game) and founded on an asymmetric exchange to man's advantage (a little betel and tobacco for a wild pig). But this material reciprocity conceals what is in fact an exchange of 'bloods': the blood with which the young *asagyam* is embellished in order to captivate the *nabasa* that is to become his *segwaag*; the blood of the quarry offered in exchange by the latter; and lastly, the blood of the dying man collected by the *segwaag* and which in turn, through a process of hypostatization, becomes a *nabasa*.

The third orientation is that founded by the *sungwaag* with its double nature: embodied or disembodied, possessed, lost or found, under control in its necessary relations with the *nabasa* or wandering among the ghosts. This psychic experience of loss expressed by so many societies has encouraged anthropologists trained in psychoanalysis to see it as the product of a fear of castration. Without reducing the representations of the *sungwaag* to this concept, it seems to me that the Yafar notion of the *nabasa* stealing the self, sorcerer attacks and especially 'ripening' (*abuk feg*) is a fitting expression of castration, either sudden or gradual, in the broad sense of the withering of the 'phallus', the latter term being taken to mean desire as a whole, the healthy, whole person (*kêfutuk*). But the danger of castration stems from two sources: *aysiri* sorcerers and, to a lesser extent, *nabasa* attacks on the one hand, and ghosts and the depths of the earth on the other. As an integral part of the social system, human aggression (by sorcerers' *sungwaag*) or attacks by the usual interlocutors of the spirit world are reminiscent of fantasies of 'arrow heads' being shot into the body: *nabasa sosoog*, or *aysiri* sorcerers' magic arrows or bone awls. These aggressors are male, active and violent. In this case, the *sungwaag* returns injured, harbouring foreign bodies which will gradually destroy the subject; the idea of ripening is not operative here. The other aspect of the fear of castration is not inscribed in the order of aggression but in that of pollution: one has only to dream of ghosts or of eating ghost foods and suspect the *sungwaag* of having delved into the depths of the earth for the self to come back 'ripe' (*abuk*) or in the process of ripening (*heweheg*) from the simple fact of having visited these regions or entities. Those who cause the *sungwaag* to wither from the acceleration of its natural evolution towards decomposition act through inertia. In the first case, the disembodied self is the victim of its own carelessness within an authorized space, an accident; in the second case, the self trespasses its assigned boundaries, which is regression.

When one recalls the opposition between the space on the surface of or just below the ground and the chthonian space proper, the first being the site of exchanges with the dead but also the scene of encounters with sorcerers, the second the dwelling place of the *ifaaf* guardians of cultivated plants and, deeper still, the site of the primordial maternal *hoofuk*, one is led to define the *sungwaag* as an entity of the person – which I have chosen to call the self – perpetually in danger of regressing towards the cosmicized mother and of confrontations with sometimes good (*nabasa*),[34] sometimes treacherous (*aysiri*) father figures. The

34. It should be remembered that the *sawangô*, female forest spirits and the spirits of deceased women, are not associated with the dangerous Archaic Mother, but are the female version of the *nabasa*, potential female interlocutors in dreams; nevertheless as they do not participate in hunting, these figures remain marginal.

desire to return to the mother[35] is a downwards pull (like the force of gravity, which makes the ripe fruit fall) against which culture erects protective barriers. The double image of the path of the dead seems to express the full ambivalence of this desire: the 'broad path' leads straight to the 'maternal hell' with no possibility of return, while a careful search for the 'narrow path' ascending to the 'villages at the top' seems clearly to express a defense against regression, which Yafar culture constantly brings into play, notably in the sphere of ritual. These two modes of the castration complex seem, however, to be closely linked if one recalls the myth of the three oedipal sons (p. 183) punished for stealing game from the womb of the earth, an irreversible return to the Mother Earth organized by their own father. Juxtaposing this myth with the fear of the *sungwaag* descending below ground relocates the Yafar problematic of castration within the context of the Oedipus complex.

The *sungwaag*'s inevitable metamorphosis into an *ifaaf* puts the self out of the running, since for the Yafar, this aspect of death appears as an inevitable castration caused by the return to the Archaic Mother. That is why, in order to become a socialized inter-locutor for living beings, the deceased had to be something else as well. And this other thing, elaborated in 'opposition' to the *ifaaf* stripped of its sociality, is the spiritual part of the two noble body substances, blood and bones: without them, the body is a mere *arfêêg*, a skin that is left to the ghost. Yafar eschatology clearly expresses this cleavage of the self between identification with the mother through a regressive return (*ifaaf*) on the one hand, and accession to the status of *nabasa* (identification with a father figure) as mediator of the maternal fecundity on the other.

If it is dangerous for the *sungwaag* to go visiting the ghosts, this is because they are at the same time close to the chthonian mother and a product of *sungwaag*. And if it is necessary to dream of *nabasa* in order to have a successful hunt, this is because the *nabasa*, as guardians and purveyors of animals, are the medi-

---

35. The fear of returning to the cosmicized womb could be interpreted as the repressed desire to identify with the maternal *imago*, itself stemming from the anxiety of being sev-ered from the mother. The fantasy of possibly fulfilling this desire through the *sungwaag* is tantamount to a transgression punished by the loss of this 'phallus' (which, once *kêfutuk* 'strong', now becomes *abuk* 'ripe') elaborated against attraction to the mother. In fact, as Kristeva shows, castration has to do not only with part of one's being, but with being on the whole. Indeed the central function of the Gungwan rite is 'to rid the subject of the fear of irreversibly engulfing his own identity in his mother' (Kristeva 1980: 79).

ators of the underground maternal world, represented in myth as
the site of the gestation of game. The noble spirits of the dead
appear as interlocutors and exchange partners, screening off the
non-socializable fertility of the depths. Furthermore, the fertile
bad Mother is guarded by Wangohra, the 'bad father', and
her sign is the *boof* tree with its deciduous fruits. Direct, non-
mediated exchange with the Mother is forbidden, and when the
relation is not mediated by a father figure, the latter is replaced
by a natural representation such as the totemic coconut palm.

To the loss of the self corresponds its re-embodiment, and the
fear of recovering a weakened self is countered by the desire to
see the *sungwaag* enriched by gifts from the *nabasa*. Its nighttime
quest for promises of animals is inscribed in the same figurative
system as its wanderings along ill-fated trails. This illuminates
the Yafars' interpretation of dreams, which, as we have seen,
is based on the alternative receive/not receive (lose). To receive
nothing is initially to be forsaken by the male forest spirits, those
mediators of blood, socialized representatives of the cosmicized
maternal principle; and secondarily it is to be abandoned by the
Mother herself, to be totally orphaned. Alternatively, to receive is
to recover a strengthened (*kêfutuk*), rejuvenated *sungwaag*, to live
under the sign of access to blood, the sign of the Mother's generosity. This obviously brings us back to food. It seems to me that
the complementary interplay between the individual and his
sungwaag underlines the analogy between exercising one's desire
and avoiding castrating regression on the one hand, and satis-
fying bodily needs and investing in cynegetic production on the
other. One is the transposition of the other, a parallel already
encountered in the myth of the Stolen Game, in which the
repressed desire for the mother is translated in terms of hunting.

Most of the rites for turning an *asagyam* into an *anuwanam* partake of this dialectic: the rite prepares the young man's *sungwaag*
to ensure the *nabasa*'s cooperation. This 'initiation' is the birth-
right of every male, from which he will draw personal advantages
(becoming a prestigious hunter) while becoming a meat producer
for the community as a whole. Hunting, formerly homicide, participation in public rites and begetting descendants are the functions
which endow every Yafar man with his status as full member of
the group. Nevertheless, there are some responsibilities – which
we have already seen as part of the dual and clan organization
(Ch. 3) – reserved for only a few individuals, which introduce

into this egalitarian structure a differentiated system of hereditary or acquired ranks which are partially mystified by the secrecy surrounding them. These functions and the principle of their transmission will be examined in the next chapter.

13

Hidden Powers

> During the day, we chat, chew betel, smoke. At night, alone, before going to sleep, we think over the 'strong words', alone, not saying anything. Then we fall asleep.
> All the strong words, I keep them deep in my mouth, in my heart. The mouth for us is like the book for white men.
>
> (Conversation with May Promp, 1981)

In the preceding chapters, we saw how hierarchical relationships are organized within the circle of close kin or in the context of marriage or production. In the next two chapters, I will deal more specifically with inherited institutional offices, but also with the more diffuse functions involved in the exercise of certain positive or negative 'powers'. The forms of power known to the Yafar can lead in opposite directions: to life or to death; one excludes the other. The 'powers of life' – to borrow an expression from Marc Augé – have to do with the management of the sacred and the use of knowledge and ritual to control the natural forces such as they appear in secret myths, but they also serve to legitimize 'political' authority, which occasionally manifests itself at the local-group level. We shall see that the credibility of authority operating at a suprakin level can only be sustained by the status derived from control of the religious domain, that is of fertility and the order of the cosmos. The socially negative 'powers of death' (Ch. 14) are manipulated more secretively and individually to destroy lives and to compromise procreation or production. Both forms of power are practised in secret, the exception being mediums, whose role, as we shall see, is not thought of as a power. This is why I will first look at the relationship between power and the sacred, and then attempt to circumscribe how symbolic control turns into a form of personalized 'political' control.

422

Secrecy: Strategies of Knowledge and Power

The notion of secrecy applies to two levels of analysis: content and strategy. The content of the secret may be qualitatively important or, on the contrary, insignificant and not really worth concealing; in this case, analysis is a matter of being familiar with religious knowledge and its sociocultural context. The means employed by those in possession of the secret as well as the function and efficacy of their strategy are, on the other hand, the object of a more sociological approach to the relations of power that fashion the social structure. Depending on their theoretical bent, anthropologists have favoured one level or the other, although the sociological approach turns out to be the more accessible since it does not require divulging the secret to the investigator. For some authors,[1] the content is of little interest, the only matter of import being the sociopolitical use society makes of it. I personally believe this problem deserves closer scrutiny, and the Yafar case provides ample evidence of a possible analogy between content and strategy. Even if what is concealed may sometimes seem futile, when it is placed in its cultural dialectic, the correlation between the signifier of the secret and the cause the discriminatory strategy is intended to serve can be seen. For the Yafar, the stakes are the same in both the semantic and social fields: the control of reproduction and relations between the sexes. Inscribed within secrecy, the sexual dialectic is the principal site of the exercise of social discrimination in view of preserving control of the coveted knowledge, from which women are excluded. As a consequence, I think that whatever is projected into esoteric knowledge or into the structure of society is composed of the same ideological problematic, and that the line between system of representations and social organization is not as sharp as some believe (something that dual organization has clearly shown). Proof of this is that the Yafar associate religious offices themselves, as well as the identity of those in charge of the rituals, with the secret content. In fact, in order to deny the very existence of a body of esoteric knowledge, the society resorts to denying the roles and offices connected with them. Even the custodians of the secret must remain anonymous. The secret is therefore not

---

1. For example Jamin 1977 or, for our region, Gell 1980. For a valuable analysis of secrecy and knowledge in Papua New Guinea, see Barth 1975, 1987.

hollow, not a simple pretext for social manipulations, it is brimming with meaning. The hidden meaning of the rites, the esoteric versions of myths, cosmological representations and the 'theory' of reproductive sexuality all comprise the core of the secret of the ritual masters, whose identity is in principle not revealed to women and young people, and whose duties consist in ensuring the efficacy of the rituals, the reproduction of nature and the true course of the heavenly bodies. To reveal their existence would already be to say something about the knowledge that must be concealed (see Juillerat 1991a).

But while the substance of the secret knowledge is formally transmitted in the framework of religious charges, it is also passed around on a less formal level and to differing degrees in part of the male community. How does this happen? First of all, this is hard to discover because of the secrecy itself and, secondly, the answer must be shaded because religious knowledge is parcelled out unequally, and its content varies from one lineage or individual to the next. Even though my limited access to the secret knowledge does not allow me to say who knows what, the overall system has gradually become clear to me, in particular beginning with the moment when, in 1981, I learned of a hitherto unsuspected system of religious charges and how they were transmitted.

I would therefore like to attempt to define the system by first of all examining the different discriminatory categories underpinning it, and then by identifying the ways in which this knowledge is communicated (whether through genealogical lines or not), which are subject to varying degrees of formalization. Although not the only mode of discrimination, the segregation of women from this knowledge remains fundamental in the sense that sexual difference underlies the main issue of secrecy. Rivalry between the male and female principles as they are represented in a process of imaginary reproduction of nature (esoteric knowledge) is never far from the surface, but it is blocked by male domination of the institutional social strategy set up to control this knowledge. It is from this discrepancy – the implicit recognition of the primacy of femaleness in reproduction, which is concealed in social relations – that the need for secrecy arises. Secrecy appears as the site of the cultural repression of that portion of knowledge which threatens to hobble and counter male power. Women appear as those to whom the men's secret is both forbidden and potentially addressed (see Zempleni 1976). The risk represented by this potentiality is the driving force behind the strategy of secrecy; and the full ambiguity of this potential comes out in the Yangis ritual, where the men, painted and masked, pretend to believe that the women believe that there are spirits under the masks, summoned from the forest by the men's magic. By risking 'discovery' in this way, the men add to the real secret of their esoteric knowledge the fictional secret of their human identity and the physical reality of spirits (see Juillerat 1991a).

More generally, the exclusion of women from male knowledge excludes them from ritual activity. Even though the women's dance has a symbolic meaning, it does not enjoy any recognized efficacy. Women do not have access to the most sacred pigments (red ochre in particular), and their body painting is reduced to a few facial designs, the rest of their bodies being left without decoration. They are also barred from any form of music-making, all instruments without exception being reserved for men, and the only songs they sing are wordless tunes during childbirth or, in rare instances, work songs accompanying the extraction of sago pith.[2]

A dividing line runs through the male community, not only between age grades but also within the category of men of knowledge (*aynaag*). The latter differentiation distinguishes those who have inherited a ritual office from those who have acquired personal prestige. These two ways of procuring status, and thus gaining access to knowledge and its ritual use, can obviously be combined. Through the very diverse personalities, the psychological factor determines, particularly among men who have not inherited a specific responsibility, a broad range of ill-defined intermediate statuses; here knowledge circulates informally, and varying degrees of non-specific ritual responsibility are acquired.

I will first analyse the inherited positions and their special responsibilities and then proceed to the non-inherited, acquired positions.

2. These work songs were in fact originally male, since they come from Waina groups, in which it is the men who strip the pith from the sago palms. The Yafar women have invented their own words to suit their gender.

Mediators of the Sacred

Inherited Religious Offices[3]

Chapter 3 presented ritual offices as they are distributed among the clans and dual units (Table 5). We must now consider their respective contents and modes of transmission.

The analysis of dual organization and its implementation in the Yangis ritual (Ch. 2) has already shown the complementary character of the two major mediators of the sacred domain, the Master (or Father) of the Sky (*oof na awaag*) and the Master of the Earth (*bəte na awaag*).[4] The first is the embodiment of the male and celestial cosmic forces as well as the male contribution to the act of procreation represented in this ritual; he is symbolically linked with the original *afwêêg* sago palm and the god W. . ., and represents the Araneri moiety as a whole. At the tribal level, he is the one who seems to be chiefly responsible for the rites governing drought and rain, which open the burning and planting seasons respectively, although these rites can also be performed at other times of the year by the Master of the Earth and, individually, by any *aynaag* (see below). The Master of the Earth, on the other hand, embodies the tellurian and maternal forces.[5] Along with all members of the Angwaneri moiety, he feels a close tie with the Primordial Coconut, and his knowledge of the myths stresses the antecedence of this totemic palm and the primacy of the female domain, whereas the Master of the Sky assigns priority to the divine couple W. . .-B. . . and the creation of first the celestial vault and then the earth (Ch. 2). *Bəte* should be understood here in its cosmological meaning and not as a territory, which is the usual meaning of the word.[6]

As we saw in Chapter 3, ritual offices may change clans, but they remain attached to one moiety or the other. The Masters of the Sky and the Earth are an inseparable pair whose cooperation

---

3. See also Juillerat 1991b. For another example from the Sepik, see Harrison 1988.

4. See Ch. 3, note 3.

5. He is supposed to control the mythic python whose trophy he keeps in a netbag (see Ch. 7, n. 25).

6. Although *bəte na awaag* is sometimes used in place of *nôô na awaag* to designate Ifêêg clan, the purported original occupant of the present-day lands, and although the expression taken out of context may lead to misunderstandings, Biyuneri clan, the main holder of the *bəte na awaag* office, is not believed to have acquired the title following a historical event.

Plate 23. Waya, Master of the Sky and the Sun for Yafar 1 – 1973 (Photo Juillerat, Musée de l'Homme collection).

in Yangis constantly recreates the cosmic and social unity of the world. Their principal duties with regard to this ceremony are to choose the date and frequency of the rite, to supervise the gathering of the materials for the masks, which they apportion between Araneri and Angwaneri according to the totemic gender of the botanical species, to recite the correct spells at the many important moments during the handling of the colours and materials, to choose the dancers for the lead roles, to direct the painting of the masks and, in general, to see that participants and visitors conduct themselves properly and that the women and children remain apart. In addition, secret rites are performed in the bush prior to the public ceremony, either by both masters

acting together, or by each separately but one always comple-
menting the other. The latter situation prevails particularly when
each of the two men goes into the bush with his wife, has
intercourse with her and collects their sexual secretions, which he
wraps in some leaves together with some vegetal *hoofuk* (sago,
tubers, etc.) and keeps until the first night of the Yangis ceremony.
Then the two bundles (each of which partakes of the two sexes
by its nature but symbolically and socially represents respectively the male and female domains) are hurled to the ground
as the two masked *êri* enter to re-enact the primordial act of
procreation by the two original deities. Here the two masters
play an instrumental role, becoming ritual actors by providing
their semen, which thus takes on something like a cosmic nature.
Both are thus an integral part of the sexual duality of the
universe and of the totemic paradigm through which, as we have
seen, the dual structure of society is legitimized. It seems that it
is their complementarity that ensures their respective statuses of
an equal footing: in the symbolic sphere, male is not superior to
female. Nevertheless, it is two men who represent sexual
complementarity in the cyclical regeneration of nature and
society, two men, one of whom serves the female portion of the
cosmos and speaks and acts ritually on behalf of all that is
female. What could be a more flagrant expression of the male
monopoly of the symbolic means of reproduction which is the
institutional stamp of men's exclusive power over life?

Theoretically there should be only one Master of the Sky and
one Master of the Earth for the whole Yafar group, but the importance given the requirement that both Yangis officiants reside
in the hamlet where the rite is held necessitated the duplication
of these offices when the single local group of some generations
ago split first into two and then into three hamlets. As a consequence there are now three pairs of masters (see below).

A second pair of offices, which do not, as far as I know, play
complementary roles in ritual, are the Master of the Sun (*akba
na awaag*) and the Master of the Moon (*wos na awaag*), also
respectively from an Araneri and an Angwaneri lineage. Unlike
the Masters of the Earth and the Sky, there is only one Master of
the Sun and one Master of the Moon for the entire society.[7] Each
is custodian of his own heavenly body and controls its path in the

7. I was told that the Punda and Umeda have homologous offices.

Plate 24. Yangis (Punda 1986): One of the two *êri* dancing during the first night of the ritual; mask topped by sago fronds of the totemic variety, orange *Rejoua aurantiaca* fruits stuck with feathers, fringe made of wild pandanus fibers, ritual penis sheath (Photo Niles, National Research Institute collection, Cultural Studies Division, Port Moresby).

sky (see Ch. 1): the sun and the moon must not deviate from their orbit nor set too fast. In addition, the Master of the Moon sees to it that his own luminary 'follows the sun' (*akba-gam ako*).

In this context, there is a myth which suggests a different origin of the sun from that given by the exegesis of Yangis (p. 53).[8] It tells how the Original Cassowary, metamorphosis of the Coconut Palm and represented as a walking coconut palm whose fruits are also eggs, used to travel in perpetual night from village to village, handing out his coconut-eggs (metaphor for the breast). Wherever he was, the inhabitants had enough to eat, but wherever he was not, they went hungry, which one day made them decide to stone the Cassowary to death. Wam, the mythical hero encountered earlier, who represents the Son (*reeg*), kept the parts of the body in a netbag (made by two sisters), called the 'Cassowary's netbag' (*kwoy na wura*) or by its secret name 'Sun's netbag' (*akba na wura*), which was kept in a house made from the Cassowary's bones. This trophy is said to have been handed down to the Yafar Master of the Sun, the last of whom (from Wamawneri clan), who died in the 1960s, still tended, in a remote spot known to only a few men, a 'sun house' (*akba na raara*) which contained an ancient netbag holding cassowary trophies, which he periodically anointed with blood from this bird. From time to time, the *akba na awaag* would spend the night there and keep a fire burning. One day the temple burned down in the absence of its custodian, who returned to find nothing but a pile of ashes. A short time later he died, and, sign of the times, the sacred house was not rebuilt nor the netbag replaced.

Whether one takes the exegesis of Yangis in which the sun is fantasised as the Coconut-B. . . deity's single unattainable breast, which the two *ifəge* try to seize by shooting their arrows, or the version with the Cassowary-Sun, born of the murder of the absent mother represented by the Coconut-Cassowary, a traveller unable to feed everyone at the same time, the meaning is the same in either case: the need to recover or preserve the warmth of the feeding mother, not to let this wandering mother become definitively 'bad', to turn the Freudian *fort* into a *da*. Stoning the cassowary is – without committing the incest that the shooting of an arrow supposes – more a case of putting an end to the

8. Another version amalgamates the sun with W's 'solidified semen', to which Wam adds some blood and one of the eyes of the mythic Cassowary.

Plate 25. Yangis: *Ogomô* (sago-palm growth spirit): emblematic mask of the dancer's clan, body painted with charcoal and white clay.

Plate 26. Man in festive dress: bird-of-paradise feathers, cowrie-shell band, pig-tusk nose and chest ornaments (*wamero*).

frustration caused by the Mother's mobility than of deliberately killing her.[9] By putting a stop to her disorderly course, she is brought under control: the now-present, now-absent Cassowary becomes a distant but warm sun, in perpetual motion, present, absent, but also perfectly under control through the very regularity of its course. The *fort/da* becomes a reassuring equilibrium.

To keep the Mother at a distance (the sky) in her idealized feeding function while protecting oneself from a return to the womb (the subterranean world[10]) is no doubt to make the best possible use of a persistent maternal image while avoiding regression.

The Master of the Sun is the custodian of this order. It is said that he must clutch the sun tightly in his fist (*ningəga-na fufukug*) in order to control its course, speed and heat. If it should ever cool down, he must 'blow on it' to rekindle its fire, or else wetness would prevail over dryness, the earth and the plants would rot, and marshes would take over the forest: 'Our mother [land and forest] must not be allowed to rot.' This relationship or identification with the sun is marked by a single rite, performed when a new *akba na awaag* assumes his charge. From sunrise to sunset, the new Master of the Sun, his body coated from head to toe with red ochre, keeps an arrow[11] fitted to his drawn bow and trained on the sun. At the same time he dances with a ritual *suh-wagmô* penis gourd (p. 260). A few helpers, partially painted with ochre, accompany him, and all recite spells in which the word *kêg*, literally 'bone', is repeated over and over, evoking the idea of dryness, of matter too hard to rot and of infinite duration; other chants are then sung to 'stop' the rivers' flow and the rain's fall. The entire rite is called *oof kêg*, literally 'sky bone'.

While the Master of the Sun ensures that men and nature receive the warmth and dryness they need, the Master of the Moon seems to play an opposite and complementary role. He is associated with cold and dew (*wos [buu]-arêmp* 'moon dew'), a condition necessary for the fertility of gardens and of nature in

9. In the myth of the stoning of the original cassowary, it is nevertheless possible to see the inevitable necessity of giving up the breast, in other words of being weaned.

10. See the Gungwan rite, Ch. 12. A parallel can also be drawn with the myth summarized above (p. 338), in which the mother *abi* wildfowl, by feeding her sons her eggs, causes the dawn to break: the sun returns with the exercise of the maternal feeding function.

11. This is the same attitude as that of the *ifəge* in Yangis, which would mean that through this rite, the Sun Master re-enacts the relation of the society he embodies with the 'cosmic breast'.

Plate 27. Fish dancers (*sawôg*). Masks painted with clan emblems, polychrome body paint.

general; but this association extends to the fertility of women as well, for a saying has it that the moon comes and 'looks at their vagina', which starts their periods. Cessation of menstruation during pregnancy and with menopause are also determined by the moon, which thus becomes an agent of the entire female cycle. The last belief sometimes causes people to point to the moon and say to a young child 'There is your father.'[12] Mythology locates the secret origin of this heavenly body in the embryo (the internal sprout floating in the milk) of a primordial coconut, which is believed to have then coated itself with sago from a palm of the *fənaw* variety (the original 'female' sago palm) to harden itself; now the coconut is the secret metaphor for the uterus.

There is also a public myth describing the moon as a mysterious agent which comes at night to complete the tasks the cultivator has begun that day (burning, planting). But when the garden begins producing, some of the food disappears every night.[13] With the help of his young son, the man discovers the moon hiding in a stream bed in the form of a sprouted coconut. He takes it home, hides it and sets siamese brothers, joined back to back, to guard it (image of a double lunar crescent); but the culture hero, Wefroog, steals it, plays with it and lets it escape, first up into a coconut palm, then into the sky.

Is the *wos na awaag* therefore the master of a male or a female principle? It is hard to say. He controls a heavenly body whose cycle is related to women's periods; but while the moon regulates conception, it is itself the product of conception, being the representation of an 'embryo'. The waning and waxing (evoked respectively by the clandestine work in the mythical clearing, then by the theft of food), one of the main features of the lunar symbol, express this potentiality of gestation and growth. But the moon-dew, sometimes metaphorically called 'moon-sweat' (*wos na ehəge*), has to do with a fecundatory water which could just as well be a representation of cosmic semen as of uterine wetness.

As far as I know, no 'moon-house' seems to have existed in the ritual domain, and no rite is mentioned for taking the title of *wos na awaag*. All I was told about was one magical hunting rite, performed by the Master of the Moon in water that had gathered in

12. The association of the moon with the biological father is also found elsewhere in New Guinea: see, for instance, Gillison (1993) on the Highland Gimi.
13. For a similar myth, see Ballini 1983: 372–3.

Plate 28. Yangis: *Fuf* trumpet-players parading around the dancing ground while the masks dance.

the hollow of a *fənaw* sago stump, a variety that replaces the coconut palm in a number of rites.

The Masters of the Moon and the Sun seem to divide the procreating and feeding principles of the naturalistic maternal function between themselves: lunar gestation and cold *versus* solar breastfeeding and warmth. In this case more than in others, it is the representation that founds the religious office. The office is so much a part of the representation that it can no longer be said to be ritual. The custodians of the sun and the moon are the personifications of these heavenly bodies in society, but this does not endow them with a material or political responsibility. They secretly carry within themselves the hidden meaning of their duties without being able to discuss them. All they know is that they are the secret bearers, in the continuity of their lineage, of a 'cosmic sign', of which they are the social equivalents. Here the ritual office is very clearly the product of the representation and does not precede it.

Next, in order of importance, come the *sawôg seeg na awaag*, the Master of the Fish Magic Plant, an office, I was told, reserved from time immemorial for the Tawank lineage of the Angwaneri moiety. This position no doubt used to consist in a relation of identity with the aquatic domain, but more particularly, by directing the Waw rite (described pp. 87–9), performed with the participation of other clans, for the renewing of fish and frogs (sometimes sago palms and their edible grubs are also mentioned). The Tawank, via their master, also used to entertain a privileged relationship with the non-human *angor* spirits of the river and guardians of water animals. Today, as the rite is no longer performed and the Tawank are reduced to two men and two women (from another line than that of the former ritual master), it is hard to tell if this Master of the Fish used to carry out other rituals or possessed and transmitted a body of knowledge that went with his office. He probably decided the time for the Waw celebration, as well as other rites associated with the *angor* spirits. Yet, in Chapter 3, we saw that Waw was primarily a collective undertaking. Here too the office is more the personification of an ecological category than a concrete authority, even when restricted to the field of ritual.

It is possible to pair off Wiyneri lineage (Angwaneri moiety) ritual duties with those of the Tawank in a Water/Fire opposition. I cannot, however, confirm this relationship on ethnographic grounds, and therefore prefer to regard them as independent. The Yafar call this ritual expert *Wiy na awaag*. Wiy is believed to be the name of an ancestor beyond genealogical record (it is effectively used as a male name), who inaugurated this office and gave his name to the lineage. One day, he is said to have miraculously rekindled a fire that was nearly extinguished, and today the man who bears this title (in fact the responsibility is shared by two cousins) is the only one who may light the torches (*wikəga*, term in which the root *wi(y)* is found + *kəga(ag)* 'sticks, branch') used in night-time ceremonies where light may not be carried to begin with. Behind the image of light springing from darkness or of the nearly extinguished fire bursting into an unhoped for flame, there is – according to my informant and friend, May Promp – the idea of coming back to life, expressed in parallel by the image of a sleeping face whose eyes suddenly open, giving new life to the whole body.[14] Moreover, the Wiyneri are also called *Wiy noofuk êri* (*noofuk* 'eyes'). It is for this sort of wonder, of light springing forth in the night, that this lineage and their Wiy Master are responsible.

The office of *fag seeg na awaag*, the Master of the (*fag*) Arrow Magic Plant, used to be held by Menaneri and Tawank (also of the female moiety) lineages, and their members were called *fag seeg na hmonik* (*hmon* or *hmonik* 'classificatory fathers'). More directly a part of group life, the role of the Master of Arrow Magic was to protect the young murderer who had committed his first homicide from 'ripening', the weakening caused to his *sungwaag*, his self, by contact with the victim's blood (see Chs 12 and 14).

Just as the Tawank enjoyed privileged relations with the water spirits, the Ifêaroog have or used to maintain close ties with the male *nabasa* spirits, considered to be the guardians of game. Even though this clan belongs to the male moiety, it is also supposed to have been responsible for the female *sawangô* spirits; but two generations ago, the master transferred this part of his duties to his sister's son, from Amisneri clan (female moiety), who in turn passed it on to his agnatic descendants. Today it is still this '*nabasa* master' who directs ritual operations at the opening of a new ceremonial cycle dedicated to these spirits and who presides over the building of the '*nabasa* house' (p. 186). The counterpart

14. May Promp also made an association with *seeing* game; but I do not know if the Wiyneri had any rite for improving hunters' eyesight or visual attention.

Plate 29. Yangis: Two men playing the big trumpets *sawye-fuf* with the five *fuf* players.

of this role in Amisneri is no longer represented, as the ceremonial cycle for the *sawangô* had already been abandoned before
the colonial administration was installed at Amanab.

I will end this list of the most significant religious responsibilities by referring the reader to the role played by certain
lineage representatives at the founding of a hamlet. Let us recall
that the title of hamlet co-founder, with the symbolic status
defined in Chapter 1, falls to a particular man and is transmitted
if possible in the same patriline.[15]

In so far as it is feasible, all the offices described above are
kept in the same male line and passed on preferentially from
father to eldest son. The younger son inherits the charge if the
elder is not deemed qualified, but more often he shares some of
the knowledge and duties with his brother: in this case he is
introduced into this assistantship more by his elder brother than
directly by his father. On the other hand, the responsibility must
never be passed to the younger brother's son, and if a younger
brother takes on an office, for example following the death of
his elder brother, succession in the next generation reverts to the
elder line if it is not extinct. Sometimes, for want of direct male
descendants or if the son is still too young when his father dies,
the charge passes to one of the sister's sons (providing he belongs
to the same moiety), but it is supposed to be returned to the
legitimate line when the son reaches adulthood. If the legitimate
line dies out, that of the sister's son or a collateral agnatic line
(possibly another lineage of the same submoiety or moiety)
acquires the office. The sister's son is usually only a stage in the
patrilineal transmission and contents himself with receiving the
esoteric knowledge, fearing to take on the actual ritual duties.

A distinction must be made between these modes of succession and the fact of sharing a ritual function. An office may be
shared between siblings or agnates for the performance of the
same rite, or such sharing may be made necessary, as I indicated
above, by the scission of the local group for the performance of
Yangis (*oof na awaag* and *bǝte na awaag*). In the last cases, different

---

15. See Ch. 3 (p. 86) for the hunting rites attached to certain patrilineages. There are
surely other ritual roles connected with specific lineages. For example, in Yangis, the figure
of the *abi* wildfowl, which appears alone in the village square in the middle of the second
night during the sacred songs, is the exclusive responsibility of a female moiety lineage.
According to the myth, this bird heralds the dawn and birth of the *ogomô*.

lineages of the same moiety are usually chosen for their place of residence, and at the same time the choice of the most qualified persons is made according to psychological criteria. Here is how the principal offices have been transmitted over the last few generations.

I. Ritual experts by local group (hamlets):
1) *Oof na awaag,* Master of the Sky:
   - Yafar 1: see Figure 38.
   - Yafar 2: see Figure 39.
   - Yafar 3: this office was held two generations ago by an Ifêaroog line, and it is said then to have passed to an Ifêêg line, even though there was a descendant in Ifêaroog. As Yafar 3 hamlet was still new, it seems in fact that the Ifêaroog had the office of *nabasa na awaag* (see p. 83) and that the Ifêêg Master of the Sky was initiated into his duties by the Sumneri or the Fuwaneri when Yafar 3 was founded. This hypothesis is confirmed by the case of the Yafar 3 Master of the Earth.
2) *Bəte na awaag,* Master of the Earth:
   - Yafar 1: see Figure 40.
   - Yafar 2: see Figure 41.
   - Yafar 3: The present Master of the Earth is a man from the immigrant Yafwayneri line (originally from Potayneri), who received his office from the Yafar 1 Biyuneri when Yafar 3 was founded.

II. Ritual experts for the whole society:
1) *Akba na awaag,* Master of the Sun:
   This office falls to Wamawneri clan as the founding clan of the ('male') Araneri moiety; it has been in the same elder line for the last four generations. As the father of the present master was too young at the death of his own brother, the interregnum was filled by a cousin from Fuwaneri clan, which is considered a younger 'agnatic' group of the Wamawneri (see myth, pp. 80).
2) *Wos na awaag,* Master of the Moon:
   This office belongs to Bwaseri clan, of the ('female') Angwaneri moiety. The last master, who died in 1981, left only a daughter, and the other branches of the clan were already extinct. The succession does not seem to have been decided and the office is in danger of disappearing. There

Plate 30. Yangis (Punda 1986): Shooting the arrows at the sun at the end of the ritual: on the right, the *anuwanam*; on the left one of the two *ifegê* in red ochre body paint (Photo Niles, National Research Institute collection, Cultural Studies Division, Port Moresby).

too in the +1 generation an interregnum master had to be provided for several years, and the 'brother' (purported agnation) Biyuneri clan stepped in.

3) *Sawôg seeg na awaag*, Master of the Fish Magic Plant: This office used to be held by Tawank clan, today extinct. It was not passed on to the still viable collateral lineage and has since disappeared.

4) *Wiy na awaag*, Master of the Torch: see Figure 42.

5) *Fag seeg na awaag*, Master of the Arrow Magic Plant: Office shared between a Menaneri line (the Menaneri are extinct) and a Tawank line.

To transmit knowledge, to teach, is *susno feg* or *mô ogfunagêg* ('to pass on the word') or simply *mô sihyaag* ('to speak the word'), and the position of teacher and the one taught are expressed by terms already examined in the preceding chapters, *asagyam* and

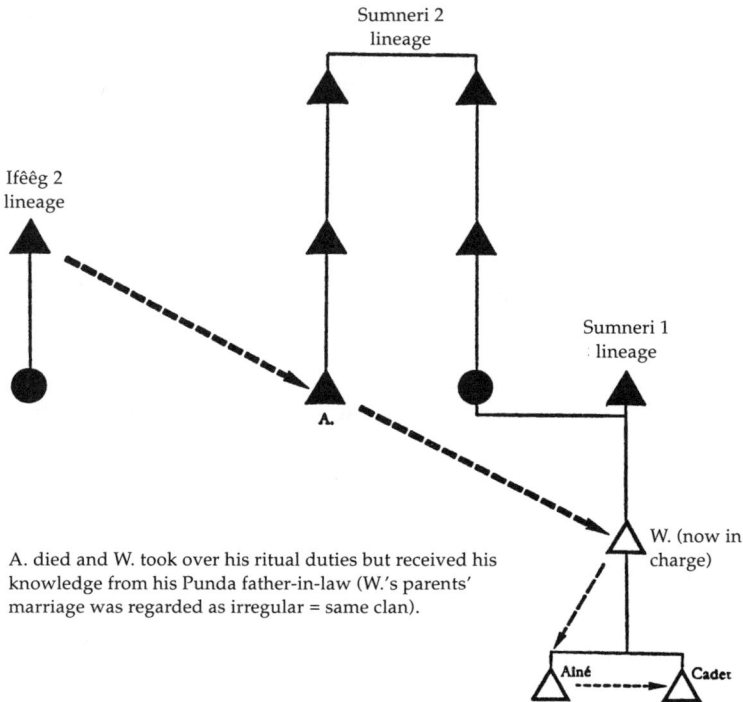

Figure 38. Transmission of the office of Master of the Sky in Yafar 1

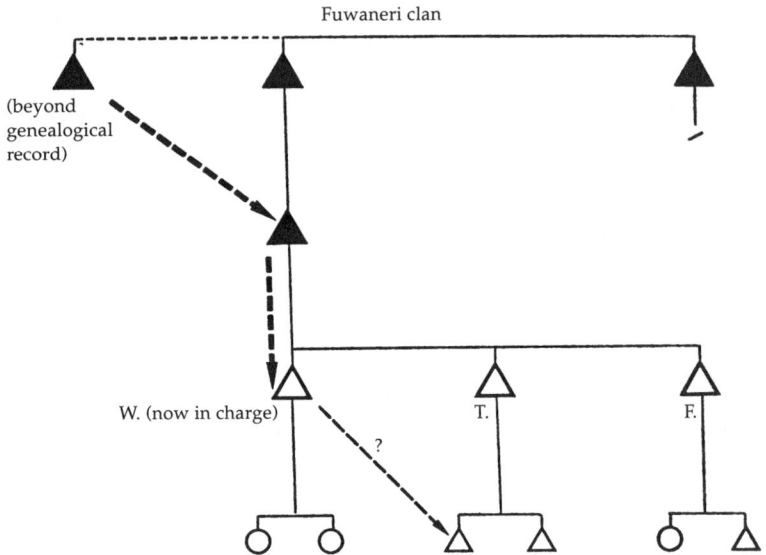

Fuwaneri clan

(beyond
genealogical
record)

W. (now in charge)

T.

F.

?

T. and F. do not share the knowledge and duties of their elder, W., so that they may continue to serve their local group as the excellent hunters they are (they own the one gun in the hamlet): an example of incompatibility between esoteric knowledge and cynegetic efficacy.

Figure 39. Transmission of the office of Master of the Sky in Yafar 2

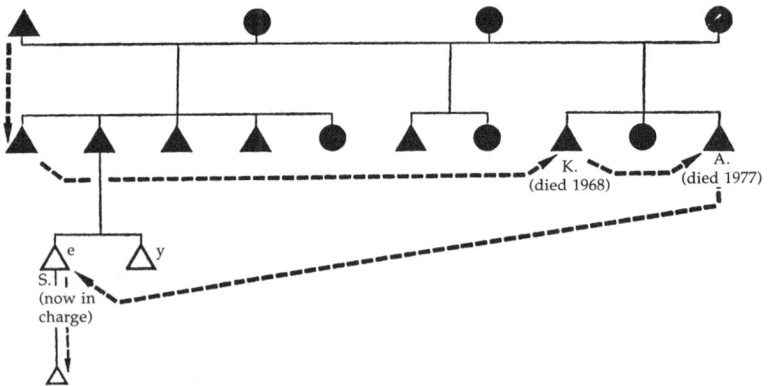

K.
(died 1968)

A.
(died 1977)

e

y

S.
(now in charge)

Figure 40. Transmission of the office of Master of the Earth in Yafar 1 (Biyuneri lineage)

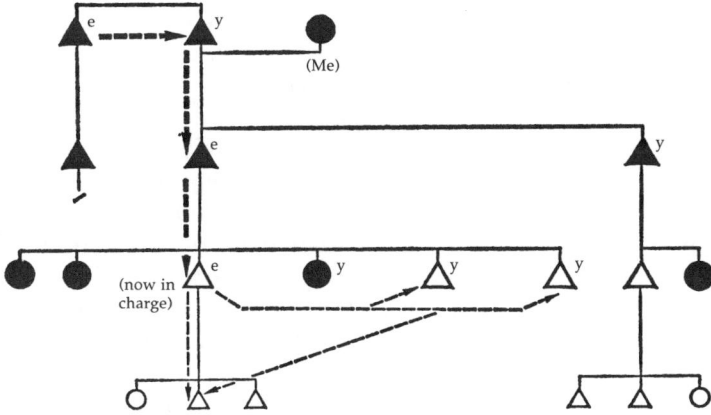

Figure 41. Transmission of the office of Master of the Earth in Yafar 2 (Sig-aynaag lineage, immigrated from Punda following a marriage with the Menaneri)

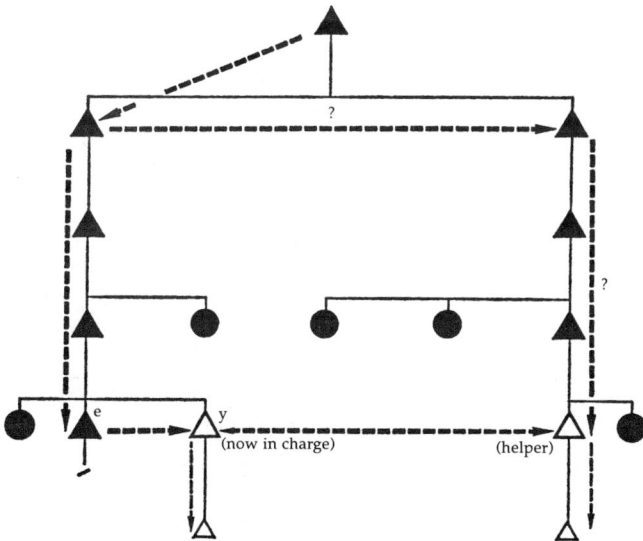

Case of an office shared by both lines of the patrilineage, although the younger line (normally forbidden) seems, in each generation, to have received part of the responsibilities collaterally from the cousins of the elder branch.

Figure 42. Transmission of the office of Master of the Torch (Wiyneri lineage)

anuwanam: *asagyam anuwanam susno fe na* 'the initiate teaches the novice'. Someone who acquires a ritual responsibility says that he 'takes (receives) the word', *mô fwag* (*ate ka mô fwak* 'I took a religious office'). Secret knowledge, the concealed word itself, is termed *kêfutuk mô* 'hard (strong) words', or *kêg mô* 'bone words', more rarely *önguk mô* 'black words', while the profane mythic tale is merely *mô bêhêk* 'empty words'. The knowledge of the Masters of the Sky and the Earth, particularly concerning the reproduction of the sago palms (Yangis) and plant *hoofuk*, is defined as *yis hoofuk* 'sago-jelly *hoofuk*'. In fact all esoteric knowledge is connected with the idea of *hoofuk* (Ch. 9), or more specifically with the image of the yam tuber, which represents 'truth', as opposed to its runners, image of the altered public versions of the myth.[16] This brings us back once more to the opposition between *hoofuk* and *taf* ('blood'): because of his knowledge, the ritual expert carries an excess of the sacred, and his cognitive proximity with the original *hoofuk* distances him from 'blood', in other words from hunting. As a consequence, esoteric knowledge and hunting are antithetical, which makes the main religious leaders say they cannot be good hunters, and good hunters say they prefer not to know anything about the *kêfutuk mô*. Sometimes this results in shunting the succession off to one of the legitimate heirs' collaterals, as he himself is 'too good a hunter', and therefore of greater use to the community in this economic function than as a recipient of esoteric knowledge. This is particularly the case for those who own a gun. His hunting activity being thus restricted, the ritual expert is provided with game by his younger brothers. This antagonism is expressed by the saying *kêg môm ne hêgêf, sês mabiyik* 'If you listen to (learn) the sacred words, you will no longer find game'. In effect, the *nabasa* game purveyors see the ritual masters' *sungwaag*, their sleep walker, as white (the appearance of *hoofuk*, of which they possess the secret knowledge) and not blood red. They turn away from it, while the dogs of these forsaken hunters will themselves devour the game they have tracked.

The transfer of the function is not marked by any ritual, perhaps because the office-holder is not himself held to be sacred; the master is not vested with a divine power nor haloed in charisma, he simply begins exercising a responsibility that derives its sacred nature from the knowledge which underpins it and

16. See 'Introduction' to *Œdipe chasseur* (Juillerat 1991a).

Plate 31. Parade of the masks at the end of the Yangis-Gungwan-Gêpôk cycle; the *ogosôk* (the one who walks in the lead) receives the bow and arrow symbolizing full masculinity and autonomy.

which gives the rite its meaning. Unlike an ordinary man, he knows the hidden meaning of the tradition he discharges; this is how he communicates directly with the realm of the sacred, but he remains at all times a layman. He is merely a mediator of the supernatural, and this mediation goes through the knowledge he receives from the preceding generation and which he will one day convey to the next. Knowledge of the myths and the exegesis of the ritual, although a necessary condition of access to the mastership of fertility, not only does not make the holder himself sacred, it increases his fragility by placing him in contact with the primordial forces, and more particularly with the cosmic deities or what remains of them, like the original female blood which is supposed to fill the bowels of the earth. The man who knows the origin of things is more liable than the ignorant man to become a victim of this privileged relationship with the world, and the anxiety of those who organize Yangis, for example, contrasts with the relaxed pleasure the younger participants take in the ceremony. Contamination by the sacred is conceived as a 'ripening' of the *sungwaag* self (Ch. 12), which can lead to death, while simple violation of the secret can occasion a 'restriction of fertility' and production for the transgressor (death of small children, bad gardens, unsuccessful hunts, etc.).

The content of the secret knowledge is in theory the same for all ritual offices. In reality, however, it seems that there are many variants, and it is hard to say whether these are due to the way the secrets are transmitted within the lineage or to the specificity of the office. It is probably a combination of the two, but I have reason to suspect that the paucity of communication between clans in matters of the sacred and the partitioning characteristic of the management of esoteric knowledge may have a lot to do with the diversity of mythic variants and their exegeses.[17] Nevertheless, the differentiation between offices remains founded more on ritual than on knowledge alone. The elements of the tradition – with the exception of clan myths of origin (Ch. 3) – are not the property of any one group, and each line may have variations unknown to the others. Today probably no one man encompasses the entire corpus of knowledge, thus corresponding to the image of 'the tree standing alone' (*mungwô rii ogo*), which describes such individual mastery.

17. This may be one of the factors explaining the lack of coherence in the religious corpus of Melanesian societies. Interclan rivalry for the control of knowledge and the resulting secrecy engender a diversity of versions and the absence of a unique 'dogma'.

How is this knowledge actually taught? There are two explanations which both contradict and complete each other. Some
maintain that the master of a charge starts transmitting what he
knows bit by bit to his son as soon as the latter marries. Others
say that only part of the exegetical corpus is communicated
in this informal manner and that the rest is taught more rapidly when the 'master' grows old and his successor is already a
mature man with children. Nevertheless it seems that global and
immediate learning over a few days or weeks is envisaged only
when replacing a ritual expert who has died suddenly without
having had time to train his disciple. In 1977, the Yafar 1 Master
of the Earth died at the age of fifty or so; as he had not completed
his successor's preparation, the latter received the remainder of
his education over a few days, so I was told, from the lips of the
Master of the Sky.[18] In other words, accelerated teaching seems
the practice above all when the teacher is not the predecessor.

Non-Inherited Religious Duties

The esoteric knowledge of religious experts is theoretically
supposed to be uttered only at the time of transmission and
otherwise remain hidden away in the memory of its custodians.
In practice, however, certain pieces of information filter horizontally to men who do not and never will hold an inherited
responsibility, but who are nevertheless deemed trustworthy by
one or another of the official keepers of the tradition. It seems
that these 'leaks' are perfectly controlled by the custodians, and
thereafter by the beneficiaries, who may in turn let something
filter to yet a third party. Whatever the case may be, every adult
male – especially if he is married and has fathered children –
knows something, sometimes very little but something, about the
origin myths and the exegesis of Yangis or other rituals. But what
exactly does he know? It is impossible to say for certain, for
everyone is conscious of his responsibilities as co-holder of a
piece of the secret and fears the supernatural sanctions that

18. This Master of the Sky had himself received his knowledge from his Punda father-
in-law, which goes to show that in spite of the partitioning of the knowledge held by lineages, there is often a break in agnatic continuity. This example points up the difference
between succession to power and the formal transmission of knowledge.

might hamper his prosperity were he to betray the secret. Despite the unequal distribution of knowledge and the reproduction of a certain elite within the male community then, there is an ongoing complicity that opposes men to women, who, the men contend, are ignorant and lacking in judgment.

Can these controlled 'leaks' from man to man give rise to less-controlled leaks in the direction of the women? It seems inevitable, although these are probably limited to isolated fragments of knowledge or sequences from myths or watered-down elements of exegesis, the moderate sacredness of which is judged not very dangerous. Furthermore older women are more likely to have a few secrets confided to them by a close male relative, especially if they have acquired a certain status by the force of their personality. It would be interesting to know to what extent this partial knowledge, once in the female community, circulates among the women and whether it gives rise to modifications or reformulations 'in the feminine'. On this point I can only note a lack of information, but it can be postulated that the women will hide from the men this portion of the sacred patrimony which they have managed to purloin, as it were. It should not be forgotten that in the past severe punishments, sometimes death, could be meted out to women who violated the law of male monopoly.

The communication of religious information depends partly on the personality of the individuals. On this basis, a sort of hierarchy of knowledge develops which is partly a hierarchy of 'outstanding personalities'. The correspondence between the two scales of value appeared so clear to me that the social conditions of the distribution and transmission of knowledge must be grounded in an assessment of a psychological order. The Yafar judge each other as individuals and assign each other corresponding statuses. Kinship plays a fundamental role on this level, but it alone cannot explain the overall system.

Knowledge goes hand in hand with its application in ritual, which is why anyone who has managed to pick up part of the secret cultural tradition tries to put it to use by taking on comparable responsibilities. Conversely, a man who would play a prominent role on the socio-religious stage must first secure access to the corresponding knowledge. To this end, he often takes the initiative of secretly questioning a renowned *aynaag* or a master in his own kinship circle.

These non-inherited ritual roles, ranging from the young adolescent to the official master, are highly varied and cannot all be listed here. They go from individual interventions, such as the lowly healing exercises consisting of simple chants and manipulations of cultivated magic plants that can be done by anyone or agrarian rites performed in a garden clearing, to the highly sacralized backstage roles in Yangis or other collective rituals which can be described as non-inheritable assistantships to the officiating master of the same moiety. While some men collect knowledge about the hunting ritual (*seeg abuk*), others are known for their expertise in horticultural rites (*aso seeg* or *aso hoofuk*). There is no clearcut opposition between the two, however, and each man learns about both domains at once, the opposition – expressed by the terms *sês* (game)/*aso* (garden) or *taf* (blood)/ *hoofuk* – being more symbolic than social. The most important rites of the *seeg abuk* (literally 'ripe magic plant') category are shared stintingly and consist in making 'ripe game appear' (see Ch. 7, p. 184). As far as plants are concerned, a certain knowledge of cultivated species is necessary to be able to organize an individual planting rite. The most common, Wabuminaag (see Ch. 6, pp. 161–2), is known by nearly all men over forty; when it is performed by a group for multifamily clearings, an experienced cultivator gathers together all the botanical specimens, magic plants and planting sticks, but he may leave the role of first planter (the one who is the first to thrust his digging stick into the freshly cleared ground) to someone else, who is *asagyam* in this task, providing he knows enough about the exegesis of the rite to make it effective. Simply reciting the spells is not enough, therefore: the operation needs to be controlled cognitively through deeper knowledge and intense concentration on the part of the officiant. The most secret rite, *aso seeg* (p. 162), is performed without witnesses and is known by only a few men, who pass on their knowledge to certain select relatives.

There was a Punda ancestor who did not drink and did not wash. The sun was hot and it did not rain, all the vegetation disappeared. Another man came and told him that he must drink and wash. He drank, and a light rain began to fall. Then he washed, and the rain fell harder.[19]

---

19. The identification of figures with a natural element seems to be the basis of the inherited 'masterships' as well. It is probable that these offices entail prohibitions concerning fire and water.

As this short account shows, there is another domain that lends itself nicely to the assumption and transmission of a ritual tradition not restricted to an inherited office, and that is weather. Two opposing effects may be sought: to make it rain or to make it stop raining. Imbalances in the natural distribution of dry and wet periods are believed to be the consequence of social disorders, of faults committed, in the area of ritual in particular. In the past, it was thought that immoderate use of water (washing,[20] drinking) could bring on heavy rains. Today people still believe that accidentally uprooting or stripping the leaves of a magic rain-making plant or mixing sago and coconut (antagonism and complementarity of the two gendered totemic species) sets off torrential rains, which are the manifestation of an excess of fertility. But in another mode of thought, persistent rain or drought are also attributed to the magic of neighbouring tribes who cast spells because they are ahead with their clearing, or have already finished burning, or again as a simple revenge on certain neighbours.

While humble individual rites (plants chewed and spat in the direction of an impending storm) can be performed by any man without danger, only certain *aynaag* accept the risks to their physical health entailed by the identification with the natural elements inherent in the more complex procedures. To call down rain or to drive it away is, in effect, to implicate oneself in a delicate manipulation of natural forces, to expose oneself to an excess of humidity (rotting) or dryness (weight loss and dehydration). The man who has this courage and risks his health for the common good derives a certain prestige from his daring. For the hamlet of Yafar 1, the only man who controls this ritual from beginning to end is the Master of the Sky. But it seems that he took on this additional responsibility over and above his inherited office. The magic ingredients used vary with the officiant's moiety. The *aynaag* of the female moiety will refer more often in his spells to 'the water of the coconut palm or of the goddess B. . .', while the Araneri officiant will evoke 'the water of the *afwêêg* sago palm and of the god W. . .'.

---

20. As far as washing goes, it used to be feared that bodily 'filth' abandoned to the river and the Mother Earth might anger the latter; only (fertile) young men and women could allow themselves to do this. Dirt, associated with the idea of *arfêêg* (sloughed skin) or *roofuk* (skin), is thus the antithesis of (maternal-terrestrial) *hoofuk*.

Below is a summary of the rain-making rite and two variants of the rite for stopping rain.

1) Rite for making rain (Araneri moiety)
The officiant works alone, without witnesses. He uproots a *hêêg bomgway* plant (*Homalomena* sp. clone), pronouncing the appropriate spells (this clone is the embodiment of rain). He wraps it up in a bundle with some *waba* bark (*Octomeles sumatrana*, a tree that grows near water) and some leaves of the Araneri totemic sago palm, *afwêêg*. Then, painted from head to toe with charcoal (in all likelihood to protect himself from this excess of humidity by a 'dry' substance), the man sits down in a stream, holding the bundle to his chest, with only his head out of the water. He chants 'Let the *waba* water appear, let the *afwêêg* water appear, let my *waba* water appear, etc.' Then 'let the water of my hips appear, let the water of my mouth appear, let the stormy sky appear. . . Let Wabuminaag's[21] penis water appear. . . May's children are hungry [other villages are named].' Then he washes his head: 'Water of the head *rurururu*, water of the nape of the neck . . .' The bundle is left in a deep hollow in the river until it rains. If later it rains too much, the bundle will be placed under the roof of the officiant's house, in the smoke coming from the fireplaces.

2) Rites to stop the rain (Araneri moiety)
a) Some earth taken in secret from the village, some red ochre, certain flowers and herbs, and the claws of two small birds are made up into a bundle. While doing this, the officiant says 'Stop! Stop the trunk water,. . .the branch water,. . .the stump water,. . .the river-clay water,. . .the *ahômp Ficus* water, etc.' Then he lists the names of the rivers and calls on them to stop flowing. The bundle is then placed under the roof of the house to dry, accompanied by spells such as 'Nenenene! (< *neheg* 'to bind', or *nehef* 'impeded, stopped'), stop the sky water. . .stop the coconut-trunk water. . . stop W's water. . .stop the flow of sago from the *afwêêg*, etc.' When the sun has returned and blazes down from on high, the officiant holds up the bundle and continues chanting. He keeps the ingredients at home and, if the drought persists too long, he will put the bundle back in the river (see rite no. 1).
b) All the inhabitants, except the *Oof na awaag* and his wife, leave the village. The man wraps up some of his wife's and his own pubic hairs with magic plants while saying 'Blue sky, black-cloud sago,

---

21. A myth shows this clearing sprite thrusting his digging stick into the ground. Local exegesis identifies the stick as his penis; planting becomes fecundation of the earth.

drizzle sago, penis-hair sago, vulva-hair sago, etc.' Then, standing beside his wife, he raises the bundle and 'stops' the different 'waters' and their persistent flow, symbolized by the claws of the various birds he names. Here too, the bundle is kept under the roof in the warmth of the home fires.

We see that rain is viewed as a male or female fecundating water, and that once again it is through the conjunction of the symbolized sexes that dryness and wetness are to be controlled. At the disposal of any experienced male, these rain-making and rain-stopping rites should theoretically be the responsibility of the representatives of the two moieties, not because dryness and wetness correspond to the two sexual poles, but because both partake of maleness and femaleness at the same time. Atmospheric balance is thus conceptualized as the optimal dosing of fertility and sterility.

Mediums
We have already seen medium possession in the context of hunting (Ch. 7). We will now examine the role and status of mediums[22] as mediators of a more familiar sacred world. In every Eri hamlet, it is the function of one or two men to allow themselves to be possessed by forest spirits, to whom they are believed to lend their 'skin' (*roofuk*). To promise animals, to receive presents from the hunter who has killed a pig or cassowary, to pronounce a diagnosis for an illness by identifying the category of spirit responsible, to give information on why a domestic pig has disappeared and where it can be found, or on the participation of a specific *nabasa* in the ceremony under preparation, such are the usual motives for the bush spirits' visits. In most cases, the visiting *nabasa* does not reveal his identity, or does so only if he is asked, and the close kin of the deceased take no special interest in his presence. This seems to be due to the fact that a dead person's spirit is not vested with the deceased's personality but represents a more abstract entity incorporated into a specific piece of land and into the natural environment as a whole. The economic and symbolic importance of hunting has raised the cult of guardian spirits of game above the worship of dead ancestors. The Eri medium is not a shaman, he does not

22. There is no Amanab term for medium. He is called the one in whom the *nabasa* 'rise up' (*fukô*).

work cures or travel in the hereafter: he is a simple 'vessel' for the spirits, the body into which they have chosen to 'rise up' in order to speak with the living, and is not regarded as possessing any special power.

After a violent shaking fit, shouting and arching his body, the medium receives or goes to fetch his bow and arrows and goes through a series of violent actions (he takes aim at his companions, shoots an arrow or two at the hunter's house), then begins to speak while vigorously smoking and chewing betel; at this point he uses a special, conventional vocabulary familiar to everyone. The seances usually take place in the evening, always in the village and preferably out of doors; they last between twenty and ninety minutes. Several mediums may enter a trance at once, but each is possessed by a single spirit at a time, although one medium may undergo several successive possessions.

The first trances appear when the individual is between the ages of twenty and thirty, and most often during the Nabasa *hug-ufa obô* rite ('to seize and bring the spirits'), that is at the opening of a ceremonial cycle dedicated to the *nabasa* in the context of the hunting cult (p. 186). The men go down to the river to call the *nabasa* by means of the appropriate rite, then bring them back to the village to usher them into the 'spirit house', which has been freshly built for the new cycle. At the riverside, the known mediums are the first to become possessed, sometimes followed by one or two novices who thus self-induce their first trance; all carry the spirits, in their bodies, back to the sacred enclosure. After his first trance, the medium retains the role for the rest of his life. In the past, there also used to be a few female mediums, possessed for the most part by female *sawangô* spirits.[23]

It is important for our purposes to grasp the opposition, with regard to social status, between fertility masters and mediums. Whereas the former acquire prestige through their knowledge and ritual responsibilities, the latter have no particular status, since their role is not founded on knowledge, apprenticeship or initiation. In fact their own identity is supposed to be effaced during the medium seance. They are supposed to be the involuntary and unwitting mediators of the spirits, who have the good

23. For more information on Eri (Amanab) mediumism and trances, see Juillerat 1975a, 1975b. For other examples of mediumism and shamanism in New Guinea, see Herdt 1989, Juillerat (ed.) 1977, Knauft 1989 and Lory 1981–82. For details on relations with spirits in the southern part of the Border Mountains, see Huber 1973, 1975.

or bad fortune (opinion is divided) to have been chosen, nor do they derive any particular benefit from this election other than a few gifts of food and betel. And even this slight advantage is denied by the native theory of possession, which claims that only the spirit feeds, leaving the medium with an empty stomach.

According to the Yafar, then, there are on the one hand, ritual masters with occult functions in contact with the most sacred entities, which endows them with implicit prestige, and on the other hand, mediums deprived of their free will during a trance, ordinary men of no outstanding position. However, if one disregards the local theory of possession and works instead with what is known about phenomena of mental dissociation, one is obliged to modify this opposition to some extent. The social role of the Yafar medium becomes no longer to establish communication passively between the spirits and the living, but to invent a discourse which, although the prisoner of a specific cultural model, is nonetheless renewed and improvised at each seance. From being non-existent, the medium's free will becomes the central phenomenon; from being a simple plaything of the spirits, the medium becomes a man who remains fully self-possessed, with an identity slightly masked by the trance when it is authentic, but totally intact if it is feigned or passes off rapidly. In this case, he is entirely free (and he alone knows it) to create situations, order healing ceremonies, make slight alterations in the number of masks by invoking the presence of a given spirit, bring to life someone recently deceased for a circle of close kin, indicate the home of a spirit on a piece of land (tree, someone's land, etc.), thus participating in updating the property map of the pantheon (Ch. 5), urge villagers to go hunting on a given piece of land and demand presents – a sort of cynegetic blackmail – of dainty dishes.[24] Yet mediums do not possess any specific knowledge, and their role is neither received nor passed on.

Ritual masters, on the other hand, bear an enormous responsibility for handing on the tradition and for the efficacy of rituals, but they have less latitude in the performance of their duties. They do not improvise discourses on the spirits or their relations with society and cannot shape the map of the forest deities or orient the dialogue between spirits and men. Their purview, further from the day to day, brings them into contact with de-

24. Clarke 1973; Devereux 1956; Schieffelin 1977.

personalized cosmic forces, spatially and genealogically remote, with which no dialogue is possible, whereas the medium's field of action is restricted to the tribal and even village territory and concerns the recently deceased and the non-human spirits familiar to hunters, which everyone encounters in their dreams. The ritual transmission of mythological knowledge certainly affords an occasion for the modification of details, for omissions and rectifications, the traditional matter appearing as a shifting narrative mass, but it may be assumed that these distortions are not deliberate and that they are certainly not part of a political strategy as is the case for mediums. What we have in reality, then is on the one hand, a prestigious position implicitly recognized by the community and based on a power and body of knowledge which have to do with controlling nature and the process of the reproduction of the world – but which does not include any direct management of mundane social reality – and on the other hand, ordinary men, with no special knowledge or status, but who, behind the misleading veil of the trance and the native theory of possession, conceal their no doubt limited but real power to organize certain aspects of social or ritual life and the forest space.

The real power of mediums is not recognized precisely because it is an integral part of their function and of the staged trance, and is thus overlooked and therefore tolerated by the group. As for the ritual masters, we shall see that the political power they do exercise lies outside their religious function and is a by-product of the status which derives from being a ritual master.

From Religious Office to Political Authority

Authority as coercive power over others is founded on status, personality and kinship ties. I will not dwell on the last area, which is obvious and has already been examined. These three factors are usually combined into a single attitude of authority, and all three must be considered conjointly to explain how relations of authority work in an 'egalitarian' and 'acephalous' society like the Yafar.

The only recognized *de jure* authority is based on the kinship system, in which the dominant figures are 'fathers' and 'mothers', elder 'brothers' and 'sisters', husbands and, to a lesser extent, mother's brothers. This type of authority is stable, permanent and self-reproducing.

A status authority emanates from the masters of fertility and their 'assistants'. In this case it is the prestige acquired through knowledge and ritual responsibilities which confers authority, a right to be listened to in areas of mundane life. The difference with kinship authority is that the authority flowing from mastership manifests itself more sporadically and especially on the occasion of disagreements or individual conflicts; the ritual master often steps in to reinforce the pressure a man is exerting on one of his younger siblings. The Masters of the Sky and the Earth can, more specifically, formulate their recriminations conjointly with regard to the man (more rarely the woman) who is held to be at fault; other men of lesser rank but respected can intervene in turn. Aside from mediating in open clashes, status authority comes into play mainly during the discussions which occupy the men most evenings in the village square. There is no question of giving and taking orders, nor of interfering in other people's families or in the organization of their work, but simply of influence, of a certain directive impact on the community that the position of ritual master plus a way with words allows him to exercise. The principal ritual masters often take the lead in collective expressions of anger, in which feelings are vented as much with the fighting stick as by the art of rhetoric (Ch. 14).

But some men manage to impose themselves on the group even if they do not have special responsibilities, and one also sees considerable differences in the temperament of those who occupy the front rank in a given hamlet. The example of Yafar 1, until 1977, is a good illustration. The dual power over the Sky and the Earth was split between two very different personalities. On the one hand, W. (Araneri moiety), a man of between 55 and 60, naturally authoritarian, highly sociable, always in the village square in the evening, voluble, respected for his opinions, somewhat quick to anger (a quality valued in a man), a good hunter and formerly active in the murder raids against neighbouring groups; on the other hand, A. (Angwaneri moiety), slightly younger, a man of few words, retiring, but listened to when he spoke, staging his expressions of anger more than truly living them, rather solitary, a good hunter and also the author of numerous successes during past homicide raids. These two men – one dictatorial, the other taciturn to a fault, one always at the centre of local group activities, the other most often marginal and discrete – nevertheless played out their complementary roles perfectly for years, even though there seemed to be no particular bond of friendship between them. Both were able to impose their views on the life of society and thus contribute to maintaining a community ethic. Nevertheless a 'diffuse authority' is also exercised in the local group outside the inherited ranks, and every man has a right to have his say. The difference is that those who hold ritual offices have more chance of being listened to. Their political authority is underpinned by their religious position. The latter does not officially give them access to the political field, but they are the ones – especially the Masters of the Sky and the Earth – whom the community expects to intervene when necessary to preserve the social order. In this way, they induce a certain respect which, in the area of public life, becomes an acceptance of hierarchy and of a temperate form of 'constraint'.

14

Bad Magic, Bow or Fighting Stick

> Bird of paradise (= woman)
> Keep stripping pith from the *yêêg* sago palm!
> Bird of paradise,
> Keep stripping pith from the *hôn* sago palm!
> I, the *yii* pigeon (= man), I watch the path,
> I, the *yii* pigeon, I keep watch along the path side.
> The Uhyay are preparing to attack,
> The Babuk are preparing to attack.
>
> (*Wesko* song)

We have come to a point in our analysis of Yafar society where it must now be clear to the reader just how important the role of relations between members of a kinship group is in constituting the ever-renewed dynamic web of social structure. Groups and the norms that provide the stable framework for their interaction exist, to be sure – these were defined at the beginning of the book – but they form a backdrop to personal relations, which constantly challenge them in their role as relevant operational units. A look at the mechanisms by which conflicts are brought out and resolved will cast a clearer light on this relationship, even though the overlapping of individual and collective references as well as the silence of informants on some matters may at times cloud our understanding of the facts.

For another society of the Border Mountains, Huber (1975) has interpreted the forms of conflict in terms of a fundamental opposition between inside and outside. When bringing intergroup relations into the understanding of the social dialectic of security, trust, violence or revenge, the articulation between self and other appears in effect to be central, but clearly it is advisable to identify the line of demarcation or, more precisely, the multiple lines of cleavage. For societies like those of the Border Mountains, where intertribal warfare almost never occurs and where there are no enemies or allies at the group level, any act of violence, whether or not it stems from a conflict, partakes of a relationship between individuals who are members of groups whose relationship does not have an absolute value: in other words, the value is not the same for all members of the groups. In Chapter 10, I showed how a man or his clan were related through earlier marriages to only some of the members of certain neighbouring tribes. This means that the line between the inside and outside of the kinship group does not fall in the same place for everyone, and when in the past the Yafar had recourse to violence, they had to consider these facts in addition to whether or not they were dealing with their own social or spatial unit, local group, agnatic group, tribe (territory), tribes related by marriage, strangers (*angôruwaag*), not to mention in the latter case *sêh* exchange partners and 'symbolic affines' (Chs 8 and 10). The three modes of aggression announced in the title of this chapter are inscribed in the double framework constituted by kinship networks and oppositions between relative inside and outside. More specifically, Yafar ideology identifies sorcery (bad magic) and killing as addressing the outside and above all as coming from outside the tribe (related or unrelated non-Yafar groups), and ritual stick fights as the appropriate way of settling conflict within the tribe. While this last type of confrontation is effectively reserved for resolving differences between Yafar and for expressing collective anger at the local-group level, we shall see that sorcery and murder did not always occur exclusively between tribes. Nevertheless, killing and sorcery, as forms of violence within the tribal community or the local group, arose from a specific conflict in which the victim was a particular person, usually himself suspected of sorcery; alternatively, violence between neighbouring tribes and between distantly related or non-related individuals could erupt independently of any immediate conflict or be triggered by non-personalized suspicions, and be aimed at a scapegoat.

After more than twenty years of government administration,[1] the Yafar now rarely resort to institutionalized violence to settle their grievances. Intertribal raids have ceased entirely and the plants once used for sorcery have, by mutual agreement, been destroyed. Only the fighting sticks still serve, though rarely, as an

---

1. At the beginning of the 1980s, when this book was written. Since then, internal dissension has once more broken out (Juillerat 1993).

accompaniment to shouting matches. People now feel relatively secure (except with respect to presumed sorcery) about neighbours or outsiders, and they respect the law of the land; but they also miss the time not so long ago when life afforded moments of daring and danger, which men now relate with a mixture of passion and good humour.

Bad Magic and its Techniques

In contrast to the relatively well-defined roles I described in discussing the powers of fertility, Yafar men dispose of other, negative powers capable of causing sickness and death in a more informal and, one might say, more democratic fashion. These practices – largely abandoned today, though still credible for those involved – which are usually filed under the heading of sorcery, comprise two categories, *agi* and *aysiri*; the first is divided into a number of different pathogenic techniques, the second is the only one supposedly capable of bringing about the death of the victim.

In both cases, the sorcerer or sorcerers work in secret and derive no reputation from their deeds. Women and adolescent boys do not have access to sorcery but may solicit the services of kinsmen. Before analysing the sociological aspects, let us first look at what goes into these techniques.

Agi Techniques

The term *agi* designates a negative symbolic category, a power that some men, more particularly in certain tribes (if one takes the Yafar point of view), succeed in employing for the purpose of inflicting harm on others through the use of a variety of techniques. This dangerous force, personalized by the Yafar under the name of Sfayow,[2] is supposed to appear occasionally in dreams as a plume of smoke rising skywards and surrounded by flames, or a cordyline with red, smoke-edged leaves: a phallic power, it could be said, associated with fire and the colour red, the dream

---

2. Sfayow is the proper name of the Yafar's only *agi*, whereas the neighbouring tribes have a variety of *agi*. In certain tribes it seems that there are several *agi* controlled by different men and transmitted through the mediation of specific magic clones.

vision of which announces an impending illness or informs a sufferer that his malady is caused by an *agi* spell. The appropriate healing rite uses a large cordyline with small green leaves edged in red called *Sfayow na rig* 'Sfayow's straight stem', which draws up the illness, thus exorcizing the patient; the stem is kept in a secret place and handled (avoiding direct contact with the skin) by the last two patients who, immunized as it were, no longer fear contamination. It is these two men, the latest *agi* victims, who preside over the rite: carrying the *Sfawoy na rig* above their heads and their bodies painted red, they draw the evil to themselves, then rid themselves of it with no harm done by bathing and remaining in the forest for a few days in order not to contaminate the others. Although personalized by a proper name, *agi* is not given as a spirit, is not localized and is not associated with the violation of taboos. Aside from its use by a human agent, *agi* can be attracted by talking about it or by uttering its name repeatedly, especially in the village, which is a 'hot' place. It is never mentioned in front of women or children, who are more vulnerable. Once the sick man has recovered, he assumes custodianship of the cordyline, which he secretly replants in an old, already harvested garden. The plant, however, is not used in the magic itself.

Under this slippery heading can be found various types of malevolent practices, each with its own variants. Here are a few of the most important.

a) *Agi wuf* or *wufôg*. The second term means 'to deposit leavings in an ill-omened place'. All variants of this practice include the use of such vestiges as remains of a meal or tobacco, betel juice or cigarette butts (sago, bodily secretions or nail parings, hairs, etc. cannot be used). The best materials are those connected with eating – although footprints can also be used when combating garden thieves – and the best items are those that have actually come into contact with the mouth. The efficacy of rites using such leavings is based on a partial identification of the material with the person's *sungwaag* (self). The person casting the spell deposits the items at the foot of an 'evil' tree while reciting a spell[3] in which he enjoins the victim's *sungwaag* to come to this

3. 'Eat the fruits of the *Ficus wawr*, eat the coconut flowers, eat the *gwengwe* bird. . . Look for a place in your house [to go and die], go with the barking of the dog [ghosts bark at night in the forest], etc.' The foods mentioned are 'ghost foods' associated with the idea of premature falling or closeness to the maternal principle (p. 373).

spot and be contaminated. As these trees (the most dangerous of which is the small *saasa* palm, *Cycas circinalis*) are regarded as ghost foods, the practice must be seen as an attempt to hasten the *sungwaag*'s transformation into a ghost (*ifaaf*: pp. 389–90), that is, as an attempt to set in motion a death-dealing process which the healing rite can stop, but which the action of an *aysiri* sorcerer can, conversely, cause to be fatal. In this event, the victim may dream about ghosts, a sign that his *sungwaag* goes down to the world of the *ifaaf* while he is asleep and is beginning to identify with them. The ailments caused by *agi wuf* are 'hot' diseases, such as fevers (*əgih*) or running sores.

b) *Agi noof* (from *noof* 'eye, gaze'), an expression which can be translated literally as 'evil eye'. The Yafar often call this kind of sorcery *agi sêh* because they consider it to be a speciality of the Sowanda, whom they do not marry but among whom they have *sêh* exchange partners (Ch. 8). The sorcerer stares at his victim, concentrating and mentally reciting spells of the type used in *agi wuf*; he enjoins the *sungwaag* to go to the 'evil' trees or to have an accident (Ch. 12). The principle is the same, then, as in *agi wuf* in so far as the magical discourse and the authority relationship between the sorcerer and his victim's *sungwaag* are concerned. In both cases, the *sungwaag* is supposed to 'ripen' and therefore become vulnerable; it will then be spotted by an *aysiri* sorcerer and killed. *Agi noof* does not kill any more than *agi wuf* does, but it weakens the disembodied self, which then becomes the perfect prey for an *aysiri*.

Agi noof can be used to cause miscarriage; it is not, to my knowledge, used for deliberate abortion, but purely as a malevolent act, one, however, that does not place the woman herself in any danger. In this case, too, the muttered spells name the species of trees whose fruits fall before reaching maturity (see above and Ch. 12).[4]

c) *Agi pafig* (*pafig* 'to kindle or poke up a fire') or *sumwasəmu* (*sum* 'following'). The aim of this type of sorcery is to send an epidemic to neighbouring groups in retaliation for a presumed *aysiri* attack having caused someone's death. Some body fluid from the cadaver of the victim is collected at the *sengêri* (p. 413)

---

4. 'Fruit of the *Ficus wawr*, let go and fall! Fruit of the *sôba* tree, let go and fall!. . .' It sometimes happens that the sorcerer, who often acts on a close relative, has second thoughts; in this event he can undo the spells by replacing 'fall' with 'hold fast'.

and wrapped in leaves with a rhizome of *Acorus calamus* or *Curcuma* (*agi wahwe, agi gaf,* etc.), clones cultivated in secret. The bundle is then burned in a fire kindled with the leaves of this plant, while enjoining the evil to 'go to the Xs' or 'to eat the Xs.' The ghost of the deceased follows the cadaver's bundle and spreads the epidemic among the neighbours. The cadaver fluids are both a metonym for the ghost (its exuviae) and a metaphor of putrefaction: the epidemic will be a dysentery-like disorder accompanied or not by fever and a cough. *Agi pafig* comes under the heading of techniques of protection against *aysiri* sorcery.

d) *Agi suwê* (*suwê* 'fire'). This is a technique similar to *agi pafig*, except that the aim is not to set off an epidemic or to counter *aysiri* sorcery, but to rid one group of an epidemic by sending it back to those suspected of having caused it in the first place. A bamboo stake is burned, and the evil is supposed to leave it when it explodes. The spells uttered during the burning enjoin the sickness to leave the community and enter the group targeted, and more specifically the bodies of its members.

e) Use of '*agi* magic plants' (*awus agi*). We have already noted the use of *Curcuma longa* and true gingers, to which must be added *Acorus calamus* and *Homalomena* spp. The Yafar distinguish a great number of clones, all cultivated, for each of these species and they have a different ritual use for each. However, one of them, planted in secret places around the edges of clearings, is reserved for sorcery. Aside from the more complex operations described above, these plants can be simply mixed into food or buried alongside a path used by the victim.

As a rule, *agi* spells appeal to the notions of rotting (ghosts) and ripening (of the *sungwaag*). The aim is to engage the victim's self in an accelerated process leading to a natural sort of death. *Aysiri* sorcery, on the other hand, is a direct attack, a murder committed on the person of the individual or his disembodied *sungwaag*.

Aysiri Techniques

Aysiri designates the sorcerer as well as his acts. The Yafar do not split the term into lexical components, but for my part, I would single out the final segment (ê)*ri* 'man', so common in other Amanab words. As for the beginning of the word, I have found only one term which is close, but which should probably be regarded as a doublet since its meaning is not easily connected with actions performed by sorcerers: *aysu* 'crying out in pain'.

The *aysiri*'s power comes from a clone of one of a variety of magic plants (see above), most often an *Acorus calamus* (*gaf*), grown in secret and called *nefôkêg*. The Yafar provide no lexical information on this term either, although one might see a derivative of *noofuk* 'eye, gaze'. The *aysiri* uses this plant primarily to strengthen his gaze as he is about to release his arrow. The ending refers to *kêg* 'bone', in this case probably a rhizome.

The discussion of *agi* has already shown the importance of the notion of *sungwaag*: the magician acts while awake to influence his victim's *sungwaag*. In the case of *aysiri*, the sorcerer can either act deliberately, while awake, against a flesh-and-blood victim, or through the mediation of his disembodied self on his sleeping victim's *sungwaag*. Whence the two registers of *aysiri* sorcery: a) the real world, in which a man deliberately performs a malevolent act using one of the techniques described below; and b) the spirit or dream world, in which the process is carried out by an *aysiri*'s *sungwaag* while he sleeps (the unintentional character of this action does not exonerate the subject). Here we find Evans-Pritchard's classic distinction between sorcery and witchcraft, even though the difference lies not in the techniques but in the two levels: reality and the imaginary respectively. Furthermore the Yafar make a causal association between the acts of the *sungwaag* and those of the real sorcerer, following the familiar principle according to which the *sungwaag*'s actions determine in part those the individual will perform the following day. But they specify that one does not always see the *sungwaag aysiri* in a dream and that sometimes, one can dream of killing by *aysiri* without necessarily wanting to. The relation of cause and effect therefore remains purely philosophical.

The *aysiri* sorcerer does not actually cause the victim to 'ripen' (*sungwaag abuk*), but takes advantage as it were of his actual state of 'ripeness'. Thanks to his *nefôkêg*, the sorcerer has the power to see if his victim's *sungwaag* is *önguk* 'black' – that is strong and healthy – or, on the contrary, *abuk* 'ripe' and orangish-red (*sawik*), weakened by contamination from the original blood or by an *agi* attack.

In using the *nefôkêg*, which is a determinant for every *aysiri* action, different possibilities can be distinguished, and primarily two separate techniques. The Yafar usually describe an *aysiri* undertaking as follows. The sorcerer or sorcerers surprise their victim, usually in a lonely spot (clearing, forest) where he may be with his family. The *aysiri* holds a piece of *nefôkêg* clenched in his teeth, having tied some of its leaves to his bow and arrow. This makes the sorcerer and his weapons invisible to any witnesses who may be with the victim, but not to the latter, who is nevertheless incapable of crying out, paralysed by both the action of the *nefôkêg* and by fear. The oncoming arrow will therefore be visible to him, but will quickly vanish into his body without leaving a wound and without causing immediate death or incapacity: the wounded person will not dare say a word about what has happened for fear of retaliation and will go back home – not without having lost consciousness for a time – and die a few weeks later of illness. As he is about to die – and only at that moment – the victim may reveal that he has been killed by an *aysiri* and identify the sorcerer if he has recognized him (this is why *aysiri* act in secret as much as possible).

In a variant of this scenario – and this is the second technique – if the victim faints before or even after the arrow is shot, the sorcerer or sorcerers go ahead with the *sosoog-na uguwôg* 'to drive in heads', a practice consisting of penetrating the victim's body in a number of places, including the natural openings; the weapon used is a long, thick awl (*rakis*) made of pig bone. Here too the attackers leave, and the victim regains consciousness, returns home and dies some time later, this time from his injuries.

Apparently shooting arrows and *sosoog-na uguwôg* were often combined. Internal injuries could exceptionally be inflicted without *nefôkêg* (not involving sorcery) by a group of men seizing their victim (*ningǝga-na kehrig* 'to seize with the hands') and manhandling him. The *nefôkêg* can also be simply pointed at the victim, who then faints. It also happens that the invisible arrow misses its mark or does not hit a vital organ: in this case, the intended victim does not die but will experience ill health, faint easily or suffer from prolonged illness. Blindness, for example, is interpreted as the result of an *aysiri* arrow having passed before the victim's eyes without hitting him.

Other secondary techniques consist of using the *nefôkêg* without direct attack. Juice from the rhizome can be put on an arrowhead which is stuck into a piece of food (tuber, areca nut); the person who eats this food then contracts an illness of the *af* type (serious lung disease), which can lead to death. The sorcerer can also throw a piece of bamboo filled with *nefôkêg* juice at the victim, a gesture that causes pain in the part of the body targeted and a drop in body temperature. Lastly the *aysiri* can exercise a pathogenic power by merely staring, thanks to the *nefôkêg* he keeps tucked away in his mouth.

Any contact the *aysiri* himself has with the *nefôkêg* requires purification, which he does by simply washing his mouth and hands.

Techniques for Identifying *Aysiri* Sorcerers

We shall see that the social dialectic of homicidal sorcery and countersorcery is based on a strategy of defense and revenge; this assumes the availability of techniques for divining the sorcerer's identity.

One such technique leads to confirmation that death was indeed due to *aysiri* sorcery. During the ritual washing of the body, the cadaver is examined for marks (Ch. 12): any blemish is supposed to have been caused by the invisible arrow. If several marks are found, it will be deduced that several sorcerers acted together or in succession, and must be identified.

Once the examination has been carried out, a group of the victim's agnates, who may be joined by one or two other close kinsmen, enlist the help of the deceased's ghost and set about looking for the *aysiri* responsible: they 'follow' it around the forest at night, leaving from the grave, while the *ifaaf* manifests itself in the form of a point of light (*gwos*, p. 390), a wallaby, the call of the great cuckoo (*Centropus menbeki*) or simply the odour of a cadaver. Ghosts of young children call attention to themselves by crying. All these signs from the dead man lead to a neighbouring hamlet and, in the event, to a particular house where the light is supposed to come to rest on top of the roof. It is said that the sorcerer, realizing that he had been discovered, used to try to escape or to drive off the ghost by loosing an arrow carrying *ifaaf awus*, a magic clone feared by ghosts. Once the sorcerer was identified (sometimes it was the first man to be seen or heard in the village designated by the ghost), the deceased's kinsmen would return home to plot their revenge: murder as a rule, combined with *aysiri* sorcery, sometimes *agi*, or again killing without sorcery.

When it was not possible to determine the exact identity of the sorcerer, an epidemic could be sent to the suspected village (see above, *agi pafig*). When revenge had been taken, the men would go back to the grave or the *sengêri* and mark the spot with ochre and betel juice after clearing the ground of vegetation. The deceased then knew he had been avenged: his ghost could descend to the world of the dead and be freed of its ties with the cadaver.

In this context too, dreams have a divinatory function: a relative can dream of the deceased, who provides clues to the name of the sorcerer. The *nabasa* forest spirit can also warn one of its human allies of the *aysiri*'s intentions with regard to him. Embodied on this occasion in an *ero* bird (of the babbler or warbler species), the *nabasa* whistles a repetitive tune (characteristic of this bird), and, each time it stops, the man asks it about the type of danger or sorcery, *aysiri* or *agi*, and the recommended counter-rite: when the bird stops answering, it means the last question is confirmed. The *nabasa* can help a man protect himself against an *aysiri* action. Or the deceased's *nabasa* (Ch. 12) can take direct revenge on the sorcerer by causing him to fall ill.

Sorcery and Social Order

The Yafar sorcerer (*agi* or *aysiri*) is neither a healer, nor a medium, nor a master of fertility; sorcery does not confer special status. Any adult male can be suspected of sorcery. He can be a co-resident or *awanəga* (a member of the same tribe) if he has good reason for avenging an injustice, but he is above all and as a general rule the 'other': maternal kinsman or affine rather than agnate, member of another hamlet rather than co-resident, non-Yafar rather than Yafar, *angôruwaag* (unrelated) non-Yafar rather than *heeheg* (relative). Nevertheless, the vast majority of accusations or suspicions of sorcery are directed towards the circle of nearby allied tribes. Within this group, it is considered that a specific motive is needed to commit an act of *agi* or *aysiri* and that having been wronged the perpetrator acts out of frustration or jealousy. Beyond this group, the accusation usually remains anonymous, the aggressor's motivations unknown. For want of a name or following an unsuccessful *ifaaf* divination (see above), a whole hamlet may come under suspicion, and the sanction will fall on one of its members at random. This makes it difficult to gather statistics on deaths from presumed sorcery, as all natural deaths today are put down to some unknown non-Yafar sorcerer. Now that the government has taken the sting out of revenge, suspicions of sorcery have become diluted by social anonymity. Nevertheless, it used to happen that a man from a neighbouring tribe with affinal links to the Yafar passed for an active *aysiri*. While he may have derived a certain prestige from this reputation, he also became the target of ever more frequent murder attempts on the part of the communities who held him responsible for a number of deaths.

Since the early 1960s fewer attempts have been made to identify *aysiri* by divination. Accusations of *agi* are sometimes lodged by someone who is fatally ill, deduced from his recent social history, like one man isolated by his family in a garden house – where his younger brother brought him food – who implicated a young man. Some time earlier, the young man had agreed to marry a widow, an agnatic classificatory sister of the sick man, who, a widower himself, wanted her to move in with him with a view to economic cooperation. He asked one of his brothers to perform an *agi* healing rite. But the community turned its back on this man, whom they reproached for certain former deeds, and no one paid any attention to his suspicions; he died a few months later, killed, it was believed, by a nameless sorcerer. All deaths of this kind, which are preceded by illness, are attributed to outside *aysiri* unless a recent conflict throws suspicion on a close relative or co-villager. In this case it is often the dying man or woman who makes the accusation, claiming to have seen the sorcerer loose his arrow (see Case 1 below).

Retaliation against a presumed sorcerer used to take the form of a killing raid, but when the technique used had been identified by a number of persons as *aysiri*, a *nefôkêg* clone and spells were used. The victim might be only lightly wounded and escape, but if he died a few months later, it was attributed to the attack. The notion of *aysiri*, then, covers everything from a simple explanation for death to a real attempt at murder combined with a magical procedure.[5] This is why it is difficult to interpret such

5. The categories of homicide by magic and homicide by aggression are therefore superposed or confused. Other authors have made the same observations in other Melanesian societies (see Marwick 1970).

Yafar statements as: 'He/they often came to kill us', 'We killed him by *aysiri*', etc. All that remains of *aysiri* today is the belief, namely that sorcery is the explanation for death; every community claims to have forsworn the practice once and for all, while accusing the others of not having done likewise. Exonerating one's own group while accusing all others is necessary if one is to go on situating death within a social logic. Even in the past, people explain, we only used *aysiri* to combat unprovoked sorcery attacks by others or to punish a serious crime committed by kinsmen (adultery, repeated serious theft, the violation of ritual secrecy by a woman, etc.). Sorcery within the group proper is claimed to be essentially defensive, legitimate and in the service of social order; it is designated by the expression *mungwaag mungwaagi*, which defines the violence as reciprocal. When one is oneself the target, however, the violence perpetrated by other groups appears as illegitimate and gratuitously offensive. The outside sorcerer, from a group allied by marriage or especially from a non-allied group, is deemed to act 'without motive' (*mungornagêm aysiri*). Nevertheless, there are cases when harmful action by a member of one's own group or another group can be recognized and the vengeance of the group attacked be approved a posteriori by renouncing retaliatory action (Case 4 below). However, it should not be forgotten that in such cases the two societies involved are linked by complex ties of kinship, and it is through this network of personal relations that an intertribal complicity may emerge against a co-resident. In most cases, though, revenge was taken in utmost secrecy, and the victim's close relatives confronted with the *fait accompli*. The opposition between self and other, between inside and outside fluctuates, and a murder in one's own village may be more remote in terms of kinship ties than one in an allied tribe which is nevertheless that suspected of sorcery. The *aysiri*, as the Yafar normally see him, is not a Yafar but belongs to the security circle, from where he strikes through the network of kin.

Despite defending the legitimacy of defensive sorcery in the interests of the group, no male Yafar would dare boast of his evil power for the sake of winning prestige. Until 1972, all mature men cultivated clones of *Acorus calamus*, *nefôkêg*, in secret places and, were therefore regarded as potential *aysiri*. A young man could easily obtain a cutting gratuitously from an older kinsman together with the magic spells that would ensure its effectiveness. It took the 1972 killing (below, Case 1) to make the Yafar community decide unanimously to destroy all *nefôkêg*: a 'brother' was punished by death for having wrongly used this power on a woman (who died of illness) – a double 'murder' had occurred in the group. Without a word to the government, the whole tribe met and buried their mortal plants, condemning *aysiri* sorcery as the greatest calamity ever. Too bad, they said, we will remain without defense against outside sorcery: the white man's law was right, they would not try to take revenge or even to identify sorcerers. From that moment, every death became an inevitable misfortune, an unpunished murder, and sorcerers were implicitly relegated to anonymity, while the dead were 'just buried', in other words without being avenged. Once inquests, divinatory or other, and all forms of retaliation were abandoned, death underwent a desocialization. But since the outbreak of internal conflict in the 1980s, it would seem that *aysiri* practices have been restored to a place of honour.

Later in this chapter, I will present some individual cases in which sorcery and murder are intertwined in the same set of events. Women can be victims, but never sorcerers (even through the agency of their *sungwaag*) or murderers. More than exonerated, they are held to be incapable of controlling these powers, and their inability to use bow or dagger is exacerbated by their lack of access to *nefôkêg* and the magic words; nor would they be capable of practising any form of *agi*. Such discrimination is consistent with their ignorance of all magic, good or bad. This being the case, they must depend on men to carry out their strategies of conflict; husbands or brothers can be commandeered to set evil doings in motion. When women marry into another group, they must assume the often uncomfortable position of having to choose between their agnate's camp and that of their affines, and, in the event, between playing a role in advancing or, on the contrary, denouncing plans for sorcery or murder. Young inexperienced men also used to resort to the services of an elder, not to mention the tactic of getting a relative in another tribe to 'kill' magically and/or physically a member of one's own village, one way of deflecting suspicion, which was discretely rewarded with a gift.

Yafar sorcery features in the list of the many 'hidden powers' that men claim exclusively for themselves. Whether it be a premeditated act by a flesh-and-blood individual or an alleged confrontation between *sungwaag*, it appears to us as rationally impracticable and ineffective. To those concerned, its ambiguous position between pure magic, or dream act, and a real attack relegates it as a technique to the field of the imaginary; and when it is accompanied by physical aggression, it is merely the illusory extension of that attack. Yet the notion as such is socially integrated, often in a dramatic fashion. By circumscribing death exclusively within the sphere of human responsibilities, Yafar culture socializes it to a degree and makes individual life a major stake in social relations.[6]

Forms of Murder

Killing raids used to be organized secretly within the same interindividual networks and the same group categories as *aysiri* sorcery. Ideally the offensive use of deadly weapons, arrows (*fag*) and bone daggers (*kas*), was forbidden within the tribe or the local group as well as between consanguines and close affines. In preparation for a raid, a few men would assemble unbeknown to the relatives of the intended victim, for fear they would warn him. Agnates, maternal kin and first-degree affines in particular were kept at a distance and only later confronted with the *fait accompli*. At that time the murderers would justify their deed, and the resulting conflict often degenerated into a stick fight. Despite this theoretical prohibition on killing within the group, several cases of murder between Yafar are attested. All originate in specific clashes between individuals, while intertribal murders could stem from a more diffuse conflict or even sometimes be the expression of violence between groups inexplicable as the evolution of a particular difference or a process of retaliation. True battles (*gehya*) are a separate case; there were a number of these several decades

6. There are other forms of bad magic that do not come under the heading of either *agi* or *aysiri*, such as the opening of the invisible underground paths leading to the cosmic maternal *hoofuk* and connected with the notion of *sungwaag abuk* ('ripe self'). When visiting an unrelated village, for instance on the occasion of a ritual, a man seeking revenge on his hosts can plant his dagger in the village soil and mutter the name of the mythical figure, Wangohra (p. 391), a sort of cannibal father figure who guards the roads to the netherworld. In so doing, he opens a passage which the inhabitants' *sungwaag* will take during sleep, only to return having become 'ripe'. It is said that one of the villagers can dream of the hole in the ground and warn the community, which will then perform a Gungwan rite (p. 380) to 'close the path'.

ago between Yafar and Sowanda, groups not allied by marriage but linked by exchange partnerships (Ch. 8). This feud originated in a dispute to be examined later (Case 7), which seems to have become a simple pretext for pursuing hostilities. As the problem of exchanging blows with relatives or affines could not arise, confrontation between whole groups became possible. As strangers but also neighbours, Sowanda and Yafar were potential enemies. This exception confirms the rule and shows, on the contrary, that the customary form of ambushes or raids by small bands on an individual or a solitary family in the forest is determined at least in part by the close-knit kinship network, which obliges homicidal designs to work in between the links in order not to be undone by far-flung solidarities. The Sowanda example also shows that *sêh* partnerships are less resistant than kinship to the outbreak of collective violence: two exchange partners were not obliged to avoid each other if they found themselves face to face on the battlefield.

Most fights or murders took place in the forest or in garden clearings. The victim or victims were surprised, often at dawn; a man suspected of *aysiri* or the author of a serious crime could be drawn into an ambush on the pretext of going hunting or gathering, and be stabbed to death by a band of distant relatives after being informed of his offense. This was *ningəga-na kehrig* 'to seize with the hands', not to be confused with *fag pəfêg* 'to kill with arrows', two forms of aggression which are opposed to *gehya* 'battle or multiple murder'.[7] A few murders took place in villages. The Yafar never practised nor were victims of hamlet encirclement (although the defensive porches on the houses, looking outwards from the village, seem to suggest this type of defence), though the Punda and Umeda are said to have made such attacks on Wamuru villages.

Lastly, I should recall the homicide taboos which link the Umeda with the Yafar as well as with a few other groups in the region. This mutual respect (which takes other forms as well, such as a taboo on marriages), is founded, as we have seen, on a common mythical uterine descent tie between groups (see pp. 18–20)

---

7. More accurately, *gehya(g)* means 'to strike repetitively or to kill down to the last man'; the same term is used for battles.

Causes and Circumstances of Murder

The notion of cause would require semantic and even philosophical precisions which have no place here. In effect, homicide should be envisaged not as the outcome of one specific cause, but as a moment of crisis in a chain of events unfolding in a particular sociocultural context. This chain can be compressed in time and involve only a few individuals or, alternatively, expand to take on a historical dimension and concern more or less well-defined groups, from which certain more directly implicated individuals occasionally emerge. Between these two extremes, any number of intermediate situations can be imagined. The 'cause' can be a real offense, an imaginary one or a divinatory act, a dream revelation, a demographic-cum-ecological situation, a belief or a general climate of suspicion determined by belief. These different elements are combined in these sequences of events and comprise a set of factors rather than causes. A murder is no more the last step in a chain of events than it is the 'effect' of a series of causes; it, too, will have its factoral consequences and will alter, perhaps for a long time to come, relations between the persons and groups involved. The killing of a man or a woman is the culminating moment in the drama of an unfolding conflict. It can occur at the very outset or, on the contrary, much later. Its expeditious manner was illustrated, for example, when a young man involved in an adulterous relationship was killed by the husband with the help of one or two 'brothers' before the rest of the community had even learned of the offense. Alternatively a man increasingly suspected of *aysiri* sorcery might come to grief only years after the first accusations.

These preliminary precautions having been taken, the precursors of homicide can be grouped into the following categories:

1) Sorcery.
   a) The victim is designated by a combination of circumstances implying that he caused the demise of someone having died recently (of a natural death).
   b) The victim is designated by divination or by revelation (accusation by someone recently deceased just before dying, dream vision, *ifaaf* divination, etc.).

    c) The victim has been suspected of practising *aysiri* for several years. The accusation stems from rumour unsubstantiated by proof or special revelations, and seems to have been determined by the victim's personality (nonconformist in matters of psychological and social values and behaviour[8]).

    d) The victim is not chosen for himself but belongs to a village suspected as a whole of one or several recent *aysiri* murders. Chance designates a scapegoat.

    e) The victim is a close male or female relative of the person formally designated and suspected of sorcery, but who cannot be located at the time.

2) Control of women and sexual offenses.

    (Under this heading, I have placed several types of conflict between men, or between a man and a woman, which centre on the woman as sexual partner or spouse, or as 'daughter' or 'sister'.[9])

    a) The victim is guilty of adultery, rape or attempted rape of the murderer's wife, 'sister' or 'daughter'.

    b) The victim is a woman who has repeatedly committed adultery.

    c) The victim is a woman suspected of having had her husband killed (by sorcery), even though he died a natural death (see 1a).

    d) The victim is a woman who has violated an important taboo concerning male ritual.

    e) The victim is a man guilty of having spied on or chanced upon a couple having sexual intercourse.

3) Problems having to do with land.

    a) The victim is a non-Yafar man caught in the act of clearing a garden or working sago on Yafar lands.

    b) The victim is caught on Yafar territory (off the main trails between villages), despite having no Yafar affines or consanguines (= suspected intention of *aysiri* sorcery).

4) Absence of open conflict.

    a) The victim is a person or family surprised on their own

---

8. Men who are taciturn or loners seem especially to have attracted suspicion.

9. See also Ch. 9, pp. 281–2.

land by men from a neighbouring tribe.
b) Two bands of men clash in battle, one of the groups having come on to the other's territory for this purpose (Yafar-Sowanda, Yafar-Punda).

The final category is difficult to isolate. In effect, for certain cases – especially when it is the outsiders who attack – informants allege an absence of motive (Howell 1975). 'A band of Wamuru men came to kill us for nothing/for no reason', they say, or more rarely, 'Hey, how about getting up an attack on the Punda?' But it is probable that these raids took place during a particular phase in the relations with one or other of the neighbouring groups, that a non-specific desire for vengeance in the wake of earlier incidents was the implicit driving force, or that a badly resolved conflict had degenerated into 'generalized violence' between whole communities. However, this does not entirely rule out the possibility of the killing raid being undertaken out of a love of adventure, the need to assert one's virility for oneself and before others, the desire to acquire a certain status (Ch. 13) and to win the right to wear the *aynaag* insignia, or simply for the pleasure of fighting and the satisfaction derived from a successful foray. When it is others who attack, it is also obvious that the assailants' motives may never be known by the group targeted, especially in the case of non-personalized suspicions of sorcery avenged by the murder of a scapegoat victim. These comments are intended to emphasize the tenuous nature of the frequent claims in anthropological writing that violence in New Guinea societies is often not motivated by conflict. Since first-hand accounts place far more stress on the anecdotal nature of the confrontations than on conflictual scenarios or psychosocial mechanisms, the anthropologist in the field often has great difficulty in tracking down the determining factors. The fact that a murder may be committed in the absence of any conflict between the protagonists does not exclude the presence elsewhere in social relations of an ill-resolved dispute or of a need for violence that has lost sight of its origins.

This brings us to the classic theme of revenge. The reader may perhaps be surprised not to have found this rubric among the factors listed above. This is because revenge, *subrana* (as opposed do *esmunam* 'without reciprocity') appeared just as obligatory and subject to the rules of honour in the case of *aysiri* sorcery as it was optional and dangerous following a murder. I have already said that the legitimacy of killing as punishment for serious anti-social behaviour was often explicitly recognized by the victim's own kin, even when it occurred between different tribes. After such a killing, the murderer's consanguines and co-residents would remain in the village with him, weapons at hand, giving battle cries and engaging in mock combat. As night fell, each family would barricade itself inside its house. In the daytime, sentinels would guard the trails. This could go on for some weeks, after which time the victim's group might send an envoy, chosen for his close kin ties with members of the murderer's village, to announce that there would be no reprisals. As a rule, the Yafar would not ask for compensation, but in some neighbouring tribes one of the victim's full brothers would demand a 'blood price', comprised of *ag* items: arrows, adzes, shell ornaments, etc.). Killing legitimized by a real or presumed offense sanctioned in this way reveals the presence of a rigorous ethic at the heart of a society which consisted not only of the tribal cell dwelling on its territory, but the entire social space defined by matrimonial exchanges and the kinship networks these engendered. In these conditions, there was no call, in most instances, for punishing murder. It was at once the culmination or revelation of a conflict that had been simmering for some time and the beginning of its resolution. But this could happen only after resentments had had time to 'settle', a process sometimes facilitated, in the case of internal strife, by the temporary dispersal of the local group (Ch. 1).

The devalued status of revenge for a 'legitimate' murder is thus the complement of the high value placed on revenge for an *aysiri* attack. Yet when it comes to avenging murder by murder, Yafar ethics seems torn between an eye for an eye (*mungwaag mungwaagi*) and respect for the person thus expressing his solidarity. For instance, a man seeking to avenge the physical killing of his father, brother, maternal uncle, male cross cousin or sister's husband was looked up to and could even be encouraged by the victim's wife or sister. But someone who nursed his rancour without taking action or who expressed the desire to avenge a more distant relative was said to be 'not thinking straight' or 'to have a bad heart (thought)'. Similarly, revenge that targets the real murderer and is not content with a substitute victim is more readily accepted. Nevertheless, a man who renounces vengeance is considered wise, for in so doing, he contributes to the restoration of social order. The influence of the immediate circle of a man mourning a close relative – and of whom the murderer's co-residents would say *Or ning-nag, ba fe bof* 'He is sad [he is thinking], therefore he is preparing to come [to take revenge]' – was considerable, and the little information I was able to glean on this subject indicated that women played a decisive role. If a first murder was rarely avenged, the escalation of successive reprisals between two clans or villages was even more unlikely. Men used to take a certain pleasure in occasionally crossing the threshold of fear and slipping from hunting into homicide,[10] but excessive violence in an individual was frowned upon, and efforts to bring peace were continually being made. The five-murder rule (often reduced to three or four) for the right to wear pig-tusk ornaments is itself a sign of a certain moderation in the social management of violence. Nor did every man have a taste for combat, and several who lived through these periods of insecurity never killed a human being. They sometimes went along on raids, but were never the first to fire, contenting themselves with merely shooting or stabbing a victim who was already fatally wounded. Even today they are teased about having 'cheated' by claiming the right to wear the insignia of true killers. Still more rare were those who systematically refused to take even a passive part in murder. They are sometimes designated by the term *aynaag* because of their age or knowledge, but they are held in a certain contempt. As for the others, the number of murders for which they claim credit, men, women and sometimes children together, remains, in every case I recorded, less than ten.

Yafar women never took part in raids or battles, unlike the Waina, whose women often followed their husbands and brothers into the fray.

Sorcery and Murder: Some Case Studies

In this section, I will present a few cases selected from Yafar accounts meant (except in the first case) to entertain the listener

---

10. Note that the same magic plants were used to stimulate the hunter and help him confront a wounded animal and to fire the courage of the murderer on the trail of his victim.

with the tale of an attack, a battle or a murder. The causes of the conflict are only mentioned briefly, if at all. Nor, in most cases, are the social ties between the protagonists made explicit. My complementary inquiry into the conflictual relations between the persons or groups involved often met with strong reticence on the part of my informants, a reserve which sought to shut the foreigner out of the private social life of the group and to preserve the image of a united community. I will begin with the most recent case (1972), to my knowledge the last real murder committed among the Yafar, which, as I mentioned above, triggered the collective decision to put an end to *aysiri* sorcery.

Case 1 (*aysiri* and *fag pəfêg*) (Figure 43)

A kills a cassowary and gives a large portion to his wife W's parents: M, his father-in-law, and T, his mother-in-law (M and T are members of X lineage, an immigrant branch of a Potayneri clan). R, T's clan brother, receives only a small portion of boneless meat. He demands more from M and T, who refuse him. Shortly thereafter, W falls ill and dies two weeks later. Before dying, she claims to have seen, after the sharing of the meat, R shoot an *aysiri* arrow at her while she was out gathering firewood with a small boy (the child did not see anything, in conformity with Yafar theory on sorcery). She did not dare speak out for fear of retaliation on the part of R. The information is kept secret in part, but M talks it over with his Yafar and Potayneri agnates and with his mother's brother; T in turn informs only her few agnates (Z clan) from the same village (whereas most of the Z live in one of the two other Yafar villages). Anger is riding high, and it seems that R gets wind of the accusation directed at him. A short time later, M, R's maternal uncle, and a Potayneri man from M's lineage, catch R up a tree in the forest and kill him (not without having duplicated the work of the arrows by an *aysiri* rite). The victim's funeral is held hurriedly, and the two other Yafar hamlets are informed, after the burial, that R has killed himself falling out of a tree. The deceased man's agnates are mistrustful, for they are aware of the problem of the division of the cassowary meat. They conduct a discrete investigation, find M's footprints[11] leading to the tree and determine the day of the murder.

---

11. Any man having left his footprints in the mud can be identified with near certainty by his close relations.

Once they are convinced of the proof of the crime, and without lodging a formal complaint with the Administration, the Z and other relatives of R call together all the men from Yafar and Potayneri (from the closest hamlet in which the Yafar have numerous relatives and from where M's line originated) and present their suspicions. M's uncle is the first to own up, followed by his nephew, who takes responsibility for the murder. After numerous speeches on the abominations of *aysiri* sorcery, all present decide to meet again the next day and to bring all the evil plants still under cultivation. The next day a big hole is dug in the forest and the *nefôkêg* are buried.

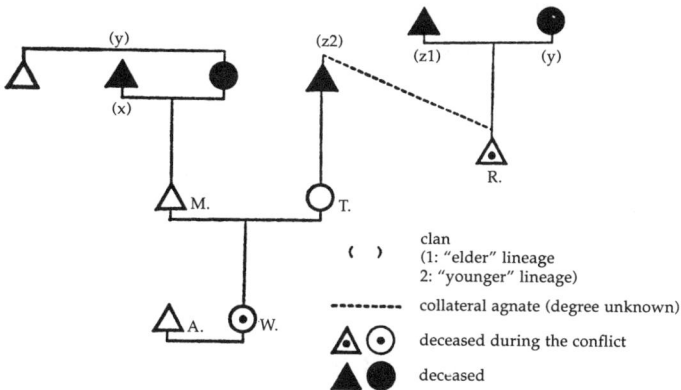

Figure 43. Conflicts: Case 1

This tragic case is a good illustration of categories 1a and 1b, defined above, that is of instances in which the role of chance is rejected and the individual finds himself a prisoner of coincidences, in this case reinforced by an accusation whose underlying motivations I was not in a position to understand. The logic of the scenario quickly transforms suspicions into certainties, all the more as R's demands concerning the division of the meat, as a classificatory father-in-law of M, were partially founded and therefore indirectly confirm the possibility of revenge. Furthermore, the victim W was perfectly situated in the genealogical chain, namely between A, the hunter (her husband), and M (her father) who was responsible for refusing to redistribute meat to R. In addition, as R and T belonged to two lineages of Z clan, the *aysiri* murder of a grand-daughter by her classificatory matrilateral great uncle was plausible (descent in the direct line would

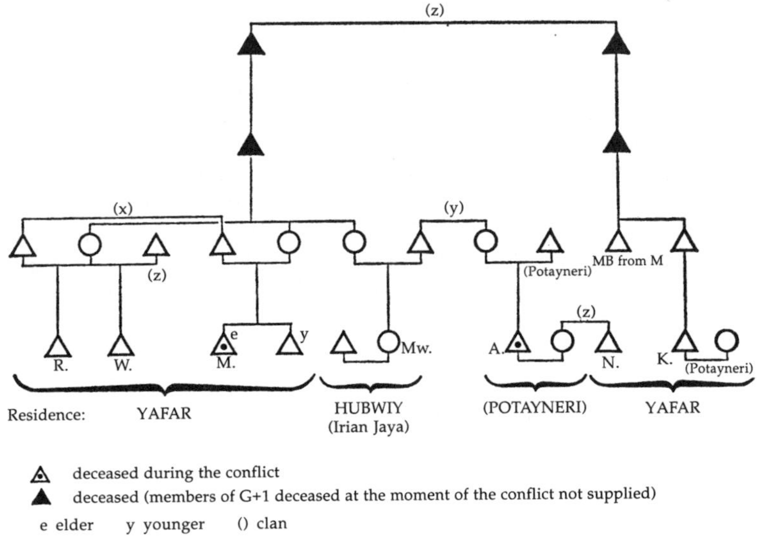

Figure 44. Conflicts: Case 2

have made the deed less likely). To this must be added the valorization of hunting as an activity and of the distribution of the product as a social relation, as well as the prime importance of affinal ties in this kind of distribution. It should be noted that the speeches condemning sorcery and the destruction of the *nefôkêg* are in themselves an implicit justification of R's murder.

Case 2 (*aysiri* and *ningǝga-na kehrig*) (Figure 44)

Mw, a Y clanswoman, marries in Hubwiy, in Irian Jaya. Her husband pays compensation of a single *wis* set of shell ornaments to Mw's 'brothers'. Two men who have contributed to the education of Mw, an orphan, each politely offer to leave the *wis* to the other: A, a Potayneri and Mw's cross cousin, and M, a Yafar from X clan and Mw's matrilateral parallel cousin. M finally accepts the present. The rest of the incident is described as follows, with some events obviously being reconstructed a posteriori. A is said to have changed his mind and decided to 'kill' M by *aysiri* (an invisible arrow), and then, with the help of other Potayneri men, to have surrounded M in his garden and to have 'driven in the heads' (*sosoog uguwôg*). Before dying some time later, M denounces A. The Yafar follow M's ghost, who effectively leads them to A's house. Reprisals are organized: the victim's classificatory maternal uncle is to be the first to 'shoot' an invisible *aysiri* arrow at A, an action then repeated by M's younger brother and by one of his agnatic cousins. By shooting him with magic arrows, they 'summon' his *sungwaag* to the trail and be definitively and physically killed. Finally W and K, two Z clansmen (K married a woman from A's clan), lure A (who suspects nothing and has not yet been physically attacked) into an ambush. K is afraid (perhaps because of his affinal tie with A) and begins to shake. Fearing that A might notice, W tells K to stay out of sight with the other Yafar who are to kill M. W goes alone to meet A.

W had told A: 'Take your dog and come with me; N (A's wife's full brother, a Yafar from Z clan) has shot a pig (that needs tracking).' A takes along his big netbag to carry his share of the kill. The two men banter back and forth and smoke. W gives A's dog some sago jelly. Then they set out into the forest with A's wife. W's Yafar accomplices shout as though they are driving a pig towards the men. A meets his brother-in-law, N, and asks: 'Well, where's this pig?' At that moment R (an agnate of M and W's half brother) grabs him from behind, and another Yafar blocks his path. They accuse him of killing M. A replies: 'You must be joking?' M's younger brother steps up and stabs him with a *kas*. A Babuk man, on a visit to the Yafar, also stabs him. N (who has gone off somewhere) hears the shouting and comes running. They tell him they have just killed his brother-in-law. (Told by Woy, 1973)

A's real responsibility in M's death is doubtful, as it is not clear whether the latter suffered a physical aggression from the 'heads' (bone awls thrust into the natural openings of the body) or whether this was a symbolic attack or a later narrative invention. The boundary between real and imaginary is sometimes difficult to establish when dealing with accounts of acts of sorcery. The motive of the presumed *aysiri* 'murder' (the *wis* ornament) seems highly implausible, and A's words before being killed point to his innocence. The solidarities driving this tragedy are manifested by the interventions of M's maternal uncle, his younger brother and his two agnatic cousins (R and W). The fact that N had not been told of the plan, whereas he himself was the bait, shows that the brother-in-law relationship is based on obligatory trust and that N would have been morally obliged to warn A. Aside from the victim, N is no doubt the most unfortunate of those involved because of the role of unwitting 'traitor' in which he is cast. K's position is ambiguous, for he feels an obligation to his agnate W, himself under obligation to R, whereas he is at the same time the agnatic third cousin of N and of A's wife, which makes him a classificatory brother-in-law of the victim. In these circumstances, his discomfort and his withdrawal from the scene are understandable.

Case 3 (*aysiri, ninga-na kehrig, fag pəfêg*) (Figure 45)

> W, an Aynunkneri man, comes and 'kills' S, a Muwagneri woman married to a Yafar, Mo. S's ghost shows the Yafar the way and leads the men to W's house. P (a Yafar and Mo's matrilateral parallel cousin) and Mi (a Muwagneri) shoot an *aysiri* arrow at W. Later they seize him, drive in the 'heads' and magically enjoin him to take the trail to Yafar (where he will be physically killed). The Yafar are waiting on the trail. W comes along (his wife is visiting the Yafar at the time). He chats and has a smoke with the Yafar. One of the Yafar men, H, K's father, claims to have diarrhoea and keeps leaving the group. In fact he is going for other Yafar men, who conceal themselves close by. He makes several of these trips. The Yafar surround the group on the trail. Seeing they are now close, I (a Yafar man) lays hold of W. Everyone lends a hand. One man stabs him with a *kas*, the others follow suit. M grabs the bow of the man accompanying W and breaks it. This man runs off. W, injured, is released, he tries to escape. They shoot after him. He dies. The Yafar break out in *imisio* cries (shouts of victory) and return to the village. A Yafar woman, W's wife (who has learned of the murder), tries to strike one of the killers with an adze. Someone takes it and throws it aside. The Aynunkneri come to the murder site, cut some carrying poles and bear W away. (Told by Woy, 1973)

As is often the case, the account of the event, which I have transcribed as it was told, begins with the justification, in other words by formulating the guilt of the murder victim, whereas the proof by divination, which preceded the justification in the sequence of events, is mentioned only afterwards. Then comes a short description of counter-sorcery (invisible arrows and 'heads') performed by S's close relatives. No doubt lacking in objectivity on this point, the account seems intended to show the power the Yafar have at their disposal and that they used it 'legitimately' and effectively, since W obeyed the magic order to go along the trail. The way he is described as innocently chatting with the Yafar on the path concurs with the Yafar theory that the

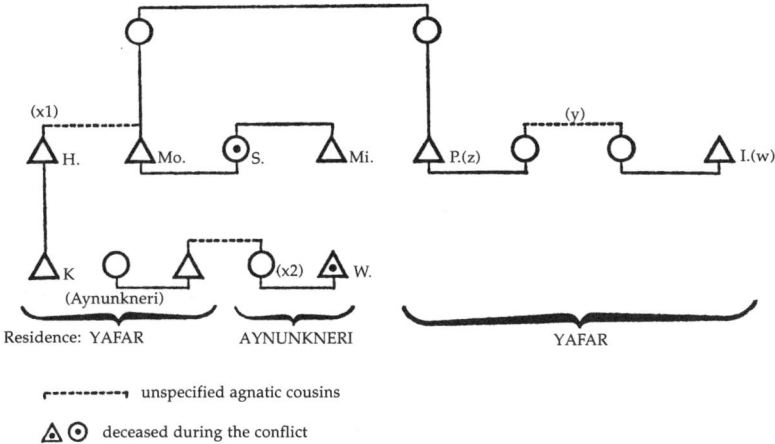

Figure 45. Conflicts: Case 3

victim, having fainted, does not realize what is happening. The rest of the scenario is typical of homicide by ambush.

As for solidarities, the same ties are found as in the earlier cases: agnates, matrilateral cousins and affines. The last relationship in this case is present by its absence: Mo, W's classificatory father-in-law, and his son are not mentioned in the counter-sorcery procedures – even though they are the husband and the son of S – and do not take part in the killing.

Case 4 (*aysiri* and *fag pɔfêg*) (Figure 46)

Below is Woy's account of the murder of Y (which took place shortly before the Amanab station was established and which has already been discussed above), a Potayneri man sought by the Yafar, who held him responsible for numerous *aysiri* attacks. This man seems to have been a bit peculiar, which is no doubt at the origin of the suspicions; his polygamy (three wives present at his death) might also be seen as a sign of power. A few days before the murder, Y had been knifed during a public rite held by the Yafar and had managed to escape from his aggressors. This is the reason for the allusion to his *ifaaf* (or *sungwaag*), his 'self', who keeps watch above his shelter and holds death at bay.

Tomorrow we intend to go and kill a man (Y). Each man goes home to get some food and we meet outside the village (so that the women from the target village who are married with Yafar will not find out). First of all we spend the night in the forest. Early the next morning, when the *kwimpi* birds start singing, we get up. We advance, waving firebrands (it is still dark). We go up to Y's garden shelter. His *ifaaf* is watching from the roof and ducks back into the shelter when it sees us. We surround the shelter without making a sound. W wants to be the first to shoot, but A beats him to it and looses his arrow. Then W fires. We kill the children. Y's second wife (a Potayneri) runs away. M (a Yafar man from Z clan) gives chase, shoots her and she goes of with the arrow in her. Y's first wife (a third agnatic cousin of W) tries to flee, but we hold on to her and reassure her, for she is one of our 'sisters'.[12] F stabs Y with his *kas*, but Y, who has already been hit by several arrows, is nearly dead. F cheats, and later will put on the *wamero* (pig-tusk ornament). The child of Y's first wife has escaped. Y is my mother's brother, that's why I didn't shoot, I just watched. Y's third wife (a Potayneri) also ran off. We take the arrows and the netbags from under the shelter. Y's eldest son has heard our *imiso* cries from the village. He shouts that he wants to block our path. But we shoot at tree stumps and yell to frighten him. He gives up. We didn't kill Y for nothing, he had killed many of our 'brothers'. We go to tell his brother-in-law, S, a Yafar, what has happened. We didn't tell him ahead of time for fear he would come and help Y. The Potayneri bring carrying poles and take away Y's body. The Potayneri did not come to take revenge later. They recognized that Y had killed us with sorcery. (Woy, 1973)

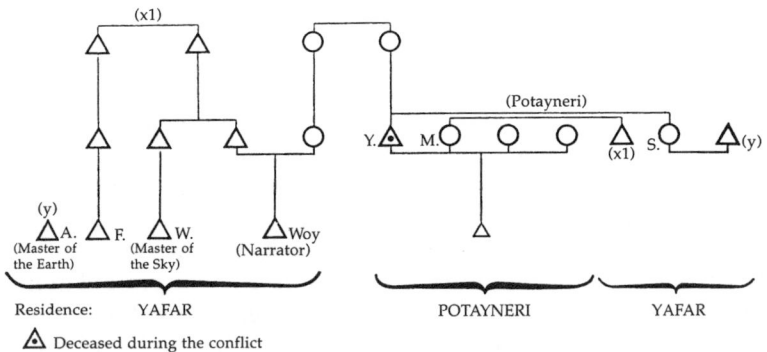

Figure 46. Conflicts: Case 4

12. A third agnatic cousin of the narrator.

No doubt it is not without significance that the two men who vie to shoot the first arrow, W and A, were the Masters of the Sky and the Earth (Ch. 13) and in all likelihood needed to confirm their status by acts of bravery. Once again solidarity between agnates comes to the fore (lineage X 1), while the narrator's position as second-degree uterine nephew forbids his attacking his uncle, even though he may take part in the raid; and the victim's brother-in-law, as in the preceding examples, is informed only after the event.

We now come to the category *gehya* 'collective combat, battle'. Kinship ties are less decisive here, since the confrontations do not arise from personalized disputes, but from some violation of land rights. The following accounts provide information primarily on the techniques of combat and the apparent disorder stemming from the dense forest environment, on the surprise effect produced by the assailants, as well as on the absence of fight leaders. To my knowledge, groups never arranged to do battle together. Rather than a 'targeted' killing (*pǝfêg*), *gehya* implies the engagement of two specific tribal groups, although it has occurred that members of the attacking group who happened to be visiting the Yafar have sided with their Yafar maternal kin or affines against their own residential group, while avoiding battle with their close kinsmen.

Case 5 (*gehya*)

The Punda come on to our lands to work sago palms. The Yafar try to catch them in the act. The Punda constantly change work sites and go back to their village every night. One day the Yafar hear a group of Punda coming along the trail (on Yafar territory). They block the way: some Yafar set a lookout on the trail, others hide in the undergrowth. Afram (a Yafar) goes down the trail and waits. The Punda arrive. Afram shoots at the first man, Sum, and calls his own kinsmen as he runs away; the Punda give chase. As he runs, Afram injures himself in the testicles with one of his own arrows. There is fighting everywhere. Sum dies. The Yafar go home, the Punda carry Sum away, shooting after the Yafar. Afram was not hit. (Told by Woy, 1973)

Case 6 (*gehya*)

We (a small band of agnates from Yafar) go to wait for bandicoots at the foot of a wild pandanus. I kill a bandicoot. Resay shoots an *afwah* bird. Then we go to fence Fewô's garden. This is when we hear the *bubwere* bird's alarm call. Someone says 'The Punda must be coming (to attack us).' We go on fencing the garden. Fewô and Uw go to gather some *Gnetum gnemon*, cook it and eat it there. All the Punda are coming, not one of them has stayed in the village. A group from Yafar 2 is working sago. Among them, Suig is cutting stakes to split a sago palm he has felled. The Punda have spotted them and encircle the sago grove. When Suig comes back with his stakes, the Punda shoot him in the thigh. He tries to take his bow but is hit by two more arrows. He flees. Rafay, his sister's husband, is in the bamboos (too far away to help). Our group, from Yafar 1, still fencing the garden, hear the Punda shouting. We take our bows and go. Two Yafar 2 men are already hit. We try to block the Punda's path. We hear them singing the *taf sangêk* (a killing song). In our group, Rapô has his dog, it runs ahead to meet the Punda. They recognize the dog and shout 'Yafar 1 is here!' Wiy, an adolescent, runs back to the village, pursued by some Punda. We have blocked their path, and the Punda are milling around in the forest looking for a way out. The fighting is disorganized, everybody shooting pretty much at random. In the village, Tapô is getting ready to come to our aid: he paints his face with charcoal and puts on *rəge* (*Selaginella* sp.) (so that the arrows will miss him). Ibni is hit in the leg. Waya gets his bow caught in the vines as he runs and a Punda grabs it. Waya comes running in my direction and takes my bow. One Punda tries to sneak up behind the Yafar, but Mafa (Yafar 1) sees him and shoots him in the chest. He runs off. The Yafar matrilateral kin among the Punda hide so that they won't be recognized. (Woy, 1973)

The first of the two clashes (case 5) focuses on two small groups, a handful of Punda stealing the Yafar's sago and the Yafar landholders assisted by a few kinsmen. Case 6 involves a broader conflict in which the entire Punda group is present, while the surprised Yafar pull together what they can of their numbers, regardless of individual solidarities; they feel assailed as a tribal group. The Punda attack, which occurred around the time the Amanab administration was established (1961), is not set in a particular context of conflict and, according to the Yafar I questioned, did not have any specific cause.

I will close these case studies with an account of the feud which divided Yafar and Sowanda three generations ago, the character of which, as I mentioned above, is exceptional for the region. At the time, the Yafar were still living in the village of Sahya (Ch. 1). These two societies did not intermarry but did practice institutionalized barter or *sêh*. As a result, they found themselves in a relationship which contrasted with the ties the Yafar entertained with their other neighbours. It was therefore easier for a dispute to degenerate into a feud in which the declared goal of each camp was physically to exterminate the other. It is of prime importance to note that the immediate cause of the conflict was precisely the intention of a Yafar man, Wara (Menaneri clan, now extinct), to marry his two daughters to Sowanda men and to take up residence there himself, at their invitation. The exact circumstances of this arrangement are no longer known among the Yafar; some maintain that Wara did not have enough sago on his Yafar lands, but it is probable that there were ties predating this arrangement inscribed in the context of *sêh* exchanges. Wara had even taken his daughters for a prematrimonial stay with their future husbands and fathers-in-law. This deliberate violation of the rule of not marrying Sowanda was viewed very badly by the Yafar in general and by Yur, Wara's younger brother, in particular. Most of the Sowanda sided with Wara, since they gained two women in the bargain, whereas the dominant practice was endogamy, which restricted their choice in marriage.

Some informants spoke of a specific field in which the confrontations took place on the boundary between tribal lands, but it seems that the spot was not clearly defined and was simply somewhere along the border. The battles between the two groups are said to have occasionally been planned in advance, but this detail does not appear in the two accounts that follow. The Yafar–Sowanda feud was of short duration, limited to a few important *gehya* and a number of scuffles. Sowanda losses are said to have been much higher than those of the Yafar (according to the latter).

Here are the two accounts. In the first, the battle is the result of a trap laid by the Yafar. It had been agreed that the problem of Wara's daughters would be discussed between the two parties. Instead, there was an attempted massacre, and Wara and his daughters were recaptured by force. The second account tells of a later battle in which the Yafar found themselves at a disadvantage and lost one of their men.

Case 7a (*gehya* between Yafar and Sowanda [Suara] – first account)

...then Yur tells his people that they have to settle this affair, re-
capture Wara's two daughters and take them back to Sahya. All the
Yafar agree and send a message to the Suara (Sowanda) to come to
a meeting place between the two territories with their women and
to bring sago jelly. 'We will bring jelly, too, and we will exchange,
(with the intention of making peace).' The Yafar set out and build a
fire at the meeting place. The Suara arrive and ask 'Where are your
women?' – 'They're coming', reply the Yafar; but they are lying. The
Suara are there with their women and children. Now the Yafar surround the Suara, splitting into small groups, some armed with bows
and arrows, others with *kas* daggers, and others unarmed. But one
group of Suara is not under control, ten or so. Some Yafar notice this
group and decide there are not enough of them. Mwayif (a good
fighter from Sumneri clan) says 'There are enough of you, I'll take
care of that group.' On the Yafar side, Inwey is very tall. On the
Suara side, Buwô too is very tall. Someone goes to fetch Inwey to
take care of Buwô. Inwey looks Buwô over and motions that it will
be alright. He watches him. Yur (Wara's younger brother) makes the
round of the groups and comes back to the fire. Mwayif is sitting in
front of the fire with his bow in one hand, drying some tobacco on a
log. Yur says 'Have you got an areca nut?' Mwayif puts the wrong
end of his cigarette in his mouth (from nervousness). Then the Yafar
attack a Suara group and kill one of them with a *kas*. Inwey shouts
out the name of his river and grabs Buwô (see note 14); another Yafar
shoots him in the chest. Buwô takes Inway down with him. Buwô
sees that the arrow doesn't have any barbs: he pulls it out and stabs
Inwey with it. Inwey moves off and shouts 'Ah! I'm not a cassowary
to be eaten with sago! Get out of here!' Buwô goes, but is caught by
Mwayif, who kills him. Some of the Suara leave. Yur makes another
round of the battlefield killing as many men, women and children
as he can. Agwe and Mwayif go looking for new victims. Inwey is
left sitting on the ground with the arrow in him.

Now Yur takes command of his brother Wara, his wife and his two
daughters. Wara is shaking and resists. Yura tells him 'We are going
home now.' Wara wants to go and break the trumpets at Sahya
so that the Yafar won't be able to celebrate their victory. Wara and
his younger brother, Yur, each take a different path. They hurry. Yur
is the first to reach Sahya while Wara is only a hundred metres away.
Yur takes the trumpets and hides them in the garbage pit. Wara looks
for them and then gives up. Soon the rest of the Yafar can be heard
arriving and giving the *imiso* cries.

Everyone gets ready for the rite and the celebration. The *fag seeg na awaag* (the Master of the Murder Rites; see p. 438) places ashes on some *kofay* banana leaves (see above) and holds a *yuu* (blunt) arrow in one hand. The Yafar arrive. Each fighter is designated according to his exploits and his weapons. The *fag seeg* master performs a rite (*sês abugum* 'ripe game') on each of them. Then the warriors circle the village square shouting and the master takes aim at each one ritually with his *yuu* arrow and then relaxes his bow. After which he mingles with them. Then the trumpets are played all night. The Potayneri join the Yafar and blow the trumpets with them. The second night the same thing. (Told by May, 1981)

Case 7b (*gehya* between Yafar and Sowanda [Suara] — second account)

The Babuk (who were already living in their present-day village when the Yafar were still in residence at Sahya) go to their gardens on the Amunwo's land. They notice that the Suara have made a large collective garden on land belonging to them. The Babuk come and say to the Yafar 'We saw that the Suara have made a big clearing on Amunwo lands. Come with us, let's surprise them. We'll surround the garden and kill them.' The Yafar and the Babuk go, together with several Potayneri kinsmen. They see the Suara garden and sneak up to it. But no one is there: the Suara have stayed in the village. So the Yafar, Babuk and Potayneri crowd into the garden and begin picking all they can. The garden is full of men from everywhere. The Suara have left a *mesöw* tree standing in the middle. A *riksik* bird lands on it and gives its alarm call. Some Suara hear it and come to check. They see the Yafar and their allies in the garden and run to call the Suara from all the other hamlets. They blow their trumpets: 'Beee! beee! beee!. . .' and shout 'They've come to attack us, they've come to attack us!' The Suara gather. A man from Naikur hamlet gives the first war cries and goes to wait on the trail; another Naikur follows suit. Then it is the turn of a man from Sabo hamlet, then another, again from Sabo. The rest follow. The Kwiner give a shout and join the others; the Wasaw give a shout and join the others. A great number of Suara are ready now. From the garden the Yafar hear them shouting one after the other. They leave the garden and go and stand on the trail. 'Let's surround them down by the Afaag river.' They arrive on the Samenag land and wait; they roll cigarettes. They have surrounded the spot. The two adversaries are now face to face, the Yafar, Babuk and Potayneri well fanned out and blocking the path.

Fiyêy (Ig[13] clan) and Manga (If), two Yafar, go down to meet the Suara and wait at the river. Fiyêy hides near a *se* tree, while Manga lies in wait near by. Now the Suara can be heard coming and shouting: 'Wee wee wee wee.' They take no care in coming and suddenly find them selves face to face with the Yafar. Fiyêy shoots the first arrow and shouts 'Mafunk! Mafunk! Mafunk![14] eee! eee!' The wounded Suara cries out in pain. The man behind him steps aside to get out of Fiyêy's line of fire but is hit by an arrow from Manga, who shouts the name of his river 'Pwanksunk! Pwanksunk! Pwanksunk! eee!' The rest of the Suara arrive: the unwounded men are in front, the wounded behind. In the ensuing fray, arrows fly in all directions. The Suara ask their rear guard 'What shall we do?' The others reply 'The Yafar haven't left, they're waiting for us' – 'OK, wait there. . .' The Suara try to encircle the Yafar. Then they ask their adversaries 'Who are you?' – 'We are Yafar, Babuk and Potayneri!' The Suara turn around and shout to those in the rear 'The Yafar, Babuk and Potayneri are blocking the path!' The Suara are about to go home, but one of them notices Mawya, a very tall Potayneri, and asks 'What group does that possum head (fur head-dress) sticking up over there belong to?' – 'That's Mawya, a Potayneri', he is told.

Then the Suara fall back a short distance and perform a rite to improve the chances of their attack: they uproot a *woog* tree, stand it up and spit magic plants and betel on to it (to cool the enemy's body, whose *sungwaag* will then become 'ripe'; see below p. 495 and Chs 7, 12). The Suara then attack and repel their enemies, who fall back; the Suara pursue them and gain ground. During the attack they shoot Yêy (a Yafar from Wi clan). 'Yaaa yaaa! Leave me here, I'm hurt too bad, let the Suara finish me off!', he cries. But his 'brothers' carry him away. Some of the Yafar and their allies flee, leaving the others behind. The Suara have split their adversaries into two groups, and they now turn on those who remain. A pitched battle is engaged. Having picked up the arrow fallen from Yêy's body, a Suara shouts 'He's badly wounded, leave him to us!' But the Yafar bear Yêy off. Soon they come to the place of the two *nabasa* (forest spirits), Ay and Kafway (Yafar spirits on Yafar land). They cross the Feromung-na and Wahwemp-na streams and come to the San river (Yafar land). There Ibyan (Wi clan) crosses at a spot he believes to be shallow and falls into the water over his head. He calls for Manga. The latter looks at him and waits: he is afraid the Suara will come from behind and seize the occasion to kill them. In effect, Musgor (a Suara) comes up over the bank, sees Ibyan but not Manga, and prepares to shoot

13. For a list of abbreviations of clan names, see Ch. 3, Table 4.
14. As he loosed his arrow, a fighter would sometimes shout out the name of a water course on one of his presumed ancestral lands with which his clan felt identified.

him. Manga promptly looses his *kus* arrow. The Suara flees, the arrow sticking into him. Ibyan goes under from time to time, then comes back up. Manga sees his headdress of croton leaves and cordyline emerge from time to time. 'Help me!' cries Ibyan. Manga holds out his bow and jerks him up on to the bank. Ibyan gets up and walks off dripping. The Suara continue their pursuit for a while and finally give up at the Buu river. Others have already turned back.

Some of the Babuk have gone back to their village. Others, 'brothers-in-law' of the Yafar, help the latter, and a few Potayneri carry Yêy, who has died in the meantime. Other Yafar and some Potayneri have gone ahead. Night is falling, and the group, hampered by having to carry Yêy, decide to make camp. They suspend the body tied to its carrying poles between two trees and make a shelter further down the slope. They have neither fire nor food. During the night, Yêy's ghost talks with other Yafar ghosts who come calling. The Yafar and Babuk wake up and think the Suara have returned. They pounce on their weapons and wait: nothing. They go back to bed, then hear voices again, pounce on their bows. Several times like that during the night; it's the ghosts playing tricks on them. At dawn some of the men go ahead to announce the news to the village. The women then prepare sago jelly, coconuts, etc., and take some fire; with other men, they come to meet the fighters. They arrive at the camp. Every-one eats, warms themselves, chews betel and smokes. The Babuk carry Yêy with the help of a few Potayneri, and come to Sahya. The funeral takes place rapidly and the Potayneri and the Babuk leave for home. (Told by May, 1981)

I have quoted these accounts at length because they give some idea, with their spontaneity and the permanence of certain de-tails, of the resolute but disorderly way in which these battles take place. The story of the *gehya* with the Sowanda is no longer a matter of personal memories; these have become oral traditions handed down for some fifty years. Stress is laid on the importance of cunning, of the silent plotting behind innocuous appearances, the better to erupt in unfettered violence. The point is not to cause suffering but to lay the adversary low, 'militarily' as well as demo-graphically; the ambush set for the Sowanda women and children (7a) is a vivid illustration. Despite the gaps and discrepancies in the accounts, one can still see how the fight was organized with-out benefit of any leader or general staff. The oldest or the most dynamic men would suggest a tactic which met with immediate consensus. In account 7a, Yur, more personally involved as the paternal uncle of the two girls to be recovered from the Sowanda, seems also to play a supervisory role in the operations. The order that is imposed on the strategy is only the start of the battle, for the adversary's unpredictability, as well as the impossibility of visually encompassing all or even part of the operations, soon result in the scattering of the troops and the gradual dislocation of the forces. Men find themselves alone or in clumps of twos and threes, some wounded, pursued or pursuing, regrouping from time to time to reestablish a fleeting front, which promptly dissolves.

Gehya never resulted in territorial loss or gain. Lands along the Yafar-Sowanda border are underexploited and have never been an object of contention (as was the case with the Potayneri and Punda, but only by means of isolated murders). Even though often among the victims, women and children were never captured by the victors. The idea of booty was, as a general rule, unknown. The issue was the fighting forces and the very presence of the respective groups in their social and physical existence of the moment and their potentiality for growth to come.

Murder Rites

In the Yafar's symbolic system, murder is defined as on the one hand, an act of bravery which requires a self-induced state of aggressiveness in order to be carried out, and on the other, a 'hot' relationship with blood, which seems to be experienced as a transgression. We have also seen (Ch. 12) that it is productive of status and prestige, and is ritually rewarded with the bestowing of insignia. These two registers, symbolic and social, of the exercise of violence meet in some of the ritual measures surrounding homicide. Among these are the individual precautions taken by fighters or murderers; collective propitiatory rites (symbolic murders), whose function is to 'excite the heart' of the participants; and lastly, the post-combat ritual for victory, protection and social gratification, which is of an initiatory nature.

The notion of daring and endurance is expressed by the term *kêfutuk* 'strong, hard', already encountered in the discussion of the fate of the *sungwaag* (p. 373). Before engaging in a killing raid or a *gehya*, a man would abstain from eating soft foods (notably sago jelly, replaced by roasted sago). Pork was also proscribed for reasons that are not altogether clear, whereas cassowary and other species could still be eaten. In order not to aggravate his future identification with blood, the fighter would not consume either betel or pandanus juice, both red foods. Lastly, he abstained from sexual intercourse in the days immediately preceding the confrontation. Some men would also paint themselves with charcoal, the blackness of which is associated with the concept of *kêfutuk*, but, according to some, with invisibility as well. Others would, on the contrary, enhance their appearance with ornaments.

Prior to engaging in collective warfare, propitiatory rites were often performed, in which the killing was acted out beforehand, or during which participants consumed a little blood mixed with magic rhizomes to 'heat up' the heart and make the men aggressive. These symbolic procedures were no doubt effective, in the sense that they induced a state of excitement which manifested itself by violent shaking, called *kêg afǝgêk* 'shaking the bones'.[15] Here are the two rites which were described to me as being the most common:

a) A young man wanting to commit his first murder shoots an arrow into a ripe (red) dwarf pandanus fruit in a garden.[16] Then he calls to his aid the other men concealed nearby. They all surround the pandanus and throw themselves on the fruit, which they stab with their *kas*. The fruit is cooked by the novice, and each man filters part of it through his hands (using the customary technique). The resulting juice is not drunk but is mixed with the magic rhizomes (*Acorus calamus: gaf kukugu*) of clones used to induce aggressiveness (the most venerable plants of which are grown secretly by the *fag seeg na awaag*, the 'Masters of the Arrow Magic' of Menaneri and Tawank lineages; see Table 5) and a piece of dried human blood, which the experienced men would keep in the hollow of their bone dagger. Lastly, betel would be chewed with a small quantity of these different ingredients.

b) A *woog* tree, which has reddish sap, is uprooted and summarily replanted in the sand on a riverbank. A hole is dug around the tree so that river water will collect. Charcoal is thrown in, together with a piece of dried human blood and magic rhizomes. Each participant drinks some of this water and spits it back out, jumping around in a

---

15. But this symptom is often mentioned as a sign of fear before the attack.
16. The Waina-speaking groups used to perform the same type of rite on a pig killed by hunters.

frenzy and giving 'war cries'. The men face off in two groups, corresponding to the Araneri and Angwaneri moieties. In the evening, the *fuf* trumpets are played in the village.

The second account (7b) of the *gehya* between Yafar and Sowanda shows that this rite may be performed during the battle itself. It seems to have two purposes, 'to excite the heart' and to cool the enemies' *sungwaag*. In effect, spells are uttered at the same time to bring about the adversary's 'ripening' either by directly naming the potential 'enemy' groups, or by metaphorically citing the names of game animals. Hunting and homicide meet at many points through the expression of the same symbolic referents.

A murder or an arrow striking an adversary is greeted with *imiso* cries, also emitted when a wild pig is brought down or a tall tree felled. But on their way home, the group of fighters (therefore especially for *gehya*) sing the *taf sangêk*, the 'blood song'. This makes mention of a small marsupial *sawye* which is said to drink the victim's blood:

Sawye sawye!	Sawye sawye!
Ang' taf rəbe	Lap the blood from the ear
Bos' taf rəbe	Lap the blood from the nose
Noof' taf rəbe	Lap the blood from the eyes
Hur hur hur hur hur	(= *huguk* 'big, fat': allusion to the cadaver's bloated belly)

The returning fighters were welcomed by the men and women. The *fag seeg na awaag* (p. 438) would have prepared banana leaves covered with ashes that the killers would trample and then circle, to 'cool' their bodies, but also to fortify their *sungwaag* which, through contact with blood, had become 'ripe'.[17] Every novice murderer, even if he was physically unscathed, was made fragile by the momentary 'ripening' of his 'self' and consequently needed to protect himself against *aysiri* sorcery and even against insect bites and stinging plants. Nevertheless, through repeated killings, the fighter would gradually become immune to the ripening process, and his *sungwaag* would, on the contrary, grow *önguk* 'black'. At first, killing made the murderer vulnerable, but eventually it

17. It should be remembered that *abuk* means both 'ripe' and 'red'.

would fortify him, rendering him so *kêfutuk* that someone who was afraid of killing and stayed behind in the village was said to become 'ripe' and open to sorcery. It is necessary to go through the critical phase of ripening to be free of this threat. What we seem to have here is an encounter between two contradictory processes: contact with blood, which starts the 'self' down the path of rotting; and the acceptance of an act of courage, which, conversely, strengthens the identity of the subject capable of conquering his own fear. The second, deliberate initiative cancels the first process, which is akin to natural contamination.

The function of the *fag seeg na awaag* seems to have consisted mainly of ridding (with the aid of a clone kept by his line) inexperienced killers of the contamination incurred by their contact with blood. After the rite for 'cooling' the body, several weeks would be allowed to pass during which game was amassed before proceeding with the distribution of the warriors' insignia. The pig-tusk ornaments,[18] especially the *metiy* (the forehead decoration), were briefly placed by the officiant on the forehead of each warrior, and then finally on that of the *asagyam* (pp. 398–400) who was receiving the insignia for the first time following (in principle) his fifth killing. At this time the ritual master would recite the spells evoking the power of aggression over outside tribes, named lands, game and even relatives designated by classificatory terms; this last point confirms that violence is also exchanged within the kinship network. Older men would add feathers indicating the sex of the victims killed to the ritual insignia. The next night a Gepôk rite (pp. 187–9) would be held, then the trumpets would be sounded for several more nights.

Resolution of Internal Conflict: Fighting Sticks and Words

The third means of expressing or resolving conflicts, ritual combat – duels and/or collective engagements – with fighting sticks was practised exclusively within the village, between kinsmen.

---

18. The *metiy* is a decoration worn on the forehead and made of sections of pig tusk which have been cut off and filed down. The *wamero* is a chest ornament made of pig tusks and is still worn. To these should be added upper-arm bracelets made of pairs of tusks tied together and the nose decoration fashioned from filed tusks passed through the septum with the sharp ends turned upwards, touching the cheekbones (*anəngu*).

The protagonists were co-villagers among whom might also be found a few outside Yafar or more rarely relatives from other tribes. The causes of these engagements were always fairly minor conflicts. In principle only men took part, although it is said that in former times women were more courageous and sometimes used to lend a vigorous hand to a husband or a brother.

The fighting stick, *maruwô*, is made from a bent branch of the tree of the same name (*Garcinia* sp.), also used for the handles (*maruwaag*) of stone adzes (*maar*) (Juillerat 1983b), but it may also be the actual handle of an adze from which the head has been removed. The sameness of the material and the similarity of name clearly indicate that the *maruwô* was originally a *maar* adze used as a hand weapon, without its contusive component. The moderation and self-control with which this society seeks to contain the violence present within kinship and residential groups is evidenced by the very semantics of this technical relationship. The Yafar make a distinction between a duel (*maruwô na bəgaag ahfeg* 'to quarrel with the stick') and a col-lective engagement (*maruwô hagêk*, from *hagêg* 'to apportion'). In fact, although the quarrel may begin with a clash between two men, a group of relatives armed with their *maruwô* will promptly rally around each combatant and every man will be able to express his point of view verbally while brandishing his stick and stalking back and forth. Two camps will form, according to individuals' ties with one protagonist or the other. But sometimes (Case 1 below) the duel, normally limited to one or several simultaneous exchanges of blows, takes place in the course of the general fray and does not necessarily involve the two main adversaries, or men directly concerned by the dispute, or even men who are in disagreement. Blows are sometimes exchanged between men who have nothing personal against each other but who find themselves on opposing sides and suddenly decide to clash briefly as a way of venting their anger. However, the majority of the participants – and every man in the village feels under an obligation to participate – do not wield their *maruwô* to do violence but merely brandish it as a way of lending force to their arguments. In this case, the stick becomes the symbol of attack, without a specific physical objective, merely an extension of the moving body, one of the components of the whole style of conventional behaviour which can be defined as the social expression of anger. The spontaneous aspect of the *maruwô hagêg* or of the duel, is significant: combat is not a 'judicial' procedure set up to choose between the protagonists or to decide which side is right – it is neither a trial by arms nor a test. The technique is subject to rules, however: the two men must face each other, advance rapidly, *maruwô* raised, and each strike a single blow at a time, on the back, below the shoulder blade (which means that the blow must be struck laterally). The contusive portion of the weapon, called the 'jaw' (*kawuk*), is that part to which the adze blade is normally hafted. If the rules are respected, the blow is not dangerous and leaves only a superficial wound. If one of the adversaries hits another part of the body, the other is entitled to do the same, but there is no referee. It used to happen that a blow might deliberately or involuntarily miscarry and fracture a bone. Even more rarely a man in the heat of his rage might go so far as to strike his adversary on the head. But any death occurring in the wake of such injuries was necessarily ascribed to the prior action of an *aysiri* sorcerer.

Here too, government influence has introduced a social inhibition into the management of physical violence: the *maruwô* are brought out on to the village square less and less frequently and, when this does occur, they are usually restricted to the semiological function noted above.

Among the conflicts that can lead to a *maruwô hagêg*, we find:

a) Refusal to recognize another's land or land-use rights: repeated thefts from gardens, refusal to respect ownership signs (bunches of leaves deposited beside gatherable produce), fishing without the required permission, a domestic pig killed in the forest by a hunter, etc.
b) Disputes over the use of *eney* darts (arrowheads stuck in the ground: gardens, paths, access to a reserved gatherable product), the purpose of which is to identify a chronic thief.
c) Dissension over the distribution of a product (especially game).
d) Sexual offenses: adultery, attempted seduction, etc., or disputes stemming from a husband's mistreatment of his wife.
e) Dissension over an accusation of sorcery that casts doubt on a kinsman, or following a murder.

I witnessed the use of *maruwô* by the Yafar on only two occasions. Only in the first case was there an exchange of blows, and then only one; the second took the form of a collective expression of anger in which it was impossible to tell which side the actors were on and whether or not they experienced the event as socially antagonistic.

Case 1 (1971)

There had been a Gungwan (p. 380). Instead of being taken into the forest and tied to a *gungwan* bush, in accordance with the rules of the ritual, the masks were left in the enclosure. The next day some children took them and played with them. Late in the afternoon, a few *aynaag* noticed and began to express their disapproval publicly and with increasing vehemence. One of them was blamed because the others had been counting on him to see that the masks were taken into the forest; he had not felt it necessary, judging that the rite was not important enough. While the tide of anger rose, and one after another high-ranking men (in particular the Masters of the Sky and the Earth) held forth on ritual and social order, on the deadly danger incurred by the community and on respect for tradition, the villagers went up into their houses and came back with their *maruwô*. People were scattered about the village square, with only the oldest men giving loud vent to their revolt, while the young men remained calm, their fighting stick at rest. Suddenly the Master of the Sky and a younger man from his clan clashed, and two nearly simultaneous dull blows were heard, while the women cried out. The physical and verbal demonstrations went on for another fifteen minutes. Then a certain peace settled over the crowd and smiles began to appear. The Master of the Sky told me that only men were capable of expressing such anger, and that the women 'didn't know how'. Then one of his young clan brothers took up a general collection to appease ('to pay') the wrath of the Master of the Sky.[19] The latter received what amounted to some two Australian dollars.

The next day the masks were stood in the forest, even though people maintained, out of pure convention, that it was too late and that sooner or later, all the Yafar would die.

---

19. Only later, when I learned that the man was the Master of the Sky, did this wrath payment appear to me as an act appeasement addressed to the celestial powers through the person of this master. We saw in Chapter 2 that the male Sky was sometimes attributed with the power to strike humans with the *maar* adze (one of its attributes). For a more detailed example of compensation for resentment, see the Kaluli Gisaro rite (Schieffelin 1976).

Case 2 (1973)

> A woman came back to the village one afternoon and complained to
> her husband that a young man, K (a bachelor from the same village
> and the couple's future son-in-law), had tried to seduce her. She had
> been gathering *Pometia pinnata* fruits and said that K came by and
> gave her to understand that he wanted to have intercourse with her.
> She said she had had to insist before he would go away.
>
> The news spread through the village and the surrounding vicinity,
> and in the late afternoon some men began holding forth with vehe-
> mence, not on K's presumed offense, or on the veracity of the facts,
> or the value of the accusation, but on the necessity for social and
> sexual morality in general. In the midst of his diatribe, one man
> ran back to his house, grabbed his *maruwô*, and returned to pick up
> where he had left off. Soon everyone was there, not scattered about
> (as in the first account) but packed together, fighting sticks raised
> and hopping up and down in a frenzy. Every so often an *aynaag*
> would break away and, bellowing his revolt and declaiming the
> rules of good conduct, would stride back and forth like a warrior
> in the midst of battle, slapping his hip like an archer loosing his
> arrow. Meanwhile, a few young men who had worked on the plan-
> tations in the 1960s attempted – more timidly and often in Pidgin –
> to restore peace, recalling the principles of the 'white man's order':
> 'There must be no more fighting with sticks, there's a "law" now (*i
> gat lo* in Pidgin); it's no longer like it used to be, when we would
> "kill" each other – today everyone must keep calm (*sindaun gut*).'
>
> After half an hour, the group dispersed and, a bit shamefaced, some-
> one came over to me to explain that no one was really angry and
> that it was all just a 'game', a show.

In both cases it is the threat of 'disorder' rather than the 'fault'
committed that stirs people's anger. In the event, the problem for
the Yafar is not to apportion responsibility or sanction the trespas-
sers (although these two aspects can be discussed beforehand). In
the first example, the community is expressing its indignation at
the lack of respect for the rite and the danger this represents for
the group. In the second case, it is the social order that is called
into question by a simple suspicion, with few grounds as it happens, and which seems to be of no real interest to anyone: the
young man was not reprimanded and barely had to explain himself to the husband, and this was before the anger began to swell.
Later he joined the others, *maruwô* in hand, ill at ease with an
obligatory 'rage' that he did not feel.

Feelings have no doubt not always been so conventional, though. In another case of which I learned indirectly, a violent quarrel broke out following an incident in which a child was injured by a steel axe head flying off its handle during use. The child's father wanted compensation through striking the clumsy user with an axe. He was stopped by, among other things, the mobilization of all his co-villagers, *maruwô* in hand, then by a call for help to Yafar from the other hamlets who were kinsmen of the protagonists. In this case, the collectivity armed with its fighting sticks appears more as a means of prevention, a bulwark or protective barrier against excessive violence.

It would be hard to overemphasize the importance of words in the procedure of the *maruwô hagêg*. For all that homicide, with or without sorcery, was often committed without uttering a word, it is inconceivable to imagine a group of men brandishing their *maruwô* or engaging in duels in silence. On the contrary, speech is paramount, even if every man does not feel entitled to verbalize his resentment or even to feel it. Each individual armed with his stick is there by duty and occupies his place out of solidarity with his close kin. But there is a sharp contrast between the *aynaag* moved by a partially self-induced anger which goes on to become authentic in the end, and the more or less bored adolescent waiting for it all to be over. As for the content of the diatribes, despite a few references to the events which sparked the crisis, the recurrent form is that of general declarations about what is good and bad, about blameworthy behaviours that endanger the community's permanence and unity. These ethical rules are familiar to everyone, and the *aynaag*'s speech (which here resembles the reprimands we talked about in Ch. 13) is in this sense more expressive than persuasive.

Lastly, we need to identify the principles underpinning the system of inter-individual solidarities which, in the event of a serious dispute, momentarily divides the local collectivity into two camps clustered around the main actors. In the first place, the Yafar forbid duelling between maternal uncle and uterine nephew, cross cousins and brothers-in-laws of the first degree, as well as between father and son. Alternatively, two full brothers may fight each other.[20] When this happens, all their 'brothers',

---

20. See above, p. 124, on the opposition between sameness and difference in the organization of social relations.

in the broad sense of the term (including cross cousins), team up according to elder (*etanǝnga*) and younger (*sumninǝnga*), the 'elder brothers' siding with the elder, the 'younger brothers' with the younger. The 'brothers' in the middle (*öruk-inaag*) divide themselves between the two camps. Difference of age takes precedence over generation, and a young paternal uncle will side with the 'younger brothers'. This device permits discrimination within the homogeneous kinship category of agnates and inversely echoes the mandatory solidarity between maternals and close affines. Sisters' husbands necessarily go to the aid of their wife's brothers, and *vice versa*. But at the same time, a man has a duty to defend his *segwaag*, (pp. 360–63) and if, for instance, the dispute arises from a marital conflict between his *segwaag* sister and her husband, he may exceptionally take sides against his brother-in-law. Such cleavages last only the time of the conflict, however; the groupings they determine change from one *maruwô hagêg* to the next and do not constitute stable alliances.

Whether it is the way the *maruwô* engagements develop or the way solidarities line up, one cannot help noticing how little attention Yafar rationality pays to examining the facts or truthfulness of testimonies. Preserving the sociosymbolic order counts more than ascertaining the truth. As a member of a society preoccupied with unity, the individual, normally so free in his social choices, finds himself, at these times of crisis, hedged in by his obligations and forced to occupy the place that falls to him by definition.

The analysis of these three forms of social control through violence has clarified their organization in terms of in-group/out-group. In effect, the notion of social boundary is to be taken in two dimensions and in varying degrees. The dimensions are the local or tribal group and the kinship network. The fluctuating degrees of near and far refer, at the first level, to the boundaries of the hamlet, the tribe and the social space as a whole, including adjacent societies; and at the second level, to the greater or lesser degree of consanguinity or affinity between individuals regardless of their respective group membership. It is within this double dialectic that strategies of aggression must be organized. These structural principles are summarized in Table 23.

	Groups or social spaces				
Degree of kinship	Same hamlet or tribe	Same social space of alliance (another tribe)	Outside groups	Outside groups, *sêh* exchange partners (Sowanda)	Symbolic 'consanguine' outside groups (Umeda)
Privileged close kin (MB/ZS, c.c., F/S, WB/ZH)	P	P	–	–	–
Other close kin (1st and 2nd degree)	M	S (S/H)	–	–	–
More distant kin	M (S/H)	S/H (M)	–	–	–
Non-kin	M (S/H)	S/H	S/H	S/G	P

H: individual homicide; G: *gehya* feud; S: presumed *aysiri* sorcery; M: *maruwô* stick fights; P: prohibition on violence. (Parentheses indicate that the type of aggression is rare.)

Table 23. Modes of violence as a function of socioterritorial units and kinship

The psychosocial motivations behind violence seem, in the majority of situations, to come under the heading of 'defence' (I prefer this term to 'paranoia', used by some authors). Killing as punishment for sorcery, possible vengeance and stick fights are governed by a defensive social reflex against aggression from without or within, and against the danger of internal sociosymbolic disorder. Belief in the 'other's' sorcery is in itself a defence against death, which threatens the perenniality of the 'self'. Whether the defensive strategy is directed at the other as group or as individual or is used within the local or kinship group, it all comes down to the same phenomenon, despite the choice of techniques and the variable number of individuals committed. The Yafar's defensive violence grows out of a sentiment of vulnerability ill-concealed by the culturally valued and socially approved behaviours that typify manly acts of bravery: physical fragility in the first place, rooted in climatic, dietary and pathogenic conditions engendering a high rate of mortality, a state of affairs entailing an unstable demographic situation in which population decline follows on the heels of hard-won growth; and social fragility in the second place, due to the atomization of the tribes, the mobility of local groups and their propensity towards scission.

Compared with other New Guinea societies, in which the economic and political motives for conflict are more visible and used to determine endemic warfare between certain large groups (especially in the Highlands), the Border Mountain peoples have no place in their social systems for rivalry (between 'big men' for instance) over power or land, which is apt to engender a calculated use of violence (see however Juillerat 1991b). Violence, for the Eri, tends to insinuate itself into the normal lines of communication, or rather tends to be one of their components: the function of killing or of stick fights is, on the whole, to favour the resumption of relations which have momentarily been compromised and to foster the continuity of exchange within the social zone of alliances, whereas conversely, the Yafar-Sowanda feud was meant to drive the latter out of this socialized space. In both of these apparently contradictory orientations, the concern was to preserve a certain arrangement of social and symbolic relationships, both inside and outside the society.

Part IV

Fracture and Change

The last part of this work is comprised of a single chapter dealing with the twin themes of the changes introduced by colonization and the response elaborated in turn by the Yafar, which gave rise to the emergence, in 1981, of a millenarian cult. In Chapter 14, I analysed the process of internal fracture and the measures taken to prevent these breaks; but this analysis dealt with mechanisms that were part and parcel of the traditional sociopolitical system. This is why the present chapter can be seen as a continuation of the preceding one: from internal conflicts and their resolution, we now move on to the transformations induced by contacts with the outside and to the ensuing search for a new sociocultural identity.

The broader spatial and temporal vision imposed by the colonial context places Yafar society in a regional framework and a historical context of which it is largely unaware. Seen on this new scale, closer to our own history, the Yafar are just one more dot on the map, one more case of a people confronted by Western encroachment. But it will be only when the Yafar have been restored again to their own dimension, through an examination of their millenarian ideology using the ethnographic approach that has been mine throughout the book, that I will close this final chapter.

15

Contact: Colonization, Independence and Identity

At the second moon, he will come. He will have a new language and an awesome voice. When they hear him, the Yafar will fall down and be taken with convulsions. They will clench their netbags in their teeth to stop from crying out. Black clouds will hide the sun at noon.

(Yafar 1981: conversation on the millennium)

Every anthropologist who goes into the field is confronted with the transformations occurring in the society under study, those already completed and marked by the definitive disappearance of certain cultural features, or those in process, of which the observer is at once a witness and one of the many agents. In writing this book, I have sometimes hesitated between the present and the past, so numerous were the behaviours and ideas that, in the present transition from one generation to the next, were yielding to more 'modern' concerns. This break between generations is only partial, however, for while the young people (especially the young men) are more vehement in demanding access to a certain purchasing power, however feeble, their 'fathers' are just as concerned with procuring European goods; and while the elders remain firmly attached to traditional values (socioeconomic as well as religious), the younger generations continue to take part in rituals, to collect sacred knowledge and, for the most part, to reject the modest prospects of economic development held out to them. The 'Cargo Cult', which I will analyse later in the chapter, attracts men and women of all ages, for it represents the fusion of old cultural values and a millenarian utopia in a new material and spiritual world. As elsewhere, change came initially through the rapid abandonment of institutions such as murder and accusations of sorcery, induced by the coercive action of the colonial government, and later through the slower and more fluctuating loss of other cultural practices, in the areas of ritual and burial, for example. Lastly, on a third level, contact with the authorities and missionaries, experience on plantations and more recently the opening of a government school in the Yafar territory (not to mention the periodic presence of the anthropologist himself), have set in motion a deep and more insidious long-term metamorphosis of mental and social habits. The recent onset of these processes as well as the general lack of mission influence on the northern Eri have obviously much to do with the Yafars' perplexity in the face of the changes occurring in their immediate area and their nation as a whole.

In the first section of this chapter, I will attempt to reconstruct the history of contact by first of all situating the Yafar and neighbouring groups in the broader spatial and chronological framework of the region's colonial history (Rowley 1972) and then going on to draw some parallels with Yafar oral tradition concerning the same period. I would like to stress from the outset that the colonization of this part of the world was shaped by its geographical position on the border which, until the early 1960s, ran between Australian New Guinea and the part of the island under Dutch administration, later known respectively as the State of Papua New Guinea and Irian Jaya, which belongs to Indonesia.

Colonization of a Border

In Search of a Meridian

It took over sixty years of hemming and hawing, political wrangles, astronomical measurements and expeditions into the interior before agreement was finally reached on the exact location of the border which was to divide New Guinea in two. It is due to this leisurely pace, primarily of a political order, on the part of the colonial powers that, until the early 1960s, some 3,500 inhabitants of the northern Border Mountains were, for better or for worse, 'forgotten'. In the nineteenth century, the Netherlands, Great Britain and Germany had agreed that 141° east longitude was to serve as the north-south border: the Dutch would take the western part, while Great Britain and Germany would share the eastern side of the island, the dividing line being 5° south latitude. In 1895,

Great Britain and the Netherlands signed a convention for the southern half of the border, but Germany was in no hurry to do the same for the northern half, notwithstanding repeated requests on the part of the Dutch. In 1910, a German-Dutch expedition was finally organized to take astronomical measurements and thus establish the precise position of the 141st meridian. There were already discrepancies between the readings of the two teams for the northern coastline; furthermore, the Netherlands had a preference, at least for the stretch between the coast and the Sepik, for a natural boundary corresponding to waterways that would later be easy to locate. This expedition was aborted on its way inland before achieving its goal. Several months later, another attempt was made, having followed the Sepik upstream, to find a tributary that could serve as an international frontier west of the Border Mountains, but in vain. In the course of these trials, the expedition had circled this massif to the west and south without penetrating the interior. Two years later, the Dutch team submitted a secret report to their government detailing the economic resources of the northern border region, the most important of which were birds of paradise (hopes of finding oil, on the other hand, were disappointed[1]). Until 1924, when the feather trade was banned, hunters from the Netherlands, Australia, Indonesia, Melanesia and other parts travelled these regions, triggering the rapid expansion of the colonial government seat, Hollandia, which reached 700 inhabitants in 1923, later to drop to 30 or 40.[2] To the east, Vanimo – which had been founded to tighten control on the contraband trade of bird-of-paradise feathers – also declined in importance.

By 1914, Germany had lost its colonies, and Australia was asked to take over the administration of the northern half under the supervision of the League of Nations. Not much progress was made between the wars, as the Australians did not seen any urgency in administering the northern boundary. Nevertheless, an 'exchange of notes' took place in 1936, following a more accurate localization of the boundary on the coast. The border

---

1. In the 1970s, copper, gold and silver mines opened along the northern border on the Indonesian side.
2. E. Mayr, *Birds of Paradise* (1945), cited by van der Veur 1966: 81. I have taken the bulk of my information on the colonial history of the border area from this author. The reader can also consult Ryan 1970 and Galis 1956–1957, the latter for Dutch penetration of the area. For the southern part of the border, see Schoorl 1993.

was shifted to the east and, in spite of a few divergences between Australian and Dutch geographers, a boundary marker was erected just west of the coastal village of Wutung, where it stands even today, indicating the international boundary line between Indonesia and Papua New Guinea.

It was not until 1956 that the Dutch managed to take accurate astronomical readings at Jaffi, a station located some ten kilometres west of the border and at the same latitude as the Yafar, and not until 1961 that they repeated the measurements at Waris, which turned out to be a mere 150 metres inside Dutch territory. But it was only in August 1962,[3] when the transfer of western New Guinea to Indonesia was decided by the New York Agreement, that Australia finally decided to cooperate actively with the Netherlands in taking a large number of readings that would enable them to draw a definitive border and establish the colonial affiliation of numerous villages that had been left in doubt. The virtual partition of the preceding century had at last become a material fact just as the Dutch were completing their final withdrawal, and it was with Jakarta that Canberra settled the last details of the territorial delimitation. But we also know that the boundary problems have been replaced by border problems of a different order, namely those occasioned by clashes between Melanesian guerrillas and the Indonesian army, and by the growing numbers of Irianese refugees crossing over into Papua New Guinea (Osborne 1985; Tapol ed. 1983).

The Yafar between Two Enclaves

Meanwhile, what was happening in the field, and in particular among the Dera, Amanab, Waina and Walsa language groups (Map 1)? Aside from a few fleeting contacts between nearly every village in the region and bird-of-paradise hunters from the west, and more rarely from the east, after the First World War (probably between 1920 and 1924), nothing of note happened until 1950, after the creation of the two nearest Dutch stations, Waris (1948) and Jaffi (1952). Perhaps before, but more likely after the establishment of Waris, steel axes and machetes began finding their way into the region along the numerous exchange routes.

3. This Act was 'confirmed' by a dubious referendum in 1969, itself ratified by the UN in 1975.

By 1949, Dutch Catholic missionaries began extending their activities east as well as west of the invisible border, while the Protestants of the Unevangelized Field Mission controlled the area west of Jaffi. K.W. Galis, a Dutch government anthropologist, mentions in a 1956 report several Dera-speaking villages east of the boundary line as being under Catholic influence, but says nothing of any penetration of Amanab-speaking villages. In particular, the Catholics founded a centre at Amgotro, across from the present-day Passionist Mission Center in Kamberatoro (Amanab District). They set up schools in many villages and even came to Yafar homes for the children (their parents soon took them back). Ryan writes elsewhere that the Dutch Catholics 'had established partial or total control over approximately forty villages on the Australian coast' (working mainly out of Waris and Amgotro) and had penetrated as far as twelve miles east of the border (Ryan 1970: 94).

With the Australians totally absent from the northern half of the Border Mountains until 1959–1960 (by 1951 they controlled the southern portion of the range from the Green River Station, or Abau), the Dutch government was free to extend its influence eastwards fully aware that they were trespassing at some point and with the tacit consent of the Australians. It was in this way that what came to be called the Waris and Jaffi enclaves were formed (Map 5). According to van der Veur (1966: 104), the Waris enclave (Olenda, Wainda and the Walsa speakers) had fifteen villages and 1662 inhabitants; the Jaffi enclave (Dera speakers) had ten villages and 866 inhabitants. Ryan, however, includes the Amanab-speaking villages in the Jaffi enclave. Map 5 shows clearly drawn eastern borders which certainly had no counterpart on the ground. The southern part of the Waris enclave is shown as being 'under the influence' (not 'administration') of the Dutch and as corresponding to the Waina-speaking groups. To the southeast, the map leaves the Eri (Amanab) region blank, with the note 'not under administrative control': the Yafar are located north of this last area. In fact, they received, probably in 1956, one (and at the most two) visits from a Dutch administrator, who appointed a *'korano'* and an *'erbasa'* to represent the Government (terms derived from the Indonesian [?] equivalents of the Australian New Guinea *luluai* and *tultul*). It is hard to say whether these patrols came from Waris or from Jaffi, as the Yafar were easily reached from either station. The presence of the

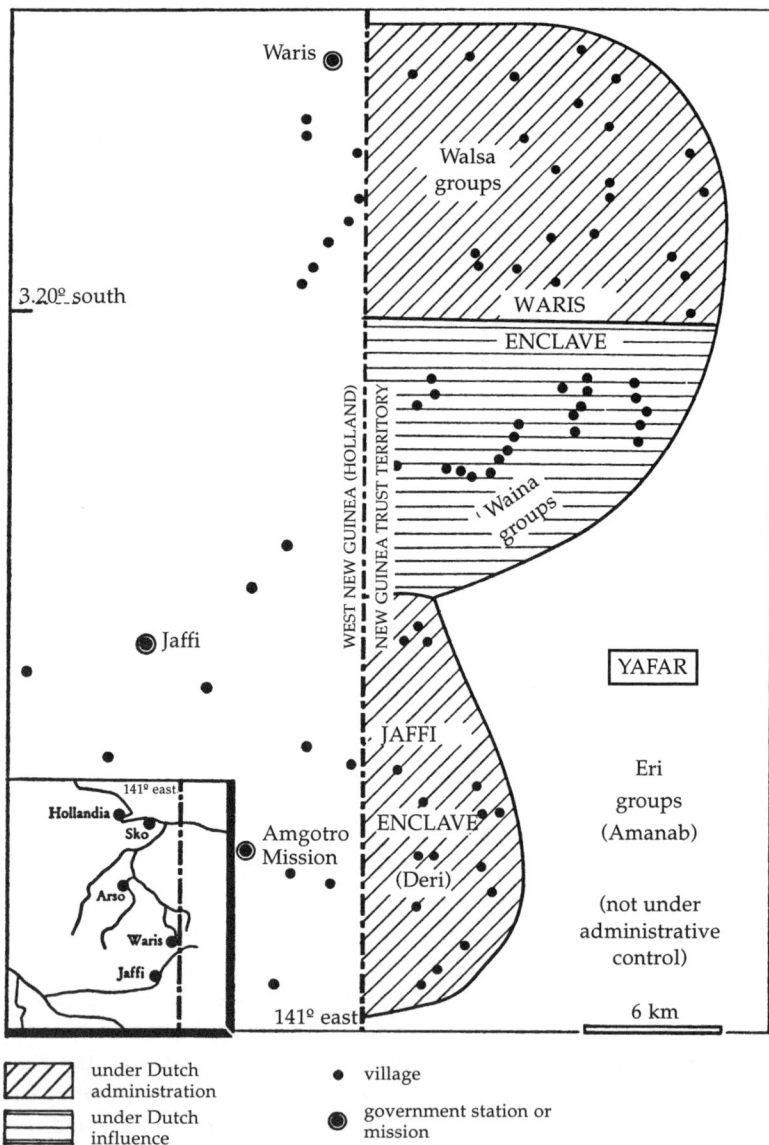

Map 5. Waris and Jaffi enclaves before 1960 (after van der Veur and the Department of Geography, School of Pacific Studies, Australian National University)

Dutch in the two enclaves is attested from the early 1950s; in June 1956, this situation was even sanctioned in the presence of the Governor of Hollandia by the Sepik District Commissioner, who said that he 'would appreciate the present situation, in which the Dutch authorities are in control of this area, to be perpetuated, until the boundary line has been definitely established by a boundary commission' (quoted by van der Veur 1966: 101).[4]

By the time the Australians arrived, the Dutch had left a deep Catholic imprint on the Dera and the Walsa, where they had taught some of the young people to read and write. The Waina had shown more reticence and several times had ambushed Dutch patrols from Waris (Willey 1965). The northern, north-eastern and central Eri had kept to themselves, while those in the southeast lived along the Australian zone of influence at Green River and near the Dutch zone in Jaffi.

From Australian Settlement to Independence

It was not until Indonesia had decolonized and recolonized western New Guinea that Australia finally to decide to move into the Border Mountains. For the Eri group, the Protestant Christian Mission in Many Lands (CMML) was the first to build; they did so in a clearing at Amaraf (Amanab) in 1959, followed a year later by the Administration, which completed a landing strip. In 1962–1963, Imonda patrol station was opened in the former Waris enclave, between Bewani and the northernmost point of the Border Mountains, which today administers the Waina, among others. At about the same time, in 1964–1965, the Passionist Mission built its Kamberatoro station in the former Jaffi enclave. The Yafar had received only one visit from the Australian side, from a Green River doctor, but the population was not vaccinated until after the founding of Amanab. Regular administration of the central and northern Eri did not come until 1960.

Unlike the Waina tribes, the northern Eri more or less accepted colonial penetration and the new regulations imposed on them. The Dutch-appointed *'korano'* and *'erbasa'* were replaced by the *luluai* and *tultul* selected by the Australians, who put a radio receiver in each village so that people could learn Pidgin. But five

---

4. On Dutch influence on the Waina, see Gell 1975: 2–4; Willey 1965.

more years passed before the Local Government Councils and elected councillors were in place. A council was elected for the Amanab ward in October 1965, and 94% of the voters turned out.[5] Each group or 'village' of the area elected a councillor (in Pidgin *kaunsol*) as well as one *komiti* (from 'ward committee member') from each hamlet to assist him.

In the early 1960s, the recruiting of manual labour for the European copra and cacao plantations of the Bismark Archipelago began to reach the central and northern Eri, whereas the southern and southeastern groups had been under contract since 1953, to the Green River Station.[6] Some fifteen young Yafar men left, and a few signed on for a second and final two-year contract at the end of the 1960s. All hiring was subsequently banned throughout the region, as the Government wanted to preserve the labour force, which they needed to open and maintain the Sepik-Vanimo road; moreover, the approach of self-government, planned for 1973, lowered the hiring rate throughout the country.

After the installation in 1964 of a Department of Agriculture representative, the government began encouraging the populations of the Amanab region to try a few cash crops (pepper, small chilli peppers, hevea or India rubber), as well as some crops to supplement their subsistence production (dry-farmed rice, pineapple, fish-farming, poultry and even some European breeds of pig). A few experiments in growing rice were tried with the eastern and southern Eri, but were rapidly abandoned. Of the many projects announced in 1967 in an Amanab patrol report (wells, agronomy studies, agricultural field experiments, a market in Amanab, fish-farming and even the transformation of traditional agriculture), only fish-farming met with any success, in some of the southern villages; and a weekly market was effectively opened in Amanab in the 1970s to give local station employees the possibility of procuring fresh produce and the villagers a new source of income. People from the more remote villages gave the experiment a try and then dropped out because of the distance

---

5. Amanab administration report. For the new National Parliament and the political context of the time, see Rowley 1972, White 1972.

6. In October 1970, there were for Amanab district (total population 3,226), a total of 169 'absent workers' (no women). For the Northern Eri in the same year, there were forty absent workers (no Yafar) out of a total population of 748 (Aynunkneri, Yafar, Potayneri and Wamuru). In 1969, however, fifteen Yafar were still on the plantations out of a total population of 168 (Amanab administration reports).

they had to walk and frequent bad sales, which forced them to give or throw away their produce rather than carry it home again. As for the cash crops, the Eri's only success was the small hot peppers, particularly between 1975 and 1980.

The most spectacular source of income in the region was the native gold present in the streams of the villages to the east of the station. The collectively managed income was most often used to set up village shops, most of which were not long in going bankrupt because of overextension of credit to kinship networks. Unfortunately no nuggets have been found in the streams running through central and northern Eri lands until very recently.

The entire region will remain economically handicapped until the Sepik-Vanimo road is completed. The first non-air link with the outside will no doubt be along the Sepik, while the northern section will remain blocked by the Bewani Range. Once the northern route is opened to the coast, however, it will also be an invitation to rural exodus, which can only lead to urban unemployment and the much-feared arrival of urban 'rascals' in the interior.

Plate 32. Australian patrol officer taking the census (1971).

After the Catholic schools in the two enclaves, the CMML at Amanab opened a primary school (taught in Pidgin) in 1960, replaced in 1964 by a government school where the teaching is done in English. Ten years later, a second public school opened its doors to the northern Eri, at Yafar 2. In 1982, three Yafar boys were continuing their secondary education in Aitape, on the coast.[7] In the area of health, the infrastructure put in place after 1960 (the Amanab Health Centre, run by a medical officer from outside the province with the help of a few health workers, and an Aid Post at Yafar opened at the same time as the school) is insufficient, and the only doctor for the province (still usually a foreigner) working in Vanimo, as well as his district officers, rarely visit the villages. In the 1960s and 1970s, the CMML periodically sent around a nurse, who examined the children brought to her.

The missionary phenomenon in this region is something of a special case. As I have said, the Anglo-Saxon Catholics had the advantage of 'ground' already prepared along the border by their Dutch counterparts from Amgotro and Waris. The CMML Protestants, solidly established in the Torricelli Range, came into the Green River area in the early 1950s, then into Amanab and Imonda after 1960. In Amanab, their main activity is a Bible school for boys from all over the district who already have some schooling; there they are 'trained' as Bible teachers before leaving to exercise their ministry, for the most part in their home villages. The concentration of the Amanab mission work considerably hindered village evangelization, especially to the north. The Australian missionary merely maintained relations with the villages in the vicinity of the station or those that could be reached on motorcycle. Certain southern Eri groups, especially the Nayneri, who, shortly after the founding of Amanab, hosted a family from the Summer Institute of Linguistics (Graham and Graham 1980),[8] were deeply affected, while the northern Eri were not even superficially introduced to Christian influences until the late 1970s.

The colonial history of the region visibly does not lack diversity, especially if one adds the contacts between the border villages

7. They returned to the village after four years of schooling. One of them went to Finshchafen to study to be a health worker, but died upon his return to New Guinea; another left to look for work in Madang and did not return.

8. This institute sends Protestant missionaries throughout the world to translate the Bible into the vernacular. Although their official function is to study languages, they often do missionary work on the side.

and their allies on the Indonesian side (who spoke the same native language, but used Bahasa Indonesia as their *lingua franca* rather than Pidgin). Nevertheless, the Yafar usually remained outside the white men's discrete rivalry for domination. The brief period of plantation hiring and the ensuing frustration of the next generation, condemned to listen to the memories of their elders, exacerbated the feeling of being consigned to the dustbin of history. In such conditions, the 1973 self-government phase, and then independence in 1975, could be nothing more for the Eri (with the exception of a very few salaried positions: gendarmes, school teachers, station employees) than abstract pieces of information whose only concrete counterpart was the replacement of Australian administrators by native officials from other provinces and by greater difficulty in finding even part-time work at the station. In spite of a few information campaigns before and after independence, aimed at the villages and local councils, the changes promised by the end of colonialism at the national level were neither understood nor perceived positively at the hamlet level. And the drop in job availability and purchasing power (in the mission or private shops in Amanab) which preceded or accompanied this transition period did not help the district government get its message across.

The Yafar Experience of Transition

Now that the historical context has been outlined, let us return to the Yafar. To paint a faithful picture, after their own accounts, of their experience of these first contacts and their feelings over the longer term about the process of a duplicitous transformation from which they do not always gain what they have hoped is too long and difficult an undertaking to do any more than evoke here. The Yafar experience the breaching of their own sociocultural limits and the encounter with men and habits from far away not only as a hope of acceding to material goods from the West, but as a symbol of renewal. Their perception of this foreign world is filtered by cultural imaginary representations; the Whites' material wealth, knowledge and power are interpreted in terms of representations of fertility, death and the universe. But at the same time, the Yafar listen to these foreigners talking about industry, production, mankind and his history, and they can only react with uncertainty, a mixture of desire, trust, incredulity and rejection. The dream, in 1971, of one former plantation worker under thirty – first councillor, ready to head back to the coast under any conditions, fervent follower of the 1981 Cargo Cult, critical of power but waiting hand and foot on visiting administrators – is symptomatic of this ambiguity. 'I learn that the *kiap* (patrol officer) is on his way to the village by way of Potayneri. Immediately I take my bow and arrows and leave the village in the opposite direction, on my land. I tell all the men and women I meet that the *kiap* is coming and to go back to the village right away. But I run away into the bush.'

Against the unchanging backdrop provided by this internalized form of their relationship with colonial and postcolonial power, recent Yafar history can be divided into three periods: the already old memories of the pre-government era, the era of Australian colonization, and lastly the years from independence to the present day.

The Yafar are not the only ones with memories of the bird-of-paradise hunters who, at various times, hunted the hill country as well as the Bapi plain. Among them were 'Whitemen' (in reality Indonesians) that the Yafar called '*Eber*' (southern Eri '*Aber*' or '*Apier*'),[9] from Dutch New Guinea, accompanied by carriers and Melanesian policemen. All spoke the same language, of which the Eri villagers have retained some thirty or so words, most of them recognizable as Indonesian, as well as the names of many of their visitors, among whom one woman. The Yafar received the *Eber* on two occasions; one of these visits lasted some five months, during which the hunters scoured the area and met with hostility from the Waina, on whom they are said to have been forced to use their guns. The *Eber* carried 'European' food with them, but they also purchased local produce with cowry shells, oblong white or round blue beads, manufactured items such as small knives, fabric and shirt buttons used as ornaments in place of cowries. Sometimes they stole from gardens. They also had steel axes and machetes, but did not leave any of these behind; in the southern groups, however, the rape of a woman was sometimes compensated by the gift of an axe. Around the same

9. From the Biak-Numbor term *amberi*, which the Melanesians of this area and later all West Irian Melanesians use to designate the Indonesians; the word has a pejorative connotation and means 'someone who hides wicked intentions behind flattering speech' (Tapol ed. 1983: 13).

time, the Yafar were visited twice by Melanesian hunters who had come alone from the east (the Sepik plain) and whom they called *'Ranay'* (southern Eri *'Nanay'*). In all of the villages, the *Eber* attempted to adopt children (no doubt for domestic service), which sometimes incited the Yafar women to take to the bush with their youngest offspring. The men of knowledge, for their part, secretly performed rites to send the Whites (the *Eber* and, later, the first administrators), back to where they came from, namely to the *mwig rabô*, 'the original white clay', a metaphor for *hoofuk* (Ch. 9), to the primordial place where they were supposed to keep the 'cargo' in eternal darkness.

The Second World War went almost unnoticed by the populations of the region despite the allied forces using the Abau clearing (the future Green River) as a secondary air base. This proximity probably had something to do with an air battle that drove the Yafar into the forest; later they watched tracts rain down from the sky, probably announcing Japan's surrender in 1945 and addressed to the many Japanese refugees hiding in the forests of Melanesia.

The introduction of the first Dutch axes, through trade with the Walsa via Ifêêg and Hubwiy allies (Map 2) and later by direct exchange with their Sowanda partners, brought changes to the local economy, at least in its technical aspects. Shortly after the establishment of Waris, at the end of the 1940s, these products began to wend their way east of the border via a chain of exchanges. The Yafar could obtain an axe from the Walsa for one large netbag (made by the women) or one large yam for planting. But their kin ties with the Kumwaag also obliged them to send some of the axes southward. The stock of metal tools was still low in 1960 when they came under Australian administration, and the Yafar had no money to supply their needs in Amanab. It was not until the first contract workers returned from the plantations (in 1964–65) that every cultivator had at least his own axe.

Indeed it was not until after the 1950s (see above) that the northern Eri – recruited, by an agent paid by the head, to work on the Australian plantations on the Gazelle and Buka peninsulas – took this step. While those who stayed behind would pay visits (quaking at the idea of crossing territories where they had no kinsmen) to the new Amanab station as a place of curiosity or possibly temporary work, a few young Yafar were being thrown into violent contact with the world of Western production and relations of exploitation. They shared this experience with men from other parts of Papua New Guinea for whom this was not the first time and from whom they learned Pidgin. 'Plantation stories' tell of 'good Whites' or 'bad Whites' who ran the plantations, which meant those who provided good food and respected working hours or those who gave out nothing but rice and vegetables and made their workers split coconuts late into the night by torchlight. There are also tales of fights among Melanesians, of braving the 'boss boy' and of complaints to the Administration when a worker would learn from a friend that his contract had been up for some months and he had the right to return home. Illness introduced some to the 'comforts' of the hospital and the efficacy of Western medicine. This is one of the arguments frequently advanced for returning to the city. Alternatively, the Yafar did not take to beer, unlike many workers who, following the Australian custom that had been adopted by the Melanesians, turned the weekend drinking spree into a social ritual subsequently carried over to the village. The more personal memories have to do with sexuality, homosexual advances, prostitution by schoolgirls and more experienced women who knew how to command respect. This venality as well as the relative sexual freedom on the coast contrasted sharply with the strict social control of Yafar society.

The first to leave paid the price of homesickness, some trying to run away when the plane set down in Wewak and return home on foot, taking several weeks to cover the distance that had required a mere hour by air (see Gell 1975: 4–5; Juillerat 1979). The ten Yafar came back from this trip to the *'tesin'* (plantation, coast, city) with a little money, some clothes, axes, wooden chests for storing their belongings and other manufactured goods. These items were given out to the family, to brothers and brothers-in-law, but readapting to the close community life back home was often difficult: some signed on again. Only one Yafar failed to return and is said to have married in Rabaul. In such cases, the contract worker becomes an urban job-seeker and works here and there for as long as the job lasts; he goes from the 'security' of the contract to what is called in Pidgin *wok mun*, work by the month.

In contrast to the *luluai* who, like the *korano* before them, were chosen among the men of the group who had already achieved a certain status, the councillors elected from 1965 on needed to speak Pidgin if they were to take part in local Council meetings. It was therefore the *boi*, that is young men back from the plantations, who took over the job. Between 25 and 35 years of age, the village *kaunsol* felt imbued with a power symbolized by the medal awarded to him by the government. In particular, he organized work on the roads (every Monday) and supervised village hygiene, accompanied the patrol officer on his rounds and presented him with the 'village book' in which he wrote down his observations. However, the village saw to it that he did not overstep his prerogatives and was ready to react at the first sign of excessive force: the *kaunsol* is supposed to be on the villagers' side and merely to pass on the Administration's orders. In the traditional power structure (Ch. 13), he is neither obtrusive nor in competition, but belongs to another order. Most local (tribal) elections among the northern Eri are by consensus and not by secret ballot: the voters, having come to an agreement beforehand, prefer to announce the name of their choice to the administrator in public when he comes around. This system places women – who have the same voting rights as the men – at a disadvantage, as it does those who side with the visible majority out of a spirit of conciliation or from fear of internal disorder. A decision concerning the whole society can be taken only through the public airing of all arguments. The secret individual vote is not compatible with the customary conception of life in society.

The announcement, in 1973, of the imminent 'arrival' of an enigmatic being, *'self gavman'* (self-government), cast a shadow of doubt over the tranquil, ambiguous relationship obtaining between the Yafar and the colonial administration. Something, or someone, was going to come and upset the status quo, which the villagers saw as protecting their rights, and might even threaten their control over their natural resources. They imagined one or two tall men from the coast taking over their crops and sago palms, 'killing' their women and children, and machines (images inspired by bulldozers seen on the plantations) levelling the countryside and cutting down the forest. Opinion was divided and fears varied, but some even feared a return to the marshy plains of the beginning of the world. For others, *self gavman* became the name of a lone figure, of a terrifying dictator. At the other extreme from this enslavement fantasy, national autonomy went unremarked on the local level and was concretized only by the total disappearance of Australian patrol officers after independence.

Plate 33. School at Yafar in 1976 (founded in 1974), flying the flag of independent Papua New Guinea.

Following the opening of the school in 1974 and the small aid post at Yafar 2, change broke out at the heart of Yafar society. The first northern Eri children were learning to read and speak English. At the same time Yafar 2 was turning into a regional meeting place, due to the aid post and the weekly convergence of parents who came to maintain the 'station'. Each year another teacher would arrive from the coast, move in and set up a new class, while a district health worker bandaged wounds and administered antibiotic shots or chloroquine pills. Teaching the children to read and write was fairly easy, despite the dissatisfaction of some head teachers. Opinion had been polled before hand, and most of the Yafar and their neighbours sent their sons, and to a much lesser extent their daughters, to acquire this foreign learning, even though they were unaware of its content or its purpose. Certain families sent only some of their sons to school, and kept the others at home to help in the garden; the girls too were kept home largely for economic reasons, as a mother unaided would find it difficult to keep up the housework and chores, work sago and look after young children.

The Yafars' reaction to modern health care deserves special attention. Their acceptance of medication but refusal, in cases of serious illness, to consult or call in the health worker can be explained by two types of factor: the conception and social practice of illness on the one hand, and their fear of being caught up in a vulnerable state by the outside world and dying far from the family on the other hand. I have already explained (Ch. 12) that illness is regarded as a desocializing process once it immobilizes the person or makes them physically (both in terms of strength and appearance) incapable of working or communicating. The sick person is the first to begin the marginalization, by staying at home, refusing to speak, being fed by the domestic group but receiving practically no visits. In these circumstances, neither the brothers nor the sons will send for the health worker (or the anthropologist), nor will they consider having the patient transported to Amanab; it is the patient himself who will request that no one be told of his state. If he thinks he has merely been attacked by *nabasa* spirits or perhaps by non-fatal *agi* sorcery, the appropriate healing rites should suffice, though pharmaceutical remedies may be accepted if they happen to be offered. But when a person sees himself sinking, he may suspect that he is the victim of an *aysiri* sorcerer and that there is no cure. Here too,

Western medicine is accepted but not actively sought. The cultural attitude towards sickness is therefore characterized by passivity. There is no fussing or commotion around a sick person, as with the Waina, for instance; on the contrary, people ignore him or do not speak of him. Such conditions do not automatically favour information reaching the nearest medical help. How many people have died since 1974 without the Yafar 2 aid post (a distance of thirty and sixty minutes respectively from the other hamlets) receiving the slightest request for aid? There is one exception: the Yafar are much more concerned about the health of their children than that of adult parents. Further away, Yafar 3 hamlet is also something of an exception: there more than elsewhere the sick are hidden away when the health worker comes through.

This cloak of silence thrown over the sick person can also be explained by fear of the outside world, motivated in the event by the risk that the patient might be sent first to Amanab, then to Vanimo and even on to Wewak. To leave one's village in a weakened state, with a *sungwaag* that might be 'ripe' (pp. 372–5), is to hand oneself over to foreign sorcerers. And to die away from one's land, with no contact with the family, is to be exiled forever, to die and leave one's *nabasa* and ghost with no social or territorial roots – to die away from home is to be irrevocably separated from one's group, from one's kinsmen living and dead, to be deprived of those highly valued exchanges with the living that are transmitted through hunting and mediumism. It is not Western medicine as such that is rejected, though; rather, the exile it sometimes requires is incompatible with the fate of humans after death. The fear of sorcery inside the Amanab hospital also explains why no Yafar wants to go there: furthermore the trail is impracticable for someone in a weakened state, and the sick are never carried on litters. For a Yafar in the mid-1990s, to be seriously ill is still to try to escape the notice of government health officials, to proceed calmly with the rituals advised by dream revelations or by mediums, and to stay at home and wait to recover or to die. As the sick often say: 'This is my village; if I am meant to die, I will die and be buried on my forest land.'

Personal relations between the Yafar and government employees, in the person of the health worker and various teachers, reproduce in part the ambiguity characteristic of their relations with administrators. Yet the latter are both geographically more distant and more powerful: the Yafar owe them nothing. In Yafar 2, people with a child at school or who have been cared for by the health worker feel bound by a more socialized relationship: they make presents of garden produce, betel or a bit of game. Government employees are authorized to hunt on Yafar land. The Yafar make the trip to Amanab, for a small sum or for nothing, to pick up supplies the teachers have ordered from the coast. But in private they grumble about these tasks, criticising the methods of one teacher or another and expressing doubts about the professional competence of the *dokta boi*. However, when one of the government representatives hails from the Amanab area, a certain feeling of brotherhood grows up. Still treated with skepticism in his functionary role, he is at the same time a *wan tok*, a friend. If he is unmarried and stays for several years, the Yafar may even offer him a wife. One of the teachers is a Wofneri (a village near Amanab) married to a Yafar woman. This was the first marriage contracted outside the usual networks.

Money entered northern Eri society in 1960, by way of temporary station jobs and through the plantation workers. Since the 1970s, the road has been the main source of income; yet there are no women on the lists of jobs drawn up by the administration. Alternatively, in the late 1970s, growing small peppers gave women a chance to earn their own money, even though many were content just to work alongside their husband. This modest and irregular income was spent on expendable items and, on occasion, saved. How much was saved and for how long are hard to determine, as everyone always claimed 'not to have any money'. Nevertheless people do keep money in the house or in their netbags, not to speak of some savings accounts taken out with the representative of the national bank in Amanab, a form of savings that had already been encouraged by the colonial government. Proceeding from the Administration, the only local source of revenues, the Yafar's income flows in the main back to Amanab, the only place to spend money,[10] and nearly all of it at the Protestant mission shop, where villagers from the area line up to buy clothing, soap, matches, batteries or rice. The mission is supplied from Wewak by the Protestant Churches' airline (whose only purpose is to connect the various mission stations) and sells to the local

10. In 1981 there were six shops registered at the Amanab station (Patrol Report, Amanab), most of which carried only a few basic products. The Protestant mission trade store was the only one able to renew its stocks before they ran out.

populations with what seems to be a comfortable profit margin when prices on the coast are compared with those of the shops in the interior. The lack of local competition in the case of most articles is another factor favouring this flourishing trade. And the difficulty the unschooled Eri have in counting their money and checking change (they often complain of being short-changed by the mission sales people) diminishes their already minute purchasing power.

In contrast to these small purchases scattered over the year, there are more important expenses which cannot be met with individual savings if these are not completed by village solidarity. Two situations call for such a request: the purchase of a shot-gun[11] (approx. 120 kinas in 1981, i.e. US$ 150, and more than twice that in 1984), and, since 1981, the necessity of paying room, board and school fees for the few students attending high school on the coast (around 150 kinas, or US$ 190, per student per year, including travel). Between the income and the outlay, and parallel to eventual savings, money circulates within the community and becomes an object of exchange very like traditional items. In spite of plans announced in 1981 to set up a shop in Yafar 2 which would be supervised by the teachers, and another small business open intermittently and run by the health worker, in the mid-1980s the Yafar had not yet taken in the idea of investment and returns. For them, money was still something that came from Europe, part of the 'cargo' which is controlled exclusively by Whites.

What will happen to Yafar culture under the pressure of these changes? The integration of new needs has a distracting effect which diverts attention, the young people's in particular, from the old values, although this process has not as yet reached the stage of explicitly depreciating the native culture. The government, notably under Michael Somare,[12] encourages people to rediscover the value of regional cultures and to maintain non-Christian symbolic and ritual complexes. The missions obviously do not go along with this. The CMML is increasingly endeavouring to make the Eri feel guilty by preaching a Manichean ideology in which local religious practices are placed on the side

---

11. Shot-guns and cartridges have been banned since the mid-1980s (see Ch. 7).
12. Head of the Papua New Guinea government from 1973 to 1978, and again from 1982 to 1985.

of Evil, of the Devil even,[13] and sorcery is seen either as a real power or a stupid belief, but not as part of the social system. It is not so much as dispensers of the Christian faith that the missions play an insidious role, however, but through the production in their Bible School of young zealots who, sent to villages throughout the province, go on to become the agents of an intolerant brand of Christianity determined to bring down the local cultural edifice. Formerly in direct contact with the locality and its people, today's missionary now works out of his home; he recruits his disciples, indoctrinates them and then sends them back to their villages, while partially financing his institution by selling local populations overpriced European products that are not always indispensable. And so a sham Christianity coupled with a simplistic moral teaching ill-adapted to the societies it is addressing is gradually creeping into even the most remote villages. Nevertheless, a trip I took through the nearby plain in 1973 convinced me that notwithstanding certain overzealous and authoritarian 'pastors', the local cultures were making a concerted effort to carry on in spite of and with this new element.

Although the Yafar live relatively close by, they receive only one or two visits a year from a student pastor, often extremely fearful of meeting these 'pagans', whom he suspects of diabolical activities; on this count, the missionaries' ethnocentric indoctrination finds fertile soil in the fear of the sorcery. Until the 1970s the entire population met evangelization with complete indifference, and it was only in 1986 that I heard a young Yafar confess his desire to go to Bible School. The elders saw the missionary's discourse as an alternative that ran counter to their own conceptions of the world, and the young people, although less knowledgeable about their own culture, often rallied to their elders' rejection. In the last few years, though, some young people have been lending a perplexed ear to their visitors' sermons. But they are still far from the example of their Wamuru neighbours who – according to the Yafar – collectively decided to adopt Christianity around 1980, apparently at the urging of their councillor. The Yafars' resistance can be explained in part by Cargo Cult rumours from western New Guinea, which do not explicitly refer to the Bible and which were concretized in the 1981 movement.

13. See the testimony of a CMML missionary from Lumi who – having been a long-time follower – has begun to criticize his colleagues severely for propagating this ideology (McGregor 1975).

When one has spent a total of over thirty months in such a small society, and this over a span of some fifteen years, one cannot help becoming involved in the ongoing process of change by becoming part of one's own object of study. This was all the more inevitable in my own case since, during these periods, I was constantly present and in permanent contact with the people. Unlike the administrator and the missionary, who exercise power at a distance, the anthropologist is close to the people and eschews any kind of power. Of course this does not mean that he is neutral or that his hosts are indifferent. A relationship has grown up between a community whose contact with the outside world is recent and a single individual, but one who represents a far-away, rich society. Essentially it is through this role as symbol, as the site on to which my hosts projected their frustrations and desires, that I see my primary involuntary role among the Yafar. Inevitably I left a whole arsenal of manufactured gifts, rapidly rendered useless, handed out European food and money to those who worked with me and, by placing my gun at the disposal of the community, enabled them, in 1971 and 1973, to distribute many times the normal amount of wildfowl. But these material advantages, of necessity distributed with a calculated parsimony – and which inevitably gave rise to grumbling –, were linked with the symbolic role the Yafar had tacitly assigned me. In a society which never engages in competitive deferred exchanges (like those carried on by 'big men' in other parts of Melanesia), but which does invest heavily in the desire for 'cargo', the anthropologist cannot help but consent to the role of dispenser of goods or partner in occasional exchanges that is expected of him (for instance, I was asked to pay for local food in European goods rather than with money). When I arrived in 1970 – even before they knew me – I had been invested with an enormous potential of wealth and generosity. Needless to say, my relationship with the Yafar has not been restricted to this kind of request. But running through the moments of privileged communications and the ties of friendship, there was always to some extent this expectation, this unsatisfied desire, which a small gift sufficed to fulfil. Even more than the thing, what was important was the gesture, going from my world, characterized in the Yafar mind by the effortless production of wealth, towards their own universe, doomed to confinement and poverty. It should be recalled that the Yafar expect the same type of symbolic gift from their forest spirits through dream experiences (Ch. 7).

I seemed to have little influence in social matters or relations with the authorities, and the Yafar rarely consulted me. They asked me very few questions about Europe or my family. The presence of my wife Michèle in 1978 situated me as part of a couple, which turned out to be necessary for unlocking certain relationships as well as items of ethnographic information not hitherto forthcoming. When, in answer to their questions on the origin of Western manufactured items, I told them about industrial production, they listened with incredulous concentration, but when I tried to tell them about my life in Paris, they promptly brought me back to more accessible preoccupations. The few times I intervened in favour of certain openings for local development, my comments on the economic and political background of the colonial plantations (the workers back from the Bismarck Archipelago were unaware of the geographical and commercial destinations or the use of the copra they produced) or my occasional allusions to nearby western New Guinea and its recent history may have helped broaden the Yafars' horizons. But on the whole, I usually maintained a non-interventionist attitude, which no doubt both limited my role as an agent of change and preserved the symbolic character of my status.

To what extent can a symbol bring about change? That is the question, but I have no clear answer. The anthropologist may have precipitated the external orientations already present in Yafar culture. This he will have done through what he himself represents, but also by exhibiting his 'cargo', this mandatory attribute of all Westerners. This association links the white man with *hoofuk* (Ch. 9), because to have access to wealth is to exercise control, not over production in the Western sense of the word, but over primal fertility. The European anthropologist (like the Australian administrator minus his power) is to a certain extent the embodiment of this notion. Someone said to me one day: 'When you are here we feel good, we find game and we are healthy; when you go away we get sick and we die.' And when a high-ranking old man burst into tears when I left in 1981, it was because, above and beyond any personal ties, this separation meant a loss of security. With his stocks of food, his presumed knowledge (which he is unwilling to divulge) of how to (re)produce wealth, his generosity and his retention, the anthropologist in one sense resembles a guardian of fertility, that is to say, a *nabasa*.

The link between symbol and change may perhaps be found in the fact that the anthropologist, by living in the host community, enables it to live this relation from the inside and in everyday life. This relational ordeal generates new experiences on the social and psychic levels rather than economic or cultural change. The anthropologist opens the way for a more intense experience of the other, equivalent and inverse to his own experience; and just as this relationship leaves traces in him, it probably also leaves traces in the host society.

Neither the modernization processes set in motion by the government, nor the missionary activities, nor the long stretches of plantation work altered the traditional social structure. With the exception of the defusing of violence by the 'pacification' movement, and the Yafars' own relaxation of exchanges between *sêh* after the introduction of steel axes and the clashes between Yafar and Sowanda, the socioeconomic system remained unchanged. The area of communication had grown, but the alliance network and the boundaries of the kinship circle remained as they were. Yafar society had received stimulations from the outside and had accepted a school on its territory and an anthropologist in its villages, but this did not call into question the internal organization of exchanges or rank or the function of the bulk of ritual.

It was not until a new beacon began winking on the other side of the Indonesian border, broadcasting the 1981 cult in the direction of the Yafar, that the society, with no official urging, began to examine itself more critically and to question certain of its fundamental precepts.

The 1981 Millenarian Movement

This cult, the outcome of the contact situation in general and very likely of the Melanesian uprising against Indonesian power west of the border (Osborne 1985; Tapol ed. 1983), was to my knowledge the first in Amanab District. Apparently the Yafar episode is only one local aspect of a phenomenon that runs the length of the border,[14] or at least the stretch between Waris-Imonda and

14. Millenarian movements originating in Irian Jaya have also been discovered along the coast as far north as Aitape (see Losche 1990: 398–9).

Kamberatoro. A similar cult is said to have grown up on either side of the border in the vicinity of Waris. Here I will simply look at the concrete form of the movement in the Yafar cultural context, where it was introduced through alliances entertained by several Yafar clans with the two Irianese villages of Ifêêg and Hubwiy (Map 2).

News had reached the Yafar as early as 1977–1978 (although I heard nothing of this at the time) of contacts between Melanesian Irianese and Umeda. Internal conflict is said to have prevented the cult taking hold in Umeda, but vague unsubstantiated reports had already reached the Yafar of promises of wealth and the necessity of partially abandoning subsistence gardening. It was in 1981 that Yafar 3, then Yafar 1 and 2, began organizing secret men's meetings and nighttime rallies. Several trips to see their distant allies (ten to twelve hours' walk) in Ifêêg and Hubwiy were undertaken (only the young men went) to obtain additional information on the underground site further west where their dead were supposed to manufacture European riches. The whole cult was kept strictly secret, and I was able to gather my information only due to the discrete cooperation of a few friends.

Mythic References: Fertility and 'Cargo'

It has often been written that Melanesian 'cargo' cults validate the belief in the supernatural origin of the white man's wealth by readapting ancient myths to new circumstances.[15] What anthropologists have perhaps not satisfactorily brought out, on the other hand, is the specific symbolic association underlying this identification. For the Yafar, there is a clear continuity between their vision of maternal fertility, accessible only through oedipal transgression, as shown by the exegesis of the myth of The Stolen Game (see Ch. 7, p. 183 and secondarily Ch. 11, p. 352), and the fantasized vision of the 'cargo' in a blood-spattered cavern, guarded by a bloody male figure, by *bos* (from 'boss') who maintain the link with the outside and by armed men (an image apparently inspired by the Irianese rebels), who watch the door. The narrow entrance is wedged between two 'bones' of the

15. See, for example, Burridge 1960, Jeudy-Ballini 1988, Lattas 1992, Lawrence 1964, Panoff 1971.

mother divinity's pelvis (also called the 'mother' and the 'father'), already represented by the roots of the *ahômp Ficus* in the profane version of the myth. When the millennium comes, the bones will spread, either letting out the dead and the 'cargo' or letting in the chosen members of the cult. The myth did not need much touching up to identify European goods with game, a scarce product in a subsistence economy; all that was needed was to add that along with his three elder sons, the angry father buried in the underground gallery (profane version) or in the uterus of the Cosmic Mother (esoteric version) the 'Western' manufactured goods that were originally part of their cultural heritage. Already in the earlier version, the paternal punishment banished the 'oedipal' sons back to the female *hoofuk*, while the father denied himself access by blocking the entrance. In the 'cargoist' complement to the myth, the sons are also endowed with the wealth that they are now going to be able to reproduce at will. With hindsight, the Yafar experts claim that upon seeing the first Whites, they understood that these were probably the descendants of the Three Sons.[16] In this way, the 'cargo' was integrated into the continuity of a single tradition which embraced the Yangis imaginary representation of the birth of the *ifəge* (p. 53) or the father's secret of the origin of game (i.e. procreation), as well as the discovery of modern riches and the resurrection of the dead fantasized as childbirth. According to this revised version, Whites are the descendants of the eldest line, whose wealth the three Melanesian ancestors had taken down into the bowels of the Mother Earth, obliging their father and their youngest brother themselves to fashion the traditional objects handed down even today. In this inverted version of the story, in which the steel axe is designated by the term *mwig maar* 'original adze', the 'cargo' is wealth which has been diverted from its true cultural line of inheritance.

The mental image of the gift received which we have already encountered in hunting ideology, dream interpretation and the relationship with the anthropologist attains its maximum dimension in the millenarian vision. This time the expectation was focused not only on a passing portion of the primal treasure trove, not on a product, but on the entirety through access, with the

---

16. According to some versions, the underground gallery where the father shut up his three sons came out in Australia.

help of the dead, to the buried site where all merchandise is produced. This place had a secret name, which I will not divulge
here, but it could be designated by the expressions usually employed for the original source of life, *mwig kəbik* 'original place'
(in Pidgin *'as ples'*), namely 'placenta place', *mosuwô taf kəbik*, or
'delivery bark place', *mosuwô kəfe* (on which women give birth),
'original kaolin place', *mwig rabô kəbik*, or even more simply, *hoofuk kəbik* (Ch. 9); the members of this cult lived their spiritual
quest as a 'search for the bark and the placenta'. Once they had
acquired enough book learning in special 'schools' and had been
accepted by the guardians of the place, the chosen Yafar would
be able to enter. They would descend, naked as new-born babes,
and there they would recognize the familiar voices of their dead
relatives behind the bloody faces, make love to beautiful women
and see the piles of wealth and money. Two broad paved roads,
one for each moiety, would lead out towards the Yafar villages.
Christmas 1981 was somewhat doubtfully announced as the
likely date of the millennium.

The desire for European goods is therefore inscribed in a cultural continuity, despite the unprecedented break produced by
contact. Any production of goods not under human control from
start to finish (growth of tubers, or sago palms, reproduction of
game, formation of the human foetus) is explained by a principle
that can never be integrated into experience, namely the *hoofuk*.
The white man's wealth naturally falls into this category; it is
even, by its particular sophistication, an expression of the highest
level.

The mythic loss of the 'cargo' is explained by a transgression,
but not the one that might be expected. In effect, through a striking inversion of the transgression in the oedipal paradigm, the
myth of The Three Sons makes the father responsible (through
his excessive anger and his refusal to recognize the filiation of his
elder sons) for the loss of this wealth, whereas ultimately, his
'incestuous' children are banished from society, excluded, but
wind up with the 'cargo' and the *hoofuk*. Now at last their claims
to the game appear legitimate and the father's rage a mistake,
just as today the Yafars' quest for the original wealth is validated
by the purported White monopoly.

The Attempt to Reconstruct a Social Identity

Although some anthropologists (see especially Burridge 1960, 1971; Kilani 1983; Worsley 1973) rightly claim that the anticipation of 'cargo' is not always the main component of Melanesian millenarian and messianic cults, in the Yafar case it appeared as the cornerstone. And yet this seemingly materialistic desire hid a more spiritual searching, which is none other than a permanent quest for a means of mastering fertility. However, the cult, as manifested among the Yafar in 1981, cannot be reduced to this dimension. The society was examining its position and its rights with respect to the Westernized world, but it was also examining itself. This self-questioning did not concern the social structures as such, but rather the ethical values underpinning social relationships. It was, furthermore, part of an overall strategy which the cult members were trying to perfect in order that their community might appear worthy of being chosen in the eyes of the father-figure who controlled access to the *hoofuk*. This bloody figure would see the Yafar men coming through a sheath of coconut petiolar fibre (symbol of the uterus) and would let in only those who were good. Another version presents a man, head of the cult west of the border, who was supposed to recognize the moral quality of the members by viewing them in a mirror (those whose wives were menstruating and who showed up red would be turned back). People also spoke of a great prophet, a sort of messiah (see the chapter epigraph), who would visit the Yafar and address them in a voice that would make them tremble, while the sun at its zenith would grow black and a devastating wind would sweep away to the sea all those who fled into the forest. Such perspectives called for the moral restoration of society, which was the object of the periodical 'meetings' which assembled the men and women in the village square of Yafar 1. The people of Yafar 3, closer to Irian Jaya and allied with the Ifêêg and the Hubwiy, always attended, and one of them, the cult leader, would conduct the meetings and do most of the speaking. He would hold forth on general principles concerning community and family solidarity, bodily cleanliness, child care and the danger to the society of all forms of aggressiveness or asociality. Anyone looking for a fight was to be met with silence. Quarrelling couples had to make up, and their marital conflicts were laid before the audience by witnesses for the two sides. Those who persisted in the practice of sorcery would be recognized, on the day, by their risen victims. If the whole community did not adopt this new conduct, they would be 'covered by fog' (*rangôk kagwôg*; see the parallel with relation to game, p. 196), and the 'cargo' would never be found.

Although the women formed a group apart, they had the right to speak out in public and, for the first time, appeared to parti-cipate on an equal footing in collective demonstrations. The new identity seemed set on abolishing sexual discrimination in daily life and within the couple, but not in the control of knowledge: esoteric discussions were for men only, and only men would have access to the 'cargo' and would be responsible for its dis-tribution. Women might speak out, but in fact only men went in for speech-making. Never have I seen the Yafar place such value on words: after speeches by the leader and his helpers, other men – including young ones – would hold forth on one principle or another of the new law of society. Delivered with great feeling, each speech ended with a collective approbation in the form of an enthusiastic 'Yesa!'. The passive listener who did not voice his approval loudly was suspected of individualism and implicit col-laboration with the Amanab government against the new faith.

From time to time, the moral rigour was reinforced by a military-style discipline, with cult members coming to attention and saluting each other. The young men about to leave for the allied Irian villages were reviewed by the leaders, who inspected their dress and gave them a talk. It was on one such occasion that an Ifêêg 'brother-in-law', on an exceptional visit, seemed to me to behave more like an army recruiter than a kinsman. These men imagined themselves coming back from the western New Guinea cult 'schools' uniformed and armed with guns. One glimpses the impact produced on the Yafar imagination by the military patrols in this border region, when the troops camped on the outskirts of villages and had their supplies dropped in by parachute.

The hierarchy that emerged in the developing cult should be placed in the context of the 'hidden powers' analysed in Chapter 13. The principal leader is the only exception to the corres-pondence between traditional ritual responsibilities and the new powers. And this is no accident: to begin with the cult was intro-duced on the personal initiative of one man, who had in-laws among the Ifêêg and the Hubwiy and who had just given his agnatic niece in marriage there. His frequent visits to his Irianese allies made him, together with his fellow clansmen, a potential propagator of the cult. For the rest, it was his personal qualities that made him a leader. His difficulty in readapting to village life upon return from the plantations in the 1960s (he 'ran amok', as it were, and his co-villagers had to tie him up and hold him in the smoke to exorcize him) can be seen as an early sign of his prophetic calling. The other cult leaders appeared later, in an effort to structure the movement, and it is not surprising that these were chosen whenever possible from among the ritual masters or their lineages.

What other roles were there in the 1981 movement? The cult headquarters were in Yafar 3, but its leader had to be represented by counterparts in the other two residential groups. In Yafar 1 this was the Master of the Earth (also a medium), in Yafar 2 the youngest brother of the Master of the Earth. One is immediately struck by the parallel between the symbolic context attaching to the former office, in particular the relationship with the Mother Coconut and the chthonian depths, and that surrounding the nature of the 'cargo' as defined above. Two other roles were ensured by younger men, but their meaning is not absolutely clear. According to one informant, the representatives of the first role, 'the guardians of the women', stayed behind in the village during cross-border expeditions, while the heads of the latter group, 'the guardians of the dogs' were supposed to be the advance party, going ahead to 'prepare the way' and to gather information from mysterious figures in the most remote villages (something that was never done during my stay). Once again one glimpses an analogy with hunting and the dog on the trail of game, running back and forth between his master and the quarry. The two new roles per residential group were represented as follows:

Guardians of the women
Yafar 1: the eldest son of the Master of the Sky, heir to the office
Yafar 2: the first younger brother of the Master of the Earth
Yafar 3: the Master of the Earth himself

Guardians of the dogs
Yafar 1: the former first councillor, highly respected despite his youth and a younger brother with no official role but enjoying guaranteed prestige
Yafar 2: the heir to the (abandoned?) title of Master of the Sun

Yafar 3: the only adult representative of Tawank lineage, former
depository of the magic for multiplying fish (*sawôg seeg
na awaag*).

Here again the choices were the result of a compromise
between the individual personality and the position occupied in
the traditional power structure.

After what was said earlier about the Yafars' disillusionment
with national independence, and also in view of the armed struggle of the Melanesian people of western New Guinea against the
colonial power in Jakarta, it is easy to see the whole paradox of
the cult. The fight for independence to the west, disappointment
with independence and nostalgia for the 'good white man' to the
east: two opposite reasons meet in this millenarian anticipation,
a disappointed hope in this case too, but one which henceforth is
inscribed in Yafar culture and will be ready to spring back to life
at some time in the future. Although politically contradictory,
these two versions of the movement find a common denominator
in (obvious) economic frustration, but also in the quest for a recognized identity. As for the Irianese side, I know nothing about
the circumstances in which the cult came about nor how long
it has existed. It seems to be part of a broader context of liberation movements and to have taken on a more properly religious
dimension in the border villages, while at the same time being
manipulated for purposes of recruitment. The Yafar know very
little about events west of the border (until the 1980s they had not
even heard of the name Indonesia), and their Ifêêg and Hubwiy
allies appear to them as the impassable threshold on an imaginary trail they have never walked. The political permeability of
the border contrasts here with the impenetrable security of the
kinship circle. The exaltation produced by the idea of a new era
founded on riches, equality with and separation from the Whites,
and communion with the dead ended, in late November 1981,
with what seems to have been felt as a failure. The last expedition
had been cut short, and the Yafar had come home complaining
that they had been cheated.

To build a strong new identity by seizing control of the production of the lost 'cargo', independently of but parallel to the
Whites, but also to impose a new moral code on the group in
order to be worthy of entering the 'original place' – these seem to
have been the guiding principles of the cult. The 'cargo' is at once

an end and a means; the attempts at reshaping society through the public meetings (which appear to have been inspired by the Western missionary ethic, but again may only be an idealized vision of social relations) were explicitly aimed at pleasing the guardians of the deceased and of the riches, but also at consolidating an individual and collective 'ideal ego' that had been severely shaken. Over and above the anticipated material advantages, the 'opening of the way' would also endow the Yafar with their true strength while gradually bringing them into a broader community as the millennium advanced. Dependence can only be overcome by abundance, and the significant stipulation of the 'cargoist' dogma that Blacks would henceforth have their own source of riches, while the Whites would keep theirs, reveals a desire for equivalence – to use R. Bastide's term (1975: 153) – not for rivalry.

The socio-religious enterprise just described developed little by little and is perhaps still only in its infancy. Through their cross-border contacts and internal consultations, the Yafar gave the impression of being engaged in a veritable quest, proceeding by trial and error, by contradictions and corrections. The cult experience had its ups and downs, in a constant process of becoming, and that is no doubt its main strength, more than its anticipation of the millennium as such, which, from a psychosocial point of view, merely serves to validate their search for identity. This is perhaps what certain Western observers failed to see when they voiced surprise at the perseverance of cult followers despite their successive failures to receive the 'cargo'.

I will end this chapter with a few comments on the validity, for the Yafar, of an alternative between 'cargo' cult and economic development.[17] The cult grew up against the backdrop of reluctance to invest in the various possible cash crops (mainly hevea at the time) proposed by the government. The spatio-political dualism (west-foreigner-millennium/east-government-no outlets) which placed the cult in a dichotomous world view favoured the momentary rejection of development. The rare fields of immature hevea planted by a few young Yafar were left untended, and peppers, still a prosperous crop in 1978–1979, were totally aband-

17. On the problem of the validity of this alternative, see Kilani 1983. For other comments about development in the Border Mountains, see Peter 1990.

oned (despite an upturn in the market, which had momentarily collapsed). Shortly after the last cross-border expedition mentioned above, the department of agriculture representative from Amanab came to advise the villagers on their hevea crops: the majority of the few Yafar concerned did not even take the trouble to go to their nearby fields. In 1981 several men even decided not to clear new subsistence gardens. The cult, then, had a tendency to hold back productive work in general. No doubt, the alternative between millenarian movement and development need not feature openly in all cults of this type, but the evident contradiction between the two orientations can appear on the ground, especially in those regions recently contacted, where change is still a new experience.

And yet the notion of work, and even of 'hard work', was part of the millenarian 'programme'. It said that along with acquiring special knowledge, there would have to be a period of hard work before the inactivity that would be authorized by the control of riches. When I left the region, in November 1981, the government was announcing a programme of intensive work on the Sepik-Vanimo road and the arrival in Amanab of the corresponding machines.[18] Certain Yafar saw in this the 'hard work' that was to precede the next stage in the cult. And so the district administration, although somewhat disqualified because of its limited financial means, was suddenly seen as furthering the conditions indispensable for the subsequent acquisition of the 'cargo'. The local Member of Parliament, a Nayneri (southern Eri), is even said to have encouraged this idea and is supposed to have declared his confidence in a coming age of abundance.[19] The roadwork was accepted because roads are a symbol of elsewhere, whereas village fields represent a sentence of decisive sedentarization. By the end of 1981, the young generation could think of nothing but escaping from the closed circle of the subsistence economy as well as from the everlasting social space which seemed to be shrinking in a world which, they heard, was becoming ever more vast. Looking back, this violent rejection of their ancestral lands, associated with disillusionment with the cult, appears to have been a passing phase. When I last visited

18. Nothing had changed in 1986.
19. At least this is what was retained by a few Yafar who attended one meeting organized by the MP.

the Yafar, in 1986, this rejection had abated and a new hamlet had been founded, which, despite the many residential splits in the rest of the society, seemed to announce a relative stabilization over the middle term. Nevertheless, a rise in the number of cases of tuberculosis in the region has recently compromised this evolution (Juillerat 1992b).

Conclusion

An organization founded – like that of the Yafar – on defensive atomization and strong internal solidarity seems to determine a lack of strong institutions or social relationships. The predominance of diffuse exchanges within the security circle, or the clear preference for symmetrical exchanges (barter or marriage by direct exchange), the absence of a traditional currency as well as of stockpiling for later redistribution or collective exchanges, like the very limited circulation of goods on the occasion of outstanding events (marriages, funerals, etc.), comprise a set of facts, all of the same nature, which suggest that Yafar culture has invested in something other than the construction of a complex system of social relationships. This something is socialized nature – supernature – with which humans entertain intense relations. An important part of this social and psychic investment has to do with the natural forces or socialized entities located *extra muros*, outside society itself; and it emerges that it is with this parallel world that the community has developed its need for reciprocity in particular. A Yafar man feels at ease in this benign forest with which he has established a codified system of exchanges. Negative or dangerous forces are relegated to the subterranean depths or somewhere beyond the territorial boundaries (or they come from within society itself via sorcerers), while community lands and even the more distant hunting grounds are places of highly valued communications with the invisible. Even a young person acquires his adult status by confirming his symbolic control over natural fertility; 'initiation' is replaced by what is first of all simply a ritual whose purpose is to have the novice approved by the spirit guardians of fertility, and it is only in this roundabout way, through the mediation of nature, that the acquisition of social status is ensured. The idea of initiation is also symbolically *represented* in the Yangis festival, where only two actors (one for each moiety) embody the initiate. This could explain the absence of initiation rites as a device for social integration through the elder men's direct action upon the younger. The same holds for authority and powers: society masks the institutional side in favour of secrecy and its effectiveness as a two-pronged strategy for the perpetuation of the male ideology and for the proper governance of nature. As the vessel of esoteric knowledge, secrecy applies to everything including the identity of those who know; to reveal its implicit political value would be tantamount both to letting women in on precisely what it is that sets them culturally apart from men and to revealing the mechanisms of male dominance. In short, this continual integration of nature into society contributes to hobbling sociopolitical development. One of the founding principles of Yafar society seems to be this twofold phenomenon whose contradictory orientations are welded together in their complementarity.

These conditions ensure that the 'political' dimension of social life remains a prisoner of 'infrasocial'[1] categories, such as sex and age, of descent reckoning or of the founding kinship relations, as an experience and a representation that is at once individual and collective, psychological and social. Bastide (1972a: 222–4) has shown that psychoanalysing a culture is in no way tantamount to reducing the social to the psychic, but requires identifying the 'transformation rules' which have enabled the psychic structure to reproduce itself in the sociocultural structure and conversely the latter to produce meaning in individual thought (see Green 1995). As far as the Yafar are concerned, we have seen how often their conceptual system, assembled from infrasocial structures, recurs on many levels. Indeed it seems that nearly all the principles of organization use, to various degrees, one 'key-representation' or another (see Juillerat 1993a; Ortner 1973), and are often its most direct expression. Group structures, alliance systems, forms of young male 'initiation', rituals for protecting a person or reproducing totemic units, etc. – all of these processes refer to descent reckoning (institutional agnatic or uterine), to the relationship with the real or mythic mother, to the oedipal transgression and its regulations, to the temporal irreversibility of the social order, to the transcendental relationship with the male or female 'bloods' etc. In conjunction with this, we have seen how female

---

1. By this term I designate not that which is not yet in the social domain, in the full sense of the term, but that which constitutes its foundations.

pollution, the expression of the sacredness ascribed to women's fecundity, is filtered through these infrasocial categories and transformed into a partially controllable power by being declared the effect of the improper social use of *hoofuk*. This manifestly coherent complex of signifiers is expressed by countless metaphors borrowed from nature: social categories and basic family relationships are projected on to the cosmos, while the universe is 'introjected' into the social group. One contains the other in the image man fashions of this relationship. And yet the question of the primacy of one over the other is worth raising; for, while the sexualization of the world, or the inscription of male descent reckoning mediated by the mother in the trajectory of the sun, assigns primacy to the social sphere and kinship over a simple explanatory vision of the universe, the personification of the cosmic forces in certain hereditary roles, and therefore in certain individuals, seems to proceed from an opposite principle (Juillerat 1992b). Might there be, then, a chain of factors which, starting from infrasocial experience, is ultimately projected on to a cosmological and mythic vision which reproduces its structures, even though certain cosmic principles may also be socially reintegrated in accordance with the meaning with which they have been endowed by this projection and no doubt in accordance with their physical role in nature as well (e.g. the balance between wet and dry). This, at least, is what seems to emerge from this integrated exchange between nature and society. Generally speaking, then, it is by attempting to control nature that society seeks to ensure its own continuity.

But this symbolic construction is only secondarily the expression of a quest for material efficacy, and representation prevails over belief here. Religion is not a technique serving production; the true driving force behind the conceptual elaboration does not lie in the quest for economic profitability, but elsewhere. Were profitability the only concern, the transmission of ecological knowledge and techniques, the preservation of the domestic plant pool and the exercise of a rationality constantly tested by reality would be sufficient. But while an overly strict economistic approach is not the solution, neither is systematic sociological reductionism. Both are the handmaidens of a functionalism, or – as Sahlins (1976) says – a utilitarianism incapable of replacing the semantic value of cultural categories.

Of the infrasocial categories mentioned above, the one that is apparently the simplest but which triggers the most heated discussions and the sharpest differences is that of male-female relations and their representations. I will not try to propose a theory applicable to all New Guinea groups, but I would like to end this book with a few remarks suggested to me by the Yafar material.

The first is that the real relationships (social, familial, economic, etc.) between men and women are partially determined by mental and cultural representations of sexuality and procreation. However, from time to time they manage to break free of these and in this case are governed by other, more objective factors (e.g. rational aspects of the sexual division of labour). Although reproductive sexuality is founded on the complementarity of sexual roles (dual organization), it is also characterized by a flagrant disproportion between the male role – episodic and unencumbered by the process of gestation-feeding – and the female role, defined by the lasting nature of motherhood (Yangis). The woman is distinguished from the man by the fact that she is the *site* of gestation.[2] If one accepts the idea that human reproductive sexuality is experienced as an intrusion of nature into society, it follows that the largest non-socializable share of the procreation process falls to women. It is not woman as a person or a social category that is placed on the side of nature, but her capacity to bear children, her procreative function. Subsequent to the processes that transform this biological fact into a central representation of culture, man, inasmuch as he stands outside this phenomenon, makes it into an object of social control. Female fecundity appears to be managed by the male community in the alliance *system*, which does not mean that the woman is not allowed her say in *individual* choices. The opposition between female continuity and male discontinuity is reproduced in the ideal model of the marriage cycle determined by the closure ending the marriage prohibitions (Figure 32), but this opposition is at the same time reversed on the one hand, by the dominance of patriliny and the status of exchange units accorded to agnatic groups, and on the other, by the male monopoly of the fertility ritual, in which men set themselves up as the organizing subject, as masters of

2. On the idea that the cultural differentiation of women is based on their procreative function (and not on anatomical sex), see Héritier 1984–1985.

predominantly female natural fertility.[3] Even hunting as an exclusively male endeavour fits into this paradigm: certainly it is a male activity because it requires exercising a degree of violence, but also because game comes from the Mother Earth and is guarded by male spirits, whom the hunter undertakes to charm by exchange and with whom he will be identified after death.

'Male domination' is therefore exercised over nature first of all as the feminized site of reproduction. Men reserve hunting and the distribution of game for themselves, just as they act on women with the purpose of incorporating into their own descent group the child that will be born; and if they alone know how to play musical instruments and to perform rituals, it is because this too is part of the dialogue with nature's fertility.

Some will say that these are only pretexts for imposing men's political domination on women, that the paradigms of the imaginary representations merely provide the means of subordinating women in the organization of production and power. And yet Yafar social organization does not seem to substantiate this explanation. Their sexual division of labour (Appendix B) is fairly well balanced; although land-holding rights are handed down *de jure* through men, in fact women cannot be left landless. The distribution of produce is highly egalitarian, the single exception being game; only this last point appears as an abuse, which nothing but the men's global claim on the entire sphere of hunting could justify in the eyes of those involved. Aside from this crucial element, there is no economic discrimination between men and women, nor is there any between seniors and juniors. The systems of reciprocity, attribution and redistribution to younger siblings, solidarity and sharing between members of the household level any differences that may be present in the initial stages of the production process.

Relations between the sexes in socio-economic organization are thus marked more by complementarity than by inequality, even though they are accompanied by a minimum of intercommunication. Domination is exercised primarily over nature and over what appears as specifically natural – that which cannot

3. The Yafar idea, discussed in Chapter 9, that the father should have frequent sexual intercourse with his wife during the first half of her pregnancy (so that the child will develop properly, but also to mark it with the stamp of his paternity) can also appear as a device by which men recover some of the duration of gestation, thus compensating for the episodic nature of their biological role.

be socialized – in society, not over the individuals or the goods within the society. Constraint, when and where it is exerted, is episodic and used as a means, not as an end or a system.

While the dominant ideology is largely restricted to men's claims on female fecundity through the exercise of social and ritual control, the development of a system of symbolic exchanges with nature can be seen as a guarantee that the balance of power in society will remain if not equal, at least complementary and will not go on to become a political strategy in the hands of any one social category or group.

Appendix A: Linguistic Note

Phonology

The Amanab phonological system is the object of a study by Henry Tourneux (CNRS) based on my recordings of the Amanab lexicon.[1] Certain minor problems need checking with an Amanab speaker, which my colleague was unable to do. Nevertheless, the phonological tables below correspond to my own experience of the language, and additional details provided by Tourneux, for whose collaboration I am grateful, have allowed me to clear up certain ambiguities. I have only one reservation, and that concerns the vowel *oe/ooe* (which I have placed in parentheses); I am not personally convinced that it is relevant and will assimilate it to /ô/ or /u/, depending on the case (this sign is therefore not used in my transcriptions).

Vowels

	Short			Long	
i	[ə]	u	ii		uu
ê	ö	ô	êê	öö	ôô
e	(oe)	o	ee	(ooe)	oo
	a			aa	

Comments:
 – the [ə] is a schwa which replaces a vowel that has been dropped (but which can sometimes be identified in certain speakers as /e/ or /a/).
 – 'mute vowels in unaccented final position' (H.T.). The only one is /ɨ/, which is pronounced like an *ɨ* that has lost its voicing.

---

1. This lexicon has recently been filed with the *Melanesian Archives* at the University of California at San Diego (Juillerat 1994).

– 'It would seem that the place of the tonic accent is non-predictable, in other words that it is relevant in Amanab. It is characterized by a more emphatic articulation and a slight lengthening of the vowel' (H.T.). It is particularly noticeable in the syllable preceding a mute vowel (*'êrɨ*) or following a schwa (*bə'sa*); the accent has not been marked in this work.

Consonants
1) In initial and intervocalic positions (the sounds in square brackets indicate the various phonetic realizations of the phonemes):

	Back	Central	Front
Voiceless	p [p]	t [t]	k [k]
Voiced	b [b, ᵐb]		g [?g, g, γ]
Fricatives	f [ɸ]	s [s, ts]	h [h]
Nasals	m [m]	n [n]	ng [ⁿg]
Semi-vowels	w [w]	y [y]	
Retroflex		r [ ]	

Comments:

a) 'Historically, /r/ probably comes from a **d*. However, synchronically, it does not correlate with voicing (it can appear in final position when the opposition is neutralized in favour of a voiceless pronunciation); this is why I have not placed it with the voiced consonants' (H.T.).

b) 'Before a mute vowel, /b/ may be pronounced [ᵐb or ᵐp] and /ng/ may be pronounced [ⁿg or ⁿk]' (H.T.).

2) In final position. 'In this position the opposition voiceless/voiced is neutralized' (H.T.).

p [ᵐp]	t	k [k⁻, g]
f	s	h
m	n	ng[ⁿk]
w	y	
	r	

'One is obliged to recognize that the final consonant raises a serious problem because of the presence of a mute unstable vowel, so that it is not always possible to tell whether it is truely a final consonant or a final vowel. Whence, too, the difficulty of telling whether the *k/g* opposition in final position is really neutralized. This will explain some of the hesitations in my notation' (H.T.).

Comments:

a) The voiceless/voiced opposition is usually neutralized in favour of the voiceless pronunciation, except following a long vowel. In the latter case, I have kept *-g* in the spelling

e.g. *awaag* (*/awaak/*)

b) In all verbs there occurs an opposition which I have noted *kag/kak* ('to go' / 'has gone'). Tourneux sees this as simply a special case of a); for him there is an opposition between long/short vowel *kaag/kak* (*/kaak/* ~ */kak/*).

c) After a voiced consonant, the mute vowel *i* is often reduced to a slight palatalization. In this case I have written

ag, wog, instead of *agi, wogi.*

Verb Clusters

Personal subject pronouns for the singular, dual (verb prefix *ah-*) and plural are distinguished by different pronoun suffixes for the objective case. The endings for the tenses recorded are:

Infinitive or present indicative	*-g*	*-g*	'to eat'
Preterite	*-k*	*ne-k*	
Conditional and polite imperative	*-i*	*ne-i*	
Subjunctive	*-m*	*ne-m*	
Future, conditional	*-f*	*ne-f*	
Immediate future, intentional	*-gêm*	*ne-gêm*	
Continuity of action or state	*-fêm, -fum*	*ne-fêm*	

The root alone is used for the categorical imperative,

e.g.   *ne!*   'eat!'

and before a pronoun or an auxiliary

e.g.   *ne fe-g,*   '*to eat*'

Affixes are often used to convey specific semantic values. For example:

atê-perfective (completed action)	*atê-ka-k*	'he has gone'
sa-desiderative	*ka sa-nangô-m*	'I want to see'
-hyaag repetitive	*ne-hyaag*	'to eat in a repetitive way and without stopping' (animals)

A number of verbs are composed of two separate roots, which makes it possible to describe processes with great precision.

ex.: *fego < fe + ogo* 'to be busy + to be standing'
      kosungo < ko + sungo 'to cut + to place, set down'

Noun Clusters

Nouns do not have singular and plural. For certain classes of noun, however, such as terms for persons (kin terms, for instance), suffixes may be used to indicate number

e.g.	*angwangunguk*	'a single wife'
	angwaningik	'two wives'
	angwabuguk	'several wives'

In certain contexts the objective case is shown by the ending *-m*.

e.g. *ka təta-m pfê-g*   'I kill a pig'

Appendix B: The Sexual Division of Labour

Production Techniques

Horticulture-Arboriculture

Clearing undergrowth		W
Felling trees	M	
Primary burning	M	(W)
Secondary burning	M	W
Planting	M	W
Harvesting	M	W
Transporting shoots or cuttings and produce	M	W

Sago Working

Felling and preparing the trunk	M	
Building the filter		
Setting up the frame	M	
Attaching the troughs and filter		W
Stripping the pith and filtering		W
Removing and wrapping the sago starch	(M)	W
Transporting the sago for storing in river	M	
Transporting the sago for consumption		W

Gathering

All products (but see also Ch. 7)	M	W

Hunting

All game, including butchering	M	

Fishing

Collective use of fish poisons	M	
Individual use of fish poisons	M	(W)
Bailing	M	W
Use of bait and bow and arrow	M	

Pig-Raising

Capture of wild piglets	M	
Raising and domestication (see Ch. 7)	(M)	W

Manufacturing Techniques

Tools and Weapons

Adzes and sago pounders: stones obtained through outside exchange		
Hafting, sharpening	M	
Tools and weapons made from bone and tusk	M	
Bows and arrows	M	
Digging sticks	M	
Wooden tongs for burning and household tasks	M	W
Scoops for bailing	M	W

Miscellaneous

Smoking baskets	M	
Fish traps	M	
Twine and netted objects		W
Women's skirts		W

Penis sheaths	M	
Limbum containers	M	W
Bark cloth	M	W
Musical instruments		
(manufacture and use)	M	
Ritual objects, masks, etc.		
(manufacture and use)	M	

Architecture

Bush and garden shelters	M	
House		
Procuring the timber and making the		
frame	M	
Roof		
rafters	M	
gathering and transporting sago folioles		W
thatching	M	
Suspended fireplace		
framework and ties	M	
gathering clay		W
installation and fashioning	(M)	W
Garden fences, ritual enclosures, etc.	M	

Household Chores

Cooking		
Sago	(M)	W
Other vegetable produce	M	W
Game	M	
Fish	M	W
Gathering firewood		W
(ringbarking trees : M)		
Fetching water		W
Childminding	(M)	W
Village upkeep		W

Appendix C: Kinship Terms

1. *awaag* Address *aya*	'father': real father
eteeg awaag	'father's elder brother' (lit. 'elder father'): father's elder brother, father's parallel cousin whom he calls *eteeg* ('elder brother')
sumnik awag	'father's younger brother' (lit. 'younger father'): father's younger brother, father's parallel cousin whom he calls *sumnik* ('younger brother')
2. *afaag* Address: *naya*	'mother': real mother, mother's sister, mother's female cousin[1]
eteeg afaag	'mother's elder sister' (lit. 'elder mother'): mother's elder sister, mother's parallel cousin whom she calls *eteeg* ('elder sister')
sumnik afaag	'mother's younger sister' (lit. 'younger mother'): mother's younger sister, mother's parallel cousin whom she calls *sumnik* ('younger sister')
3. *h(u)mon* Address: idem	'classificatory father': father's brother or cousin, mother's cross cousin, father's sister's husband, mother's sister's husband, etc.
4. *afahmom* Address: idem	'classificatory mother': mother's sister or female cousin, father's female cross cousin, father's brother's wife, mother's brother's wife, etc. (this term covers *afaag* in its classificatory sense)

1. When the term 'cousin' is used without further qualification, it means both parallel and cross cousin.

5. *at (atôk)*	male and female ego: mother's husband
Address: idem	male ego: wife's child
6. *atôk*	m/fE: father's younger brother; 'adoptive
Address: idem	father': any male kinsman in the first
	ascending generation (G+1) feeding or
	having fed ego
atôk awaag	father's younger brother or 'adoptive
	father' (specifies direction of relationship)
atôk reeg	elder brother's son (mE) or 'adoptive son'
	(idem)
atôk röögunguk	elder brother's daughter (mE) or 'adop-
	tive daughter' (idem)
7. *reeg*	'son': son, brother's or male cousin's son
Address: *nuwik*	(mE), female cross cousin's son (mE),
	sister's or female cousin's son (fE), male
	cross cousin's son (fE)
8. *röögunguk*	'daughter': daughter, brother's or male
Address: *papyo*	cousin's daughter (mE), female cross
	cousin's daughter (mE), sister's or fem-
	ale cousin's daughter (fE), male cross
	cousin's daughter (fE)
9. *abungunguk, abik*	m/fE: 'grandfather': father's or mother's
Address: *apiy*	father mE: 'grandson (granddaughter)':
	son's or daughter's child
abiniga	m/fE: male collaterals in G+2
	mE: male and female collaterals in G-2
10. *asagunguk, asaag*	m/fE: 'grandmother': father's or mother's
Address: *ata*	mother
	fE: 'grandson (granddaughter)': son's or
	daughter's child
asanənga	m/fE: female collaterals in G+2
	fE: male and female collaterals in G-2
11. *sumwagunguk*	m/fE: 'great-grandfather': male lineal
	consanguines in G+3
	mE: 'great-grandson (granddaughter)':
	male and female lineal consanguines in
	G-3
sumwanənga	m/fE: male collaterals in G+3
	mE: male and female collaterals in G-3

12. *nerete*
Address: idem

mE: 'brother': brother, half-brother, parallel cousin

13. *haneruk*
Address: idem

fE: 'sister': sister, half-sister, parallel cousin

14. *eteeg*
Address: idem

'elder' (male or female): ego's first-born same-sex sibling, same-sex half-sibling whose mother was taken in marriage before ego's, ego's parallel cousin whose father is ego's father's first-born brother or whose mother is ego's mother's first-born sister

etanəŋga
Address: idem

'elder' (male or female): ego's elder (but not first-born) same-sex sibling, ego's same-sex parallel cousin whose father is ego's father's *etanəŋga* or whose mother is ego's mother's *etanəŋga*

15. *sumnik* (or *sumni-gunguk*)
Address: *sumnik*

'younger' (male or female): ego's last-born same-sex sibling, same-sex half sibling whose mother was taken in marriage after ego's, ego's same-sex parallel cousin whose father is ego's father's last-born brother or whose mother is ego's mother's last-born sister

sumninəŋga
Address: idem

'younger' (male or female): ego's same-sex (but not last-born) sibling, same-sex parallel cousin whose father is ego's father's *sumnik* or whose mother is ego's mother's *sumnik*

16. *nisag*
Address: idem

fE: 'brother': brother, male parallel cousin

17. *weerik*
Address: idem

mE: 'sister': sister, female parallel cousin

18. *magawô*
Address: idem

'cross cousin' (male or female): all children of the women ego's father calls *weerik*, or of the men ego's mother calls *nisag*. See above note Ch. 11 note 8, p. 307 on the term *taway*

19. *nonoog*
Address: *aw*

'maternal uncle': mother's brother

nonanənga	'maternal uncle': man (other than the mother's real brother) whom ego's mother calls *nisag*
20. *rabik* Address: idem	mE: 'uterin nephew or niece': sister's child
rabiniga	mE: 'classificatory uterine nephew or niece': child of a woman ego calls *weerik* (other than his real sister)
21. *amagunguk* Address: *ama*	m/fE: 'paternal aunt': father's sister fE: 'fraternal nephew or niece': brother's child
amanənga	m/fE: 'classificatory paternal aunt': woman whom ego's father calls *weerik* (other than his sister) fE: 'classificatory fraternal nephew (niece)': child of a man (other than his real brother) whom ego calls *nisag*
22. *kowaag* Address: idem	'father-, mother-, son-, daughter-in-law': wife's father or mother, husband's father or mother, son's or daughter's spouse
kowanənga	collateral of a *kowaag*
23. *rəgaag*	husband
24. *angwaag*	wife
25. *guweeg* Address: idem	mE: 'brother-in-law': wife's brother or cousin, sister's or cousin's husband
26. *mamunguk* (or *maminiga*) Address: idem	fE: 'sister-in-law': husband's sister or cousin, brother's or cousin's wife
27. *abwari* Address: idem	mE: 'sister-in-law'; wife's sister or cousin fE: 'brother-in-law': sister's or cousin's husband
28. *riyagunguk* (or *riyanənga*) Address: idem	mE: 'sister-in-law': brother's or cousin's wife fE: 'brother-in-law': husband's brother or cousin
29. *habugni* Address: idem	mE: wife's sister's husband

Glossary[1]

aba	filtered sago (raw or cooked); cleared space
abi	wildfowl, *Talegalla* ? *jobiensis* Meyer
abuk	red; ripe
afaag	mother (ref.)
aftur	disembodied psychological component of the person endowed with feelings of envy
afwêêg	sago clone, totem of the Araneri ('male') moiety of Yafar society
ag	object made locally or manufactured (as opposed to *teh* 'food')
agi	form of non-homicidal sorcery
ah-	dual prefix
akba	sun
akba na awaag	Master of the Sun
angaag	handle; food offering to a spirit
angô	segment meaning 'woman, female' or 'peripheral, outer'
angômêg	young fertile woman
angor	non-human river spirit
angôruwaag	outsider, member of a non-allied village
angwaag	wife
angwafik	woman
Angwaneri	'woman's people' (*angô na êrɨ*), 'female' moiety of Yafar society
anuwanam	state of someone already having undergone a given experience, of being initiated to something
Araneri	'man's people' (*ara na êrɨ*), 'male' moiety of Yafar society
arfêêg	epidermis, sloughed skin, film of any kind

1. Only the terms that appear regularly in the text are listed here; for a more complete lexicon, see Juillerat 1994.

asagyam	state of someone never having undergone a given experience, of being a novice at something
aso	garden, clearing
at	mother's husband
atôk	adoptive father, adopted child; father's younger brother
awaag	father, master, owner
awanənga	member of the same tribe
awtinaag	old, ancient
awus	magical plant (generic term)
aya	papa, father (add.)
aynaag	man of knowledge, elderly man
aysiri	sorcerer or homicidal sorcery
baha	reddish stone; flake of this stone used as a sago-pounder blade
bêêbɨ (bêêmpɨ)	vine, *Calamus* sp., used in making the Yangis masks; in cosmology it marks the path of the sun
bəsa	coconut petiolar fibre, used to filter sago or as a canvas which is painted to make certain Yangis masks
bəte	earth, ground, land
bəte na awaag	Master of the Earth
boof	Bot. the tree *Rejoua aurantiaca* or its orangish fruits (for ritual use)
busuk (bus)	white
buu	water, river, rain
b(w)ehyaag	to stand up, to grow
bwêr	apparatus for filtering sago pith
efêfêy(ik)	sides of the waist, below the ribs, the loins
emwêêg	vagina
êrɨ	man, person, people
esik	widow, widower
esmunam	without reciprocity, gratuitously
eteeg	sibling or elder same-sex parallel cousin, first-born of the same sex
fango	bow
fango-inaag	'in the bow', male or female matrilateral cross

	cousin, *magawô* [offspring of the brother of the ancestral sibling pair: see *nay-inaag*]
fənaw	sago clone, totem of the ('female') Angwaneri moiety; euphemism for the totemic coconut palm
fuf	wooden trumpets (generic term)
fufuk	the primary couple of the five *fuf* trumpets
fut	the beetle, *Rhynchophorus* sp., which produces the *nibik* sago grubs; primordial, ancient
gaf	Bot. *Acorus calamus* (cultivated magical plant)
-gam	suffix indicating direction
gehya(g)	to kill down to the last man; battle
ging	notched pole leading up to the house porch
gingêg	petiol; to open a path; to paint
gungwan	Bot. *Antiaropsis decipiens* or *A. toxicaria* (shrub); name of a rite for protecting the disembodied self (*sungwaag*)
gungwe	Bot. iron tree: *Intsia palembanica*
guweeg	brother-in-law (reciprocal; male ego)
haneruk	classificatory sister (female ego); women exchanged in marriage
heyfu	female pollution
heyfu-inaag	'in the *heyfu*', polluted by menstrual blood or childbirth
hôn	little stone, rock, cliff, boulder
hoofuk	pith of the palm or the banana tree; flesh of tubers; fertility principle; esoteric knowledge associated with plant reproduction
humon(ik)	classificatory father
hwagi	sago pounder, the blade is made from a stone flake
hwatiy	Bot. *Areca catechu*, areca; areca nut
hwig	penis
hwis	semen
ifaaf	ghost, non-socialized part of the deceased
ifêêg	original, primordial; a clan name
ifəgê	three-pronged arrow for hunting birds; name of the ritual figures known as 'children of the blood' which appear at the end of the Yangis rite (< *ifêêg êri*, 'original person/man')

ifya-minaag	from *ifêêg-meeg-inaag* 'origin-hole-in'; first wife in a polygynal family
imiso	yodelling cries anouncing a victory: homicide, hunting, felling of a tree
-inaag	suffix: 'in'
me-inaag	(from *meeg* 'hole') inside, in the interior
wa-inaag	(*wa* 'on')
ira	women's dance consisting of making the skirt swing from side to side; a public rite
ka	the personal pronoun 'I'
kag	to go
kaga	rattan platter or basket for smoking meat
kagwôg	to cover, to block (a path), to prevent
kas	bone dagger
kêfutuk	solid, hard; resistant to illness or sorcery; brave; sacred
*kehrag,*pl. *kehrig*	to seize, grab
kêg	bone, bones; pit; hard wood
kê-ruur	from *kêg ruwar* 'child of the bones': entity that comes from the bones of the deceased
keeg	Bot. palm sheath; hard envelope; empty tin can
kəbik	site, place, spot; village, hamlet
kəfe	black palm sheath, or limbum, used to make mat to sleep or sit on
kəgaag	branch; marriage cycle closed in the fourth generation
kowaag	spouse's father or mother; son- or daughter-in-law
kwimpɨ (*kwibɨ*)	Ornith. *Centropus menbeki* (great coucal), black bird of ill omen, incarnation of ghosts (*ifaaf*)
kwoy	cassowary
kwoyrêmp	young cassowary that still has its striped feathers
maar	stone adze formerly used for felling trees
mabiyik	characterized by repeated lack of success in hunting; someone who is no longer accepted by the guardian spirits of game
magawô	cross cousin
maruwô	adze handle or L-shaped stick used as a fighting

	stick; Bot. *Garcinia* sp. (used to make these sticks or handles)
mawank	dog
meeg	hole, cavity
mengêk	mouth
mesoog	head, crown, top
məna	path, trail
mô	speech
mogasəngaw	enclosed space under the house where a woman who is menstruating or has just given birth is isolated
moog	stump, base, origin
mosuwamp	placenta
mosuwô, mosuwaag	navel, umbilical cord
mööfuk (mööf)	sterile, unmarried
mööf raara	unmarried boys' house
mungwô, mungwaag	one, lone, same
mwaywey	spell cast on a hunter to keep him from finding game (to make him *mabiyik*)
na	sago palm (generic term); of, with (suffixed to name)
nabasa	male forest spirit; spirit of the deceased that comes from the blood; guardian spirits of game
nabasa raara	see *raara*
narik	big
nay	string skirt; outer layer of the young sago frond used to make the string for skirts
nay-inaag	'in the skirt', male or female patrilateral cross cousin, *magawô* (see *fango-inaag*)
naya	mama, mother (address)
neg	to eat, drink, chew (betel); metaphorically, to have sexual relations
nefôkêg	*Acorus calamus* (*gaf*) clone used in homicidal sorcery (*aysiri*)
nerete	classificatory brother (male ego)
ningəgaag	the hand
ningəga-na kehkig	'to seize by the hands', to seize someone with the purpose of killing him having lured him into an ambush

nihik	meat, flesh of a fruit
nisag	brother or male parallel cousin (female ego)
nôô (nôwô)	forest land far from the village, hunting ground
nonoog	maternal uncle
noofuk (noof)	eye, gaze
nööngêk (nöönguk)	rotten
ogo	to stand
ogohyaag	to make a repetitive vertical movement; to dance with a ritual penis sheath (*-hyaag*: see Appendix A)
ogomô	the sago spirit of growth; a ritual figure of Yangis
oof	the sky, the firmament, the cosmic top
oof na awaag	Master of the Sky
önguk	black
öruk	heart; centre, middle
pəpak	screen made of palm fronds; ritual enclosure
pugug	to appear, to show oneself, to go out
raag	feathers, (animal or human) hair
raara	house, shelter
aso raara	garden shelter
nabasa raara	'spirit house', ritual shelter in the *pəpak* enclosure; ceremonial cycle dedicated to the *nabasa*
rabik, rabiniga	uterine nephew, niece
rangôk	fog
rangôk kagwôg	'covered in fog', 'blind' to game, having been the victim of a *mwaywey* spell
rangwarik	members of either of the two gandmothers' clans, with whom marriage is prohibited
reeg	son
rəgaag	husband
rii	tree (generic term)
roofuk (roof)	skin, bark, peeling; *roofêg*: to peel, to skin (ritual)
röögunguk	daughter (kinship term)
rumurik	the back
rumuri-kêg	the backbone, spinal column
ruwar	child; descendant, offspring of –.

sa (ritual: *say*)	coconut palm, coconut
sabaga	two
sangêk	sacred song, chant
sawangô	female forest spirit; spirit of deceased women that comes from the blood
sawangô raara	now abandoned fertility rite dedicated to the *sawangô* spirits (see *nabasa raara*)
sawôg	fish; category of ritual Yangis figures
sêh	non-kin exchange partner
sês	game, edible animal
seeg	category of magical plants, mainly for hunting
segwaag (*segwôg*)	privileged (exchange) partner among one's kins men or forest spirits
sengêri	funeral shelter in which the enshrouded corpse suspended from its carrying pole is concealed
səsêg	flower
sibɨ	black sap of the iron tree (technical uses and symbolic association with blood)
sig	tip, end of an object
sosoog	imaginary arrowhead introduced into the body of a victim
sosoog uguwôg	'to drive in the heads' (technique of *aysiri* sorcery)
sööbɨ	Bot. variety of black areca palm; black areca sheath, limbum; container made from these sheathes
suhêêg (*suh*)	ritual term meaning 'fertile' and 'black' (leaves, skin etc.)
suh wagmô	black ritual penis gourd
sum	following, coming after (in space or time)
sum-inaag	second (third, etc.) wife in a polygynous family
sumneri	from *sum na êri* 'people who come afterwards'; designates a group regarded as 'younger': a clan name
sumnik	younger same-sex sibling or parallel cousin
sungwaag	a person's self (soul) which leaves the body in sleep
suwê	fire; metaphor for 'blood'
suweeg	smoke
suweegik	pollution emanating from a woman who is menstruating or pregnant

taf	blood
taway	male or female third cross cousin allowed as a spouse at the end of a cycle
teh	food
təta	wild pig
tot, totom	breast, milk
-wa	suffix: on
wagmô	Bot. *Lagenaria* sp. gourd; decorated penis sheath made from an ovoid gourd; see also *suhêg*
wahmuh	domesticated pig
wahwe	Bot. *Curcuma* sp.; rhizome of this plant; yellow paint made from this plant
wanwe	secondary growth, tall grass
wanweri	secondary forest
ware	wild canes (Pidgin: *wail pitpit*)
wêsik	small
we	tie(s), bond(s); rattan used in building; weeping, lamentations
weerik	sister, female paralel cousin (male ego)
wesko	from *we sungo* 'to put lamentations'; song accompanied by hour-glass drums
wos	moon
wos na awaag	Master of the Moon
wura	netbag
wurag	uterus (metaphorically associated with *wura*)
-ya	suffix: on top of, above, on the surface
yis	sago jelly

Bibliography

Baal, J. van 1966. *Dema: Description and Analysis of Marind Anim Culture*. The Hague, Martinus Nijhoff.

Bachelard, G. 1975. *La Formation de l'esprit scientifique: Contribution à une psychanalyse de la connaissance objective*. Paris, Librairie Philosophique J. Vrin.

Ballini, M. (see also Jeudy-Ballini) 1983. L'Identité sexuelle et ses représentations chez les Sulka de Nouvelle-Bretagne. Thèse de doctorat de troisième cycle. Université de Paris X-Nanterre.

Bamberger, J. 1974. 'The Myth of Matriarchy: Why Men Rule in Primitive Society', in M. Z. Rosaldo and L. Lamphere (eds), *Woman, Culture and Society*. Stanford, Stanford University Press.

Barrau, J. 1958. *Subsistence Agriculture in Melanesia*. Honolulu, B.P. Bishop Museum Bulletin no. 219, 111 p.

Barth, F. 1975. *Ritual and Knowledge among the Baktaman of New Guinea*. Oslo, Universitetsforlaget; New Haven, Yale University Press.

— 1987, *Cosmologies in the Making: A Generative Approach to Cultural Variations in Inner New Guinea*. Cambridge, Cambridge University Press.

Bastide, R. 1972a. *Sociologie et psychanalyse*. Paris, Presses Universitaires de France (2nd revised edition).

— 1972b. 'Rêve et culture', in his *Le Rêve, la transe et la folie*. Paris, Flammarion.

— 1975. 'Le Millénarisme comme stratégie de la recherche d'une nouvelle identité et dignité', in his *Le Sacré sauvage et autres essais*. Paris, Payot.

Bateson, G. 1958 [1936]. *Naven: The Culture of the Iatmul People of New Guinea as Revealed Through a Study of the 'Naven' Ceremonial*. Stanford, Stanford University Press.

Bettelheim, B. 1954. *Symbolic Wounds*. Chicago, Free Press.

Bourdieu, P. 1980. *Le Sens pratique*. Paris, Editions de Minuit.

Bulmer, R. 1967. 'Why is the Cassowary not a Bird?', *Man* (n.s.) vol. 2, pp. 5–25.

— 1968. 'The Strategies of Hunting in New Guinea', *Oceania* vol. 38, no. 4, pp. 308–18, also in L.L. Langness and J.C. Weschler (eds), *Melanesia: Readings on a Culture Area*. Scranton etc., Chandler, 1971.

Bulmer, S. 1975. 'Settlement and Economy in Prehistoric Papua New Guinea: A Review of the Archaeological Evidence', *Journal de la Société des Océanistes* no. 46, pp. 7–75.

Burridge, K.P.L. 1959. 'Siblings in Tangu', *Oceania* vol. 30, pp. 128–54.

— 1960. *Mambu, a Melanesian Millenium*. London, Methuen.

— 1971. *New Heaven, New Earth: A Study of Millenarian Activities*. Oxford, Basil Blackwell.

Clarke, W.C. 1973. 'Temporary Madness as Theatre', *Oceania* vol. 43, no. 3, pp. 198–214.

— 1976. 'Maintenance of Agriculture and Human Habitats Within the Tropical Forest Ecosystem', *Human Ecology* vol. 4, no. 3, pp. 247–59.

Condominas, G. 1980. *L'Espace social à propos de l'Asie du Sud-Est*. Paris, Flammarion.

Cooper, A.B., J.J. Lauvergne, G. Mazynicz and A.R. Quarterman 1981. 'Pig Husbandry in Papua New Guinea: A Bibliography 1983–1979', *Annales de Génétique Sélective Animale* vol. 13, no. 3, pp. 301–30.

Coppet, D. de, 1976. 'Jardins de vie, jardins de mort en Mélanésie', *Traverses* nos 5–6, pp. 166–77.

Craig, B. 1969. Report to the Wenner-Gren Foundation for Anthropological Research of the Upper-Sepik Ethnographic Expedition of 1968. New York.

— 1988. 'Art and Decoration of Central New Guinea', Aylesbury (U.K.), Shire Publications.

Crocombe, R.G. 1974. 'An Approach to the Analysis of Land Tenure Systems', in H.P. Lundsgaarde (ed.), *Land Tenure in Oceania*. Honolulu, University Press of Hawaii.

Darmon, P. 1977. *Le Mythe de la procréation à l'âge baroque*. Paris, J.J. Pauvert.

Descola, P. 1986. *La Nature domestique: Symbolisme et praxis dans l'écologie des Achuar*. Paris, Editions de la Maison des Sciences de l'Homme (English translation, *In the Society of Nature: A Native Ecology in Amazonia* (N. Scott trans.), Cambridge, Cambridge University Press 1994).

Devereux, G. 1956. 'Normal and Abnormal: The Key Problem of Psychiatric Anthropology', in J.B. Casagrande and T. Gladwin (eds), *Some Uses of Anthropology: Theoretical and Applied*. Washington, The Anthropological Society of Washington.

Douglas, M. 1967. *Purity and Danger*. London etc., Routledge & Kegan Paul.

— 1975. 'Couvade and Menstruation', in *Implicit Meanings: Essays in Anthropology*. London etc., Routledge & Kegan Paul, pp. 60–72.

Dumont, L. 1971. *Introduction à deux théories d'anthropologie sociale: Groupes de filiation et alliance de mariage*. Paris and The Hague, Mouton.

— 1978. 'Communauté anthropologique et idéologie', *L'Homme* vol. 18, nos 3–4, pp. 83–110.

Favret-Saada, J. 1978. *Les Mots, la mort, les sorts: La sorcellerie dans le bocage*. Paris, Gallimard (English translation, *Deadly Words: Witchcraft in the Bocage* (Catherine Cullen trans.), Cambridge etc., Cambridge University Press, and Paris, Editions de la Maison des sciences de l'homme 1980).

Fischer, H. 1983 [1958]. *Sound-producing Instruments in Oceania* (translated from the German by Ph. W. Holznecht). Boroko (Port-Moresby), Institute of Papua New Guinea Studies.

Fortune, R. 1963 [1932]. *Sorcerers of Dobu*. London, Routledge & Kegan Paul.

Freud, S. 1900. *The Interpretation of Dreams*. In vol. 4/5 of the standard edition of the complete psychological works of Sigmund Freud. London, Hogarth Press.

Fried, M.H. 1975. *The Notion of Tribe*. Menlo Park (California), Cummings.

Galis, K.W. 1956. *Ethnografische notities over het Senggigebied (district Hollandia)*. Hollandia, Gouvernement van Nederlands Nieuw Guinea, Kantoor voor Bevolkingzaken.

— 1956–1957. *Ethnologische survey van het Jafi district*. Hollandia, Gouvernement van Nederlands Nieuw Guinea, Kantoor voor Bevolkingzaken.

Gell, A. 1971. 'Penis Sheathing and Ritual Status in a West Sepik Village', *Man* vol. 6, no. 2, pp. 165–81.

— 1975. *Metamorphosis of the Cassowaries: Umeda Society, Language and Ritual*. London, Athlone Press and New Jersey, Humanity Press.

— 1979. 'Reflections on a Cut Finger: Taboo in the Umeda Conception of Self', in R.H. Hook (ed.), *Fantasy and Symbol*. London etc., Academic Press.

— 1980. 'Order or Disorder in Melanesian Religion?', Correspondence, *Man* vol. 15, no. 4, pp. 735–7.

Gennep, A. van 1981 [1909]. *Les Rites de Passage*, Paris, A. & J. Picard.

Gillison, G. 1993. *Between Culture and Fantasy: A New Guinea Highlands mythology*. Chicago and London, The University of Chicago Press.

Glasse, R.M., and M.J. Meggitt (eds) 1969. *Pigs, Pearlshells and Women: Marriage in the New Guinea Highlands*. Englewood Cliffs (N.J.), Prentice-Hall.

Godelier, M. 1973. 'Le Concept de tribu: Crise d'un concept ou crise des fondements empiriques de l'anthropologie?', *Horizons, trajets marxistes en anthropologie*. Paris, Maspero.

— 1982. *La Production des Grands Hommes: Pouvoir et domination masculine chez les Baruya de Nouvelle-Guinée*. Paris, Fayard (English translation in *The Making of Great Men. Male Domination and Power among the New*

Guinea Baruya (R. Swyer, trans). Cambridge, Cambridge University Press and Paris, Editions de la Maison des sciences de l'homme 1986).

Graham, G. and D. 1980. A revised statement of Amanab phonemes. Ukarumpa, Summer Institute of Linguistics, unpublished.

Green, A. 1977. 'Atome de parenté et relations œdipiennes', in C. Lévi-Strauss (ed.), *L'Identité*. Paris, Grasset.

— 1992. 'The Œdipus Complex as *Mutterkomplex*', in B. Juillerat, *Shooting the Sun: Ritual and Meaning in West Sepik*. Washington, The Smithsonian Institution Press.

— 1995. *La Causalité psychique: Entre nature et culture*. Paris, Editions Odile Jacob.

Groves, C.P. 1983. 'Pigs East of the Wallace Line', *Journal de la Société des Océanistes*, no. 77, pp. 105–19.

Harrison, S. 1988. 'Magical Exchange of the Preconditions of Production in a Sepik River Village', *Man* (n.s.) vol. 23, no. 4, pp. 319–33.

Haudricourt, G.A. 1964. 'Nature et culture dans la civilisation de l'igname: L'origine des clones et des clans', *L'Homme* vol. 4, no. 1, pp. 93–104.

Herdt, G.H. 1981. *Guardians of the Flutes: Idioms of Masculinity*. New York, McGraw-Hill.

— 1989. 'Spirit Familiars in the Religious Imagination of Sambia Shamans', in G. Herdt and M. Stephen (eds), *The Religious Imagination in New Guinea*. New Brunswick and London, Rutgers University Press.

Héritier, F. 1979. 'Symbolique de l'inceste et de sa prohibition', in P. Smith and M. Izard (eds), *La Fonction symbolique*. Paris, Gallimard.

— 1981. *L'Exercice de la parenté*. Paris, Ecole des Hautes Etudes en Sciences Sociales/Gallimard/Le Seuil.

— 1984. 'Stérilité, aridité, sécheresse: quelques invariants de la pensée symbolique', in M. Augé and C. Herzlich (eds), *Le Sens du mal: Anthropologie, histoire, sociologie de la maladie*. Paris, Editions Archives Contemporaines.

— 1984–1985. 'Le Sang du guerrier et le sang des femmes: Notes anthropologiques sur le rapport des sexes', in 'Africaines. Sexes et signes', *Cahiers du GRIF* no. 29, pp. 7–21.

— 1994. *Les deux sœurs et leur mère: Anthropologie de l'inceste*. Paris, Odile Jacob.

Hiatt, L.R. 1971. 'Secret Pseudo-procreation Rites among the Australian Aborigines', in L.R. Hiatt and Jayawardene (eds), *Anthropology in Oceania: Essays presented to Ian Hogbin*. Sydney, Angus and Robertson.

Hocart, A.M. 1970. *Kings and Councillors*. Chicago, The University of Chicago Press.

Hogbin, I. 1970. *The Island of Menstruating Men: Religion in Wogeo, New Guinea*. San Francisco, Chandler.

Hogbin, I., and P. Lawrence (eds) 1967. *Studies in New Guinea Land Tenure.* Sydney, Sydney University Press.

Howell, R.W. 1975. 'Wars without Conflict', in M.A. Nettleship, R. Dalegivens and A. Nettleship (eds), *War, Its Causes and Correlates.* Paris and The Hague, Mouton.

Huber, P.B. 1973. Identity and Exchange: Kinship and Social Order Among the Anggor of New Guinea, doctoral dissertation, Durham, Duke University.

— 1975. 'Defending the Cosmos: Violence and Social Order Among the Anggor of New Guinea', in M.A. Nettleship, R. Dalegivens and A. Nettleship (eds), *War, Its Causes and Correlates.* Paris and The Hague, Mouton.

— 1979. 'Anggor Floods: Reflections on Ethnogeography and Mental Maps', *The Geographical Review* vol. 69, no. 2, pp. 127–39.

— 1980. *Organizing Production and Producing Organization: The Sociology of Traditional Agriculture*, Development Studies Centre Monograph no. 11, Canberra, Australian National University.

— 1990. 'Masquerade as Artifact in Wamu', in N. Lutkehaus *et al.* (eds), *Sepik Heritage. Tradition and Change in Papua New Guinea.* Durham (North Carolina), Carolina Academic Press: 150–159 (Actes du Symposium international sur le Sépik, Bâle, 1984).

Iteanu, A. 1983. *La Ronde des échanges: De la circulation aux valeurs chez les Orokaiva.* Paris, Maison des sciences de l'homme, and Cambridge, Cambridge University Press.

Jamin, J. 1977. *Les lois du silence: Essai sur la fonction sociale du secret.* Paris, Maspero.

Jeudy-Ballini, M. (see also Ballim) 1988. 'Entre le clair et l'obscur: les transformations de l'histoire', *L'Homme* (n.s. 'Le Mythe et ses métamorphoses') vol. 28, nos 2–3 , pp. 237–51.

Juillerat, B. 1971. *Les bases de l'organisation sociale cher les Mouktélé: Structures lignagères et mariage.* Paris, Institut d'Ethnologie.

— 1975a. 'Transe et langage en Nouvelle-Guinée: I. La Possession médiumnique chez les Amanab', *Journal de la Société des Océanistes* no. 47, pp. 187–212.

— 1975b. 'Transe et langage en Nouvelle-Guinée: II. Du symptôme au rite', *Journal de la Société des Océanistes* no. 49, pp. 379–97.

— 1975c. 'Objets du Haut-Sépik, Nouvelle-Guinée (Amanab et Kwomtari)', *Microfilms* no. I 74 099 117, Paris, Institut d'Ethnologie, Musée de l'Homme.

— 1977. 'Terminologie de parenté iafar: Analyse formelle d'une nomenclature de type dakota-iroquois', *L'Homme* vol. 17, no. 4, pp. 5–53.

— 1978a. 'Techniques et sociologie de la couleur chez les Iafar', in S. Tornay (ed.), *Voir et nommer les couleurs.* Nanterre, Université de Paris X, Labethno.

— 1978b. 'Vie et mort dans le symbolisme iafar des couleurs', in S. Tornay (ed.), *Voir et nommer les couleurs*, Nanterre, Université de Paris X, Labethno.

— 1979. 'En route pour les plantations', *Journal de la Société des Océanistes* no. 64, pp. 209–12.

— 1980. 'Order or disorder in Melanesian religion?', *Man* vol. 15, no. 4, pp. 732–7.

— 1981. 'Organisation dualiste et complémentarité sexuelle dans le Sépik occidental', *L'Homme* vol. 21, no. 2, pp. 5–38.

— 1983a. 'Note sur les rapports de production dans l'horticulture-arboriculture yafar', in M. Panoff (ed.), 'Tubercules et pouvoir', *Journal d'Agriculture Traditionnelle et Botanique Appliquée* vol. 29, nos 3–4, pp. 285–93.

— 1983b. 'L'essartage chez les Yafar', *Journal d'Agriculture Traditionnelle et de Botanique Appliquée* vol. 30, no. 1, pp. 3–35.

— 1984a. 'Culture et exploitation du palmier sagoutier dans les Border Mountains (Nouvelle Guinée)', *Techniques et Culture* (n.s.) no. 3, pp. 43–64.

— 1984b. 'D'*Acorus* à *Zingiber*: taxinomie et usage des plantes cultivées chez les Yafar de Nouvelle-Guinée', *'Journal d'Agriculture Traditionnelle et de Botanique Appliquée* vol. 31, nos 1–2, pp. 3–31.

— 1988. '"Une odeur d'homme": Evolutionnisme mélanésien et mythologie anthropologique à propos du matriarcat', *Diogène* no. 144, pp. 67–91 (English translation: '"An odor of man", Melanesian Evolutionism, Anthropological Mythology and Matriarchy', *Diogenes*, 144, pp. 65–91).

— 1990. 'The Couple Between Male Ideology and Cultural Fantasy in Yafar Society (West Sepik)', in N. Lutkehaus *et al.* (eds), *Sepik Heritage: Tradition and Change in Papua New Guinea*. Durham (Nth Car.), Carolina Academic Press (Actes du Symposium international sur le Sépik, Bâle, 1984).

— 1991a. *Œdipe chasseur: Une mythologie du sujet en Nouvelle-Guinée*. Paris, Presses Universitaires de France.

— 1991b. 'Complementarity and Rivalry in Yafar Society', in M. Strathern and M. Godelier (eds), *Big Men and Great Men: Personifications of Power in Melanesia*. Cambridge, Cambridge University Press, pp. 130–41.

— 1992a. '"The Mother's Brother is the Breast": Incest and its Prohibition in the Yafar Yangis' and 'Epilogue', in B. Juillerat (ed.), *Shooting the Sun: Ritual and Meaning in West Sepik*. Washington, The Smithsonian Institution Press.

— 1992b. 'L'Univers dans un hameau: Cosmologie et histoire chez les Yafar', *Etudes Rurales* (n.s. 'La Terre et le Pacifique') nos 127–8, pp. 159–76.

— 1993. 'L'Air, le feu, le son: Fabrication et usage des trompes de bois et des tambours dans les Border Mountains (P.N.G.)', *Baessler Archiv*, (Neue Folge) pp. 413–44, ill. (English translation 'Air, Fire, Sound: The Construction and Use of Trumpets and Drums in the Border Mountains (P.N.G.)', *Kulele* vol. II, 1996, National Research Institute, Cultural Studies Div., Music Dept. Port-Moresby).

— 1994. *Amanab-English Lexicons and Texts*. La Jolla, Melanesian Archives, University of California at San Diego (microfilms).

— 1995. *L'Avènement du père. Rite, représentation, fantasme dans un culte mélanésien*. Paris, Editions de la Maison des sciences de l'homme / Editions du CNRS.

Juillerat, B. (ed.) 1977. '"Folie", possession et chamanisme en Nouvelle-Guinée', *Journal de la Société des Océanistes* (n.s.), pp. 56–7.

— 1992 (ed.). *Shooting the Sun: Ritual and Meaning in West Sepik*. Washington, The Smithsonian Institution Press.

Kaberry, P.M. 1967. 'The Plasticity of New Guinea Kinship', in M. Freedman (ed.), *Social Organization: Essays Presented to Raymond Firth*. London, Frank Cass.

Kelly, R. 1977. *Etoro Social Structure: A Study in Structural Contradiction*. Ann Arbor, University of Michigan Press.

Kelm, A., and H. 1980. *Sago und Schwein. Ethnologie von Kwieftim und Abrau in Nordost-Neuguinea*. Wiesbaden, Franz Steiner.

Kilani, M. 1983. *Les Cultes du cargo mélanésiens: Mythe et rationalité en anthropologie*. Lausanne, Editions d'En-Bas.

Knauft, B.M. 1989. 'Imagery, Pronouncement, and the Aesthetics of Reception in Gebusi Spirit Mediumship', in G. Herdt and M. Stephen (eds), *The Religious Imagination in New Guinea*. New Brunswick and London, Rutgers University Press.

Koch, K.F. 1974. *War and Peace in Jalemo. The Management of Conflict in Highlands New Guinea*. Cambridge (Mass.), Harvard University Press.

Kristeva, J. 1980. *Pouvoirs de l'horreur: Essai sur l'abjection*. Paris, Le Seuil.

Langness, L.L. 1974. 'Ritual, Power and Male Dominance in the New Guinea Highlands', *Ethos* vol. 2, no. 3, pp. 189–212; also in R.D. Fogelson and R.N. Adams (eds), *Anthropology of Power*. London etc., Academic Press, 1977.

Lattas, A. 1992. 'Skin, Personhood and Redemption: The Double Self in West New Britain Cargo Cults', *Oceania* no. 63, pp. 27–54.

Laurie, E.M.O., and J.E. Hill, 1954. *List of Land Mammals of New Guinea, Celebes and Adjacent Islands*. London, British Museum of Natural History.

Lawrence, P. 1964. *Road Belong Cargo: A Study of the Cargo Movement in the Southern Madang District, New Guinea*. Manchester, Manchester University Press.

— 1984. *The Garia: An Ethnography of a Traditional Cosmic System in Papua New Guinea*. Manchester, Manchester University Press.

Laycock, D.C. 1975. *Languages of the Sepik Region*. Canberra, Australian National University, Pacific Linguistics, Series D, no. 26.

Leeden, van der, A.C. 1960. 'Social Structure in New Guinea', *Bijdragen tot de Taal-, Land- en Volkerkunde* no. 116, pp. 119–49.

Lemonnier, P. 1981. 'Le Commerce intertribal des Anga de Nouvelle Guinée', *Journal de la Société des Océanistes* nos 70–1, pp. 39–76.

— 1993. 'Le Porc comme substitut de vie: formes de compensation et échanges en Nouvelle-Guinée', *Social Anthropology* vol. 1, no. 1A, pp. 33–55.

Lévi-Strauss, C. 1958. 'L'analyse structurale en linguistique et en anthropologie', *Anthropologie Structurale*. Paris, Plon, (English translation 'Structural Analysis in Linguistics and in Anthropology', in *Structural Anthropology*. New York, Anchor Books, pp. 29–53 1967).

— 1967 [1947]. *Les Structures élémentaires de la parenté*. Paris and The Hague, Mouton (English translation, *The Elementary Structures of Kinship* (James Harle Bell, John Richard von Sturmer and Rodney Needham trans.). *Boston, Beacon Press* 1969).

— 1973. 'Réflexions sur l'atome de parenté', *L'Homme* vol. 13, no. 3, pp. 5–30; also in *Anthropologie Structurale Deux*. Paris, Plon, pp. 103–35 (English translation 'Reflections on the atom of kinship', in *Structural Anthropology*, vol. 2. New York, Anchor Books 1976).

— 1984. *Paroles données*. Paris, Plon .

Lewis, G. 1980. *Day of Shining Red: An Essay on Understanding Ritual*. Cambridge, Cambridge University Press.

Lewis, I.M. 1971. *Ecstatic Religion. An Anthropological Study of Spirit Possession and Shamanism*. Harmondsworth (U.K.), Penguin Books.

Lincoln. J.S. 1970 [1935]. *The Dream in Primitive Cultures* (New Preface by G. Devereux). New York and London, Johnson Reprint Corporation.

Lory, J.-L. 1981–1982. 'Quelques aspects du chamanisme baruya (Eastern Highland Province, Papouasie Nouvelle-Guinée)', *Cahiers ORSTOM, Série Sciences Humaines* vol. 18, no. 4, pp. 543–59.

Losche, D.S.B. 1990. 'Utopian Visions and the Division of Labor in Abelam Society', in N. Lutkehaus *et al.* (eds), *Sepik Heritage: Tradition and Change in Papua New Guinea*. Durham (North Carolina), Carolina Academic Press.

Loving, R., and J. Bass, 1964. *Languages of the Amanab Sub-district*. Port Moresby, Department of Information and Extension Services.

Lowie, R. 1948. *Social Organization*. New York, Holt, Rinehart and Winston.

McGregor, D. 1975. The Fish and the Cross. Auckland, unpublished manuscript (copy deposited in the library of the Musée de l'Homme).

Malinowski, B. 1948. *Magic, Science and Religion, and Other Essays*. New York, Free Press.

Marshall, M. (ed.) 1981. *Siblingship in Oceania. Studies in the Meaning of Kin Relations*. Ann Arbor, Association for Social Anthropology in Oceania, University of Michigan Press.

Marwick, M. 1970 [1964]. 'Witchcraft as a Social Strain-gauge', in M. Marwick (ed.), *Witchcraft and Sorcery*. Harmondsworth, Penguin.

Mead, M. 1970–1971 [1940]. *The Mountain Arapesh* (vols 2, 3). New York, American Museum of Natural History, Natural History Press.

Mendel, G. 1972. *Anthropologie différentielle*, Paris, Payot.

Moore, S.F. 1964. 'Descent and Symbolic Filiation', *American Anthropologist* vol. 66, no. 6, part 1, pp. 1308–20; also in J. Middleton (ed.), *Myth and Cosmos: Readings in Mythology and Symbolism*. New York, American Museum of Natural History, Natural History Press, and Austin and London, University of Texas Press.

National Census 1980. *West Sepik Province. Preliminary Field Counts*. Port Moresby.

Oliver, D. 1967. *A Solomon Island Society. Kinship and Leadership among the Siuai of Bougainville*. Boston, Beacon Press.

Oosterwal, G. 1959. 'The Position of the Bachelor in the Upper Tor Territory', *American Anthropologist* vol. 61, pp. 829–38.

— 1961. *People of the Tor*. Assen, Royal van Gorcum.

Ortner, S. 1973. 'On Key Symbols', *American Anthropologist* vol. 75, pp. 1338–46.

Osborne, R. 1985. *Indonesia's Secret War: The Guerilla Struggle in Irian Jaya*. Sydney etc., Allen and Unwin.

Panoff, M. 1971 (April). 'Il faut qu'un mythe soit ouvert ou fermé', *Esprit* (n.s. 'Le Mythe aujourd'hui'), pp. 707–22.

Patrol reports and government census: Amanab, Green River.

Peter, H. 1990. 'Cultural Changes in Gargar Society', in N. Lutkehaus *et al.* (eds), *Sepik Heritage: Tradition and Change in Papua New Guinea*. Durham (North Carolina), Carolina Academic Press.

Pouwer, J. 1960. '"Loosely Structured Societies" in Netherland New Guinea', *Bijdragen tot de Taal-, Land- en Volkerkunde* vol. 116, pp. 109–17.

Rand, A.L., and E.T. Gilliard, 1967. *Handbook of New Guinea Birds*. London, Weidenfeld and Nicolson.

Rappaport, R.A. 1984 [1968]. *Pigs for the Ancestors: Ritual in the Ecology of a New Guinea People*. New Haven and London, Yale University Press.

Roheim, G. 1950. *Psychoanalysis and Anthropology*. New York, International Universities Press.

Rowley, C.D. 1971 [1965]. *The New Guinea Villager: A Retrospect from 1964*. Melbourne, Cheshire Publishing.

Rubel P.G., and A. Rosman 1978. *Your Own Pigs You May Not Eat.* Chicago, University of Chicago Press.

Ryan, J. 1970. *The Hot Land: Focus on New Guinea.* Melbourne and Sydney, Macmillan.

Sahlins, M. 1974. *Stone Age Economics.* London, Tavistock.

— 1976. *Culture and Practical Reason.* Chicago and London, University of Chicago Press.

Sanger, P., and N. Sorrell, 1975. 'Music in Umeda Village', *Ethnomusicology* vol. 19, no. 1, pp. 67–89.

Schieffelin, E.L. 1976. *The Sorrow of the Lonely and the Burning of the Dancer.* New York, Saint-Martin Press.

— 1977. 'The Unseen Influence: Tranced Mediums as Historical Innovators', in B. Juillerat (ed.), '"Folie", possession et chamanisme', *Journal de la Société des Océanistes* (n.s.) nos 56–7, pp. 169–78.

Schoorl, J.W. 1993. *Culture and Change among the Muyu* (translated from the Dutch). Leiden, Koninklijk Instituut voor Taal- Land- en Volkenkunde.

Schwimmer, E. 1973. *Exchange in the Social Structure of the Orokaiva: Traditional and Emergent Ideologies in the Northern District of Papua.* London, Hurst.

Stanek 1983. *Sozialordnung und Mythik in Palimbei: Bausteine zur ganzheitlichen Beschreibung einer Dorfgemeinschaft der Iatmul, East Sepik Province, P.N.G.* Basel, Ethnologisches Seminar der Universität und Museum für Völkerkunde.

Strathern, A.J. 1968. 'Descent and Alliance in the New Guinea Highlands. Some Problems of Comparison', *Proceedings of the Royal Anthropological Institute* 1968, pp. 37–52.

— 1971. *The Rope of Moka. Big Men and Ceremonial Exchange in Mount Hagen, New Guinea.* Cambridge etc., Cambridge University Press.

Tapol Association (ed.). 1983. *West Papua: The Obliteration of a People.* London, Tapol Association.

Testart, A. 1986. *Essai sur les fondements de la division sexuelle du travail chez les chasseurs-cueilleurs.* Paris, Ecole des Hautes Etudes en Sciences Sociales, Cahiers de l'Homme.

Tourneux, H. 1983. Notes résumées sur la phonologie de la langue amanab (Papouasie Nouvelle-Guinée). Paris, unpublished manuscript (see Appendix A).

Turner V.W. 1969. *The Ritual Process: Structure and Anti-structure.* London, Routledge & Kegan Paul, and Harmondsworth (U.K.), Penguin Books, 1974.

Tuzin, D.F. 1976. *The Ilahita Arapesh: Dimensions of Unity.* Berkeley etc., University of California Press.

— 1980. *The Voice of the Tambaran: Truth and Illusion in Ilahita Arapesh Religion.* Berkeley etc., University of California Press.

Veur, P.W. van der, 1966. *Search for New Guinea's Boundaries: From Torres Strait to the Pacific.* Canberra, Australian National University Press.

Voorhoeve, C.L. 1971. 'Miscellaneous Notes on Languages in West Irian, New Guinea', in *Papers in New Guinea Linguistics* no. 14. Canberra, Australian National University Press, Pacific Linguistics, Series A 28.

Vos, G. de, 1975. 'The Dangers of Pure Theory in Social Anthropology', *Ethos* vol. 3, no. 1, pp. 77–91.

Wagner, R. 1972. *Habu: The Innovation of Meaning in Daribi religion.* Chicago, University of Chicago Press.

— 1984. 'Ritual as Communication: Order, Meaning, and Secrecy in Melanesian Initiation Rites', *Annual Review of Anthropology* no. 13, pp. 143–55.

White, O. 1972 [1965]. *A Parliament of a Thousand Tribes: Papua New Guinea: The Story of an Emerging Nation.* Melbourne, Wren Publishing.

Willey, K. 1965. *Assignment New Guinea.* Brisbane, The Jacaranda Press, and San Francisco, Tri-Ocean Books.

Williams, F.E. 1976. *The Vailala Madness and Other Essays.* London, Hurst (first published in *Journal of the Royal Anthropological Institute of Great Britain and Ireland*, no. 62).

Wilson, M. 1957. *Rituals of Kinship among the Nyakusa.* London, Oxford University Press.

Worsley, P. 1973 [1957]. *The Trumpet Shall Sound: A Study of 'Cargo' Cults in Melanesia.* London, Paladin.

Wurm, S.A., and S. Hattori (eds). 1981. *Language Atlas of the Pacific Area, Part 1: New Guinea Area, Oceania, Australia.* Canberra, Academy of the Humanities (in collaboration with the Japan Academy).

Zempleni, A. 1976. 'La Chaîne du secret', *Nouvelle Revue de Psychanalyse* no. 14, pp. 313–24.

List of Films

Juillerat, B. 1977. *Un jardin à Yafar.* Paris, CNRS Audiovisuel, 16mm, 95 min; commentary in French.

— 1983. *Le sang du sagou.* Paris, CNRS Audiovisuel, 16 mm, 55 min; commentary in French.

Owen, C. 1976. *The Red Bowmen.* Port Moresby, Institute of Papua New Guinea Studies, 16 mm, 58 min (in collaboration with A. Gell).

Index